CLASSICAL TOWN HISTORIES

GENERAL EDITOR: W. B. STEPHENS

THE ANTIQUITIES
OF CANTERBURY

THE ANTIQUITIES OF

CANTERBURY

BY

WILLIAM SOMNER

With a new Introduction by
WILLIAM URRY

This edition originally printed for
R. Knaplock, 1703
Republished 1977 by EP Publishing Limited

PUBLISHER'S NOTES

The first edition of this work appeared in 1640, a new title-page was printed in 1661, but the author had not completed his own revision when he died suddenly in 1669. The Rev. Nicholas Battely completed the work and the volume reprinted here is his revised second edition of 1703. Battely incorporated the author's and his own corrections, transferred some material to the Appendix, added the author's posthumous pamphlet *Chartham News*; and enlarged the work by including his own ecclesiastical history *Cantuaria Sacra* as a self-contained 'Second Part' of the new edition. The new title-page giving details of both parts, and the text of *The Second Part: Cantuaria Sacra* have been omitted from this reprint. The Errata from the end of the Second Part for the First Part only have been inserted after the Table at the end of the reprint. The plates specially engraved for the Second Part which also illustrate the text of the First Part have been included in this reprint after the text. The only known portrait of William Somner, a facsimile of his signature and his father's notarial sign, and an engraving of his monument have been inserted in the new Introduction. A list of all the plates in the order in which they appear in the text has been compiled for this reprint.

The text and plates for this volume have been reproduced from the Kent County Library copies nos. 7513, 41925 and 7873, in the Maidstone and Dover Divisional Libraries and the Headquarters Library. The portrait of the author and the engraving of his monument have been reproduced from Kent County Library copies of *A Treatise of the Roman Forts and Ports in Kent* and *A Treatise of Gavelkind*, 2nd. ed., 1726, nos. 53025 and 104512 in the Canterbury Divisional Library. Full details of these are deposited with Kent County Library. The document showing the notarial sign of William Somner (senior), from the Canterbury Cathedral Archives and Library Z 1 10 folio 333 is reproduced with the permission of the Dean and Chapter of Canterbury Cathedral.

The Publishers wish to thank Mr. Dean Harrison, Kent County Librarian and his staff, and the Dean and Chapter of Canterbury Cathedral and their Archivist, Miss A. Oakley, for their valuable assistance.

No directions are given in this work for the arrangement of the text and plates; and these have been placed in the order usually found in most copies of the work. In the Appendix, pages 42, 49, 52 and 78 seem always to be incorrectly numbered 24, 52, 49 and 87. Page 14 is sometimes incorrectly numbered as page 4. The sequence of the text is always unaffected by the errors of pagination.

British Library Cataloguing in Publication Data
Somner, William
    The antiquities of Canterbury, or, A survey of
    that ancient city, with the suburbs and
    cathedral . . .—2nd ed. revised and enlarged.
    —(Classical town histories).
    1. Canterbury, Kent—Antiquities
    I. Title   II. Battely, Nicolas   III. Series
    936.2'2'34   DA690.C3
    ISBN 0–85409–843–7

The text and plates in this volume have been reduced to 88 per cent of the original size.

ISBN 0 85409 843 7

Printed in Great Britain by The Scolar Press Limited, Ilkley, West Yorkshire

SOMNERUS. GULIELMUS.

MORIBUS ANTIQUIS.

MBurghers delin. et sculp.

INTRODUCTION

William Somner and his 'Antiquities'

A remarkable group of men had an origin in Canterbury within the century between Reformation and Civil War. They numbered the dramatist Christopher Marlowe (d. 1593); John Lyly (d. 1606), author of the best-selling novel *Euphues*; Stephen Gosson, the puritan controversialist (d. 1624); and Richard Boyle, 'Great Earl of Cork' (d. 1643). To these, born in the city, may be added William Harvey, the anatomist (d. 1657), and Robert Cushman (d. 1625), the grocer's assistant who was mainly instrumental in hiring the ship *Mayflower*. Harvey and Cushman (both of Kentish origins) underwent education and apprenticeship respectively in Canterbury.

William Somner stands high amid this diversity of talent and it is curious that he has never attracted a serious biography. A great discouragement has been the destruction of his papers in the fire at the Cathedral Audit House in 1670, the year after his death. There was a second, less well-known destruction of documents relating to Somner and his family in the air-raid of June 1942, though fortunately notes of their contents survive, while some letters to his distinguished correspondents are available. Moreover, as a busy official he left masses of administrative documents in his beautiful but difficult handwriting. Happily at least part of his historical collections, with his books both printed and manuscript (some of medieval date), had been transferred to the Cathedral library and escaped damage in 1670.[1]

White Kennett compiled a *Life of Mr. Somner*, prefixed to the Rev. James Brome's edition of Somner's *Roman Ports and Forts in Kent* (1693). Kennett was himself a distinguished antiquary whose father, Basil Kennett, had known Somner personally. White Kennett was at this time Vice-Principal of St. Edmund Hall, Oxford, where he had been an undergraduate, and dated his *Life* of Somner with great precision from '*Edm. Hall Oxon. Feb.* 15. 1693'. Edmund Gibson, from the adjacent Queen's College, supplied learned footnotes to the edition of *Roman Ports*.[2]

Kennett's *Life*, however, though written in stately Stuart prose, with much charm and enthusiasm for its subject, is of limited value, for it is commonly vague, discursive, inaccurate and lacking in such essential features of a biography as sound personal chronology. In fact it is less a *Life* than a manifesto for the value of contemporary antiquarian studies. Kennett may perhaps be excused for a faulty compilation, since he lived far from Kent, had few materials to work upon, and was out of immediate contact with those who harboured fleeting recollections of the great antiquary and who could have supplied personal memories and touches. James Brome can less be excused, for as incumbent of Newington near Folkestone he was living only a few miles from Somner's widow and children. Brome (who enjoyed a name as a travel writer) had wished the task of writing a memoir on to Kennett upon the excuse of a 'retir'd life, and want of access to books', yet he was no more than a ride from the Cathedral library at Canterbury.

Kennett is vague about Somner's origins, and commends him for not advertising them. The father proves to be another William Somner (son of David Somner), Registrar of the Canterbury Consistory Court, baptized at Boxley near Maidstone in 1572 and brought up not far away at Debtling. He reached Canterbury when about nineteen around the year 1591 and was apprenticed to lawyers in the Consistory Court, then conducted beneath the north-west tower in the Cathedral nave.[3] He had left his heart behind him, for in October 1594 he went to Maidstone and on 22nd of the month married the twenty-year old Anne Winston, then of that town, who had been born at Linstead, near Faversham. William Somner the antiquary, her son, owned a medieval glossary once in the hands of Giles Winston, an objectionable Canterbury attorney, so perhaps there is a family connection with him.[4]

In the absence of much personal information about the mother of William Somner, we may proffer what we do know, and observe that she was, like many ladies of the day, unlettered and unable to sign her own name.[5] She was near neighbour of and acquainted with Mrs Susan Fludd, the mother-in-law to Izaak Walton, and it is possible that William Somner met the author of the *Compleat Angler*. Walton liked to cultivate clerico-legal circles, and for his *Life of Richard Hooker* obtained a copy of Hooker's will 'attested under the hand of William Somner, the Archbishop's Registrar for the Province [sic] of Canterbury'.[6] Walton probably used the copy of Hooker's will issued in 1600 for probate purposes by Somner senior. Both Izaak Walton the angler, and William Somner the antiquary were in accord over the excellence of Fordwich trout, remarking respectively that they are 'accounted rare meat', and that they 'beare away the bell'. Walton was intimate with Meric Casaubon, Prebendary of Canterbury, the antiquary's friend and patron.[7]

In a court case of 1622, the elder William Somner gave evidence and provided additional news of his movements. Entries of baptisms (underlined by the evidence) show that the young couple started married life in St. Margaret's parish in Canterbury. Their child George Somner was christened in that church on 17 February 1597, while a William Somner followed on 5 November 1598.[8] The father, advancing in his career, was admitted Proctor in the Consistory Court on 7 June 1597,[9] and about then moved into St. Alphage parish, dwelling in the building with the sign of the 'Sun', the wooden structure still standing on the Sun Yard in Sun Street.[10] It seems once to have been known as the 'Splayed Eagle', and as such would have been the boyhood home of John Lyly, author of *Euphues*. Baptisms appear in the St. Alphage Register, of Henry Somner (1600), Mary (1603) and of John (1605).

After a sojourn of about five years, the Somner family returned to St. Margaret's parish, clearly moving into the large house with an overhang, today with a classicized front, numbered 5 Castle Street. At that time the house bore a sign, like the previous residence, namely the 'Crown'.[11] The house has a singular feature for it spans the three Canterbury parishes of St. Margaret, St. Mildred and St. Mary de Castro. Here was born another William on 30 March (according to family tradition), in the year 1606. Probably he was baptized at St. Margaret's, but in the absence of the parish register or of the Bishop's transcripts for that particular year, we are uncertain. The baptism is at any rate not noticed in any other of the central parishes. A sister, Mabel, was born in 1615 and baptized at St. Mildred's, Canterbury.

There can be no question but that the child William, born in 1606, is the antiquary. Kennett debates the point and the *Dictionary of National Biography* settles for the earlier date in 1598, but the child baptized then must have died, while the family perpetuated the Christian name. William Somner (the younger) himself resolves the question, for during a court case in November 1663 he said that he was born in Canterbury, had lived there *ab incunabulis*, and was then 56 years of age, which points to the later date of 1606 but suggests that the famous historian had forgotten precisely how old he was, and was a year out.[12]

The young Somner grew up in an atmosphere of ecclesiastical law as suitors or clients came and went, for the 'Crown' was not only his father's office, but the centre of much diocesan business. Somner, senior, (as disclosed in his own Consistory Court records) was called upon to write wills, and occasionally agitated relatives induced him to ride far out into the countryside to take down a testament at a bedside.

William Somner, the younger, probably first attended school at one of the numerous small private establishments of which only a bare trace remains in local archives. He went on to the King's School, where his headmaster was the redoubtable John Ludd, with his famous boast of 37 Masters of Arts of his own bringing up. But Somner's stay at the school can hardly have extended much beyond the age of thirteen or so, when he was taken away and apprenticed to his father's occupation.[13] The transition was easy, for he worked at home. The court archives were kept in the house, useful not only for reference to cases, but as sources of precedent, and in due time as a mine of information to the growing antiquary about medieval Canterbury, for the earliest Consistory register went back to the year 1396. Somner's interest in antiquity must indeed have fermented at an early age. Clearly the *Antiquities* published in 1640, when he was 34, written not in learned leisure but in the spare time of a busy professional life, can hardly have taken less than twenty years to compile.

In his career as an ecclesiastical lawyer the grade to be aimed at was that of Notary Public. There seems to be no record of his admission to the grade available, but on 3 April 1623, when he was just seventeen years of age, William Somner, junior, gave evidence in a case styling himself *Notarius Publicus*.[14]

He would henceforth be much in demand, representing people in the church courts, in a period when those institutions interfered to a now unbelievable degree in private lives. For instance, Sir James Hales of Reculver, a sworn officer of His Majesty's Privy Chamber, no less, early in 1626 sought the services of the Notary Somner, not yet twenty, to extricate himself and his lady from a charge of non-attendance at church.[15] A Notary's word was as good as that of two ordinary witnesses. Somner could now draw up Notarial Instruments, that class of solemn legal document, adorned in great days during the Middle Ages with complex individual notarial signs. Such a sign, of William Somner, senior, is reproduced in this volume with attestation written out in the hand of his son, William, the antiquary.[16]

Several men connected with Canterbury influenced Somner's development as a scholar. These included William Laud, Archbishop of Canterbury, whose patronage of learning was marred by his tactless and overbearing rule, contributing so much to political troubles of the time. One of Laud's more ill-advised projects was an effort to impose conformity with the Church of England upon the French and Walloon Protestant refugees, of whom there was a very large community at Canterbury, worshipping in the Cathedral crypt. They were sober, disciplined and industrious, keeping their own poor and also providing employment for many native English. Few were anxious to see them disturbed but Laud could not keep his fingers off them. A commission was instituted to deal with them, including somewhat unenthusiastic members like Dean John Bargrave and Meric Casaubon B.D. (and later D.D.), the classical scholar, Prebendary of Canterbury (see below). The commissioners, among whom was Sir Nathaniel Brent, the Commissary, met delegates from the refugee churches in the Somners' own house in Castle Street, on 19 December 1634.[17] The Archbishop had and has but few admirers. However he stirred a devotion in the heart of William Somner, who, when he came to publish his *Antiquities*, dedicated it in a fulsome address to Laud. But Laud deserved and still deserves adulation from scholars, for today they benefit from his great benefactions in manuscripts reposing in libraries like the Bodleian. William Somner, deeply learned in the history of the diocese, was of value to the Archbishop in resolving questions relating to benefices.[18]

Another influence upon Somner was Prebendary Meric Casaubon, son to the immensely learned Isaac, the refugee from France living in Geneva, enticed to this country by James I. Meric produced theological works and editions of the classics. He dwelt, the scholarly ornament of the Cathedral Chapter, in a house flanking the Mint Yard, where William Somner was certainly a visitor. It was Casaubon who directed Somner's footsteps towards a study of Anglo-Saxon. Yet another inspirer of studies (according to Somner's *Preface*) was Thomas Denne, Esquire, who may be identified with the Counsellor-at-Law (and later Recorder) to the Canterbury Corporation, a member of the distinguished Kentish legal family.[19]

William Somner developed enthusiasm for at least one field-sport. His passion for archery made him overstep bounds of prudence, though his publisher indulged him. He went off at a tangent in the *Antiquities* on the subject and in the Appendix reprinted in six sides of print *An Apologie for Archery* taken from Bingham's *Notes on Aelians Tacticks*.[20]

No doubt Somner lived at home in Castle Street all these years. He was 28 before he married, late for the age. On 12 June 1634 he espoused Elizabeth Thurgar of the Archbishop's Palace precinct, a member of a Cambridgeshire family.[21] Two children of the union have been traced, Elizabeth Somner who was unmarried at the date of her father's death in 1669, and Ann who married Richard Pising, a goldsmith—an unsatisfactory son-in-law, with erratic movements, if anything can be read into the language used of him in William Somner's will.

The next landmark in Somner's career was admission on 20 March 1638 as Proctor of the Consistory Court. His father had been admitted at 25, but the younger man was over thirty before promotion. Present on the occasion in court was Sir Nathaniel Brent, the Commissary, with William Somner, senior, as Registrar. William Somner, junior, appeared, flourishing a mandate from Archbishop Laud, enjoining his admission. The Commissary duly complied, but at once a question of precedence arose with Leonard Browne, N.P., admitted Proctor at the last court day. It was agreed by Browne that Somner might occupy a place to his right, whereupon Somner expressed his gratitude. All this question of protocol is now of course lost upon us, but clearly it must have meant a lot to the parties concerned.[22]

Within this year the father died. He had prepared his will on 11 July 1637. Various legacies were made to the children and to servants. A surprising bequest for a supposedly pacific official was of armour, assigned to George. The principal legacy, the house in Castle Street, devolved upon George Somner, as the eldest surviving son. He had evidently no wish to live in it, and sold it to William, who had spent much if not all of his life there, and was probably dwelling in the building with his young wife. Probate was effected on 21 September 1638 in the presence of William Somner, N.P., junior, acting in his official capacity.[23]

The office of Registrar was open to purchase. Somner could not succeed his own father, since two bidders had already obtained reversion to act jointly. It must have been galling when on 27 February 1639 Benjamin Holford, N.P., and Richard Cobb, N.P., attired in official robes, were established as joint-Registrars in the court place in the Cathedral nave, and even more galling when the couple arrived in Castle Street to take over the accumulated archives of the court. They turned everyone out of the depository even including William Somner himself. Eventually he was admitted and required to make an official record of proceedings.[24]

It seems very likely, however, that Holford and Cobb left the records and the office where they were, and where they had been for 30 or 40 years, in which case things went on very much as before. It seems that Somner was living in the house in the years after 1639, for in 1669, when writing the pamphlet *Chartham News*, he remarked that his next neighbour in Castle Street, 'within these thirty years' had found Roman remains when sinking a cellar.

At this time Somner must have been hard at work completing the *Antiquities*, with

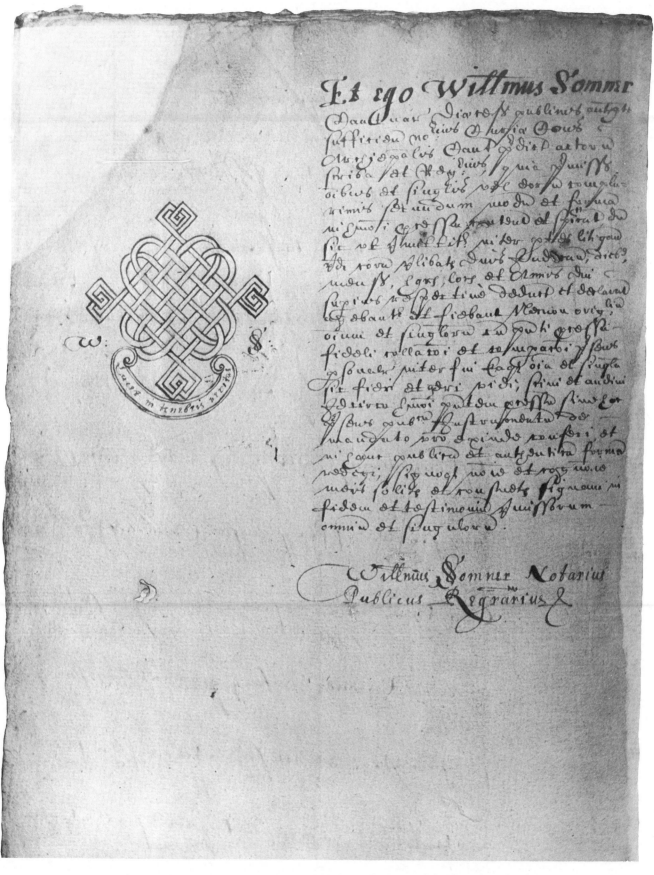

Notarial sign of William Somner, senior, Notary Public and Registrar of the Canterbury Consistory Court, with attestation written out in the hand of his son and assistant, William Somner, junior, Notary Public, the antiquary

proof-correcting and journeys to London to see the publisher-printers. The work was finally brought out in 1640, and in the same year Somner, the fierce local patriot, had the gratifying experience of being admitted as a Freeman of Canterbury by gift.[25] He had actually made application, and would have expected to pay fees, but as the minute shows, he was accorded the Freedom on the grounds that he was now Deputy Registrar to the Archbishop (a fact not noticed in the records of the Consistory Court). Another minute, under date 14 April 1640, discloses that at the City Council meeting on that day, William Somner, Deputy Registrar to the Archbishop, presented to the city his book *The Antiquities of Canterbury*.

Little need be said of the *Antiquities* as the volume speaks eloquently for itself and its author. After the adulatory address to Archbishop Laud, Somner offers his own Preface, in the form of a charming apologia for the study of history in general, and of local history in particular. The author's passionate affection for his native city stands out in every line. He tells with tremendous relish the story of Cicero's visit to Syracuse, where he asked after the tomb of their famous resident, Archimedes. To Cicero's contempt this was only discovered after clearance of vegetation in the overgrown local cemetery, 'as if a man should scoffingly object to us here of Canterbury', that the graves of local heroes could not be identified. Canterbury Cathedral is more splendid than almost any other (Somner clearly mentally omits 'almost') in the realm, and likewise is richer in the 'unvaluable' (i.e. of non-bullion value) archives to go with the buildings.

The inspiration of the volume is obviously Stowe's *London*, in turn inspired by Lambard's *Kent*. Indeed some of the internal order is the same, for Somner follows the other topographer's subject matter, as in *antiquity, city walls*, to the *city ditch and defences*. Somner's chapters on *wards, parish churches, ecclesiastical government*, and *temporal government*, are clearly modelled on those in the London volume.

The *Antiquities* appeared at a most unhappy moment, on the eve of the Civil War. Copies remained unsold at the Restoration in 1660, and to clear the stock it was put out with a new title-page 'pasted over the old' (see Battely's Preface, below). By the end of the century there was call for a new edition. There were now many more readers than before the wars, but less ponderously learned, and Somner's heavy ballast of Latin documents was now not so welcome. Nicholas Battely, Vicar of the nearby Bekesbourne, decided to bring out a new edition, catering for the public of the time. He transferred the Latin evidences to the appendix for the greater part (often with translations), but left some of Somner's learned mannerisms still standing in the text. In effect Battely's performance is a work of popularization. His explanation of his methods should be studied in his Preface below. To Somner brought up to date, Battely added his own *Cantuaria Sacra* not reproduced here. As its title indicates, it is mainly concerned with the ecclesiastical side of local history.

During the Civil War Canterbury suffered grievously. The Cathedral underwent a desecration in August 1642 effected by Colonel Sandys and his ruffianly troopers.[26] What William Somner suffered during the episode hardly bears contemplation but a more systematic attack was to follow the next year. Acting on authority of Parliament, commissioners 'for abolishing monuments of idolatry', numbering the Mayor and the Recorder with the local puritan fanatic, the Rev. Richard Culmer, called Blue Dick from his gown with its unclerical colour, entered the building, hot upon mischief. The middle-aged vandals did not know where to start, and in an excess of refined cruelty, as the psychopathic Culmer gleefully records, they used a copy of Somner's recently published *Antiquities of Canterbury* to find their way around.[27]

'The book was a card and a compass to sail by in that Cathedral ocean of images. By it many a popish picture was discovered and demolished.'

One wonders if the Mayor had actually brought along the copy presented with glowing pride to the Corporation three years before. The terrible story of destruction is well-known, largely through Culmer's own account, *Cathedrall Newes from Canterbury*, by which the author damned himself to perpetual infamy. One medieval masterpiece after another was annihilated by the barbarians.[28] Somner must have been distraught.

A principal casualty in the Cathedral was the new font, given in 1639 by Dr. John Warner, Bishop of Rochester. Kennett says that the materials were carried off by the rabble, that Somner retrieved the fragments and was rewarded by his daughter being the first to be baptized when the font was re-established in 1660. But there are divergent accounts and the chronology seems unsatisfactory.[29] Kennett also says that at this time Somner concealed the Cathedral archives, depositing some in unsuspected hands, keeping some in his own custody, and redeeming some from needy soldiers, which suggests that certain were seized during the dragonnade of August 1642.

As far as we know Somner played no part in the disturbances which occurred in Canterbury in 1647 and which developed in the following year into a general royalist outbreak. The origin of the affair was a parliamentary decree that Christmas should not be celebrated. At Canterbury defiant shopkeepers kept closed, while the puritan Mayor went up and down trying to make them open up. A riot ensued and for a few days disorder reigned. The next May parliamentary judges came down to conduct the Assizes at Canterbury and to deal with the prisoners taken in the Christmas affray. These prisoners numbered distinguished local residents like the lawyers Sir William Man and Francis Lovelace, with Alderman Avery Sabine, the woollen-draper, who had tried to keep the peace. There were two sessions, one at the Guildhall for the City, and another at the Castle for the county. The bloodthirsty Justice Wilde, (who had only just hanged, drawn and quartered a royalist in the Isle of Wight) gave vent to an intemperate attack upon the prisoners, but was quietened down by his colleague, Justice Cresheld. The Grand Jury threw out the indictment. At once real rebellion flamed. Parliament sent troops into Kent under General Fairfax, who defeated the royalists in a furious battle at Maidstone on 1 June 1648. Canterbury now remained the centre of revolt. Three columns approached, Fairfax from the west, with Colonel Rich and Colonel Hewson, whose regiment had been badly mauled at Maidstone, coming from the south. With only 1,300 men to defend the long perimeter ($1\frac{1}{2}$ mile round the walls), surrender was inevitable. Terms, not unreasonable, were agreed with Fairfax at Faversham on 9 June 1648, and the next day the enemy marched into Canterbury under General Ireton. The city gates were pulled off their hinges and burnt, while a stretch of wall was overturned. Captured arms from the county to the number of 3,000 were laid out in the Cathedral, while 300 horses were led in to be stabled there.[30]

The Somner family suffered grievous loss in the rising. George Somner, the elder brother, no doubt attired in some at least of the armour left him by his father, the Registrar, charged at the head of a royalist detachment in Olantigh Lane, close to Wye, and was killed in action.[31] The rebellion was finally subdued with bloody retribution across the Thames at Colchester. William Somner's name is not found among those who turned out on behalf of the King. Yet, as Kennett says, while his 'profession and genius had less adapted him for arms . . . he was no less zealous to assert the rights of the Crown, and the Laws of the land, by all the means which his capacity could use'. He acted in his own way with great courage, setting to work upon an anonymous poem (where it must be confessed his passion outdistanced his Muse), entitled *The In-securitie of Princes, considered in an occasional meditation upon the Kings Late Suffering and Death*, produced in quarto by a printer who does not identify himself. Hardly had the head of Charles fallen, when the book *Eikon Basilike* went into circulation, bringing a revulsion against the judicial murder. Somner went to work again with more verses, under the heading *The Frontispiece of the Kings Book Opened*, again anonymous but anonymity in the small world of printers was easy enough to pierce. However, no trace of reprisals is found.

It may be asked, in the face of a breakdown in his professional world, what William Somner lived upon in these years. The disciplinary side of the church courts had gone, while there was no more litigation for him to handle over tithes, matrimony or defamation, where he had once drawn fees. However, the local courts in their probate aspect were still functioning in the late 1640s so some income may have been available from professional charges. But there is a suggestion of collapse thereafter, when wills were no longer copied into registers.[32]

A weary decade dragged by with terrors for antiquarians, for the horrors of destruction accompanying the dissolution of the monasteries in the 1530s were almost re-enacted. At one stage a motion was actually brought for the demolition of fifteen great cathedrals. First upon the list was that of Canterbury yet some vestige of commonsense prevailed and no action was taken. But William Somner had something else to occupy his mind. If barbarism was abroad, so was a surge of antiquarian interest. The Kentish gentleman, Sir Roger Twysden, gave up warfare and devoted himself to his great collection of ancient historians, still valuable today and not superseded, the *Scriptores X*, brought out in 1652. The distinguished Canterbury antiquary, Somner, could hardly be left out of the project, and contributed his much-lauded word-list of obsolete terms, in some 80 folio pages headed

'Glossarium: in quo obscuriora quæque vocabula . . . copiosè explicantur . . . *Gulielmo Somnero* Cantuariensi, Auctore.'

A vaster project was under way, namely *Monasticon Anglicanum*. Roger Dodsworth has accumulated enormous transcripts relating to northern monasteries. William Dugdale, the Herald, was collecting materials elsewhere in the realm. Again Somner could not be left out. At the appeal of the compilers, he sent up the charters of Christ Church, Canterbury and of St. Augustine's Abbey, 'with the ichnography of the Cathedral, the draught of the monastery and other sculptures'. He 'furnisht them with the original charter of King Stephen to the abbey of Faversham, then in his hands . . . and then accepted the office imposed upon him, of bearing a peculiar part of the burden, by translating all the Saxon originals, and all the English transcripts from the itinerary of Leland . . . into plain and proper Latin'. Drawings sent up by Somner were prepared by Thomas Johnson, a member of the Canterbury family of artists living for many years in St. George's parish. Somner told Dugdale that one drawing would cost ten shillings. Wenceslaus Hollar himself engraved some of the plates.[33]

The first volume of the enormous enterprise appeared in 1655. There seems to have been some feeling abroad that Somner's contribution to *Monasticon I* was in fact more substantial than it was. Six Kentish or Canterbury poets got to work and produced an amusing set of verses belauding the great tome. The verses were printed in sheets, a copy of which is inserted (as Kennett says) into the magnificent large-paper copy of *Monasticon I*, with its gilt vellum covers, its gleaming and goffered fore-edges, still in the Chapter library. The versifiers salute Somner as joint-compiler with Dodsworth and Dugdale. Richard Fogge Esq. of Dane court unambiguously heads his Latin effort *In Monasticon . . . a Rogero Dodswortho, Gulielmo Dugdalio, & Gulielmo Somner . . . editum*. Dr. Frederick Primrose, the Canterbury physician, starts off in similar terms, bringing the three names together, as does John Boys of Hode. Joshua Childrey, the Faversham schoolmaster, provides a charming imitation of Chaucer, addressed 'To the right ylered Clerks, Dan *William Sompner* & c. on her makelesse werke, hight *Monasticon*'. Neither in the heading, nor in more than 60 lines of verse do Dugdale and Dodsworth even get a mention, *proprio nomine*.

The loss of William Somner's letters, his 'in' file, at the Audit House fire of 1670 becomes even more harrowing when his relationships to the great antiquaries of the day are reviewed. Sometimes letters from Somner can be found addressed to such scholars. Dugdale sent him a copy of his *History of Embanking and Draining* as a token of help given. On 11 April 1662 the Canterbury antiquary acknowledged the work, promising to promote the sale, 'but it is (you know) a dull and dead time'.[34] The letter concludes with best wishes to be sent on to a whole galaxy of mutual antiquarian friends, Mr. Goddard, Captain Ashmole, Sir John Marsham, 'and the rest of my noble friends and benefactors, especially my patron Mr. Spelman'.

Somner was known to the great international scholar Francis Junius who wrote to Dugdale from the Hague in January 1656 sending his service to John Rushworth (compiler of the *Historical Collections*) and to Mr. Somner, 'with other lovers of Antiquities'.[35]

White Kennett gives a long list of scholar-gentry, local and nation-wide, whose regard was gained by Somner. Sir Roger Twysden with whom Somner collaborated in the *Scriptores X* 'exchanged intimate visits'. Kennett provides a noble roll-call of these Kentish country gentlemen 'who had affection to virtue and good letters', who contracted relations with Somner and, if the language may so be interpreted, supported him or his learned projects.[36]

A well-defined picture emerges of William Somner as a generous scholar anxious to share his enthusiasms with others, whether with a mature researcher such as Dugdale or a more youthful enthusiast like Anthony à Wood, who wrote from Oxford on 21 February 1662 to Somner, respectfully introducing himself as a young antiquary, asking for transcripts relating to the extinct Canterbury College. Despite his correspondent's dubious (and to Somner disadvantageous) postal arrangements, Somner had despatched from Canterbury by 21 March all that was needed by his enquirer.[37]

The growing interest in English antiquities had drawn attention to one glaring want in the *apparatus criticus* of the day, namely an effective dictionary of Anglo-Saxon. Studies in the tongue had long been in progress, indeed since the days of Elizabeth I, at the hands of men like William Lambard. The general public had access to sermons of Bishop Wulfstan printed in handsome Old English type by John Day, in Foxe's *Martyrs*. Somner had long been interested in the language and certainly it engaged him through his pre-occupation in the early history of Canterbury. Prebendary Meric Casaubon relates in a delightful passage in his *De Quatuor Linguis* how he came to study Anglo-Saxon charters.[38] On his appointment to his stall at Canterbury he started looking at the muniments, and with awe discovered the ancient documents in the Cathedral treasury. At this juncture he came into contact with William Somner, who was making a start in the language. Casaubon claims to have urged upon Somner the compilation of a dictionary. Already by 1653 the question of special types for this dictionary was under discussion.[39] Sir Henry Marsham in his *Propylaeum* to the *Monasticon* (1655) remarks that Somner was preparing his Saxon-Latin dictionary for the press.

Wealthy collectors gave admission to their hoards. Somner was accorded admission to the library of Sir Simonds D'Ewes, and worked there upon the great Anglo-Saxon verse *Genesis* (now B.L. MS. Junius XI).[40] Sir Thomas Cotton entertained him in his house at Westminster for some months 'to collect and digest his Saxon Dictionary', when Somner gained access to the Saxon *Orosius* (now Tiberius B. 1. 1), and other treasures of that collection.[41]

Sir Henry Spelman, a leader among the antiquaries and a man of means, took a practical step and established a readership in the tongue based upon 'a sufficient yearly stipend, with presentation to the benefice of Middleton, nigh *Lin Regis*'. The first Reader was the Cambridge linguist, Abraham Wheelock, who justified his appointment by producing a version of Bede and other like works. He made promise to work up a dictionary, but had not done much by the time of his death in 1653. Roger Spelman, grandson to the founder, on whom the patronage had devolved, planned to assign the readership to the Rev. Samuel Foster, 'a learned and worthy divine'. Archbishop James Usher, however, urged the allocation to William Somner, and Spelman deferred to the judgment of the great ecclesiastical historian, though Somner, with characteristic delicacy refused to accept without approval from Foster, who contented himself with the office of incumbent of Middleton.[42]

The financial provision must have been very welcome indeed to Somner at a low point in his career, with income from much of his normal professional activities in suspense. It can hardly be claimed that the readership supported him while at work on the *Dictionary* since it came to him near the end of his labours, close upon publication, but it must have re-imbursed him. The great work of scholarship appeared in two volumes in 1659 from the Oxford Press, with the title *Dictionarium Saxonico-Latino-Anglicum*.[43] Ælfric's Saxon Grammar was published under the same covers. A group of friends, including again Joshua Childrey and John Boys of Hode, got together and produced a clutch of learned and humorous verses celebrating publication of the *Dictionary*, parallel to those produced to mark publication of *Monasticon*. As in the case of that work, a set of the verses may be found inserted into the Cathedral library copy of the *Dictionarium*.

The *Dictionary* was an extraordinary achievement, an instance of scholarship carried out into wide and obscure fields with no substantial predecessors to provide a foundation, though Somner's meagre materials, as Kennett says 'might have exercised a Critic, sooner than instructed a Novice'. Not only is it a pioneer effort, but it reached a singular degree of perfection at a first effort. Says Kennett:[44]

'certainly, if we look back on the first attempts of this kind, in all the ancient and modern tongues, we shall find no one *Nomenclature*, in it's pure beginning so copious, and so exact, as this of Mr. *Somner*.'

No dictionary can ever be complete. Fresh materials came Somner's way, naturally through publicity provided by his own work. The bulk swelled continuously, and additional words and corrections were inserted into an extra-leaved copy (still to be seen at Canterbury). However, a new edition was not brought out in his lifetime.

It is a source of pride to Kentish antiquarians that the shire boasted of its own system of tenure, namely Gavelkind. Its chief feature was the equal partition of ground between heirs, and its attractions were less apparent to estate owners than to antiquaries. Many of the former had their lands disgavelled by Act of Parliament, as shown by lists included in William Lambard's *Perambulation of Kent*. The custom of Gavelkind remained to torment lawyers and owners until 1926. Clearly there was a need for an exposition of the custom, and Somner, both as a good antiquary and a good patriot, set about supplying the want. He had completed the work by 1647, but it was not until 1660 that it saw the light as *A Treatise of Gavelkind*. A second edition was called for in 1726 and was produced by the faithful White Kennett.

At some moment in the 1650s William Somner's troubles were sharpened by the loss of his wife, Elizabeth, with whom he had, as White Kennett says, 'liv'd in love and peace about thirty [read twenty?] years'. Parish registers were then being kept only intermittently, and her entry of burial seems not to have survived.[45]

Politically the days were dark, but the military government as imposed by Cromwell was too alien to Englishmen to last. William Somner, who seems to have remained quiescent in earlier crises (apart from his publication of anonymous poetry), found a new boldness. With other local men he promoted a petition at Canterbury for a free Parliament. The unrepresentative body calling itself by that name, however, took immediate action and bundled him and fellow-petitioners into the castles of Dover and Deal. By February 1660 William Somner 'the proctor', in company with such an old offender as Sir William Man, with Mr. Masters from St. Paul's parish, and with 'old Mr. Boyce' (John Boys, the versifier?) is listed as a prisoner within the chilly battlements of Deal.[46]

On 25 May, however, Charles II arrived at Dover to take possession of his kingdom, and in pious language thanked the Mayor of the town for the gift of a Bible. At Canterbury he was greeted in the suburbs by the Aldermen and City Councillors, probably in the region of Oaten Hill or Dover Street. A golden cup, containing gold pieces, worth £250 was presented to the Monarch, together with yet another Bible, richly bound. There was still a further present, again another book. William Somner, choking with royalist fervour, offered to the King 'on the bended knees of his body' a handsome large-paper copy of the *Antiquities of Canterbury* of 1640. What Charles said about this book or whether he regaled himself with it stands unrecorded, but at any rate the volume was taken into the royal collection, bound in blue morocco and stamped with the king's arms. Somehow, though printing was not carried out nearer than London, Somner had managed to get a special extra dedicatory leaf printed for insertion, with a declaration of loyalty accompanying the humble offer of the book.[47] The actual copy, it should be noted, still survives, and reposes today in the Henry Huntington Library in California.

William Somner settled down at once to the welcome task of establishing the *status quo ante bellum*. This involved re-activating the church courts. On 15 July 1660 the old Consistory Court register, with its last entry dated 1 June 1643, was fished out, and business re-started with never a glance at the seventeen-year gap.[48] The returned Dean and Chapter made William Somner their Auditor or Agent, and he and his employers set about recovering lost income with a will that made them extremely unpopular. Yet there seems to be some suggestion that Somner was actually involved in collection of Cathedral rents at Ladyday 1660. Had he compromised and worked in effect for Parliament which had expropriated the Chapter's estates?[49]

Somner must have been excited and happy at this stage. For the time being there was no Archbishop, so the administration of spiritualities devolved upon the Chapter *sede vacante*. The joint Registrars Holford and Cobb seem to have faded from the scene. On 14 July 1660 the Chapter appointed as Registrar William Somner who now found himself exercising his father's old office. But the appointment was only temporary, and when Archbishop Juxon was enthroned he too had a candidate, George Juxon, clearly a kinsman. However, this man and Somner were made joint-Registrars from 6 October 1660.[50]

Somner now enjoyed two offices satisfying to his tastes. White Kennett provides him with another, that is '*Keeper* of the *Archives*' of Canterbury Cathedral.[51] The precise title seems not to have existed at that date, but Somner would have performed such a function *ex officio* from 1660, and his long-standing love of the muniments meant that for long years before then he had kept a tutelary eye upon them.

The appointment as Auditor it seems carried with it the right to a house in the Precincts. In November 1661 Somner was still being paid at the rate of £12 per annum by the Chapter in lieu of a house. The map of the waterworks prepared in 1669 shows that the house was sited in what had been the southern aisle of the ancient monastic Infirmary, the front of the building framed in giant 12th-century arches. It may have suited Somner's antiquarian tastes but it was deep in the shadow of the great church, and perpetually deprived of sunlight.[52]

Meanwhile William Somner had remarried, on 1 December 1659. The new wife, Barbara Browne, was widow to Edward Browne, Master of the King's School, and daughter to John Dawson, 'a great sufferer in the long rebellion' as Kennett calls him.[53] The new Mrs. Somner seems to have been much younger than her husband. Baptisms appear in the Cathedral register: Barbara, daughter of Mr. William Somner, was baptized on 11 September 1660. It is this infant, who it is claimed, was the first baptized at the restored font. The next child was William Somner, baptized on 3 November 1661; next was Francis, baptized on 16 August 1663. He died an infant, being buried 27 May 1664. The last child was John Somner, baptized on 1 July 1666, when his father was just 60. Kennett says (1693) that Barbara the daughter died unmarried. William went to Merton College, Oxford, and became Vicar of Lyminge in Kent. John Somner practised surgery in the area, and dying in 1695 when only 29, was buried beneath a handsome ledger stone in the chancel at Elham, bearing the Somner arms (see below), and declaring him to have been 'Son of the Learned Mr. William Somner of Canterbury'.[54]

William Somner seems to have lived on terms of friendship with his brother John, who had followed the trade of a tailor, with a business next to Christ Church Gate, where he appears to have prospered. John Somner had been made a city Freeman in 1658, but had refused office as a City Councillor during the Interregnum, and was apparently deprived of his freedom. He had been re-elected a Freeman of Canterbury after the Restoration (22 January, 1661) for his part in persuading Archbishop Juxon to give new doors for the city gates to replace those burnt by the parliamentary troops in 1648. The Archbishop also provided handsome new doors (still surviving) for Christ Church Gate to succeed those destroyed in the troubles.

John, like William, was a good friend of the Cathedral. He donated works of Richard Hooker, Lancelot Andrews, and others, as well as the folio edition of Richard Burton's *Anatomy of Melancholy*, to the new Cathedral library built by Juxon to replace the ancient library destroyed in the war. John also acted as an on-the-spot supervisor of work in progress on the library building.[55]

William had achieved eminence as an author, John was quite prosperous, and it occurred about this time to the brothers that they should seek the distinction of gentility and acquire a coat of arms. They applied to Sir Percy Bysshe, Clarenceux Herald (an old antiquarian contact of William's, probably on the heraldic visitation in Kent), and on 25 August 1663 were granted the handsome coat *Ermine, two chevronels or.* John, though the elder, bore his coat with a crescent for difference.[56]

Friendly feelings between John Somner and the Canterbury Corporation were soon marred. He had conceived the generous notion of building, at a cost of over £400, a market house for the city. This was to be on the site of the ancient High Cross destroyed by fanatics during the Commonwealth, and was to have an open lower storey, a large upstairs room for public meetings and assemblies of the city trade-companies, with a loft for grain for the poor against time of dearth. The Somners, for William was concerned too, made a modest request of some use of the premises during their lifetimes. But mean people intervened and the brothers' generosity was thrown back in their faces, though not before the Market House was actually completed.[57] The building served the city well, for it acted on the ground floor as a butter market (and as such has given a fresh name to the little square previously called Bullstake), and upstairs as the local theatre until its replacement by another market house in 1790. The Somner family seems to have claimed some rights in the structure as late as 1734.[58]

Kennett paints a picture of William Somner in his latter days as a local patriarchal figure, the doyen of Kentish antiquaries. He shows him appearing at the School, selecting likely lads as King's Scholars, and noting those to be sent on to the universities. In this period, too, he was appointed as Master of St. John's Hospital, outside the Northgate of Canterbury, and may be found assiduously defending its interests (with those of Harbledown Hospital) in letters to Miles Smith, Archbishop Sheldon's secretary.[59]

Here we may well repeat the delightful apostrophe set in Kennett's Stuart prose:[60]

'Mr. *Somner* . . . prosecuted the duties of his office with prudence and integrity. *An office* (as he calls it) *laudable, and enough honourable.* And when he had *any hours reliev'd from the business of his calling,* those he devoted to his beloved search into the mysteries of time: to which by the nature of his profession, he seemed the more determined; he himself observing, *that to the studie of Antiquities his particular calling did in some manner lead him.* He lov'd much, and much frequented the *Cathedral* Service; where after his devotions were paid, he had a new zeal for the honour of the *House,* walking often in the *Nave,* and in the more recluse parts, not in that idle and inadvertent posture, nor with that common and trivial discourse, with which those *open Temples* are vulgarly profan'd: but with a curious and observant eye, to distinguish the age of the buildings, to sift the ashes of the dead; and, in a word, to eternize the memory of things and Men. His visits within the City were to find out the Ancestors, rather than the present inhabitants; and to know the genealogie of houses, and walls, and dust. When he had leisure to refresh himself in the

Suburbs and the fields, it was not meerly for digestion, and for air; but to survey the *British bricks*, the *Roman ways*, the *Danish hills* and *works*, the *Saxon Monasteries* and the *Norman Churches*. At the digging up foundations, and other descents into the bowels of the earth, he came often to survey the Workmen; and to purchase from them the treasure of Coins, Medals, and other buried reliques, of which he informs us, *that many were found in almost all parts of the City, some of which came to his hands.* Whenever he relaxt his mind to any other recreation, it was to that of shooting with the long bow, which no doubt he lov'd as much for the antiquity, as for the health and pleasure of that manly sport.'

Though he would not be considered old today William Somner was mature indeed by contemporary standards. He was in fact near his end, but went on working and writing to the last. He attended court as Registrar on 17 March 1669, but thereafter failed to make appearance. By now he was terminally ill. At this time he told his wife that in all his life he had never been let blood nor taken physic.[61] However, they called in the local doctor, John Bale, at the very end.

Late in his life William Somner was working upon an acute essay called *Chartham News*. John his brother had acquired some ground at Chartham on the Stour a few miles above Canterbury, where workmen digging a well encountered certain strange and monstrous bones. Somner embarked upon a discussion, and here we have the spectacle of an acute mind grappling with preconceived notions derived from biblical chronology. How did the beast get to Chartham? What geographical changes had happened? Somner got a limner to make a drawing but it appears that only a view of the teeth is now available (as the engraving in *Chartham News*). Somner thought the animal must be an *equus fluvialis* or hippopotamus. The pamphlet was published in 1669 and reprinted by Battely with the *Antiquities* in 1703, and the engraving is reproduced below.

March 30 was William Somner's birthday. It is inconceivable that a man who had spent all his life writing wills, proving wills, and using them as historical evidence should not have made his own with all proper formality years before. Perhaps he changed his mind dramatically about legacies at the last moment. His own effective will was made on this day 30 March 1669, at the last moment, not in proper form but *nuncupative*, by word of mouth.

He gave to his eldest son William (now aged seven), the house in Castle Street, to pass to him after the death of Barbara Somner, the child's mother. He discloses that he has ground at Chartham, like his brother John. He gave to his daughter Elizabeth by his first marriage the sum of £250, and to her sister Ann, wife of Richard Pising, goldsmith, the sum of £100 due from one Mr. Vaughan, who was to succeed him in his Registrar's place, a valuable insight into traffic in offices in those days. Twenty shillings were to be given to Mr. Stockar, minister of St. Alphage. The residue (after payment of miscellaneous minor legacies) was to go to Barbara the wife and her children which he had by her. His brother John Somner was named as executor, and the verbal will was attested by him with John Bale M.D. and Leonard Browne, his colleague for endless years in the church courts, now an Alderman of Canterbury.[62]

Within the course of his birthday William Somner died, and was carried on 2 April to burial at his old parish church of St. Margaret, where he was laid to rest in the north aisle. The Chapter made what was both an attempt at a wise acquisition for their Library and a generous benefaction to the widow, in a payment of £100 which they gave her for William's papers, taken round the corner to the Audit House but with disastrous results as we know.[63] Barbara Somner did not long bemoan widowhood, for by licence dated 31 January 1671 she married the Rev. Henry Hannington, widower, vicar of Elham. He died in 1691.

For years no monument was erected above the remains of the great antiquary, a fact deplored by White Kennett in 1693:[64]

'I cannot but admire and lament, that such learned ashes should lye without a letter on them: that he who rais'd the memory of so many great names, should

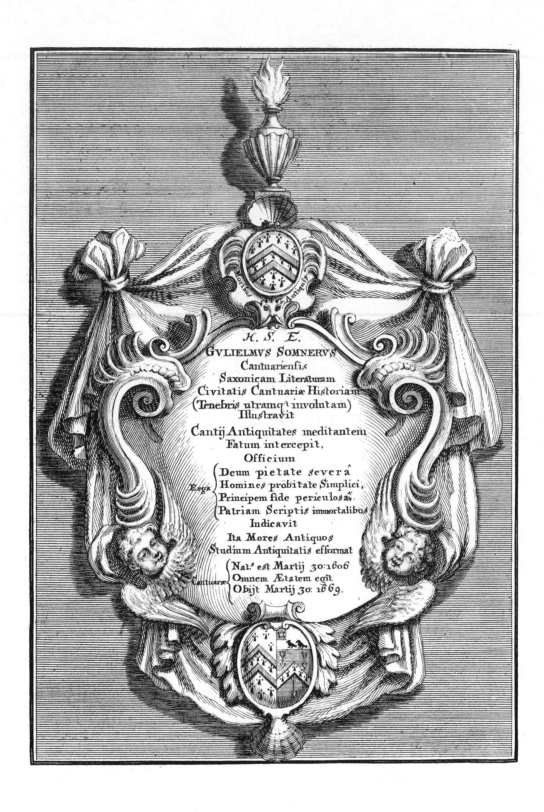

The author's memorial in St. Margaret's Church, Canterbury, from A Treatise of Gavelkind, *2nd ed., 1726*

himself sleep in a place forgotten: and after all his labours, to eternize the tombs and epitaphs of others, should have no such decent ceremony paid to his own dust. Sure the time will come, when some grateful monument shall be erected for him, either by someone of his family, whom providence shall enable to pay that duty: or by some one generous lover of Antiquities: or by that Capitular body, to whom he did such great service.'

Barbara Somner, now Hannington, soon took the hint, and at her own costs, in her widowhood, commissioned the handsome memorial still to be seen in St. Margaret's Church, 'in Memory of her beloved Husband'. There is no doubt where her affections lay. She had been married three times, but at the end demanded to be laid to rest, as she said, 'in the grave of William Somner my husband'.[65]

William Somner's *Anglo-Saxon Dictionary* of 1659 may have been regarded by his contemporaries as his *magnum opus*, but it was a foundation-work, has long since been superseded, and pride of place in Somner's writings today must go to his *Antiquities*.

Somner's book is certainly not only the earliest, but also the best and most scholarly in that age among historical accounts of an English provincial borough and of its great ecclesiastical monuments. White Kennett recites a list of testimonials, sharpened by some very harsh judgments on works in the same field. Richard Izaac's *Exeter* (1681), is nothing but 'a dry collection, full of mistakes'; John Davies's *Cathedral Church of Durham* (1672) is 'an ignorant and pitiful legend', to repeat but two of his censures. On the other hand Somner's *Canterbury* earned wholesale approbation from the scholarly world. Meric Casaubon called it 'a pious and laborious work, and highly useful, not only to those who desir'd to know the state of that once flourishing City, but to all that were curious in the ancient English history'. John Burton, the editor of the *Antonine Itinerary*, refers anyone wanting to know about Canterbury to 'courteous Mr. Somners description of it', Richard Kilburne, the surveyor of Kent, touches only briefly upon Canterbury, 'because Mr. William Somner had so elaborately, judiciously and fully wrote of the same, and there was left but little . . . which he had not there set down'. Thomas Philpot, 'who had reason to envy him', acknowledges in *Villare Cantianum* that 'Canterbury hath . . . exactly in all the parts and limbs of it been describ'd and survey'd by Mr. Somner', and does not want to compete with the latter's work, 'pencilled out in so large and exquisite a volume'.[66]

The *Antiquities* has had only one real imitator,—in Edward Hasted's section on Canterbury in his vast *History and Topographical Survey of the County of Kent*.[67] Apart from Hasted, Somner has a minor competitor in William Gostling, who produced his *Walk in and about the City of Canterbury*, (published in various editions from 1774 to 1825), but this lacks deep scholarship, and for its more solid elements draws upon William Somner. Perhaps the enormous wealth of Canterbury in terms of architecture, archaeological remains, manuscript books, archives and chronicles is enough to deter would-be writers of any general account of the city's history.[68]

The *Antiquities*, especially as revised and enlarged by Nicholas Battely in the edition of 1703 (made use of by Hasted and here reproduced), still stands as a unique contribution to the general history of Canterbury. It is a happiness of local historians that, however slight, their work is never entirely replaced and by the time another comes to rewrite their particular effort, the original has assumed an antiquarian value all of its own. Somner's *Antiquities* (at the other end of the scale) remains especially important not only in this way, as a register of so much that has been lost since his own days, but still as a fascinating piece of reading all in its own right, especially with the modest metamorphosis effected by Nicholas Battely.

INTRODUCTION

Nicholas Battely and his Kinsfolk: A Note[69]

The editor of Somner's *Antiquities* was but one of a learned family with a taste for antiquarian studies. Nicholas Battely had an elder brother, John, and a younger, Thomas. The three were sons to Nicholas Battely, an apothecary of Bury St. Edmunds, and each became an undergraduate of Trinity College, Cambridge. There was a sister Ann, aged 50 at her death in 1714 (according to her monument at Bekesbourne, Kent, where her brother Nicholas became incumbent).

The eldest, John Battely, was born in 1646. He matriculated in 1662, was B.A. by 1666 and M.A. by 1669, becoming a Fellow of his college. He took orders in 1675 and was appointed chaplain to Archbishop Sancroft, who collated him to the rectory of Adisham in Kent, south-east of Canterbury. At the same time John Battely became Chancellor of Brecknock, though his pluralism (in this case hardly reconcilable with a Kentish incumbency), gave him misgivings upon his deathbed. In 1688 he became Master of Eastbridge Hospital at Canterbury, where he is remembered as a wise administrator and as a good and generous benefactor. Likewise in 1688 he became Archdeacon of Canterbury and Prebendary of the Cathedral.

John Battely was an excellent Latinist, and on arrival in Kent threw himself into a study of local antiquities. He collected Roman coins and pottery, acquired particularly at Richborough and Reculver, the Saxon Shore forts. He wrote up his finds in an engaging and humorous tract, *Antiquitates Rutupinæ*, in the form of a colloquy between himself and other chaplains in Sancroft's service, likewise with antiquarian tastes, namely Henry Maurice and Henry Wharton. The tract 'generally admired for the elegance of the Latin'[70] was published posthumously in 1711 and republished by Oliver Battely, the writer's nephew and son to Nicholas, who under the same covers printed John Battely's *Antiquitates Sancti Edmundi Burgi* (1745). It was published in abridgment and translation in 1774, by the Rev. John Duncombe, who embodied collections relating to Eastbridge Hospital left by Nicholas Battely into his *Three Archiepiscopal Hospitals*.[71] John Battely was twice married but left no issue. He died 10 October, 1708, at the age of 61.

Nicholas Battely, brother to John, and editor of Somner's *Antiquities* was baptized at St. James, Bury St. Edmunds on 14 June 1648. He was admitted as Pensioner at Trinity College, Cambridge on 30 March 1665, and matriculated in Lent, 1667. He was B.A. within the year 1668-9, and M.A. in 1672 as from Peterhouse, whither he had removed himself. He was Fellow of that college from 1670 to 1704. He vacated his fellowship on taking orders in the Diocese of Ely on 18 September 1675. He was Rector of Nowton, Suffolk from 1680 to 1685, and of Greeting St. Olave by 1681. He secured the living of Ivychurch in Romney Marsh, Kent in 1685, becoming at the same time Vicar of Bekesbourne, three miles from Canterbury. A tiny population in either cure left him ample time for research, profitably put to use in the Canterbury archives so close at hand, both for his revision of Somner and for his own *Cantuaria Sacra* which bears witness to original work among the plenitude of Canterbury MSS. At Ivychurch, over 25 miles from Bekesbourne, he no doubt put in a curate.

Nicholas Battely married Ann, daughter of Oliver Pocklington of Brington, Hunts. She died in 1716, aged 60 according to her grave-slab in Bekesbourne church. There were at least two sons of the marriage. The elder was John who attended the King's School, Canterbury. He too entered Trinity College, Cambridge (at the age of 17). He was B.A. 1708-9 and M.A. in 1712. He became Fellow of his college in 1711, having taken orders. He held livings in East Anglia. He was sufficiently esteemed by his uncle the Archdeacon to be recipient under his will of the latter's collection of antiquarian specimens.[72] The younger John died in 1741. His kinsfolk eventually gave the collection to the library of Trinity College.

The younger son of Nicholas Battely was Oliver (clearly taking a name from his maternal great grandfather). He was born in 1696 and matriculated at Oxford as from Christ Church, on 8 June 1716 at the age of 19. He was B.A. by 1720 and M.A. in 1724. He graduated B.D. in 1734 and served as Proctor in 1731. He ended life as Prebendary of Llandaff. As indicated above he made a valuable contribution to antiquarian studies by producing an edition of his uncle's historical remains.

Thomas Battely, the third son of Nicholas the apothecary of Bury St. Edmund's, born in 1655, seems to have left no literary traces of himself. He may be identified with the Thomas graduating B.A. as of Trinity College, Cambridge in 1677–8.

There are handsome memorial slabs to be seen in Bekesbourne church, to Nicholas Battely, placed by his widow, Ann; to Ann Battely, placed by her son John, the Archdeacon; and a wall monument to Ann Battely, styled sister to John the Archdeacon.

Edm. Hall. Oxon.
Feb. 15. 1977

William Urry

NOTES

Abbreviations

A.C.	*Archaeologia Cantiana*
BAC	Borough Archives, Canterbury, in Cathedral Library
CAC	Cathedral Archives, Canterbury, in Cathedral Library
DAC	Diocesan Archives, Canterbury, in Cathedral Library
K.	*The Life of Mr. Somner* by White Kennett, prefixed to J. Brome's edition of Somner's *Roman Ports and Forts in Kent* (1693)
Misc. Gen. Her.	*Miscellanea Genealogica et Heraldica*
PRC	Probate Records of Canterbury deposited in Kent County Record Office, Maidstone
s.a.	*sub anno*

For marriage licences, see J. M. Cowper, *Canterbury Marriage Licences*, series I, etc.

1. MSS. of Mr. Wood, optician, Sun St., Canterbury, mostly destroyed in house of Mr. Cleaver, auctioneer, Church St., St. Paul's, Canterbury, in air raid, June 1942. I had taken notes of some Somner items, and others were luckily removed to survive today in the Supplementary MSS, Canterbury City Records. The collection also contained original water colours by F. W. Fairholt, used in B. Faussett: *Inventorium Sepulchrale* (1856). The Cathedral Audit House stood in the angle between Choir and Treasury, close to the Library. For Somner's MSS., see Batteley's Preface, below; *Report Royal Comm. on Historical Manuscripts* ix, appendix, i, p. 125, and C. E. Woodruff, *Catalogue of Manuscript Books . . . Canterbury* (1911), nos. 79–98. It is strongly emphasised that the account of William Somner below by no means exhausts the available materials, and a much longer study could compiled. Acknowledgments must be made to William Parry Blore, Chapter Librarian (d. 1948), for notes and for long discussions on the life of Somner. A typescript list of Somner's printed books compiled by C. E. Woodruff, among Cathedral library catalogues, appears to be very far from complete.

2. See G. V. Bennett, *White Kennett, 1660–1728* (1957). Kennett's own copy of Somner's *Antiquities* (1703) is in my hands.

3. Kent County Record Office, PRC 32/52, fol. 78; *Misc. Gen. Her.* ser. ii, V, p. 99; the evidence of W. Somner, senior, in court case of 1622 is in DAC, X. 11. 19, ff. 124–5. The baptism is taken from DAC, Transcripts.

4. Chapter Library, Canterbury, Lt. MS. D 2. As attorney Winston once conducted a case against Christopher Marlowe: BAC, J / B / 391.

5. DAC, X. 11. 14, ff. 176–8.

6. I. Walton, *Lives* (*Hooker*, appendix). See C. J. Sisson, *Judicious Marriage of Richard Hooker* (1940).

7. *Compleat Angler* ('Fordidge Trout'). The text varies between editions: *Antiquities* (1640), p. 45; *Antiquities* (1703), p. 25.

8. DAC, Transcripts, St. Margaret, Canterbury. The original register, cited by Kennett, (*K.*, p. 102), no longer survives.

9. DAC, Y. 3. 15, fol. 461.

10. DAC, X. 11. 19, ff. 124–5.

11. Wood MSS. (see note 1, above), deed of sale, G. Somner to W. Somner, 1639– now in Canterbury City Records. Some inhabitant of the house (a servant?) secreted a hoard of silver coins running down to 1644 beneath the floorboards of an upper room, found in 1947 and declared treasure trove.

12. *K.*, pp. 2, 101, 102; DAC, X. 11. 8, s.a.

13. *K.*, pp. 4–5.

14. DAC, X. 11. 14, fol. 108.

15. *A.C.* xxv (1902), pp. 49–50.

16. Plate 2, facing p. (viii)

17. F. W. Cross, *History of the Walloon and Huguenot Church at Canterbury* (Publications of Huguenot Society of London, xv, 1898), pp. 99, 522. Brent lodged at the house when in Canterbury (A.C., xxv, p. 52).

18. L. B. Larking (ed.), *Proceedings Principally in the County of Kent* (Camden Society, O.S., lxxx, 1862), pp. 138–9.

19. For Casaubon's house, see *Antiquities* (below), p. 110; C. E. Woodruff, 'Parliamentary Survey . . . in the time of the Commonwealth', *A.C.* xlix (1937), pp. 19 sqq; plan opp. p. 195. Somner's other friend, T. Denne, has been given a poor character, 'a lawyer of some repute', but 'subtle, resourceful, unscrupulous': D. Gardiner (ed.), *Oxinden and Peyton Letters, 1642–1670* (1937), p. xxiii.

20. See Battely's Preface, below.

21. R. Hovenden (ed.), *The Register Booke of . . . the Cathedral Church . . . of Canterburie* (Harleian Soc. 1878), s.a.

22. DAC, Z. 2. 1, fol. 100.

23. PRC 32 / 52, fol. 78; *Misc. Gen. Her.*, ser. ii, V, p. 99.

24. DAC, Z. 2. 1, unfoliated.

25. J. M. Cowper (ed.), *The Roll of the Freemen of the City of Canterbury from A.D. 1392 to 1800* (1903), under *Gift*; E. Hasted, *History and Topographical Survey of the County of Kent*, xii (1801), p. 646. It may be noted that this local patriot does not seem to know of the distinction between Men of Kent and Kentish Men: see *Antiquities*, below, p. 1.

26. C. E. Woodruff and W. Danks, *Memorials of the Cathedral and Priory of Christ in Canterbury* (1912), p. 324 (Dr. Paske's letter).

27. R. Culmer, *Cathedrall Newes from Canterbury* as reprinted in G. S., *Chronological History* (1883), p. 313. Somner is alluded to as Proctor (p. 289).

28. The amount of imagery (on Culmer's evidence) which had survived the Reformation seems astonishing: see *ibid.*, pp. 311 sqq.

29. E. Lee Warner, *Life of J. Warner, Bishop of Rochester* (1901); D. Gardiner in *Canterbury Diocesan Notes*, no. 104 (1937) and C. E. Woodruff (*ibid.*, no. 106, 1937). Somner was reimbursed in 10s. at the Restoration by the Chapter, for bringing the font and ironwork in from the town: J. W. Legg and W. H. St. J. Hope (eds.), *Inventories of Christchurch, Canterbury* (1902), p. 269.

30. Pamphlets: *Canterbury Christmas* (1647), and *Articles of Agreement between . . . Fairfax and the Kentish Forces* (1648); A. M. Everitt, *The Community of Kent and the Great Rebellion, 1640–60* (1966), chapter VII; W. Gostling, *A Walk in and about the City of Canterbury* (1777 edn.), p. 8. Prints of the 18th century indicated that the stretch lay in the S.W. quadrant, but this was already ruinous in the 16th century.

31. *K.*, p. 90. The episode is mentioned in the epitaph of George's son-in-law John Petit (1700)

at Margate: *Misc. Gen. Her.*, ser. ii, V. p. 120. See *Cal. of Committee for Advance of Money*, part 3, pp. 1315–6.

32. See H. R. Plomer, *Index of Wills . . . Canterbury* (Kent Archaeological Soc., Records Branch, vi), part ii (1920). For the latest study of probate during the Commonwealth see the papers by C. Kitching in *Journal of Soc. of Archivists*, v (1976), pp. 283–293, 346–356; D. M. M. Shorrocks, 'Probate Jurisdiction within the Diocese of Canterbury', *Bulletin of Inst. of Hist. Research*, xxxi (1958), pp. 186–195.

33. *K.*, p. 68; W. Hamper (ed.), *Life Diary and Correspondence of Sir W. Dugdale* (1827), p. 288. See schedule of letters therein. For the whole antiquarian group; see D. C. Douglas, *English Scholars* (1939, 1943), *passim*.

34. British Library, Add. MS. 33,924, fol. 54.

35. Hamper, *ut supra*, Letter C.

36. *K.*, pp. 108–9, 116–7.

37. Bodleian MS. 25218 (307).

38. *K.* p. 29; M. Casaubon, *De Quatuor Linguis* (1650), pp. 140 sqq.

39. Bodleian MS. 854, lvii, fol. 60, Dr. G. Langbaine of Queen's to Dugdale.

40. I. Gollancz (ed.), *The Cædmon MS. Junius XI* (1927), pp. xiv sqq.; Woodruff, *Catalogue, ut supra*, no. 81 (3); *K.*, p. 109.

41. Woodruff, *Catalogue*, no. 81 (2).

42. *K.*, pp. 73–4; 107–8.

43. *K.*, pp. 22–32; 70–87.

44. *K.*, p. 85.

45. *K.*, p. 103.

46. *Cal. State Papers, Domestic, 1659–60*, pp. 329–30.

47. Hasted, *op. cit.*, pp. 648–9. The extra, dedicatory, leaf is inserted into a copy of *Antiquities* (1640) in the Bodleian Library. Another copy there contains a cutting from the catalogue of T. Payne the bookseller for 1796, advertising the presentation copy for sale. Perhaps it had been discarded as a duplicate from the royal collection, removed to the British Museum.

48. DAC, Z. 2. 4, unfoliated.

49. CAC, Register Z, fol. 18; Domestic Economy, no. 91; *A.C.* x (1876), pp. 93 sqq.

50. CAC, Register Z, fol. 34. The registers show Somner active at this time, as in riding to a Lathe meeting at Dymchurch in the summer of 1663: CAC, Register 27, fol. 128. He calls himself Chapter Clerk on occasion: *ibid.*, fol. 132.

51. *K.*, p. 92.

52. DAC, Treasurer's Accounts, s.a. See *A.C.* xlix (1937), map opp. p. 195.

53. *K.*, p. 103; *Register Booke of the Cathedral Church, ut supra* (note 21), s.a.; C. E. Woodruff and H. J. Cape, *Schola Regia Cantuariensis* (1908), p. 112. The marriage settlement for Somner and his second wife has survived in Wood MSS. (see note 1, above), now in Canterbury City Records.

54. *K.*, p. 103; *Misc. Gen. Her.*, ser. ii, V, pp. 121–3.

55. BAC, Minute and Account Books, s.a.; Chapter Library, Canterbury, Lit. MS. E 40 (Benefactors' Book), s.a.

56. *Grantees of Arms* (Harleian Soc., lxvi, 1915), p. 238; *Visitation of Kent, 1663–8* (Harleian Soc., liv, 1906), p. 152. The chevronels appear as gules on William's monument (see below). Archbishop Sumner (clearly a descendant of William or John) bore them as did *his* descendant, Warden Sumner of All Souls College, Oxford (d. 1951). The arms appeared on the latter's funeral scutcheon, probably the last displayed in Oxford.

57. J. Somner, *True Relation . . . Concerninge the New Market House* (1666); W. Gostling, *op. cit.*, appendix v.

58. S. Rosenfeld, *Strolling Players and Drama in the Provinces* (1939), section on *Canterbury*.

59. *K.*, p. 100; Bodleian MS. 28183 (Sheldon Letters), 128, 133, 137.

60. *K.*, pp. 8–10.

61. DAC, Z, 2. 5., s.a.; *K.*, p. 101.

62. PRC 17/58, fol. 94.

63. *K.*, pp. 103–4.

64. *K.*, pp. 102–3.

65. PRC 32/58, fol. 94; *Misc. Gen. Her.*, ser. ii, V, p. 100. A smaller plaque was erected beneath the main monument, and renewed in 1831. It adds minor details. Somner's monument stands astride a lateral wall introduced into the aisle when the church became the local Deaf Centre. The lateral wall was jammed against the lower monument with scant respect. A transcription had been made by myself. For the text of the main monument, see Kennett's edition of *A Treatise of Gavelkind* (1726) and *Misc. Gen. Her.* as above.

66. *K.*, pp. 19–21.

67. First published 1778–99; 2nd edn., 1797–1801, reproduced in facsimile by EP Publishing, Ltd., with introduction by A. M. Everitt, 1972. The Canterbury section comprises volumes xi and xii.

68. There is no modern definitive study of Canterbury as a whole. Aspects have been treated, as in R. A. L. Smith, *Canterbury Cathedral Priory* (1943), or in W. Urry, *Canterbury under the Angevin Kings* (1967). There are large numbers of articles scattered in periodicals, and an extensive corpus of primary materials among the publications of record societies.

69. Except where otherwise stated the following is based on J. Foster, *Alumni Oxonienses* (1887–92); J. A. Venn, *Alumni Cantabrigienses* i (1922–7); and *Dictionary of National Biography*. For members of the family buried at Bekesbourne, see Hasted, *Kent* (2nd edn.), *op. cit.*, ix, pp. 273–274. There was an 18th-century calf-bound volume in the stock of Mesdames Carver and Staniforth, booksellers of Burgate St., Canterbury, which, if memory serves aright, contained memoranda relating to the Battely family of Bury St. Edmunds, with notes relating to *Cantuaria Sacra*. The shop with the stock was destroyed in bombing late in 1940. British Library, Add. MS. 22,665 contains a version of *Antiquitates Rutupinae*.

70. Gostling, *op. cit.*, p. 311.

71. *Bibliotheca Topographica Britannica*, Vol. I, xxx (1785).

72. See *Antiquitates Rutupinae*, introduction *Lectori S.*

LIST OF PLATES

Number   Facing page

Plates in new Introduction

1   Gulielmus Somner, moribus antiquis, M. Burghers del. et   (v)
     sc. Portrait of William Somner from *A Treatise of the Roman
     Ports and Forts in Kent*, 1693

2   Notarial sign of William Somner, senior, Notary Public   (viii)
     and Registrar of the Canterbury Consistory Court, with
     attestation written out in the hand of his son and assistant,
     William Somner, junior, Notary Public, the antiquary

3   The author's memorial in St. Margaret's Church, Canter-   (xvii)
     bury, from *A Treatise of Gavelkind*, 2nd ed., 1726

Plates in *The Antiquities of Canterbury*

4   A view of Canterbury, J. Kip sc.   Title-page

5   The mapp of Canterbury, 1703   1

6   Summi Altaris in Ecclesia cœnibitica Scī Augustini Can-   25
     tuariensis cum reliquiarum scriniis circumstantibus et in-
     scriptionibus in veteri ejus exemplari insertis, Figura. A
     drawing of the High Altar in the monastic church of St.
     Augustine, Canterbury, with the shrines of relics standing
     round it and their inscriptions, as inserted in an ancient
     manuscript belonging to that monastery. [Elmham's
     Chron., Trinity Hall, Cambridge, MS. 1]

7   Fossil teeth found at Chartham, Canterbury, 1668   192

Plates from *Cantuaria Sacra*
by Nicolas Battely

These plates appear at the end of the book. For reference
purposes, page numbers (1–16) have been added.

8   The west prospect of the Cathedral Church of Canterbury,   1
        J. Kip sc.
                        (See text p. 91)

9   The Ichnography of the old Church before Lanfranc. The   2
        shrine of Thomas the reputed Martyr and his bones
                    (See text pp. 85–86)

10   Ichnographia Ecclesiæ Cantuariensis a Lanfranco con-   3
        structæ cum Choro Conradi. Ichnographia Cryptæ
        Eccles: Cantuar: Plans of the Cathedral and Crypt built
        by Lanfranc, with the Choir completed by Prior Conrad
                (See text pp. 86–87, 139–140)

11   The South Prospect of the Cathedral and Metropolitan   4
        Church of Canterbury. Tho. Johnson delin. W. Hollar
        fecit
                        (See text p. 91)

12   The Ichnography of the Metropolitan Church of Canter-   5
        bury. Tho. Johnson delin. W. Hollar fecit
                    (See text pp. 91–101)

13   The Monument of King Henry IV and his Queen. J. Kip   6
        sculp.
                        (See text p. 100)

14   The Monument of Edward the Black Prince   7
                    (See text pp. 99–100)

15   Viro Honorabili . . . Figuram hanc Tumuli Thomæ,   8
        Ducis Clarenciæ, Iohannis, Comitis Somersetiæ et Mar-
        garetæ eorundem Uxoris. D.D.D. F.S. W. Hollar fecit.
        Tomb of Thomas, Duke of Clarence, John Beaufort, Earl
        of Somerset, and Lady Margaret, successively their wife
                        (See text p. 100)

16   The Tomb of A.-Bp. Walter Reynold. The Tomb of A.-Bp.   9
        Hubert Walter
                    (See text pp. 131 and 127)

Number   Page

Plates from *Cantuaria Sacra*
(continued)

17   The Tomb of A.-Bp. John Stratford   10
              (See text p. 133)

18   The Tomb of A.-Bp. Simon Sudbury. J. Collins delin. &   11
      sculp.
              (See text pp. 134–135)

19   The Tomb of A.-Bp. William Courtney. The Tomb of   12
      A.-Bp. Theobald. J. Collins delin. & sculp.
              (See text pp. 135–136 and 123–124)

20   The Monument of Henry Chichely, Archbishop of Canter-   13
      bury. E. Taylor delin., 1703
              (See text p. 136)

21   The Tomb A.-Bp. John Kemp. J. Collins delin. & sculp.   14
              (See text p. 137)

22   Ichnographica Descriptio omnium tum locorum ædium   15
      infra Ambitum Ecclesiæ Christi Cantuariensis. Tho. Hill
      delin. Ichnography of Canterbury Cathedral and the
      Precincts
              (See text pp. 101–113)

23   The Prospect of the Reliques of the Abbey of St. Austin   16
      Canterbury from the high Tower of Christ Church in the
      same Citty. Tho. Johnson delin. D. King sculp.

S. Sep. fe.

THE
ANTIQUITIES
OF
CANTERBURY.

OR,

A Survey of that Ancient CITY,
with the Suburbs and Cathedral.

Containing principally Matters of *Antiquity* in them all.

Collected chiefly from Old *Manuscripts*, *Lieger-Books*, and other like Records, for the most part not before Printed.

With an *APPENDIX* here Annexed:

Wherein (for better Satisfaction to the Learned) the *Muniments* and *Records* of chiefest Consequence, are faithfully exhibited.

All (for the Honour of that *Ancient Metropolis*, and his good Affection to *Antiquities*) Sought out and Published by the Industry and Good Will of

WILLIAM SOMNER.

The Second Edition, *Revised and Enlarged by* Nicolas Battely, *M. A.*

CHARTHAM-NEWS:

Or, A Brief Relation of some strange Bones there lately digged up, in some Grounds of Mr. *John Somner's*, of *Canterbury*: Written by his Brother Mr. *William Somner*, late Auditor of *Christ-Church, Canterbury*, and Register of the Archbishop's Court there, before his Death.

To which some Observations concerning the *Roman* Antiquities of *Canterbury* are added. Together with a Preface, giving an Account of the Works and Remains of the Learned Antiquary Mr. *William Somner*, by *N. Battely*.

The FIRST PART.

LONDON:

Printed for R. KNAPLOCK, at the *Angel and Crown* in St. *Paul's* Church-Yard. MDCCIII.

To the Moſt Reverend Father in God,

WILLIAM

By the Divine Providence,

Lord Archbiſhop of CANTERBURY, his Grace,

Primate of all *England*, and Metropolitan; One of the Lords of His Majeſty's Moſt Honourable Privy Council, and Chancellor of the Univerſity of *Oxford*.

May it pleaſe Your Grace,

AS without the concurrence of divers good reaſons to induce me, I had not preſumed to preſent unto Your *Grace* the following *Diſcourſe*: So I conceive it very fitting, and my bounden duty, to give Your *Grace*, and the world, an Account in brief, of the inducements whereby I have been animated to appear in this kind before Your *Grace*. The chief whereof hath been, and is, Your *Grace*'s intereſt both in the *Author*, and in the *Work*. In the *Author*, as ſubſiſting in his place and profeſſion, under *God*, chiefly by your *Grace*'s Favour and Goodneſs. In the *Work*, in a double reſpect: the one, as it is a Diſcourſe of *Antiquities*; Your *Grace*'s tranſcendent and unpattern'd care and coſt for the Collection whereof, of all ſorts, from all parts, crowned by Your ſingular Piety and Nobleneſs in diſpoſing them to the good and ſervice of the Publick; as they are thankfully acknowledged and worthily celebrated by all the Lovers of *Antiquities*; ſo do they give Your *Grace* an eſpecial intereſt to the fruits of all their Labours who are that way inclined. The other, as it handleth more eſpecially the *Antiquities* of two ſuch *Particulars* as are of very near relation to Your *Grace*, the *Church*, and *City* of *Canterbury*. Theſe reaſons (may it pleaſe Your *Grace*) not to trouble You with more, in all Humility I hope may prevail with Your *Grace* for Your patience and pardon of this preſumption: and though not procure Your *Grace*'s acceptance and protection of the *Work*, yet Your excuſe of the *Author*'s boldneſs, who moſt humbly craves it at Your *Gracious* Hands: and with his hearty Prayers, both for the long continuance of Your *Grace*'s Health and Happineſs here, to *God*'s Glory and the good of His *Church*, and for Your endleſs bliſs hereafter, proſtrates both Himſelf and His Labours at Your *Grace*'s Feet with that Reverence which becomes

The Meaneſt of Your Grace's Servants,

WILLIAM SOMNER.

THE

THE
Preface to the READER.

*I*T is the observation of some ancient Philosophers, (who also prove it by divers good Arguments) that all men, for the most part, have a natural desire to Immortality. But this we all know by common approv'd experience, that Man that is born of a Woman is of short continuance. He cometh forth like a Flower and is cut down, he flieth also as a shadow and continueth not. *Some therefore who knew not of any other world after this, in defence of Nature's ways and providence, maintained, (a) that she had in some manner satisfied the desire of man in making him* generative. (b) For *that man in some sort may be thought yet* alive, whose Progeny is living. As I may say in the words of Cassiodore (c), *with little alteration. But if there be any immortality in this, it can be but an immortality of the Body, not of the Mind, the best and chiefest part of Man. The immortality of the mind (all that it is capable of in this world, which though it be not immortality properly, yet may certainly much conduce to allay the complaints of mortal men concerning their shortness of life) doth, as I conceive, especially depend from that* (d) Remembrance of things past, *and* Foresight of things to come ; *which the* Latin Orator *speaks of.*

As for the first, he certainly that knows no more of the world (the time of a man's life being so short as it is) than what hath happened in his time, though he may be in years, and perchance very old in regard of his body, yet in regard of his mind and knowledge, he can be accounted but a very child. Which is the very answer that an ancient Ægyptian *Priest and Antiquary gave to* Solon, *concerning the* Grecians *of his time ; that they were all, the best and ancientest of them, but very babes and children.* (e) *And his reason was, because none of them could say any thing of the state of their own Countrey, beyond their own and their Fathers memory : whereas the* Ægyptians, *out of their ancient holy Records, could tell them many memorable things, both concerning* Greece *in general, and the state of their then famous* Athens *in particular, for many hundred, if not thousand, of years before. If therefore a man living in a place of note, can by his industry, out of undoubted Records and Monuments, (if such be the happy condition of the place, that it afford them) certainly find, what have been the several* both material Alterations (as in respect of Buildings, and the like) and Historical Events, *that have happened to it for divers ages before, and can derive the present times and places that he lives in, by a continual series of chances and alterations from such or such a beginning, I do not see (if knowledge be granted to be the life of the* Soul, *as the Soul is the life of the Body) but he may reckon his years according to the proportion of his knowledge, accounting himself to have lived so many years, as he is able truly and historically to give an account of.*

Now for that other part of immortality, which is (f) the foresight of things to come, *even this hath such dependance of the former, as that he that is well vers'd in the knowledge of things past, may probably foresee what will happen in time to come. As for example: It was no difficult thing for one of the* (g) ancient Grecians *(who lived in the days of* Pythagoras, *and was one of his Auditors) having observed the course of the world, and what had already happened to* Greece *it self, and to other places in that kind, to foretell of old* Greece, *then flourishing, that the time would come when it should be the seat of* Ignorance and Barbarism; *as it is at this day. Upon the same grounds of former ages experience, did another of the Ancients both foresee and foretell, above a thousand years before any such thing happened, the discovery of a new world, in these remarkable words of his ; which in* English *run thus :*

(a) Plato in Symposio sive Convivio. (b) Nam quodammodo ipse putatur vivere, cujus progenies vivit. (c) Variar. l 8. c. 2. (d) Memoria præteritorum, & Providentia futurorum. (e) Plato in Timæo. (f) Providentia futurorum. (g) Ocellus Lucianus de Universa Natura, c. 3 p. 45.

The Preface to the Reader.

Dr. *Heylin's* Cofmography, in the beginning of *America*.

(a) In the laft days an Age fhall come,
Wherein the all-devouring foam
Shall lofe its former bounds, and fhew
Another *Continent* to view.
New Worlds, which Night doth now conceal,
A fecond *Tiphys* fhall reveal ;
And frozen *Thule* fhall no more
Be of the Earth the fartheft Shore.

As the knowledge of ancient things is pleafant, fo is the ignorance as fhameful, and oftentimes expofes men to the fcorn and contempt of ftrangers. (b) Tully *relates of himfelf, that being fent with authority to* Syracufa, *a* quondam renowned City *of* Silicia, *for his own private fatisfaction, he enquired of the chiefeft of the City about the fepulchre and monument of their famous* Archimedes ; *who (through fhameful ignorance of their City-Antiquities) denied that he had any. But* Tully *knowing the contrary by what he had read, and by good luck remembring fome certain Verfes that mentioned fome particulars of his Monument, whereby it might be known from others, taking along with him thofe* venerable blocks *(who, as ordinary worldly men, had no care but for their profit, no curiofity but for their belly) he repaired to the place, being near the City-gates, where ancient fepulchres and monuments were moft frequent, and fo neglected (whereby you may judge of the temper of the Inhabitants) that they were almoft all overgrown with thickets and bufhes. But the place being cleared by men that were on purpofe fet on work, he found at laft by help of the forefaid directions, the monument that he fought, with the very marks (a* Sphæra *and a* Cylindrus *) and the infcription (though new half worn out, more through neglect than age) that he looked for. And fo, to the great fhame of that City, and the inhabitants thereof (noted abroad for their luxurious life and great excefs in all worldly things) concludes with thefe upbraiding infulting words :* (c) Thus the nobleft and alfo once moft learned City that ever was poffeffed by the *Greeks*, had not known the Monument of their Citizen, who was one of moft acute parts, if they had not learnt it from a Native of *Arpinum*. *As if a man fhould fcoffingly object to us here of* Canterbury, *that he was fain to come out of* Wales *or* Scotland, *of purpofe to fhew us the Monument and place of Burial of fome one of our famous Abbats, or renowned* Archbifhops, *whofe credit and bounty, when living, had redounded much to the honour and benefit of the City.*

For thefe and the like reafons, my thoughts and affections having ever much inclined to the fearch and ftudy of Antiquities, *(to which alfo my particular calling did in fome manner lead me) I have more particularly, as bound in duty and thankfulnefs, applied my felf to the Antiquities of* Canterbury, *the place of my birth and abode. And to me this was a fufficient motive why I fhould of all other places defire to know the Antiquities and former eftate thereof. But why any man elfe, that is an* Englifhman, *fhould have the fame defire, other reafons may be given, very confiderable, if I be not much deceived : As firft, the Antiquities thereof.* Antiquity's *due and proper* Epithet *is* venerable. *Now the intereft which our City hath in that venerable badge and cognizance, is not unknown ; it being acknowledged for one of the moft ancient Cities in the Kingdom.* (d) Becaufe the City of *Canterbury* is one of the ancienteft Cities in *England* ; *is no other language than is frequently found in the Charters, and fuch private Acts of Parliament, as (making that a main motive to the Grant) have conveyed any* Favour *or* Franchife *to the City or Citizens. Secondly, the great fame and repute that it hath had abroad, for reafons that will appear by this Treatife ; and thereupon the great refort of ftrangers, from all Nations under heaven, (which, in probability, gave occafion to the Proverb of* Canterbury-tales *) to the number fometimes, as fhall be fhewed, of a hundred thoufand at once. But the chief reafon,*

(a) ——————Venient annis
Secula feris, quibus Oceanus
Vincula rerum laxet, & ingens
Pateat tellus, Typhyfque novos
Detegat orbes : nec fit terris
Ultima Thule. *Senec. in Med.*
(b) Tufcul Qu. l. 5.　　(c) Ita nobiliffima Græciæ civitas, quondam verò etiam doctiffima fui civis unius acutiffimi monumentum ignoraffet, nifi ab homine Arpinate didiciffet.
(d) Quia civitas Cantuariæ eft una de antiquiffimis urbibus Angliæ.

in my judgment, ought to be, because from thence first the Faith of Chrift *was propagated and derived unto other parts of the Realm of* England *; after the* Saxons *our forefathers were become Lords and Poffeffors of it. When the* Romans *had conquered* Greece, *they did not use them as they did other Nations commonly by them fubdued, but with all love and refpect,* Athens *efpecially, which they had in honour (fay ancient* (a) Geographers *of thofe times ;) and, in token of their refpect, fuffered them to enjoy their ancient* Laws, Liberties, *and* Form of Government, *as though they had not been conquered.* Tully *gives the reafon :* (b) Since we are come to govern thofe very men from whom Civility (almoft peculiar to themfelves) feems to have been deriv'd to the reft of the World ; we ought certainly to fhow it moft particularly to thofe, of whom we have received it. *And do not all pioufly-affected* Englifh *owe fo much honour and refpect to the place, from whence the light of* Chrift's *glorious Gofpel firft fhined unto their fore-fathers, as to defire to be acquainted with the prefent and paft eftate of it ?*

I have fpoken of Religion *only, but I might add* humanitatem, [*as it fignifies* N. B.] Learning *and good* Literature *too. For with* Religion *came* Learning : *and in the days of* Theodorus VII. *Archbifhop of* Canterbury, (*if publick Schools wherein all good* Arts *and* Sciences, Philofophy *efpecially, are learnedly taught and profeffed, make an* Univerfity) Canterbury *was a famous* Univerfity ; *yea, and was afterwards a pattern (as fome have written and publifhed) for the erection and foundation of a famous* Univerfity *in this land.*

This work is chiefly collected from old Manufcripts, Leiger-Books, *and other* Records *of credit, exhibited to me for the moft part by the Treafury of our* Cathedral ; *which, as it exceeds moft of the Realm, if not all, in beauty, ftatelinefs, and magnificence of Building ; fo in this particular kind of unvaluable treafure, is, as I conceive, inferior unto none. With the help of* Spot's *Hiftory of* Canterbury, *mentioned of* Balæus, *and of* John Twine's *Collections of the Antiquities thereof, fpoken of by him in his* Commentaries, de rebus Albionicis, &c. *could I but have gotten them, I fhould perchance have brought the work to more perfection ; but with the helps I have had, I have done my beft endeavour that nothing might be ftrange or unknown that carries with it any fhew of* Antiquity, *either in the* Church, (*as the moft eminent place of all*) *or in the* City *and* Suburbs *thereof.*

If the Work *may not deferve thine acceptance (*Courteous Reader*) for it felf, let then the* Author's *love to* Antiquities, *his thankful intentions towards the* place *of his birth, education, and* prefent abode, *and the* encouragement *of worthy friends, ferve for his* Apology. *If otherwife it give thee fome content, and mine endeavours prove acceptable unto thee, I fhall defire thou wouldft be thankful to them, without whofe help, as I had not been able, fo without whofe* encouragement *I had neither been willing, thus to have adventured forth in publick ; as namely,* Dr. Cafaubon, *one of the Prebendaries of this Church, and* Thomas Denne Efq; : *to whom, for their great and ready favour and furtherance herein, I were confcious of much ingratitude and want of ingenuity, if I fhould not acknowledge my felf exceedingly beholden. Such as it is I commend it to thy favourable acceptance, (*friendly Reader*) and fhall add no more but the beft wifhes and refpects of*

Thine to ferve thee,

William Somner.

(a) Strabo Geograph. p. 398.   (b) Cum ei hominum generi præfimus non modo in quo ipfa fit, fed etiam à quo ad alios pervenifle putetur humanitas : certè iis eam potifsimùm tribuere debemus, à quibus accepimus. Lib. 1. Ep ad Qu. Fratrem, Ep. 1.

A

PREFACE

TO THIS

New Edition.

MR. William Somner *collected the Antiquities of* Canterbury *in a time of Peace, while (as yet) the Church flourished under the Government of King* Charles I. *and under the Conduct of Archbishop* Laud, *to whose Patronage he dedicated this Work, which he published* Anno 1640. *But before this Year was ended, a dismal Storm did arise, which did shake and threaten with a final overthrow the very Foundations of this Church: For upon the Feast of the* Epiphany, *and the* Sunday *following, there was a riotous disturbance raised by some disorderly People, in the time of Divine Service, in the Quire of this Church: And altho' by the care of the Prebendaries a stop was put to these Disorders for a time, yet afterwards the Madness of the People did rage, and prevail beyond resistance. The venerable Dean and Canons were turned out of their Stalls, the beautiful and new erected Font was pulled down, the Inscriptions, Figures, and Coats of Arms, engraven upon Brass were torn off from the ancient Monuments ; and whatsoever there was of beauty or decency in the Holy Place, was despoiled by the outrages of Sacrilege and Prophaneness. During those distractions of our Church and State, this Book was so disagreeable to the then prevailing Powers, as that the best Fate which the Book or its Author could at that time expect, was to lie hid, and to be sheltered under the Security of being not regarded. After an end was put to the Great Rebellion, the whole Impression of this Book was not sold off, and the Author seems to have designed to have put forth a new Edition of it ; hereupon the Bookseller, to revive the Sale of this Treatise, caused a new Title to be printed* Anno 1662, *and to be pasted over the old Title Page : Hence it has been thought, that there have been two Impressions of this Book already, which is a Mistake. Mr.* Somner *did not live to give the World the new Edition, as he intended, and the whole Impression has been long since sold, so as this Treatise has been bought at a dear Rate, whensoever it has been accidentally met with in a Bookseller's Shop : Hence a Second Edition has been much wanted and desired : And to supply this want I have used my best endeavours.*

In this New Edition the Reader has Mr. Somner's *Antiquities of* Canterbury *whole and entire, without any Alterations, except where Mr.* Somner *with his own Pen has corrected, altered, blotted out, or added, in order to a Second Edition : All which Alterations or Corrections are observed by me ; and whatsoever he has added (except where it is only a word or two) the Addition is enclosed in a Parathesis or Crochet [ ] after this manner, with* W. S. *added to it. And whereas this Treatise was not so absolute and compleat, but that it did admit of some farther Amendments and Enlargements, I have, here and there, added, as there seem'd occasion, some Annotations : All which are included in the like Paratheses or Crochets, with* N. B. *added thereunto.*

I have transferred into the Appendix, or Margin, all the Latin Records, Charters, Instruments, Quotations, and Sentences, and have translated most of them into English, some of them word for word, some of them according to the Sense ; and of some of the Records I have given no more than the general Sum or Title. I have found these Translations a toilsome piece of Work ; and herein I consulted more the benefit and delight of my Reader, than mine own ease. I wish Mr. Somner *himself had done this to my hand ; for he was an absolute Master of interpreting obsolete Words and Terms. I fear I may have committed some Mistakes or Improprieties in some Expressions:*

where-

wheresoever any such Mistake has passed, I beg that the courteous Reader would gently correct it with his Pen. I have been so just and punctual to Mr. Somner, as not to omit the meanest Word or Expression, such as inter aliâ, sed in callem regredior, ipse vidi, *and the like; all which I have transmitted to the Margin. If I had been minded to have taken any liberty with that Author, I would have omitted the long Citation out of* Ælian, *concerning* Archery; *but I did forbear that or any thing else, which some, perhaps, may think might have been conveniently left out.*

By the leave of the Reverend the Dean and Canons, I had free access to the Registers and Records of Christ-Church, (*which Kindness and Favour I do hereby acknowledge with all gratitude*) *and hereby I have had an opportunity of examining and comparing almost every one of the Charters and Instruments, which Mr.* Somner *had made use of; and where I found any Word or Sentence which was to be corrected, altered, or supplied, I have put it in the Margin. I had also the use of Mr.* Somner's *own Book, which he had prepared in order to a Second Edition. The Writer of Mr.* Somner's *Life, in the Catalogue of his* Posthumous Manuscripts, *has these words,* His Antiquities of Canterbury interleav'd with very large Additions. *This is a gross Misinformation, which brings this new Edition under a great disadvantage; for Expectations have been raised to see considerable Enlargements in this Work from the Author's own Learned Pen: And who may be blamed when Men find themselves disappointed herein? Mr.* Somner *has corrected with his own Pen very many* Errata *of the Press; and a few Mistakes, which were his own Mistakes, and not of the Press. He has altered a few Expressions, and blotted out or added a word or two, to make the Sense more easie. He has transferred his Dissertation concerning the Etymology of* Herbaldown, *from the Appendix into the History, and has reviewed that whole Discourse: Whereas he had mentioned the Exercise of Archery in three several places, he will have them joined altogether without alteration, in this new Edition. He has given some additional Thoughts concerning* Ethelbert's Tower, *some other small Additions, and two or three Charters in the Appendix. This is all that can be expected from Mr.* Somner's *revisal of his own Work; and the Reader shall find every particular thereof in this new Edition.*

I will here subjoin an account of all the Works of this Learned Man, that have been published, or that remain in Manuscript in the Library of the Cathedral Church in Canterbury.

Anno 1640. *He published the* Antiquities of Canterbury, *which he had finished in the* 33d *Year of his Age.*

Anno 1650. *His* Animadversions *upon some old* German Words, *were made publick by his singular good Friend Dr.* Meric Casaubon, *who had sent him a Collection of some old* German Words, *taken out of an Epistle of* Lipsius *to* Schottus, (Epist. Cent. III. ad Belgas Epist. XCIV.) *desiring him to consider what near affinity they did seem to bear to the* Saxon Language. *In a few Days, such Notes and Animadversions upon those Words were returned, as were thought worthy to be printed at the end of the Commentary of Dr.* Casaubon de linguâ Saxonicâ.

Anno 1652. *He compiled the Learned Glossary annexed to the* X. Scriptores, *which was this Year published. At this time also he was assisting towards the bringing to the Press the* Monasticon Anglicanum, *with some other good Services to the Common-Wealth of Learning, whereof the Writer of his Life does give a just account.*

Anno 1659. *His* Saxon Dictionary, *the true and lasting Monument of his Praise, came forth. This was a Work of incredible Labour to himself, and of singular Benefit to the World.*

Anno 1660. *His* Treatise of Gavelkind *was now printed. It had lain by him finished twelve Years, namely, during the Confusions of the Civil Wars in* England. *But the same Year that it pleased God to put an end to the Great Rebellion, Learning did revive, and this Treatise came abroad, so compleat, as it did not afterward admit of one Correction (the* Errata *of the Press being excepted) from his own Pen, nor of any one Alteration or Addition, tho' he lived several Years after he published it. I take notice hereof, to correct a Misinformation which is given in the Catalogue of his Posthumous Works.*

Anno 1669. *His Treatise called* Chartham News *was the last thing that he wrote; for as soon as he had finished it, his last Sickness, attended by Death, came so speedily upon him, as to leave him neither Time nor Strength so much as to read it once over: For which reason we may look upon it as one of his Imperfect Works. It was published by his Brother within a few Months after his Death.*

Anno

A PREFACE to this New Edition,

Anno 1693. The Treatise of the Roman Ports and Forts in Kent *was printed at* Oxford, *with some Annotations upon it by* Dr. Gibson, *and his Life prefixed by* Dr. Kennet. *It had been easie to have supplied, from the Registers of this Church, some Records or Charters mentioned by the Author, which are wanting in it, as in particular the Charter concerning the Port of* Sandwich, &c. *Among Mr.* Somner's *Manuscripts, there is a Fragment which he calls* Goodwin-Sands; *This was by him inserted into his Treatise of the* Roman Ports and Forts, *where it is published. I will here take occasion to add, That the emergency of the* Goodwin-Sands, *and the building of* Tenterden-Steeple, *seem to have been coetaneous, which might give occasion for the* Old Man *(as is reported) to say,* That Tenterden-Steeple was the cause of the Goodwin-Sands.

Anno 1694. A Discourse of *Portus Iccius, wherein the late Conceits of* Chiffletius, *in his Topographical Discourse thereof are examined and refuted:* The Judgment of *Cluverius concerning the same asserted and embraced; and the true site thereof more clearly demonstrated by* William Somner. *This is the Title of the Manuscript in* English. *Some Years after he had finished this Treatise, he put an* Addendum *at the end of it. This Discourse was done into* Latin *by the Reverend and Learned Dr.* Edm. Gibson, *and printed at* Oxford. *The Translator has faithfully done his part, and has given much credit to the Discourse, by attiring it in the old* Roman Dress, *a Garb most suitable to a Discourse upon such a Subject. It is certain, that both these Treatises,* The Roman Ports and Forts in Kent, *and the* Portus Iccius *were, many Years before the Author's Death, finished in the same form in which he left them. And I have been credibly informed, that his very good Friend, the judicious Dr.* Meric Casaubon *did advise him to forbear making them publick. These (I think) are all the Pieces of his Works which have at any time been printed.*

He has left in Manuscript a short Discourse, which he stiles, Littus Saxonicum per Britanniam. *The design of it is to overthrow the Opinion of Mr.* Selden, *in his* Mare clausum (L. 2. c. 7.) *concerning this Shore, and to vindicate the Opinion of* Ortelius, Cambden, Merula, Cluverius, *and other Geographers. This might be very conveniently annexed to the* Portus Iccius, *and would be received, as* Fragment, *worthy of the Name of its Learned Author.*

I will now give an account of the other Remains of Mr. W. Somner, *which he has left behind him; and I will lay open in the first place the largest of all his Manuscripts, which has this Title,* Observations upon the Commissary of Canterbury, his Patent of that Commissariship. *The Writer of his Life informs the World, that it is* A large Discourse concerning the Original Jurisdictions, Privileges, Laws, &c. *of the Spiritual Court. Great Expectations are raised hereby, far beyond what this Treatise can answer; for great part of it was inserted by the Author into his* Antiquities of Canterbury; *and the rest is not fitted for publick Use. I will here give a particular account of it, that whosoever shall desire to peruse it, or any part of it, may be rightly informed of what he may expect to find in it.*

This Discourse was (I suppose) the first Fruits of his Labours, the beginnings of his Study of Antiquity. It was composed in the time of Archbishop Abbot, *a little after the Death of King* James I. *upon the Patent of Commissariship granted to Sir* Nathanael Brent. *Upon the word* Archbishop *he proposeth to shew the Antiquity of Archbishops in general, of our Archbishops in particular, and of their number in* England. *He discourseth concerning the Title,* Totius Angliæ primas, *upon the Bishops of* St. Martin's; *concerning the Original of the* Consistory-Court, *of Rural Deans, &c. All which is inserted into his* Antiquities of Canterbury: *Only in the Manuscript there is a Copy of the Charter of King* William I. *for the separation of the Ecclesiastical from the Secular Courts, which, he says, he did forbear to print, because it had been several times publish'd.*

Upon the word Clergy *he has the whole Discourse concerning the Privilege, which is commonly called* The Clergy, *which is to be seen at large in his* Appendix *to his* Antiquities. *He comments also upon the stile* Dean and Chapter; *from hence he supplied himself with whatsoever he has written, concerning the Foundation and Antiquity of this Metropolitical Church, and the Deans and Priors thereof. Thus it appears, that a very great part of the Treatise is already publish'd by him in his* Antiquities.

He discourseth also upon the several Ecclesiastical Courts of our Archbishops, the Arches, Audience, &c. *And he declares, That whatsoever he has observed concerning these Courts, their Rights, and Jurisdictions, is collected from Archbishop* Parker's *Antiquities of Britain; as also concerning* Surrogates, Proctors, Apparitors, Sommoners, *from whence he derives his own Name.*

The

A PREFACE to this New Edition

The remaining parts of the Treatise contain a Commentary upon these Heads, Coercion by Ecclesiastical Censures, as Suspension, Excommunication, Interdiction, and Sequestration, Absolution of Persons deceased from Excommunication, Matrimonial Causes, Illegal procuring or holding of Ecclesiastical Benefices, Blasphemy, Perjury, Incest, Drunkenness, concerning the Sanctuary, the Probate of Wills, Administration of the Goods of the Deceased, Executorship; and he is large in justifying the Fees due to the Officers of Ecclesiastical Courts. He speaks of the Confirmations of Grants or Patents, by the Dean and Chapter, and of private and of authentick Seals.

In fine, upon the restrictive Clause in the Commissary's Patent, Citra tamen legum & Statutorum hujus Regni offensionem. *He takes occasion to make some mention of Parliament and Convocation, where he writes thus :*

"Parliament *signifies as much as* Collocutio *or* Colloquium *; agreeable where-
"unto is that of* Cook (Comment. upon *Littleton,* fol. 110. a.) *Parliament* (says
"he) *is so called, because every Member of that Court should sincerely and discreetly*
"Parler le ment, *for the general good of the Commonwealth. This Court* (a) *was*
"anciently before the Conquest called, Michil Sinoth, Michil Gemot, Ealsa
"Witenagemot, *that is, the Great Court, or Meeting of the King with the Council of*
"his Bishops, Nobles, and wisest of the People. I learn from Mr. Selden (Titles of
"Honour, Part II. c. 5. §. 23. p. 721. 726.) *that once under King* Edward II. *the*
"Official of the Archbishop of Canterbury, and the Dean of the Arches, were by
"Writ among other Regular Barons of that Age summoned to Parliament. Proctors
"also of the Clergy *(as* Cowel *affirms,* Interpret. verbo, Proctors of the Clergy)
"howsoever of late Days the case is altered, had place and suffrage in the Lower House
"of Parliament, as well as Knights, Citizens, Barons of the Cinque-Ports, and Bur-
"gesses ; for so it plainly appeareth by the Statute Anno 21. R. II. c. 2. & c. 12.
"And sithence they were removed, the Church (saith he) has daily grown weaker and
"weaker, &c. *Thus he. The cause (it seemeth) why at first the House of Convocation*
"was dismembred from the Lower House of Parliament was this : Whilst the Pope's
"Power extended it self to this Kingdom, and took place amongst us, the Clergy then
"(b) was no true Member of the Commonwealth, and therefore there was no reason
"that the Convocation should have the Privileges of Parliament, when it was distorted
"from it, and assembled without it by vertue of the Pope's Legate's Writ ; and so the
"power and purpose of it was foreign, and justly came within the compass of a Præ-
"munire. This was the cause why the Convocation in those Times was disjoined
"from the Parliament. But now this Cause is taken away and ceaseth : Sith it is now
"assembled with the Parliament, by the same Writ with the King ; and the Parliament
"is not compleat without it, being one of the Three Orders, and that State which makes
"it have competent Power in matters Ecclesiastical, that it is not a meer temporal Court ;
"which being so, the effect in all reason ought to cease ; and therefore though heretofore
"it was a Member, whose Nerves were wrested, distorted, distracted, and racked from
"its natural Head, by extension to a Foreign ; yet there was no dissolutio continui
"(as Physicians speak) from the Head, and therefore not from the collateral Members :
"and seeing it was but a discontented discontinuance that did cause it to be suspected
"and suspended, it being now again contracted and knit most firmly to the Head, is
"united as closely to the Members, and may safely exercise and enjoy all the Power and
"Privileges that did of right belong unto it, with the Parliament.——Our King's Ma-
"jesty apprehending thus much, was graciously pleased to consider of the restitution of
"this discountenanced and disabled House of Convocation. A very worthy Consideration
"(saith Downing, who very rightly commemorates it) seeing it is as nearly and
"dearly annexed to his Supremacy as the Parliament is : For His Majesty having two
"Capacities (c) of Government in him, the one Spiritual, the other Temporal ; by both
"these he hath Supremacy, and this Supremacy is chiefly exercised in the calling, pre-
"siding over, and dissolving of the Great Assembly of the Three States ; which High
"Court is not competently correspondent to both the Powers in the King, unless the Par-
"liament consist collective of Spiritual and Temporal Persons, which it hath anciently
"(if the Book De modo tenendi Parliamenta be authentical ;) for he makes the
"Upper House to consist of Three States, the King's Majesty, the Lords Spiritual, and
"Temporal ; and the Lower House of the Knights, Procurators of the Clergy, and the
"Burgesses ; which both answer the King's mixt Supremacy : So that as he is Supre-
"mus Justitiarius totius Angliæ, in relation to the Temporalty ; so he is Supremus,

---

(a) *Cook.*   (b) *Downing's* Discourse, Concluf. 3. p. 70.   (c) *Ridley's* View of Ecclesiastical ws, p. 140.

A PREFACE to this New Edition.

" or (*as* Conftantine *truly intituled himſelf in the Council of* Nice) Ἐπίσκοπος τῶν
" Ἐποκόπων, *in reſpect of the Spiritualty. Hitherto of Parliaments. Theſe are the
words of Mr.* Somner, *which I have tranſcribed as a Sample of the whole Diſcourſe.
I will now lay aſide this Treatiſe, and take another of his Manuſcripts into my hand;
to which the Catalogue of his Poſthumous Works gives this following Title :*

Collections out of ancient Manuſcripts and Records, relating to the City
and Church of *Canterbury,* and to other Towns and Churches in *Kent. Some
curious Perſons may deſire to know what Treaſures are contained in theſe Collections ;
and for their Satisfaction, I will acquaint them that herein are contained :* 1. *The
Charter of King* Edward IV. *granted to the City of* Canterbury, *Anno* 1460.
2. *Anſwers to the Articles of Enquiry made by the Commiſſioners of King* Henry VIII.
*concerning the Eſtates, Goods, and Revenues of ſome Hoſpitals and Chanteries, particu-
larly of the Hoſpital of St.* Thomas *the Martyr of* Eaſtbridge, Maynard's *Spittle,
(the Inventory of the Goods belonging to the Chapel is printed in the Antiquities,)*
Prince Edward's *Chauntery in the Undercroft in* Chriſt-Church, *St.* John's *Hoſpital without North-gate, the Hoſpital of the Poor Prieſts, Sir* William Roper's *Chantery in St.* Dunſtan's *Church, the Hoſpital of St.* Jacob *in* Thanington, Herbaldown-
Hoſpital and Chantery, Wingham *Collegiate-Church, the Chanteries of the* Bleſſed
Lady *and St.* Stephen *in* Aſh, *the united Chanteries of the* Bleſſed Virgin *and the*
Holy Trinity *in* Reculver, *the Chantery of the* Holy Croſs *in the Chapel of the Bur-
rough of* Hoth, *the Chantery of our* Bleſſed Lady *in the Pariſh of* Heron, *our* Lady-
Church *in* Dover, *St.* Bartholomew's *Hoſpital by* Dover, *St.* Martin's *in* Dover,
and Archbiſhop Arundel's *Chantery.* 3. *Tranſcripts out of* Thorn, &c. De Tranſlatione Sti. Auguſtini, Littera Regis ad Archiepiſcopum de reſtituendâ Abbatia,
(*viz.* S. Auguſtini,) Reſcriptum Archiepiſcopi ad Dominum Regem de eadem.
Privilegium Greg. Pap. IX. Scriptum de Capella de Dane in Thaneto. Ap-
propriationes Eccleſiæ de Elcham Scholarib. de Merton Oxon. & Eccleſiæ de
Hedcrune Hoſpitali de Oſpring. Decretum D. Archiepiſc. Cantuar. ut Inhabitantes de Hearne contribuant reparationi Eccleſiæ de Reculvre. Confirma-
tio cartæ Theobaldi per Gregorium Papam ſuper dona Obedientiariorum, in
qua quædam de Prioratu B. Martini Dovor. Confirmatio Cœmiterii S. Pauli
Cantuar. De Capella de Shorn vel Thorn. Excerpta ex ſcedis D. Doctoris
Caſauboni de Sigillis, &c. Carta Huberti Archiepiſc. Cant. Conſervatoris
Poſſeſſionum Canonicorum Prioratus S. Gregorii Cant. (*This is inſerted into the
Monaſtic. Anglican.*) Donatio Manerii de Dene in Inſula Thaneti Monaſterio
S. Auguſtini. Compoſitio inter Abbatem & Conventum S. Auguſtini & Tenentes
eorum de Menſtre & Hengrave in Thaneto. *Theſe are the Titles of all the Records that
are tranſcribed into this Book of Collections, and good part of them are publiſhed in* Thorn, *&c.*

The Catalogue of Mr. Somner's *Poſthumous Manuſcripts, directs me next to a Volume, in which are contained,*

Large Extracts out of the Chronicle of *William Thorn,* with other Extracts
out of the Obituary of *Chriſt-Church, Canterbury,* and *Rocheſter,* with Collections out of the *Saxon* Annals. *This Title promiſeth much. I will forbear to mention his Extracts out of* Thorn's *Chronicle, that Book being now printed. I will account for the reſt in order.*

1. Excerpta ex Gotcelini libro de Tranſlatione S. Auguſtini Anglor. Apoſtoli & Sociorum ejus, in Bibliotheca Deuveſiana. *Concerning this Treatiſe, ſee
the Preface to the Second Part of* Ang. Sacr. p. 7.
2. Excerpta ex vet. libr. Mſ. olim Eccleſiæ Chriſti Cantuar. modò in Bibliotheca Comitis Arundel, cui Titulus, Regiſtrum ſive Martyrologium Eccleſiæ Chriſti Cant.
*The greateſt part of theſe Excerpta out of the Obituary, may be ſeen now printed
in the Firſt Part of* Angl. Sacr. pag. 55, &c. Dies Obituales Archiepiſcoporum
Cantuarienſium, & p. 137, &c. *in the Hiſtory of the Priors. The reſt are the Obits
of ſome Benefactors to the Church, who were received into the Fraternity ; and the
chief of them are theſe which follow :*

Chriſtian de Haghe *gave ſixty Marks* Sterling, *and* John *her Husband gave ten
Marks toward the building of the Refectory.*

b

John

A Preface to this New Edition.

John Tyece *gave five hundred Marks out of three Messuages, viz. the* Crown *in* St. Andrew's *Parish, the* Rook *in* St. Mary Bredne, *and the House in which he lived.*

William Lwyte *gave fifty Marks out of a House in the Parish of* St. Elphege.

Osbern Bygge *(besides divers other Benefactions, which are there recorded) gave seventy two Mansions in the City of* Canterbury, *&c.*

John Bokynham, *Bishop of* Lincoln, *came to this Church, and lived here twenty four Weeks at his own Costs, and died in the Prior's Lodgings, called* Master Homers. *By his Will he gave to the Church* 40 l. *to* Thomas Chillenden, *then Prior,* 40 l. *to every Monk that was a Priest* 13 s. 4 d. *to every Monk not of the Order of Priesthood* 6 s. 8 d. *He appointed that a hundred Pence should be given to a hundred poor People, to every one a Peny, annually on the anniversary of his Death for ever, &c. He constituted Prior* Chillenden *to be his Executor, who out of his Goods which were sold, purchased Ornaments and Vestments for this Church, to the value of* 240 l. *the particulars whereof are recited in the Obituary.*

John Beaufort, *Earl of* Somerset, *Brother of King* Henry IV. *was buried in this Church, having been admitted into the Fraternity of this Convent.*

Alexander Hawkin, *who had been Secretary to several Priors forty Years, gave a hundred and fifty Pounds, towards the South Steeple, a new Bell, and towards the new Roof of the Martyrdom.*

Robert Bourn, *Commissary to several Archbishops, gave eighty Pounds in Gold.*

John Bryan, *Stone-cutter in the new Work of the Church twenty Years, gave by his Will twenty Marks.*

King Richard II. *forgave two Corrodies of thirty Marks, and the Forfeitures of their Tenements in* London, *to the value of a thousand Marks; and gave them Licence of Mortmain, without Fine or Fee, to purchase Lands or Rents to the value of* 200 l. *and to appropriate to themselves the Churches of* Godmersheim *and* Mepham; *and moreover gave above* 1000 l. *Sterling towards the Fabrick of the High Altar, and of the Nave of the Church, besides rich Jewels and Gifts, which he at several times offered at the Shrine of St.* Thomas *the Martyr, and at the Altar in the Chapel of the Blessed Virgin in the Undercroft.*

John Lovel, *Rector of the Parish of St.* George *in* Canterbury, *gave a silver Salt-seller for the use of the President's Table in the Refectory.*

Anne Tatreshade *gave to the Fabrick of the Church* 140 l. *and to the High Altar a Censer of pure Gold.*

William Brenchesly, *Knight, gave to the Fabrick of the Church* 100 l.

John Wymborn, *Commissary of this Church, gave* 200 Marks *for the purchase of Lands, for the use of this Church and Convent: Also* 100 Marks *towards the building of the new Kitchen: Also* 60 Marks *to the Convent: Also* 40 s. *to the Sacrist for the Steeple: Also all his Cups and Silver-Plate for the use of the Table of the Master: Also two Acres of Meadow for the use of the Cellrer: And all his Books to the Library, viz. two Books of Decrees, and two Books of Decretals, and two Books of* Innocent, *and* Notabilia de jure civili; *besides other Benefactions.*

Prince Edward *is recorded to have given several Jewels, Vessels and Images of Gold, rich Vestments, &c. which are recited in the Obituary.*

King Edward I. *granted several Liberties and Privileges, gave several Jewels, Images, and Vessels of pure Gold, of inestimable value: And he either sent, or personally offered every Year upon the Day of the Martyrdom of St.* Thomas *three Florens of Gold, which the Obituary calls his* Chevage.

King William *the Conqueror restored almost all the Lands which had been wrongfully taken away from the Church as* Raculfre, *&c. Of this matter, See* Selden's *Notes upon* Edmer's *History,* De placito apud Pinendenam. *Page* 197.

Lewis *King of* France *gave an hundred Muyds of Wine yearly for the use of the Convent, &c. This Charter, with his Letter of Fraternity from the Convent, may be seen in the last Page of the Appendix to* Reyner's Apostolat. Benedictin. in Anglia.

Sir John Denam *gave an Image of Silver gilt, valued at* 60 l.

Hugh Manimot *gave the Church of* Quenyngate *in* Canterbury, *and eleven Mansion-Houses to this Convent and Church.*

The Lady Mabilia Gobioron *gave towards the building of the new Chapel of the Virgin* Mary 14 l.

Robert Clyfford *of* Welle, *Esq; Brother of* Richard Clyfford, *Bishop of* London, *gave* 400 Marks, *and his silver Plate, &c.*

3. Excerpta

A Preface to this New Edition.

3. Excerpta ex Veteri libro Mf. fc. Regiftro (ut infcribitur) temporalium Ecclefiæ & Epifcopatus Roffenfis abbreviato.

The greateſt part, if not all, theſe Excerpta *are publiſhed in* Anglia Sacra. *fc.* P. I. *yet I may recommend them to be examined and compared by any one who will undertake to write the Hiſtory of the Church of* Rocheſter.

4. E pervetuſto Libro Mf. in Bibliotheca Cottoniana, Orofii hiftoriam continente quâ præfcriptâ tractatuloque de menfibus addito, ftatim fequitur manu Saxonica, ut cætera, exarata, Chronologia Saxonica, cui hic titulus, manu nupera præfixus, Chronica Saxonica Abingdoniæ ad Annum 1066.

Then follows a tranfcript of that whole Chronicle. Theſe are all the things that are contain'd in that Volume of Collections. As to the reſt of his Saxon Tranſcripts, *and his Annotations or Amendments upon ſome printed Books, the Reader may conſult the Catalogue of his Works ſubjoined to the end of his Life.*

THE

A

TABLE

OF THE

CHAPTERS

Contained in the First Part.

THE Antiquity *of* Canterbury, *and the* Names *of the* City. Page 1
    The City-Wall *and* Gates *therein.* ——————— 4
The Ditch *encompassing the* City-Wall. ——————— 17
The Castle. ——————— 18
The River. ——————— 20
The Monastery *of St.* Augustin. ——————— 25
The Church *of St.* Martin. ——————— 34
The Mote. ——————— 35
Long-Port *and the* Nunnery *of St.* Sepulchre. ——————— 36
The Hospital *of St.* Laurence. ——————— 38
———— *of St.* Jacob. ——————— 41
———— *of St.* Nicolas *at* Herbaldown. ——————— 42
Hakynton, Barton, *and* Jesus-*Hospital.* —— 47
The Priory *of St.* Gregory. ——————— 48
The Hospital *of St.* John. ——————— 50
Westgate-*Street.* ——————— 51
The Division *of the* City *into* Wards. ——————— 52
Westgate-*Ward. The* Grey-Friars. ——————— 54
The Black-Friars. ——————— 57
The Hospital *of* Eastbridge. ——————— 60
The Exchange, Mint, Jury, *and* Guild-Hall. ——————— 63
Newingate-*Ward. The* Augustin-Friars. ——————— 67
Northgate-*Ward.* Stable-Gate, *&c.* ——————— 69
Northgate-*Ward, the* Hospital *of* Poor-Priests, *the Island with* Mayner's
    Spittle, *and* Cotton's Hospital.   }71
Ridingate-*Ward, the* Dungeon. ——————— 75
Burgate-*Ward.* ——————— 79
The Cathedral. ——————— 81
The Archbishop's Palace, *&c.* ——————— 101
The Archbishops. ——————— 113
The Priors. ——————— 139
The Archdeacons. ——————— 150
Parochial Churches. ——————— 153
The Ecclesiastical Government *of the* City. ——————— 171
The Temporal Government *thereof.* ——————— 178
Chartham News. ——————— 186
The Appendix.

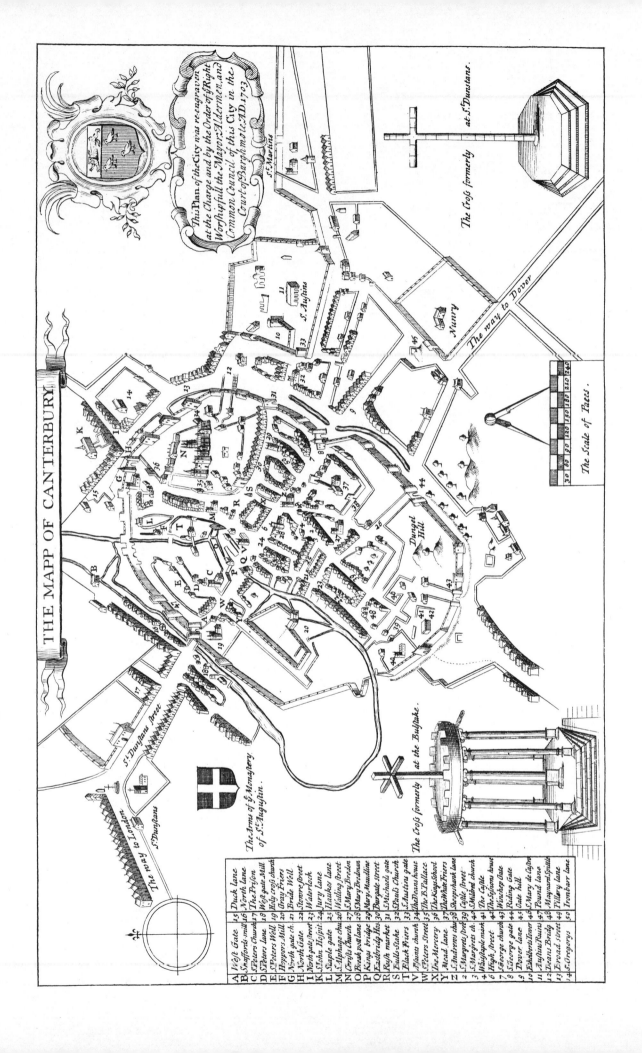

THE MAPP OF CANTERBURY

This Plan of the City was re-engraven at the Charge and by the Order of y.e Right Worshipfull the Mayor Aldermen, and Common Council of this City in the Court of Burghmote A.D. 1703

S.t Martins

S.t Austins

Nunry

The way to Dover

The Cross formerly at S.t Dunstans.

The Scale of Paces.

30 60 90 120 150 180 210 240

The way to London

S.t Dunstans

S.t Dunstans Street

Dungel Hill

The Arms of y.e Monastery of S.t Augustin.

The Cross formerly at the Bulstake.

A	West Gate	15	Duck lane
B	Swaffords mill	16	North lane
C	S.t Peters Church	17	The Prison
D	S.t Peters lane	18	West gate Mill
E	S.t Peters Well	19	Holy crofs church
F	Hoppers Mill	20	Gray Friers
G	North gate ch:	21	Bride Well
H	North Gate	22	Stowre street
I	North gate street	23	Waterlock
K	S.t John Hospit:	24	Jury lane
L	Staple gate	25	Maukes lane
M	S.t Alphage chu:	26	Watling street
N	Crofs Church	27	S.t Mary Bredon
O	Frank pollane	28	S.t Mary Bredman
P	Kings bridge	29	Mary Maudlin
Q	Eastbridg Ho:	30	Burgate street
R	Rush market	31	S.t Michaels gate
S	Eadls-Stake	32	S.t Pauls church
T	Black Friers	33	S.t Austins gate
V	Manis church	34	the Deans house
W	S.t Peters Street	35	The B.t Pallace
X	The Mercery	36	The Kingshead
Y	Mead lane	37	The White Friers
Z	S.t Andrews chu:	38	Shepsbank lane
1	S.t Margarets street	39	Caftle street
2	S.t Margrets ch:	40	S.t Mildred church
3	Wayfaple mart	41	The Caftle
4	High street	42	The Sejsions house
5	S.t George street	43	Winchep Gate
6	S.t George gate	44	Riding Gate
7	Dover lane	45	Oate Hill
8	Ethelberts Tower	46	S.t Mary de lafro:
9	Austins Ruins	47	Pound lane
10	Deans Bridg	48	Maynard Spittle
11	Broad street	49	Pillory lane
12	S.t Gregorys	50	Ironbar lane

THE
ANTIQUITY
OF
CANTERBURY.

SO great and Universal is the Respect that is worthily given to venerable Antiquity, that not any one Ornament sets off any place, whether City or other, with greater Lustre, or more proclaims and applauds their Judgment that first selected the place for Habitation, than the true and known Antiquity, and long Duration of the place.

Now no one thing almost of this nature that Discourse shall offer to the Consideration of an *English-Man*, especially a *Kentish-Man*, shall find more vulgar Belief, nor is better grounded in Tradition, than (my main Motive to the ensuing Treatise) the Antiquity of this our City. And than it, what more celebrated in (the living Monuments of their deceased Authors) our Stories and other like Works of *English* Writers ? For brevity sake (which I shall study throughout my whole Discourse) the Testimonies only of two, Mr. *Cambden* (*a*), our modern *Chorographer*, and *Henry of Huntingdon* (*b*), one of our elder Historians, as sufficient to justify so known a verity, shall suffice for instance. Who, in the places here marginally quoted, have set and left the Note and Mark of Antiquity upon the place. And no marvel, when as in the *English-Saxons* time, and even in the beginning of their Heptarchy, it was the head or chief City of the *Kentish* Kingdom, and the King's Seat. (*c*) *The chief City of King Ethelbert.* So venerable *Bede. The head of the Empire.* So others call it. *In the Famous City, which by an Ancient Name is call'd Dorovernia*, is the close of a Charter, of *Kenulph*, King of *Mercia*, in the Year of Grace Dcccx.

Names of the City.

AS for the further Discovery of the yet greater Antiquity of the Place, if any shall desire it ; let him consider with me in the next place, the Names that former times have known it by. As the *Saxons* of old (*d*) call'd *Kent*, Cant-ᵹuaꞃ-lanꞇ (*i.* the Country of the Men of *Kent*:) So the name which they gave to this our City was Canꞇꞃaꞃa-byꞃıᵹ, and Canꞇꞃaꞃa-ꝥıc, (*i.* the *Kentish* Men's City, Court, or Borough:) A Name well agreeing with that of *Cair Kent*, or *Caer Kent* (the City of *Kent*) as *Nennius* and the *Britains* called it. What time the *Roman* Empire extended it self hither, it was of them called *Durovernum* ; haply from the British, *Durwhern*, rendered by my Author (*e*), a swift River, such as our *Stoure* is : or else (as one (*f*) will) from *Thorowbourne*, because of the River's running through the City. With very little variation from which *Roman* name, you may find that our elder Historians, *Bede*, and others called it *Dorovernia*, and *Derobernia* : and that you see before, in the Year Dcccx. was called (*g*) *the Old Name* ; and yet long afterwards continued it in use, even until that of *Cantuaria*, better answering to the *Eng-*

(a) *Britannia.* In *Kent.*   (b) *Hist. lib. 6. An. Dom.* 1011
(c) *Imperii Regis Ethelberti Metropolis. Eccles. Hist l. 1. c. 25   Caput Imperii,* &c. *Florileg. al A. D.* 556. *In civitate famosa, qua antiquo vocabulo* Doroverni *dicitur. Cart. Antiq.*
(d) *Cambden* in *Kent.*   (e) *Cambden ubi supra.*   (f) *Twyne. De Reb. Albion. l. 1. p.* 113.
(g) *Antiquum Vocabulum.*

lifh-Saxon, Cantwarabyrig; and from about the *Norman* Conqueſt hitherward, more frequently than the other; and in time altogether taken up and uſed, made it give her place. But of our City's Name ſee more if you pleaſe in the *Antiquit. Britan. pag.* 34.

Canterbury in being in the Romans time. Clearly then *Canterbury* had an exiſtence in the time of the *Romans* Empire here. Let me add, and before in the preceeding *Britains* time too, as to me ſeems ſomewhat evident from hence, that the Roman *Durovernum*, is ſeemingly no other than the Latin rendring of the Britain *Durwhern*; by which or near a like Name (moſt probably,) the *Romans* found it call'd by the *Britains* at their coming. However the mention of it in the Emperor *Antonine's Itinerary*, more I take it, than Fourteen hundred Years old, and the many pieces of *Roman* Coin, both of his, and alſo of preceeding, and ſucceeding Emperors, found almoſt in all parts of the City; (ſome whereof are come to my hands) are evident tokens of the Place's great Antiquity. A thing not doubted of a far more learned, and judicious Surveyor of our City, Mr. *Cambden* (*a*), in whoſe opinion it was famous in the *Romans* time.

One ſtrong Argument whereof amongſt the reſt, are the preſent Remains of a double Military way of theirs; the great Stone-cauſeys, I mean directly leading from two of their Famous Havens, *Dubris* and *Lemanis*, that is, *Dover* and *Lymne*; unto this our City, tho former by *Barham down*, the latter by *Stone-ſtreet.*

Elder than Rome. Of whom founded. But (will ſome ſay:) what make I loitering here? It is neither in the *Saxon*, nor yet the *Roman*, neither the intervening *Britains* time, that we are to expect the finding of our Cities Original. It's much elder: *Rome* it ſelf not ſo old. Indeed I Read that one *Rudhu-dibras* or *Lud-hudibras*, a King of the *Britains*, almoſt Nine hundred Years before our Saviour's Incarnation, was our City's Founder. So ſays the Author of the *Britiſh* ſtory, a Writer, though by the beſt of our Antiquaries (*Cambden* eſpecially) for the generality of his Hiſtory exploded as fabulous; yet in this particular followed by divers Men of Judgment, and good Antiquaries too (*b*): with what warrant, as I cannot determine, ſo neither will I examine, but leave it as I find it to the ſcanning of others. So much for our City's Original and Antiquity.

Now what was the general State and Condition of it in either the *Britains*, *Romans*, *Saxons*, or *Danes* times: No Man may exact or expect any Account of me, in regard no Hiſtory, or other Record enables me to ſhow it. The Survey taken of it in the Conqueror's time, and recorded in the Book of Doomſday (*c*), is the firſt and moſt Ancient Deſcription of it any where extant. A Tranſcript or Extract whereof, is preſented in the *Appendix* Numb. I. There Read if you pleaſe.

[But before the Reader turns to the *Appendix*, I will remind him, That this and all other Tranſcripts of Doomſday-Book, do not lie open to the Apprehenſion of every One. The matter contain'd in it thro' diſuſe, is hard to be underſtood, and the terms of it are grown obſolete. I have therefore conſulted his Eaſe and Benefit, ſo far as to give the whole of it in *Engliſh*, together with ſome Annotations, for the explaining ſome particular Words and Paſſages of it. I have followed the ſenſe and interpretation of Dr. *Brady*, a Man moſt Learned and knowing in theſe things, who in his (*d*) *Hiſtorical Treatiſe of Cities and Boroughs*, has printed ſome lines of the beginning of this Record; from whence I have noted two or three various Lections, in the Margin of the Latin. The Tranſcript is as followeth.

KENT.

" IN the City *Canterbury*, King *Edward* had one and fifty (*e*) Burgeſſes, paying Rent, and two hundred and twelve others, under his Privilege and Ju-

---

(*a*) *Britannia.* Of *Canterbury*, in *Kent.*   (*b*) *Author Antiquit Brit. Lambard. Holinſhead. Stow. Speed.*   (*c*) Why ſo call'd, ſee Sir H. *Spelman's Gloſſary*, and the Interpreter, *in hac voce.*
(*d*) *Lond.* 1690.
(*e*) Theſe Burgeſſes ſeem to have been ſuch as exerciſed Free Trade, according to the Liberties and Privileges granted them by the King, for which they paid the King a *Gablum*, a yearly Rent or Tribute-Money. To this agrees what Dr. *Brady*, in his fore-nam'd Treatiſe (*p.* 47.) writes of a Free Burgh, which he ſays was a *Town of Free Trading*, a *Merchant Guild or Community*, without paying

" riſdiction,

" rifdiction, of forty Shillings Rent. (*a*) Now the Burgeffes paying Rent are
" nineteen. Of the other two and thirty, which were formerly, Eleven in the
" City-ditch are wafted : And the Archbifhop has feven of them ; And the
" Abbot of St. *Auguftin* has the other fourteen, in exchange for the Caftle.
" And there are yet ccxii. Burgeffes under the King's (*b*)Privilege and Jurifdicti-
" on, iii Mills paying Rent, cviii. Shillings.   There were viii. Acres of Mea-
" dow, which were wont to belong to the King's Legates or Officers. And a
" Thoufand Acres of Wood, not bearing fruit, from which Iffue xxiv. Shillings.
" In the time of King *Edward*, the whole was worth li. pounds. And it was
" worth fo much when *Aamo* the Sheriff received it. Now he that holds it, pays
" (*c*) xxx. Pounds of Money, refin'd and weigh'd, and xxiv. Pounds of Money
" by tale : Over and above all thefe, the Sheriff has cx. Shillings.
" A certain Monk of the Church of *Canterbury* has taken away two Houfes
" of two Burgeffes , the one without , the other within the City. Thefe
" were built on the King's Way.
" The Burgeffes had xlv. Manfions without the City, of which they had
" (*d*) Rent and Cuftom, but the King had the Jurifdiction and (*e*) Protection-
" Money. The Burgeffes alfo themfelves had of the King xxxiii. Acres of Land
" or Meadow for their (*f*) Guild, *Ranulphus de Columbeis* holds thefe Houfes and
" this Land : Befides thefe, He had fourfcore Acres, which the Burgeffes held
" of the King by (*g*) free Tenure. He holds alfo v. Acres of Land, which
" belong of Right to a certain Church. For all thefe the fame *Ranulph* voucheth
" the Bifhop of *Baieux* (*h*) for his Protector.

---

ing *Toll, Paffage, Pontage, Stallage,* &c. And being free from certain *Fines* or *Mulcts,* from Suit to
Hundred or *County-Court,* or *being prefented,* or *anfwering there,* or *any where elfe, but within their own
Burgh, except in Pleas of the Crown* ; with other *Liberties, Privileges,* and *Cuftoms,* according to the
Tenor of particular *Grants* and *Charters.* According to which *Liberties* and *Privileges,* They who
exercife *Free Trade* are called *Free Burgeffes.* Upon account of thefe Liberties, a *Toll* or *Cuftom* was
paid by them to the *Prince* or *Lord* of the *Burgh,* which in procefs of time became a *Fee-Farm* Rent,
or an Annual Compofition in a ftated Sum of Money.

(*a*) Whereas, in the time of King *Edward*, before the *Norman* Conqueft, there were in the City
II. *Burgeffes* of the King's Demefne, which paid him Rent ; now when *Doomfday-Survey* was taken,
They were reduc'd to XIX ; for XI. of them were fallen into Decay, VIII. of them were become
the Archbifhop's Demefne, and the other XIV. of them were affign'd over to the Abbot of St. *Auguftin,* in Exchange for the Caftle that did formerly belong to that Abbot.

(*b*) Dr. *Brady* does here explain the Term *Soca,* to be *Money paid for their Liberties and Privileges,*
that is, The Fine paid to the King for it ; whereas the Word is ufually underftood of the *Liberty* or
Power it felf, which was granted them. *See* Dr. *Brady's* Preface *to his* Hiftory, *fol.* 61. The Meaning here feems to be, *The King had the Franchife.*

(*c*) This Diftinction of Money, *refin'd, weigh'd,* and *by tale,* does not feem to arife from falfe *Coy-
ners* or *Clippers* of Money, but was occafion'd by the feveral *Mints* which were then allow'd of in
England. From fome of which there might come forth, probably even by Miftake, and not of Defign, bad Money, deficient either in *Weight* or *Finenefs.* Money by Tale, was paid by the Number
of the Pieces, without examining the Weight or Finenefs. Money weigh'd was receiv'd by the
Scale, without numbring the Pieces, or examining the Finenefs. And Money Refin'd, had paffed
through the purifying Fire, and was reduc'd to the true Standard. The Manner of Proving and
Examining the true Value of Money minted, before it paffed from the Mint, fhews how liable
the Mint Mafters were to be miftaken in the Value of their Coin. For the Proof was, by well
mixing together in one Heap, the whole Sum that was minted at a time : Out of the Middle of
the Heap as much was taken, as weighed XII. Ounces ; the Pieces were told, and were allow'd to
pafs Currant, if they did not want or exceed fuch or fuch a number of Pence in the whole XII.
Ounces. And according to this Tryal, the whole Sum minted at the fame time was either to pafs
currant, or to be new minted. The whole of this Matter is related in a MS. Regifter, formerly
belonging to the Monaftery of St. *Edmund's-Bury,* called *Pinchbeck,* and is too long to be inferted
here. The *Gloffary,* fubjoin'd to the *Parochial Antiquities* of *Ambrofeden,* informs us, That *Libra ad
numerum,* is *a Pound in ready Money,* oppos'd to *Libra urfa & penfitata* (rather *arfa & penfata*) a
Pound-weight in folid Metal. If I miftake not our Expofitor, he means, That a Pound of Money by
Tale, was Money ready minted ; and that a Pound by *Weight,* was a Lump of folid Metal, before
it was coin'd. Herein he difagrees from Sir *Henry Spelman* and *du Frefne.*

(*d*) By *Rent* and *Cuftom* in this place is probably meant *Forfeitures* and *Toll.* Dr. *Brady's* Hift. *of
Boroughs, p.* 10 *in the Margin.*

(*e*) Tallage was due and paid by the Burgeffes to our Ancient Kings, in Confideration of Liberty granted to them.

(*f*) Merchant- or Trading-Guilds, Communities and Societies in Burghs were granted them by
the King's Charters. Dr. *Brady,* ib p. 17.

(*g*) *Alodium* is Propriety or Lands holden *optimo jure,* free from any Works of Servitude or
ufual Preftations, which though they are not properly under the King's Dominion, yet are under
his Protection. Dr. *Brady.*

(*h*) The Meaning is, He held them of the Bifhop of *Baieux,* who was his Warrant for his Poffeffion. Dr. *Brady.*

" *Ralph*

" *Ralph de Curbeſpine* has four Houſes in the City, which a certain Concubine
" of *Harold* has held : The Juriſdiction and Protection-Money whereof belongs
" to the King ; but as yet he has never had it.

" The ſame *Ralph* holds xi. other Houſes of the (*a*) Biſhop of *Baieux*, in this
" City, which has belonged to (*b*) *Sbern Biga*, and pays xi. ſhillings, xi. pence,
" and a half penny.

" Through the whole City, *Canterbury*, the King has Juriſdiction and Pro-
" tection-Money, except of the Lands of the Churches of the *Holy Trinity*, and
" St. *Auguſtin*, and of Queen *Eddive*, and *Arnold Cild*, and *Eſter Biga*, and *Si-*
" *ret de Cilleham.*

" It is agreed concerning the ſtraight Path-ways, which have a paſſage in
" and through the City : Whoſoever commits a Treſpaſs in them, ſhall be fin'd
" to the King : Likewiſe concerning the ſtraight Roads, without the City, even
" to the diſtance of one League, three Perches, and three Foot. If any one
" therefore ſhall dig or ſet up Stake or Poſt, within any of theſe publick Ways,
" within or without the City, the King's Bailiff proſecutes him, whereſoever
" he ſhall go, and ſhall Levy a Fine on him for the uſe of the King.

" The Archbiſhop lays Claim to Forfeitures made in the publick Ways with-
" out the City, where his Land lies on both ſides. A certain Bailiff, *Bruman*
" by Name, in the time of King *Edward*, took Cuſtom of Foreign Merchants
" in the Lands of the Churches of the *Holy Trinity* and St. *Auguſtin*, who after-
" ward in the time of King *William*, acknowledged before Archbiſhop *Lan-*
" *franc*, and the Biſhop of *Baieux*, that he took it againſt Right, and declar'd
" upon his Oath, That theſe Churches did quietly enjoy their Cuſtoms in the
" time of King *Edward* : And from that time, both of theſe Churches have
" quietly enjoyed their Cuſtoms, in their own Lands, by the Judgment of the
" Barons, before whom it was pleaded. *N. B.*]

The City-Wall, *and Gates therein.*

WHen *Canterbury* was firſt encloſed with a Wall, I think, is no where to
be found in Story, or other Record, either private or publick. Tokens of the Walls good Antiquity are the *Britiſh* Bricks, to be ſeen at *Riding-*
gate, at the Gate alſo now done up, ſometime leading from the Caſtle-yard to
Wencheap, and at *Queningate*, or rather (if you will) at the place in the Wall,
where once the Gate ſo called ſtood, and is now alſo made up. But in greateſt
plenty, upon the Bank on either ſide the River behind St. *Mildred's* Church in
the Remains of the Wall there. And that the City was walled in before the *Nor-*
man Conqueſt, is evident by the Teſtimony of *Roger Hoveden* (*c*), who relating
the Siege and Surprizal of the City by the *Danes*, in the time of King *Etheldred*,
Anno Chriſti 1011. tells us, that (amongſt other particulars of the *Daniſh*
Cruelty, wreaked on the poor *Engliſh* People of the City) many of them being
by the *Danes* caſt headlong from the Wall of the City met with Death in the
precipice.

This may be further proved by ſeveral Records of our Cathedral, making
mention of this Wall in the *Engliſh Saxons* time (*d*). But that I may not ſeem to
loyter, I purpoſely paſs them by, and proceed to elder Evidence. Now the
firſt and moſt ancient Hiſtory of our City-Wall (I conceive) offers it ſelf in
King *Ethelbert's* Charter of the Site of the Monaſtery called (from him, for
whoſe ſake it was founded of King *Ethelbert*) St. *Auguſtin's*, dated *Anno Chriſti*
Dcv. The Ground ſet out for that intent being deſcrib'd to lie (*e*) *under the*
Eaſt Wall of the City of Canterbury. A plain Argument of the City's Walling
at that time, and (as I conjecture) Archbiſhop *Parker's* Warrant for his ſaying,
(*f*) *This City was compaſſed with a Wall, &c.* where he reports the Donation
of this City, with the Royalty thereof by King *Ethelbert* to *Auguſtin.* And
that it was then Walled, may hence be farther argued, that as *Edward* the Con-
feſſor long after, is ſaid to build St. *Peter's* Church in *Weſtminſter* without *Lon-*

(a) *Odo,* **Biſhop of** *Baieux*, was Brother to King *William* the *Firſt*, and by him created Earl of
Kent.   (**b**) *Esbern.*   (c) *A nal. Par. prior.*   (d) *In Archivis Ecclesiæ Chriſti.* Cantuar.   (e) *Sub orientali muro Civitatis.*   (f) *Hanc muro cinctam,* &c. *Antiq. Brit.*
pag 34.

don-City-Wall purposely for the place of his own Sepulture (*a*): So one main End of the Work, of that *Agustinian* Monastery, was (as both *Ethelbert* and *Augustin* in their several Charters intimate) that it might be a Cemitary or place of Burial for them and their Successors; the Kings and Archbishops of the place for ever. And why? but even because of the then Unlawfulness of Burial within Cities, and other Walled Towns; a thing by that Law of the twelve Tables, which said, (*b*) *Thou shalt not bury or burn a dead Man within the City,* flatly forbidden. Tho the *Saxons* in likelihood regarded not that *Roman* Law, yet St. *Augustin* being a *Roman* did. So have I briefly trac'd our City-Walls, to the furthest of their known Antiquity.

But by the way, I may not conceal from you, what suspicion there is of (these Heralds of our City Walls Antiquity:) the *Ethelbertine* Charters to be fictitious and counterfeit. Sir *Henry Spelman,* that learned and worthily admired Antiquary, hath that opinion of them. And indeed, there is a Note to be found in the Records of our Cathedral (*c*) which confirms the suspicion. It tells us that until *Withred* (King of *Kent*) about the Year of Grace Dcc. that Church did peaceably enjoy its Lands and Liberties, only by Ancient Custom, without any Charters or other written Muniments. Could it now be truly added, that *Withred*'s is the first and most ancient Muniment of that Church, judging of the one by the other, this would give great cause of Suspicion of the Truth of those *Ethelbertine* Charters. But in regard, that several Muniments of elder times than *Withred*'s, as one of King *Edbald* Son and Successor of *Ethelbert,* and two of *Cedwalla* the *West-Saxon,* made to this very Cathedral, are to this day extant, being registred at length in the Leigers of that Church (I speak (*d*) what I my self have seen) and, if judgment may be given by the agreement of the hands, even by the very pen of the Author of that Note, there is more cause in my judgment to suspect that Note of falsity, than those Charters, which it may seem to question, of Forgery.

But the noble Knight sets before you (if you please to peruse them) other Reasons for his Opinion. I refer you to them, and them to your consideration: and so pass on to further discourse of our City Wall. Which I conceive carries yet greater Antiquity, than hitherto hath been spoken of. For if (as *Huntingdon* affirms it was) *Canterbury* were one of the 28 Cities infamousing this Island in the *Britains* times, and of them called *Kair-Chent,* taking this note along with us, that *Kair* (*e*) with them signified a wall-defenced Town or City, we need not doubt but it was walled in their times. And so much for the Walls Antiquity; now I pass to after-accidents that have betided it.

The City (as I have given you a former touch) being by the *Danes,* in the days of King *Ethelred,* besieged, taken, and with the Cathedral (as all our Chronologers agree) burnt and utterly wasted; the City Wall (no doubt) being the City's best security against a like surprisal, if it should still have stood, was not spared by that all-wasting enemy.

I read that Archbishop *Lanfranc,* in the Conqueror's time, was a great Benefactor to the Repair of it. So saith Mr. *Lambard* (*f*), and so *Stow,* followed by *Speed.* But no other story mentions it, no not that of his life and acts written by (his successor) Archbishop *Parker.* But so they say. Take it as I find it. When or by whom soever it was repaired, it is plain by the Monk of *Malmesbury,* that in his time, which was about the year of Grace 1142. in the Reign of King *Stephen,* it was walled round. For he saith (*g*) it was then a City much renowned (amongst other things) for the Walls whole and undecayed enclosing it round about. Which being so, and no violence offered them afterward that we read of, I marvel somewhat that there should be need of that fortification of the City with Walls in *Richard* the first's time, as it seems there was: For the King being (it should appear) taken prisoner in his return from the Holy Land, his Mother Q. *Alianor,* out of her care in her absent Son's behalf, of this amongst other (as it seems) weak parts of the Kingdom, takes order for the Fortifying of it: as by her Letters (*h*) of the following tenor

---

(a) *Post alios v'd Cambd in Middlesex.* (b) *Hominem mortuum infra urbem ne sepelito neve urito.* (c) *Vide Dom Hen. Spelman. Tom.* I. *Concil. pag.* 125. (d) *Ex proprio visu.* (e) *Caius de Antiquitat Cantabrig. lib.* I. p 50. (f) Perambulation of *Kent.* In *Canterbury.* (g) *De gest. Pontif lib.* I. *in Prologo.* (h) *In Archivis Ecclesia Cant.*

may appear, written (it seems) at the instance and for the security of the Cathedral Monks, fearful that this one act of their assistance in the work of the City's Fortification, might infringe their liberty of *Burgbote*, and being drawn (*a*) into a president, become a prejudicial example, effectual to compel them to the like in future time, as of the nature of a leading case. The Charter it self is transcrib'd into the *Appendix*. Numb. II.

The import of the Charter was to this purpose, That " inasmuch as it ap-" pear'd requisite, that the City of *Canterbury* in those troublesome times should " be fortified with Ditches, Walls, and other Fortresses, and that all should be " compelled to labour in this Work ; some Vassals or Men under the protecti-" on or patronage of the Prior and Convent of the Church of *Canterbury* did " labour in the same Work, not of right nor of custom, but at the instant En-" treaties of the Queen. Whereupon the Queen having due regard to the " Liberties and Immunities belonging to the said Church, and those that are " under the Protection thereof, did Grant and Promise to the Convent of the " same Church, that the labouring of those their Vassals in that work, which " urgent Necessity and the Queen's interposing by her Entreaties, had moved " them unto, should never hereafter turn to the damage of the Church, and " the Vassals thereof, or to the prejudice of their Liberties and Charters of " Immunities granted and confirmed unto them by many Kings. Witnesses to " this Charter were *H.* Archdeacon of *Canterbury* and *Petrus Blessensis*, &c.

With like caution I find the same Monks, a while after help forward the City's defence another way. For in King *John's* time, *Rich.* 1. immediate successor, the Citizens after much suit to the Monks, prevailed with them at length, to sell them of their wood to make hurdles or wattles withal, for the defence of their City. They are indeed (as I am informed (*b*)) things of especial good and known use for such a purpose, in divers respects, but chiefly serviceable, rightly used, for the securing of a Wall against Ramms and such like engines of assault and battery. Consider of this further, after you have read these Letters (*c*), which I may call the Monks acquittance, or protection.

[These Letters now mentioned are transcrib'd in the *Appendix*, Numb. III. and remain yet in the Registers of the Church of *Canterbury*, and run in this Form, *N. B.*] " To all to whom this present Writing shall come, *Hubert de* " *Burgo*, Justiciary of our Lord the King, greeting. Know ye, That at our " Petition, and at the Petition of the Citizens of *Canterbury*, the Convent of " *Christ*-Church in *Canterbury* did sell to the Citizens of *Canterbury* some of " their Wood to make Hurdles or Wattles, Keys or Spiles, for the defence of " the City. And in as much as it appear'd to us evidently by the Charters of " our Lord King *John*, and his Predecessors, that the said Convent were not " bound to help in the Fortifications of the said City ; left the said Sale of " Wood should hereafter tend to the prejudice of the said Monks and their " Church, we do protest and declare, by these our present Letters under our " Seal, the Right and Liberties of the said Monks and their Church, so far as " concern the said Sale of Wood. Farewell.

The prototype is yet remaining in the Cathedral, where I have seen it with the Seal appendant. The like to that (of the Author's) represented in figure in the last Edition of the Remains, *pag.* 209, and in the Map of *Kent*.

I read nothing of our Walls afterward till *Rich.* 2. days, who (as *Thorne* reported by Mr. *Lambard* (*d*) saith) gave 250 Marks towards the ditching, and inclosing of the City , and in whose Reign , (*e*) *after the Royal Pattern* , that renowned Patriot Archbishop *Sudbury* is said to have built the Western-gate of the City, together with the Wall, lying between that and the North-gate, commonly called the long Wall, and was purposed (some say) to have done likewise about all the City (*f*), if he had lived. The rest of the Wall (it seems) either tottering, or being quite decayed at that time. Insomuch as *Simon Burley* (Warden of the Cinque Ports) advised that the Jewels of *Christ*-Church and St. *Augustin's*, should for more safety be removed to *Dover*-Castle (*g*).

(*a*) *In consequentiam.*   (*b*) *Vide Gloss. D. H. Spelman in verbo Hurditiam.*   (*c*) *In archivis Ecclesia Cant.*   (*d*) Peramb of *Kent*, in *Canterbury.*   (*e*) *Regis ad exemplum.* (*f*) *Wever* of ancient Funeral Monuments, *pag.* 225.   (*g*) *Lambard Peramb. in Cant.*

What coft in reparation it had afterward beftowed on it, was chiefly raifed by the general Tax of the City. For it appears by the Book of *Murage* in the City-Chamber, that the whole City in the time of *Hen.* 4. was taxed and affeffed to the repair thereof: Towards the fuftaining of which Charge, both for the prefent and future, and the Citizens incouragement to proceed in that worthy undertaking, that King, by his Writ of Privy Seal, gives them both a licence of Mortmain, for the purchafing of twenty pound Land *per annum* to the City for ever; and alfo grants them all waft Grounds, and places lying within the City, to ufe and difpofe of for their beft Advantage, likewife in perpetuity. For your better fatisfaction, take here a tranflated Copy of the Writ, as I have it from the Records of the Chamber.

" *Henry* by the Grace of God, King of *England* and of *France*, and Lord of
" *Ireland*; to all People to whom thefe prefent Letters fhall come, Greeting.
" Know ye, that where our Well-beloved, the Citizens of our City of *Canterbury*, Motives.
" (as we hear) have begun to fortifie and ftrengthen the fame City as well
" with one Wall of ftone, as with a Ditch. We confidering the fame City to
" be fet near unto the Sea, and to be as a Port or entry of all Strangers into
" our Realm of *England*, coming by the fame parts; fo that it hath need of
" the more ftrength. Of Our efpecial Grace, and for the honour of God;
" and by the affent of our Counfell, have granted and given licence to the
" fame Citizens, that they may purchafe Lands and Tenements to the Value Grant.
" of twenty pound by the year within the faid City. To have and to hold to
" them and their Succeffors, Citizens of the aforefaid City, in help towards
" the building and making of the fame Wall and Ditch for ever. The ftat.
" made of Lands and Tenements not to be put to Mortmain, or for that the
" faid City is holden of Us in Burgage notwithftanding. Provided that by in-
" quifitions thereof, in due forme to be made, and into the Chancery of Us
" or of Our Heires, duly to be returned, it be found that it may be done with-
" out hurt or prejudice to Us or to Our Heires aforefaid, or to any other:
" And moreover, in confideration of the premiffes of Our more fpecial Grace,
" We by the affent of Our faid Counfell, have granted and given licence to
" the forefaid Citizens, that they all Lands and places voyde and wafte with-
" in the forefaid City may dreffe up, arrent and build up. And the fame
" Lands and places fo dreffed up, arrented and builded, they may have and
" hold to them and to their Succeffors aforefaid, in help and relief of the fame
" Citizens, and in maintenance of the premiffes and other Charges to the
" fame City hapning for ever: without let of Us or of Our Heires or Mini-
" fters whatfoever they be, the ftat. aforefaid; or for that the faid City is
" holden of Us, in Burgage as it is abovefaid notwithftanding. Saved al-
" wayes to Us and to Our Heires the Services thereof due and accuftomed. In
" Witnefs whereof We have caufed thefe Our Letters Patents to be made.
" Witneffe Our Selfe at *Weftminfter* the fifth day of *May*, in the fourth Year
" of Our Reign.

The better and more eafily to eftimate and judge of the Charge of which work, I find that the Year before (3 *Hen.* 4.) the Compafs and Circuit of the Wall was meafured, and a Note thereof taken and regiftred in the Records of the Chamber. Let me prefent you with the Copy of it, in the identity of words and language that I find it. See in the *Appendix* Numb. IV.

The Meafurement of the Walls about the City of Canterbury, *made by* Thomas Ickham, *an Honourable Citizen of the faid City, in the Third Year of the Reign of King* Henry.

Firft from the little Gate called *Quyningate* unto *Burgate* xxxviii Perches, and the Gate, *Burgate*, contains one Perch.
Then from the faid Gate *Burgate* to *Newingate* xxxvii Perches, and the Gate, *Newingate*, contains one Perch.
Then from the faid Gate *Newingate* to *Ridingate* xlviii Perches, and the Gate, *Ridingate*, contains one Perch.
Then from the faid Gate *Ridingate* to *Worgate* lxxxiii Perches, and the Gate, *Worgate*, contains one Perch.
Then from the Gate *Worgate* to the Water behind S. *Mildred's* lxi Perches, and the Bank of the River there contains iv Perches.

Then

Then from the Bank of the River to *Weftgate* cxviii Perches and a half, and the Gate, *Weftgate*, contains one Perch.

Then from *Weftgate* to the end of the Wall, which is called the *Long-Wall*, containing lix Perches, and a quarter of a Perch.

Then the Water, which is called the *Stour* from that Wall to the Wall which is called *Waterlock*, contains xviii Perches and a half.

Then the Wall from that place to *Northgate* contains xl Perches, and the Gate, *Northgate*, contains one Perch.

Then from the Gate *Northgate* to *Quyningate* contains lxix Perches, which is towards the Priory of *Chrift*-Church *Canterbury*.

The Total Sum is Dlxix [that is, 569] Perches, and a fourth part of a Perch.

[But it is mifcaft. It is, befides the Gates and the Bank of the River, 572 Perches and a quarter.

To which add the Six Gates and the Bank of the River 10 Perches, fo the whole Compafs of the City is 582 Perches, and a fourth part of a Perch, befides *Quyningate*, which was a very fmall Gate. N. B.]

This *Thomas Ickham*, by the way, the Wall-meafurer, was Alderman of *Burgate* in the fourth Year of *Hen.* 4. and dying the twenty fixth of *May* , 3 *Hen.* 5. was buried in *Chrift-Church* (a). Others of his Name and Family, (I take it) lye buried in St. *Peter*'s Church in *Canterbury*, as I fhall fhow hereafter.

By this Record, you may perceive that the whole Wall between *Weft*-gate and *North*-gate was not then built, as now we fee it is. For on either fide the River, the Wall, by this Record, clearly breaks off, fo that there is an interjected diftance of eighteen Perches long between the one, and the other Wall. And indeed it will eafily appear to but a flight Obfervation, that fo much of the Wall as ftands and is made up in that then (as I fuppofe) unwalled part, namely, between the Poftern and the Waterlock, next *North*-gate, through which in Arches, with a Port-clofe, the River now paffeth from Abbots Mill, is in the ftone-work much different from the reft of the Wall, and fhews not in any part the leaft wrack or decay, as the other doth. It feems then that Archbifhop *Sudbury* built not all the long Wall.

But enough of the Wall, unlefs the City of latter time had more tendred her own credit and fafety in keeping it better repaired. In pity and juft reproof whereof (whether in this City, or any other) I crave leave here a little to enlarge my felf. A City's Afpect is much blemifhed by ruinous Edifices; efpecially publick, and in places moft obvious to the eye. Now what more publick and obvious than the City-Wall? Againft this deformity the Civil Law very carefully provides, which fays, (b) *That a City ought not to be blemifhed with ruinous Edifices.* As likewife do the Laws of this Land: Statutes being made 27, 32, and 33 *Hen.* 8. to remedy fuch deformities in many of our Cities, and this in particular. If this move not, know then, that our *Englifh* Towns and Cities are taxed, and have a Note fet on them publifhed to the World in Print, for their notorious defect of Walls and Bulwarks. (c) *Nations are expos'd* (faith the French *Tholofanus*) *to the prey of Foreigners, which have not Cities walled and fortified; as appears from* England *and the* Scythian *Countries: for their Ports being once ftorm'd, and an Entrance and Paffage being laid open, all the reft quickly yield,* &c. Thus he, and leaves it not fo, but a while after hath it up again: (d) *'Tis a thing known to all, that* England *and other Nations have fo often changed their Kings and Lords, becaufe there are in them none or very few Cities and Caftles fortified. That it may be efteem'd a moft certain Rule, that an entrance into thofe Countries being once obtain'd, they are prefently fubdu'd.* Thus he, much to the Difcredit of our Nation; but defervedly I doubt, and fufpect our particular neglect and defect in this kind, partly gave the occafion. As we tender then our own, and our

(a) *Liber MS. in Archivis Ecclefia Cant.* (b) *Civitas ruinis non debet deformari. Fin. ne quid in loc. pub. lib.* 43 *ff. lit.* 8. (c) *Expofita funt nationes praeda exterorum, quae non habent muratas aut munitas Civitates, ut de Anglia, & Scythicis liquet nationibus: Cito enim, expugnatis portubus, ingreffu & aditu patefacto, omnia cedunt reliqua, &c.* De Repub lib 1. cap. 3 num. 5
(d) *Eftque res notiffima, Angliam aliafque regiones toties mutaffe Reges & Dominos, quod nulla aut pauciffima funt in eis urbes & arces munita: ut fit axioma certiffimum, ingreffu in eas Regiones obtento, ftatim dominationem earum fequi.* Eod. lib. cap. 5 num. 3.

Countries credit; as we refpect our particular commodity in point of fecurity and beauty, both which it will at once bring unto our City, let us with our Forefathers, as good Patriots, look better to our Walls.

But I fear I fpeak too late. (*a*) The Malady is of that growth by the want of applying timely remedies, that, I think, it is now become incurable. Such danger, fuch detriment attends, and is begotten by delay. Yet let me not feem tedious, whilft I remember what fome yet living cannot have forgotten, that not long fince the cure was in part worthily attempted by a noble Citizen, (*b*) Mr. *J. Eafday* by name, fometime one of our Aldermen, who in the time of his Mayoralty, well hoping his Succeffors in the place, would likewife have fucceeded him in this his exemplary Piety and commendable Endeavour for the Repair of the City-Wall, to his great Coft, being a Man but of an indifferent Eftate, began the Repair thereof at *Ridingate*, and therein proceeded fo far, as where you may find his Name infcribed on the Wall. A Work left for future Ages to follow, none having hitherto vouchfafed it their imitation. But I forbear, becaufe I lift not to be fatyrical.

In this Wall are to the number of twenty one Turrets, or fmall Watch-Towers orderly placed, the moft of them (thanks to God) of no ufe now-a-days; but in many Mens judgments, fuch, as with no great Coft, if it might ftand with the Wifdom of the City, might make, what we much want, convenient Peft-houfes, and Receptacles for the poor vifited People of the City, many times either endangering the publick fafety by their ftay in their Houfes, or elfe hazarding their private welfare abroad for want of fuch or like accommodation. I have done with the Walls.

The Gates.

THE Gates of the City come next to be confidered of. The Wall at this day admits of only Six (except the three Pofterns) anfwering to the number of the Wards, *Burgate, Newingate, Ridingate, Worthgate, Weftgate,* and *Northgate.* Anciently we had another, a Seventh Gate, which was called *Queningate,* whereof mention is made in the foregoing note of the meafurement of the City-Wall. I will briefly fpeak of them all, beginning with that whereof I find eldeft mention, *Burgate,* or *Burrough-gate.*

Burgate, or *St. Michael's Gate.*

THE firft of King *Ethelbert's* Charters dated in the Year of our Redem- *Burgate.* ption 605, tells us of this Gate; bounding out the intended fite of Saint *Auguftin's* Monaftery, (*c*) *South to Burgate-way,* faith the Charter. It was afterwards, and ftill is otherwife called Saint *Michael's*-Gate, from the Church fo called fometime neighbouring to it. About the Year of Grace 1475, this Gate was new builded, at whofe Charges is to be feen upon the Gate without, where you may find the principal Benefactors, worthy Citizens in their times, thus memorized, (*d*) viz. *John Franingam, John Netherfole,* and *Edm. Minot.*

By this Gate lies the Road between the City and *Sandwich,* and the border- A common ing parts, and that only by *Long-port* at this day: whereas in former time Foot-way there was alfo a common Foot-way lying through St. *Auguftin's* Church-yard, fome time by the Gate at either end, the one yet ftanding againft St. *Paul's*-ftreet, called through St. Church-ftreet, at the one end; and the other directly oppofite to it, where a Auguftin's new Gate was lately made, opening into St. *Martin's*-ftreet. Befides Tradit- Church-yard. on, which retains the memory of this common Way, the Wills (*e*) of fome of our Townfmen buried in St. *Auguftin's* faid Church-yard, make mention of it, by appointing and laying out their Burials in (*f*) *the Cemitery of St.* Auguftin *in the High-way,* and the like. And in or about the beginning of *Hen.* 6. Reign, I find there arofe a great debate, ending in a Suit in Law, between the City and the Abby concerning Limits; occafioned chiefly by the Citizens

---

(a) *Serò medicina paratur, &c.* (b) *Anno Domini* 1586. (c) *In meridie via de Burgate.* (d) *Per Johannem Franingam, Johannem Netherfole, & Edm Minot.* (*) *Penes Regiftrum Confiftor. Cantuar.* (f) *Cemiterio S. Auguft. in alta via.*

challenge, and the Monks denial of this Way, to lye and be within the Liberty and Franchife of the City. The quarrel happened in the time of the Bailiffs, who in their paffage to and from St. *Martins* by that way, with their Maces, the Enfigns of their Magiftracy, born up before them, fo diftafted the Monks, that on a time meeting them and their company upon the place, and not prevailing with them (*a*) *by words*, or by force of argument to defert their and the City's claim in that behalf; impatient of the affront, they attempted it (*vi*,) or by force of arms, endeavouring by ftrong hand to force them from the place, but being the weaker party, were put to the worft. To fuit then they go, but the iffue what it was I cannot learn; only I have feen (and have a Copy of) an Argument drawn and framed on the Monks part, and in defence of their Limits and Liberties, to the doing whereof the premifed difference gave the occafion. However, the way continued and lay common till our memory. And here, in all probability, lay the moft ancient Road between *Burgate* and St. *Martins*, it meets in fo ftrait a Line, the Roads at either end, whereas *Long-port* Road lies wide of them both, more South from the Abby; the Road being fo turned of purpofe (as I conceive) to make more way, and give larger fcope for St. *Auguftin*'s Church-yard. And (which moves me moft) the firft Site of the Abby is bounded South to *Burgate* way, and not to *Long-port* (*b*). But leaving this Gate, come we now to the next.

Newingate, or St. *George his Gate.*

NEwingate, otherwife from the Church fo called ftanding hard by it, St. George's-Gate. This Gate was new built much about the time that *Burgate* was. For thus I read in the Will of one *William Bigg* of *Canterbury*, (*c*) a Benefactor to the Work, *Anno* 1470, *Item, I give Ten Pounds to the making and performing of St.* George's *Gate, to be paid as the Work goeth forward.* But it took not the name of *Newingate,* that is, *Newgate,* from this new building of it, but was much more anciently fo called. For about the middle of the Eleventh Century, in a Bull of Pope *Alexander* 3. to the Monks of *Chrift-Church,* I read thus; (*d*) *The Church of St.* George *of* Newingate, *in the City of Canterbury.* Yet by the name of it it fhould not be of any great antiquity. And indeed I conceive it to be of a later foundation than any of the other five, and that it was built (as *Newgate* in *London* was upon an occafion not much unlike (*e*)) chiefly for a more direct paffage into the heart of the City from *Dover* Road. Whereas the more ancient Road and Paffage into the City from *Dover,* lay by the next Gate, whither I am going.

Ridingate.

RIdingate, an ancient Gate, and mentioned in the Records of St. *Auguftin*'s Abby, in *Anno Dom.* 1040, thus; (*f*) Eadfinus *Archbifhop gave to St.* Auguftin *five Acres of Land by* Radingate, *and one Acre of Meadow belonging to the faid Land, on condition that the Monks of St.* Auguftin *fhould make a fpecial Commemoration of him in their Oraifons.*

By this Gate (I fay) anciently lay the *Dover*-road, or rather the *Roman* Port-way, or military Way between *Dover* and *Canterbury;* the like whereof lay between (*g*) *Limen* and the City. (As probably alfo between it and the reft of the *Roman* Ports, to wit, *Reculver, Richborough,* and *Newenden;* places all where the *Romans* planted their *Caftra Riparenfia,* as I may not unfitly call them, for the defence of the *Saxon* Shore:) Of the which former two, one upon *Barham* Down, and the other upon the Downs by *Horton* and *Stowting;* is, in ancient Evidences called *Dunftrata.* 1. The Street-way on the Hill or Down. The *Veftigia* of the latter, is that long continued hard Way, called

---

(a) *Verbis.*   (b) *Vide Char.* 1. *Ethelberti.*   (c) *In Archivis Regiftri Domini Archidiaconi Cantuar.*   (d) *In civitate Cantuar. Ecclefiam Sancti Georgii de Newingate.*   (e) *Survey of London, pag.* 35. *ult. Editionis.*   (f) *Eadfinus Archiepifcopus dedit Sancto Auguftino quinque acras terræ Radingate & unum pratum pertinens ad terram prædict' : hac conditione interpofita, ut monachi S. Auguft. haberent ejus memoriam in orationibus fuis fpecialem. Thorne in vitis Abbat. S. Auguftini. Cant.*   (g) *Cambd.* in *Kent,* of *Portus Lemanis,* and *Stone-ftreet.*

Stoneſtreet, and of the other the abrupt pieces of a fair Cauſey upon *Barham* Down ; a Way more ſtraight and direct than that now uſed, lying by *Whitings*-way, or rather *Whiteway* (for King *John*'s Charter to St. *Radegund*'s Abby, by *Dover*, calls it, (a) *The white Way* ;) whither the Road was turned (as is probably conjectured) for the frequency of Robberies and Murders committed in *Woolwich* Wood, through which the former Way lay and lead. But to our Gate again ; which, I ſuppoſe, took its Name from this Port-way or Road-way. *Ridingate* being no other but the Road-gate. Which conjecture is made much more probable, if not the matter put out of all doubt ; partly by the Tokens of Antiquity, the *Roman* or *Britiſh* Bricks as yet to be ſeen about it : And partly by the Name of the Street leading from it into the City, called to this day *Watlingſtreet*, one of the four famous Ways or Streets which croſſed and quartered the Kingdom. *Ermingſtreet*, *Ikenildſtreet*, and *Foſſe*, being the other three, which *Mulmutius Dunwallo* is by ſome ſtoried to have made, I know not how many hundreds of Years before Chriſt. So *Holinſhead*. But of Mr. *Cambden*, who hath a large diſcourſe of them (b) much more probably attributed to the *Romans*. I proceed.

St. *Edmund*'s Church.

By this Gate was ſometime ſtanding a Church, called the Church of St. *Edmund* (c) the King and Martyr ; otherwiſe from the Gate by which it ſtood, St. *Edmund*'s of *Ridingate* ; built by one *Hamon* the Son of *Vitalis*, one of thoſe who came in with the Conqueror (d). This Church was ſtanding near within the Gate ; for I have read an old Deed bounding out an Houſe, one way to the Street leading to St. *Edmund*'s Church from *Tiern-Crouch* (that is, the Iron Croſs which ſometime ſtood at the *North*-end of *Caſtleſtreet*, at the meeting of the four Wents) but the Church is now ſo clean gone, that the leaſt *Veſtigium* of it appears not. I read (e) that upon the declining of it, in the Year of our Lord 1349. it was united to St. *Mary Bredne*, by the then Commiſſary of *Canterbury*, ſpecially authorized thereto by the Ordinary, who were then the Prior and Convent of *Chriſt-Church*, in the vacancy of the See, by Archbiſhop *Bradwardine*'s death, with conſent of the Nuns of St. *Sepulchres*, who were Patrons of it, it being given them long before by the Abbot and his Convent of St. *Auguſtine* ; whereof their domeſtick Chronicler (f) hath theſe words. (g) "*In the Year of our Lord* 1184, Roger *Abbat and the Convent of this Monaſtery,* "*have granted to the Nuns of St.* Sepulchres *in* Canterbury, *the Church of St.* "Edmund *of* Ridingate, *in Frank Almoign* ; *yet ſo as the ſaid Nuns in acknowledg-* "*ment of the Right which the Abbot and Convent of St.* Auguſtin *have in the ſaid* "*Church, ſhall offer yearly upon the Altar of St.* Auguſtin, *on the ſame Saint's day,* "*Twelve-pence, as a Rent, towards the repair of their* Organs. *And for the per-* "*formance of this* ; *the Prioreſs and Supprioreſs have ſworn fidelity in the preſence of* "*many Witneſſes in our Chapter-houſe.* Thus he. Let me only acquaint you that over this *Ridingate*, was ſometimes, and that in the memory of many yet living, a Bridge lying upon the Underprops or Buttreſſes yet ſtanding on either ſide the Gate, by which when it ſtood, a man might have continued his walk from the leſſer to the greater *Dongehill*, and *è contra*, but it is decayed and gone. And ſo I walk on to *Worth-gate*.

Bridge over *Ridingate*.

Worthgate.

Worthgate.

OF which I can ſay but little, and the rather becauſe I am not as yet perſwaded to be of their Opinion, who think that *Winchepgate* that now is, and ſo called, is the ancient *Worthgate*. For my part, I rather conceive the gate now diſgated ſometime leading out of the Caſtle-yard into *Winchep* to be *Worthgate*, becauſe it is both the more ancient Gate in all appearance, carrying a ſhew of greater Antiquity than the Caſtle it ſelf in the perfect Arch of Britiſh Brick which it hath, not ſampled of any other about the City ; and

---

(a) *Alba via. Lib. Abb. S. Radegundis.*   (b) *Britannia. Romans* in Britain, pag. 63, 64, 65. *Engliſh* Edition.   (c) St. *Edmund*'s Church.   (d) *Lib. Hoſp. S. Laurentii prope Cant.* (e) *Lib. Eccleſ. Chriſti, Cant.*   (f) *Thorne in vitis Abbat. S. Auguſtini.*   (g) *Anno Dom.* 1184. *Rogerus Abbas & Conventus hujus Monaſterii conceſſerunt eccleſiam beati* Edmundi *de* Redingate *in puram & perpetuam elemoſynam Monialibus S. Sep. Cant. Ita tamen quod Moniales prædictæ in recognitionem Juris quod S. Aug. habet in prædicta eccleſia de red. 12 denarios de ipſa eccleſia ſingulis annis reddent ſuper Altare S. Aug. in die ipſius Sancti ad organa reparanda, & ſuper hoc tam Prioriſſa & Supprioriſſa in Capitulo noſtro fidelitatem juraverunt multis teſtibus præſentibus.*

in its ruins retains the *veſtigia* of a gate, both for ſtrength and beauty of good reſpect. Beſides, by it the Road is continued, directly from *Caſtleſtreet* into *Winchep,* and *è contra* : whereas *Winchepgate* carries no ſhew of the leaſt Antiquity ; and, beſide ſtands wide of *Winchep,* making the Paſſenger wheel about and fetch a compaſs to come to it. Beſides, obſerve the Name, which I ſuppoſe taken up and given it ſince the building of the Caſtle, *Worthgate,* that is (as I conceive) the Caſtle-gate, or gate by the Caſtle : Worth (as ſome interpret it (a) ſignifying a Fort : or elſe *Worthgate,* quaſi *Wardgate,* from the conſtant watch and ward (commonly called Caſtle-guard:) anciently kept in the Caſtle and *Barbican,* for the ſafeguard of it and the City, whereof ſome ancient Evidences have taken notice, as (amongſt other) one of S. *Radeg.* Abby (b), made in *Ric.* 1. or King *John*'s time, concluding thus. (c) *This purchaſe was made at that time, when* William *of* Heſheteford *was Warden of the Caſtle of* Canterbury, *and at the ſame time* Theoricus le Vineter *was Præfect.*

London Road. But leaving this matter, let me tell you, that, according to traditional report, *London* Road lay anciently by this Gate, until *Boughton* way, as the more direct, came into requeſt; which it did but lately as they ſay, how truly I know not, but not improbably, (if for no other reaſon) becauſe of the priſon kept of old firſt in the Caſtle, and afterward at or near St. *Jacob*'s (whereof more anon) places moſt likely of the greateſt thorough-fare. But as a thing uncertain I leave it with a (d) freedom for the Reader to believe as much of it as he pleaſeth, until further enquiry ſhall enable me to give him better ſatisfaction. But for certain, of old, in perilous times of Hoſtility, all Strangers coming by *Dover,* and thoſe Eaſtern Coaſts from foreign Parts, being denied the common thorough-fare of the City, were put to ſeek *London*-Road, by a Lane leading to it not far diſtant from this Gate, of ſome called Strangers Strangersway. Way, of others Out-aliens Way, which croſſeth the Road at St. *Dunſtans* Croſs a little on this ſide of *Cockering ferm.* Of this Gate I have nothing more to ſay in this place, becauſe I ſhall have a ſecond occaſion for it, when I come to the Caſtle. I paſs therefore from it to *Weſtgate.*

But firſt will it pleaſe you to hear my ſecond Thoughts, touching the Roads lying by this Gate, to and from *London* ?

Some haply will more readily adhere to this Opinion, becauſe Mr. *Cambden* (e) ſeems to be in a manner of their Mind, by making *Lenham* (in his interpretation) the ſame with the Emperor *Antoninus* his *Durolevum* mentioned in his *Itinerary,* as one of the manſions or ſtations upon the road lying in his time between *London* and *Richborough.*

Mr. Cambden's opinion touching Lenham examin'd. But therein (I take it) Mr. *Cambden* is miſtaken : If you will hear my Reaſons, firſt let me give you the Stations or Manſions which the *Itinerary* mentions lying in the road between *London* and *Richborough,* with the diſtances between the ſtages, and the total ſum or number of Miles in the whole journey, taking beginning from *London.*

Noviomago, m. p. x.
Vagniacis, m. p. xviii.
Durobrovis, m. p. ix.
Durolevo, m. p. xiii. (f)
Duroverno, m. p. xii.
Ad portum Ritupis, m. p. xii.
} *In toto* lxxiv.

Let me add alſo the Stages (and their diſtances) between *London* and *Dover,* and between *London* and *Lim,* with the Totals alſo of their Miles, as the ſame *Itinerary* ſets them down.

Item, à Londinio *ad portum*
Dubris, M. P. 66. *ſic.*
Durobrovis, m. p. xxvii.
Duroverno, m. p. xxv.
Ad portum Dubris, m. p. xiv.

(a) **Remains of Sirnames** *in verb.* Worth. *pag.* 93. (b) *Lib* Abb. S. Radegund.
(c) *Hæc emptio facta fuit iſto tempore quo* Willielmus *de* Heſheteford *habuit wardam Caſtelli* Cant. *& eodem temp.* Theoricus le Vineter *fuit præfectus.* (d) *Fides penes lectorem eſto.*
(e) Britannia, *In* Kent. [(f) vii. *in* Tab. Peutigeriana. W. S.]

Item, à Londinio ad portum
Lemanis, M. P. lxviii. *fic.*
Durobrovis, m. p. xxvii.
Duroverno, m. p. xxv.
Ad portum Lemanis, m. p. xvi.

Now the firſt of theſe Stages between *London* and *Richborough* (*Noviomagus*) Mr. *Cambden* conceiveth to be that which is now called *Woodcote*, a little Village near *Croydon* in *Surrey*. The next (*Vagniac.*) he takes for *Maidſtone*, a Town well known in *Kent*. The third (*Durobrovis*) for *Rocheſter* City. The fourth (*Durolevum*) for *Lenham* in *Kent*. The fifth (*Durovernum*) for *Canterbury* City, and the next and laſt (*Portus Ritupis*) for *Richborough* near *Sandwich*.

As for the third and two. laſt of theſe Stages, there is no cauſe of doubt (as I conceive) but he hits them aright : the *Quære* reſts then only upon the other three. Now it will, I think, be eaſily granted that the *Roman* Roads between Port and Port, and between one great Town and another, were made and laid out as direct and ſtreight as might be (*a*) : and that for the Poſts and other Travellers both better direction, and alſo more ſwift and ſpeedy diſpatch of the Journey ; to facilitate whoſe paſſage they invented and made thoſe Cawſeys, whereof we have in many places the remains to this day. And that the Road or Port-way between *London* and theſe Port-Towns was ſtreight and without much winding, appeareth plainly by the total of the Miles, not only between them (eſpecially between *London* and *Dover*, being reckoned but at 66, a diſtance which it holds almoſt to this day, though the *Engliſh* be longer than the *Italian* Miles:) but alſo, if you mark it between *London* and *Rocheſter*, and between *Rocheſter* alſo and *Canterbury*, the former being 27, the latter 25. If this be ſo, the Traveller goes much awry and out of his way, that ſetting out of *London*, and bound for *Richborough*, goes firſt eight or ten Miles wide of *London*, to *Woodcote* : from thence to *Maidſtone* ſome 24 Miles aſunder : and from *Maidſtone* makes to *Rocheſter*, (obliquely all the way, without gaining a ſtep nearer his Journey's end, when he is there :) and then quatering again returns into *Maidſtone* Road, and ſalutes *Lenham*, and ſo makes forward. He that takes his way thus, ſhall find it little leſs than 80 of our Miles between *London* and *Richborough*.

The Caſe thus ſtanding, ſuffer me to give my weak Conjecture, how the Road might lye in the *Romans* time ; and to tell you whereabout I gueſs theſe Stations, Manſions, or Stages that the *Itinerary* ſpeaks of, were ſeverally ſeated, and may now probably be found.

As for the firſt then, being *Noiomagus*, or *Noviomagus*, and that ſeated Ten Miles from *London*, I cannot conceive how it ſhould be a Stage for this Road, and lye wide of *London*, as *Woodcote* doth, ſo many Miles, and conſequently ſet the Traveller at as great a diſtance from the place whither he is bound (*Richborough*) as when he firſt ſet out of *London*. Conſidering this, and the diſtance between *London* and *Rocheſter*, by the *Itinerary*, I ſhould rather place it about *Crayford*, much about ten Miles from *London* : [and the rather, in regard the Termination of the Name, *Magus*, ſhews it to be ſeated by a Ford or River's ſide, according to *Cluverius* in his *Germania Antiqua*, l. 1. p. 64, 67. *W. S.*]   *Noviomagus.*

As for *Vagniacæ*, the next ſtage, 18 Miles from *Noviomagus* (ſaith the *Itinerary*, not without a miſtake, I believe of 18 for 8 Miles, it being by the ſame *Itinerary*, but 27 between *London* and *Rocheſter*) I ſuppoſe it might ſtand about *Northfleet*, diſtant about 8 Miles from *Crayford*, and about as many Miles from *Durobrovis* or *Rocheſter*, the next Stage upon the road, and which I think *Nennius* rather intends by his *Caer Medwag*, in his Catalogue of Cities, than *Maidſtone*.   *Vagniacæ.*

The 4th and next Stage after *Durobrovis*, *Durolevum*, 13 Miles (by the *Itinerary*, [but in the *Peutigerian* Table no more than 7. *W. S.*]) diſtanced from *Durobrovis*, I take to have been ſeated not far from *Newington*, a Village on the Road between *Rocheſter* and *Canterbury* : In this particular not a little ſtrengthen-   *Durolevum.*

(a) *Hæ via ſumma rectitudine tanquam protenſa linea, per quacunque locorum incommoda, tanta latitudine ducta ſunt, &c.* Twyne de Reb. Albionic. lib. 2. pag 152.

ed and upholden in my conjecture by the multitude of *Roman* Urns lately found in digging there, at such place as is already discovered and discoursed of by the learned *Meric. Casaubon,* then Batchelor, now Doctor in Divinity, my ever honoured Friend (*a*). [There is one Reading of the *Itinerary* by *W. Har-rison* in his first Edition of his Description of *Britain,* where the distance from *Durobrovis* to *Durolevum* is 8 Miles, which agrees so nearly with the *Peutingeri-an* Table, as to strengthen Mr. *Somner's* Conjecture, that *Durolevum* was *New-ington* or not far from it : And it is not an improbable Conjecture, that the old *Durolevum* being devoured by Time and Age, a new Town or Village being built at or near the same place might thence have the name *Newington.* N. B.]

If any shall stumble at the disproportion of Miles between it and *Durover-num* (*Canterbury*) let them know there is even as great between *Lenham* and *Canterbury.*

Why it should be called *Durolevum,* I am altogether ignorant. What if I conjecture (because the *Itinerary* lays out the Road from *London* to *Richborough,* and not *è contra*) from having the River or Water (of *Medway*) on the left hand of it, as by the Inhabitants tradition, *Newington* sometime had, and with-in about 2 Miles of it yet hath ?

If any looking for better Remains of a *Roman* Station, shall object the mean condition of the present Village, such may know that *Newington* hath been a place of more note in time past than now. I read of a Nunnery there of an-cient time, whereof and of the pristine estate of the place, please you to read what *Thorne* hath written.

(*b*) He says, " At the Maner of *Newington* there were formerly *Nuns,* who
" were in possession of the whole Maner, to wit, That which the Lord Ab-
" bat of St. *Augustin* holds, and that which the Heirs of *G. de Lucy* hold , and
" that which the Heirs of *B. de Ripariis* do hold, besides that which *Richard de*
" *Lucy* purchased of *Brunel de Middleton,* and then that Maner was taxed for
" one *Ploughland* in *Middleton.* It happened afterwards, that the Prioress of
" that Monastery was in the Night Strangled in her bed by her Convent, and
" then drag'd into a pit, called *Nonne-pet.* This being discovered, the King
" seiz'd upon the Maner, and kept possession of it, and removed the rest of the
" Nuns to *Shepey.* Afterwards King *Henry* substituted certain secular Canons
" and gave them that whole Maner with xxviii weigh of Cheese out of the
" Maner of *Middleton.* Some time after, one was Kill'd amongst them, of
" which Murder Four of them were found Guilty, and the other Two not
" Guilty, who by Licence from the King gave their Portion to St. *Augustin's,*
" the other five Portions remain'd in the King's hands, untill he gave them to
" *Richard de Lucy,* his Chief Justice. Hence the Abbat of St. *Augustin* held
" the two said Portions, until he made an exchange of it together with xi*s.* v*d.*
" yearly Rent in the Hamlet of *Thetham,* which Hamlet was afterwards the
" possession of the Abbat of *Feversham,* by the gift of the said *Richard de Lucy;*
" so the Abbat of *Feversham* became answerable for the said Rent. Others
" say, That those Canons in the time of King *William* the Conqueror had so
" Offended, that all their Goods were seiz'd upon by the King as Forfeited,
" who gave the above said two Portions to the Abbat of St. *Augustin's* : But
" which of these two Stories is the truer, I leave the Reader to judge.

Craving pardon for this digression, and leaving *Worthgate,* I come now as I promised erewhile, and as the order of my method requires, to *West-gate.*

Westgate.

Westgate.

EDmerus the Monk of *Canterbury* shortly after the Conquest, names unto us this and the *Northgate* of the City, telling us of Archbishop *Lanfranc's* founding a double Hospital, the one for Leprous, without the former, and the other for aged and impotent without the other gate (*c*). This of *Westgate* be-ing decayed (as I have told you) was re-edified by Archbishop *Sudbury* in

---

(*a*) **Notes upon** *Marcus Aurelius Antoninus's* **meditations,** *pag.* 31, *&c.*   (*b*) See the *Ap-pendix,* Numb. V.   (*c*) *Edmer. Hist. Novorum, lib.* 1. *pag.* 9.

Rich. 2 time. It hath its Church by it called Holy Crofs (with this addition, from the Gate:) of *Weftgate* [built where now it ftands about the fame time with the Gate, in fupply of a former, which being built over the old Gate was pulled down with it, as fhall be more fully fhewed hereafter. A Record of the Foundation of the prefent Church may be feen in the *Appendix*. Numb. LXXIII. *W. S.*]

Prifon there.

The fame Gate the fureft and largeft about the City, and therefore, and in refpect alfo of the chief thoroughfare under it, is at this day the common Gaol or Prifon of the City, both for Malefactors and others, and hath been fo (as I fuppofe) almoft ever fince the new building of it: but certainly from the 31 of *Hen.* 6. For then (as *Edw.* 4th in his Charter recites) he granted it to the City by his Charter, in thefe Words: (*a*) *The keeping of his Gaol at the* Weftgate *of his faid City of* Canterbury *for Prifoners then in prifon, or hereafter to be imprifoned within the fame City and Suburbs, for whatfoever Crime or Caufe taken or to be taken, to be detain'd in the fame by Themfelves or their Officers,* &c. The Town Prifon being immediately before its remove thither kept in another place, to wit, before the now Town-Hall or Court-Hall (whereof more hereafter:) as formerly it was at another place, to which I am copioufly directed by the Records of Chrift-Church, which fhew it to have ftood in the heart of the City, hard by St. *Andrews* Church, on the North-fide of the ftreet, even where fince and now our Corn-market is kept; which the boundary of a houfe of *Chrift*-Church fituate thereabouts anciently thus difcovers. (*b*) *In the Parifh of St.* Andrew *between a Lane, by which they go to the Prifon of the City of* Canterbury, *which is toward the Eaft.* And another thus: (*c*) *In a corner, as they go from the Church of St.* Andrew, *toward the prifon of the City.* This latter Houfe I take to be that where Mr. *Taylor* the Linnen-draper lately dwelt, which is a Church-houfe, and it feems was anciently, a Corner-houfe, that being but lately put up which now ftands between it and the Corn-Market.

This Prifon in thofe days was known by the Name of the *Spech-houfe*. (*d*) *Nicholas of* Wiltfhire, *Prifoner in the Goal of the City of* Canterbury, *called the Spech-houfe, died,* &c. fay the Crown-Rolls, 11 *Ed.* 2. And whilft it was kept there, the Lane, now called *Angel*-lane, to which toward the *Eaft* it abutted, called, (*e*) *A fmall Street near the* Spech-houfe, and Spech-houfe-lane. For a Townfman in his Will, dated 1404, proved (according to an old Cuftom of the City) before the Bailiffs of the place, devifeth his Tenement in St. *Mary Magdalens* Parifh, in *Spech-houfe*-lane (*f*); which of neceffary confequence, muft be this, there being no other Lane in that Parifh that leads to the *Spech-houfe*.

Another Prifon.

The fame Records of the Cathedral inform me of a yet more ancient common Gaol or Prifon than this, belonging to the City; which in the time of Prior *Benedict*, about 450 Years ago, they call, (*g*) *The new Prifon of the City.* It ftood (fay they) in a part of that which was afterwards the *Auguftin* Friars Seat; fince the diffolution, become the Dwelling-houfe (after many others) of Captain *Berry*; having then a Lane leading to it, from St. *George's* ftreet, called *Lambertflane*, afterward *Brewerflane*, and (*h*) *The Street which leadeth to the old Gaol.* [*In St.* George's *Parifh at the old Gaol.* N. B.] For, the Compofition made in the Year 1326, between thofe Friars, and the then Parfon of St. *George's* (whereof more hereafter) bounds out their feat in this manner. (*i*) *In the Parifh of St.* George *in* Canterbury; *near a certain lane, called* Brewerflane, *namely, between the faid lane and the Tenement of* Thomas *of* Bonynton, *toward the North, and a certain place called* Eald-gaol, *that is, the old Gaol, and the tenement of* Cecile *at the Gaol toward the Weft,* &c. To which add the Boundary of the

---

(*a*) *Cuftodiam Gaiolæ fuæ de Weftgate prædict. Civitatis fuæ Cantuar. ad prifones tunc incarceratos & extunc incarcerendos infra eandem Civitatem & fuburb.pro quocunque crimine feu caufa captos feu capiendos, detinendos in eadem per fe vel Miniftros fuos,* &c.   (*b*) *In parochia S. Andreæ, inter venellam per quam itur ad carcerem Civitatis quæ eft verfus Eaft.*   (*c*) *In angulo ficut itur ab ecclefia S. Andreæ verfus carcerem Civitatis. Rental. vet. Ecclef. Chrift. Cantuar.*   (*d*) *Nicholaus de Wiltfhire Prifo in Gaola Civitatis Cant. vocata* Spech-houfe, *moriebatur,* &c.   (*e*) *Parvus vicus juxta* Spech-houfe.   (*f*) *Liber. Civitat. Cant.*   (*g*) *Novum Carcerem Civitatis.*   (*h*) *Vicus qui ducit ad veterem Gayolam.* [*Apud antiquam Gayolam in parochia S. Georgii. MS. Eccl. Cant.* N. B.]   (*i*) *In parochia S. Georgii Cant. juxta quandam venellam vocat. Brewerflane, viz. inter præd. venellam, & tenementum Thomæ de Bonynton verfus North, & quendam locum vocat. Eald-gaole, & tenementum Ceciliæ at Gayole verf. Weft,* &c.

House, then of the Monks of *Christ-Church*; now the Dwelling-house of Mr. *Peter Piard*, and some others; which in the same Records is thus laid down. *(a) Between the High-way toward the North, and the old Gaol toward the* South. This Note added to the former, plainly points out the Situation.

And now, *(b) I return to my purpose*, hoping this digression is neither in point of Antiquity impertinent, nor in point of Method preposterous, being ushered in by so fit an occasion. Our Forefathers, whose Wits the frequency of Invasion prompted to all manner of warlike Invention, used to secure their City Gates against Assailants; not only with a Port-close to let down before it, but also with a warlike device built over it; through which they could let down any offensive thing against the Enemy approaching to assail it. A Gate so fortified, was called *Porta machecollata*, from *machecollare*, or *machecoulare*; which (saith my Author *(c)*) is to make a warlike defence over a Gate or other passage like to a Grate, through which, scalding Water, or ponderous or offensive things may be cast upon the Assailants: Thus he. After this manner were, and are our two principal Gates built, this of *Westgate*, and in imitation thereof, that of *Newingate*, with each of them a Port-close, like as *Burgate*. Now to *Northgate*.

Northgate.

Northgate.

THis Gate stands under a part of St. *Mary*'s Church, which is built over it upon the Wall, and to distinguish it from the other *Mary*'s of the City, hath this addition from the Situation (of *Northgate*). Under the Quire or Chancel whereof, is a Vault, with an open space or lope-hole in the Wall, fashioned like a Cross. It was sometime an Hermitage, but is now belonging to the Parsonage.

Queningate.

Queningate.

COme we now to *Queningate*. But where shall we seek it? There is none of the Name at this day; and few know where it stood. I sought as narrowly for it as for Ants-paths, and at length having found it, will shew you where it was. It stood against the Priory of *Christ-Church*, saith our Wall-measurer, distanced from *Northgate* (saith he) 69 Perches, but saith an Elder Record of *Christ-Church*, 71 Perches. By these Descriptions, it must needs have stood near the place of the now Postern-gate, against St. *Augustin*'s. And indeed a Remanent of *Brittish* Bricks laid and couched Arch-wise at a place in the Wall, a little *North*-ward of the Postern, shows the very place. A small Gate it was, (*(d) The little Gate of* Queningate, saith *Ickham*;) but I will assure you a very ancient one; as not only the Bricks betoken, but the Records of St. *Augustin* prove it; which tell, that one *Domwaldus*, in the Year 760, gave to that Abby certain Land within *Queningate*. The very Name hath Antiquity in it, signifying the King or Queen's Gate; being haply *Ethelbert* and his Queen *Bertha*, their passage from their Palace near adjoyning to the several places of their divers Devotions: The one (if *Thorn* say true) at St. *Pancrace* (so afterwards called;) the other at St. *Martin*, whereof more hereafter *(e)*.

St. *Mary* of *Queningate* Church.

Where the Church or Chappel stood, that had its Name from this Gate, being called St. *Mary* of *Queningate*, I cannot well tell. That such a Church it had is most certain. I trace it in many Records (some 450 Years old and more) of *Christ-Church*, which had the Patronage of that and St. *Michael* of *Burgate*, confirmed to them in and by a Bull of Pope *Alexander* 3, and in many like Bulls since. The Parson thereof in the Year 1381, as those Records inform me, made an Exchange of it and *Burgate*, to which it was an annexed Chappel, for *Pertpole* Chantery in *Pauls*. This being certain, it is no less sure that it stood not far from the Gate, by the name of it; yet not very near, it is like, because the Bounders of the City-Wall and Ground under it, between *Northgate* and *Queningate*, and between it and *Burgate*, granted to *Christ-Church*, neither of them mention it: And *Ickham*'s measurement saith, *Queningate* stood,

---

(a) *Inter Regiam stratam versus North, & veterem Gayolam vers. South.*   (b) *In callem regredior.*   (c) *Coke* upon *Littleton, lib. 1. cap. 1. sect. 1. pag. 5.*   (d) *Parva porta de Queningate.*   (e) *In St. August.*

(a) *Toward the Priory of* Chrift-Church, not *towards* or *nigh the Church* or *Chappel of* Queningate. [By this paffage in an old Deed, recorded in a Leiger-Book of St. *Auftin's, viz.* (b) *Of a certain Meffuage in St.* Paul's *Parish, near* St. Mary's *of* Queningate *Church,* it feems to have ftood without the City-wall *W. S.*] But for want of more certainty I muft leave it, untill I am better inftructed where to find it. [I have feen in an ancient Charter the Boundaries of a Meffuage, which feems to give fome light into our fearches for the place where this demolifhed Chappel once ftood; in thefe words: (c) The Meffuage was bounded *with the Wall of the City* Eaft: Queningate-*Chappel on the* South: *And* Queningate-*lane* North *and* Weft. So the Chappel ftood in the Lane within the City-Wall, having this Meffuage clofe to it on the *South*-fide. *N. B.*] And fo I have done with both Wall and Gates, and come now unto (my next particular) the City-ditch. Only let me but name unto you the Pofterns, which (as erewhile I told you) were three. One againft St. *Auguftin's,* a Second at St. *Mildred's,* and the Third by the Stoure running from Abbat's-Mill.

Posterns.

The City-ditch.

OF what Antiquity this Ditch is (I confefs) I cannot well tell. In the Survey of our City in *Doomfday* Book, I meet with *Foffatum Civitatis,* but in what fenfe I do not well know. For whether the City-Ditch be there intended, or fome Siege rather or beleaguring of the City (for that fenfe the word *Foffatum* alfo carries:) it is to me fome queftion. Eleven of thofe Burgeffes (faith *Doomfday*) that were in *Canterbury* in the Confeffor's time, (d) *were wafted or come to nothing in the City-ditch.* If it had been faid eleven Burgeffes Houfes or Manfions were fo laid wafte, it had been fomewhat plain. It might have been fuppofed their Vaftation had been to make way for the Ditch. But you fee what the words are. Either there is a figure in them, or the Ditch is not fo old. If fo old, neglected afterwards. For Queen *Alianor's* Letters before prefented, fpeak of Fortifying the City, not only (e) with *Walls,* but (f) *Ditches* too, as in want of both.

Ditch about the City, how ancient.

This our Ditch (it feems) was originally of a great Breadth, 150 Foot over, as I find by the records of a fuit commenced by the City againft Archbifhop *Peckham,* in the Reign of *Edward* 1. the 18 Year, who charging upon the Archbifhop (but erroneoufly, the Jury finding it not his, but his Tenants fact) for incroaching upon the City-ditch, and ftreightning of it with Houfes built upon it about *Weftgate,* to the City's great damage and annoyance, in regard that the River running through that part of the Ditch, many times overflowed the Banks, to the great detriment of the Town-wall, make challenge to a Ditch of 150 Foot broad in thefe words. (g) "They further fay, That whereas our Lord the "King ought to have, and his Predeceffors were wont to have a Ditch encompaffing the "wall of the City aforefaid, which Ditch ought to contain beyond that wall an hundred "and fifty Foot in breadth, &c. A breadth which the prefent Ditch, I think, in no part fhews. But no marvel; for as the Wall, fo the Ditch too is in thefe days much neglected. Little more than half the Wall is now in-ditched, the reft being either fwerved, or elfe filled up, and in many parts builded upon; nay, the Wall it felf in fome places eafily fcalable, what with piles and ftacks of wood in fome, what with houfing and the like in other parts of it; a thing fatal unto fome by the fall of the Wall (*Robert Quilter, Denis Tiler,* and *Joane London,* being killed by the fall of a part of the Wall in *Ridingate*-ward, as they fate in the faid *Joane's* houfe (h)), and both very unfeemly and dangerous alfo for the City. What fays the Civil Law in this cafe? (i) "Namely, That all Edifices joining

Breadth of the Ditch.

(a) *Verfus Prioratum ecclefiæ Chrifti,* not *verfus,* nor *juxta ecclefiam* or *capellam de Quening.*

[(b) *De quodam Meffuagio in parochia S. Pauli juxta Ecclefiam S. Mariæ de Queningate. Lib. Monaft. S. Auguftini.* W. S.] [(c) *Juxta murum dicta civitatis verfus Eaft, & capellam B. Mariæ de Queningate verfus South, & venellam quæ vocatur Queningate-lane verfus Weft & North. Cart. Ec. l. Cant.* N. B.] (d) *Vaftati funt in Foffato Civitatis.* (e) *Muris.* (f) *Foffatis.*

(g) *Præterea dicunt quòd ubi Dominus Rex habere debet & anteceffores fui habere confueverunt foffatum circuens murum Civitatis præd. quod quidem foffatum debet continere extra murum illum centum & quinquaginta pedes latitudinis, &c. Liber Cameræ Civitatis Cant.* (h) Crown Rolls, *Anno* 17 Ed. 1.

(i) *Ædificia quæ vulgò parapetafia nuncupant, vel fiqua alia opera mœnibus vel publicis operibus ita fociata coharent, ut ex iis incendium vel infidias vicinitas reformidet, aut anguftentur fpatia platearum, vel minuat, porticibus latitudo, dirui ac profterni præcipimus. &c. Ædificium* 13. *de operibus publicis.*

"to

Pomœrium.   " to the Walls or publick Buildings of a City ought to be pull'd down, as dan-
" gerous in reſpect of Fires or Treacheries, or as incommodious, in caſe the
" Streets become ſtraitned thereby,· *&c.*

       Every well contrived City ſhould have a *Pomœrium.* And what is that ?
The Law *Lexicon* ſhall tell you. *(a)* " A *Pomœrium* is a certain ſpace about
" the Walls of a City, as well within as without, whereon it was not lawful
" to build Houſes to Inhabit, or Plough, leſt thereby the Defence of the
" City ſhould be hindered. The Ancients in building their Cities Conſecra-
" ted this place with the divinations of the Augures. *Felinus* the Canoniſt
more ſuccinctly defines it thus : *(b)* " A *Pomœrium* is a place, both within and
" without a City-wall, on which it was not lawful to erect any building. But
what reſpect we a *Pomœrium?* were it a *Pomarium,* or Orchard, haply it would
be better lookt unto. Witneſs the ſo much planting of the Ditch in divers
parts. What a ſhame is it for us in the mean time, that a little profit ſhould
baniſh all our care in this kind, and to ſee the greedineſs of a ſmall advantage to be a means (as it is) to betray the City at once both to danger and
deformity ? But I may forbear Cenſure : for I deſpair of its regard in theſe
days, wherein *(c)* the private Profit of ſome few, is with too many more
conſiderable than *(d)* the common good of many ; which if it find any regard,
it is but baſe and ſecundary, like that of Virtue, *(e)* after that of Gain. So
much for the Ditch.

The Caſtle.

Caſtle-gate   COme we now to the Caſtle, to which our paſſage from the City lay of
and Bridge.   old by a Bridge, and beyond that a fair Gate built at the entrance of the
Caſtle-yard or Court, as may appear by an ancient Deed recorded in the Lieger Book of *Eſtbridge* Hoſpital, concerning a piece of Land lying (ſaith the
Deed) in the Pariſh of St. *Mary*-Caſtle: *(f) Near the Gate of the Caſtle at the
head of the Bridge on the Weſt-ſide.* Afterward in the ſame Deed thus deſcribed.
*(g) Between the Highway towards the Eaſt, and the Ditch of the ſaid Caſtle toward the
South, and a certain piece of Land belonging to the Church of St.* Mary *of the Caſtle
toward the North, &c.* This Gate had its uſual Porter or Keeper. For I read
that one *William Savage, (h) Keeper of the Gate of the Caſtle in* Canterbury, was
queſtioned for taking the Daughter of *Hamon Trendherſt, (i) by Force and Arms,
over againſt the Caſtle of* Canterbury *in* Canterbury, and carrying her into the
Caſtle, and there holding her eight days and upwards *(k).* [*Hubert de Burgh*
Earl of *Kent,* had the cuſtody of this Caſtle committed to him, by a Grant or
Charter dated 12. *H. III. Philp. Villar. Cantian.* N. B.]

Caſtle's Anti-   To approach nearer to the Caſtle it ſelf, whoſe entrance (ſeemingly) was
quity.   by an aſcent of Steps porcht over on the Weſt-ſide. Some there are will tell
you that *Julius Cæſar ;* other that *Rudhudibras,* or *Ludrudibras,* long before
Built it. You may believe them if you pleaſe. For my part I ſubſcribe herein to Mr. *Cambden's* Opinion. It carries (ſaith he) no ſhew of any great Antiquity *(l),* and very probably. For in all the Sieges of our City, and the harrowing and ſacking of it by the *Danes,* at large related by our Hiſtorians, eſpecially that moſt remarkable (becauſe moſt lamentable) one in King *Ethelred's*
time, copiouſly ſtoried by *Roger Hoveden,* and our Countryman *Spott* , telling
us firſt of the Siege of the City, with the continuance of it, the treachery
by which the Enemy ſurpriſed it, and diverſe other particulars thereof ; what
is there of any Caſtle, but *(m)* deep ſilence ? It was builded by the *Normans,*
ſaith Mr. *Cambden.* Indeed both he *(n)* and *Speed (o)* inform us, that the Conqueror, for his better ſubduing and bridling of the ſuſpected parts of the

---

*(a) Pomœrium locus erat, tam intrà, quam extrà murum urbis, quem antiqui in condendis urbibus augu-
rato conſecrabant, neque in eo ullum fieri ædificium patiebantur, &c. Calvini Lexicon in verb. Pomœrium,
ex Livii libro primo.*   *(b) Pomœrium eſt locus ad intra & extra, quo ædificare non licet. De Re-
ſcriptis c. Rodulphus num.* 23.   *(c) Meum & tuum.*   *(d) Bonum & intereſſe publicum.*
    (e) Poſt nummos.   *(f) Juxta Januam Caſtri ad caput pontis ex parte Weſt.*   *(g) Inter
Regiam ſtratam verſus Eaſt, & foſſam dicti Caſtri verſus South, & quandam placeam terræ pertinent. ad
ecclesiam beatæ Mariæ de Caſtro prædict. verſ. North, &c.*   *(h) Janitor Portæ Caſtri Cant.*
    (i) Vi & armis, ex oppoſito Caſtri Cant. in Cant.   *(k) Crown-Rolls, Anno* 15. *Ed.* 2.
    (l) Britannia. In *Kent.*   *(m) Altum ſilentium.*   *(n) Britannia.* In *Cambridgſhire.*
    (o) Hiſt. in vita Conqueſt.

Kingdom, builded Castles at such places, namely at *Cambridge*, *Lincolne*, *Nottingham*, *Stafford*, and elsewhere. A piece of policy, which I find practised abroad. (a) *In the Marquisate of* Brandeburgh , *when the Citizens of* Berlin *became Seditious against their Magistrates, The Marquess* Frederick *interposing built in the City a Castle for a restraint of their Liberty.* Might not this be one of the Castles so built by the Conqueror? I conceive not : for I take it to be somewhat, but yet not much elder. Because it appears by *Doomsday*-Book, that the Conqueror had this Castle by exchange made with the Archbishop, and the Abbot of St. *Augustin's* ; who had for it, the latter 14, the former 7 Burgenses. I suppose it built in the *interim* of the *Danish* Massacre, and the *Norman* Conquest. Clearly *Doomsday*-Book hath it ; but before, it occurs not any where. Shortly after (as I find) certain of the Monks of St. *Augustin's*, quitting the Abbey in the broil between Archbishop *Lanfranc* and them, about *Guido* or *Wido* the 42 Abbat, sheltered themselves under, or within this Castle. For, of them some for their Rebellion being committed to the City Prison, by *Lanfranc's* command, (b) It was told him, that the rest, who were commanded to be gone, did go and abide *under the Castle , situated by St.* Mildred's *Church.* The next thing that I read of it is, that *Lewis* the French *Dolphin* (*Stow* is my Author) arriving in the Isle of *Thanet*, and afterward at *Sandwich*, and landing his Forces without resistance, comes to *Canterbury*, where he received both Castle and City into his subjection (c). [The Castle at this day is holden of the Manor of *East Greenwich* by Grant from the Crown. The Yards and Dikes about it contain Four Acres and one Rod of Land, and are in the possession of Mr. *W. Watson. N. B.*]

Within this Castle, in former time, there was a common Prison kept. For proof whereof I could muster up many Testimonies from Records of good credit. But, because tradition keeps it yet in memory with some, one shall suffice which I have from the Crown-rolls. (d) The Record says : " The " Escape of *Walter de Wedering*, and *Martin* at *Gate de Lamberherst*. These Prison-" ers of our Lord the King, in the Castle at *Canterbury*, sat bound in a certain " place called *Barbican*, nigh the same Castle, to beg their Bread. It happen-" ed that on *Shrove-Tuesday*, in the Reign of King *Edward* II. before Sun-set, " the same *Walter* broke the Padlock or a link of the Chain, with which he " was bound ; and drew away with him the said *Martin*, against the Will of " the said *Martin*, to the Church of St. *Maries* of the Castle, where he re-" main'd and abjur'd the Kingdom of *England* ; and *Martin* of his own accord " returned to Prison. The Prison continued here a long time after, even (as I take it) until the ordinary passage through the Castleyard, by making up the further Gate, to the end, in likelihood, the better to secure the Castle, was debarr'd. Which was done (some say) upon *Wiat's* rising, in Queen *Mary's* days ; others, upon a former insurrection in *Edward* 6th's time, called the Commonwealth ; but I think, before them both, because I meet with the Prison by St. *Jacob's*, whither (it seems) the Castle-prison was removed, in *Hen.* 8. time : Divers of our Townsmen about that time, distributing their Testamentary or dying Alms (e) *to those that were in prison nigh* St. Jacob's. It had yet a second Remove, and that even in our memory, to *Westgate*-street, where it continues. A few words now of the *Barbican*, and I shall have done with the Castle.

The Castle, it seems, (f) for the more security both of it and the City, was anciently fore-fenced with a *Barbican* or *Barbacan*. Which exotick Word, Sir *H. Spelman* thus interprets. (g) *A Barbacan is a Fort or Hold, a Mu-*

Common Prison in the Castle.

Barbican.

(a) *In Marchia Brandeburgensi, cum Cives Berlinenses in suum tumultuarentur Magistratum, Fridericus Marchio interveniens, imposuit urbi arcem frenum libertatis. Tholosanus Repub. lib.* 2. *cap.* 5. *num.* 3.
(b) *Nunciatum est ei cæteros abire jussos sub Castro (ad ecclesiam S. Miltrudis posito) consedisse. Antiq. Britan. in vita Lanfranci, pag.* 114. (c) *Stow.* Annals in King *John.* (d) *Evasio Walteri de* Wedering, & Martini *at* Gate de Lamberherst. *Prisones Domini Regis in Castro Cant. sederunt ligati in quodam loco vocat.* Barbican *juxta idem Castrum pro pane suo mendicando. Contigit quod die Martis in Carnisprivio Anno R. R. Ed. Fil. Reg. Ed. ante occasum Solis, prædictus* Walterus *fregit* * *seruram cathenæ* * F. *seri lam, cum qua ligatus fuit, & attraxit secum prædictum* Martinum *contra voluntatem ipsius Mart. ad ecclesiam beatæ Mariæ de Castro, ubi remansit & abjuravit Regnum Angliæ, & præd. Mart. rediit in prisonam ex bona voluntate.* (e) *Incarceratis prope locum* S. Jacobi. (f) *Ad majorem cautelam* (as the Civilian speaks.) (g) *Barbacan munimem à fronte Castri, aliter antemurale dictum ; etiam foramen in urbium Castrorumque mœniis ad trajicienda missilia : necnon specula, & locus ubi excubiæ aguntur. Vox Arabica.* Glossar. *in verb.* Barbacan.

nition,

nition, placed in the front of a *Castle*, or an *Out-work*. Also a hole in the Wall of a City or Castle, through which Arrows or Darts were cast out. Also a Watch-tower. It is an Arabick Word. So he. *Minshew* thus (a) : A *Barbican* (saith he) or Out-nook in a Wall, with holes to shoot out at the Enemy. Some take it for a Centinel-house, a Scout-house. *Chaucer* useth the word *Barbican* for a Watch-tower. Of the *Saxon Ber-ic-ken*; *i. e.* I ken or see the *Borough, &c.* [Had he said *Burgh-becan*, he had gone pretty nigh, for thence I could derive it, were I not convinced of its *Arabick* Original. *W. S.*] Here I will briefly prove unto you two things. 1. That there was *Barbican*. 2. The place where it stood. In a Record of the City Chamber, shewing how the Fee-farm of the City in *Hen.* 3. time was to be raised, occurs the Name of the *Barbican* in these words. (b) *From the* Barbican v s. *which are due upon account in the Exchequer.* I find also in the elder Rentals of *Christ-Church*, frequent mention of it, as a Boundary to certain of the Churches *Demesnes*, lying near it without *Worthgate*, in these or the like words. (c) *Without* Worgate, *near the Ditch del* Bayle; *but now it is called* Barbican. And the like. Now that it was is plain enough : The place where it was, comes next to be inquired. I have seen a Record of the 6. of *Edward* 2. purporting that the City-Coroner coming to do his Office upon the dead Body of a murdered Servant of the Prior of *Christ-Church*; he was not permitted, but the Body being conveyed to the *Barbican*, (d) *Without the Castle of* Canterbury, was there set upon and searched by a foreign Coroner. Now it must of necessity follow, that this place where the Inquest was taken (the *Barbican*) was without the City's liberty; but there is not near the Castle any place, save the Castle-yard, that is so. The Record (if you please to see it) is extant in my *Appendix, Numb. VI.* The Castle-yard, and Wall then, now much impaired with age; but sometime set with divers Watch-towers, four at least, and which was otherwise called the Bulwark, being the Fore-fence to the Castle, was undoubtedly the *Barbican*, or the Place and Structure, which former Ages knew, and called by that Name. I collect and conclude it also from that of (e) *the Ditch del* Bayle, *&c.* which cannot otherwise be understood than of the Ditch about the Castle-yard Wall, which (until of late that the piece of Wall was made between *Winchep-gate* and it at the one side, and the like at the other) compassed the same. Now for the better understanding of the Use and Condition of this military Structure, I refer you to *Stow's Survey of London, pag. 62,* where he speaks of the like, sometime standing without *Cripplegate*. And now I come to the *River*.

The River.

ONE Commendation that our City hath (and worthily) from *Malmesbury* (f), is the River's watering of it. This River we call *Stoure*, as did our Ancestors long ago : (g) *Between the two neighbouring Streams of the River, which is called the* Stour; are the words of a *Codicil* or *Landboc* of King *Cenulph* the *Mercian*, made to the Archbishop, and his Monks of *Christ-Church, Anno Domini* 814. (h) Long before this, a Charter of *Edric* King of *Kent*, in *Anno Domini* 686, made to the Abby of St. *Augustin*, giving certain Land in *Stodmersh*, mentioneth this River, bounding out the same to lye one way to a place called *Ford-street*, and on the other part to have (i) *the River, which is called the* Stour. And yet more anciently occurs the name. For *Sturrey*, which takes its name from this River running by it, is by that name together with *Chistelet*, granted by King *Ethelbert* himself (his Charter tells me so) to St. *Augustin's*.

River whence called S'our. What the name signifies, or whence it was taken, certainly I know not. Haply from the constant and continual stirring and swift course or motion of it, to difference it from standing Waters, whence probably the *Britain* Name of the City, *Durwhern, i. e.* a swift River; or else from *Store*, for the plenty of Water, and the many streams falling into it : as the River *Stura*, arising in the *Alpes*, one of the 30 which of the River *Po* are carried into the *Adriatick*

(a) *Dictionar. in hac voce.*   (b) *De Barbicane, 5 s. qui debentur in computo super Scaccarium*
(c) *Extra Worgate juxta fossatum del Bayle, sed nunc Barbecan appellatur.*   (d) *Extra Castrum Cant.*   (e) *Fossatum del Bayle, &c*   (f) *De gestis Pontific lib 1. in Prologo.*   (g) *Inter duos gremiales Rivos fluminis quod dicitur* Stour.   (h) *In archivis Eccles. Cant.*   (i) *Flumen quod nominatur* Stur. *Thorne in vitis Abb. S. Aug.*

Sea, whereof *Pliny* fpeaks, *lib. 3. c. 16.* is vulgarly called *Store.* Certes *Stour* is a name taken up, and given it fince the *Britains* time. For *Dur* or *Dour* was with them the common name for all Waters (*a*), (whence, as erewhile you heard, our Cities name of *Durobernia* and *Dorob.* and I take it, the name of *Dover* fprang) as haply *Stour* was with the *Saxons* for all greater Rivers. *Dour* or *Stour,* faith *Hollinfhead,* fpeaking of the *Cambridge* River, as if they were all one, or that the latter were the proper Name for that River to which the former had been given. I can but rove at uncertainties, and therefore quit the Point.

For the fource and courfe of this River, I refer you to *Holinfhead* (*b*) and *Lambard* (*c*), who will copioufly herein give you fatisfaction. Commodity hath ever her oppofite attendance. The great commodity and conveniency of our City's plantation by this River is attended by and with the difcommodity and annoyance of Inundation. But our Anceftors, the City's firft (*d*) Inhabitants, weighed not the inconvenience of the one, for the benefit and accommodation of the other. And it is an inconvenience in thefe days fcarcely confiderable, becaufe feldom happening, or that indeed can happen, in regard the City lies higher now than at the firft, having in all parts of it been much raifed at feveral times, as Cellar-diggers, and fuch like, who are much hindred in their Work by old Foundations which they meet with in their digging, daily find; occafioned (as I conceive) by the many vaftations of the City in the *Danes* time, and laftly about the Year of our Lord 1160, by cafual Fire.

The greateft Channel of this our River, ran anciently through the midft of the City, to the King's Mill. For I find Archbifhop *Peckham* charged by the Citizens with the diverting of it by certain Cuts or Trenches for the bettering of his Mill at *Weftgate* ; which the Jury found to have been done before partly in Archbifhop *Kilwarby,* and partly in Archbifhop *Boniface* times (*e*). The Channel to *Weftgate* then (it feems) became inlarged. But the firft divifion of the Stream was not then made. For that *Stour* had its courfe that way much more anciently than thofe times, is moft clear. For I find it to give name in the Conqueror's time to the Archbifhop's Mannor, fince and at this day called *Weftgate,* (from the fituation of it near that gate:) but then, from the ftanding of it by the *Stour*-fide, *Stour-feat,* the Seat by the *Stour* ; as that other part of her divided Channel gave name to the Street it runs by, called to this day *Stour-ftreet,* that is, the Street by or nigh the *Stour.*

The accommodation of the City by the fcowring and enlargement of this River, hath been a thing at feveral times attempted, but (*f*) without profit, or fuccefs worthy the Defign. About the beginning of *Hen.* 8. Reign it was projected to have made that part of the River between *Fordwich* and *Canterbury* anfwerable to *Fordwich* River, that is, fo to have cleanfed, deepned and inlarged it, that Lighters and Boats might be brought to both alike. The matter proceeded fo far, and with fuch probability of a good iffue, that the Project was allowed and authorized by Act of Parliament (*g*), of this Tenor, (which I here infert *verbàtim* and at large, becaufe, being private, the ordinary Edition of the Statutes doth not afford it.) *Projects for the River's inlargement hitherto fruftrate.*

" IN moft humble wife fhewing the King's Highnefs his true and faithful " Subjects, the Mayor, Aldermen, Citizens and Inhabitants of the City " of *Canterbury,* that where the faid City is one of the ancient Cities of this " Realm, and through the fame hath been and yet is great Recourfe of Am- " baffadors, and other Strangers from the Parties of beyond the Sea, where " alfo the Bodies of the Holy Confeffor and Bifhop of St. *Auftin,* the Apofto- " lick of *England,* and alfo many other Holy Saints been honourably humate " and fhrined ; is now of late in great ruin and decay, and the Inhabitants " thereof impoverifhed, and many great Manfions in the fame defolate ; " which ruin, decay and defolation, of like cannot be reformed, ne amend- " ed, unlefs the River that goeth and extendeth from the Town of great *Chart* " in the County of *Kent,* to the faid City, and through and fro the faid Ci- *Act of Parliament about it. Canterb.* one of the moft ancient Cities of *England.*

(a) *Cambd. Britannia.* In *Dorfetfhire, pag.* 209. *Engl. Edit. Antiq. Brit. pag.* 34. (b) Chronicle, *fol.* 20. (c) *Peramb. of Kent.* (d) *Incola.* (e) *Liber Cameræ Civitatis.* (f) *Sine fructu.* (g) 6 *Hen.* 8. *c.* 17.

" ty unto the Haven of *Sandwich*, may be so deeped, enlarged, and of Mills
" and Dams, and other Annoyances, now being in and overthwart the same
" River, between the said City and the common Crane in the Town of
" *Fordwich*, be avoided, scowred, and taken away: Which River between
" the said City and Crane, containeth in length two Miles; so that Carria-
" ges by Lighters and Boats may by the said River be conveyed between the
" said Crane in the said Town of *Fordwich*, unto the said City; which deep-
" ing, inlarging and scowring of the said River, as is before said, shall not
" be only to the profit and avail of the said City, and Inhabitants of the same,
" but also shall cause the Haven of the Town and Port of *Sandwich* to be
" deeper and larger, to the great Commodity of great Number of the
" King's Subjects. In Consideration whereof, it may please the King, with
" the assent of the Lords Spiritual and Temporal, and the Commons in this
" present Parliament assembled, and by the Authority of the same, to enact
" and establish, that the said Mayor, Aldermen, Citizens and Inhabitants of
" the said City, and their Successors, with the advice, assent and agreement
" as well of the Reverend Father in God, *William* Archbishop of *Canterbury*,
" or his Successors; and of two or three Knights, being Justices of Peace
" of the Shire of *Kent*, for the time being; as of the Mayor of the Town
" and Port of *Sandwich* aforesaid, to the said Work, at the request of the
" said Mayor of the said City for the time being, desired and called, may
" lawfully at all and every time hereafter, in such places of the said River, as
" to the said Knights, Mayors, and Aldermen shall seem convenient, deep,
" inlarge, cleanse, inhanse and scowr, and cause to be deeped, inlarged and
" cleansed the said River, with all things thereunto requisite, between the
" said Town of *Chart*, and the said City, and through the same, and fro the
" said City unto the said Crane; in such manner, as Lighters and Boats may
" have by the same River their full passage and course for carriage by the same
" to be conveyed; and without let, interruption, impeachment, disturbance or
" denial of any Person or Persons. And after such deeping, inlarging, in-
" hancing, cleansing, scowring (as is before said) done, the said Mayor,
" Aldermen, Citizens and Inhabitants of the said City, with the assent and
" consent (as is before said) obtained, may lawfully as well stop ditches, and
" make and inhance Bays, Brinks, Dams, and Walls, for the advancing and
" inhighing of the said River, as to take down, abate and put away all Mills,
" Bridges, Dams, Walls, and other whatsoever impediment lying over or
" overthwart the said River, between the said Town of great *Chart* to the said
" City, and through the same, and fro the said City to the foresaid com-
" mon Crane, and other things thereunto requisite; whereby the concourse
" of the said Lighters and Boats should be letted: And that no Action nor Suit
" therefore be maintainable, or to be had against the said Mayor, Aldermen, Ci-
" tizens and Inhabitants or any of them, or their Assigns, for the premises or
" any of them in manner aforesaid.

" Provided always, that every Person that shall be damnified by putting
" away or abating of his Mill, Bridge, or Dam, or Mills, Bridges or Dams,
" shall be reasonably satisfied therefore, for such damages, as he or they shall
" have by reason of the same, by the said Mayor, Aldermen, Citizens and
" Inhabitants of the said City, and their Successors; as the said Archbishop of
" *Canterbury* that now is, or his Successors; and the said Knights shall award,
" consider and adjudge.

Execution, which is said to be the life of Laws, was wanting here. This
Law, this Statute-law (it seems) was never so enlivened. For notwithstanding
this fair way made, I cannot tell by what infortunacy, nothing was done to
any purpose at that time. Too likely it is that the difference between the
Archbishop and the City, as it diverted him from building here, what he built
at (a) *Otford*, a stately Palace, did the mischief and nipt the project in the
bud, so that it came to nothing then, as neither did the like project afterwards.

For albeit it was revived, and in part put in practice with hopes of good
success, through the great furtherance of one Mr. *Rose* an Alderman, and

─────────────────────────────

(a) *Lambard Peramb.* of *Kent.* In *Otford.*

sometime Mayor of the City, in the late Queen's time, who was an especial Benefactor to the Work while he lived, and dying ere the Perfection of it, but well hoping it would be accomplish'd, by his Will (a), gave 300 l. towards it (a most pious act :) yet not being so well followed as behooved, through whose default I know not, succeeded now little better than before. It is now a third time undertaken, and by the good endeavours of industrious men in that forward, as not unlikely to succeed : God's blessing be upon the enterprise, and in due time crown it with Perfection.

O qui principio medium, medio adjice finem.

[Of late this River has been so cleansed and deepned, that Lighters and Boats come now up to the City laden with Coals, Stones, or any other Wares from *Sandwich. N. B.*]

I have no more to say of our River in this place, only a word or two of the Mills standing by or upon it, in and about the City, which are now but few in number, only 5. 1. *King's*-Mill. 2. *Abbats*-Mill. 3. *Westgate*-Mill. 4. *Shaffords*-Mill. 5. *Barton*-Mill: Whereas about King *Stephen's* time, I find(b), that besides these Mills, were 7 other standing all upon this River, in or not far from the City; and belonged to the Monks of *Christ*-Church, whereof the Cellerar of the place had the charge: to wit, the Mill at *Sameletesford* (now vulgarly *Shanford*) *Gudwoldsmeln, Munechemeln, Hottesmeln, Crinesmeln,* and the Mills of *Saliford,* (now *Shulford*) and St. *Mildreth.* All which Mills (I take it) are long since down, and so quite gone (except that of *Shanford*) that it is scarce known where they stood, nor hath *Christ*-Church any one Mill left her at this day. Touching these *quondam* Mills of the Church, I find in their Records Letters of *Hen.* 2. written at the suit and in the behalf of the Monks, and directed (c) to the Bayliffs of *Canterbury* of this tenor. (d) viz. *That all the Mills within and without the City of* Canterbury *should be Tried or Measured, as they were in the time of King* Henry, *my Grandfather. And those, which, since that time, have been rais'd higher to the damage of the Monks of* Canterbury, *should be brought down to the same Measure, in which they were in the time of King* Henry I. *that so the Mills, which belong to* Christ-Church, *may Grind as well and plentifully* [I suppose in respect of having a full and constant supply of Water. *N. B.*] *as they did in the time of King* Henry : *And the Damage which the Monks have sustain'd thereby, you cause to be justly made good to them, of those, by whose means the said Damage did accrue : And unless you thus do, my Sheriff for the County of* Kent *shall cause the same to be done, that I hear no more complaint for want of Justice being done them, &c.* [I take this to be grounded upon a complaint of the Monks, that some of these Mills had raised their Dams or Pools higher than usual, whereby the Water at sometimes was stopped for a while from coming down to the hinderance of the lower Mills. *N. B.*] But leaving these, let me speak of the present Mills.

As for the first, *King's*-Mill. It was and is so called because it sometimes was the King's: and was otherwise called both *Eastbridge*-Mill, and *Kingsbridge*-Mill from the near situation of it to that Bridge. *Thorne* (e) the Chronicler of St. *Augustin's* reports that King *Stephen,* being in a great straight at *Lincoln,* where he was surprised and taken prisoner by *Robert* Earl of *Glocester,* and put to a great Fine for his Ransome ; towards his relief in that Necessity, borrowed of *Hugh,* the 2 of that name, Abbat of St. *Augustin,* one hundred Marks, and in consideration thereof, by his Charter, gave to the Monastery this Mill. The effect of which Charter (saith he) was this. " King *Stephen* gave to " the Church of St. *Augustin's* the Mill, which he had within the said City " near *Eastbridge,* and the whole course of Water belonging to the said Mill, " in compensation for a Bond of an hundred Marks, which he received of " that Church in his Necessity, his Barons being present. And He granted, " That the said Church of St. *Augustin's* should have the Mill, with all the ap-

Mills upon the River.

Kingsmill.

(a) *In Registro Consistorii Cant.*   (b) *Liber Ecclesiæ Cant.*   (c) *Præpositis Cant.*
(d) *Viz. Ut omnia molendina infra Civitatem & extra * attemperentur, sicut fuerunt tempore Reg. Hen. avi mei. Et ea quæ levata altius sunt postea ad damnum Monachorum Cant. ad eam mensuram ad quam erant tempore Regis Hen.* 1. *demittantur, ut molendina Ecclesiæ Christi ita bene & plenarie molere possint, sicut molebant temp. Reg. Hen. & damnum quod inde Monachi habuerunt juste eis restaurari faciatis ab illis per quos damnum contigit, & nisi feceritis Vicecomes meus de Kent faciat fieri, ne in amplius clamorem audiam pro penuria pleni Recti, &c.*   (e) *In vitis Abbat. S. Aug.*   * *Admensurentur.*

" purtenances,

" purtenances, to the ufe of the Altar of the faid Church, as peaceably, as
" freely, as quietly, as honourably as He or any King his Predeceffor had en-
" joyed and poffeffed the fame, *&c. See the Appendix Numb.* VII. *a.* From
thenceforth the Abbey enjoyed the Mill until the time of Abbat *Clarembald,*
who made it over to King *Hen.* 2. whereof the fame Author hath thefe words
favouring of his diflike of the act. " And note that the Mill abovefaid with
" other goods and poffeffions were unjuftly alienated by *Clarembaldus* to King
" *Henry* and his Succeffors, and regranted to the ufe of his City. But the
" fame King *Henry* in recompence for this Injury, is faid to have granted ma-
" ny liberties to that Monaftery, *&c. See Appendix Numb.* VII. *b.* Afterwards when the City was granted in Feefarm to the Baliffs, by *Hen.* 3. this
Mill, as parcel, was (*a*) exprefly included in the grant. Whereof the fame
Thorne hath this note. " In thofe times the fame King *Henry* granted his City
" of *Canterbury* to the Citizens of the fame, to be governed by two Bailiffs,
" at Feeferm of lx Pounds to be paid yearly into his Treafury, with all Cu-
" ftoms belonging to the faid City, with the Mill of *Eaftbridge,* otherwife cal-
" led *Kings*-Mill. And here note that the faid Mill formerly given by King
" *Stephen* to the Church of St. *Auguftin*'s , was alienated to *Henry* then King
" of *England* by Abbat *Clarembaldus* the Intruder, and was injurioufly detain'd
" by his Succeffors, the Kings, to the ufe of his City, and at laft was by King
" *Henry* refign'd or given to the Citizens together with the Borough. *See the
Appendix Numb.* VII. *c.* Thus he.

In a caufe of Tithes brought by the Parfon of All-Saints , againft the
Miller of this Mill ; I find (*b*) the Miller brought to his Anfwer. *Who being
asked, whether he was Farmer of the faid Mill, anfwered, No, but confeffeth, that
he was a Servant of the Mayors of the City of* Canterbury, *by them there deputed.
Being further asked, he confeffed, That all the Bakers of the Town ought to grind all
fort of Grain for White-bread Toll-free ,* &c. (Appendix Numb. VII. *d.*) The
reft is wanting.

This fuit happened in the year 1366, however this paffage of it mentions
the Mayors of the City, which came not into being, by name, untill almoft
an 100 years after. Since thefe times, the cafe is altered with this Mill. For
(I take it) the City Bakers of thefe days, neither are tied to grind their Corn
at this Mill (as by this note they feem to be:) nor yet have any fuch privilege
of grinding at that Mill Toll-free, as then, for White-bread. I have but one
thing more to acquaint you with touching this Mill. And it is that one *William Bennet* a Citizen and an Alderman of *Canterbury,* about the year 1462 in
his Will, appoints his Executors to buy 300 foot of *Afheler* or *Folkftone* Stone to
make a Wharf about the King's Mill (*c*).

Abbats-Mill.   I come now to *Abbats*-Mill, the next upon the Stream to *Kings*-Mill. It
was called fo becaufe it did heretofore belong to the Abbey of St. *Auguftine.*
Whereof I find mention in King *Stephen*'s time. For then (as *Thorne* (*d*) hath
it) *Hugh,* the fecond of the name, Abbat of the place, diftinguifhing or fetting out the offices of the Monaftery, " affign'd to the ufe of the Sacrifty of
" his Monaftery the Mill called *Abbats-mill,* which he purchafed at his own
" coft, on this condition, That all Provifion of Corn for the ufe of the faid
" Monaftery be there Ground Toll-free, that the Tithe of the faid Mill be
" paid to the Almonry of the faid Monaftery, and the refidue of the Profits
" arifing from the faid Mill fhould go to the ufe of the Sacrifty. (*Appendix
Numb.* VII. *e.*) This Mill is now the Town's.

Weftgate-Mill.   I pafs next to *Weftgate*-Mill. A very old one. *Doomfday*-Book mentions it
as the Archbifhop's : but then in the hands of the Canons of St. *Greg.* The
Tithe of it was by Archbifhop *Hubert* in King *John*'s time, granted (amongft
other things) to the Hofpital of *Eaftbridge,* and that grant was confirmed by
the Prior and Convent of *Chrift*-Church (*e*). It is (the Mill) fince returned to
the Archbifhoprick, and continues a parcel of the Demefnes of the fame.

Shaffords-Mill.   As for *Shaffords*-Mill ; 'tis but little I can fay of it : yet I take it to be that
which I find anciently. *i. e.* about *Rich.* 1. time called *Scepefhotefmelne.* (*f*) With-

---

(a) *Ubi fupra.*   (b) *Lib. Ecclef. Chrift. Cant.*   (c) *Lib. Teftamentor. penes regift. Dom.*
Archidiac. Cantuar.   (d) *In vitis Abb. S. Auguftini.*   (e) *Lib. Hofp. de Eftbridge.*
    (f) *Extra Weftgate ab aquilonari parte verfus Scepefhotefmelne.*

A drawing of the High Altar in the monastic church of St. Augustine, Canterbury, with the shrines of relics standing round it and their inscriptions, as inserted in an ancient manuscript belonging to that monastery [Elmham's Chronicle, Trinity Hall, Cambridge, M.S.1]

Año Dñi MCCXL. istud altare dedicat in honore Apłoɤ Pet: et Pauli et sci. Augustini v. Kal. Nov.
Año Dñi MCCCXXV. istud altare dedicat in honore Apost: Pet: et Pauli Sci. Augustini Angloɤ Apli. et
Sci. Æthelberti Regis. Kal. Martij á Petro Epo Corbaniensi

24

out Weſtgate *on the North-ſide towards* Scepeſhoteſmelne, as in a deed of *Enſt-bridge.* The compoſition between the Prior and Canons of St. *Greg. Parſons* of Holy Croſs of *Weſtgate,* and the then Vicar in the year 1347 calls it (a) *Shefford's* Mill, and in expreſs words reſerves the Tithes thereof from the Vicar to themſelves; which clearly ſhews it to be a titheable Mill, and not within the exemption of the Stat. of 9. *Ed.* 2. *Cap.* 5. *See the endowment of the Vicarage of* Weſtgate *in the Appendix.*

Barton-Mill was ſometimes, and that (b) from old times belonging to *Chriſt-* Church, where the Monks Corn was Ground for their own ſpending within the Court. But it is now alienated, and ſo hath been ever ſince the Diſſolution. So much for the Mills. And now have I done with the River. Only let not my ſilence ſmother, or ſuppreſs that due praiſe and commendation well known to appertain unto it, for (what, but for the common Pochers it would much more abound with) the plenty of ſingular good fiſh, which it breeds and yields of divers ſorts, Trouts eſpecially; whereof thoſe at *Fordwich* bear away *Fordwich* the bell, a place of note (as *Cambden* ſaith) in that reſpect. **Trouts.**

margin: Barton-Mill.

The SUBURBS.

The Monaſtery of St. Auguſtin's.

ACcording to my propoſed method, coming now to the Suburbs: My Survey thereof ſhall take beginning at the *Eaſt* part; and therein at St. *Auguſtin's.* Concerning which I will limit my Diſcourſe to theſe two Heads or Particulars.

    1. *The firſt Foundation and following Eſtate of it.*
    2. *A Survey of the preſent Remains of it.*

margin: 1. Particular.

For the firſt. *Auguſtin* the Monk, the Apoſtle of the *Engliſh,* (as the ancient Charters of the Abby call him) Pope *Gregory* the Great's *Nuncio,* his *Alumnus,* coming over hither with his commonachal Aſſociates, and being admitted firſt into the preſence, and eftſoons into the favour of *Ethelbert,* who (c) *was the firſt Chriſtian* Kentiſh *King;* and (*King* Ethelbert *was the firſt of all the Kings of* England *that profeſſed the Chriſtian Religion,* as it is in the Bordure of the Quire-hangings of *Chriſt-Church:*) this is meant of the *Saxons,* who entred this Kingdom, and were formerly Idolaters; but the *Britains* were Chriſtians almoſt from the time of our Saviour's Death, and ſo they continued; though at this time living with their Biſhops in the remote parts of the Iſland of *Britany.* And the ſame *Auguſtin* having by his and his Fellow-labourers Preaching, both by life and doctrine, with God's cooperating Grace, at length wrought his converſion to Chriſtianity, was ſo well affected, and thankfully handled of him, that for reward of his Service, amongſt many favours, he obtained of the King his Patron, a certain piece of Ground on the *Eaſt* part of the City of *Canterbury.* Whereon afterwards, with the King's help, he built this Abby, dedicated, when ſo firſt founded, to the bleſſed Apoſtles *Peter* and *Paul,* and ſo known a while, but afterwards not (as *Lambard* (d) will) only in memory of his benefit; but from the new dedication of it by Archbiſhop *Dunſtan,* (e) *In honour of the Holy Apoſtles,* Peter *and* Paul *and St.* Auguſtine; in the Year 978 (f): From thence (I ſay) his being added to the former Tutelars, and after that, until the diſſolution, called St. *Auguſtin's.*

It may not be forgotten, that one main end of ſetting apart this Suburbian Plot of ground, and of the erecting the Abby upon it, (according to the meaning both of *Ethelbert* and *Auguſtin*) was, that it ſhould be a common Sepulchre both for them and their Succeſſors, as well in the Kingdom as in the Archbiſhoprick, for ever after. For it was not then, nor long after, the manner to bury within Cities; (the City being a place not for the dead, but the living, as it is in a Charter of *Ethelbert,* which ſhall follow anon:) and it being a thing defended, *i. e.* forbidden to bury within Cities by the Law of the

margin: Unlawfulneſs of burial with-in Cities.

(a) *Molendinum de Shefford.*   (b) *Ab antiquo.*   (c) *Rex Ethelbertus inter Reges Anglorum Chriſticola primus.*   (d) *Peramb.* of *Kent.* In *Cant.*   (e) *In honore Sanctorum Apoſtolorum Petri & Pauli, Sanctique Auguſtini.*   (f) *Thorne, in vitis Abb. S. Auguſtini.*

12 Tables: (*a*) *Neither bury nor burn a dead Man within the City.* A Law (it seems) standing till then; and long after in force here, yet more for the reason sake of it (as I conceive) fitting it to all Nations, which was the prevention of fire by burning, and other annoyance by burying the Carcass within the City, than as being any otherwise a binding law to this Kingdom, long before deserted by the *Romans*, and no way now dependent on that Empire or in subjection to it.

The further discovery of this Abby's Foundation and Original, I leave to you to make, and take (if you please) from the ensuing Transcripts of the Founders Charters, four in Number; whereof the three former are of *Ethelbert*, and the other of *Augustin*; closed and fenced (as you shall see, according to the manner of former times) with such solemn and dreadful imprecations upon the Violaters of their Piety; that (if the Charters themselves prove true and not counterfeit, as some suspect them) I for my part (how light soever some do, and will make of them) would tremble to be liable unto, for all the good, for all the gain were it never so much, that might accrue unto me by intermedling. But to the Charters, which I have taken from *Reyner*'s Copy, in his *Apostolatus Benedictinorum*; writing of this Monastery.

[The former of these is recited in an *Inspeximus* of King *Edward* III. in *Reyner* (*b*); where also are several other Charters of Kings to be found, granting or confirming Privileges to this Monastery, as of *Edbaldus* the Son of *Ethelbert*, of *Edmund*, of *Adelwolph*, of *Canute*, and of St. *Edward* the Confessor. The other three which are in the *Appendix*, *Reyner* took from *Thorn*'s Chronicle, where they are also since reprinted. They bear indeed so near a relation to this History, that they challenge a place in the *Appendix*; where they may be seen, *Numb. VIII.* (*a*). (*b*). (*c*). (*d*). They are in brief to this effect. *N. B.*]

Chart. 1.

" King *Ethelbert* gives in honour of St. *Peter*, a Portion of Land lying on
" the *East* side of *Canterbury*, to build a Monastery upon it, and in the Name
" of God adjures and wills, that this donation be confirmed for ever; with
" imprecations on the Violators of this Grant. The Portion of Land is thus
" bounded. On the *East* stands the Church of St. *Martin*; on *South Burgate-*
" *way*; on the *West* and *North Drouting-street.* Dated A. D. 605.

Chart. 2.

" King *Ethelbert* gives to God a Portion of Land, where he had built a Mo-
" nastery in honour of St. *Peter* and St. *Paul*, the Princes of the Apostles;
" with imprecations on the Violators of his donation: As in the former. The
" bounds of this Monastery are more fully expressed. In the *East* the Church
" of St. *Martin*, and thence *East*-ward by *Swennedown*, and so to the *North* by
" *Wykengmark*. Again, from the *East South*-ward by *Burewaremearke*, and so
" by the *South* to the *West* by *Kyngesmeark*, and the *West* by *Redercheep*. So
" *North*-ward to *Droutingstreet.* Dated A. D. 605. [There are added in *Thorn* an Explication of these bounds by Names that were better known; *viz.* On the *East* St. *Martin*'s Church, and so *East*-ward, by *Millehelle*; and so to the *North* by *Wibescrowch*. Again, from the *East South*-ward to *Fißpole.* So the *South* and *West* by the Highway leading from *Chaldane-crouch* even unto *Canterbury*, and so toward the *West* to *Rederchepe*, and so on the *North* to *Droutington N. B.*].

Chart. 3.

" King *Ethelbert*, Founder of this Monastery, constituted *Peter* first Abbat
" thereof, and for the increase of its Revenues, gave to it *Chistelet* with all
" its Appurtenances, Rents, Woods, Pastures, &c. also a Golden Sceptre, a
" Bridle and Saddle adorn'd with Gold, and beset with precious Stones, &c.
" *Augustine* had also enriched this Monastery with Reliques of the Apostles and
" Saints, and other Ecclesiastical Ornaments, sent him from *Rome*; and had
" enjoin'd, that himself and all his Successors should be buried therein, &c.
Dated A. D. 605.

[The Fourth Charter is called, the *Privilege of St.* Augustin; granted to this Monastery, and doth chiefly consist in Exemptions and Immunities, and in appointing it to be the only place for the Burials of Kings, Archbishops, and Princes. *N. B.*].

These auspicious beginnings had answerable proceedings. For the foundation of the Abbey thus laid, it became in process of time much advanced, both

---

(a) *Hominem mortuum infra urbem ne sepelito, neve urito.*   (b) *Apost. Bened.* p. 57.

in

in the inlargement of her Buildings, and augmentation of her Indowment. For the firft. After the death of King *Ethelbert Eadbaldus* (his fon) at the inftance of *Lawrence* the Archbifhop built a fair Church in this Monaftery which he called St. *Mary's*. After *Eadbaldus*, King *Canute* (the great Monarch of this Realm:) *Egelfine* (the Abbat that fled for fear of the Conqueror:) *Scotlandus* (whom the fame King put in *Egelfin's* place:) *Hugh Floriac* (that was of kindred to King *William Rufus*, and by him made Abbat:) were the perfonsthat chiefly increafed the building: fome beftowing Churches and Chappels ; fome Dortors and Refectories or dining places, and others other fort of Edifices *(a)*.

Now for the latter, her increafe in poffeffions and indowment, it would be too tedious a matter to particularize but the one half of the donations and grants of Lands and Revenues that were made and given by the multitude of Benefactors of all forts, who out of the heat of their Devotion to the place, for the double founders fake, the one the great inftrument of Chriftianifm brought and wrought amongft the *Saxon* people of thofe parts, the other (by God's bleffing on his endeavours) the firft Chriftian King of the *Englifh-Saxon* race, ftrived of holy Zeal, according to their knowledge to out-ftrip one another in an open handed Liberality to this Abbey. The Royal Benefactors (for I fhall omit the reft) after *Ethelbert* (as *Thorne* informs me) were chiefly thefe. King *Eadbald* his Son and next Succeffor, who gave the Manor of *Northtborne*, confifting of 30 Plough-lands. King *Lothaire*, who gave 3 Plough-lands in *Stodmerfh*. King *Withred*, who gave the Manor of *Littleborne* of 5 Ploughlands. King *Eadbert* his Son, who gave 6 Plough-lands in *Little-Mongeham*. King *Edmund*, whofe gift was 2 Plough-lands in *Sybertfweld*. *Kenewulf* King of *Mercia* and *Cuthred* King of *Kent*, who gave the Manor of *Lenham*, confifting of 20 Plough-lands and 13 Denes. King *Ethelwulf* the *Weft-Saxon*, who gave 40 Caflatos (Manfions I take it) in *Lenham*. King *Ethelbert* the *Weft-Saxon* alfo, who gave the Manor of *Merton* in *Eaft-Kent*, of 3 Plough-lands. King *Canute*, who together with the body of St. *Mildred* the Virgin of *Thanet*, gave unto the Abbey all the indowment of that late Monaftery. King *Edgar* who gave *Plumfted*, of 4 Plough-lands. *Edward* the Confeffor, who gave all the land he had in *Fordwich*.

Royal Benefactors to St. *Auguftin's* Abbey.

The fucceeding Kings, for the moft part, were rather confirmers or reftorers of the old, than contributers of new poffeffions to this Abbey. Whofe Charters (as the others) are many of them already Publifhed partly in *Reyner's Apoftolatus Benedictinorum*, and partly in *Wevers* Funeral Monuments, [and fince thefe, in the Chronicle of *Thorne. N. B.*] Wherefore I fpare their recital here. Neither will I wade or enter far into difcourfe of the once flourifhing eftate of this ancient Abbey, left I find it (as I may juftly fear it) even endlefs. For fo many were the Priviledges, fo wide the Poffeffions, and fo very great the eftimation of this Abbey, in many refpects (that of it being, of old, the felected place for the Royal and Archiepifcopal fepulture, not the leaft:) as few other in the Kingdom did or could in all points parallel it.

Only let me, ere my clofe, acquaint you from Mr. *Lambard* *(b)*, that the houfe, before the diffolution, had five Convents, confifting (faith he) of 65 Monks, Benedictines, or of the order of the black Monks of St. *Benet*, which began here in *England* with their Founder, (the nature hereof fee hereafter in *Chrift-Church:*) And, as he adds (befide Jurifdiction over an whole Lath of 13 hundreds) it had poffeffion of Livelihood to the value of 808 *l.* by year. Herein, (I fuppofe) following the eftimate of her temporalties, taxed at that fum by the Pope's Delegates, the Bifhops of *Winchefter* and *Lincoln*, *John* and *Oliver*, in the year 1292, authorifed to tax and rate the temporalties of all the Clergy, both Religious and fecular throughout the Kingdom, for the levying of a tenth thereby, which the Pope had granted to the King *(Ed.* 1.) *(c) in aid of the holy Land*. But it feems that upon the furrender and fuppreffion of the Abbey, which happened 4. *Decemb.* 29 *Hen.* 8. that eftimate was well near doubled. For (as *Speed* and *Weaver* both have it) it was then valued, as the Record in the King's Exchequer fhows, at 1412. *lib.* 4 *s.* 7 *d.* ob. q.

The Abbey, of what value.

Briefly this Abbey, and the Abbat thereof in right of his Abbaty, had *(d)*, allowance of mintage and coinage of Money, by the grant of King *Athel-*

(a) *Lamb.* Peramb. of *Kent.* In *Canterbury.*   (b) Peramb. of *Kent.* In *Cant.*
(c) *In fubfidium terræ fancta.* Lib. Ecclef. Chrifti Cant.   (d) *Cuneum monetæ.*

ſtan (a), which continued until the time of King *Stephen*, and then was utterly loſt, *Silveſter* the 45 Abbat, who died *Anno* 1161, being the laſt that enjoyed it. Whereof *Thorne* writing his Life hath theſe words. " *Memorandum*, ſaith

Appendix,
*Numb.*VIII.*e.*
" he, That this *Sylveſter* Abbat and many Abbats his Predeceſſors had a Mint
" to coin Money in the City of *Canterbury*, as appears by inquiſition made by
" *Arnold Ferre*, *Wulfine Mercer* and others who being Sworn ſaid, That a certain
" Abbat of St. *Auguſtin*'s, *Sylveſter* by name, had in the City of *Canterbury* a
" Mint for Money, and that *Elured Porre* was keeper of the ſaid Mint, on be-

**Abbat of
St. *Auſtin*'s had
Coinage of
Money.**
" half of the ſaid Abbat: And when that Abbat died, the Monaſtery was ſeiz'd
" upon and put into the hand of our Lord the King, together with the ſaid
" Mint: And no Abbat who ſucceeded, has ever ſince recovered the ſeizure
" of the ſaid Mint: And this Inquiſition was made in the time of King *Henry*
" II. and King *Richard* his Son.   The Abbat moreover was *(b)* a *Mitred Abbat*,
firſt made ſo by Pope *Alex.* 2. as the ſame *Thorne* (in the life of Abbat *Egelſine*)

**Dignified by
the Pope with
Mitre and
Sandals.**
relates.   Who ſaith that the ſame *Egelſine* being ſent on ſome Embaſſage to
Pope *Alex.* 2. in the year 1063, was there the firſt Abbat of this Monaſtery, to
whom it was of the ſame Pope permitted with his Succeſſors, the Abbats of
the place, to uſe the Mitre and Sandals, in manner of a Biſhop, the Pope thus
then pronouncing and ſaying, *(c) We decree, that the Abbat of St.* Auguſtin's *ſhall
perpetually enjoy this Dignity, to wit, out of an honourable reſpect to this ſon of the
Church of* Rome *and Apoſtle of the* Engliſh *Nation.*   He was I ſay a mitred Abbat, that is by *Cowel*'s interpretation *(d)* an Abbat Sovereign, exempt from
the Juriſdiction of the Dioceſan, having Epiſcopal Juriſdiction within himſelf.
He had place and voice not only in Parliament as a Spiritual Baron, but alſo
in the general Council, where, by the gift of Pope *Leo* ix*th*, his place was to
ſit by the Abbat *Montis Caſini (e)*.   [For this Abbat's further Dignity, what it
was before the Conqueſt, ſee the Hiſtory of *Ely* cited in St. *Henry Spelman*'s
Gloſſary in the word *Cancellarius. p.* 127. *W. S.*]   A Catalogue of theſe Abbats
and others, who living, by their learning and piety ; or dead, by the reliques
of their mortality, their deceaſed Bodies, ſome honourably intombed, others
gloriouſly inſhrined there, have enfamouſed the place, I refer you to find in
Pitſeus his Catalogue, and *Wever*'s ancient Funeral Monuments.   And hitherto
of the flouriſhing eſtate of this Abbey.

It neither may, nor will (I know) be imagined but that this Abbey taſted of
both Fortunes.   Wherefore as you have heard ſomewhat of the weal, ſo now
give me leave with what brevity I can, to acquaint alſo with the wo ; the detriments I mean and diſaſters, that have at any time abated, and at laſt fatally
obſcured and finally extinguiſhed the glory and majeſty of this once famous and
opulent Abbey.

Whereof the firſt in time and not of leaſt regard was her loſs of the long
enjoyed right and intereſt to the burials of the Kings and Archbiſhops, of
which, the former, in Archbiſhop *Brightwald*'s, and the latter in *Cutbert*'s days
were firſt taken from it *(f)*.

**Abby infeſted
by the *Danes.***
Another was the grievous and frequent infeſtation of the place by the *Danes*:
which (however their Chroniclers, for their Abbey's greater glory, ſometimes
aſcribe their ſafety, defence and deliverance from thoſe Invaders to a miraculous preſervation:) yet doubtleſs either ſuffered their violence, or at the leaſt,
and at the beſt, purchaſed their Peace (and ſo prevented their greater Calamity) at a dear rate, and with coſtly redemptions, eſpecially in that lamentable
ſpoil and devaſtation of the City under King *Etheldred*, in the year 1011. The
recorders of the tragical ſtory whereof, the elder Monks, *Henry* of *Huntingdon*,
Roger Hoveden, and others, (whoſe Pens a miracle ſo mainly tending to the
advancement of Monkery, in all likelihood could not have eſcaped) tell of
no ſuch miracle as *Thorne* will have the Abbey then reſcued and ſaved by,
which was, that when a *Dane* had taken hold of St. *Auguſtin*'s Pall or Cloak
(wherewith his Tomb was covered) it ſtuck ſo faſt to his Fingers, that by
no means poſſible he could loſe it, till he came and yielded himſelf to the
Monks, and made ſorrowful confeſſion of his Fault.   Which thing ſo ter-

---

(*a*) *Leg. Athelſtani in Archeon. Gul. Lamb. pag.*   (b) *Abbas Mitratus.*   (c) *Hunc api-
cem habere perpetuò rectorem decrevimus Auguſtinenſem, ob ipſius ſcilicet Romanorum alumpni & Anglorum
Apoſtoli dignitatem.*   (d) *Interpreter in verb. Abbat. pag 2.*   (e) *Reyner in appendice ad
Apoſtolat. Benedictin. pag* 53.   (f) *Lamb. Peramb. of Kent.* In Canterbury.

rified the reft of the *Danes*, that they defifted and ceafed from invading the Monaftery, and became chief Protectors and Defenders of it. " When the *Danes* (as *Thorn's* own words are) deftroyed the City of *Can-* *Appendix,* " *terbury* with Fire and Sword; fome of thofe facrilegious Wretches entred Numb. VIII. f. " the Monaftery, not to fay their Prayers, but to carry away what they could " lay hands upon. One of them more defperately wicked than the reft of " his Comrades, comes boldly to the Sepulchre of our Apoftle St. *Auguftin*, " where he lay entomb'd, and ftole away the Pall with which the Tomb of " the Saint was covered, and hid it under his Arm. But divine Vengeance " immediately feiz'd upon the facrilegious Perfon, and the Pall which was " hid under his Arm ftuck to the Arm of the Thief, and grew to it, as if it " had been new natural flefh, infomuch as it could not be taken away by force " or art, until the Thief himfelf came and difcovered what he had done, and " confeffed his fault before the Saint and the Monks, and then begged their " pardon. This Example of divine Vengeance, fo affrighted the multitude " of the reft of the *Danes*, that they not only offered no violence to this Mo- " naftery afterwards, but became the chief Defenders of the fame. Thus he. But (as I faid) our elder Stories have no mention of this Miracle. *Hoveden* (I confefs) naming the then Abbat of the place, fays, that he was fuffered to efcape or go his way, haply (and as it may be reafonably thought) becaufe he had ranfomed himfelf and his Abby, by compofition with the Enemy. But that your belief may not reft upon my bare and fingular opinion of this Abby's partaking with the neighbouring City and Cathedral in their *Danifh* preffures, I will ftand by, whilft the Reverend Archbifhop *Parker* gives you his, who thinking it incredible that the City fhould fo often fuffer by the *Danes*, and this Abby efcape; thus expoftulates the matter. (a) " What fhall I fay concerning " the Monaftery of St. *Auguftin's* nigh *Canterbury*, the firft and moft ancient of " all, fo lifted up with the privileges and Grants of the Bifhops of *Rome*, and " of the Kings of *Kent*, whereby they thought themfelves free from all obedi- " ence and fubjection to their Archbifhop: Yea, they claim'd this refpect, " duty, and obfervance from the Archbifhop, that the Abbat elect of this " Monaftery, when he was to receive Benediction, would not come to the " Archbifhop, but the Archbifhop went to the Abbat. Is it credible, that " among fo many Storms and Invafions of the *Danes*, whereby fo many Mo- " nafteries were overthrown, that this haughty Abby fhould remain fafe and " fecure from the *Danifh* Ravages, which fo miferably deftroyed the famous " City *Canterbury*? Thus he.

[The fame venerable Author, in the Life of Archbifhop *Dunftan*, occafio- nally mentions the pretended Miracle, whereby this Monaftery was preferved as is above related: He fpeaks of it (as there is no queftion but it was) as an idle fiction of the Monks. Concerning the efcape of this Monaftery from *Danifh* fury, I will afterwards offer a conjecture in the Supplement to the Hi- ftory of the Archdeacons. *N. B.*].

A Third and Fourth great difafter to this Abby, was the firing of it one Abbey fired. time, and the almoft drowning of it another. The former (by fire) happen- ing in the Year 1168. (b) " In the Year 1168, on *Auguft* 29, being the Feaft " of the Beheading of St. *John* the Baptift, the greateft part of this Church " was burnt, in which fire many ancient Codicils and Charters perifhed, and " the Shrines of St. *Auguftin* and many other Saints were miferably fpoiled. " In commiferation of this Misfortune, Pope *Alexander* confirm'd the appro- " priation of the Church of *Feverfham*, towards the repair of this Church,

---

(a) *Quid dicam de Monafterio Sancti Auguftini, Doberniæ, omnium primo & antiquiffimo, Romanorum Pontificum, atque Regum Cantiorum privilegiis adeo fuperbo, quibus fretus ab omni fubjectione & obedientia fui Archipræfulis, immune fe putarit? Imo, hoc officium obfervantiam, & honorem ab Archiepifcopo fibi debitum vendicavit, ut femper electus loci Abbas, cum benediceretur, non ad illum accederet, fed Archiepifcopus ad Abbatem. Credibilene eft inter tantas procellas hoc infolens coenobium tutum & à Danorum impetu liberum effe potuiffe, cum ipfam Doberniam urbem inclytam, ita mifere depopulati funt, ut fupra retulimus? Antiq. Brit. in vita Celnothi, pag. 72* (b) *A D. 1168. die decollationis S. Joannis Baptiftæ, combufta fuit ifta ecclefia pro maxima parte, in qua combuftione multæ codicillæ antiquæ perierunt, atque ipfum fere- trum S Auguftini & multorum fanctorum hujus loci flebiliter funt deformata; nec mirum cum ipfa pene tota ecclefia igne fuerat confumpta. Cujus infortunio mifertus Alexander Papa ecclefiam de Feverfham ad repara- tionem ecclefiæ fic igne confumptæ confirmavit; & ecclefiam de Menftre & Middleton ad Sacriftiam pro repa- ratione iftius ecclefiæ deputavit.*

I " thus

Abbey almoſt drowned.

" thus waſted by fire. And aſſign'd the Churches of *Minſter* and *Middleton* to
" the uſe of the Sacriſty for the repair of this Church. The latter (by wa-
" ter) in the Year 1271. (a) " In this Year, ſaith the ſame Author, on the day
" of the Tranſlation of St. *Auguſtin*, there were terrible Thunders and Light-
" nings, and ſuch an Inundation of Rain, that the City of *Canterbury* was
" almoſt drown'd. The Flood was ſo high both in the Court of the Mona-
" ſtery, and the Church, that they had been quite overwhelmed with Water, un-
" leſs the Virtue of the Saints who reſted there, had withſtood the Waters.

[The Author of the *Antiqu. Britan.* ſpeaks of this Storm and Flood as a
general Calamity to the whole City. He ſays, that it thundred and lightened
a whole day and night; in which time dark Clouds were continually gathered together. Great Torrents of Rain flowed down for many days.
Flocks and Herds were driven thereby out of the Fields; Trees were overthrown, and torn up by the roots. This Flood was followed, firſt by a general dearth and ſcarcity of all Proviſions, and afterwards by a plague and mortality. *N. B.*].

Mortmain.

7 Ed. I.

The next great Croſs which befel this Abbey, but common to it with other,
was the reſtraint of the Laity from any longer extending the hand of their
Bounty, in paſſing over their Fee to the Abbey, without ſpecial Licence of
the King, by the Statute of *Mortmain*, or the Law of *Amortization*; which
timely to moderate the before unlimited liberty of the Laity, in that kind,
likely in time to give all to God, and leave nothing, or but little, for *Cæſar*
and themſelves, by their over-forwardneſs and extreme exceſs in that kind of
operative devotion (a thing, conſidering their full perſuaſion of the meritori-
ous nature of it, nothing ſtrange) provided a convenable reſtraint, tying and
manacling the hands of the Subject for the future, from that kind of over-a-
ctive Charity, without the foregoing privity and conſent of the Prince. But
this Croſs, this Loſs was in part ſupplied, and made leſs ſenſible unto the Religious, by a piece of policy which they quickly put in ure; and that was, the
procuring not only of Privileges and Immunities from payment of Tithes, but

**Impropriati-
ons.**

alſo of Impropriations or Annexions of Churches, Parſonages I mean, to
their Houſes; which though invented, and on foot long before, upon what
pretext ſee *Hay (b)*; yet now, the other current of their gain being ſtopt,
much more abounding than ever before (c). All of them, but eſpecially the
latter, things improperly enough in the hands of the Religious, and with
cauſe enough reckoned among the 100 grievances of *Germany (d)*, but much
more improperly in the poſſeſſion of meer lay-men, as now they are moſt-
what; but generally like the gold of *Tholouſe*, not without a curſe, a croſs at
leaſt, either real or perſonal, upon the perſon of the Invader, or his eſtate,
or both, which though he either cannot or will not himſelf, yet others both
can and do ſee and obſerve to follow ſuch profaners of the Churches Patri-
mony, the improper Lay-proprietaries of Parſonages and Church-livings. (e)
[Mr. *Lambard* ſays, That this Appropriation of Benefices to the Monks *was one
amongſt many, of the monſtrous births of Covetouſneſs, begotten by the Man of*
Rome *in the dark Night of Superſtition, and yet ſuffered to live in this Day-light of
the Goſpel to the great hinderance of Learning, the impoveriſhment of the Miniſtry,
the decay of Hoſpitality, and the infamy of our Profeſſion.* Peramb. of *Kent* in *Frin-
diſbury.* W. S.] Pardon this digreſſion, and I proceed.

By the way would you be further ſatisfied concerning the grounds, upon
which Impropriations of Churches to Monks and Monaſteries firſt began, I
find them briefly to be theſe. (f) " The chief thing, the Biſhops had in view,

---

(a) *Eodem anno* (viz. 1271.) *die tranſlationis S. Aug. facta fuerant tonitrua & coruſcationes & tanta
inundatio pluviæ, ut Civitas Cant. pene ſubmerſa iſſet. Occupaverat verò aqua totam iſtam Curiam pariter
& eccleſiam, ut prope ſubmerſæ iſſent, niſi virtus S inctorum ibi quieſcentium obſiſteret.* Vid. Antiq. Brit. in
initio vitæ Kildwardbj. (b) *Aſtrum inextinctum, quaſi* 2. *num.* 9. *& ſeq. fol.* 98,99.
(c) Downing's Diſcourſe, Concluſ. 3. § 5. (d) *Fox*, Acts and Monum. Vol. 2. pag. 85.
(e) *Amicus Plato, Amicus Socrates; ſed magis amica Pietas.* (f) *Illud imprimis agebant Epiſcopi, dum eccleſias Monachis attribuerent, ut paci eccleſiaſticæ ſubſervirent. Quòd enim pleræque earum eccleſiarum in ipſis Monachorum fundis conderentur, & ab eorum ſervis, qui terram extirpatis ſilvis novarunt, fre-
quentarentur; ne quid inter Clericos & Monachos ſereretur diſſidii, poſtulabat æquitas, & concordia, ut Monachis traderentur gubernandæ. Ea cauſa cum deerat, aliam Epiſcopis ſuggeſſit charitas, ut Monachorum ſuſtenta-
tioni caveretur. Poſtremo id quoque cauſæ acceſſit, ut eccleſiæ melius regerentur, tum ob accuratiorem inſti-
tionem plebium, quibus Monachi ad omnem difficultatem praſto erant doctrinæ per ea tempora fere principatum
habentes, tum ob Presbyterorum, quos fere tunc erudiebant Monachi ſoli, delectum faciliorem. Itaque non paucæ
donationes ejus generis ſignatè cavent ut in Monachorum poteſtate ſit Presbyterorum electio, atque Eccleſiarum
gubernatio, &c.* " when

" when they affigned Churches to the Monks, was to provide for the
" Peace of the Church: For becaufe many Churches were built upon
" Grounds poffeffed by the Monks, and were frequented by their Ser-
" vants, who cut down their Woods and till'd their Grounds, left there
" fhould be any difagrement between the Clerks and the Monks, Equity
" and Peace both required, that thofe Churches fhould be committed to the
" government of the Monks: When that reafon ceafed, Charity fuggefted a
" new one to the Bifhops, namely, that Provifion fhould be made for the
" maintainance of the Monks. At laft, this alfo was added, That the Monks
" would take the beft care of thofe Churches for the good of the People, &c.
" Hence many donations of this kind exprefly provided, that the choice of
" Presbyters and the Government of the Churches, fhould be wholly in the
" power of the Monks, &c. So *Roverius* in his Illuftrations upon the Hiftory of the Monaftery of St. *John* called *Reomans.* [We in *England* have
thoughts quite different from this Author, concerning Churches appropriated
to Monks. We never find, that the Monks took good care of their Churches,
or that they were the beft Parifh-Priefts, where they were allowed to Offici-
ciate in Churches: but on the contrary, their Negligence caufed Laws to be
made, whereby they were forced to put in Vicars into their Churches, becaufe they themfelves grofly neglected to take care of them. Statut. 15 *Ric.*
II. *c.* 6. 4 *H.* 4. *c.* 28. *N. B.*] But to St. *Auguftin's* again.

    I do not remember that I have read of or met with any other much confide-
rable lofs, crofs or misfortune to have befallen this Abbey afterwards, untill
that fatal blow of utter diffolution was given it by *Hen.* 8. Little had all the 29 *Hen* 8. 24.
former Cafualties been to the ruin of this goodly Abbey, had not that fudden *Decembris.*
and tempeftuous Storm (which bare down before it all the religious Structures
of this kind throughout the Kingdom) falling upon it, brought this with the
reft, to irrecoverable ruin: whofe uncovered Walls ftood fo long languifhing
in time, and ftorms of Weather that daily increafed the afpect of her ruins,
till now laftly they are made fubject to other publick ufes, and the whole tract
of that moft goodly foundation in the fame place no where appearing, &c. as
it is in *Speed* (*a*). Yet thither let me lead you, and have your Patience whilft
I furvey the prefent Remains of the place, which is my fecond Particular
touching this Abbey.

    Amongft which, I find fcarce any of note befide *Ethelbert's* Tower and 2. Particular.
St. *Pancrace's* Chappel. But ere we enter the Sept, a word or two of that.
The fept or fite of the Monaftery yet appears and may be traced by the cir-
cuiting walls, within the compafs whereof the Eleemofinary by the Court-gate
(a place where the Alms of the Abbey, the remains of their Food being fent Almnery.
thither, were diftributed as a main part of their fubfiftence, to certain alms-
people confifting of a fociety of Brothers and Sifters, having had a Chapel to
it now defolate, and rotting in its own Ruins) was included long ago, as it
feems by a Compofition (*b*), in the year 1237. (four hundred years ago)
made between the then Archbifhop and his Archdeacon of the one part, and
the then Abbat of the other: (amongft other things) touching Jurifdiction,
and right to the co-ertion of criminous perfons of the Monaftery delinquent
in the Diocefs of *Canterbury.* (*c*) *Without the clofe or precinct of the Monaftery,*
which contain alfo the Almnery fituated without their Gate; as the compofition
wordeth it. *Hugh* the Abbat, of that name the fecond, when he divided and
diftinguifhed the Offices of his Monaftery (*d*), affigned the Church or Parfonage of *Northborne,* with the Chappels annexed to this Almnery.

    Now enter we the fept, where the firft thing in our eye obfervable (except Refectory.
the fair Hall, the late Refectory of the Monks) is *Ethelbert's* Tower. Not fo
called (as vulgar Tradition will fabuloufly tell you it was) from the building *Ethelbert's*
of it, either by him, or by others in his time. In honor and memory of him *Tower.*
I will grant it was, but yet long fince his days, being not built (I take it) untill about the year 1047. For (as it is in the private Chronicler, *Thorn*) the
then Archbifhop *Eadfin,* befide fome other acts of his bounty to the Abbey,
gave 100 Marks, (*e*) *to the building of the Tower which they were then building;*

    (a) *Hiſt. pag.* 294.   (b) *Lib. Ecclef. Chriſti Cant.*   (c) *Extra ſepta ſut Monaſterii,*
quæ continent eleemoſinariam extra portam eorum.   (d) *Thorn in ejus vita.*   (e) *Ad*
turris ædificationem, quæ tunc fuerat in conſtruendo.

meaning this Tower, as I conceive. Other certainty of the age of it, I cannot give, and so leave it with the words of *Speed* (a), who in the close of his discourse touching this Abbey, thus speaks of it. Only *Ethelbert*'s Tower (saith he) in memory and honour of the man, as yet hath escaped the verdict and sentence of destruction, whose beauty though much defaced and overworn, will witness to succeeding Ages the magnificence of the whole, when all stood compleat in their glory together. [Upon second Thoughts, under a more exact survey taken of the Structure of this Tower, I incline to think that it was sometime a Steeple, or Bell-tower annexed and contiguous to St. *Augustin*'s Church, standing by the North-side of the West-end thereof, and opening on the South-side or quarter of it, (as it is a square Piece) into the Nave or Body of the Church, as on the East into the North Isle thereof, even just as that we call *Arundel*-Steeple in *Christ-Church* doth; from which it differs but a little in the work. Of certain This and the Church, when standing, were contiguous, and there are that remember that North Isle standing in their time intire and undemolished. And thereunto (in the disquisition whereof as a thing material I was indeed somewhat curious) that the Tower of it self and until it was of late disposed into Lodgings or Lofts, made in Stories one above another, is an open or hollow piece throughout, unvaulted I mean, and without any Arch cast over within it from the bottom to the top, rendring it more fit for a Bell-tower, in respect of the scope thereby to the getting up and letting down of Bells. Now shall any man ask me, whence its name of *Ethelbert*'s Tower is derived? If I shall answer from some Bell (the prime Bell I will suppose) sometime hanging there, dedicated to *Ethelbert* or St. *Ethelbert* (for so he was called) I hope the Conjecture will not seem strange or improbable; it being a thing usual with our Ancestors in those times of Superstition, to dedicate their Bells to some Saint or other, as it were Christning them by and after the Saint's name: as (not to go far for instance) that famous Bell at *Christ-Church*, which we know and call by the name of *Dunstan*, was by the donor Prior *Molash* in King *Hen.* 6th's time, dedicated to St. *Dunstan*, a *quondam* Archbishop of the Church, and from thence the Steeple or Tower, where it hangs, to this day bears the name of *Dunstan's-steeple. W. S.*]

St. *Pancrace* Chappel.

Thorn.

     The next thing (and what else only is observable amongst these heaps of ruins) is the Chappel of St. *Pancrace*, built (as the private Chronicler makes report) before *Augustin* came; and used by the King before his Conversion to Christianity, for the place of his Idol-worship; but after it, the first that *Augustin*, after he had purged it from the Worship of the false, consecrated to the service of the true God, and dedicated to St. *Pancrace.* Wherewith the devil all enraged, and not brooking his ejection from the place he had so long enjoyed; the first time that *Augustin* celebrates Mass there, furiously assaults the Chapel, to overturn it: But having more of Will than Power to actuate his intended mischief, all he could do, was to leave the ensigns of his malice, the print of his talons, [such as I have elsewhere seen by Ivy growing and eating into old Walls, even of Stone, *W. S.*] on the *South*-porch of the Wall of the Chapel, where they are visible to this day. Thus *Thorn* tells the tale: And no better than a tale can I conceive it to be. I will grant that a Chapel of that Name, of no small Antiquity, there was sometime standing, where a good part of her ruins are yet left, built almost wholly of *British* or *Roman* Brick (infallible remains of Antiquity:) That on the Walls out-side of the South-Porch, such tokens as the Historian will have it to be the marks of the Beast, are visible enough: That of latter time this Story became vulgarly received. (*Hamond Beale*, to instance in one for many, *Anno* 1492. gives by his Will (b) to the reparation of St. *Pancrace* his Chapel within the precinct of St. *Augustin*'s Church-yard, and of the Chapel where St. *Augustin* first celebrated Mass in *England*, annexed to the former, 3 *l.* 6 *s.* 8 *d.*) But that either this was the place where St. *Augustin* first said Mass in *England*, (St. *Martin*'s was it, as *Bede* (c) will tell you:) or that the story is further true than I have granted, I cannot believe.

     To give you my Reasons. Consult venerable *Bede*'s Preface to his Ecclesi-

---

(a) *Hist. pag.* 294.
lib. I. *cap.* 26.

(b) *Penes Registrum Domini Archid. Cant.*

(c) *Eccles. Hist.*

                                             astical

aſtical Story, and you ſhall find, he there acknowledgeth his intelligence for theſe parts received, chiefly from *Albinus* the then Abbat of St. *Auguſtin's,* who with diligence inſtructed him in all things that either by written Record, or tradition of his Elders, had come unto his knowledge, any way memorable. But take his own Words. He ſays, (a) " The moſt Reverend Abbat, *Albi-* " *nus,* a Man skill'd in all kind of Learning, became, above all others, my " chief helper in this Work : Who being inſtituted in the Church of *Canter-* " *bury* by the venerable and moſt learned men, Archbiſhop *Theodore* of Bleſ- " ſed memory, and *Hadrian* the Abbat ; had diligently come to the knowledge " of all things, which were done by the Diſciples of the Bleſſed Pope *Grego-* " *ry,* both in the Province of *Canterbury* it ſelf, and in the bordering Coun- " tries alſo, either from the Monuments of Learning, or from the report of " the Aged , and tranſmitted to me concerning theſe matters, whatſoever " ſeem'd worthy to be recorded by *Nothelmus* a Religious Prieſt of the Church " of *London* , either by writing, or by word of mouth. Thus *Bede.* Add hereunto, that this was a matter ſo remarkable, an occurrence ſo much in it ſelf ; but in reſpect of the circumſtances of time and place, much more memorable. Of time : It happening ſo in the very infancy of the *Engliſh-Saxon* Chriſtian Church. Of place : Being ſuch as from an Idol-temple was become, and that but newly a Chriſtian Oratory, that, than it, there is not a thing more worthy to be kept in memory in the whole Story of times : And therefore could not have eſcaped the one, the Intelligencer (*Elbine's*) knowledge ; nor conſequently the other, the Hiſtorian (*Bede's*) pen. But, for all this, look and you ſhall find, that *Bede* is ſo far from making mention of it, that he remembers not ſo much as the Chappel. This is much. But let me add yet further : The following Chronologers, for the moſt part Monks all, paſs it over in deep ſilence. Could Fame have been (think you) ſo ſluggiſh, or ſo confin'd, that ſo famous a matter as this ſhould fall from no Author's pen, till (in compariſon) but yeſterday, till *Spot's* and *Thorn's* days ? The Caſe ſo ſtanding, (b) let him believe it that can give any credit to it, for me. And ſo I leave it.

Now being upon taking our leave of the Abby, and making our retreat, let me lead you (as the next way out) over the forgotten Sepulchres of the *Church-yard.* dead ; the ancient Cemitery ground of the Abby, and ſo out at the Gate before *Burgate.* Which great and fair Gate, with a Battlement, and that Warlike invention of Machicollation ; thus new built by *Thomas Ickham,* a Monk and Sacriſt there, at the Charge of cccclxvi *l.* xiii *s.* iv. *d.* ; called (c) *The* Weſtgate *of the Cemitery of St.* Auguſtin ; heretofore lead from *Church-ſtreet* (for ſo the Street before it hath uſually been called) into St. *Auguſtin's* Church- yard. A Burial-place, not private and proper only to the Abby, nor only free to the choice of any that deſired Burial there ; but withal untill the diſſolution, the proper and only Cemitery belonging unto divers Pariſh-Churches of the City, deſtitute of ſuch Dormitories of their own, of which the Abby had the Patronage : Such as were St. *Mary Magdalen,* St. *Andrew,* and (as I verily believe) St. *Paul* too ; however becauſe of late ſome queſtion hath been made of it, I will not contend. But what if it ſhall appear, that for more than 100 Years together, next before the diſſolution of the Abby, not one of the many Teſtators of thoſe Pariſhes have once mentioned any Church- yard of their own, either in appointment of it for the place of their Burial (as in other Pariſhes that had Church-yards it was uſual to do) or otherwiſe ; though of their Churches often ? That Scores, if not Hundreds of them have from time to time pitched on this common Cemitery of St. *Auguſtin,* for the place and purpoſe aforeſaid ? That after the diſſolution, and that Cemitery withdrawn and taken from them, not yet a Teſtator of ſucceeding times wills

---

(a) *Auctor ante omnes atque adjutor opuſculi hujus Albinus Abbas reverendiſſimus, vir per omnia doctiſſi- mus, extitit. Qui in eccleſia Cantuariorum à beatæ memoriæ Theodoro Archiepiſcopo & Hadriano Abbate vi- ris venerabilibus at eruditiſſimis inſtitutus, diligenter omnia quæ in ipſa Cantuariorum Provincia, vel etiam in contiguis ejuſdem regionibus à diſcipulis beati Papæ Gregorii geſta fuere, vel monumentis literarum, vel ſeniorum traditione cognoverat, & ea mihi de his quæ memoria digna videbantur per religioſum Londinienſis Eccleſiæ presbyterum Nothelmum, ſive literis mandata ſive ipſius Nothelmi viva voce referendo, tranſmiſit.*

(b) *Credat Judæus apella.*   (c) *Porta occidentalis Cemiterii S. Auguſtini. Sic in Compoſitione inter Abbatiam & Civitatem, in Appendice.*

K   to

to he laid in any Church-yard of their own ; but, as now to feek of a reft-ing place for their Bodies after death, peculiar to them, betake themfelves for Burial to the Church-yards of Neighbour-parifhes ? That as the fituation of two of thefe Parifh-Churches will not admit of any adjoining Church-yard ; the one like *Fanchurch* in *London* [before it was burnt down A. D. 1666. N. B.] ftanding in the midft of the Street ; the other in a throng of contiguous hou-fes ; fo the third needed none in regard of the nearnefs of it to this Church-yard of the Abbey, which in right and title (I take it) of foundation, had the patronage of it ? That it was the known Monkifh policy, for the gain fake, to draw all the Burials they could to their Abbey, and for that end probably at the Church's foundation, wittingly debarred the People of a Church-yard, to their Church : and laftly that this Abbey and Cimitery was built and fet apart for a Burial-place of old, when as yet it was not lawful to bury in Ci-ties. If thefe things (I fay) fhall be made appear and proved, as they eafily may, what judicious and indifferent man then will conceive, againft the ftrength of fo much probability and prefumption to the contrary, that thefe Churches had their proper Cimiteries adjoyning to them, however there may be fome who (in confidence of not being gainfaid, becaufe of their fome-what extraordinary age) fhall fay they had ? (*a*) But let thofe who are con-cern'd in this matter, look to it. [Since the former Edition I have met with the faculty granted for the firft confirming the prefent Burial-place of this Pa-rifh, being in *Longport* to that ufe, dated in the Year 1591. wherein (as the ground of that confirmation) is contained and deduced, that the Minifter and Parifhioners of St. *Paul*'s by their Petition had certified the Archbifhop, that their Parifh-Church *for time out of mind* had had no Church-yard at all , infomuch as they were wont from time to time to bury their Dead in the Church-yard of other Churches to their great inconvenience and expence, &c. By this the Reader may judge of their grounds, who have been fo violent and eager, fome by challenge as Parties, others by Oath as Witneffes, to evict this piece of ground from the rightful owner upon a pretence of a prefcriptive right and title to it, as Church-yard ground : Againft whom all that I fhall oppofe is only this, Truth is great and will prevail. *W. S.*] And fo I leave this Abbey.

A piece of Monkifh po-licy.

St. *Martin*'s.

St. Martin.

THE next thing after this Abbey, in the Suburbs, which I fhall furvey, is the Church of St. *Martin*, much celebrated both for the great antiquity of it, and alfo for the refort of *Auguftin* and his fellow-labourers thither to their devotions at their firft arrival (*b*), by the licence of King *Ethelbert*, imparted to them in favour of Queen *Berta* his Wife (a Chriftian, and defcended of Chriftian parentage, being the daughter of *Chilperike* King of *France*) to whom this Church built long before, to wit (as *Bede* faith) by the *Romans*, as fome fay in King *Lucius* days (*c*), and dedicated to St. *Martin*, was permitted for the place of her publick devotions. The Church indeed feems very anci-ent, being built (the Chancel efpecially) moftly of *Britifh* or *Roman* Brick, the noted reliques and tokens of old Age in any kind of building whether fa-cred or profane.

At this place afterwards. *i. e.* from Archbifhop *Theodore*'s until *Lanfranc*'s time by the fpace to wit of 349 years, there was a Bifhop's fee (*d*), who always re-maining in the Countrey, fupplied the abfence of the Archbifhop, that for the moft part followed the Court : and that as well in governing the Monks, as in performing the folemnities of the Church, and exercifing the authority of an Archdeacon. So *Lambard* (*e*). But the Chair happening void in *Lan-franc*'s time : he whether becaufe that two Bifhops were too many for one City (the very reafon which as fome fay, he gave for what he did) or by colour of that ordinance of the Council of *London* holden *An.* 1075 (*f*). requiring the remove of Bifhops Sees from obfcure rural Villages to Cities, or for that this

(a) *Videant quorum intereft.* *Ecclef. Antiquitates, cap. 6. pag.* 130. *amb. of Kent. In Canterb.*   (b) *Bede Ecclef. Hift. lib.* 1. *cap.* 25.   (c) *Vide Britan. Ec-clef.*   (d) *MS. in Archivis Ecclef. Chrifti Cant.*   (e) *Per-*   (f) *De qua vide Malmesbur. de geft. pont. lib.* 1. *pag.* 213.

Bifhop

Bishop was a *Chorepiscopus*, a kind of Countrey *Suffragan*, an order (he well knew, no doubt) for juft reafons, abolifhed abroad (*a*) : or for what other caufe it is not certain. He I fay (*Lanfrac*) refufed to confecrate any other. Neverthelefs, becaufe he needed the help of a Sbftitute, he created in his place and ftead, one of his Chaplains, Archdeacon of *Canterbury* (*b*).

In *Edward* 2. time, to wit in the Year 1321. the Parfon of this Church, and the Mafter of the Free-School of the City fell at odds about the rights and priviledges of their feveral Schools : the Parfon aforefaid, in right of his Church, and by concurrent Cuftom, challenging a liberty to the keeping of a Free-School there, which the other would not admit of, but with a limitation of the number of his Scholars ; of which more hereafter when I come to *Chrift-Church*, within the modern precinct whereof the City Free-School (as I fhall there fhew) was kept. And fo I leave St. *Martin's*. Only I wifh that for the venerable antiquity of the Church, and fometime Epifcopal eftate of the place, things that have much dignified both, it might better flourifh in the maintainance of its due rights and refpects than I hear it doth.

The Mote.

MY Progrefs next invites you to (my Lord Chief Juftice *Finch* his Seat **Mote.** or Manfion-houfe [now the houfe of the Right Honourable the Earl of *Winchelfea. N. B.*]) the *Mote*. So called now and of latter time ; but formerly, and that of old, *Wyke* : deriving its name either from that neighbour *Wic*, or *Vicus*, called *Fordwick*, upon which it borders at that place (I take it) which in the fecond of King *Ethelbert's* Charters is called *Wykingfmerke*. Or elfe being **Verftegan.** named *Wyk*, becaufe (as the word imports) it hath fometimes been a place of refuge or retreat, as it were a hold or fortrefs in fome time of Hoftility : a derivation not improbable nor improper, if we add and take this along with us, that there is a Hill hard by it in the fame Charter of *Ethelbert*, called *Sibben-down. i. e.* The Down (or Hill) of Peace, or the Down where the peace was made, intimating fome Battel or field there away fought, and afterward a truce entered, or a peace made there with the enemy. [*Stephen de Wyke* was in poffeffion of this Manor, *Ann.* 23 *H.* 3. See more of the Poffeffors of this place in *Philpot's Villare Cantian. p.* 94. *Ann.* 1333. *Richard Oxenden*, then Prior of *Chrift-Church*, (the See of *Canterbury* being void) did grant a Licence to *Stephen de Wyke's* Chaplain, to celebrate Divine Service in his Chapel at *Wyke* within the Parifh of St. *Martin's* near *Canterbury*, faving all Oblations, parochial Rights and Dues belonging to the Rector of the faid Parifh Church of St. *Martin's*. I have inferted the Inftrument it felf into the *Appendix, Numb.* IX. *a.* N. B.]

Here, or near this place, fometime lay the Chantery Lands of *Lukedale*, **Lukedale;** in our City's perambulation, called *Lokindale* ; which being deferted and left defolate, becaufe of the fmalnefs of the means, not fufficing to the maintenance of a Chantery Prieft with competent livelihood ; was paffed over to the Hofpital of St. *John's* without *Northgate*, where once I faw the Deed of Conveyance thereof, and thence took the following Brief, " The Revenues " of the Chantery of *Lukedale*, (called (*c*) *The Chantery in* Well, *called* Luke- " dale-*Chantery*) confifting of 32 Acres of Land, 16 *s.* 5 *d. ob.* 8 Cocks and " 19 Hens of Annual Rent, with the appurtenances at *Wyke* near *Canterbury*, " (which Chantery was forfaken for the fmallnefs of the means) were aliena- " ted and transferred, by *Thomas* of *Garwynton*, the Patron, with licence of " the King, and the Lord of the Fee, *i. e.* the Abbat and Convent of St. *Au-* " guftin's (within whofe Manor of *Lang-port* they were) to St. *John's* Hofpital " without *Northgate*, Anno 1384, and 38 *Edward* 3. (*d*) *That they might pray* " *for the Soul of* Reginald *of* Cornhell, *formerly Founder of this Chantery*, &c. " and others, &c. The Chantery's Foundation fhall be exhibited to you in my *Appendix, Numb.* IX. *b.*

This place our City-perambulation fetcheth within her Bounds and Liberty.

(a) *Canon. Chorepifcopi*, 68 *diftinct.*   (b) *Lamb. ubi fupra.*   (c) *Cantaria in Welle vo-cat Lukedale.*   (d) *Ut orent & celebrari faciant pro animabus Reginaldi de Cornhelle quondam fundatoris ejufdem Cantariæ, Thomæ patris dicti Thomæ, &c.*

Here

Here (or hereabouts) the Hospital of St. *Lawrence* had (haply still hath a portion of Tithes. For thus I read in the Hospital's private Leiger. (*a*) "Also "the said Hospital receives all the Tithes of a Field called *Wykesfield*, with "two Crofts there; that is to say, *Pitetokkyscroft* and *Homiscroft*, near *Fishpole*, "and lies between the High-way toward the *South*, and *Wyke* toward the *North*, "and the way that leads from the Cross of four Heads to *Trendele*, toward the "*West*, and the way that leadeth from *Fordwich* to *Fishpole*, toward the *East*.

Long-port.

Long-port.

NOW let me lead you back from the Mote to *Long-port*, the ancient and first Manor of St. *Augustin*'s Abbey, whose Bounds and Limits are still the same that you shall find and meet with in the Second of King *Ethelbert*'s foregoing Charters. (*b*) *There were* lxx *Burgesses in the City of* Canterbury, *belonging to this Maner*; saith *Doomsday*-Book. From this *Long-port* thus glanced at, let me lead you next by *Chantery-lane*, anciently called (*c*) *Newstreet*, to survey the *quondam* Chantery there, called *Doge*'s Chantery; built by an Official to the Archdeacon of *Canterbury*, and the last Parson of St. *Paul* (for in his time, and with his consent, the Vicaridge there was erected and indowed) one *Haynon Doge*, in the Reign of *Henry* 3. in the Year of our Lord, 1264. The Foundation whereof *Thorn* records; whose Words are in the *Appendix*, *Numb.* IX. *d.*

Doge's Chantery.

The Nunnery of St. Sepulchre's.

Nunnery.

STeering our Course *Southward*, we come next to the Ruins of the late Nunnery, called St. Sepulchre's, founded (not as *Wever* will, by one of the Abbats of St. *Augustin*'s; nor yet I believe to the end that *Lambard* says, *i. e.* to serve the Necessity of the Hot Monks of that Abby; but as *Thorn* reports) by Archbishop *Anselm*, upon a part of his Soil there: The same (I take it) which his Predecessor *Wilfhelem* (long before) purchased; described to lye (*d*) *Nigh a place which is called* Rethercheap, *without the Gates of* Canterbury. But let me give you *Thorn*'s Note of the Foundation. (*e*) He says, "Archbishop "*Anselm* was their Founder; and although they are situated within the "Boundaries of the Fee of St. *Augustin*, yet on the Soil belonging to the "Archbishoprick. For there was there a parochial Church, dedicated in ho- "nour of the *Holy Sepulchre*, under the Patronage of the Archbishop, having "a little Land belonging to it, which lay round about it, and it is (at this "present) evident, that they were founded there. You have the Foundation. Amongst the rest of the Benefactors, that afterwards of their Charity endowed this House with Revenues, *William Calvell* a Citizen of *Canterbury* (of whose Name there was of ancient time a flourishing Family in the City) carries the Name and Fame for the chief. After that King *Richard* 1. had given the Wood or Forest of *Blean* to *Christ-Church*, *W.* the Prior and Convent of the same (*f*), granted to this *Nunnery*, and the Prioress and Convent thereof as much Wood as one Horse, going twice a day, could fetch thence, where the Church Wood-Reeves should appoint, (as the Words of the Grant, inserted in the Margin (*g*), do declare). Which uncertainty, in the Year, 1270, the Nuns releasing, had in lieu and by way of Exchange for it, a certain part or portion of the said *Blean*-Wood, assigned and made over to them, as appears from the words of the Deed in the Margin (*h*). The which Wood retains *to*

(*a*) *Item prædict. Hosp. percipit totam decimam de campo vocat. Wikesfield, cum 2 crofts ibid. scil. Pitetok-kyscroft & Homiscroft juxta Fishpole, & jacet inter regiam Strat. versf. South, & Wyke versf North, & viam quæ ducit à cruce quatuor capitum ad Trendels versf. West, & viam quæ ducit à Fordwich usque Fishpole versf East.* (*b*) LXX *Burgenses erant in Cantuaria Civitate huic manerio pertinentes.* (*c*) *Nova Strata.* (*d*) *Juxta locum qui dicitur Rethercheap, extra portas Dorobernia. Charta Eccles. Christi Cant.* (*e*) *Harum fundator fuit Anselmus Archiepiscopus, & quanquam infra limites feodi beati Augustini sint constituta, tamen in solo Archiepiscopatus sita sunt. Erat namque ibi ecclesia parochialis in honore Sancti Sepulcri, de patronatu Archiepiscopi exiguis terris circumcincta, ubi in presenti constat eas esse fundatas.* (*f*) *Lib. Eccles. Christi Cant.* (*g*) *Summarium* [*summagium*] **Summarium.** *unum in boscis nostris bis iturum* [*habendum*] *singulis diebus ferialibus, sumendum ubicunque ministris no-* **Summagium.** *stris ad custodiam Boscorum nostrorum visum fuerit,&c.* (*h*) *Octoginta & decem acras bosci, cum solo terra, fossis & fossatis in bosco Prioris & Conventus in Blen, jacent. in longitudine inter boscum Abbatis de Faversham, quod dicitur Bosindenne versf. West, & boscum Prioris & Conventus versf. Est, & in latitudine inter boscum eorundem Prioris & Conventus, versus North, & regalem viam versus South. Lib. Memoratus.*

this

this day the Name of *Minchen*-Wood, taking its Name from the Nuns, which   *Minchen Wood.*
our Anceſtors, from the *Saxon* Mynecena, called *Minchens.* Or if any Man
chooſe rather to derive it from the Latin *Monacha,* I ſhall not contend. For
as in *Egypt,* in times paſt, they uſed to call a Monk, or any Man that became
noted for his ſingular Sanctimony of Life, *Nonnus;* ſo was it then and ſince,
as ordinary for a Nun or any like Holy Profeſſor of that Sex, to be called
Monacha, as it were a She-Monk (*a*).

In this *Blean*-Wood (as having this fit occaſion, I crave leave to obſerve)
the Priory of St. *Gregories,* and the Hoſpital of *Herbal-down,* ſometime had the
like (*b*) *Sum,* or *Seam of Wood,* or *a certain Portion of Wood,* granted ſeverally
to them. The former, by *Henry* 2, in theſe words. (*c*) *A Portion of Wood in
the Foreſt of* Blean, *for the uſe of his fire,* &c. The latter by *Richard* 1. in the
like, to wit, theſe : (*d*) *A Portion in the Wood* Sorotte, (which was part of
Blean-Wood, and is now called *Shoorth*) *for Wood for the uſe of the Brethren.* In
lieu and ſtead whereof, they had ſeverally the like quantity of 90 Acres of
Wood in *Blean,* afterwards made over to them, as the Nunnery had (*e*).

To which I return. In the Year 1184, the Church, *i. e.* the Parſonage of
St. *Edmund* of *Ridingate* was granted to it by the Abbat and Convent of St. *Au-
guſtin's,* as I have ſhewed before more at large in my Survey of that Gate.
The which Church was afterward, *i. e.* in the Year 1349, with the Nuns con-
ſent (being Patrons) united by the then Commiſſary of *Canterbury,* to the
Church of St. *Mary Bredin,* as I there alſo have noted.

Time and Superiors indulgence bringing their corruptions, Nuns, were not,   *Nuns incloſed,*
in proceſs of time, ſuch Recluſes as their Order required ; whence, and upon the Command of Pope *Boniface* 8, by his Letters written to Archbiſhop
Winchelſey and his Suffragans in that behalf (*f*), as well as by that Decretal of
his *Cap. unic' de ſtatu regularium in ſexto;* concerning the confining of Nuns to
their Cloyſter : The ſame Archbiſhop, in the Year 1305, incloſed theſe Nuns
of St. *Sepulchres,* according to that Conſtitution (*g*).

At this place, ſometime one *Elizabeth Barton,* more vulgarly known by the   *Elizabeth Bar-*
Name of the Holy Maid of *Kent,* that great Impoſtor of her time, was a   *ton.*
vailed Nun and Votareſs. Whoſe pranks and practices, or rather the Monks
and other Papaliis, by her agency, are obvious both in our Statutes and Stories. It would prove tedious to repeat the whole matter. Accept therefore,
of this Compendium of it in *Speeed's* words. *The* Romaniſts *(ſaith he) much
fearing that* Babel *would down, if Queen* Ann *might be heard againſt wicked* Ha-
man *(h), ſought to underprop the Foundations thereof with certain devices of their
own ; and that the ſame might paſs without note of Suſpicion, they laid their Forgery*   *Elizabeth Bar-*
upon Heaven it ſelf ; whoſe pretended Oracle Elizabeth Barton *(commonly called the*   *ton the falſe*
Holy Maid of Kent) *was made to be ; and the Pillars of this Godleſs Fabrick were*   *Oracle of the*
Edward Bocking, *a Monk by profeſſion, and Doctor of Divinity ;* Richard Ma-   *Romaniſts.*
ſters *Parſon of* Aldington, *the Town where ſhe dwelt ;* Richard Deering *a Monk;*   *The aſſiſters*
Hugh Rich *a Friar ;* John Adeſtone *and* Thomas Abell *Prieſts, put to their help-*   *of this falſe*
ing hands ; and Henry Gould *Bachelor of Divinity, with* John Fiſher *the Reverend*   *Propheteſs.*
Father of Rocheſter ; *imployed their Pains to dawb theſe down-falling Walls, with
their untempered Mortar. The Scribes that ſet their Pens for her Miracles, were* Ed-   *Read Statute*
ward Thwaites *Gentleman, and* Thomas Lawrence *Regiſter, beſides* Hawkhurſt   *in Anno 25*
a Monk, who writ a Letter that was forged to be ſent her from Heaven ; and Richard   *H. 8.*
Risby *and* Thomas Gould *were the men that diſperſed her Miracles abroad to the
World. This Holy Maid* Elizabeth, *made a Votareſs in* Canterbury, *was taught by*
Bocking *her ghoſtly Father, and ſuſpected Paramour, to counterfeit many feigned Tran-*   *The counter-*
ces, and in the ſame to utter many vertuous words for the rebuke of ſin ; under which,   *feiting of Eli-*
more freely ſhe was heard againſt Luther's *Doctrine, and the Scriptures Tranſlation,*   *zabeth Barton.*
then deſired of many : Neither ſo only, but that ſhe gave forth from God, and his
Saints, *by ſundry ſuggeſtive Relations, that if the King proceeded in his divorce, and*   *Edw. Hall.*
ſecond Marriage, he ſhould not reign in his Realm one month after, nor reſt in God's fa-   *John Stow.*
vour the ſpace of an hour. But the truth diſcovered by God's true Miniſters, this O-   *Holinſh.*
  Cranmer.
  Cromwell,
  Latimer.

(*a*) *Lexic. Philolog. in verb. Nonnus.*   (*b*) *Summarium boſci.*   (*c*) *Unum ſummarium
boſci in Foreſta de* Blen, *ad uſus foci in ipſa eccleſia, & in domibus eidem eccleſiæ continentibus in ipſa Civitate* Cantuar. *Lib. ecclef. Cantuar.*   (*d*) *Unum ſummarium in boſco de* Sorotte, *ad attrahenda ligna ad opus fratrum. Charta vetus Hoſpit.*   (*e*) *Lib. Ecclef. Cant.*   (*f*) *Vide* Walſingham
Hiſt. Angl. de Ann. 28 *Ed* 1, *& Anno Dem.* 1301.   (*g*) *Lib. Ecclef. Cant.*   (*h*) *The* Pope.

                                                         racle

racle gave place as all other such did, when *Chrift* by his death ftopped their lying mouths: For her felf and Seven (*a*) of her difciples were executed for *Treafon* at *Ti-burn*, and the other Six put to their Fines and Imprifonment.   Thus he.

Shortly this Nunnery was a Corporation confifting of a Lady Priorefs and Five black-vailed Nuns, whofe Habit or Apparel was a black Coat, Cloak, Coul and Vail.   It had a common Seal and all other requifites of a compleat Nunnery.   All which at length tafted of the common Calamity and Ruin of Religious Houfes in her utter diffolution by *Henry* 8.   At what time the Eftimate of her Revenues arofe unto 38 *l.* 19 *s.* 7 *d*$\frac{1}{2}$ *per annum.*

S. Sepulchres
Church. It feems the Parifh Church of St. *Sepulchre* was born down in the fame fall with the Nunnery.   For however frequent mention may be found, both of Parifh Church, and Church-yard alfo before, yet fince the fuppreffion, the place of the two latter is unknown, the limits of the other uncertain, and the Memory of all three almoft extinct.   Only that Stone-Gate by the turning on your left hand to *Dover*-Ward, feems to have been the *Weftern* Door of the Church, as I collect by this Boundary. (*b*) *Of the Land which lieth over againft the Church of the* Holy Sepulchre, *nigh a Street by which they go toward* Dudendale, *on the* South-*fide of the faid Church.*   The Boundary of the piece of ground directly over againft it.   The laft Lady Priorefs of this Houfe, by name Dame *Philip John*, [*Philippa Johanna*; N. B.] lies buried in the *North*-Ifle of St. *George's* Church, which in her Will fhe calls (*c*) *The Chappel of the Bleffed* Mary.

The Hofpital of St. Lawrence.

St. Lawrence. HAving done with the Nunnery, let us make next to St. *Lawrence*, an Hofpital hard by, dedicate to the broiled Martyr St. *Lawrence*, when firft built; which (as the private Leiger of the place fhews) was in the Year 1137, by *Hugh*, of that name the Second, Abbat of St. *Auguftin's*. (*d*) " The " Hofpital of St. *Lawrence* near *Canterbury*, was founded by *Hugo* the Second, " formerly Lord Abbat of St. *Auguftin's* Monaftery by *Canterbury*, and by the " Convent of the fame place; on the 7*th* of the Kalends of *February*, in the " Year of our Lord 1137, and in the 2d Year of the Reign of K. *Stephen*, for xvi " Brethren and Sifters, and for one Prieft or Chaplain, and one Clerk offici-" ating in the fame Hofpital.   Thus the Leiger.   This Hofpital was intended (*e*) for the Leprous of the Abby; *viz.* That if it fhould fo happen, that any profeft Monk of that Monaftery fhould be infected with any contagious Difeafe, but above all with the Leprofie, by reafon of which Sicknefs or infectious Malady, he could not live within the Precincts of the Abby, without prejudice and fcandal to the reft of the Fraternity, that then he fhould be provided for in this Hofpital of a convenient Chamber, of Meat, Drink, and Apparel, in as full a meafure as any one of his Brethren living in the Monaftery.

Alfo if it fhould fo happen, that the Father, the Mother, the Sifter or Brother of any Monk of this Monaftery, fhould come to fuch great want and indigency, as that (to the reproach of any of thefe Brethren) he or fhe be forced to ask at the Gates, the Alms of the Fraternity, that then fuch of them fo asking, fhould be provided for in this Hofpital of fufficient fuftentation, according to the ability of the Houfe, by the Advice and Confideration of the Abbat of St. *Auguftin's*, and the Mafter of this Hofpital, for the time being; as further appears by his Charter (which I have feen in the Hofpital's private Leiger) confirmed by many of his Succeffors.

After the Founder himfelf had given to the Maintenance of the Hofpital. 9 Acres of Ground upon which it was to be erected, and all Tithe-Corn of the Lordfhip of *Langport*, by his Charter in the *Appendix*, *Numb.* X. to this

---

(*a*) *Elizabeth Barton. Edward Bocking. Richard Deering. Richard Risby. Richard Mafters. Henry Gould* Two Monks.   (*b*) *De terra quæ jacet contra Ecclefiam Sancti Sepulchri juxta vicum quo iter verfus Dudindale, ex parte auftrali dictæ ecclefiæ.   Rentale vetus Ecclefiæ Chrifti Cantuar.*

(*c*) *Capella beatæ Mariæ. Lib teftamentor penes regift. Dom. Archid. Cant.*   (*d*) *Hofpitale S Laurentii juxta Cant. fuit fundatum per Dominum Hugonem fecundum quondam Abbatem Monafterii S. Auguftini Cant. & conventum ejufdem loci 7 kalend. Feb anno ab incarnatione Domini 1137. & anno regni Regis Stephani fecundo, pro 16 fratribus & fororibus, & pro uno Capellano & uno Clerico in eod. Hofp. fervien.*   (*e*) *Wever* of ancient Funer. Monum. *pag.* 255.

effect.

effect. "That *Hugo* the Second, by the Grace of God Abbat of St. *Augu-*
"*ſtin's*, and the Convent of the ſame, gave 9 Acres of Land within their Lord-
"ſhip, purchaſed, to build an Hoſpital upon, near the way that leads from
"*Canterbury* to *Dover*; on the right ſide of the way: That they had given al-
"ſo to the ſaid Hoſpital, for the Maintenance of Sick and Poor People, the
"Tithe of all ſorts of Proviſion, yearly ariſing from all the Lands belonging
"to their Maner on the right ſide of the way; and all Tithe of Wheat and
"Peaſe of all the Land which lies toward *Longport*, within their Maner, on
"the left ſide of the way. And the Bleſſing of God be upon all thoſe, that
"for the Love of God, ſhall be Charitable to the Poor and Sick in the ſaid
"Hoſpital.

The Revenues of this Hoſpital, were in proceſs of time much improved by
the benevolence of many devout People, that became Benefactors unto it.
(The whole Revenues at the ſuppreſſion being rated at 13 *l*. 7 *s*. 10 *d*.). A-
mongſt the which, one both of the firſt and moſt liberal was the Lord of *Do-*
dingdale, a Neighbour, by name *R. de Marci*, who by his Deed or Charter,
gave unto this Hoſpital in *Frank Almoigne*, the Tithes of that his whole Maner.
The Charter you ſhall have anon, when I come to *Dodingdale*. Of theſe
Tithes ſhortly after, the Canons of St. *Gregory's* endeavoured to deſpoil the
Hoſpital. For I find (a) a Petition directed to *Herbert* the Archdeacon of *Can-*
terbury, by *R. de Marci* the aforeſaid Donor, to this effect, *viz.* That he would
reſeize the Hoſpital of them as in former Years, whereas they were that Year
(b) *by force and arms*, taken from it by the Religious of St. *Gregory's*, that he
might have no cauſe of Complaint to *Richard de Luci*, (c) *whoſe Feudatary I am*
(ſaith he) *for all my Land*. Concluding thus: (d) *And be ye aſſured, that that*
Tithe, and many other Tithes of my Land, belong to my Chappelry, &c. This *Her-*
bert (to whom the Petition is directed) that you may know the Age of it,
was Archdeacon of *Canterbury* in King *Henry* 8. days (e), as *Richard de Luci*
(whom it mentions) was Chief Juſtice of the Realm about the ſame time (f).

It ſeems, this Hoſpital and St. *Gregory's* did not well agree together. For
after this, to wit, in the Year 1225, the Proctor and Brothers of this Hoſpital, ſued the Prior and Canons of St. *Gregory's*, before the Abbat of *Feverſham*,
and the Prior and Archdeacon of *Rocheſter* (the Pope's Delegates, it's like)
for the Tithes of *Molonde* beſides *Hepyntone*, to wit, (ſaith the Leiger (g)) of
80 Acres of Land of the Earl of *Gloucester's* Fee; but with what Succeſs I do
not find.

Now to *Dodingdale* Tithes again. Afterwards, in the Year 1320, *Robert*
de Malling the Commiſſary of *Canterbury*, gave ſentence with this Hoſpital for
the Tithes both of the ſame Manor, and alſo, of 300 Acres, and more, of
Land of *Thomas Chich* and his Tenents, lying within the limits and bounds of
St. *Mary Bredin's* Pariſh; upon clear Evidence of the Hoſpital's Right to the
ſame, by ancient Muniments, and otherwiſe (h). For theſe laſt-named Tithes,
of the 300 Acres and upwards, there lay a Tye of Regratulation upon the
Hoſpital. For thus I read the Leiger. "Alſo the ſaid Hoſpital receives all
"the Tithes of 300 Acres of Land, or more, of *John Chiche's*; whereof 50
"Acres lye at *Havefeld*, and the reſt nigh their own Court, and in *Mellefield*,
"nigh St. *Lawrence*: And the ſaid *John* ſhall receive of the ſaid Hoſpital, in
"Autumn, for his Servants, 5 Loaves of Wheaten Bread, and 2 Flagons and ½
"of Beer, and half a Cheeſe of the Price of 4 *d*. He ſhall receive alſo one
"pair of Doe-leather Gloves for himſelf, and one Pound of Wax-candles; and
"for his Servants, 3 pair of Gloves. [Give me leave to note a Blunder, made
by Mr. *Philpot*, in his *Villare Cantian*; where he mentions this Charter or Grant,
and tranſlates *chirothecæ ferinæ* Holiday Gloves. *N. B.*]

See the *Ap-*
pendix, Numb.
XI.

Many Benefactors I could reckon up unto you, which this Hoſpital hath
had: But let theſe ſuffice. For, it being now diſſolved, and in private hands,
I ſuppoſe there is little of the Revenues now remaining to it; although, it
ſeems (becauſe an Hoſpital) the general diſſolution took no hold of it. For
in an ordinary Viſitation of the place, in Cardinal *Pool's* time, *Anno* 1557,

---

(a) *Lib. dict. Hoſp.*   (b) *Vi & armis.*   (c) *Cujus homo ſum de tota terra mea.*
(d) *Et certum ſit vobis quòd illa decima & plures aliæ de terra mea ſunt de Capellaria mea,* &c.
(e) *Vid. Cat. Archid.*   (f) *Gloſſ. D. H. Spelman, pag* 411.   (g) *Lib. Hoſp. S. Lawrentii.*
(h) *Lib. Hoſp. Pauperum Sacerdotum.*

(long after the common diffolution) this Account, of the then State of it, is given up to the Vifitors, by the Sifters of the place (*a*).

Memorand. They being examined did fay, that Mr. *Chriftopher Hales* had a Leafe of their Land, and fince his death, from one to another, until it came to one *Tipfal*, of *London*; who did make all the fpoil of the Houfe. And they fay, there fhould be Seven Sifters, and a Priorefs, and a Prieft, found out of the profit of their Lands. The value of their Lands they efteem at xx *l.*

(*b*) *The Names of the Sifters.*

Joan Francis Priorefs.

Elizabeth Oliver.

Florence Young, not yet admitted Sifter.

The Chief Governor of this (as generally of all Hofpitals) was called (*c*) *Keeper of the Hofpital*: And he was ever one of the Monks of St. *Auguftin's* Abby.

Dodindale.   Leaving now this Martyr (or rather martyred) Hofpital, and coafting ftill *Southward*, we will next vifit *Dudindale* or *Dodindale*, (now called *Morton*) [concerning the Name *Morton*, fee *Philpot's Villare Canticum, pag.* 93. N. B.] a Manor lying within our City's liberty, known anciently and a long time together by the former of thefe Names; whether [happily like the Name of *Dug-dale, W. S.*] becaufe a Valley feated between Hills bearing out in that form, or (as *Dudley*-Caftle in *Staffordfhire* (*d*)) from one *Dudo* or *Dodo*, an *Englifh-Saxon* of that Name, that might be Lord of it, or from what other Radix or Original derived, I know not: But a Name (I am fure) by which the ancient Refidentiaries of the place (as places were wont to give Names to their Inhabitants) the Family of *Dudindale* or *Dodindale*, were of long time known, until that of latter times (as I am credibly informed) the place became the Seat of the *Mortons*, and fo loft its former Name. The Tithes of this Manor (of *Dodingdale*) *Richard de Marci* (as I told you before in St. *Lawrence*) between Four and Five Hundred Years fince, gave unto that Hofpital, by his Deed or Charter of this Tenor (*e*).

See the *Appendix*, Numb. XI. *b.*   " *Richard de Marci* to all his Leige-men, *Franks* or *Englifh*, prefent or to
" come, greeting. Know ye, that I have given and granted the Tithes of
" my Land of *Dodingdale*, to the Hofpital of St. *Lawrence*, which is nigh *Can-*
" *terbury*, in perpetual Alms, for the health of the Souls of my Predeceffors,
" and of my own Soul, and the Souls of my Wife and my Children: Where-
" fore I will and require, that the faid Hofpital fhould have and enjoy the fame
" Tithes truly, and peaceably, and freely. And I charge in the Name of
" God, and in my own Name, that the Brothers and Sifters have thofe Tithes,
" in particular, to buy Linnen-cloth, on the Feaft of St. *John* the *Baptift*,
" trufting that then they will remember me and mine in their Prayers.

The Church of *Rochefter* hath, or at leaft, fometime had, a portion of Tithes at or near this place. For as Mr. *Selden* (from the Chartulary of that late Monaftery) relates (*f*) *Haimo the Son of* Guido *of* Dudindale, confirms, (*g*) *In pure and perpetual Alms*, or *Frank Almoign*; the Gift made by his Anceftors, *Gerold* his Grandfather, and *Guy* his Father, of all the Tithes of his Land in *Dudindale*; which was afterward confirmed alfo by his Son and Heir *John*. This Tithery, at this day, paffeth by the name of *Dodingdale*-Tithery. Of which all, or fome part (it feems) lay within the Limits of St. *Mary* Caftle Parifh in *Canterbury*; as I collect hence, that (as I have it from Dr. *Tillefly* (*h*)) a Caufe was brought in the Year 1231, by *Richard, Vicar* (*i*) of St. *Mary's by the Caftle*, againft the Prior of *Rochefter*, for the Tithe of an Acre of Land, which was given by the Predeceffors of *John* of *Dudindale*, to the Priory; as by the Sentence after appeared.

Monkfdane.   Near unto this place lies another Dale or Valley called (becaufe it was parcel of the Monks demeafnes of *Chrift-Church*) Monkfdane. It lies by the place, from the dark Vaults (dungeon-like) which the much digging of Chalk there hath occafioned, called the Devil's Court-hall. Sad was the difa-

---

(*a*) *Lib. in Regiftro Domini Archid. Cant.*   (*b*) *Nomina fororum. Johanna Francis, Prior.*
Elizabeth Oliver. Florence Young, nondum foror.   (*c*) *Cuftos Hofpitalis.*   (*d*) *Cambden ibid.*
(*e*) *Lib. S. Lawrentii.*   (*f*) Hift. of Tithes, *cap.* 11 *num.* 1 *pag.* 316 *Filius Guidonis de*
Dudindale.   (*g*) *In puram & perpetuam elemofinam*   (*h*) *Animadv.* 2 Edit. *pag.* 123, & 124.
(*i*) *Sanctæ Mariæ de Caftello.*

fter which ſtands upon Record as happening at this place in King *Edward II.*
days. For (as I read in the Crown-Rolls) *(a)* " *Simon* the Son of *Adam* of
" *Colynham* and *Henry* the Son of *Henry Thetchere*, on Saturday the day after
" the Feaſt of St. *Mark* in the 17 year of the Reign of King *Edward* the Son
" of King *Edward*, were ſitting under ground in a Chalk-pit at *Monksdane* in
" the Suburbs of *Canterbury*, cutting Chalk-ſtones to make Lime : Upon whom
" by mishap the Ground fell, and beat them to pieces, ſo that they immediate-
" ly died.

St. James's, *otherwiſe* St. Jacob's *Hoſpital.*

HAving done with this place and *Dodingdale* ; let us wheel about and come St. *Jacob's.*
to St. *James*, or to St. *Jacobs*, as we now call it. An Hoſpital for Leprous Women, dedicate to the bleſſed Apoſtle St. *James*. It lies not (I muſt
confeſs) within the tether of our Cities perambulation : but yet borders upon
it, the bounds of the City lying alongſt the Hoſpital Wall ; wherefore I knew
not how to baulk it. It was built by Queen *Aleonor* wife to King *Hen.* III. ſaith
Lambard (b), followed by *Wever (c)*. Upon what ground I know not. Surely
erroneous. For of certain it was an Hoſpital before *Hen.* III. reign'd. In
[Archbiſhop *Baldwin's* time I find expreſs mention both of it and of the then
Maſter and Founder (as an old Book calls him) of it, Mr. *Feramin* by name,
to whom with the Prior of *Feverſham* Letters were directed from Pope *Clement*
the III. about the then differences between the ſame Archbiſhop and his Monks
touching the College at *Hakynton*, as may be ſeen in *Gervaſ. Dorobern.* and
ſhortly after that to wit, *W. S.*] in King *John's* time, and that toward the
beginning of his Reign (for as it appears by the Sigle, which is *H* : it was in
Archbiſhop *Hubert's* days, who died in the ſixth or ſeventh of King *John)* the
Monks, that is the Prior and Convent of *Chriſt-Church*, by their letters (as I
may call them) of protection, took it into their cuſtody, charge and patronage ;
and for the future ingage themſelves to a perpetual form of reiglement thereof,
as you may ſee by what here follows *(d)*. " Namely , That at the requeſt of See the *Appen-*
" Mr. *Firmin* ; Keeper of the Hoſpital of St. *James*, They , the Prior and *dix*, Numb.
" Convent of *Chriſt-Church*, took the ſaid Hoſpital into their Cuſtody and XII. *a.*
" under their Protection : And that they would maintain three Prieſts and
" one Clerk for the Service of Religion in the ſaid Houſe ; and XXV. Le-
" prous Women in the ſame. And that they would ſupply with all neceſſary
" Proviſions, as well the ſaid Prieſts, as the ſaid Women, out of the profits of
" the Church of *Bradegate* and other the Rents, Alms, Obventions and Poſ-
" ſeſſions of the ſaid Houſe.

Afterwards *Hen.* III. towards the augmentation of the Hoſpitals indowment
gives to it the parſonage of *Bradegate*, in words *(e)* to this effect. " That he had
" given in pure and perpetual Alms, and by his Charter did confirm the
" Church of *Bradegate* withal its appurtenencies to the Leprous Women of the
" Hoſpital of St. *James's* by *Canterbury*. So that Mr. *Firmin* during his Life
" ſhould freely enjoy the ſame, and after his Death the ſaid Leprous Women
" of the Hoſpital for ever. [As may appear by the Charters which are printed
in the *Appendix Numb.* XII. *a. b. N. B.*]

It had much other Revenues, as appears by the Inventory thereof taken and
preſented to the Commiſſioners authorized to examine ſuch matters by the
Statute 37 *Henry* 8. *Cap.* 4. Amongſt the which , one, both of the principal
and firſt, was the Farm in the Pariſhes of *Hakynton* and *Blean*, for *Firmin's*
Barton (as the fore-cited Inventory calls it) vulgarly miſcalled *Infirm-Barton,* and
of ſome, miſconceived to have appertained to St. *Auguſtin's*. Probably ſo named from that Mr. *Firmin* or *Feramin,* the *quondam* Maſter of that Hoſpital,
whereof mention is before made in each of the Precedent Charters, the Donor thereof (I take it) and (I believe) a chief Agent in the Hoſpital's Dotation, if not firſt Erection alſo. [Of whom, and of the danger both he and the

---

(a) *Simon filius Adæ de Colynham, & Hen. filius Hen. Thetchere de Cant. ſedebant die ſabbati in craſtino Sancti Marci, Anno R. R. Ed. filii Regis Ed.* 17. *in quodam loco ſubterraneo apud Monkeſdan, in Suburbio Cant. qui cedebant lapides, pro calce ibidem faciend. : quos per infortunium terra ſupercecidit, ita quòd cor-pora eorum conquaſſabantur, unde moriebantur incontinenti.* (b) Peramb. of *Kent.* In *Cant.*
(c) Ancient Funer. Monum. pag. 238. (d) *Lib. Eccleſ. Chriſti Cant.* (e) *Ibid.*

poor Hospital was in, by reason of the above-nam'd Archbishop *Baldwin's*
displeasure taken against him, because he was one of them that were design'd
to put in execution the Pope's Sentence or Decree about the College at *Hakynton*, in behalf and favour of the Monks, since it serves to vindicate the Hofpital's Antiquity, take what I have here from *Gervasius*, in his Chronicle. He
says, " That *Baldwin* so perfecuted Mr. *Feramin*, one of those that executed
" though but coldly, the Apostolical Decree against him ; having a power
" over him, as one of his Clergy, that he took from him his Oxen and his
" Sheep, his Ploughs, and all other things belonging to the Hospital of
" St. *James*, and heavily threatned him in all other respects. But *Feramin*,
" fearing left the Poor Leprous Women which liv'd in the said Hospital of
" St. *James*, should be deprived of all the Victuals and Provisions they had,
" under his Custodyship ; and knowing the angry temper of that Archbishop,
" that he would never lay down a displeasure once conceiv'd in his breast,
" was forced to make his Appeal to the Apostolical See. But notwithstanding
" this Appeal, the Archbishop ceafed not to profecute *Feramin* with so much
" violence, that there came forth a Prohibition to cut down the Corn of the
" Poor Women of the Hospital, &c. *(a)* But to proceed. *W. S.*]. The rest
of the Hospital's Revenue lay at *Egerton, Charing, Mersham, Blean, Hakynton,
Natindon, Thanington, Shadoxherst, Kingsnorth , Roking ,* and in and about the
City ; all together, in the Inventory, summed up, *(b) in clear value,* at 46 *l.*
6 *s.* 3 *d.* If any think it worth their labour to peruse the Survey of the State
of this Hospital, in every particular, as it was presented to those Commiffioners, it is in my Custody, at their Service. It payeth now no Tithe at all
(nor by Law ought to pay any *(c) for their Garden and Cattle*) but by that Survey, it evidently appears, a confideration in money in lieu of Tithe of the
site of the Hospital, paid to the Parson of *Thanington, viz.* 18 *d. per annum.*

However, the general Diffolution spared this Hospital, (as I think it did :)
yet, it seems, it did not long survive the same. For what faith the Record
(d) taken of the State of it in Cardinal *Pool's* Vifitation , holden *Anno* 1557 ?
" *Memorand.* (faith the same) that *Young* the Fermor faith, that *Freeman*, and
" one *Dartnall* caufed the Sifters to surrender the House to the King, and from
" the King this same came to the said *Dartnall*, by the King's Letters Patents ;
" and faith, that their Lands were worth a Hundred Marks by the Year ; and
" faith, that it is in divers mens hands, whereof Sir *Edward Walton* hath bought
" a great part of the Lands, which lieth about him, and he himself hath a
" Manfion-house, and a part of the Lands ; and faith that the Sifters have
" xlvi *s.* viii *d.* by the year, Penfion, and there is but one alive that he
" knoweth.

The Hospital of St. Nicholas at Herbaldown.

*Herbaldowne
Hospital.*

I Will now cross the Meadows and River, and make up to *Herbaldown*, to
take a Survey of the Hospital there. It lies alfo (I confefs) out of the
liberty of the City. Yet, for neighbourhood fake, and in regard it was built
for the Benefit of Leprous people of the City, (as I conceive :) and continues a harbour to the Aged Poor (chiefly) of the same, I have thought it worthy our Survey.

Leprofy.

Before I enter upon which (becaufe this was alfo a Lazar-houfe) let me
take a little notice of the wondrous commonnefs of that loathfome Difeafe,
the Elephantiafy, or Leprofy, in this Kingdom of old time ; which Mr. *Cambden* (*e*) thinks entred this Ifland with the *Normans.* A rare difeafe amongst us
(thanked be God) in these days ; and from what Caufe fo much abounding
as in our Forefathers, is not now of us eafily difcovered. It seems to have
been a National Malady, and accordingly, in all parts, provifion made for
receipt and relief of fuch perfons as that (as I may call it) *comitial* difeafe
had marked out for fequeftration from publick Commerce. Whereof there
were no lefs than three about this City, this of *Herbaldown* one, St. *Jacob's*

(a) *Chronic. Gervaf. Col.* 1532.   (b) *De claro.*   (c) *De hortis & animalibus. Cap.* 2.
de ecclef. ædificand. Cui adjungas velim Decreta Huberti Archiep. in Hoveden, pag. 809. *Edit. Francof.*
    (d) *Lib. Regift. D. m. Archid. Cant.*   (e) *Britan.* in *Leiceflershire.*

another, and St. *Lawrenc* a third. [All of them built without the City, from which by the wisdom of ancient times, they were excluded. See the Antiquities of *Josephus, lib.* 9. *cap.* 4. *Choppinus de Sacra Politeia lib.* 3. *tit.* 5. See also Sir *Edward Coke*'s Notes upon *Littleton, fol.* 135. *h.* Of these Lazar-houses the *W. S.*] Chief for Wealth in the whole Kingdom, and Head to all the rest, was that called *Burtonlazars* in *Leicestershire* (a). The Privileges communicable to the Benefactors (and those of the Fraternity) of which Spittle (the Baits they laid to take devout people withal) the Instrument will shew, if you peruse it; which you may find in the *Appendix, Numb.* XIII.

But enough of this, Come we now to the Hospital it self. Whereof let me first give you the Foundation, as *Edmerus* hath it. (b) Who having immediately before mentioned the Foundation of St. *John*'s Hospital without *Northgate,* says, " That this Hospital was built by Archbishop *Landfranc,* on the side of " a hill at a further distance from the *Westgate* of the City, than St. *John*'s " Hospital was from the *Northgate* of the City, That it was assign'd for the " use of the Leprous; and so contrived, that the men, as in other like Hos- " pitals, were kept seperate from the Society of the women. By his appoint- " ment also, whatsoever the Sick wanted, according to the quality of their " disease, was provided for them, out of his own Substance; and the Care " hereof was committed to men, whose diligence, kindness, and patience in " looking after the Sick, no one could doubt of. Thus he. By which it appears who was the Founder, the Time also, and End or Intent of the Foundation of *Herbaldown* Hospital. My Author, you see, specifies not the Indowment setled upon it by the Founder. With your leave I will supply that omission, and shew you both what the Original Endowment was, and how afterwards improved.

Archbishop *Richard, Becket*'s immediate Successor, in a Charter (c) (which I have seen) of his to this and St. *John*'s Hospitals, relating first their erection, by his Predecessor *Landfranc,* shews, that he endowed them with Sevenscore Pound *per annum.* to issue and arise out of his Manors of *Reculver* and *Boĉton,* that is, to either Hospital after an equal Division 70 *l. per annum*: This now was the Original Endowment of both these Hospitals; with which the same *Richard*, finding them scarce well able to subsist, in augmentation added 20 *lib. per annum* more to their former means; payable out of *Reculver* Parsonage. Which 160 *l.* continued afterwards constantly paid unto them, and unaltered, until Archbishop *Kilwardby*'s days. For so it appears by an Exemplification, made of certain Charters of those Hospitals, under the Seal of *Thomas Chicheley,* Dr. of the Decrees, Archdeacon of *Canterbury,* and Prothonotary to the Pope, and Signed by his (d) *Register* and (e) *Actuary*: Namely, that from *Becket*'s time downwards until *Kilwardby*'s, these two Hospitals had, and received by equal divisions, yearly, 240 Marks, or 160 *l.* of the Archbishop's Chamber, saving, that 20 *l.* of it was paid them of the Parson of *Reculver.* This, *Kilwardby* misliking, withdraws their Stipend, and in Lieu assigns and appropriates over to them his Parsonage of *Reculver,* with the Chappels annexed. But for some Inconveniences (that of the Leprous condition of the people of this Hospital the main, rendring them both unable and unfit to attend and intermeddle in a Tithery; especially so remote:) his next Successor *John Peckham,* alters and revokes, what he (*Kilwardby*) had done, and redintegrates the Hospitals into their former Estate. Archbishop *Stratford* afterwards gets the King (*Edward* 3.) of whom this Parsonage held *in capite,* by his Charter, to appropriate it (f) to the Archbishop's Table; yet charged with that old Payment or Stipend, which *Simon Islip* afterwards with consent of the Chapter, the Prior and Convent, confirms unto them; and that (for the better strengthening of their Title, maintainable as yet only by Customary Right, having no sufficient (g) *written Title* to shew) by his Charter in Writing,

---

(a) *Idem ibidem.* (b) *Hist. Novor. lib.* 1. *pag.* *Remotius verò quam à Boreali ab Occidentali porta Civitatis ligneas domos in devexo montis latere fabricans,* (meaning *Lanfranc*) *eas ad opus leprosorum delegavit, viris, quemadmodum in aliis, à fœminarum societate sejunĉtis. His nihilominus pro qualitate sui morbi omnia quibus egerent de suis ministrari constituit, institutis ad hoc peragendum talibus viris de quorum solertia, benignitate ac patientia, ut sibi quidem videbatur, nemini foret ambigendum.* (c) *Inter chartas Hosp. S. Johannis extra Northgate.* (d) *Registrorum Costas.* (e) *Actorum Scriba.* (f) *Mensæ Archiepiscopali.* (g) *Jus scriptum.*

whereby

whereby to recover it, if at any time denied or detained: Ever since which time they have peaceably enjoyed the same. These things I thought good the rather to deduce, that I might vindicate that false Aspersion, wherewith some of the old People of these Hospitals, ignorant altogether of the premised Passages, are wont to deprave some of the Archbishops of former times, for depriving them of this and that Manor; and I know not what other means, revenues and indowment, wherewith, they say, and will tell you, their Houses were at first so richly endowed, as they cannot think their Prior of old time, any less Man, forsooth, than a Lord Prior, I wot. But thus others have told them, and they think they may take it up upon trust, and say as much after them.

I shall not insist on the specification of the other Revenues of this Hospital, whereof, by the Charity of former times, it hath a pretty Competency: *Eilgar* at *Bourne* and *John* of *Tonford*, Neighbours to the place in their time, being the prime (I take it) of the secular Benefactors; as King *Henry* III. was of the Royal, who gave to the Poor here, 20 Marks a Year, out of the City Fee-farm, payable by the Chamber.

This Hospital's ancient Governor, now called a Master, was a Dean: For to a very ancient Deed of the Hospital (amongst other Witnesses) one *Benedict* in the first place subscribes, with this addition of *(a)* at that time Dean of St. *Nicholas*. Pope *John* 23 *(b)* by his Bull, discharged this Hospital of payment of Tithes *(c)* Gardens, &c.

Hitherto, and enough of the Care taken for their Bodies, and the furnishing of them with the Necessaries of this Life. Next, of the provision made for their Souls, and their Christian Instruction that might prepare them for that better one to come,

St *Nicholas* Church.

Adjoyning to this Hospital is an indifferent fair Church, lately (as the Hospital) by the Cost of the Reverend Master, Dr. *Jackson*, much beautified; which sometimes was a Parish Church, and hath in it a Font (an ancient one) and about it a Church-yard (the Badges and Characters of a Parochial Church) and in the account of the State and Condition of the Hospital, given to the Commissioners upon the Statute 37 *Henry* 8. *cap.* 4. it is avouched to be a Parish Church, and to have Parochial Rights; and Archbishop *Stratford*'s appropriation of it to *Eastbridge* (whereof anon) calls it *(d)* the Parish Church. It was indeed the Church of the Parish of St. *Nicholas* at *Herbaldown*; the bounds, extent and continent whereof I have not hitherto met with: only once I saw a Deed registred in the Lieger of *Eastbridge* Hospital, 400 years old and upwards, mentioning a piece of Land, abutting Eastward to the High-way leading to the *Barton* of *Westgate* (i. e. *Westgate*-Court) from *Tonford*, therein said to lie in the Parish of St. *Nicholas* of *Herbaldown*. A Parsonage it once was; payeth Procurations to this day as a Parsonage, and by the same Name was in the year 1292, at the general Valuation of all Ecclesiastical Livings in this Diocess *(e)*, valued at 9 Marks *per Annum*, (more than most of the Parsonages in and near about the City were rated at), and accordingly the Tenths set at 12 *s.* And the ancient Incumbent thereof (as a Parson and Parsonage are Relatives) was a Rector, or in the phrase of our Municipals) a Parson. *Anno* 37 *H.* 3. one *Thomas Walsham*, by his Charter granted *(f)* to *William* the Brother of *Gilbert*, [Parson of St. *Nicholas* of *Herbaldown*, for his Parsonage Mansion 'tis like, a certain Croft by the Bounders of it, seeming to be the same that was afterwards assign'd and set out for the Dwelling of the Chantery-Priest; of which afterwards; *W. S.*] unto which Deed one *Luke* the then Parson of St. *Michael* of *Herbaldown* (amongst others) was a Witness. To this Church, and the then Presbyter thereof (the Parsonage and Parson, as we since phrase it, of St. *Nicholas*) *Theobald* the Archbishop, by his Charter attested by *Walter* the then Prior of *Christ-Church* (amongst others), granted the Tithes of his and his See's Mannor of *Westgate* *(g)*. The Parsonage thus improved, a Successor of *Theobald*, *John Stratford*, in the year 1342, 15 *Ed.* III. upon his novel Ordination of the Hospital of *Eastbridge* in *Canterbury*,

---

(a) *Tunc temporis Decanus de sancto Nicolao.*   *(b)* *Inter Chartas Hospitalis:*   *(c)* *De hortis, virgultis & animalium nutrimentis.*   *(d)* *Ecclesiam Parochialem.*   *(e)* *Lib. Ecclef. Christi Cant.*   *(f)* *Prout in Charta quad. hujus Hosp.*   *(g)* *Lib. de Eastbridge.*

and in and by the fame Charter, annexed and appropriated to that Hofpital (the Deed or Charter whereof I purpofe fhall follow in my Survey of *Eaft-bridge :*) But becaufe it fhould feem that Church had been the Hofpital Church of St. *Nicholas,* wherein the Poor there had the Sacraments and Sacramentals miniftred unto them by the Incumbent for the time being, (it was built for them, as Archbifhop *Parker* fays, by *Lanfranc* their Founder), the Appropria-tor, *Stratford,* to prevent and provide againft all damage and detriment which that Appropriation might occafion to St. *Nicholas* Hofpital, obligeth *Eaftbridge* Hofpital to the finding (not of a Vicar, the Living was too flender to maintain one, but) of a Chaplain, who fhould officiate and minifter to them (*a*) *Divine Service* (as the forefaid Inftrument will fhew :) In this, Archbifhop *Wittlefey* afterwards finding fome inconvenience, *Anno* 1371, erects a perpetual Chan-tery ; the Chantery Prieft whereof (becaufe of the danger of converfing with the Hofpitalers, being Leprous People many of them) feated and houfed apart, *viz.* over-againft the Hofpital Gate, and endowed with a competency of Re-venue, partly from the one, partly from the other Hofpital; was charged with Cure of Souls, and to that end tyed to perpetual Refidence upon it, as the In-ftrument of that Chantery's erection and dotation (to be fought in my *Appen-dix)* more at large will fhew. In this wife things ftood with the Church of St. *Nicholas* afterward until the latter end of *Hen.* 8. or beginning of *Edw.* 6. Reign. About which time the Chantery and Chantery Prieft vanifhed. Since when, the Church continuing to the Hofpital, the Poor are ferved there (*b*) *in Divine Offices,* by one in Orders, a Member of the Houfe.

(margin: Herbaldown Chantery.)
(margin: Numb. XIV.)

I was willing to enlarge my felf in this matter the rather, becaufe the ftate of this Church enquired into by fome, but unknown of moft, I would make as evident as my Reading and Obfervation had enabled me. And fo I have only a Tale to tell you from *Erafmus,* touching an old Ceremony ufed heretofore in this Hofpital (as *Wever* hath abridged it), and I fhall take leave of it. In this Houfe (faith *Wever* (*c*)) was referved the upper Leather of an old Shooe, which had been worn (as they gave it out) by Saint *Thomas Becket ;* this Shooe, as a facred Relick, was offered to all Paffengers to kifs, fair fet in Copper and Cryftal.

What he there adds of a Priory of Black Canons, which (as he faith) was originally annexed to this Hofpital by *Lanfranc* the Founder, is but a Tale. The Man was miftaken in this, as he is much out in many other things about this City. The Priory, I wot, by him intended, is that of St. *Gregory* without *Northgate,* over-againft St. *John's* Hofpital there of *Lanfranc's* Foundation, to which it was not annexed neither, much lefs to *Herbaldown,* but an Injunction only laid upon the Canons of the place to minifter unto the Poor of St. *John's* in things appertaining to their Souls health, and in Rites of Burial, as in pro-per place I fhall further fhew.

[Before I leave this place left my Reader fhould fwallow an error in the Etymology of its Name, give me leave to fay fomewhat here of the Original thereof. *Herbaldown* by *Canterbury* (faith Mr. *Lambard* (*d*)) in *Saxon ,* ꝥepebelæpdune, that is, *The Hill where the Army was betrayed :* as if he had met with that *Saxon* name of the place in fome ancient Record or Monument of the *Saxon* times, which I am verily perfuaded he never did, and that for divers reafons. Firft, becaufe that as this name ꝥepebelæpdune hath no ground in Story (no Chronicle of ours that ever I faw recording any fuch occurrence as the betraying of an Army either there or any where elfe thereabouts.) So Mr. *Lambard* is filent in the inftancing or fpecifying of any fuch matter, for the illuftration of the name. Next as a charter of King *Henry* I. which is one of the firft and eldeft deeds or charters of the Hofpital there, calls the Hofpital (*e*) *the Hofpital of the Forreft or Wood of* Blean, without any other proper name ; fo fuch other of that Hofpital's evidences, as makes any men-tion of its proper name conftantly call it as we do at this day *Herbaldune* or the like : I could inftance in a multitude, but for brevity fake I will limit my felf to a few of the eldeft as moft likely to give the trueft expreffion of the Name. *Henry* II. then in two feveral charters of his to this Hofpital, the one

---

(a) *In divinis.*   (b) *In divinis.*   (c) Ancient Fun. Monum. *pag.* 259.
(d) Peramb. of *Kent,* p. 318.   (e) *Hofpitale de Bofco de Blean.*

of xx. Marks *per Ann.* out of the City Fee-ferm , continuing to this day : the other of a portion of fewel out of the wood, now called *Shoorth* expreſly makes his grant, (*a*) to the Leprous of *Herbaldown* , as likewiſe doth Archbi-ſhop *Theobald* , both for his penny a day granted to the Hoſpital out of his Manor of *Liminge* and for the Tithes of *Weſtgate*-Court, by him granted to the ſame Hoſpital. Archbiſhop *Stratford* afterward annexing to the Hoſpital of *Eaſtbridge* in *Canterbury*, the Church of St. *Nicholas* here calls it (*b*) the *Pariſh Church of St.* Nicholas *of* Herbaldown. *Herbaldown* then doubtleſs is the very right name of the place. Which having cleared, enquire we next , when firſt and why the name came up ; that is, from what antiquity and upon what grounds the place became ſo called at the firſt. We are to conſider then that the *quondam* extent and continent of *Blen-wood* , or of the Forreſt of *Blen* as I have ſeen it called in ſome old Deeds ; (*c*) *very great part whereof is turn'd into Fields and Paſtures*, was much larger than of late, and at this day from that Charter of *Hen.* I. to this Hoſpital abovementioned it may be more than probably infer'd, that it did extend and ſtretch it ſelf unto the very Hoſpital : for it not only calls it (*d*) *the Hoſpital of* Blen-wood, but withal grants and gives unto the Hoſpitallers liberty to Aſſart, Stock, or Grub up and riddaway 8 (*e*)Perches of Wood on all ſides (or round about) the Hoſpital. For your better ſatisfaction ſee here the Charter it ſelf recited Ver-batim, (ſee the *Appendix*, Numb. XIV. 6.)   " *Henry* King of *England* to the " Archbiſhop of *Canterbury*, and to the Sheriff and to his Barons, and to his " Officers and to his Subjects of *Kent*, *French* and *Engliſh*, greeting. Know " ye that I have given and granted for the love of God, and for the Soul of " my Father and Mother, and of *Maud* the Queen and of *William* my Son " and for the pardon of my Sins, in increaſe of the Hoſpital of *Blen-wood*, " Ten Perches of Land on every ſide round about the ſaid Hoſpital to be " grubbed up and tilled : And I will and ſtraitly command , that thoſe, who " inhabit in that place, be under my Protection, that no one ſhall injure or " moleſt them. Witneſs *William* my Almoner and Chaplain, &c.

Here you ſee Power and Licence granted to quit and clear the Hoſpital of ſuch Wood as was about it , Ten Perches every way. By which and like courſes for the disforeſting of the place, and fitting it for Tillage and Her-bage the Hill or Down of Wild and Woody, becoming plain Fields or Paſture ground : Hence I ſay the Hill or Down, to diſtinguiſh it from the neigh-bouring Hills or Downs as yet continuing Wild or Woody, took the name or began to be called by the name of *Herbaldown*, that is, the Paſture-down, or the down of Herbage or Tillage, like as *Wertsbergh*, a City in *Germany*, ſo called, ſaith *Verſtegan* (*f*), from the abundance of Wurts or Herbs, which grew about the Hills ſides by that Town, is in Latin called *Herbipolis* (*g*).

Or (to inſtance in an Example nearer home) as that *Bocton* near *Lenham* in *Kent*, for diſtinction ſake from the other three *Boctons* in that County , hath this addition of *Malherb*, from a kind of bad Herbage proper to the place, as I am told. *Ita mihi videtur*, &c. This is my opinion ; or to ſay with Learned but Modeſt *Covarruvias*, (*h*) in a like doubtful Caſe : " By theſe Reaſons, I " become of this opinion, being ready to yeild to the opinion of any one that " ſhall bring better and ſtronger Reaſons : For in doubtful Caſes, it is not " good to adhere contumaciouſly to a conceived opinion, ſo to refuſe to yield " to the judgment of moſt Learned men. So I ſay, this is my opinion, but with ſubmiſſion to better judgments, being very willing that other men ſhould take or leave it, as they pleaſe, and ſhall ſee cauſe. Give me leave to con-clude this diſcourſe of the place with the words of the forenamed Mr. *Twyne*, (ſometime an Alderman and Mayor of our City) concerning *Blen-wood* : He

---

(*a*) *Leproſis de Herbalduna.*   (*b*) *Eccleſiam parochialem ſancti Nicolai de Herbaldowne.*

(*c*) *Cujus hodie pars bene magna in agros & paſcua complanatur*, as *Twine* hath it, *de rebus Albionic.* l. 2. p. 101.   (*d*) *Hoſpitale de Boſco de Blen.*   (*e*) In the Charter X.   (*f*) Reſtitu-tion of decayed Intelligence. *pag.* 238.

     (*g*) —————— *Urbemque petunt, cui nomen ab herbis*

         Eſſe putant linguæ vulgaris origine tractum.   Ligurin l. 5.

(*h*) *Part.* 1. *Relect. in cap. Alma mater*, &c. *Tom.* 1. *p.* 411. § 11. *His rationibus animum induxi meum, ut hanc opinionem in hâc quæſtione probarem, facillimè admiſſurus cujuſlibet ſanioris ſententiam & quæ , his probationibus excluſis fortioribus & melioribus conſtet. Etenim in re dubiâ nequaquam decet ſemel conceptis opinionibus ita contumaci animo adhærere, ut doctiſſimorum virorum judicia recuſare nitamur.*

ſaith,

faith, (*a*) " Why fhould I fpeak of *Blen-wood*, a Wood near *Canterbury* of no
" inconfiderable bignefs, full of Thorns; thick with Wood; a good part
" whereof is at this day turned into Fields and Paftures; in which in the me-
" mory of our Fathers, wild Boars were hunted and killed : A Wood fit for
" Bears to breed in; in which are now holes for Foxes and Badgers. *W. S.*].

Hakynton.

MY Progrefs being Circular, I am bound next for St. *Stephen*'s or *Hakyn-* Hakynton.
ton. Whither my next way lies (by *Beaufhern*, anciently as ftill a par- Beaufherne.
cel of the Demefnes of poor Priefts Hofpital in *Canterbury*) over St. *Thomas*'s St.ThomasHill.
Hill. Where I will ftay you no longer than whilft I may give you the derivation of the Hill's Name. The Inventory of Rents and Revenues of *Eft-*
bridge Hofpital prefented to the Commiffioners upon the Statute 37 *Henry* 8.
cap. 4. calls it *Thomas Becket*'s Hill. And that (I fuppofe) either becaufe the
greateft part of the Demefnes or Endowment of that Hofpital, built by Archbifhop *Becket*, and to this day called (*b*) *The Hofpital of St.* Thomas *the Martyr*
of *Eaftbridge*, lay as it doth ftill, about that Hill; or elfe from a Chappel
fometime ftanding thereaway, called St. *Thomas*'s Chapel; whereof in a
Deed of *Eaftbridge*-Leiger of divers Quit-rents (*c*) *without* Weftgate, I read
as followeth. (*d*) *Nigh a Field in which had ftood a new Chapel of the bleffed*
Thomas *the Martyr*. [This it feems, being the Chapel built by Archbifhop
Baldwin, in *Henry* 2. time, upon his difappointment at *Hakynton*, mentioned
of *Gervafe* the Monk of *Canterbury*; who tells us, that in the Year 1187 " the
" Archbifhop returning to *Canterbury*, changed the place defign'd for the ere-
" ction of his intended Chapel, from the Church-yard of St. *Stephen*'s to a
" Field before St. *Dunftan*'s Church, and that at the firft beginning to dig the
" foundation there, fuch a Tempeft of Hail happened as the like had not
" been feen before in *Kent*. (*e*) *W. S.*]
[That this Chapel gave the Name to the Hill, may eafily be granted.
N. B.]. So much of that. Now for *Hakynton.*
I might here enter into a large difcourfe of the fierce Quarrel that happened between *Baldwin* the Archbifhop, and his Monks, the Prior and Convent
of *Chrift-Church*, about a College by him intended to have been erected at
this place, which (the caufe of their oppofition) would mainly have damnified the Monks, had the Project fucceeded. But the Story is delivered by fo
many hands already, and that fo fully and at large, that (not defirous to
make my Book fwell with other mens labours) I purpofely fpare the recital
of it; and refer the Reader for fatisfaction, to the *Antiquitates Britannicæ*, the
Catalogue of Bifhops, to the Acts and Monuments, and *Lambard*'s Perambulation. I my felf alfo fhall have occafion to give a touch upon it hereafter.
in the Life both of the fame *Baldwin*, and of *Alanus* the Prior.

Barton *and* Jefus *Hofpital.*

I Pafs from *Hakynton*, and croffing the Meadows and River at *Barton*, (fome- Barton.
time a Manor of *Chrift-Church*, and that which *Doomfday*-Book calls *North-*
wood) from (it may feem) the fometime woody condition of fome part of
the foil; in fpeaking whereof *Lambard* (*f*) commits fome errors, efpecially
in faying the Manor was long time in the poffeffion of certain Gentlemen of
the fame name, *&c.*) I come next to the Suburbs without *Northgate*. Where
after we are paft *Jefus* Hofpital, a Spittle for the Poor ferved there with Jefus Hofpital.
good annual allowance by the Founder, Sir *John Boys* Knight deceafed,
(whofe Monument placed by his Tomb againft the *North*-Wall of the Body
of *Chrift-Church*, further fets forth what he was:) the Priory of St. *Gregory*'s,

---

(*a*) *Quid referam fylvam Blenam Cantuariæ vicinam, magnitudinis non contemnendæ, fiqua alia fenta
atque frondofa, cujus hodie pars bene magna in agros ac pafcua complanatur, in qua Patrum noftrorum memoria apri venatione conficiebantur, & non ineptam fane ad urfos gignendos, quæ modo vulpium ac taxo-
num luftra opacat, arbitrimini, &c. De rebus Albionicis.* l. 2. p. 101.
(*b*) *Hofpitale Sancti Thomæ martyris de Eaftbridge.*   (*c*) *Extra Weftgate.*   (*d*) *Juxta*
campum in quo nova capella beati Thomæ Martyris fuerat.   (*e*) *Gervaf. Dorober Col.* 1491.
(*f*) Perambulation of *Kent* in *Norwood.*

and tho oppofite Hofpital of St. *John's* minifter unto me much matter of Survey.

The Priory of St. Gregory's.

I Shall firft, from *Edmerus* (a), give you their foundation joyntly, and then treat feverally, firft, of the Priory of St. *Gregory*, then of the Hofpital of St. *John.*

(b) " Without the *Northgate* of this City, Archbifhop *Lanfranc* built a fair " and large Houfe of Stone, and added to it feveral Habitations with a fpaci- " ous Court, contriv'd in the beft manner for the benefit of thofe that fhould " dwell therein. This building he divided into two Parts; and defign'd one " part for Infirm Men, the other part for Infirm Women. He provided them " with Food and Raiment at his own charge: He appointed Officers, who " fhould fee that they wanted nothing, and that the Men and Women fhould " not come at one another. On the other fide of the way, he built a Church " in honour of St. *Gregory,* wherein he appointed Canons, who fhould be bound " to order the courfe of their Lives according to certain Conftitutions or Ca- " nons, and who fhould Adminifter to the Infirm People of the aforefaid " Hofpital whatfoever was neceffary for the good of their Souls; and take " care alfo of their Burial. For thefe he provided fo much Lands, Tithes, and " Rents, as feem'd fufficient for their Maintainance. Thus *Edmerus.*

St. *Gregory's.*

The Priory (to begin with that) was you fee a Houfe of regular Canons, otherwife called (from their habit, which was a white Coat, and a linen Rochet, under a black Cope, with a Scapuler to cover their head and fhoulders (c)) black Canons: of the order of St. *Auguftin,* as appears by the Catalogue of the Monafteries of that order (amongft which it is reckoned for one:) which coming in and compounding with the King (*Edw.* I.) about a fubfidy (for a general denial whereof by the whole Clergy, regulating themfelves by the Pope's conftitution, and their Archbifhop's example, they were by Parliament excluded from the King's protection, and their Goods pronounced confifcate to the King) obtained letters of protection (d).

It was (I take it) the firft houfe of Regular Canons in the whole Kingdom. Sure I am it was erected long before the Priory (of the fame order) at *Nofthill* in *Yorkfhire,* which *Reynor* (e) faith was the firft the Kingdom had, being built (as he delivers) by *Adelwold* or *Ethelwolph, Henry* I. his Confeffor, that firft (if we may believe him) brought the order into this Land.

What Number of Canons here were required by the Foundation, I know not, but in a Vifitation (f) of the Priory by Cardinal *Bourchier,* only Five give up their Names with the Prior; who indeed then complained of the paucity of his Canons, which (as he lays the fault) was occafioned by the diminution of their Revenues, or (in his own words) their Lands, Tenements and Rents.

Concerning this Priory, in the Book of *Doomfday,* in the Archbifhop's Manor of *Store-feat* or *Weftgate* (as we now call it) thus I read: (g) *And therein are further* xxxii *Dwellings, and one Mill, which the Clerks of St.* Gregory's *hold as belonging to their Church. And there remain* xii *Burgeffes, who pay them* xxxv *Shillings; and the Rent of the Mill is* v *Shillings.* The fame *Doomfday* in another place, under the Title of the City mentions the fame thing, but

---

(a) *Hift. Novor. lib.* 1 *pag.*   (b) *Extra aquilonalem denique portam urbis illius lapideam domum decentem & amplam conftruxit, & ei pro diverfis neceffitudinibus hominum & commoditatibus habitacula plura cum fpaciofa curte adjecit. Hoc palatium in duo divifit, viros viz. variis infirmitatum qualitatibus preffos uni; parti verò alteri fæminas fe malè habentes inftituens. Ordinavit etiam eis de fuo veftitum, & victum quotidianum; Miniftros quoque atque cuftodes qui modis omnibus obfervarent ne aliquid eis deeffet, neque viris ad fæminas, vel fæminis ad viros accedendi facultas ulla adeffet. Ex altera verò parte viæ Ecclefiam in honorem beati Gregorii Papæ compofuit, in qua Canonicos pofuit, qui regulariter viverent, & præfatis infirmis quæ faluti animarum fuarum congruerent cum Sepultura miniftrarent. Quibus etiam in Terris, in Decimis, & in aliis redditibus tanta largitus eft, ut ad fuftentationem eorum fufficientia effe viderentur.*   (c) *Polyd. Virg. de Invent. Rer. lib.* 7. *cap.* 3.   (d) *Reyner Apoftolat. Benedict. in Appendice. pag.* 66.   (e) *Apoftolat. Bened. pag* 158.   (f) *Lib. Regiftri Confiftor. Cant.*   (g) *Et inibi funt iterum* xxx. *& ii. manfuræ & unum molendinum, quæ tenet clerici fancti Gregorii ad eorum ecclefiam. Ibique manent* xii. *Burgenfes qui reddunt eis* xxxvj. *& molendinum reddit* vs.

with fome little variation ; thus : (*a*) The Archbifhop has within the City of *Canterbury* xii Burgeffes, and xxx Manfions ; which the Clerks hold of the Village, towards the maintenance of their Guild, or belonging to their Society. And they pay xxxv *s.* and the Rent of one Mill is v *s.* This Priory had Indowment, confifting (as *Edmerus* fhews) as well in Tithes as Temporalties. As for their Titheries, in the Year 1292, (at what time their Temporalties in *Canterbury*, *Natyndon*, *Hugevelde*, *Chertham*, *Tanintone*, and *Herbaldown*, were together valued at xxv *l.* xv *s.*) they were thefe ; the Parfonages of *Taninton*, *Weftgate*, *Northgate*, St. *Dunftan*, *Natindon*, *Livingfborn*, *Waltham*, *Elmefted*, *Betrichedenne*, *Stallesfield*. Together with certain Titheries in *Goldftanefton*, *Berham*, *Plukele*, and *Riffeburn* (*b*). The whole Revenue every way, Mr. *Lambard* reckons up to but 30 *l.* falling much fhort of *Speed*'s Eftimate, which is 166 *l.* 4 *s.* 5 *d.* Whether of them is miftaken, I leave it to them to inquire, that pleafe to fearch the Record.

As for any remarkable Matter or Occurrence concerning this Priory, until the Suppreffion, I read of none befide the firing of it in King *Stephen*'s days. (*c*). Anno 1145. *This Year, on the Second day of* July, *the Church of St.* Gregory *in* Canterbury *was burnt. W. S.*(*d*)]

As appertaining, fo alfo adjoyning to this Priory, before and until the diffolution, (yea and after too) was a Cemitary or Church-yard, not proper only to the Priory, for the Burial of the Domefticks, but which was (whether of Right, or by Courtefy only, I know not) common to others alfo with them, and thofe not the Hofpitallers only, (the Reafon why they were till very lately deftitute of any Church-yard within themfelves) but alfo the Parifhioners of *Northgate*, their Neighbours, of which Church this Priory had the Patronage ; who did conftantly by their Wills appoint their Burials in that Church-yard, and never mention other of their own : It faring with them as with thofe other Parifh Churches of the City ; which belonging fome to *Chrift-Church*, fome to St. *Auguftin*'s, had their want of Church-yards fupplied by thofe *Monafteries*. This at St. *Gregory*'s continued to the Parifh of *Northgate*, after the diffolution, until (as the tradition goes) Sir *John Boys* the late Tenent to the Priory obtained to appropriate, and inclofe it upon exchange of the modern Church-yard Ground for it with the Churchwardens of *Northgate* for the time being. It continued (I fay) till then to the Parifh for a Burial place, *de facto* ; but was not acknowledged theirs of Right. For at a Vifitation (*e*), holden in the Year 1560. it is from *Northgate*, by the fworn men (among other things) thus prefented ; *viz.* That Mr. *May* doth withhold part of the Church-yard, *&c.* This Mr. *May* (it feems) was then Tenent to the Priory : Who in defence of himfelf, being convented upon this prefentment (*f*) *produced the King's Letters Patents*, (as the Act of the Court runs) *by which it appears, that the Church-yard is the Hereditary Right of the moft Reverend* &c. Afterward, *viz. Anno* 1573, at another Vifitation (*g*), it was from the fame place thus prefented ; to wit, That their Church-yard is not decently kept ; neither can they bury in it unlefs they pay 2 *d.* for an old Body and 1 *d.* for a Child.

It hath been a thing much controverted between the City and this Priory, whether it be of the Cities liberty or not. Now not out of any defire I have to ftickle in the matter, but for manifeftation and maintenance of a truth herein the beft I am able, unto which by occafion of the places furvey, I am in a manner engaged, I fhall without partiality deliver what, in matter of fact, I know may conduce to the clearing of this doubt and quieting the debate. In the year 1269. *Ann.* 53 *Hen.* III. I find (*h*) the Prior of St. *Gregory*'s, by the fame Writ with the Prior of *Chrift-Church*, the Abbat of St. *Auguftin*'s and others, after a legal difcuffion of the cafe by enquiry and verdict of felect men of the City, and voycinage, acquited by the Kings writ of tallage, *i. e.* of being within compafs of tallage with the City. Befides in the Argument drawn up by the Abbat of St. *Auguftin* in defence of

Controverfy between the City and St. Gregory's.

(*a*) *Archiepifcopus habet infra Civitatem* Cant. xii. *Burgenfes, & xxx. manfuras quas tenent clerici de villa ingildam fuam, & reddunt* xxxvs. *& unum molendinum reddit* vs. (*b*) *Lib. ecclef. Chrift. Cant.* (*c*) Lambard *Peramb. of* Kent *in* Canterbury. (*d*) *Hoc anno* 1145. *Combufta eft Ecclefia S. Gregorii Cantuar.* vi. *nonas* Julii Gervaf. Dorobern. W. S.] (*e*) *Lib. Confiftorii* Cant. (*f*) *Exhibuit literas Regias patentes per quas patet cimiterium effe jus hæreditarium Reverendiffimi, &c.* (*g*) *Lib. ejufdem Confiftorii.* (*h*) [See Adam Chillenden *among the Priors of* Chrift-Church, *where is a Record relating to this matter. W. S.*]

O

him-

himself and his Abbey againſt the City, challenging the Abbey and ſome of her neighbouring demains to be of and within the liberty of the City in *Hen.* VI. time, amongſt other heads thereof (that it might not ſeem ſtrange, that the Abbey being in the Suburbs, and ſo near the City-wall, ſhould neverthelefs be exempt from the Franchiſe of the ſame,) by ſhewing how the matter ſtood in the ſame ſtate with other like places about the City : this Priory is pleaded to be as without the Walls, ſo without the liberty alſo of the ſame City in theſe words, *viz.* (a) " And alſo there are ſome places, as " near the Walls of the ſaid City, as are thoſe places, which are contain'd, " in the aforeſaid Articles of the Bailiffs aforeſaid, which always were with- " out the ſaid City, the precinct, liberty, or Suburbs of the ſame, namely, " the ſtreet of *Weſtgate*, the ſtreet of St. *Martin* , the Priory of St. *Gregory*, " the Hoſpital of St. *John* of *Northgate*, &c. In *Henry* VIII. time certain Articles were concluded between, the Prior of this houſe and the Convent of the ſame on the one party, and the Mayor and Commonalty of the City of the other party, for the compoſing of this difference about the temporal Juriſdiction of the place. Which compoſition, from the Records of the chamber, I ſhall in my *Appendix* preſent the Reader with. *Numb.* XIV. e.

But leaving theſe things, and the houſe, I come next to the ground lying behind it, ſometime the Canons Orchard or Garden : where are yet ſtanding or rather falling (and yeilding to time) the ruins of an old Chapel, a Barn I wot of late, dedicated to that once reputed holy Martyr St. *Thomas* of *Canterbury*, and called (as I find by the Will (b) of one *William Harry* of St. *Martin, Ann.* 1461. who gave a Legacy unto it) (c) *The Chapel of the Brotherhood of St.* Tho- mas *the Martyr, ſituate in the Garden of St. Gregory's.* I will cloſe this diſcourſe of St. *Gregory's* with the following *memorandum*, touching the water-courſe of *Chriſt-Church* running through this part of it. (d) " *Memorandum*, ſaith a Book " of *ChriſtChurch*, concerning a Charter of the Prior and Convent of St. *Gre-* " *gory's* by *Canterbury* making particular mention of this matter, wherein it is " expreſſed, That they ſhall preſerve, as far as they can, a Water-courſe of " the Prior and Convent of *Chriſt-Church* in *Canterbury* , which runs through " their Orchard ſafe and free from damage ; and that they ſhall grant free " Liberty of Ingreſs, Egreſs, and Regreſs through their Court and Gate to " the Workmen of *Chriſt-Church* as often as it ſhall be neceſſary for them to " repair the ſame Water-courſe. [In the ſame agreement it is further added, " That they ſhould ſend in Dinner-time into the Refectory of *Chriſt-Church* " a Baſket of the beſt fruit on or before the 15th day of *September* , every " Year; and ſhould further pay the Sum of Eightpence, as a yearly Rent " for a ſmall piece of Land there, belonging formerly to the Archdeacon. " *N. B.*] Dated in *July, A. D.* 1227.

St. John's Hoſpital.

I Return now to the Hoſpital, whoſe foundation being premiſed, her do- tation ſhould follow : but what I might here ſay of it, is already ſaid and may be ſeen in that of *Herbaldown*, the other twin as I may call it, for their parity as well in time as manner, both of their erection and original endow- ment. This of St. *John's* was fired in *Edward* III. time, as I find by certain Letters of the Hoſpital under their ſeal, framed after the manner of a Brief, and directed to all Prelates in general, wherein they in pitiful manner deplore their miſerable eſtate occaſioned (as they ſay) by a late lamentable fire hap- pening in their houſe, which had waſted their Hoſpital and adjacent Edifices, in the which were more than 100 poor People ſuſtained, with deſire of their

---

(a) *Ac etiam quod ſunt aliqua loca adeo prope muros Civitatis prædictæ ſicut ſunt loci in prædictis arti- culis ballivorum prædict' &c. contenti quæ ſemper fuerunt extra prædictam Civitatem, præcinctum, liberta- tem aut ſuburbia ejuſdem, viz. vicus de Weſtgate, vicus Sancti Martini, Prioratus ſancti Gregorii, Hoſpi- tale Sancti Johannis de Northgate, &c.* (b) *Penes regiſtrum Conſiſtor. Cant.*

(c) *Capella fraternitatis Sancti Thomæ Martyris exiſten' in orto Sancti Gregorii* (d) *Me- morandum de carta Prioris & Couventus Sancti Gregorii Cant. ſpecialem mentionem facien. & extriſſum quòd aquæductum Prioris & Conventus eccleſiæ Chriſti Cant. per pomarium ſuum tranſeuntem ſalvum & il- læſum quantum in eis eſt conſervabunt, & permittent operarios dicta eccleſiæ Chriſti Cant. quotiens neceſſe fuerit ad eundem aquæductum emendandum per Curiam & portam ſuam liberum habere ingreſſum & egreſ- ſum, &c. Dated Ann. 1227·*

charitable

St. *Thomas's* Chapel.

Chriſt-Church Water-courſe.

St. *John's* H- ſpital.

charitable relief, letting them know (as the moſt perſwaſive Rhetorick of that age) what indulgences had been granted to their benefactors by ſeveral Archbiſhops and Biſhops of former times.

This Hoſpital hath a fair Chapel to it decently kept, wherein divine Ser- **Chapel.** vice is ſaid, the Sacraments adminiſtred, and God's Word preached to them of the Houſe. Their preſent Chaplain's Stipend is the ſame with his Predeceſſors of old, 8 *l. per annum.* The Chapel hath had ſome domeſtick Benefactors. Amongſt others, one *William Garnar*, who in the Year 1511. by his Will (a) gave 40 s. to the mending of the Steeple, and 4 *l.* for a new Bell. *John Roper*, another, who in the Year 1526, by his Will (b) took order with his Executor for the new building of the ſide Chancel's *Eaſtern* Window ('being the Window, as he calls it, of our Lady's Altar) proportionable and correſpondent to that of the Quire. The Chappel affords theſe Monuments of ſome Note; as of *Alice Aſhburnham*, whoſe Monumental Inſcription is in the Margin (c).

She lieth in the ſame ſide Chancel; in the ſaid Eaſt-window whereof ſome words are yet legible (d).

In the Quire-window is the Epitaph of one *Hyllys* (e).

It is a very brave Window, having in ſo many Panes, every of the Twelve Apoſtles pourtrayed, with the ſeveral Articles of the Creed that they are ſaid to make.

In the *South*-window is a Memorial of *W. Septvans* (f).

Archbiſhop *Stratford* erecting and endowing the Vicarage of *Northgate* Church, expreſly reſerves and excepts from the Vicar thereof the Tithes of this Hoſpital in theſe words: (g) *The Oblations and Obventions of the Hoſpital of* Northgate *only excepted.* In what Caſe and Eſtate the Commiſſioners upon the Statute 37 *Henry* VIII. *cap.* 4. found the preſent Hoſpital, were it not too tedious of recital, I would here ſubjoin. I ſuſpect a fleecing of it as of other like places by the Sacrilegious Pilferers of thoſe ravenous and wretched times, ſet upon the ſpoil even of (what the Proverb might have ſtav'd them from) the very ſpittle it ſelf. I could inſtance in ſome particulars wherein it ſuffered, but my haſt will not permit me.

Weſtgate-Street.

I Have now ſurrounded the Suburbs, yet having hitherto ſaid nothing of **Weſtgate-** *Weſtgate*-Street, the Suburbs (I mean) lying without *Weſtgate*, exempt from **ſtreet.** the Liberty and Franchiſe of the City, give me leave here to give it a place apart, and therewith to finiſh my Survey of the Suburbs, and then I ſhall enter the Walls.

I have ſeen a preſentment in Eire, inrolled in the King's Exchequer of the 21 of *Edward* I. wherein (h) (*among other things*) this Street (*Weſtgate*-Street) is preſented and avouched, how truly I know not, to have anciently belonged to the Citizens of *Canterbury*, ſubject with the City to Tax and Aid; but in King *John*'s time to have been taken from the City by *Hubert* the Archbiſhop, to the City's great damage; in regard Merchants and men of Worth and Eſtates withdrew themſelves thither, and there hous'd themſelves, and were defended of the Archbiſhop, againſt the City's impoſitions. But whether this part of our City's Suburbs, were not from all Antiquity, as now it is, clearly exempted from the Franchiſe and Liberty thereof, becauſe part of the Archbiſhop's Manor (and Hundred) of *Weſtgate*, as we now call it, or of *Stourſeat*, as of old it was named, diſtinct from the City-Hundred (as it ſeems it was no other of old) may deſerve Inquiry and Conſideration; and the rather (ſith *Doomſday*-Book records, that the Archbiſhop then challenged to have (i) *Forfeiture in Ways without the City, on both ſides where the Land of the*

(a) *Penes Regiſt. Conſiſt. prædict.* (b) *Ibidem.* (c) *Orate pro anima Aliciæ Aſhburnham filiæ & hæredis Willielmi Tooke armigeri & Aliciæ Woodland uxoris ejus & antea fuit uxor Thomæ Roper Gent. quæ obiit* xvii. *die April. Anno R. R. Hen.* 8. xv. *& Anno Domini* 1524. *Cujus anima, &c.* (d) *Orate pro ——— Rooper & pro bono ——— Thomaſinæ uxoris ejus ——— Domini* 1529. (e) *Orate pro bono ſtatu ———Hyllys fratris iſtius Hoſpitalis & Prior, qui ab hoc ſeculo migravit, qui feneſtram iſtam fieri fecit, Anno Domini* 1474. (f) *Orate pro animabus Domini Willielmi Septvans & —— conſortis ſuæ.* (g) *Oblationibus & obventionibus Hoſpitalis de* Northgate, *duntaxat exceptis.* (h) *Inter alia.* (i) *Forisfacturam in viis extra Civitatem ex utraque parte ubi terra ſua eſt.*

Archbishop lies ; because the Archbishop, in Right of his See, is (a) Lord of the Soil on either side this Street. It makes much for this what *Edmerus* (b) said upward of 500 Years agone ; That in the Lands of the Archbishoprick throughout the Kingdom, by an ancient Custom and Usage, the Archbishop hath the sole managing of things as well Human as Divine. But enough of the Street.

Ferry. Somewhat I have heard of a *Ferry* sometime at this place, belonging, as I am told, to the Archbishop, who did arrent it out for 16 *d. per annum.* But I have seen no Record to warrant the relation, and therefore no more of that until I be better instructed.

The Archbishop and the Citizens , both (as bound by Oath, if I mistake not) standing in the defence and maintenance of their Liberties ; the one of his See, the other of their City, have anciently much differed about Liberties here, but now and of a long time, all such matters have been well accorded and setled between them ; wherefore because I much desire they should ever so continue, (c) professedly I decline the discourse of their Quarrels, lest I seem to rub up old Sores.

Having now done with *Westgate*-Street, I will take the next Way into the City, and that is by *Westgate.* But ere we pass or enter further than the Gate, I must, according to my proposed Method, premise and say somewhat of the Wards of the City.

Division of the City into Wards.

Number and names of the Wards.

THE Wards of our City at this day are, as (I take it) they ever were, nor more nor less than six in number. In name distinguished and differenced from each other, by the names of the six principal Gates, that is, 1. *Westgate*-Ward. 2. *Newingate*-Ward. 3. *Northgate*-Ward. 4. *Worthgate*-Ward. 5. *Burgate*-Ward, and 6. *Ridingate*-Ward. Of that number at first, haply in imitation of the Shires division into 6 Lathes , whereof it did of old consist.

Their original.

Of the first division made of the City into Wards, neither written Record, nor unwritten Tradition makes any mention. But I conceive it very ancient. The whole City (it seems) in the Conqueror's time, was but one intire Hundred. For *Doomsday*-Book speaking of the Churches Manor of *Barton*, which it calleth *North-wood*, saith it was (d) of the Hundred of *Canterbury*, as the very words are. If so, it was not long ere a sub-division made of it, haply for more easy and good Government; into divers several Hundreds, namely into the six Wards or Hundreds now under our Survey. For the more ancient appellation and term given to those our Cities modern sub-divisions of Wards, was Hundred, as almost all our eldest deeds and other like evidences do witness, which generally, close with a *memorandum*, that they were first made and recorded in the Hundred of that Division (as in the Hundred of *Westgate*, *Burgate* , and so alike for the rest) and afterwards in the Burgmote of the City. Another term they had somewhat varying from the other in sound, but of synonymal sense and signification with it, which was *Bertha*, a frequent phrase in our ancient evidences.

These Divisions, *Fitz-Stephens*, in his description of *London*, endeavouring to parallel it, all he could, with old *Rome*, calls Regions. Every of these Divisions, Hundreds, Wards, Regions, was committed and intrusted , for reiglement, to an Alderman, one in office and authority, the same (I take it) with (e) the Hundreds Ealdor, as our Ancestors would phrase it.

I will spare all discourse touching (what many men's interpretation hath made of vulgar knowledge) the word, Alderman, both Name, and Office, in general, derived, traduced and descended unto us from great antiquity, and confine my self to speak of those only set over our City Wards. Whose antiquity I conceive to be from about *Richard* I. time ; the generality of these Aldermen being said to be of that ages production (f) (four hundred years old and upwards.)

(a) *Dominus fundi.* (b) *Hist. Novor. lib.* 1. (c) *Ex professo.*
(d) *De hundredo de Cantuarberia.* (e) *Præpositus Hundredi.* (f) *Vide D. Hen.*
Spelmanni *Glossar. in hac voce.*

Thefe

These Aldermen, every of them, had and kept within their Ward, and haply (as the Jews held theirs (*a*)) at their several Gates , a Court holden every three weeks, which was called of our anceſtors ſometime the Hundred-Court, ſometime the Wardmote, that is, the meeting or aſſembly of the **Wardmote.** Hundred or Ward, or the Portmote, as the Juriſdiction was called *Port-ſoka*.

Their Office, from their name, was called an *Aldermanrie*; which it ſeems **Aldermanrie.** was not (as now) elective, but as free-hold either demiſable or deviſable , (*b*) *at the will and pleaſure* of him or her that held the ſame : or if neither demiſed, nor deviſed of him nor her in life time, but indiſpoſed at death, then as inheritance and fee, deſcended to the next Heir at law ; and thence it was that (as I find) moſt of the ſame *Aldermanries* continued in a name and family, through many deſcents and ſucceſſions, as that of *Burgate* to the *Chiches*, of *Northgate* to the *Polres* or *Pollers*, as we now write it, of *Newingate* to the *Digges*, of *Worthgate* to the *Cokyns*, afterward to the *Tiernes*, of *Weſtgate* to the *Brownes*, and ſo of the reſt.

This laſt of *Weſtgate*, was in 10 *Richard* II. given by the Will (*c*) of *Henry Garnate* to *Sara* his wife. It ſometimes was in the Abbat of St. *Auguſtin*'s poſſeſſion, who (as *Thorne* tells me) Anno 1278. gave it to Mr. *Nicholas Doge*, (*d*) *To have and to hold the ſame with all it's appurtenances, as well within the City of* Canterbury *as without, in the Suburbs of the ſame or elſe where of the ſaid Abbat and Convent for ever, paying therefore yearly into our Treaſury* x l. *Sterling for all Services, ſaving the ſuit of the* Burgmote *of* Canterbury, *which for that reaſon he is bound to hold.* As *Thorne*'s words are. Before this, *i. e.* in the beginning of *Henry* III. time, I find (*e*) it enjoyed by one *William* (as he writes himſelf) *Ciſſor Domini Regis*, the King's Taylor, I take it. But of late days it was the *Brownes*. Whoſe then ſeat and inheritance (before the *Septvans*) was the Manor of *Milton*, or *Middleton* by *Canterbury* (from whence ſo called is of vulgar conjecture :) and continued to the name of the *Brownes*, until of late the inheritrix married to *Robert Honywood* Eſquire, Son of that famous *Mary Honywood* (of whom I leave you to take further information, if her fame ſave you not the labour , from her Monument's Inſcription or Epitaph in Dr. *Hakewill* (*f*)) and father of Sir *Robert Honywood* of *Charing*, and Sir *Thomas Honywood* of *Marks*-Hall in *Eſſex*, whoſe it now is, the anceſtor of whom Sir *George Browne*, in *Richard* III. days, taking part with *Lancaſtrian Henry* VII. was, by Parliament, deprived for it of this *Aldermanry*, but his Heirs ſoon after, *i. e.* in the 1 *Henry* VII. repoſſeſſed of it.

I inſiſt the more upon this *Aldermanry*, becauſe I conceive it to have been, if not abſolutely the chief, yet one of more reſpect and conſequence than the reſt ; which were all bought or otherwiſe gotten into the City , and made eligible by the Mayor and Commonalty early to that this was, which (it ſeems) came not in until about the time of the New ordination made by *Henry* VII. which appoints two Aldermen to every Ward. In ſome reſpects alſo it differed from the reſt, which (I take it) were held only by Freemen and inhabitants of the *Franchiſe*, whereas this was holden neither by one nor t'other, a great inconvenience to the City , as in the fore-cited act of Parliment (1 *Richard* III.) in the preface of it, is ſuggeſted. So much of the Wards in general. Which, it ſeems by an ancient Record (*g*), were annexed and appertaining to the Fee-Ferme paid by the City to the King , of whom they held *in capite*. You ſhall find a copy of it in my Appendix, Numb. VI.

Now of each of them in ſeveral, beginning, becauſe I ſtaid you (as you may remember) at *Weſtgate*, with *Weſtgate*-Ward; and obſerving and ſurveying ſuch things (as I ſhall do likewiſe afterwards in the reſt) as occur therein any thing worthy of note or Memory : ſaving that I ſhall reſerve the Churches to a future mention by themſelves.

(a) *Deuter. Cap.* 21. *ver*: 19. *& cap.* 16.　(b) *Ad libitum.*　(c) *Lib. Camera Civitatis.*　(d) *Tenend' & habend' eandem cum omnibus appendiciis tam in civitate Cant. quam extra in ſuburbio ejuſdem vel alibi, de præfato Abbate & Conventu in perpetuum, reddendo inde annuatim in theſaurario noſtro.* xl. *ſterlingorum pro omnibus ſervitiis, ſalva ſecta Burgmoti Cant. quam ob eandem cauſam facere tenet* [*lege tenetur.*]
(e) *Lib. eccleſ. Chriſti Cant.*　　　(f) *Apology. lib.* 3. *cap.* 5 *Sect.* 7. *pag.* 224.　　　(g) *Record. de An.* 19. *Rich.* 2.

Weſtgate Ward.

MArching on therefore from the Gate into the City, by the high Street (that, I mean, terminated by this Gate at the Weſt, and by the oppoſite *Newingate* at the Eaſt-end) we have on this ſide *Kingsbridge*, on either hand of tis a Gate that leads us to a ſeveral ruined Monaſtery. That on the right hand late the bare-footed Franciſcans, or the Minorite-Obſervant-mendicant-Gray-Friers. The other on our left, late the Minors alſo, or the Prædicant-black-Friers.

The Gray-Friers.

Gray Friers

I will begin with the Gray-FF, or Franciſcans. So called from *Seraphical* St. *Francis* the inſtitutor of their Order. The legend of whoſe life and miracles, becauſe too tedious for my intended ſhort method, and too too fabulous moſt what, I doubt, for your belief, for mine I am ſure; I have thought good rather to overpaſs in ſilence, than to trouble either my ſelf to write, or you to read the rabble of fopperies (if no worſe) that are written of it and them, legible in *Matt. Pariſ. Polyd. Virg.* but more largely in Owen's genealogy of Monks, &c. the *Chronicon Minorum*, and elſewhere.

Leaving therefore (I ſay) their Founder and Patron, I come to the Friers *(a)* themſelves. They were called Minors or Minorites, from the humility and lowlineſs of mind which by the preſcript of their Founder they ought ever to have: Obſervant, to diſtinguiſh them from a looſer ſort of Franciſcans, than whom theſe were more careful and obſervant to keep the ſtrict Rules and Orders of St. *Francis*, and were therefore alſo called Regular Franciſcans : Mendicant, becauſe pretending to Evangelical Perfection, and therefore profeſſing wilful Poverty, they ſubſiſted chiefly upon Alms ; which they uſed, with the Predicants, *Auguſtins*, and *Carmelites*, to ask and receive *(b)* from door to door; whereby *(c)* chiefly Friers were differenced from Monks, who kept home, and lived upon their own in common : Gray, from their Habit, (which (in imitation of their Founder *(d)*), was a long Gray Coat down to their heels, with a Cowl or Hood ; and a Cord or Rope about their Loins, inſtead of a Girdle. Their Governor's proper Name and Stile was *Guardianus.* *(e)* " The Monks in former times, (ſays one) did not live " all together under one Roof, but had little Cottages built up and down " through the Mountains and Foreſts. This Cuſtom of Solitarineſs being " left off, they began afterwards to dwell in Societies, fram'd by political " Conſtitutions ; one of them being choſen as Chief or Governor, who ſhould " rule and govern them and preſide over the Monaſtery. The *Greeks* call'd " him *Archimandrita*, and *Cœnobiarcha* ; but we commonly call him *Abbat* : " Altho in proceſs of time, it came to paſs, that the Orders of Monks being " multiplied, the Titles alſo of him that preſided over the Monaſteries, were, " in like manner, multiplied : Hence the *Dominicans* call him, the *Prior* ; the " *Franciſcans* call him, the *Guardian* ; the *Trinitarians* call him, the *Miniſter.*

Theſe *Franciſcans* came firſt into *England* about the Year 1224. in King *Henry* III. Reign ; as did the *Dominicans* *(f)* [ſeven Years *(g)* before them, *viz. Anno* 1217. *N. B.*]. How or where they were afterwards entertained with Proviſion, and Accommodation of Houſing, I find not until the Year 1270. By which time, it ſeems (whether by their Piety, or Policy, I know not) they had ſo inſinuated themſelves into the favour of a devout and worthy Citizen, and of a flouriſhing Family then in the City (as ſtill in the County)

(a) *Qui dicantur Monachi & qui Fratres, item & quo diſtent. vide Panor. ſup. cap. Cum qua. ext. De judic. l. 2. Decretal. & conſil. 27. parte ſecunda.* (b) *Oſtiatim.* (c) *Duaren. de Beneſic. l 1. c 23.* (d) *Polyd Virg. ac. Invent Rer. lib. 7. cap 4* (e) *Monachi olim non omnes ſimul commorabantur, ſed domunculas ſparſim per montes & ſaltus ſtructas habebant : quo derelicto, inceperunt poſtea ad modum Reip. in communitate habitare, uno eorum electo velut principe & gubernatore, qui eos regeret & gubernaret, praeſſet Monaſterio, quem Græci appellabant archimandrita & cœnobiarcha, nos vero communiter vocamus abbatem, lice temporis lapſu factum ſit, ut, multiplicatis monachorum ordinibus illorum nomina etiam multiplicata ſint : unde apud Dominicanos vocatur Prior, apud Franciſcanos Guardianus, apud Trinitarios miniſter.* Barthol. Cartagena. *in expo. titul. jur. Canon. lib. 3. titul. 35.* (f) Harpsfield. *a Hiſt. Eccl. Angl. ſæcul. 13. cap. 11.* (g) *Knyghton.*

one *John Digg*, or *Diggs*, then an Alderman, and 12 Years before (1258) and also 3 Years after (1273.) one of the Bailiffs of the City, whom *Wever* miscalls Sir *John Diggs*, that he purchased for them the Island in *Canterbury*, then called *Bynnewith*, and shortly after translated them thither. (*a*). Whence the place, this Island might derive the Name of *Bynnewith*, if I may conjecture, I shall tell you, either from a composition of [a *British* word *Guith*, or a *Saxon* word *With*, join'd with the *Saxon* word *Binnan*; W. S.] signifies within; and *With*, an Island or Separation, as it were the Island within, in distinction of it from an Island sometime lying without the City by *Westgate* Northward, called simply *With*; whereof in the elder Rentals of *Christ-Church*, mention is made thus: (*b*) *A small Island without* Westgate, *toward the* North, *called* With. Or else *Binnewith quasi Bine-with*, the double Island; indeed it is no other, and an ancient Rental of *Christ-Church* (which once had Ground, Houses, and Fee here) speaks of Rent in St. *Peter*'s Parish, payable (*c*) *Of Two little Islands, where was* Crinemilne. For thereabout sometime stood a Miln of *Christ-Church*, so called; unto which the Lane in St. *Peter*'s called *Mead-lane*, and of *Speed* in his Map of the City, miscalled *Maidenlane*, did lead; and from thence was called *Crinemelne-lane*. For in an exchange, *Anno* 1294, made between *Christ-Church* and St. *Austin*'s, three Tenements in St. *Peter*'s Parish in *Canterbury* being granted to the *Abby*; one of them is thus described and bounded. (*d*) " A certain Tenement lying " in a great Garden of the said Abbat, nigh the Land which belongs to the " *Minor Friers* of *Canterbury*, on the *South* side, in a Lane called *Medlane*, and " which formerly (saith the Deed) was called *Crine-Mill-lane*. But may it not more probably be called *Binnewith* (that is, *Binney-Island*) from the same *radix* with the Mead or Meadow-ground by it, called to this day *Binney-Meads*, as the Bridge thereaway which we call *Bingley*-bridge is rightly called *Binney-*brigde, from the *Saxon Binnan ea*, signifying (as I said) within or between the Water; because [like to that which some call a *Mediamnis* or *Interamnis. W. S.*] lying and inclosed within or between our *Stour*, or River's double Channel, bounding it on either side. Whence the Codicil or *Landboc* of *Cenulph* the Mercian that gave that Ground to the Church, copied in my *Appendix, Numb.* XV. thus describes it to lye: (*e*) *Between two not far distant Streams of the River, which is called the* Stour. Which Mr. *Lambard* reads thus; (*f*) [as it is in the Margin; corruptly (I suppose) which cannot be well understood in any Signification otherwise, than of the Spring-head of these Streams or Currents *N. B.*]; and accordingly would send us further up the Stream, to find out this Ground about our River's Spring-heads; whereas the very Name yet remaining, shews it to lye here.

I may not so leave the Place's Name. For though ancient and even obsolete with us, yet of so much note with our Ancestors, as it served to give Name to a Family of Citizens, sometime the Residentiaries of the Place, and from thence called the *Withs*, or (as more frequently) the *Binnewiths*, whereof one *John Binnewith* about the beginning of H. 3. Reign was a Benefactor to *Herbaldown* Hospital, where I have seen his Charter with the Seal appendant, in the circumference of it thus circum-inscribed, SIGILL. IOIANNIS DE WITD. And one *Arnold Binnewith* was, *Anno* 1221, and also again about the Year 1227, one of the Bayliffs of the City (*g*). The Friers having gotten possession of the place, both the Island and her former *Incolæ* or Inhabitants, soon after lost their Names. But leaving that, I proceed.

The Friers being here seated, and many Houses and much Ground of the Fee of *Christ-Church* Monks lying within the *Ambitus* or Precinct of their Monastery, they (it seems) made bold to usurp them as their own, because within the Confines of their Seat, and so *de facto* made themselves absolute Lords and Possessors of the Island. The Monks seeing the common People much inclined to favour them, and not willing to incur theirs, lest it might bring with

Binnewith.

A Family of *Binnewiths.*

(*a*) *Emit Insulam vocatam Bynnewight in Cantuar. & locum Portæ super Stour-street ad opus Fratrum Minorum, & tempore opportuno transtulit Fratres ad illam*, as *Wever* from *Leland*. Ancient funeral Monum. pag 134 (*b*) *Parva Insula extra Westgate, versus Aquilonem, vocata* With.
(*c*) *De duabus parvis Insulis ubi fuit Crinemilne.* (*d*) *Viz. quoddam tenementum jacens in magno gardino dicti Aobatis, juxta terram fratrum Minorum Cant. ex parte Australi, in venella quæ dicitur Medlane, & quæ olim vocabatur Crinemelle-lane. In Lib. ecclef. Cant.* (*e*) *Inter duos gremiales rivos fluminis quod dicitur Stour.* (*f*) *Inter duos genitales rivos, &c.* (*g*) *Lib. Hosp. de Eastbridge.*

it

it tho Peoples difpleafure alfo, make a virtue of, as it were, a neceffity ; and to fhew themfelves as forward in Charity toward them, as the common People, after the Friers (by their connivance 'tis like) had been a pretty while in poffeffion, without paying or yielding to the Monks their accuftomed Rents and Services, which their *quondam* Tenants were bound to pay, *viz. Anno* 1294. by Compofition, remit unto them all Arrearages and Duties paft *gratis*, or *intuitu charitatis*, as they phrafe it, and for the future make them an abatément of almoft the moiety of the Rent; as the Compofition will fhew; which (becaufe it fets forth in fome fort the ftate of the Ifland, and how it was peopled before the Friers time) being tranfcribed from the Records of the Cathedral, I will give in my *Appendix*, in the Words of the Record. The Sum of which is as followeth.

Numb. XVI.

" *A. D.* 1294. It was agreed between the Prior and Convent of *Chrift-*
" *Church* in *Canterbury* on the one part, and the Guardian and Convent of the
" Minor Friers on the other part, That whereas the Prior and Convent of
" *Chrift-Church* had divers Tenements of their Fee, fituate within the Precinct
" of the faid Minor Friers, *viz.* a Tenement formerly of *Samuel* the Dyer, for
" which was paid them the Yearly Rent of vii *d. qu.* Alfo a Tenement former-
" ly of *Beringer* in *With*, for which xii *d.* Rent was paid. Alfo a Tenement of
" the fame *Beringer* in *Ottemod*, Rent v *d.* Alfo a Tenement formerly of *Serona*
" of *Bocton*, Rent vi *d.* Alfo for Rent of *Wibert*, formerly Prior of *Chrift-Chrift*
" nigh *Ottewell*, for which was paid xii *d.* Alfo a Tenement of *Stephen* the Son
" of *Lewin Samuel*, for which was paid xviii *d.* They freely remitted all Arrea-
" ges of the faid Rents for the faid Tenements, on condition that the faid Mi-
" nor Friers caus'd to be paid for the faid Tenements to the Monks of *Chrift-*
" *Church* in full for all Services and Demands, the Yearly Sum of iii *s.*
" Rent, *&c.*

How this might ftand with their Founders Rule and their own Vow, I fee not. For confult their Rule delivered articulately in *Matt. Paris*, and you fhall find them clearly debarred and difabled, both by their Vow of Poverty, and by exprefs Prefcript befide from all (*a*) *Propriety.* (*b*) " The Brethren or Friers
" may appropriate (faith the Rule) nothing to themfelves, neither Houfe, nor
" Ground, nor any kind of Subftance : And as Pilgrims and Strangers in this
" World, ferving the Lord in Poverty and Humility, they go and beg Alms
" with Confidence, *&c.* Whence that of *Durand.* (*c*) and others, (*d*) *The Men-*
" *dicant Friers are uncapable of Poffeffions.*

Gray Friers privileges.

Thefe *Francifcans* or Minorite Friers being a great Prop to the Papacy, were profecuted by feveral Popes with many Privileges, Immunities, Indulgences, and what not Graces, that might affure them the Pope's faft Friends, and faithful Sons and Servants. Befide their Exemption and Immunity from Epifcopal and all other ordinary Jurifdiction, in matter of Tithes they were privileged from Payment of any, either of their Houfe, their Orchard (or Garden) and the Nutriment, *i. e.* the Herbage or Agiftment of their Cattel, as in the Decretals (*e*). They had withal in matter of Burial *liberam fepulturam* (paying the fourth part of the Obventions to the Parifh Church) ; whofoever would, might elect and have their Church or Cœmitery for his place of Burial (*f*). And that was a thing whereof multitudes were ambitious; and the rather, becaufe they were made believe, that whofo was buried amongft them, efpecially if in the holy and virtuous Habit of a Frier, fhould not only be fecured from evil Spirits that' would elfe haply difturb the quiet of his Grave, but alfo be as fure to go to Heaven. [I have read of feveral Perfons of high Degree, ambitious to live, dye, and to be interred in this Habit. *Gregory* IX. coming to the Papacy, was the firft Pope that put it on, who frequently wore it, and willed to be buried in it. Pope *Martin* the IV*th* was likewife buried in the fame Habit, as were alfo divers Kings, by name *James* and *Alphonfus* Kings of *Arragon*, and many other Eminent Men befide, whereof the Reader may inform himfelf from *Landmeter* (*g*), as likewife from the Bee-hive of the *Romifh*

(*a*) *Peculium.*   (*b*) *Fratres nihil fibi approprient, nec domum, nec locum , nec aliquam rem. Et tanquam peregrini & advenæ in hoc faculo, in paupertate & humilitate Domino famulantes, vadunt pro elemofyna confidenter, &c.*   (*c*) *Specul. jur. de monach. ftat. lib.* 4. *Part.* 3 *n* 7.
(*d*) *Mendicantes funt poffeffionum incapaces.*   (*e*) *Nimis prava.* 12. *de exceffib. prælat.*
(*f*) *Cap. Dudum. de fepult. in Clementin.*   (*g*) *De vetere Clericorum & Monachorum habitu. Part.* 2. *c.* 7.*Pag.* 123.

Church,

Church, *lib.* 1. *c.* 2. *W. S.*] There is authentick Record of many worthy Perſonages, and of Worſhipful Families that have been here interred : The Catalogue of whom *Wever* (*a*) hath collected, and delivers, but under a wrong Title, ſaying they were buried in the White, whereas he ſhould have ſaid the Gray Friers ; as I can make good to the ſatisfaction of any that makes a doubt hereof.

As for Benefactors to this Monaſtery, I find theſe. One *William Woodland* of Holy Croſs Pariſh, *Anno* 1450, by his Will (*b*) gave 5 *l.* toward the Reparation of their Church, and 5 Marks beſide to the repairing of their Dortor. *Hamon Beale,* a Citizen, and in his time twice Mayor of *Canterbury,* chuſing their Church for the place of his Burial, as *Iſabel* his Wife had formerly done, gave 40 *s.* in Money to the Convent. Indeed (to be ſhort) almoſt every Teſtate dying Man of the City and neighbouring Parts of any Worth, remembred theſe Friers : The *Dominicans* alſo and the *Auguſtines* of this City, in their Wills with ſome Legacy, more or leſs. One domeſtick Benefactor I meet with, one *Richard Martin,* the Guardian (I take it) of the Houſe, who in the Year 1498, by his Will (*c*) gave liberally both to the Church and Convent. He was (as it ſeems by his Will) Parſon alſo of *Ickham,* and Vicar of *Lyd* in *Kent.* But what may he mean by writing himſelf (as he doth) Biſhop of the Univerſal Church ? A Title ſo cryed down and condemned as Antichriſtian by Pope *Gregory* the Great. I conceive he was a Titular Biſhop ; a Biſhop in Name and Title only ; endued with the Order, but not with the Juriſdiction Epiſcopal, having no particular Charge to intend, but generally Officiating as Biſhop in any part of the Chriſtian Church. Theſe Titular Biſhops were frequent with us in thoſe days. About the ſame time one *Thomas Wells,* the Prior of St. *Gregory's* by *Canterbury* ; in his Will (*d*) writes himſelf Biſhop of *Sidon.* He was a Titular Biſhop likewiſe ; an Order as excepted againſt by ſome, ſo defended by others of the *Trent* Council ; whereof I leave you to inform your ſelf further (if you pleaſe) from *Tholoſanus* (*e*) and others. The Uſe made of them (I take it) was to ſupply the Dioceſan Biſhops abſence in ſuch Affairs Epiſcopal as theſe ; to wit, Conſecration of Churches, and Church-yards, and their Reconciliation, conferring of Orders, Confirmation of Children, and the like.

Titular Biſhops.

But to our Friers again. *Hugh Rich* the Guardian, or (which is all one) the Warden (as the Statute (*f*) calls him) of this Convent, was one that conſpired and ſuffered with *Elizabeth Barton* the Holy Maid of *Kent* ; whereof before in my Survey of that Nunnery.

This Monaſtery had, as the place ſtill hath, a double Gate and Way to it ; the one called (*g*) *The Eaſt-gate,* the other (*h*) *The North-gate* ; that in *Stourſtreet,* in *All-Saints* Pariſh, this in *High-ſtreet,* in St. *Peter's* Pariſh.

Let me but acquaint you, that *John Peckham* Archbiſhop of *Canterbury,* in *Edward* I. time, was firſt a Frier, and the Provincial of this Order ; and I have done with the *Franciſcans* or Gray-Friers.

The Black Friers.

Leaving theſe then, I come next to the other ſort of Minors, the *Dominican,* Black, Preaching Friers. Preaching, becauſe they were the only Preachers of all the Friers : Black, becauſe of their Habit (*i*), which was a black Cope and Cowl over a white Coat : *Dominican ,* becauſe St. *Dominick* was their Founder ; a Holy man (they ſay) contemporary with St. *Francis* ; and whoſe Diſciples (the firſt Friers of this Convent) were even coætaneous with the *Franciſcans* of this City, coming both hither much about the ſame time. It is ſaid of them, that King *Henry* III. at their coming received them kindly (ſo did *Stephen Langton* alſo the then Archbiſhop (*k*) :) and placed them at *Canterbury,* where (it ſeems) he built them this late Monaſtery, which was the firſt that the Kingdom had of that kind. Hence, and from this

Black-Friers.

1492.

(*a*) Of ancient funeral Monuments. *pag* 238.   (*b*) *In Regiſt. Conſ. Cant.*
(*c*) *In Regiſtro memorato*   (*d*) *In eod. Regiſt.*   (*e*) Syntag *juris univerſi Lib.* 15.
cap. 12. *n.* 44.   (*f*) *Anno* 25 H. 8 *cap.* 12.   (*g*) *Porta Orientalis.*
(*h*) *Porta Borealis.*   (*i*) *Polyd. Virg. de Invent. Rer. lib.* 7. *cap.* 4.   (*k*) *Harpsfield.*
Hi. Eccleſ. Anglic. Sæc. 13. *cap.* 11.

ground (I fuppofe) *Wever* takes his Warrant for attributing the erection of this Houfe to *Henry* III, The Title proper to the Governor of the *Domini-cans,* was Prior. Like the *Francifcans,* they and the Monks of *Chrift-Church*, in the fame Year with the other (1294.) came to Compofition about divers Houfes and Lands lying within their Precinct.

The Church-yard of this Monaftery was the place of Rendevous, defigned by the Citizens of *Canterbury* confpiring a Revenge to be taken of the Monks of *Chrift-Church,* for refufing them their aid, and to join with them in the finding and furnifhing of Twelve Horfemen, impofed on the City by the King, (*Edward* I.) for his Expedition againft the Rebellious *Lewelyn Fitz-Grif-fin* Prince of *Wales*; which *Stow* (a) (much miftaken in the time and fome other Circumftances) thus relates. " About this time (faith he, fpeaking of " the 1 of *Edward* III.) the like Stir was made againft the Monks of *Canterbury*; " whereof I find recorded as followeth. King *Edward* preparing an Army in- " to *Scotland,* commanded the Bailiffs and Citizens of *Canterbury* to furnifh him " Twelve Horfemen, and fend them to *Newcaftle*; toward which Charge the " Citizens required aid of the Monks; who anfwered them, that without the " affent of the King and their Archbifhop they would not agree thereunto, " for fo much as the Kings of *England* had founded their Church in free and " perpetual Alms. Whereupon, *William Childham* Bailiff, and many Com- " mons of the City affembling themfelves in the Preaching Friers Church- " yard, confpired and fwore againft the Monks, as followeth:

1. That they would overthrow the Pentifes, Windows, and Miln, belong-ing to the Monks.
2. That no Citizen fhould dwell in any Houfe belonging to the Monks.
3. That all Rents belonging to the Monks of *Canterbury* fhould be gathered to the Ufe of the Commons.
4. That no man fhould fend or fell to the Monks any Victuals.
5. That they fhould feize all the Horfes and Beafts that came into the City with Carriage to the Monks.
6. That all fuch Monks as came forth of their Houfe fhould be fpoiled of their Garments.
7. That a Trench fhould be caft, to ftop all men from going in or coming out.
8. That every Pilgrim fhould at his entring fwear that he fhould make no Offering.
9. Alfo that every of thofe Commons aforefaid, fhould wear on their Finger a Ring of Gold that belonged to *Thomas Becket.* Thus he. [But by the good means of *Robert Kilwardby,* then Archbifhop, the Citizens were pacified, and their fierce Attempt timely fuppreffed. *W. S.*]

This Church-yard is in part now become the (b) *Artillery-Ground* for our Young Artillery of the City.

Wever's Collection of Ancient Funeral Monuments will acquaint you of divers Perfonages of Note and Quality buried here.

Fraternities of Parifh Clerks. At this place the Parifh Clerks of the City once had and held a gild or fraternity, commonly called the Fraternity of St. *Nicholas.* I have my dire-ction for this, from the following legacy of one *Richard Cram* fometime of this City, who by his Will (c), dated 1490. gave to the Fraternity of St. *Ni-cholas* kept by the Parifh Clerks of *Canterbury*, in the houfe of the Friers Preachers of *Canterbury* vi s. viii d. as his very words are. Of thefe Frater-nities, our City hath had divers; amongft which that of the *Smiths* newly re-vived, is the moft ancient. The elder rentals of *Chrift-Church* bounding out fome Land of theirs lying without *Newingate,* make mention both of it and of certain ground belonging to it, in thefe words: (d) *The Land which belongs to the Gild, Fraternity, or Company of the Smiths.* This and all other like Fra-ternities (if the Diffolution of the Monafteries fpared them, yet) the Sta-tute of 1 *Edward* VI. *cap.* 14. took hold of, and diffipating the focieties, feized on all their goods and endowment. If any defire further information touching them and their antiquity, I refer them to Sir *Henry Spelman*'s *Gloffa-ry* (e).

_____

(a) **Annals** *in Ed. III. Vide Antiquit. Brit. in vita* Rob. Kilwardby *Archiep.*   (b) *Campus* *Martius.*   (c) *In Regiftro Confift. Cant.*   (d) *Terra quæ pertinet ad gildam fabrorum.*
(e) *In Verb. Gilda.*

This Monaftery had a treble paffage to it, namely by three Gates, one, and that the moft private, that opening before the Street by St. *Alphege* Church a fecond by the Waterlock, the third in St. *Peter*'s ftreet (as we call it) built (it feems) not long before the 30 of *Edward* III. for then thefe Friers, by their Charter or Deed pafs over to the Hofpital of *Eftbridge* a place, fhops and garden lying towards the Weft and North, *(a) Between our new Gate and the paffage or entrance to our Church in the Parifh of St. Peter, &c.* as in *Eftbridge* Book; in another part of the Book thus defcribed and bounded. *(b) In the Parifh of St.* Peter *in the City of* Canterbury *between a Garden and Manfion of the Predicant Friers towards the North and Weft, and a certain Lane called* Brekye-pot-tif-lane *toward the Eaft.*

Approaching to an end of my difcourfe touching thefe Friers, I cannot (me-thinks) clofe better than with *Matthew Paris* his relation of the controverfy, in or about the year 1243. happening between them and the *Francifcans*, which together with his Glofs (which he adds) upon it and them, is to this Effect:

A Controverfy *between the* Francifcans *and* Dominicans.

" HAving made mention of other Difcords, he fays, And left the World
" fhould feem free from difquiets and confufions multiplied on every
" fide, there was in thefe times a Controverfy ftrongly debated between the
" *Francifcans* or Minor-Friers and the *Dominicans*, or Preaching Friers;
" whereat many are fill'd with admiration. For thefe feem to have chofen the
" way of perfection, namely Poverty and Patience. The Preaching Fri-
" ers afferted, That the inftitution of their Order was more ancient, and on
" this account they claim'd the Preheminence, that their Habit alfo was
" more decent, and that they defervedly had both their Title and Office
" from Preaching. The Minors anfwered, That they had chofen a way of
" life more Severe and Humble for God's fake; and thereby were to be
" efteemed more Excellent becaufe more Holy: And that the Brethren might
" and with leave ought to pafs from the order of Preaching Friers to their
" Order, as from a lower to a better and higher Order. The Preaching
" Friers contradicted what they faid to their face, telling them, That altho'
" they, the Minor Friers, go bare-foot, in a poor vile Habit, girt
" about with Cords, yet they were not forbidden to eat Flefh, even in
" Publick, unto all fulnefs and plenty. From all which the Preaching Fri-
" ers being forbidden by their Rules, do abftain, and for thefe Reafons they
" could not pafs to the Order of the Minors, as to a higher and more ftrict
" Order; but rather the contrary. In like manner as between the Templars
" and Hofpitalers in the Holy Land, fo between thefe Friers, the enemy of
" Mankind fowing his Tares, there is rais'd a heavy Scandal, and in as much
" as they were Scholars and reputed Learned men, the Scandal became too
" too dangerous to the Univerfal Church. And which is to be efteemed
" a difmal Prefage, for three or four hundred Years or more, the whole
" Monaftical Order have not had at any time fuch a fudden rife to fo great a
" height, as the Order of thefe Friers, who within lefs than Four and
" twenty years laft paft, built their firft Manfions in *England*, which appear
" now like the ftately Palaces of Kings. Thefe are they, who lay out in-
" eftimable Treafures in Magnificent Buildings, which are daily Enlarged
" and in high Walls, tranfgreffing with all Impudence the Rules of their
" Order, paffing over the boundaries of Poverty, the foundation of their
" Profeffion; according to the Prophefie of *Hyldegarde*, They diligently
" attend upon Great and Rich Men dying, where they know there is plenty
" of Wealth, not without injury and damage to the Ordinaries, that they
" may fill themfelves with Booty; they extort Confeffions, and procure Wills
" and Teftaments to be made privately; recommending themfelves only
" and their own Order to the Charity of the Teftators, and preferring them-
" felves before all others. Hence it comes to pafs, that no Believer now
" thinks, he can be faved, unlefs he be guided by the directions of thefe

---

(1) *Inter novam portam noftram, & introitum ad ecclefiam noftram in parochia fancti Petri, &c.*
(b) *In parochiâ fancti Petri Civitatis Cant. inter gardinum & manfionem fratrum prædicatorum Cant. verfus North & Weft, & quandam venellam vocat' Brekyepotiflane verfus Eaft.*

" Fri-

" Friers, either the Preaching or the Minors. They are careful to gain
" Privileges; in the Courts of Kings and Nobles they are Counſellors, and
" Chamberlains, and Treaſurers : They are ever thruſting themſelves in for
" ordering the concerns of Marriages : They are buſy to put in execution all
" Papal Exactions, and Extortions. In their Preaching, they are either ful-
" ſome Flatterers, or bitter Reprovers, or betrayers of private Confeſſions,
" or unwary or unwiſe in their Reprehenſions. They alſo ſlight and deſpiſe
" the Authentick Orders, which were conſtituted by the Holy Fathers, name-
" ly St. *Benedict*, and St. *Auguſtin*, and the Profeſſors of thoſe Orders, as ap-
" pear'd in the cauſe of the Church of *Scardebure* : They repute the *Ceſtertian*
" Monks to be rude, ſimple, half-laymen, and mere ruſticks; the Black
" Monks, to be proud and Epicures. Thus he.

[Having given the ſenſe of the Author in Engliſh, the Reader if he pleaſeth, may conſult in the works of *Matthew Paræ*, the words in Latin, to
which I ſhall rather refer him, than to the *Appendix*, N. B.]

I have but only to tell you, That *Robert Kilwardby*, afterwards firſt Archbiſhop of *Canterbury*, and then advanced to a Cardinalſhip, was firſt a Frier of
this Sect of the *Dominicans*, and I leave them.

Eaſtbridge or *Kingsbridge* Hoſpital.

Eaſtbridge Hoſ- MY Progreſs in this Ward, brings me next to *Eaſtbridge* or *Kingsbridge*
pital. Hoſpital. An ancient Spittle, and as now known (Chriſten'd, as it were)
by the Name, ſo firſt erected and endowed by the Charity and Piety of St. *Thomas Becket* in *Hen.* 2. time; and thence to this day called the Hoſpital of St. *Thomas* the Martyr of *Eaſtbridge*. For this we have the Teſtimony of Archbiſhop
Stratford, a Succeſſor of his; who upon his novel Ordination of the Hoſpital,
and in the Charter thereof, (as ſhall be ſeen in the *Appendix*,) acknowledgeth
him the firſt Founder and Endower of it. For other Record either of the
Foundation of the Hoſpital it ſelf, or of the intent wherefore it was erected,
beſides that Charter of *Stratford*, is not, nay in his time (as it ſeems by him)
was not extant, or to be found. The reaſon probably why the Record of the
State of it, taken by the Commiſſioners upon the Stat. of 37 *Hen.* 8. *cap.* 4.
aſcribes the Foundation unto *Stratford*; whereas he (as his Charter will declare) did but reſtore the Foundation, and give Laws and a Form of Government to it, to ſupply the former which were loſt, and ſo the Hoſpital in ha-
zard of Confuſion for want of them; as you ſhall eaſily perceive by the Tranſcript or Copy of it, if you peruſe it, which is in the *Appendix*, Numb. XVII.

By this Record you may ſee who was both the firſt and ſecond Founder of
Eaſtbridge Hoſpital: The ancient Rules and Ordinances preſcribed to it; the
Union and Annexation made of St. *Nicholas* of *Herbaldown* Church to it, into
which the Leiger ſhews the Maſter's Induction and Inveſtiture by the Commiſſary of *Canterbury*, by Mandate from (the Appropriator) Archbiſhop *Stratford*.

I muſt now look back to the Times intervening theſe two Founders. In
which I find (a) *Hubert* the Archbiſhop in King *John*'s time, an eſpecial Benefactor to this Spittle; giving to it the Tithes of *Weſtgate*-Mill, of a Mill and
two Salt-pits at (b) *Herewic* (in or near *Whitſtable*, I take it); of a Windmill in
Raculfre, and of another Windmill in *Weſthalimot* in *Thanet*. [*Lambard* ſays,
that *Herewick* is a Borough within the Hundred of *Weſtgate*. N. B.] This, with
the Confirmation of the then Prior and Chapter of *Chriſt-Church*.

Cokyn's-Hoſpi- In this Archbiſhop's time, there was another Hoſpital neighbouring unto
tal. this of *Eaſtbridge*, called *Cokyn*'s Hoſpital (c), built and founded by one *William
Cokyn* a Citizen of *Canterbury*, and of a worthy Family, whoſe Name in his
Poſterity did long ſurvive him in this City; ſome of whom were Bayliffs of
the City in their time. The Hoſpital was dedicated to St. *Nicholas*, and (the
Virgin and Martyr) St. *Catherine*, and ſtood ſometime in the Pariſh of St. *Pe-
ter* in *Canterbury*, almoſt directly oppoſite to the now Black-Friers Gate; hav-
Cokyn's Lane. ing had a Lane by it aforetime called *Cokyn*'s-Lane, now ſhut up and built up-

---

(a) *In lib. privato hujus Hoſpitalis.*   (b) [*Hugo de Herewick filius Simonis de Herewick. Antiq.*
Carta Eccleſ. Cant. N. B.]   (c) *Ibidem.*

on, often mentioned in *Eastbridge* Book, and not forgotten of some yet living. I collect by Charters which I have seen, that the Founder lived by that Lane. And find that for 18 marks *de gersuma*, or for the consideration of 18 marks, he purchased of *Stephen* the Priest, and *Godesman*, the Sons of *Richard Mercer* of *Canterbury*, with the consent of their Widow-Mother *Cicely*, a Messuage next adjacent to his own, thus in the Deed or Charter described : *(a)* " All that " Messuage with its Appurtenances, which is Forty two Foot broad towards " the King's High-way, and in length so far as reacheth from the King's " High-way even to the River which is called the *Sture*. Which said Messuage " lies next to a Stone-Messuage of the said *William*, and to a Messuage of *Wal-* " *ter* the Merchant, in the Parish of St. *Peter*. Having purchased this Mes- suage, he either builds there a new Hospital, or else converts his Purchase into one. Afterwards, by his Charter *(wherein he saith the Hospitals of St. Nicho-las*, St. *Catherine*, and St. *Thomas* of *Eastbridge* in *Canterbury*, were united, haply and probably by Archbishop *Hubert*, and that union by Pope *Innocent* confirm-ed *)* entitles these Hospitals to all his Lands, Possessions, and Chattels, and makes them his Heirs. This done, and one *Godelman* Son of *Richard* the Mer-chant, challenging an Interest in the Soil where the Hospital stood ; for 7 *s.* Consideration he is bought out, and makes a Charter to Archbishop *Hubert*, acknowledged in a full *Burgmote* of the City, of release of all his right there-unto. *(b)* That is, *Of the land* (as his words are) *in which the Hospital is built, which* William Cokyn *Founded , which lies between the lands late of* William Co-kyn *and the land of* Thomas *the Merchant, namely, from the King's high way unto the* Stour. The Priory of St. *Gregory* (it seems) had some interest here also. For *Robert* the Prior and his Convent of the place, did by their Charter made to the Hospital confirm, *(c) The Donation which* William Cokyn *made to the Brethren of the Hospital of St.* Nicholas *and St.* Catherine *and St.* Thomas *the Martyr of* Eastbridge, *of that Messuage, which is in the Parish of St.* Peter, *lying next to the Hospital of St.* Nicholas *and St.* Katherine *towards the West, which is in our tenure*, as the Charter runs. *Eastbridge* Hospital being thus (*i. e.* by union or consolidation) possessed, and become owners of *Cokyn's* Hospital ; it ceased soon after (I take it) to be used as an Hospital, or in the way of an Hospital, and was hired and rented out. In the year 1238. *Peter* the then Rector or Keeper of *Eastbridge* Hospital, and the Brothers of the same, grant and demise to one *William Samuel* a parcel thereof, to wit, *(d) The whole Tene-ment with all the Edifices of Wood or Stone and all the appurtenances which lye in the Parish of St.* Peter *in* Canterbury, *between the house of* Osmund Polre, *which is on the East-side,and the lane which is called* Cokyn's-lane *which is on the West-side, and the High-way which is one North-side, and the Sture which is on the South-side.* The lane there (by the way) was as yet open, as you may see ; and that it might continue so, hearken to what follows in the Deed. *(e) It is moreover agreed between the aforesaid Parties, That neither the aforesaid* Peter, *nor his Brethren, nor his or their Successors, nor the said* William, *nor his Heirs, nor his or their Assigns, shall stop up the said Lane, but both parties may have free use of Ingress and Egress through the said Lane.* So much for *Cokyn's* Hospital : and now I return to *Eastbridge*.

Stephen Langton the next Archbishop after *Hubert*, by his and his Convents Charter *(f)*, confirms unto this Hospital, the gift of *Blean* Church or Par-sonage, made unto it by the Patron, *Hamon Crevequer*, after the resignation of it by the till then incumbent Parson, *William Crevequer*. Whereupon the Ma-ster or Keeper of the Hospital, became afterwards Parson there, to whom *Blean* parson-age And parson-age house.

(a) Totum illud messuagium cum omnibus pertinentiis suis, quod habet in latitudine versus cheminium in Domini Regis 42 *pedes, & in longitudine quantum extendit à cheminio Domini Regis, usque ad aquam quæ dicitur Sture. Quod vero messuagium adjacet proximo messuagio lapideo prædicti Willielmi, & messuag. Walteri mercatoris in parochia sancti Petri.* **(b)** *De terra in qua Hospitale fundatum est quod Willielmus Cokyn fecit, quæ jacet inter terram quæ fuit W. Cokyn, & terram Thomæ mercatoris, scil. à magna via regali usque ad Sturam.* **(c)** *Donationem quam Willielmus Cokyn fecit fratribus Hosp. Sancti Nicholai, & Sanctæ Catherinæ, & Sancti Thomæ martyris de Eastbridge, de illo messuagio quod est in parochia Sancti Petri proximo adjacen' Hosp. Sancti Nicholai & Sanctæ Catherinæ versus West, quod est in tenura nostra.* **(d)** *Totum tenementum cum ædificiis supra positis tam ligneis quam lapideis & omnibus pertinentiis suis quod jacet in parochia Sancti Petri Cant. inter domum Osmundi Polre quæ est ex parte orientali, & venellam quæ appellatur Cokyncslane, quæ est ex parte occidentali, & Regiam stratam quæ est ex parte Aquilonari, & Sturam quæ est ex parte Australi* **(e)** *Præterea ita convenit in-ter partes prædict' quòd nec prædict' Petrus, nec fratres nec successores eorum, nec prædict' Willielmus, nec hæredes sui nec sui assignati poterint prædict' venellam obstruere, quin utraque pars possit uti commodè via prædicta venella eundo & redeundo.* **(f)** *Liber memorat.*

R and

and to the Brothers of the Hofpital the fame *Hamon*, by another Charter grants (*a*) *all that Meffuage with the appurtenances, which was* Lefwin's *the Prieft, Parfon of the faid Church, and which was afterwards the Archdeacon's of* Petter's, *Parfon of the faid Church, and which was afterwards* William's *de* Crevequer, *Parfon of the faid Church* : that is, the Parfonage houfe. The Parfonage thus to the Hofpital, affigned and confirmed in *proprios ufus*, that is, appropriated, Archbifhop *Iflep* afterwards, induced by many reafons, Founds a perpetual Vicarage there, indowing it in fuch wife as the Charter or Inftrument thereof in my *Appendix*, will demonftrate, *Numb.* XVIII. [The date of this Inftrument fhews, that it was *Simon Sudbury*, not *Simon Iflip*, who founded this Vicarage, in the year 1375, and in the firft year of his Tranflation to the See of *Canterbury* : And in the Inftrument it's faid, that *Simon Iflip* late Archbifhop was dead. *N. B.*]

Blean Vicarage

At this place (the *Blean*) lay the moft of this Hofpital's Demeans and Revenews. Amongft which the principal (I take it) is the Manor of *Blean* given (*b*) to the Hofpital by *Thomas de Roos de Hamlack* , *Ann.* 33 *Edward* III. the fame Man (I take it) whofe death *Walfingham* thus mentions in the year 1399. (*c*) *In the fame year, Lord* Thomas de Roos, *in his return from the* Holy Land, *died in the Ifland of* Cyprus *in the City* Paphos, *through the badnefs of the air of that Countrey* : Says he. By probable conjecture, he dwelt at *Chilham* Caftle, from whence the year before, his Mother *Margery* Lady *Roos* daughter of *Bartholomew* Lord *Badlefmere*, and Widow of *William de Roos de Hamlack*, who as a benefactor to the work, hath his name and effigies fet up and pourtrayed in a Window of the Chapter-houfe at *Chrift-Church*, dates a Charter of her's to the Mafter of this Hofpital, and at her prefentation, as Patronefs in the year 1349, the See of *Canterbury* being then void, one *Osbertus* is admitted by the Prior and Chapter. (*d*) *To the free Chapel of the Bleffed Virgin* Mary *in the Caftle of* Chilham, there perfonally to ferve and officiate as a perpetual Chaplain (*e*). This by the by.

The very next year after this gift of the Manor of *Blean*, by *Thomas de Roos*, *viz. Ann.* 34 *Edward* III. one Sir *John Lee* Knight by his Deed or Charter (as I find by a Copy of it in the Leiger of the houfe) gave to this Hofpital one meffuage, 180 acres of Land, 27 *s.* rent of affife, 9 Cocks and 21 Hens (*f*) *in the Village of* Blean, *for the Increafe of Works of Piety in the faid Hofpital.*

With leave and liking of Archbifhop *Langham*, a certain Chantery in the Church of *Livingsborne*, that is *Beaksborne*, founded in the Year 1314. by one *James* of *Bourne*, with the Revenues of the fame was tranflated to this Hofpital by one *Bartholomew* of *Bourne* (*g*). [This was done in the Year 1362. not by Archbifhop *Langham*, but *Iflip*; as appears by the Inftrument whereby Archbifhop *Sudbury* confirms the fame. See the *Appendix*, *Numb.* XIX. *N. B*]

There was fomtime a Windmill ftanding near the Nunnery without *Ridingate*, which this Hofpital held by the Grant of the Nuns there (*h*). The very place of Situation whereof was (*i*) *In a quarter of an Acre of Land, in little* Foxmold, *toward the Weft, in the Hundred of* Ridingate. So go the Words of the Deed. The Conditions mutually agreed upon at the time of the Grant, were, That the Nuns bearing the Fourth part of the Charge of the Mill, fhould reap the Fourth part of the Profit of it, and have their own Corn ground there for them when they would *gratis*, or of free Coft. And the Hofpital to find a way to it (*k*) from the Road or High-way by it. And this about King *John*'s time.

By the Bull of Pope *Honorius* ([it was certainly fo. *N. B.*] I take it) the Third, this Hofpital was privileged of and from paying Tithe (*l*) of their Gardens (*m*).

(*a*) *Totum meffuagium cum pertinentiis quod fuit Lefwini facerdotis perfonæ ejufd' ecclefiæ, & quod poftea fuit Archidiaconi de Petters perfonæ ejufd' ecclefiæ, & quod poftea fuit Willielmi de Crevequer perfonæ ejufdem ecclefiæ.* (*b*) *Liber memoratus.* (*c*) *Eodem Anno Dominus Thomas de Roos dum reverteretur à terra Sancta in Infula de Cypro civitate Papho, tactus aeris regionis incommodo, diem claufit extremum. Cambden* in *Kent.* Englifh Edition *pag.* 334. (*d*) *Ad liberam capellam beatæ Mariæ in Caftro de Chilham.* (*e*) *Liber Ecclef. Cant.* (*f*) *In villa de Blean. in augmentum operum pietatis in eodem Hofpitali, &c.* (*g*) *Vide copiam fundationis Cantariæ de Eaftbridge in Appendice.* (*h*) *Lib. hujus Hofpitalis* (*i*) *In quarta parte unius acræ in parva Foxmold verfus Occidentem, in hundredo de Ridingate.* (*k*) *A Chemino magno Regali.* (*l*) *De hortis.* (*m*) *Ibid.*

The

The City Chamber hath a Record dated the 7 *Richard* II. *Anno Domini* 1391. whereby it appears that the Mafter of this Hofpital ought to repair, erect, and fuftain the Neighbour-bridge, *i. e. Kingsbridge.* The Account of the Hofpital's Eftate given up to the Commiffioners upon the Statute 37 *Hen.* VIII. *cap.* 4. chargeth the Mafter with the paving alfo of the Street there.

The Hofpital hath a neat handfome Chappel [dedicated to our Lady *W. S.*] to which have belonged two Bells to ring to Service. So it is reported to thofe Commiffioners, by the Parfon and Church-wardens of *All-Saints :* Who fay withall, that the faid Hofpital (as their own words are) is a Parifh-Church, wherein there is continually miniftred all Sacraments and Sacramentals to the pcor People thither reforting, and to the Keeper of the faid Hofpital and his Houfhold, and all other remaining within the Precinct of the fame by the Chantery Prieft, *&c.* Truth is, this Chapel was ferved heretofore by a Chantery Prieft, which had x *l.* vi *s.* viii *d.* yearly wages, befides his Manfion or Dwelling, which was that at the Weft-end of the Hofpital, whereof the Statute 1 *Edward* VI. *cap.* 14. for the fuperftitious quality of it, hath long fince deprived it. However, to fatisfy the inquifitive, I have given the Foundation a place in my *Appendix.* I have nothing further to fay of the Chappel, but that one *Creffy* a *Jew* building againft the head of it that Houfe which yet ftands there, and now belongs to *Chrift-Church* ; (to which upon the expulfion of the *Jews*, it was, with other given by the King;) he was fain afterwards to agree with the Hofpital, that he might have their fufferance for the ftanding of it, and had it in Writing, the Charter whereof dated in the year 1236. I have feen in a Leiger of *Chrift-Church* intituled (a) *A Charter of Releafe*, made by *Peter* the then Rector, and the Brethren of the Hofpital of St. *Thomas* of *Eaftbridge Canterbury*, to *Creffy* the *Jew*, (b) *of all complaints on occafion of a Houfe or Foundation, or Wall, which he built on the Eaft-fide, againft the Head of our Chapel ; fo as he fhall never be called in queftion for it either in the Court Chriftian, or Secular,* &c. as the Deed runs.

Chapel at Eaftbridge.

Chantery there.

Numb. XIX.

For brevity and difpatch fake, I balk and fpare the mention of much of this Hofpital's Indowment. But there is yet a parcel more which I may notfo pafs over ; and that is of certain Tenements in *All-Saints* Parifh, fituate between the Sign of the George Weft, and the Queens-head Eaft, in the *High-Street.* Thither then I will make next : But firft for fome fatisfaction to them that cannot underftand the Foundation of the Houfe formerly laid down in Latin. I defire firft to fet down the State of it, in which it ftood at Cardinal *Poole's* Vifitation of the place, *Anno* 1557. taken in *Englifh. viz.*

Memorandum, They are bound to receive way-faring and hurt Men, and to have 8 Beds for Men, and 4 for Women, to remain for a Night and more if they be not able to depart ; and the Mafter of the Hofpital is charged with the Burial, and they have 20 Loads of Wood, yearly allowed, and 26 *s.* a year for Drink. [*Memorand.* There was 10 *l.* Land a year with a Manfion, which the Prieft always had for Officiating in the Chappel, taken away by the King ; and that it is the Head Church to *Cofmus Blean* ; but they have no Ornaments but Organs. *Origin. Vifitat.* Book of Archdeacon *Harpsfield. N. B.*]

The Exchange, Mint, Jury, and Guildhall.

NOW to the Tenements which haply feem to be fo mean as fcarce worthy of any Notice. True : But for what hath fometime ftood here, and into the place whereof they have fucceeded, I think fcarce a place in the City more remarkable, if at all fo memorable ; which was an Exchange, a Royal Exchange. *Cambium Regis* ; mention whereof often occurs in the old Rentals and other Records of *Chrift-Church* ; whofe Tenement (now the George) is anciently bounded Eaftward to this Exchange. It was ftanding, it feems, untill *Edward* III. days, and in likelihood received its fatal period from him. For he in augmentation of the Hofpital's endowment, gave it (c) to the then Mafter of *Eaftbridge*, by name, *Thomas New* of *Wolton*, for life, and afterwards to his Succeffors for ever. Which *Thomas*, fhortly after, dividing

Exchange.

(a) *Carta Remiffionis.*   (b) *De omnibus querelis occafione domus vel fundamenti vel muri quam in parte orientali in capite capellæ noftræ ædificavit, ut nunquam queftio movebitur in Curia Chriftianitatis vel feculari, &c.*   (c) *Lib. de Eaftbridge.*

it

it (it ſeems) into Tenements, hires them out in Fee-ferm to ſeveral Tenents, *viz.* one part thereof to the then Commiſſary of *Canterbury, Thomas Maſon* by name.

Append. Numb.
XX. a.
" A certain piece of Land with a Houſe built upon it, and Walls and other
" its Appurtenances, which was part of the Tenement called *La Chaunge*, or
" the *Exchange*, lying in the City of *Canterbury*, in the Pariſh of *All-Saints*,
" together with a Paſſage or Entrance leading from *Highſtreet* on the South-
" ſide, through a great Door of the ſaid place into it, between the Tenement
" of the Heirs of *William Child* toward the Eaſt, and the Tenement of the
" Prior and Convent of *Chriſt-Church Canterbury*, toward the Weſt, and the
" Tenement of *Edmund Horn* toward the North, and the Tenement of the
" ſaid *Thomas de Walton*, which is part of the Tenement called the *Exchange*,
" toward the South. This *Anno* 43 *Edward* III.

The other part or reſidue thereof, unto one *William Silkenden* and *Joan* his
Wife, in theſe Words, to wit : " A certain place which is part of the Tene-
Append. Numl.
XX b.
" ment which was called the *Exchange*, and which our Lord the King that now
" is, gave unto me for the Term of my Life, and to my Succeſſors for ever ;
" for the increaſe of the Endowment of the ſaid Hoſpital. In which place
" there is a Storehouſe, two Solars, and one Room between them like a Hall,
" with a certain piece of a Garden lying at the end of the ſaid Storehouſe,
" which lies all together , and are ſituated in *All-Saints* Pariſh in *Canterbury*,
" between one part of the Tenement called the *Exchange*, which now Mr.
" *Thomas Maſon* holds of me by demiſe toward the North ; and another part
" of the ſame Tenement, the *Exchange*, which the ſame Mr. *Thomas Maſon*
" holds of me by Livery, and certain Shops which belong to the Hoſpital to-
" ward the Weſt, and the Tenement of the Heirs of *William Child* towards
" the Eaſt, and the *Highſtreet* toward the South : Alſo three Shops of the ſaid
" Hoſpital with a ſmall place lying longways between the ſaid Shops, and in
" the Tenure of the ſaid Mr. *Thomas Maſon* ; which alſo he holds of me by de-
" miſe on the Northſide, and a certain old Paſſage or Entrance into the Tene-
" ment called the *Exchange*, on the Eaſt-ſide, and the *Highſtreet* toward the
" South, with one Stone Wall, which is at the end of the ſaid place and Shops
" from the Tenement of the ſaid Mr. *Thomas Maſon*, in a direct line to the
" Gate of the ſaid entrance or paſſage on the left hand of thoſe that go
" in by the ſaid Gate. This was *Anno* 47 *Edward* III. Both which Demiſes
I was deſirous to expreſs at large, becauſe I have not ſeen any other Record
that ſets forth at all what kind of Building this Exchange was.

Antiquity of
its ſtanding
here.
For the Antiquity of its continuance here before the ſuppreſſion ; I cannot
ſay much. In the ſixth year of *Henry* III. *Ann. Dom.* 1222. I meet with the
King's Exchange at *Canterbury*. For *Henry* the third (*Stow* (a) is my Author)
in the ſixth year of his Reign, wrote to the *Scabines* and men of *Ipre*, that he
and his counſel had given prohibition, that none *Engliſh*-men, or other, ſhould
make change of Plate, or other maſs of Silver, but only at his Exchange at
London, or at *Canterbury*.

Shortly, there was ſometime a family in our City, which from their neighbourhood or other relation to this place, took name from it, and were ſirnamed *De Cambio.*

Mint.
An exchange relates to a Mint, or place of mintage and coinage of Money ; but of old, as will appear by the Statute, *anno primo H. 6. cap.* 4. they
might not be together, but were kept apart, and a place there was ſometime
neighbouring to the Exchange, on the other ſide of the ſame ſtreet, even
there where now the Inn called the *Crown* or ſome part of it ſtands where our
Mint was kept. (b) *In a corner of the Mint toward the Eaſt*, is part of the
boundary to that which is the dwelling-houſe of *Iſaac Clerk*, [now Alderman
Webb. N. B.] The Officers and Miniſters retaining to this Mint, had their
houſing hard by it in ſome Tenements of *Chriſt-Church*. Whence in their old
rentals is frequent mention (c) *Of the Mints* ; or *Offices belonging to the Mint in
the Pariſh of St.* Mary Bredman. This Mint (I take it) was ſilenced about the
ſame time with the Exchange, for of latter years I find no mention of it. [I
have ſeen a Charter (d), in which mention is made of a Mint-Office in the
Pariſh of St. *George* over-againſt the pillory of the City. *N. B.*]

(a) Survey, *pag.* 351. *ult. edit.*   (b) *In angulo monetaria verſus Eaſt.*   (c) *De
monetariis in Parochia Sanctæ Mariæ Bredman.*   (d) *In Parochia S. Georgii contra magnam co-
mum Sancti Dunſtani de monetaria juxta pillorium civitatis. In Archivis Eccleſ. Cant.* N. B.]

From

From what antiquity it had stood and been kept at this place I know not. Antiquity of it. But amongst the places where King *John* in his letters makes mention of Mints kept in *England*, this City is one *(a)*, and hath been so (I suppose) for many Ages. King *Æthelstane* appointing out the places for Mints, and the number of Minters throughout the Kingdom *(b)*, begins with *Canterbury*, to which he allowed seven Minters : a greater number than to any other place in the Kingdom, except *London*, which was allowed to have Eight. Of these seven, four were the King's, two for the Archbishop, and the seventh for the Abbat of St. *Augustin's*. The Archbishop's Mint (it seems) is yet elder. For Mr. *Selden* in his notes upon *Edmerus*, and *Speed* in his History make mention of two several Coins, one of Archbishop *Plegmund* under *Alfred*, the other of *Celnoth* under *Ethelwolf* extant, and presented in figure, by *Speed* the latter, by *Selden* the former. When or how the Archbishop lost or left off his mintage here, I do no where find. Of the time when the Abbats ceased I have shewed before out of *Thorne*, in my Survey of St. *Augustin.*

Amongst other pieces of antique (*Roman, Britain, Saxon, Danish* and *Norman*) Coin which I have met with and reserve, some were stamped in this Mint, I take it, in this City, of certain the Reverse of the Coin saith so ; I have withal a piece or two of *Henry* VIII. coined at *Canterbury*, not here ; but as I conceive at the place now called the Mint by the Court-gate of *Christ-Church* ; where after the Dissolution he coined Money for the service (they say) of his *French* Wars. Ever since which time, the place therefore retains the Name of the Mint, and the Court or Yard which it incloseth is called the Mint-yard. So much for the Mint.

Retreating a little from this place, on the same side of the Street there is a *Jews* in *Cant.* place where sometime the *Jews* that of old, for a long time together, were suffered to dwell amongst us in most of our chief Cities, kept their residence ; being housed in this Street and in the Lane by it, from thence to this day called *Jury-lane* ; the same (I take it) which of old I find called *Little-pet-lane (c)*. There was of their Houses hereaway to the number of almost Twenty. All which, together with their Synagogue, or (as more frequently called) *(d)* their School, upon their general Banishment out of this and all other parts of the Kingdom, in *Edward* II. days (at what time their Number amounted unto 16511 *(e)*) as confiscate, escheated to the King ; and by him were eftsoons , some of Gift, some otherwise alienated ; some to one, some to another, but the most (to the number, *viz.* of at least 12. and a void piece of Ground which was *(f)* [or rather which belong'd to the Community or Fraternity of the *Jews*, intimating as if they were a Corporation or politick Society. *N. B.*] the *Jews* in common) to the Monks of *Christ-Church (g)*. Their Synagogue or School stood about where now some part of the Saracen's head [now the King's head. *N. B.*] Tavern doth, as appears by the Record of *Christ-Church* : Which have this bound to certain Fee of the late Monks hard by it ; namely, *(h)* " The Land in the Parish of *All-Saints*, between the great " Street, which is toward the North, and the School of the *Jews*, which is " toward the South ; nigh a Lane which leads from the said Street towards " St. *Mildred's* ; being that ground (I take it) whereon the Forepart (to the Street-ward) of that which is now the Saracen's head Tavern, being in show newer than the back-part, was afterward built. To which ground the very next House above (the Mitre) is bounded West-ward, and called *(i) the House nigh the School of the Jews* ; thus explained in the Rental : *(k) The Stone House which is over-against the Land where the School of the Jews is situated, toward the West.* By all which I collect and verily conceive, that the now Stone Parlour of the *Saracen's*-Head, [now the new *King's* -Head. *N. B.*] mounted upon a Vault and ascended by many Stone-steps (as the *Jewish* Synagogues and Schools were always built aloft *(l)*) is the remains of a good part of that which was our *Canterbury Jews* School or Synagogue.

---

(1) *Stow.* Survey. *pag.* 46.   (b) *Lambard* Archæonom.   (c) *Rental vet. eccles. Cant.* (d) *Schola Judæorum.*   (e) *Matt. Westm. de anno* 1290   (f) *Communitatis Judæorum Civitatis.* (g) *Lib eccles Christi Cant.*   (h) *Terra in parochia omnium Sanctorum inter magnum vicum qui est versus Aquilonem, & Scholam Judæorum quæ est versus Austrum, juxta venellam qua itur à prædicto magno vico versus Sanctam Mildritham.*   (i) *Domus juxta scolam Judæorum.* (k) *Domus lapidea quæ est contra terram ubi scola Judæorum sita est versus Occidentem.*   (l) Moses and *Aaron. lib.* 2. *cap.* 2. *pag.* 80.

I could

I could here very much enlarge my ſelf in giving you the Story of the *Jews* firſt advent or entrance into this Land, their time of continuance here, with their behaviour and dealings during that time, and the cauſes, reaſons, and motives for their expulſion at laſt : which were chiefly two ; their immoderate uſury ; and their barbarous practice of crucifying, at places where they abode, any Chriſtian's Child they could get about *Eaſter* time. But I am prevented herein by many others that have ſeverally divulged theſe things already to the full ; as *Harpsfield* and *Stow*, but more exactly and moſt elaborately and like himſelf, our learned *Selden*, *Purcaſes* guide and Author for a purpoſed diſcourſe of this kind ; wherefore I forbear, (a) *Leſt I ſhould repeat what has been ſaid before* : only adding what I have ſeen noted, (but how truly I know not) that the *Jews*, when living here, were ſuch notorious Uſurers that Uſury among the Chriſtians, became called *Judaiſm*. (b) *For the Premiſes the Abbat acquitted the donor of 28 s. in Judaiſm, inſtead of a fine* : as it is in an old Deed. And they ſtill continue this trade whereſoever they become, whereby they grow rich even to envy every where , yet (as one ſaith (c)) many of the Chriſtians do uſe them under hand in improving their unlawful rents to their utmoſt proportion. [The *Jews* in *England* were grown numerous and wealthy. Uſury, in exacting unreaſonable intereſt upon the loan of Money was their practiſe or trade, and became ſo notorious, that Judaiſm in ſome ancient Charters (d) ſeems to have been a term or name for Uſury, and has been ſo interpreted by the learned *du Freſne. N. B.*]

Now a word or two of the Gild-hall (or Court-Hall, as we call it) and my Survey of this Ward is at an end. Here then, as in the fitteſt and moſt convenient place, being the principal Street of the City, is the Court, Tribunal, or place of Judicature of the City, ſeated and kept ; where diſtributive Juſtice in both Civil and Criminal Cauſes of ſecular Nature, ſorting to the cognizance of that Court, is adminiſtred. Vulgarly we call the place the *Gildhall*. The Etymology and derivation whereof is from the *Saxon* (or old *Engliſh*) word *Gild*, ſignifying a Society or Corporation. Here is a Court kept every Monday throughout the Year, for Law-Matters and for the deciding of Differences, and righting of Grievances between Party and Party : And on every other Tueſday a Court of Burgmote holden beſide, for Meeting and Treaty about the Affairs and good Government of the City. It had not the Name of the *Gildhall*, until (as it were) of late Years. That Name of it occurs not in any Record that I could yet meet with, until the 26. of *Henry* VI. who then in his Charter of the Change of the Bailiffs into a Mayor, makes mention of this Tribunal by that name, granting ((e) *among other things*) that the Mayor ſhall hold Pleas (f) *in the Guildhall of the ſaid City*, as his words are. Aforetime it was commonly called and known by the name of the Spech-houſe ; and the common Gaol or Priſon of the City, ſince removed to *Weſtgate*, being then kept by it, that is, in that part of it which is to the ſtreetward, was from its adjacency to it, ſo called alſo. For proof both of one and t'other read the following Notes, extracted from certain Witneſſes Examinations, *Anno* 1414. taken in a Cauſe of Defamation, between a Couple of the City (for calling one the other Thief ; a Crime and Calumny wherein the defamed of thoſe days did uſually after purgation, right himſelf in Court Chriſtian) and recorded in a Book of Depoſitions remaining in the Office (g). Whereof one is this. One Witneſs ſaith (h) *That he once ſaw* John Copherſt *in a certain Houſe called the* Spech-houſe, *ſituated nigh the Lyon Inn in* Highſtreet *in* Canterbury, *in the Pariſh of* St. Mary Bredman. Another ſays this. *For theſe words*

Usury called judaiſm.

Gildhall.

Spech-houſe.

(a) *Ne actum agerem.*   (b) *Pro præmiſſis Abbas donatorem acquietavit de 28 s. in Judaiſmo, loco gerſumæ.*   (c) *Sandy's* Relation of Religion, *&c.*   [(d) *Cujus tempore empta fuit grangia du Korely & domus obligata in magnis debitis in Judaiſmo Monaſt. Anglic. T.* I *p.* 339 *Nec in Judaiſmo pignori obligare præſumant. T.* 11. *p.* 10. *Sex marcas ſterlingorum ad acquietandam terram prædictam de Judaiſmo, in quo fuit impignorata. Ibid p.* 665. *Judaiſmus videtur uſurpari pro Judæorum menſa nummularia ſive uſuraria. Car. du Freſne N. B.*]   (e) *Inter alia.*   (f) *In le Guildhall Civitatis prædict.*   (g) *Regiſt. Conſiſt.* Cant.   (h) *Dicit quod Johannem Copherſt ſemel vidit in quadam domo vocat' Spech-houſe ſituat' juxta Hoſpitium Leonis in alto vico Cant. in parochia Sancta Mariæ Bredman. Occaſione hujuſmodi verborum dictus Thomas fuerat arreſtatus ad priſonam vocat' pech-houſe in alto vico Cant. ſituat' & ibidem dictus T. B. movebat querelam contra eum ad ſummam decem marcarum. coram Ballivo & juratis dicta villæ. Interrogatus penes quos opinio dicti Tho ſit. denigrat' dicit apud Ballivos Cant. Jo. Brown & Will. Bennet, & apud omnes Burgenſes pro tunc exiſtentes in domo vocat' Spech-houſe Cant.*

the said Thomas *was arrested or imprisoned at the Prison called the* Spech-house, *situated in* Highstreet *in* Canterbury. *And there the said* Thomas, *as Plaintiff entred his Action against him, to the Sum of* X *Marks, before the Bailiff and Jurats of the said Village.* A Third and the last, *Being asked with whom the Reputation of the said* Thomas *was defamed; replies : Before the Bailiffs of* Canterbury, John Brown *and* William Bennet, *and before all the Burgesses of* Canterbury , *who at that time were present in the House called the* Spech-house.

The Town-Court hath not always been kept at this place ; but as now it is, and of long time hath been here, so both it and the Prison were formerly kept together elsewhere, and that (I take it) at the place of the now Corn-Market, and were then also called the *Spech-house* (of which before at large:) Very properly did they stand contiguously together, if *Tholosanus*'s (a) judgment in this point be to be followed ; who saith, (b) Prisons are built contiguous to Tribunals, as well for the safe Custody of those that are to be tried, as for the easy bringing them before the Judgment-Seat. Thus he. But why the place of Judicature called the Spech-house ? Properly, some think, from the arguing and debating of Matters there, not without much Sermocination. And not unlikely. With as much congruity (I dare say) as *Forus* is of *Isidore* , derived *à fando,* from speaking. But I leave it, and this Ward, and proceed (up the Street) to *Newingate-*Ward.

Whence called the Spech-house.

Newingate-Ward.

The AUGUSTIN *Friers.*

IN which what is most remarkable of us, are the remains of the *Augustin* Friers, whereunto a reasonable fair Stone Gate in St. *George*'s street leadeth ; the now Mansion or Habitation of Captain *Berry* , [now *William Turner* Esq; N. B.] after many other mesne owners, since the suppression : before which time it was the seat of the *Augustin* (as I said) *Eremite, mendicant Friers. Mendicant* because it was one and the first of the four Orders of begging Friers : *Eremite* and *Augustin,* because St. *Augustin,* that famous *African* Father (they say) was their founder, who being and living (c) in the Wilderness, erected and instituted their Order, and prescribed them a rule of living; about which they and the Regular Canons are at contestation, as you may read elsewhere. They were otherwhile and of some called also the *White-Friers.* (though properly and strictly the Carmelites are understood by that Epithete) because that they do wear (d) a long white Coat of cloth down to their heels all loose, with a cowl or hood of the same, when they are in their Cloisters; however when they go abroad, they wear a black Coat over the other, with another Cowl, having both their Coats then bound close to their bodies, with a broad leather girdle or belt, saith *Owen.*

Augustin Friers

The generality of these Friers came first into *England,* from *Italy,* about the year 1252. saith *Bale.* These in particular came hither, and setled themselves here, about the year 1325. For that very year the then Archbishop of *Canterbury* sends and directs these his mandatary letters (e) concerning them to his then Commissary, to this Effect.

" That whereas the Friers of the Order of St. *Augustin* had built themselves
" a Chapel, and tolling a Bell had publickly celebrated Mass in the same,
" and had received oblations (as it was affirm'd) due to the Parochial-
" Church, without License from the Archbishop and the Chapter of *Christ-*
" *Church,* contrary to the Privileges granted to the Archiepiscopal See and
" the Metropolitical Church , The Commissary was commanded to make
" enquiry into these matters, and to inhibit by an Ecclesiastical Interdict the
" Friers from celebrating Mass in that Chapel, and to cite them to appear
" before him, &c.

See the *Append.* Numb. XXI.

For the Friers (f) having purchased and gotten possession of a house or tenement and appurtenances , in the Parish of St. *George* in *Canterbury* of one

---

(a) *De Republica. lib.* 2. *cap.* 7.   (b) *Juxta tribunalia & continentes sint carceres qui ad custodiam judicandorum ædificari debent , tuti & contra vim omnem muniti ut inde facilius & cum minori periculo ad judicium duci & reduci possint.*   (c) *In Eremo.*   (d) *Owen's* Genealogy of Monks, &c.   (e) *Liber Eccles.* Cant.   (f) *Lib. ecclef. Christi Cant.*

Thomas

Thomas of *Bonynton* (a) bounded out as followeth, *viz.* by a certain Lane, sometime called *Lambertslane*, afterwards *Brewerslane*, that is, between the same lane, and another tenement of the said *Thomas* toward the North, and a certain place called *Ealdgaole*, and the tenement of *Cicely* at *Gayole* toward the West, and the tenement of *Thomas Chich* toward the East, and the tenement of *Thomas Clement*, and of the Hospital of Priests toward the South : the Friers I say, having purchased and gotten possession of this tenement ; forthwith build them a Church, and therein erect Altars, and all of their own authority : So busily bestirring themselves, that both the Monks and the Parson of St. *George* were in danger to be prejudiced in their several interests, the one (the Monks) to an annuity of 20 *d. per Ann.* payable to them (that is the Prior and Covent of *Christ-Church* ;) the other (the Parson) to the Tithes and other rights Ecclesiastical payable to him, out of the said Tenement. At length within a year after or such a matter, the Monks and they came to composition for their annuity, of whom they obtained a remission and release of all arrerages thereof past, so as the Friers see to the due payment of it for time to come. The Parson also, *John* of *Natyndon* by name, after he had (for the timely prevention of his own and his Churches prejudice, by the Friers alteration of the state and property of that late house, which beside (b) *first fruits tithes and oblations,* yielded him and it other commodities before the Friers time) brought his action against them before *John Badesley* the Chancellor, and *Robert de Weston,* Auditors of Causes under the then Archbishop (*Walter Reinolds*) to the end to compel them by course of Law (as but right and reason required) to secure him and his Church against detriment and deterioration in this behalf ; he, I say, the Parson came also to composition with them : in and by the which the house is quietly yielded and confirmed to the Friers, with liberty to make their abode therein, and to get their Chapel, Oratory or Church and Altars already erected upon the place, and also a certain plot of ground laid out for a Churchyard, to be dedicated : and 9 *s.* to be yearly paid by them, for and in lieu of all dues, to the Parson of St. *George* for the time being for ever ; whereof the one moiety at *Midsummer,* and the other at *Michaelmas* ; subjecting themselves to the Archbishop, or any other Judge ordinary, or delegate, for compulsion, in default of payment. The Parson being tyed to obey (c) *under pain of Excommunication,* and the Friers, (d) *under pain of Interdict.*

The Friers afterward (e) enlarging their seat by purchasing of *John Chich* of *Canterbury,* (f) a certain place or Court, within the Parish of St. George *in* Canterbury, *lying upon the High-way or Street at the Cloth-market,* upon part of which they built their outward Gate : In the year 1356 they enter into obligation, and do bind themselves and their house to the Prior and Cnovent of *Christ-Church* (of whose Fee it seems it was a part) to pay them 2 *s.* 4 *d. per Ann.* for it. And thus have I shewed you when, and in what manner these Friers came to house first, and afterward compleatly seated themselves here.

John Capgrave.   A great Ornament afterward to this place, and to the whole Order, was *John Capgrave* in his time ; that is *Anno* 1484, or thereabouts ; a famous Frier of this House, [Provincial of that Order. *W. S.*] and a great Writer ; the Catalogue of whose Works may be seen in *Pitseus,* who is very large if not lavish in his Commendation for a Man of most excellent Parts.

As for Benefactors to this Monastery, of note, I read of but two. The one a Widow-woman, one *Amabilia Gobyon,* who made choice of these *Austin*-Friers-Church for her place of Sepulture, and gave by her Will (g) ten Marks to the Repair thereof. This in the Year 1405. The other one Sir *John Fineux* Knight, who in *Henry* VII. time became a most liberal Benefactor to the place, as, if you peruse the Instrument (h) in the *Appendix, Numb.* XXII. will appear unto you.

The importance of which Instrument is to this effect : That Sir *John Fineux,* Lord Chief Justice of the Pleas in the Reign both of King *Henry* VII.

(a) [*Pat.* 17 *E.* 11. *memb.* 18. *Part.* 11 *Philp. Vill. Cantian. N. B.*]   (b) *Primitias decimas & oblationes.*   (c) *Sub pæna excommunicationis.*   (d) *Sub pæna interdicti.*
(e) *Lib. Eccles. memorata*   (f) *Quandam placeam seu aream infra prochiam Sancti Georgii Cant. existen' super stratam Regiam apud Clothmarket.*   (g) *Penes registrum Consist. Cant.*
(h) *Ms. penes meipsum.*

and

and VIII. whom they highly commend as a Person of singular worth and excellency, had of his Bounty expended much more than the Sum of xl *l.* in repairing their Church, Refectory, Dormitory, and Walls. Out of gratitude to so liberal a Benefactor, they agreed that one of their Brethren should every day celebrate the Mass of the Blessed *Mary* for ever, at the Altar of the Blessed Virgin, for the Souls of Sir *John Fineux* and *Elizabeth* his Wife, of King *Henry* VII. and Archbishop *Morton,* &c. Dated *November* 28, *A. D.* 1522.

Hitherto and enough of the *Augustin* Friers. Having formerly discoursed at large of the old Gaol or Prison sometime standing about this place, for avoiding of repetitions I forbear all further discourse of it here; and so finish with this Ward, finding nothing more observable in it, except the goodly Conduit there; which, because of a future occasion which I shall have to make mention of it, I shall deferr to speak of here.

Northgate Ward.

Stablegate: The House of the Templars; And the House of the Black Prince's Chantery Priests.

THis Ward offers and affords three remarkable Places to our Survey; and they are, 1. The place called *Stablegate.* 2. The *quondam* House of the Templars. 3. The late House of the Black Prince's Chantery Priests.

I will begin with *Stablegate.* A Borough or Hamlet by the Charter of *Stablegate.* *Henry* VI. made to the City, excepted from the Franchise of the same, as being a parcel of the vill of *Westgate,* and of the fee and liberty of the Archbishop, to whom of old it hath belonged: It being taken for the very place where *Augustin* the first Archbishop of *Canterbury,* and his Company were entertained and seated by King *Ethelbert,* before he resigned to him his Royal Palace. As *Thorn* informs us. For here *Augustin* sojourned at first, and to this place he obtained the Privilege of being a Sanctuary; a place of Refuge for Criminals, even after they were indicted, if they could flee unto it, where they should be under the sole Power of the Archbishop, which was their protection. [The words of *Thorn* are in the Margin *(a)*, but Mr. *Somner* has entirely omitted a material Clause, of which I shall take notice by and by. *N.B.*]

Whence it took the name of *Stablegate,* I am as yet ignorant. Some surmise from the Staple of Wooll which anciently was kept in the City. *Canterbury* being one of the places where by the Stat. 27 *Edward* III. it was ordained to be kept, and the only place that two Years before (25 *Edward* III.) the same King appointed for the keeping of it at, for the honour of St. *Thomas (b).* If so, then is there a mistake in the writing of it *Stablegate* for *Staplegate.* [But our Countryman *Darel* in his Itinerary, derives the name of the place from the *Saxon;* in which Tongue, he saith, it signifies as much as *(c) the ease of a Passage, or the rest or end of a Journey, or the laying down of a Burden.* For it was, saith he, the place appointed for Strangers or Travellers. *W. S.*]

[*Thorn* does assure us, that this was the reason, why it was called *Stablegate,* " Because *(d)* those which had been wearied with carrying their Burdens in the " way, at this place for a long time after, were Unladen and *Stabled:* for " which cause that same place is called *Stablegate* unto this very day. Just after *Thorn* had related, (as Mr. *Somner* has quoted) where *Augustin* and his Domesticks did sojourn, until the Conversion of the King, these words follow, which I have added in the Margin, and (I know not how) this whole Clause is en-

---

(a) *Concessit eis locum habitationis in civitate Doroberniæ situatam, viz. infra parochiam Sancti Ælphegi, ex opposito regiæ stratæ versus Aquilonem; per murum [per quam murus N. B.] Palatii Archiepiscopalis in longitudine se extendit, in quo Augustinus cum suis Domesticis usque ad conversionem Regis hospitatus est. Fuerat tunc temporis quasi oratorium pro familia Regis ut ibi adorarent & Diis suis liberos [l. libamina N.B.] immolarent. Sanctus verò ille hospes tanta hospitium suum voluit libertate promovere, & ab exactionibus quorumcunque perpetualiter acquietare, quòd neque Civibus in tallagiis & assisionibus quoque modo debeant respondere, vel eis subsidium aliquid præstare: sed Archiepiscopo in omnibus subjacere, & suum Palatium firma libertate gaudere. Ita ut si fures vel homicidæ vel alii quamvis indictati situm de Stablegate valeant introire, ut in ecclesia, libertate gaudebunt.* (b) Stow Survey pag. 496. ult. editionis.

(c) *Transitûs quies sive itineris vel sarcinorum depositio.* (d) *Illa tamen quæ per viam extiterant sarcinis honustata, loco prædicto longo postea tempore stabulata sunt; ob quam causam usque in hodiernum diem situs ille Stablegate vocatus est.*

tirely

tirely omitted by Mr. *Somner*; which would have led him to the true reafon of this name. And I add, this has continued ever fince to be the way to the Stables of the Archbifhop, of the Prior, and of the Convent of *Chrift-Church*. N. B.]

Edmund Sta-
blegate.

There was fometime a family in our City, who from their habitation either at or near this place, were furnamed *De Stablegate*, and of *Stablegate*, whereof one *Edmund Stablegate* (the fame man I take it that *Lambard* fpeaks of. Per-amb. of *Kent*, in *Bilfington*) in the 42. *Edward* III. was a Bailiff of the City. For to a Deed or Charter of *Nicholas at Crouch*, made to the Hofpital of *Eaft-bridge* ((*a*) *whereby he quitted his intereft in a tenement and garden in St. Peter's Parifh*) this *Edmund*, by the title of one of the Bailiffs of the City is, with others, a witnefs. He had alfo a feat or habitation in the Suburbs by *Natindon*, limitaneous to the City's Franchife thereaway, as the perambulation thereof will fhew.

Houfe of
Templars.

I leave *Stablegate*, and pafs to the houfe of the Templars. An order of Knights that began in the year 1118. Thefe Knights Templars (faith *Stow*(*b*), fpeaking out of *Matthew Paris*, of the Temple in *London*) took their beginning about the year 1118 in manner following. Certain noble Knights bound themfelves by vow in the hands of the Patriarch of *Jerufalem*, to ferve Chrift after the manner of Regular Canons, in chaftity and obedience, and to re-nounce their own proper Wills for ever: the firft of which order were *Hugh Pagan* and *Geffrey of St. Audomar*.

And whereas at the firft they had no certain habitation, *Baldwin*, King of *Jerufalem*, granted unto them a dwelling place in his Palace by the Temple, and the Canons of the fame Temple gave them the ftreet, thereby to build therein their houfes of Office, [that is, houfes for Offices. N. B.] and the Patriarch, the King, the Nobles, and the Prelates, gave unto them certain revenues out of their Lordfhips.

Their firft profeffion was for fafeguard of the Pilgrims, coming to vifit the Sepulchre, and to keep the high-ways againft the lying in wait of Thieves, &c. About ten years after, they had a rule appointed unto them, and a white ha-bit by *Honorius* the fecond, then Pope; and whereas they had but nine in num-ber, they began to increafe greatly. Afterward in Pope *Eugenius* time, they bare Croffes of red Cloath, on their uppermoft garments, to be known from others, and in fhort time becaufe they had their firft Manfion hard by the Temple of our Lord in *Jerufalem*, they were called Knights of the Temple.

Many Noblemen in all parts of Chriftendom, became brethren of this Or-der, and builded for themfelves Temples in every City or great Town in *England*, but this (faith my Author) at *London* was their chief houfe, which they builded after the form of the Temple near to the Sepulchre of our Lord at *Jerufalem*. They had alfo (faith he) other Temples in *Cambridge*, *Briftol*, *Canterbury*, *Dover*, *Warwick*, &c.

That in *Canterbury Stow* fpeaks of, was fituate in *Northgate* Parifh, in or near *Waterlock-lane* (the Lane, I conceive, under the Town-wall, and leading by *Northgate*-Church within, down to the River running from Abbots-Mill. For I read (*c*) of a Meffuage, which in the Year 1271 was given to St. *Auftin's* Abby, by one (*d*) *Edmund of the Exchange*; *fituated in* Waterlock-lane, *in the Parifh of* Northgate, *near the Houfes of the Templars*, &c. When this Sect of the Templars was abolifhed, and why, as alfo what became of their Poffeffi-ons, you may find elfewhere.

Princes
Priefs.

Leaving them then, I fhall fhow you next where the Black Prince's Chan-tery Priefts were once houfed, and fo I fhall have done with this Ward. Their Houfe ftood, I may fay it yet ftands (for fo I take it, in part it doth) very near, if not in the place, where fome part of the Templars Habitation was fituate. But let me firft fhow you that fuch a Houfe there once was, and that I fhall do from the Charter or Deed of this Prince's Chantery's Founda-tion; in which are thefe words: (*e*) *For an abode of the faid Priefts, we have af-*

((a) *De quieta clamatione juris fui in quodam tenemento cum gardino & pertinen' fituat' in parcchia fancti Petri Cant. inter curtilagium de Eaftbridge verfus Eaft, & murum lapideum fratrum minorum Can-verfus Weft, continen' in longitudine à regia ftrata verfus North ufque ad aquam del Stour verf. South 136 pedes, & in latitud. 46 pedes.)*   (b) Survey pag. 438, and 439   (c) *Thorn in vitis Abbat. Sancti Auguftini.*   (d) *Edmund de Cambio fcituat' in venella de Waterloke in parochia de Northgate, prope domos Templariorum, &c.*   (e) *Pro mora fiquidem dictorum facerdotum affigna-vimus quendam habitationis locum juxta elemofinariam dicti monafterii in quo conftruetur, &c.*

fign'd

fign'd a Dwelling-place, near the Elemofynary of the Monaftery of Chrift-Church ; *in which a Houfe fhall be built for them,* &c. Wherewith concurreth the relation of the Priefts themfelves, (one of them at leaft) to *Henry* VIII. Commiffioners ; which hath thefe words of it : Alfo the faid Prince *Edward* gave to the faid Chaplains and to their Succeffors for ever, a Houfe in St. *Alphies* Parifh ; the yearly Value of it is xx *s*, *&c.*

Next let me obferve unto you, that over an ancient Stone-porch, opening to the Lane leading you from *Stablegate,* Weftward ; towards the Lane turning to Abbats-Mill, there are yet undefaced the Black Prince's Arms, obvious to the eye of any obferving Paffenger. And fo by this time (I hope) the place is fufficiently difcovered, and my Task for this Ward abfolved.

Worthgate Ward.

The Hofpital of Poor Priefts ; *now the* Bridewell : *The Ifland* With : Mayner's *Spittal ; and* Cotton's *Hofpital.*

COming now to *Worthgate*-Ward ; the firft thing I fhall furvey there, is the *quondam* Hofpital of Poor Priefts. A Spittal firft built and founded by *Simon Langton* Archdeacon (and Brother of *Stephen Langton* Archbifhop) of *Canterbury* about the Year 1240 Not (it feems) altogether of his own Purfe, but chiefly by and with the Alms and Charity of pious and devout Benefactors. (*a*) *Which Hofpital the fame Archdeacon is faid to have built with the Charitable Benevolence of divers People,* faith *Thorn,* relating the Foundation of this Spittal. It was (I conceive) intended for a place of Succour and Relief to poor Priefts, *i. e.* Chaplains, Curates, and otherlike unbeneficed Clerks ; chiefly thofe (I fuppofe) that either by Age or other Infirmity, were difabled for the performance any longer of their Holy Function abroad in the World, and therefore were here accommodated with a Chapel (wherein to pray, fing, and celebrate for their Benefactors, and to perform other Divine Duties) contiguous to this their Habitation ; dedicate as their Hofpital to the Bleffed Virgin ; whofe firft Fabrick was not as now, of Stone. One *Thomas Wyke* (Mafter, I take it, of the Hofpital) *Anno* 1373, new built it of Stone ; but it is now made and parcelled out into Dwellings and Work-houfes.

Shortly after the Hofpital's Foundation perfected, at *Langton* the Founder his inftance, the then Abbat and Convent of St. *Auguftin's* granted to it the Parfonage of *Stodmarfh,* of their Patronage. Of which Grant my Author (*Thorn*) gives the Copy ; which is in the *Appendix,* Numb. XXIII.

The Tenour of the Grant was to this effect : " That at the inftance of *Si-* " *mon de Langton* Archdeacon of *Canterbury,* they paffed over to the Hofpital " of poor Priefts ; fituated in the Parifh of St. *Margaret's,* by a perpetual " Grant, the Church of St. *Mary* of *Stodmarfh,* of their Patronage, with the " profits of four Acres of Land. [The Mafter or Governour of the Hofpital in thofe Letters, is termed *Syndicus. N. B.*]

To this Parfonage, not long after, to wit, *Anno* 1271, another was added ; that I mean of St. *Margaret* in *Canterbury,* given to this Hofpital by the Donors that the former, or if you will (as the private Leiger of the Houfe hath it) by *Hugh Mortimer,* then Archdeacon, (*b*) the See being void, with confent of the Patrons, the Abbat and Convent aforefaid. *Thorn* informs us, " That in the Year of our Lord 1271, the Church of St. *Margaret* in *Canter-* " *bury* was given to the Hofpital of Poor Priefts there ; in free and perpetual " Alms, by R. Abbat of St. *Auguftin's,* which was of their Patronage. And " that the Syndic or Prieft of the Hofpital, fhall not purchafe or appropriate " to themfelves, any Lands, Rents or Tenements, within the Parifh of " St. *Margaret,* of the Tenents of the faid Abbat and Convent, without their " fpecial leave. And the Syndic of the Hofpital for the time being, in ac- " knowledgement of the Right and Jurifdiction of the Abbat and Convent " in the fame, fhall fwear Fealty to them, in their Chapter, when he fhall be

Marginal notes:
Hofpital of Poor Priefts.

Chapel.

Grant of St. *Margaret's* Church. *Append. Numb:* XXIV.

(a) *Quod Hofpitale idem Archidiaconus diverforum elemofinis dicitur fundaffe.* (b) *Authoritate ordinaria.*

" requi-

" required. And that as oft as the Abbat shall pass by the said Church, the
" Bell shall toll.

I shall not further insist on the particulars of this Hospital's Demains and
Revenues, saving the Island behind it, and a forgotten Milne sometime both
Medmilne. neighbouring and belonging to it, called *Medmilne*; either, I take it, because
situate by the Meadows, *quasi Meadmilne*; or else because standing about mid-
way, between St. *Mildred's* Mill on the one, and *Eastbridge* on the other side,
quasi Middlemilne. [which seems to be the plain reason of the name. N. B.]
Before the Hospital's erection it was the proper Mill of one *Lambinus* or *Lambin*; from either his Birth-place or Parentage, sirnamed *Flandrensis* or *Fleming*,
who dwelt where since and now the Hospital is seated; and living there, gave
to *Eastbridge* Hospital, besides 14 Perches of his Land lying in *With*, an Annuity of one Quarter of Wheat out of the said Mill; of which Gift, I once
took this Note from *Eastbridge* Book. (a) " The Grant of *Lambin* the *Fleming*,
" the Son of *Adam* of *Berghes* to the Hospital, of one Seam of Wheat from
" his Mill, called *Medmilne*, and 14 Perches of Land, which lye in *Binne-*
" *with*, between the Lands or Tenement of *Samuel* the Dyer, toward the
" North, and the Land of *Godard* the Miller toward the South, upon the Ri-
" ver *Stour*.

The Poor Priests afterwards succeeding *Lambin* in his Seat, succeeded him
(it seems) in this Mill also. For in the Year 1325, a Controversy arising between the two Hospitals about this Mill (b), and that brought before *Robert de
Malling* then Commissary of *Canterbury*; He, (c) *the Cause being first heard*, adjudged the Mill to the Hospital of Poor Priests. It stood charged nevertheless
with a Resolute of certain Bushels of Wheat to *Eastbridge* Hospital, which, it
seems, by my Inventory of the present Hospital, taken in *Henry* VIII. time,
was four Bushels. For in the recital there of the Rents Resolute, yearly going out of the same Hospital, this is one. *Item*, To the Hospital of *Eastbridge*
in *Canterbury*, in Wheat four Bushels.

Island. Now, as for the Island behind this Hospital, and lying between it and the
Friers, called by a *British* word *With*, it was sometime belonging to this Hospital, serving the Poor Priests for a Garden; but aforetime appertained partly
to *Christ-Church*, and partly to several private Men; Whereof one Family
long ago, took their Sirname, and from this their Habitation were called the
Withs or *Binnewiths*; as some of those were (as you have seen before) which
inhabited the Neighbour *With* or Island, the late Gray-Friers Seat. Part if not
all the Island anciently lay in the Parish of St. *Margaret*. For the elder Rentals of *Christ-Church* who had Rents here, make mention of several Tenements
and parcels of Ground here, as of and within that Parish. And the private
Leiger of this Hospital so mentions the House of one *Solomon* of *Binnewith*,
Way to the *Anno* 1239. At or about which time, the common and ordinary Way or Pas-
Island. sage to this Island, was by the now little and straitned Lane leading from
the Street before the Hospital, (called *Stourstreet*) to the common Washing-
place on the North side of the Hospital; and from thence over the *Stour*, by
a Bridge crossing the Stream. For the Situation of that which is now the
Dwelling-House of *Peter Noble*; (then one *Robert de Hotwel's*) on the North
side of the Chapel is in an ancient Rental of *Christ-Church* described thus:
(d) Between the House sometime of *Lambin Fleming* (which I told you is now
the Hospital) on the one side, and the Lane as you go to *With*, or to the
Island on the other. In another Rental thus described. (e) *The Tenement which
is between the Chapel of the Priests toward the South, and a certain Lane which
leads to the Island of the said Hospital, toward the North, and the High-way toward the East.* And that on the Lane's other side thus: *In the Parish of St. Mary of Bredman, between the Stonehouse of* Samuel *the Dyer, toward the North, and*

(a) *Carta Lambini Flandrensis filii Adæ de Berghes, Hospitali de una summa frumenti de molendino suo
quod vocatur Medmilne, & 14 perticatis terræ meæ quæ jacet Binnewytt inter ter.* [ten.] *Samuelis tinctoris
versus North, & terram Godardi molendinarii vers. South, super Sturam Cant.* (b) *Liber sancti
Lawrentii.* (c) *Causâ prius cognitâ.* (d) *Inter domum quæ fuit Lambini Flandrensis &
vicum sicut itur ad With.* (e) *Tenementum quod est inter capellam Hospitalis sacerdotum versus
South, & quandam venellam quæ ducit ad Insulam præd' Hosp. vers. North, & regiam stratam vers. East.
In parochia sanctæ Mariæ de Bredman inter domum lapideam Samuelis tinctoris vers. Aquil. & domum Rober-
ti de Hotwell vers. Austrum, interjacente quadam venella quæ itur versus Stur, & regiam stratam vers.
Orien. & Stur versus occiden.*

the Houfe of Robert *of* Hotwell *toward the South; a certain Lane lying between, by which they go to the* Stour *; and the High-way toward the Eaft, and the Stour toward the Weft.* Which firft defcribed Houfe was fometime belonging to *Chrift-Church ;* of all Right and Title to which Houfe (or Challenge thereof) the Poor Priefts *Anno* 1242. coming to be Neighbours to it, (and their Neighbourhood, it feems, of the jealous Monks fufpected) make a Charter *(a)* of Releafe to them, namely (as the words of it are) *(b) Of their Right in certain Land, and a Houfe at* Hottewell, (for fo, it feems, the place was called) *which is near the Bridge on the North fide ;* to which they put *Simon Langton* the Archdeacon's Seal, becaufe they had then (as they fay in their Charter, by reafon, I take it, their Hofpital was but newly founded) no Seal as yet of their own. Hottewell.

The late Owners of the Gray-Friers have exchanged this Houfe (which was theirs) with the City, for that Ifland ; which now goes with the Friers, and is parcel of the fame.

But now to our Hofpital again, which I find clearly to have ftood out, and efcaped the general Diffolution unfuppreffed. In Queen *Mary's* days, *Anno* 1554, the Masterfhip thereof with the Rectory of St. *Margaret,* which went ftill with it, was conferred upon one *Hugh Barret,* prefented thereto by the Patron, *Nicholas Harpesfield* the Archdeacon, to the Dean and Chapter of *Chrift-Church,* Ordinaries, or Keepers of the Spiritualties in the Sees then vacancy; who gave the prefented Inftitution with Letters mandatary to the Archdeacon or his Official for his Induction. Whereof a Book of that Church keeps the Record, which I have transferred into the *Appendix ;* and in *Englifh* runs thus : The Hofpital
fpared by the
Diffolution.

Numb. XXIV.
b.

" *July* 27, *A. D.* 1554. *Hugh Barret* Prieft was admitted to the Hofpital of
" Poor Priefts in the City of *Canterbury,* and to the Rectory or Parochial
" Church of St. *Margaret,* in the faid City, appropriated to the faid Hofpital;
" void by the death of *Nicholas Langdon,* laft Incumbent there. To which
" Rectory and Hofpital he was prefented by the Venerable Mr. *Nicholas Harps-*
" *field* L. L. D. Archdeacon of *Canterbury,* the true and undoubted Patron of
" the faid Hofpital and Church. He was inftituted Governor, Mafter, or
" Rector of the fame ; and cononically invefted in all the Rights and Ap-
" purtenances of the fame ; and had the Cure of Souls committed to him, with
" a *Salvo* of the Capitular Rights, Honour, and Dignity of the Metropoliti-
" cal Church of *Canterbury :* An Oath alfo being made by *James Canceller,* the
" Proctor of the faid *Hugh Barret ;* that he would obferve the Statutes and
" Ordinances of the faid Hofpital, according to its Foundation ; and an Oath
" alfo of Canonical Obedience being made, *&c.* There iffued out a Man-
" date to the Archdeacon or his Official for his Induction, *&c.*

But afterward, to wit, *Anno* 17 *Eliz.* (and not before) this Hofpital was diffolved, being then furrendred to her Majefty, by *Blafe Winter* the Mafter, *Edmund Freak* the Patron, and *Matthew Parker* the Ordinary ; and eftfoons granted by the Queen to the City, whereunto ever fince it hath belonged, and is called *Bridewel* Hofpital : *Bridewel,* becaufe of the Houfe of Correction there kept: and Hofpital, both for the old Name's fake, and becaufe of a certain number of Boys (poor Townfmens Children) kept there in an Hofpital way. Of the aforefaid royal Grant, my *Appendix* fhall give you a Copy, if you defire the fight of it. So much of this Hofpital. Of the State whereof in 37 *Henry* VIII. whilft it yet was *(c) in being,* if any defire fatisfaction, I fhall be willing to them give a more exact Account from good Record thereof, which I can produce. When furren-
dred Bride-well.

One thing being very pertinent to our Difcourfe of this Spittle, fince I wrote the Premifes coming to my knowledge, and therefore hitherto omitted; I defire leave to mention here, though the place in fome refpect be indeed improper : And that is, That in the interim of this Hofpital's Foundation, and the Appropriation of St. *Margaret's* Church unto it ; the Parfon and the Hofpital with confent and confirmation of the Abbat and Archdeacon, did come to compofition about the Tithes and other Ecclefiaftical Rights and Duties of this Hofpital. A Copy whereof, taken from a Leiger-Book of St. *Auftin's,* you fhall find in my *Appendix,* Numb. XXV. b.

(a) *Liber ecclef.* Cant.   (b) *De Jure fuo in quadam terra & domo apud Hottewell qua eft*
juxta pontem ex parte aquilonari.   (c) *In effe.*

I come next to *Maynard's*, or more rightly, *Mayner's* Spittle; so called from the Founder, one *Mayner*, sometime a Citizen of *Canterbury*, dwelling in St. *Mildred's* Parish (*a*): And that (as I have good inducement to avouch) in *Henry* II. days. A Man, in his time, (it seems) of noted Wealth, and (I suppose) therefore, and to distinguish him and his Family from another Family of *Mayners*, which were Dyers about the same time; sirnamed *Dives*, and so styled and called in ancient Writings that make mention of him; *viz.* (*b*) *Mayner le Rich*, an addition whereby his Succession or Posterity were known and called after him, by name *Ethelstane* and *Wiulphus*, *Wilulphus* or *Winulphus*, (for so variously is he written) his Sons; and afterward, *Maynerus*, his Grandchild (I take it). Of which the Two former lived in *Richard* I. and King *John's* days, (and in the first of King *John*, *Winulphus*, who lived where Alderman *Sabin* now dwells (*c*), was one of the *Præpositi* of the City) and the latter in *Henry* III. in the Thirteenth Year of whose Reign he was alike Governour of the City,

I find (*d*) the Hospital called both *Hospitale Mayneri*, and *Hospitale Winulphi* [*Wiulphi*]. For this cause (I conceive) that the Patronage of the Hospital, though the first Founder were dead, yet continued to the Son. And so *Maynerus* the Father dying, the Hospital took name afterwards from *Winulphus* the Son, the succeeding Patron; whilst as yet the City had not the Patronage, Power, or Government of it. Or else thus: The Foundation was imperfect in the Father's days, and became afterward either perfected or bettered by the Son; and so it gained the name of *Winulph's* or *Wiulph's* Hospital; which latter name it hath now clean lost, and is known only by the former.

The Hospital hath a neat little Chapel to it (of late incumbred and endangered too, by part of a House and a Chimney put up against it) which together with the Hospital was dedicate to the Blessed Virgin (*e*).

As for the Endowment, Possessions, and Goods of this Hospital and Chapel, what they are now, or at first were, I know not; but what they were in *Henry* VIII. days, you may learn from this following Inventory taken of them and delivered up to the Commissioners upon the Statute 37 *Henry* VIII. *cap.* 4.

MAYNARD's Hospital.

The house and the Garden is by estimation one half Acre and the Rod.

Item, in the *Spittle*-lane they have three Tenements, the Rent of them all is yearly ⎱ xiii s.

Item, in *Castle-street* be two Tenements, the Rent is yearly of both   vi s.

Item, in the same *Castle-street*, in the Parish of St. *Margaret's*, they have one Tenement by the year ⎱ vi s. 8 d.

Item, in the same Street, other three Tenements all by the year at   xv s.

Item, in the same Street, other three Tenements by the year all   ix s.

Item, in *Wincheape* one Tenement, by year   iv s.

Item, in *Waterlock*-lane, in the Parish of St. *Margaret*, there they have two Tenements by the year ⎱ x s.

Item, they have three little pieces of Garden rooms, every of them goeth for 12 d. by the year ⎱ iii s.

Item, they have a little stripe of Ground leading them from their Wood unto the King's High-way ⎱ ii s. iv d.

Item, they have a Wood called the *Brotherhedds*-Wood, in the Parish of *Fordwich*, containing by estimation Six Acres.

In the Chapel.

Item, one Chalice.

Item, two Masers bound with Silver.

Item, two Candlesticks for two Tapers of Latten.

Item, one Corporas and the Case.

Item, two Vestments and two Albs.

Item, one painted Cloath for the forefront of an Altar.

Item, one Bell.

Item, one great Chest in the Chapel.

(*a*) *Rentale vetus ecclesiæ Christi Cant.*   (*b*) *Maynerus Dives.*   (*c*) *Rentale eccles.* *præd.*   (*d*) *Sic in Archivis ecclesiæ præd.*   (*e*) *Ex Archivis memorat.*

Adjoyning

Adjoyning to this Hospital, or rather within it is another like Hospital, ere- *Cotton's Hof-* &ed of late by one *Leonard Cotton* Gentleman, sometimes an Alderman and *pital.* Mayor of this City : whose commendable Piety is as yet so fresh in memory, and his Will so obvious to any that will search the Office for it, and therein the nature and condition of the foundation so largely set forth, that it shall not need my further mention.

Rindingate-Ward.

The Dungeon.

WHerein the *Dungeon*, a Manor lying in this Ward, so called, challen- *TheDungeon.* geth the next place in our Survey : whose name Time (I perceive hath sported with, calling it sometime *Danzon* and *Dangon* (*a*) *all our Land which we had at* Dangon [Danzon] as in an old Deed of St. *Lawrence:*) as also *Dangun*, ((*b*) *in the field, which is called* Dangun, as in a Deed of 47 *Hen.* III. And, (*c*) *a little piece of my Land with the appurtenances, lying at* Dangun, as in a Deed of 14 *Edward* I.) Likewise *Daungeon* (*juxta le Daungeon, or near the* Daungeon, as in old Rentals of *Chrift-Church:*) and *Dungeon* (so *Roger Brent* of *Canterbury* in his Will (*d*) dated *Anno* 1486 mentioning his Manor there, cal- leth it, and so do we at this day, and the Hill hard by *Dungeon*-Hill:) Names much alike all. And as the Manor (I take it) derived its name from that of the neighbouring Hill ; so the radix and original of that, I conceive to signi- fy the *Danes*-work : and therefore corruptly called *Dungeon*-Hill for *Danian*-Hill, or *Danes*-Hill : and that because it was either theirs against the City, or con- trariwise the City's against them. For my part, I conceive first that it was the proper work of the *Danes*, (the great and frequent molesters, invaders and wasters of our City:) and that probably at such time as they beleaguered the City in King *Etheldred*'s days, which stood out against them and their Siege twenty days, and then was not mastered (*e*) by open force, but by base trea- chery surprised : if we may follow *Henry* of *Huntingdon*; *Osborne* (*f*) that was (and writ the story) many years before him, making no mention of any Trea- son that the other faith was plotted or practised in the winning of the City.

Next I am persuaded (and so may easily, I think, any one be that well observes the place) that the Works both within and without the present Wall of the City, were not Counter-works one against the other, as the vulgar opinion goes ; but were sometimes all one entire plot containing about three Acres of Ground, of a triangular form (the Out-work) with a Mount or Hill intrenched round within it. And that, when first made and cast up, it lay wholly without the City-wall ; and hath been (the Hill or Mount, and most part also of the Out-work) for the City's more security, taken and walled in since : That side of the Trench encompassing the Mount now lying without, and under the Wall, fitly meeting with the rest of the City-ditch ; after either side of the Out-work was cut thorough to make way for it, at the time of the City's inditching, as I suppose, it cannot seem unlikely to have been, to any that shall considerately mark and examine the place.

[*W. S.* Here, as in a fit and proper place, (this, I mean, the *Dungel*, as we use to call it ; being the known place of common resort for such of the City as affect the Exercise of *Archery*) let us observe by the way, the Alteration of *Archery.* the Times in point of Martial and Military Weapons. The Bow (the long Bow) and the Bow-man ; we all know, were those which did the Deed, and bare away the Bell in martial Brunts, in former times; the Bow, then the prime Weapon for offensive Service, and the chiefest Instrument War knew, wherewith to try the Mastery ; the Gun and Gunshot being but of late (tho it may be thought too soon) invented ; and yet so cry'd up and magnified, by Martialists especially, that the Bow the whilst is quite rejected with con- tempt as useless, and doom'd and deem'd at best, as only fit for men of peace in way of recreation to sport withal. Now being grounded in a good opini- nion of *Archery*, my self, and not unwilling to vindicate the under-valuation

---

(a) *Totam terram noftram quam habuimus ad* Dangonem [Danzonem.]   (b) *In campo qui vocatur* Dangun.   (c) *Particula terrae meae cum pertinen' jacent' apud* Dangun. (d) *In Regiftro Confiftorii Cantuarien.*   (e) *Aperto Marte.*   (f) *Angl. Sacr.* P. II. p. 135.

A worthy
Commendati-
on of it See
the like in Mr.
Carew's Survey
of *Cornwall.*

of it with other men, I defire here to recommend to my Reader a worthy
and judicious Elogy or Commendation of (*England's* ancient Glory) *Archery*;
not my own, nor yet any mere *Mercurian's*, one able to judge only by The-
oretical Speculation; but a learned Difciple's both of *Mars* and *Mercury*, one
equally experienced in both Warfares the armed and gowned: Mafter *John
Bingham*, I mean, in his Notes upon *Ælian's Tacticks*; where he plays the part
of a moft Judicious Advocate for difcarded *Archery*. The Book is now
fomewhat dear and fcarce, and therefore to fave their labour and coft (of
fearching the Original) who can endure to fee defpifed Archery commended
according to its worth, I fhall prefent them with a true copy of that paffage
verbatim as it there lies. *pag.* 24, and fo forward.

An Apology for Archery; by Mr. John Bingham, *in his Notes upon*
Ælian's *Tacticks, pag.* 24, *&c.*

ARrows] *Archers have always been of fpecial efteem for the field, and preferred
before the other kinds of light-armed. Many Nations have been commended for
their Skill in Shooting. Amongft the* Grecians *the* Cretans *were (of ancient time)
fole Archers; (a) as* Paufanias *witneffeth: Yet was not their Service equal with the
Service of the* Perfians. *For* Xenophon *confeffeth, that the* Perfian *Bow over-reached
the* Cretan *a great way; and that the* Rhodians *with their Sling out-threw the Cretan Bow. Of the* Carduchans, *a People, through whofe Country the* Grecians *paffed at their return out of* Perfia, *(b)* Xenophon *writeth thus:* They carried no
other Arms, than Bows and Slings. They were excellent Archers, and had
Bows well nigh three Cubits long, Arrows more than two Cubits. When they
fhot, they drew the String, applying their hand fomewhat toward the neither
end of the Bow, fetting their left foot forward. With their Arrows they pierced both Targets and Curates. *The* Grecians *putting Thongs to the midft of
their Arrows, fent them back at the Enemy inftead of Darts. The fame in effect is reported by (c)* Diodorus Siculus. *Of the* Parthian *Horfemen* Appian *faith:*
When *Craffus* commanded the Light-armed to disband, and go to the Charge,
they went not far, but meeting with many Arrows, and being fore galled
with them, they retired ftraight, and hid themfelves amongft the armed, and
gave beginning of diforder and fear; reprefenting to the fight of the reft the
force and violence of the Shot, that rent all Arms they fell upon, and made
way as well through Bodies that had the beft, as the worft furniture defenfive;
giving mighty and violent ftrokes from ftiff and great Bows, and forcing out
the Arrow boyfteroufly with the compafs and bent of the Bow. *(d)* Plutarch
hath the very words that are in Appian. *The* Indians *alfo were good Archers; albeit
not much praifed by* Q. Curtius. *(e) He faith,* Their Arrows were two Cubits
long, which they deliver out of their Bows with more labour than effect: for
as much as the Arrow, whofe whole efficacy is in lightnefs, becometh altogether unwieldy by reafon of the weight. *And yet he telleth,* That *Alexander* at
the Affault of the principal City of the *Mallians*, was ftruck thorough his Curace into the Side, beneath the Paps, with an *Indian* Arrow: *with whom (f)*
Plutarch *and* Diodorus Siculus *accord. (g)* Arrian *addeth, the Wound was fo
deep, that his Breath was feen to iffue out together with his Blood. The* Goths
and other people of the North, that invaded the Roman *Empire, had their chief Vi-
ctories againft the* Romans *by the help of Bows and Arows. (h)* Vegetius *(before
alledged) fpeaketh it plainly:* So our Soldiers, *faith he,* unarmed both Bodies
and Heads, encountring with the *Goths*, were oftentimes wholly defeated and
flain with the multitude of their Arrows. *I may not pretermit the praife of our
Nation in this Skill. Our own Stories teftify, that the great Battels we gained againft
the* French, *were gained by the joynt-fhooting of our Archers principally. And that
the* Englifh *have heretofore excelled in Archery and Shooting, is clear by the teftimony
even of Strangers. (i)* Cicuta *(whom I named before) commending the ufe of Bows,
as neceffary for the fervice of the field (and that long after Guns were invented) pre-*

(a) Paufan. *in* Atticis 40.   (b) Xenoph *de exped* Cyti. *lib.* 4. 322 C.
(c) Diod. Sicul. *lib.* 14. 411.   (d) Plutarch. *in* Craffo.   (e) Curtius *lib.* 8.
353.   (f) Plutarch *in* Alexan. Diod Sicul. *lib* 17. 614.   (g) Arr. *lib.* 6. 129. E.
(h) Veget. *lib.* 1. *cap.* 20.   (i) Aurel. Cicuta *de difciplin. mil. lib.* 2. 206.

ferreth

ferreth the English *before all other, and setteth him down as a Pattern for other to follow. And (a)* Patricius *disputing of the violence of Arrows, doubteth not to affirm, that an* English Arrow, *with a little wax put upon the point of the head, will pass through any ordinary Corslet or Curace. Howsoever the Credit of Bows is lost at this present, with many great Soldiers, yet have they of ancient time been highly prised. (b)* Vegetius *saith, how great advantage good Archers bring in fight, both* Cato *in his Books of Military discipline, doth shew evidently; and* Claudius, *by augmenting the number of Archers, and teaching of them the use of their Bows, overcame the Enemy, whom before he was not able to match.* Scipio Africanus *(the younger) being to give Battel to the* Numantines, *that before had forced a* Roman *Army to pass under the yoak, thought he could not otherwise have the better, unless he mingled chosen Archers in every Century. And (c)* Leo *the Emperor in his Constitutions military, hath this Constitution amongst other; You shall command all the* Roman *Youth, till they come to Forty years of Age, whether they have mean skill in Shooting, or not, to carry Bows and Quivers of Arrows. For since the Art of Shooting hath been neglected, many and great Losses have befallen the* Romans. *And in another place : (d) You shall enjoin the Commanders under you, in Winter, to take a view, and to signify to the* Turmarches *(Colonels) how many Horse, and what kind of Arms the Soldiers under their Commands stand in need of; that necessary Provision be made, and the Soldiers be furnished in time convenient. But especially, you are to have care of Archers; and that they who remain at home, and have vacation from War, hold Bows and Arrows in their Houses. For carelesness herein hath brought great damage to the* Roman *State. So* Leo. *This of old time was the Opinion of the* Romans, *concerning Archers. How we are fallen out with them in our days (the skill of the Bow being a Quality so commendable, and so proper to our Nation) I know not, unless Fire-weapons perhaps have put them out of countenance. And surely, it may not be denied, that the force of Fire-weapons of our time, doth far exceed the height of all old Inventions for annoying the Enemy. And when I have given them the first place, I will not doubt to give the second to Bows and Arrows; being so far from casting them off, that I would rather follow the wisdom of the* Grecians; *who albeit they esteemed Arrows the best flying weapons, yet thought it not amiss to hold in use Slings and Darts. Every weapon hath its property; and that which is fit for one service, is not so fit for another. The Fire-weapons have their Advantages; they have also their Disadvantages. Their Advantage is, they pierce all defence of Armour, and lighting upon a place of the Body, the wound whereof endangereth life, they bring with them certain death. Their Disadvantages are, they are not always certain; sometimes for want of charging, sometimes through overcharging, sometimes the Bullet rowling out, sometimes for want of good Powder, or of dryed Powder, sometimes because of an ill dryed Match, not fit to coal, or not well cocked. Besides they are somewhat long in Charging, while the* Musketeer *takes down his Musket, uncocks the Match, blows, proyns, shuts, casts off the pan, casts about the Musket, opens his Charges, chargeth, draws out his Scouring-stick, rams in the Powder, draws out again, and puts up his Scouring-stick, lays the Musket on the Rest, blows off the Match, cocks, and tries it, gards the pan, and so makes ready. All which Actions must necessarily be observed, if you will not fail of the true use of a Musket. In rain, snow, fogs, or when the Enemy hath gained the wind, they have small use. Add that but one rank (that is the first) can give fire upon the Enemy at once : For the rest behind discharging, shall either wound their own Companions before, or else shoot at random, and so nothing endanger the Enemy; the force of a Musket being only available at point blank. Contrariwise, the disadvantage of Arrows is in the weakness of the stroke, which is not able to enter a Curace, that the Foot or Horse now use. Yet can no Weather be found wherein you may not have good use of Bows : Rain, snow, wind, hail, fogs, hinder little, (especially the string of the Bow being not too wet) nay rather profit. Because in them you can hardly discern, much less avoid the fall of the Arrow. As for quickness in delivery, the Bow far excelleth the Musket. A good single Archer is able to give five Shot in exchange for one of the Musketeer; and that with such certainty, that you shall not hear of an Archer that misseth the delivery of his Arrow, where*

(a) *Patrit. Parall. parte secunda, lib. 3. pag. 37.*   (b) *Veget. lib. 1. cap. 15.*   (c) *Leo*
ap. 6 §. 5.   (d) *Leo cap. 11. § 49.*

X   *the*

the Musketeer ofteen faileth, by reason of the Accidents and Impediments before by me rehearsed. Joyn, that a whole Squadron of Archers being embattail'd, may shoot at once together; which only the first Rank of Musqueteers may do. And make the case there were a hundred Musketeers, and a hundred Bow-men each digested into ten Files, each file containing ten men; the Bow-men shall be able to shoot at once a hundred Arrows (all their Arrows) for ten Bullets given by the Musketeers, namely those ten of the first rank discharging alone. It must not be pretermitted, that the Bow and Quiver both for marching, and all service, are lighter and of less labour to use, than a Musket, which is no small advantage in Arms and fight. To conclude, the Bow-men may be placed behind the armed Foot, and yet in shooting over the Pha-lange annoy the Enemy before joyning, and (a) all the time of Fight, even whilst they are at push of Pike; where the Musketeers, there placed, must either idlely look on, or else playing with his Musket, most of all endanger his own Friends. Neither is the force of Arrows so weak, as is imagined, no not in the arming of our days. For the Pike albeit he have his Head and Body covered, yet are his Legs, and Feet, his Arms, and Hands open to Wounds: any of which parts being wounded brings a disability of service. To say nothing of his Face and Eyes, before which the showers of Arrows falling like a tempest without intermission, must needs breed a remediless terror, and make him think rather of saving himself, than offending his Enemy. The Musketeer being also unarmed is as subject to the shot of Arrows, as the Archer is to the shot of the Musket; and the Arrow touching any vital part, as much taketh away life, as doth the Musket. Lastly, a Horse-man for his own person (I must confess) is safe enough from the danger of Arrows by reason of his Armour; but his Horse, being a fair and large mark, and having neither Barbe, nor Pectoral, nor ought else to hide his Head or Breast, how can he escape Wounds? Witness our fields in France, *where our Archers always beat the* French *Horse, being barbed, and better armed, than our Horse are, at this day. And for the bloudy effect of Bows the story of* Plutarch *is worth the rehearsing. He, in the life of* Crassus *hath thus: (b) The* Parthians *op-*posing the Cataphracts against the *Roman* horse, the other *Persians* galloping here and there dispersedly, and troubling the face of the field, broke up from the bottom, Hills of Sand, that raised infinite dust, whereby the *Romans* lost their sight and voice; and thronging together, and thrusting one another were wounded, and died not a simple, or quick Death but tormented with convul-sions and pangs of Grief, wallowing up and down in the Sand, to break the Arrows in their wounds; or else endeavouring to pluck out the hooked heads, which had pierced Veins and Sinews, renting afresh themselves, and adding Torment to Torment: so that many died in this manner, and the rest became unprofitable. And when *Publius Crassus* desired them once more to charge the Cataphracts, they shewed their Hands nailed to their Targets, and their Feet fastned to the Ground, whereby they were unable either to Flye or Fight. *These wonders did the* Parthian *Bows, which notwithstanding were not to be compa-red to our ancient* English *Bows, either for strength, or farr shooting. And that we may not seem to rely upon antiquity alone. (c) The Battel of* Curzolare *(commonly called the battel of* Lepanto*) fought in our days betwixt the* Turks, *and* Christians *by Sea may serve for an experience of the service of Bows and Arrows. In which there died of the Christians by the Arrows of the* Turks *above five thousand, albeit they were in Galleys and Ships, and had their blinds pretended to save from sight, and mark of the* Turks, *whereas the Artillery of all sorts of the Christians consumed not so many* Turks: *notwithstanding the Christians had the victory. Now then for us to leave the Bow, being a weapon of so great efficacy, so ready, so familiar, and as it were so domestical to our Nation, to which we were wont to be accustomed from our Cradle, because other Nations take themselves to the Musket, hath not so much as any shew of reason. Other Nations may well forbear that, they never had. Neither* Italian, *nor* Spaniard, *nor* French, *nor* Dutch, *have these five hundred years, been accounted Archers. It was a skill almost appropriated to our Nation. By it, we gained the battels of* Cressy, *of* Poitiers, *of* Agincourt, *in* France; *of* Navarre, *in* Spain: *By it, we made our selves famous over Christendom. And to give it over upon a conceit only (for no experience can say that our Bow was ever beaten out of the field by the Musket) will prove an imitation of* Æsop's *Dog, who carrying a piece of flesh in his mouth over a River, and seeing the shadow in the wa-*

(a) *Plut. in Sylla.*   (b) *Plutarch in Crasso.*   (c) *Patric. paral. mil. part 2. p. 39.*

ter, snatched at the shadow, and left the flesh. I speak not this to abase the service of Muskets which all men must acknowledge to be great; I only shew there may be good use of Bows, if our Archers were such as they were wont: which is not to be despaired, and will easily come with Exercise.

But leaving that, a word or two more of the Manor of *Dungeon,* which was sometime the *Chiches*; a Family of Gentlemen, for many Generations known in our City, though now extinct to one poor Spark; to whom the Aldermanry of *Burgate* appertained. Of which *Thomas Chich* (whose name in an old Character, together with his Effigies are set up in the West Window, as his Coat is in the Chancel, in Stone-work, of St. *Mary Bredin's* Church) was *Anno* 1259 (*a*), and again *Anno* 1271, one of the Bailiffs of the City, as was also *John Chich* in the 23. and again in the 26. year of *Edward* III. After the *Chiches* it was the *Brents,* then the *Butlers,* and shortly after the *Hales,* now *Henry Lee's* Esq. [See *Philpot's Villare Cantianum,* pag. 94. *N. B.*]

Chiches a Family.

This Ward affords me nothing else observable, wherefore I leave it, and betake my self to the next.

Burgate Ward.

WHerein I shall observe first the Market-cross, at the *Bull-stake*; and thereof let me give you the true Antiquity from a Rythmical brazen Memorial, fastened to one of the Columns, which is this:

Bull-stake.

John Coppyn of *Whitstabell,* in great Devotion,
And *William Bigg* of *Canterbury,* in Christ's Passion
Did do make this Cross, in Heaven God them solace.
Mcccc. and xlvi. in the Year of Grace.

[It was pulled down by Mr. *John Pollen, Anno* 1645. who was then Mayor of the City, and who coined Farthings of the Lead, wherewith this Cross had been covered. *N. B.*]

This Cross (it seems) was built to supply the decay of a former, standing here. For in the Story of Archbishop *Stratford's* troubles, recorded in the *Antiquit. Brit.* my Author makes mention of a Writ of Summons against the Archbishop, set up at Noon-day, (*b*) *at the high Cross without the Gate of the Priory of* Canterbury.

Now for the Name of the place, the *Bull-stake*: Which it took from the baiting and chasing of Bulls there; by an ancient Order and Custom of the City, used by the City Butchers, before their killing; not so much (if at all) for pleasure, as to make them Man's meat, and fit to be eaten; which Bull's Flesh, without such baiting and chasing, is not held to be.

At this place (the *Bull-stake*) is a Market holden twice a Week, *viz.* every Wednesday and Saturday throughout the Year; plentifully serving the City and Neighbouring parts with houshold Provision of Victual, of divers kinds, especially of Poultry, and that (*c*) from ancient days: Whence in a composition (*d*) between *Christ-Church* and St. *Augustin's* Monks, made *Anno* 41 *Edward* III. that part of the Street by it, *i. e.* between it and the now Lane called *Angel-lane,* is termed le Polettria, the Poultry (*e*) *In a certain Messuage of the said Prior and Convent, with a Warehouse and Shop belonging thereunto, in the Parish of St.* Andrew's, *in the* Poultry, *situated between the Highway or Street toward the North, and other Tenements of the said Prior and Convent toward the South, and a certain Lane called* Clement's-lane *toward the East, and a certain publick place called the* Bull-stake, *toward the West*; as it is in the Composition.

The Poultry.

Offa King of *Mercia* in the year 785, gave unto *Ealdberht* his Minister, and his Sister *Seledrith* the Abbess, (*f*) *the street which is called* Currington *in the City of* Canterbury, *in the North-side of the Market-place.* Where to find this Market-place I know not. But here (as in a place which I have purpos-

---

(a) *Record. Eccles. Cant.*   (b) *Ad crucem excelsam extra portam Prioratus Cantuariensis. Antiq. Brit. in vita Stratford, pag.* 224.   (c) *Ab antiquo.*   (d) *Lib. Eccles. Cant.*

(e) *In quodam Messuagio cum cellar. & shop. ad idem pertinen. dictorum Prioris & Conventus in parochia Sancti Andreæ Cant. in le Polettria situat inter Regalem stratam vers. North & alia tenementa ipsorum P. & C vers. South, & quandam venellam vocat. Clementslane vers. East, & quandam placeam communem vocat. le Bolstake versus West.*   (f) *Vicum qui dicitur Currington in urbe quæ dicitur Doroverensi, in aquilonali parte venalis loci.*

Markets in the City and Suburbs.

ly referved, as moft proper for it) let me fhew unto you what feveral Markets and Market-places our City had of old. For, as we now fee they are, and like as the Philofopher in his Politicks (a) in like cafe requires, where he faith, *Thefe Markets are to be kept in diftinct places for the better conveniences of Trafick: There is one place to be affign'd for Sheep, another for Oxen to be offered to fale. In one place the Butchers, in another place the Bakers are to have their Stalls, according as the City or Town will beft admit of.* So have our Markets been of old, kept apart, each commodity almoft having a diftinct place to be vented in. As (for example) firft Poultry, and other like provifion here at the Bull-ftake.

Wheat-market.

Upwards, *i. e.* without *Burgate* in St. *Paul's* Parifh, was of ancient time a Wheat-Market (b) *of a certain Tenement at the Wheat-market, and of new Shops, which are at the Wheat-market in the Parifh of St.* Paul's, as in old Rentals of *Chrift-Church*, mentioning their now houfes, at and about the corner on your left-hand without *Burgate.* A Deed or Charter of Lands given to St. *Auguftin's*, by one *Dunwaldus* in the year 760 makes mention of a Market-place by *Quenegate* in thefe words: (c) *A Vill now fituated in the Market at* Quenegate *of this City of* Canterbury. Come we back again, and at the *Red-well*, by the Palace back Gate, there was another Market, commonly called and to this

Rufh-market.
Cloth-market.

day remembered by the name of the Rufh-market. In St. *George's* ftreet, about the *Auguftin* Friers Gate, there was a Cloth-market kept (a touch whereof I have given before in fpeaking of thofe Friers) whence the Lane now called *Iron-barr-lane*, was then called and defcribed, (d) *the Lane which leadeth from the Cloth-market toward* Burgate. The fame Lane (by the way) was fome-

Thorough-hall Lane.

time called *Thorough-hall-Lane*, whether or no from a houfe in or by it of *Chrift-Church*, called in their old Rentals, (e) *St. Dunftan's Hall*; I leave to conjecture. Below this Cloth-market, was as it is ftill, the Flefh-market, or Flefh-fhambles for Butchery ware. To the repair whereof, and for paving the Street thereaway, Alderman *Bennet* by his Will (f) *Anno* 1462, gave x *l.* Thus occafionally induced, let me obferve that the City in thofe days lay generally unpaved, and fo continued a good fpace of time afterwards. But in 17th year of *Edward* IV. by a particular Act of Parliament made for that pur-

Act of Parliament for paving the Streets.

pofe, order was taken for the paving of the principal Streets, as by a copy of the fame Act, which you may find in my *Appendix* will more fully appear, Numb. XXVI.

Fifh-market.

Yet lower down (to return to our Market-places) to wit, in the High-ftreet, befides St. *Mary Bredman's* Church, was wont in time paft to be kept a Fifh-market. (g) *In the middle of the Market, where Fifh is fold, nigh the Church of* St. Mary Bredman, as I find in the examination of a witnefs, mentioning where certain words of defamation were uttered by one that was fued for them, in *Anno* 1414 (h). This Fifh-market (it feems) was of long continuance kept here. For in a Deed of *Chrift-Church*, dated 1187, mention is made of a houfe, (i) *fituate in the Parifh of St.* Mary's, *which is called the Church of the Fifh-mongers in* Canterbury, paffed over to the Church (in exchange for another) by the Nuns of St. *Sexburgh* in the Ifle of *Shepey.* And before that, *Odo* the Prior of *Chrift-Church* leafed out (k) *the manfion of* Lambert Gargate *nigh Fifh-mongers-Church, to wit, that part which is next to the Church,* &c. as the Demife runs. Now I conceive this to be the Church intended by thofe Deeds. And fo, as it is now, from the Bread-market by it called St. *Mary Bredman's* Church, it was more anciently called St. *Mary Fifhman's* Church. I proceed.

Oaten-hill.

Upwards, a little without *Newingate*, at *Oaten-Hill*, now the City's place of Execution, was that commodity of Oats, fometime vented; as at the fame place before Salt was fold, whence it was called *Salt-Hill* (l). It had a Market Crofs to it: for I read of (m) *the Crofs at* Oat-Hill. The place hath a Crofs ftill, but it is ill marketting at it.

(a) *Ariftot. 7. Politicor. cap.* 12.　　(b) *De quodam tenemento apud Wheat-market; De novis fhoppis quæ funt apud Wheat-market in parochia Sancti Pauli.*　　(c) *Villam unam, quæ jam ad Quenegatum urbis Doroverniis in foro pofita eft.*　　(d) *Venella quæ ducit à Cloth-market verfus Burgate. Rentale vetus Ecclef. Chrifti Cant.*　　(e) *Aula Sancti Dunftani.*　　(f) *In Regiftro Domini Archid. Cant.*　　(g) *In medio mercati ubi venduntur pifces Cant. juxta ecclefiam beatæ Mariæ Bredman.*　　(h) *Ex Regiftro Confiftor. Cant.*　　(i) *Situat. in parochia Sanctæ Mariæ, quæ vocatur Ecclefia Pifcariorum in Cant.*　　(k) *Manfium Lamberti Gargate juxta Fifmannccherich, ubi ipfe Lambertus manere folebat, fcilicet partem illam quæ eft proxima Ecclefiæ, &c.*　　(l) *Rentale vet. Ecclef. Chrifti Cant.*　　(m) *Crucem de Oat hill.*

Not

Not far hence, to wit, by the Nunnery, at the meeting of the four Wents or Ways there, another Market was kept, or the former continued thither; whence the Field over-againſt the Nunnery, Southward, now almoſt all over digged for Chalk, is anciently called Market-field *(a)*. Here were, as not far hence yet are, Cattel bought and ſold, eſpecially (at this day, Bullocks, Oxen, and the like: Whence (as I conceive) the Market took its name at firſt of *Re- thercheap*; which being a compound of two *Saxon* words, *Hrythera* and *Ceape*, may be rendred in *Latin, Forum armentorum,* and in *Engliſh,* the Drove-market; hnýẟeꝑa in the *Saxon* ſignifying a Drove of Oxen, or ſuch like big Cattel. Whence in a *Latin* Charter of *Cuthred* King of *Kent,* made to Archbiſhop *Wl- fred,* which I have ſeen in *Chriſt-Church, Campus armentorum* is engliſhed, hꝑý- ẟꝑa leahᵹ. For the antiquity ſake of this Market, I cannot but take notice of the mention made of it in the ſecond of King *Ethelbert*'s Charters to St. *Augu- ſtin*'s Abbey.

Rethercheape.

There was yet another Market, and that of old was kept in *Wincheape*. A Market haply for Wines: For ſo the Name imports: [Unleſs any ſhall chuſe to fetch it from the Wents or Ways there meeting, as if it was *Went-cheap*. W.S.] *Cheap* ſignifying a Market; whence the name of *Cheapſide* in *London, Chepſtow* in *Monmouthſhire,* and other like Market-places; as Chapman, for a Trader there. Our words alſo of Cheapning, Chopping (as chopping and changing) and of Shop, anciently written uſually (in Lawyers *Latin*) *Choppa,* as alſo of *Lieu-cope* (ſignifying a Sale or Bargain made upon the place) have thence all their derivation; ſpringing from the *Saxon Radix,* which is *Ceap,* ſignifying Wares or Merchandiſe, and *Cyppan,* to buy *(b)*. This Market had its Croſs too, and that ſtanding within Man's memory, upon the Green before the Street, built of Stone, with a Croſs-houſe about it, and was called *Barnacle*-Croſs. But there is neither Market, nor Market-Croſs there now. 'Tis true there is hard by, a Croſs; but (as that other at *Oaten-hill*) it ſpoils their marketing ever after that once Market thereat. And therefore let us haſten from it.

Wincheape.

Barnacle Croſs.

Cathedral and Pariſh Churches.

HAving briefly ſurveyed our City's Wards, the Order of my propoſed Me- thod requires, in the next place, my Survey of the Cathedral, and Pariſh Churches of and about the City. Firſt then of the Mother Church (the Ca- thedral) and then of the Daughters. The former indeed the thing which I ac- count the chiefeſt Glory both of the City, and my preſent Survey thereof. Which *Malmesbury (c),* haply not knowing how to commend enough, amongſt the many Commendations which he gives our City, (as, for the Situation and exceeding Fertility of the Soil adjoining, for the ſoundneſs of the incloſing Walls, for the Rivers watering it, for the commodiouſneſs of the neighbouring Woods, for the vicinity alſo of the Sea yielding ſtore of Fiſh to ſerve it, for the noble and generous Diſpoſition of the People, as well of it as of the Coun- trey, prone and propenſe to offer Courteſy to others, and impatient of any In- jury offered to themſelves, and the like) ſays no more of the Church, but this. After the Converſion of the *Engliſh* to Chriſtianity, the prime Epiſcopal See was fixed at *Canterbury,* and there continues. Saving that anon after he adds; There is the Archbiſhop's chief Seat, who is the Primate and Patriarch of all *England.* But I cannot ſo contain my ſelf: Yet for my more methodical Pro- ceeding, much being to be ſaid of this Metropolitan Church, my whole Diſ- courſe thereof ſhall be referred to theſe Heads.

Malmſb. com- mendation of *Canterbury.*

1. *The Antiquity of the Foundation, and the Nature thereof.*
2. *The Hiſtory of the Church's Fabrick.*
3. *A Survey of the preſent Church, with the Monuments therein, as alſo of the more Ancient Buildings throughout the Precinct both of it and the Palace, with the Ambitus, or Precinct it ſelf.*
4. *A Catalogue of the principal Benefactors to the Church.*
5. *A Catalogue of the* { 1. *Archbiſhops,* 2. *Priors,* 3. *Archdeacons,* } *of the Church.*

(a) Lib. S. Lawrentii, & Rentale Eccleſ. Cant.   *(b) Cambden. Spelman.*   *(c) In* *Prolog. lib. 1. de geſtis Pontif.*

The

The Antiquity and Foundation of Chrift-Church.

1. Particular. TO begin with the firft; The Antiquity and Nature of the Foundation. In the former of which I fhall be brief, that fo I may not (a) make needlefs Repetitions of what others, many others, for even vulgar fatisfaction, have already faid upon the Point, as *Bede, Parker, Cambden, Lambard*; a few of the many that have largely and worthily written hereof. It may not be expected, nor will it (I conceive) become me (b), after fo many famous Writers to undertake the Narrative of thefe things. Neither can I in this matter fay what is not vulgarly known already. And (c) fuch needlefs Repetitions will not pleafe I know in fuch dainty Times as thefe. Yet not altogether to put you over to other Mens Inftructions, and to let you fee that the ancient Leiger-Writers of the Church, in Thankfulnefs to the Founder, keep him and the Foundation in memory; I fhall here by way of Corollary, or (to fpeak in the Language of mine own Profeffion) *ex fuperabundanti*, over and above what is abfolutely needful, produce and prefent unto you a treble Note faithfully taken from the Leigers, which doth memorize both one and t'other. The one thus penned, (as in the *Appendix*, Numb. XXVII. *a, b, c.*) informs us, that [" The Foundation of

Append Numb. XXVII. *a.* " *Chrift-Church* in *Canterbury* was laid by *Lucius* the firft Chriftian King of the " *Britons*, in the time of the *Romans*: The Monaftical Order was firft inftituted " in this Church by St. *Auguftin*, the Apoftle of the *Englifh* Nation; who as foon as " he had obtain'd an Epifcopal Chair in this City, with the aid of the King " repair'd the Church, built here (as he had been informed) by the Believing " *Romans*, and dedicated it in the Name of God our Saviour, and our Lord " *Jefus Chrift*; and appointed this to be a Seat for himfelf and his Succeffors. " And here he built a Monaftery alfo. For King *Ethelbert* had given him his " Royal Palace, with the whole City; where St. *Auguftin* and his Monks li- " ved together in common, after the Pattern of the Holy Difciples of our " Bleffed Lord, &c. W. S.]

Numb. XXVII. *b.* The Second is to this effect. " King *Ethelbert*, who was converted to the " Chriftian Religion by St. *Auguftin*, A. D. 596. gave him his Palace in the " City of *Canterbury*, for his Habitation, and for his Succeffors, together with " the old Church, which had been built there in the times of the *Romans*; " and which *Auguftin* himfelf, after he had been confecrated a Bifhop at " *Arles*, dedicated to the Name of our Holy Saviour. By vertue of Authority " from the See of *Rome*, King *Ethelbert* appointed, that in this Church Monks " fhould for ever obferve the Monaftick Order, namely, left the Preaching of " the firft Monks, by whom Chriftianity was planted in this Nation, fhould " ever flip out of their memories, &c.

Numb. XXVII. *c.* The Third tells us, " King *Ethelbert* in the 35. Year of his Reign being " converted to the Faith of *Chrift*, by St. *Auguftin*, did forthwith give his Pa- " lace within the City of *Canterbury* to him and to his Succeffors for ever, that " they might have there a Metropolitical See, to the end of the World. St. *Gre-* " *gory* decreed and confirm'd, that this See fhould be the firft of the whole " Kingdom; that where the Chriftian Faith was firft received, there alfo " fhould be a primacy of dignity. This Gift was granted by the King, *A.D.* 597.

Thus the Leigers, (d) Witneffes indeed in their own cafe, but in regard of the many confentient Teftimonies (if not of themfelves) of indubious credit. So much for the Antiquity.

Now the nature of the Foundation appears from thefe Extracts, plainly fhewing the intention both of *Auguftin, Ethelbert*, and *Gregory* to be, to make it (as it afterward became) both a Monaftery and a Cathedral, or rather a Cathedral-Monaftery. The better to underftand me, you muft know, that (as *Reyner* (e) hath it) fince and from the time that Chriftianity was firft embraced by the *Saxons* inhabiting this Ifland, there have been in *England* two forts of Monafteries the one Cloiftral, the other Cathedral. (f) Thofe were call'd

---

(a) *Dictum dicere.*   (b) *Poft tot Homeros fcribere Iliada.*   (c) *Crambe bis cocta.*
(d) *Teftes domeftici.*   (e) *Apoftolat. Benedictin. tract. 1. Sectio 1. §. 17 pag. 77.*
(f) *Etenim duo genera cœnobiorum habuit Anglia, à prima fidei Chriftianæ receptione: unum clauftralium duntaxat, aliud verò Cathedralium; vocabantur clauftralia, in quibus fub Abbate aut Priore, Abbatem proprium non habente, occupabatur conventus in divinis officiis, actibufque regularibus ad perfectionem fingulorum Monachorum acquirendam ordinatis, fine onere & cura regiminis diœcefani. Cathedralia verò, quorum Abbas erat Epifcopus, & conventus erat capitulum cathedralis ecclefiæ, atque adeo Monachi erant canonici cathedrales, ad quos omnia munia pertinebant, quæ in ecclefiis cathedralibus fæcularibus, ad fæculares canonicos fpectare dignofcuntur, &c.*

Cloy-

Cloyftral, who were governed by an Abbat, or where there was no Abbat by a Prior. Thofe were Cathedral, where the Bifhop was Abbat, and the Convent was the Chapter of the Cathedral Church; and fo the Monks were Cathedral Canons, performing all thofe Offices which fecular Canons are wont to perform in fecular Cathedrals. Of the which latter fort was this our Monaftery, a Cathedral-Monaftery. [But this diftinction, tho' offer'd by one who was well skill'd in the Monaftical Orders, both in *England*, and beyond Sea, feems liable to fome exception. For I do not remember, that in Cathedral Monaftries, the Bifhop was ever reputed as Abbat; but the Prior, who was inftead of an Abbat, chief over the Monks. And the Capitular Acts did run alike in the fame form, as well in Cathedral as Clauftral Monaftries; *Abbas & Capitulum, Prior & Capitulum*; which is, *The Abbat, or, the Prior and the Convent or Chapter. N. B.*] *Chrift-Church a Cathedral Monaftery.*

Now of what Order this *Auguftin* and his Monks were, and confequently this Foundation originally was, is of fome made difputable in thefe days; the received Opinion, until now of late, without queftion affirming them *Benedictines*, or Followers of the Order of the black Monks of St. *Bennet*. The Adverfaries of which Opinion haply, are fufficiently anfwered in *Reyner's Apoftolatus Benedictinorum*, &c. to which I refer the unfatisfied. Now what kind of Order this of St. *Benet* was, will beft be learned from the Story of it's Author, St. *Benet* himfelf. Take here, therefore, a Relation thereof, borrowed for the more part of *Polydore Virgil* (a).

Authors vary in the Year, but agree that in the Fifth Century or Age of the Church, one *Benedictus Nurfinus*, a man born in *Umbria*, a Region in *Italy*, having led fome certain years a folitary life in thofe defart places, at length retired to *Sublacum*, a Town diftant forty Miles from *Rome*; whither many People (by reafon of his great fame, and integrity, and holinefs of life) reforted unto him. But within a while he departed thence, and repaired to *Caffinum*, an ancient City in that Region; where he built a Monaftery, and in a very fhort time gathered together all fuch Monks as then wandred here and there in the Woods and Defarts of *Italy*, and gave them certain Rules and Statutes to obferve and keep, and withal bound them to three feveral Vows: (by the Example of St. *Bafil*, who had prefcribed them in the Eaft-Country to certain Monks of his, about the Year 383. which *Bafil*, was the firft that gave Rules or Orders unto Monks:) The one of Chaftity; the Second of Poverty; the laft of Obedience. To live chaftly, to poffefs nothing, and to obey their Superiors Commands. Again, *Benet* gave unto his Monks, a new kind of Habit; he appointed them alfo a certain Form of praying, and intending to allow them but mean Commons, prefcribed them a new Rule of Abftinence. You have the Story. *Story of St. Bennet.*

By the way, this congregation of St. *Benet* grew by little and little to be fo great, that it is almoft incredible. There were no Monafteries (faith *Reyner*(b)) amongft the *Englifh* from the time of King *Edgar*, till the time of *William* the Conqueror, but *Benedictines*. Yet in the end there hapned fuch a Schifm among them, that it was and ftill is divided into many Families, as the *Cluniacenfes, Camalduenfes, Vallifumbrenfes, Montolivitenfes, Grandimontenfes, Ciftercienfes, Sylveftrenfes, Cœleftini*, and diverfe others, who are now adays either united with other Orders, or elfe quite extirpated and abolifhed. Thofe that were firft inftituted by this Saint (as they themfelves confefs, faith *Polydor* (c)) are thofe that now adays wear a black loofe Coat of Stuff reaching down to their heels, with a Cowl or Hood of the fame which hangs down to their fhoulders, and their Scapular fhorter than any other of thofe Monks: and under that Coat another white Habit as large as the former, made of Stuff or white Flannel, and Boots on their legs. They fhave their heads, except one little round circle which they call their Crown, and perpetually abftain from Flefh, unlefs when they are fick, &c. This Order (faith *Reyner*) came firft into *England* with *Auguftine* the Monk, Archbifhop of *Canterbury*. So you have in brief both the ftory of St. *Benet*, and the condition of his order: wherewith if you will be further acquainted, I refer you to the Decrees or Conftitutions of it, recom- *Benedictines their Habit.*

(a) *De Invent. Rerum, l. 7. c. 2.*   (b) *Apoftolat. Benedict. tract. 1. §. 1. fect. 1. pag. 11.*
(c) *Ubi fupra.*

mended

mended by Archbishop *Lanfranc* to the observation of his Monks of this Church, (whereof *Reyner*'s forecited book affords a copy ;) and to the *Ceremoniale Benedictinum.* And so have I done with the first Head or Particular, and proceed to the next.

The History of the Church's Fabrick.

THE records of the Church, concurring with the common opinion of our Historians, tells us of a Church in *Canterbury,* which *Augustin* at his first arrival here found standing in the East part of the City. A work (saith *Bede (a).)* of the ancient faithful or believing *Romans.* This Church *Augustin* had of gift from King *Ethelbert,* which after his consecration at *Arles* in *France* he commended by special dedication to the patronage of our Blessed Saviour. Whence it afterward became called *(b) The Church of our Blessed Saviour.* [I must here interpose and observe, That the Church, which St. *Augustin* Found at his first arrival in the East part of the City, was St. *Martin's* Church. For this Church, dedicated to our Saviour, stands not in the East part, but, as it were, in the middle of the City, and undoubtedly was built, as the other Church of St. *Martin's* was also, by the faithful believing *Romans. N. B.*] All extant Stories, Coucher-books or Leigers, and Records that ever I could yet see, afford no remarkable matter concerning this Fabrick (the miraculous preservation of it from the injury of all Weathers then very tempestuous in neighbouring parts, whilest it was in Roofing, at the Prayer of Archbishop *Odo,* only excepted *(c)*) from the time of this her infancy, until that lamentable *Danish* demolition of it in the days of King *Ethelred.* When a common fire

The Cathedral burned. kindled by that implacable insatiable rout of *Danish* divelish Furies, malicing not the persons only, but for their sakes, the place too, consumed both it and the City : whereof see a full relation (if you please) in my *Appendix* taken from *Osbern* the Monk of *Canterbury,* and never before Printed. *(d)* [This dismal Calamity which befel the Church and City of *Canterbury,* is related by several of our Historians at large, and almost in the same words, as if they had copied it from one another. *(e)* It was so remarkable, that I think no Pen, which records the Transactions of those times, has omitted it : Nor shall it be here passed over in silence. Mr. *Somner* did refer us to the Relation of it in *Latin,* in the *Appendix* of the former Edition from *Osbern,* which then had never been Printed : But the same Story being related by several others ; and *Osbern* being also of late Printed, *(f)* I shall now ease the *Appendix* of it, and refer those, who desire to consult the Narration at large, to the Author himself ; and the Margin directs where to find him. *Osbern* indeed is the most Authentick Writer of this relation, that we can rely upon ; and, which will further account for my dismissing him from the *Appendix,* I will give an abridgment of the long Story in *English,* as I receive it from the Pen of *Osbern.*

A. D. 1011. in *September,* the *Danes* with a numerous and well arm'd Fleet came to *Sandwich;* there Landing, they made their way directly for *Canterbury ;* which they forthwith Encompassed and Besieged. They carried on the Siege with all vigour, using all war-like means either to Batter, or to scale the Walls, or by throwing Fire to set the City in a Flame : And on the 20th day of the Siege, this last way took effect : for a fire being kindled in some Houses that were nearest to the Walls, was so encreased by a strong South-wind , that the whole City was presently all in a Flame. The Citizens were brought into a miserable streight : for before them they saw the Enemy ready to enter with Sword in hand. Behind them they saw the Flames not only devouring their Houses, but, which was far more dreadful, ready to devour their Wives also and Children. Hereby private Affection and a tenderness of Compassion prevailed so far over them, as to neglect the publick Safety. They forsook the defence of the Walls, ran to their own Houses to pluck their Wives and Children out of the Flames, who in the same hour were to be exposed to the more merciless fury of the Enemy. For whilst they were busied amongst the Ashes of their houses, the City was broken up : the Enemies entred : Then a terri-

---

(a) *Ecclesiast. Hist. lib. 1. cap.* 33. (b) *Ecclesia S. Salvatoris.* (c) *Malmsb de Gest.* *Pontif. lib* I· *pag.* 201. *Edit. Francof.* (d) *See Angl. Sac. Part* 2 *p.* 133, *&c.* (e) *Match.* *Westm Florent. Wigorn. Symeon. Dunelm. Jo. Brompt Rog. Hoveden, &c.* (f) *Angl. Sac. Vol.* 2. *p.* 133.

ble noife of Shrieks and Cries on the one fide, of Trumpets and Shouts on the other fide, was lifted up to the Heavens, fo as the very foundations of the City feem'd to be fhaken. And now, Who can conceive in his Thoughts, what fad Confufions overfpread the whole City? Some fall by the Sword, fome perifh in the Flames, fome are thrown headlong over the Walls, and others in a manner more fhameful than is fit to be expreffed, are put to death. The noble Matrons are drag'd by the Hair of the head through the Streets, to extort from them a confeffion of hid Treafures, which they never had, and then were caft into the Flames. Little Children were torn from their Mothers Breafts; fome of them were carried about, ftuck on the tops of Spears; others were laid under the Wheels of Carriages and crufhed all to pieces. The Venerable Archbifhop, who all this while had ftaid in the Church, in the midft of his weeping Monks, could no longer endure to hear of the calamities of the miferable People, rufheth out of a fudden from the Church, runs among the heaps of flain Bodies into the midft of the Enemies, cries aloud, *Spare,* O *Spare,* &c. They feiz'd upon him, bind him, ftop his Mouth that he fhould not fpeak, beat and abufe him; they force him back to the Church, and there make him ftand and fee a moft difmal Tragedy: For before his Eyes, many are put to feveral kinds of cruel death, that he might behold Death in the moft frightful Shapes, before he came to dye himfelf. The Church is rifled, and fet on fire. The melted Lead ran down upon the heads of the Monks. They come out and are prefently put to the Sword. In this flaughter the Monks and People, Men, Women, and Children were decimated, nine were flain, and one faved alive. The Archbifhop was carried away alive, kept in Prifon for fome time and then put to death. This is the Relation which Mr. *Somner* gave in *Latin,* and I have given it (and more briefly too) in *Englifh. N. B.*]

Shortly after which vaftation, the Church arofe again, and was (I read) by **Re-edified.** *Agelnoth* the Archbifhop (at whofe coming to the See it was begun to be repaired after that *Danifh* fpoil) entirely brought to perfection (a). About which time, to wit, in the year 1023, haply by the fame Archbifhop's procurement, (for being well beloved of the King, he perfuaded him to many worthy acts) (b) and not unlikely for recompence and expiation of the late fpoil of the Church, made by the King's Countrymen the *Danes* ((c) *and endeavouring alfo to reconcile all the* Englifh *unto himfelf, by the perfuafion of Queen* Emma, *he confer'd many Donations upon them;* they are the words of *Matt.* of *Weftminfter* of King *Knute* in that very year 1023) *Knute* gave the Port of *Sandwich* (or rather **Sandwich.** reftored it, for King *Egelred* or *Ethelred* had given it 44 years before) to this Church. A thing thus recorded in one of the Liegers of the place (d) " In " the year 1023 King *Kanutus* gave unto *Chrift-Church* in *Canterbury* the Port of " *Sandwich,* with his Crown of Gold, which is yet preferv'd in the head of " the great Crofs in the nave of the faid Church. He gave that Port to the " Monks with the Toll of the fame Village, and with wreck of Sea and all " other Cuftoms belonging to the faid Port. Which Gift *Hen.* II. afterward renewed and enlarged, granting to the Monks by his charter, (e) " the Cuftom " of the Port of *Sandwich* on both fides of the water, that is, from *Eadbur-* " *gate* unto *Merksfleet,* and a ferry-boat, &c. as I have it in the Church Records: all which (f) *excepting their Houfes and Keys, and a free Paffage in the Haven, in a little Boat, called a* Vere-boat. [I fuppofe it is a fmall Ferry-boat. *N. B.*] and free liberty for themfelves and their men to buy and fell Toll-free, were of the Monks, in exchange (g) *for* lx. Libratæ *of Land* in fome other convenient place in Kent, refigned to the King that then was *Edward* I. and that *Anno* 18. *Regni fui,* to wit, *Anno Domini* 1290. [Dr. *Brady* (h) obferves, That thefe Privileges

---

(a) *Antiq. Brit. in ejus vita, pag.* 94. [(b) *Vide Ingulph. Hift. Fol.* 507. *Lond Edit.* W. S.]
(c) *Anglos quoque omnes, hortatu* Emma Regina, *fibi reconciliare ftudens, multa eis donaria contulit.*
(d) *Anno* 1023. Kanutus Rex dedit Ecclefia Chrifti in Dorobernia portum de Sandwico, cum corona fua aurea quæ adhuc fervatur in capite crucis majoris in navi ejufdem ecclefiæ. Portum illum dedit Monachis cum thelonio ejufdem villæ, wrecco maris & omnibus aliis confuetudinibus ad portum illum pertinentibus.

(e) *Confuetudines portus Sandwici ex utraque parte aquæ, viz. ob* Eadburgate *ufque ad* Merkesfleete, *& naviculam ad transfretandum, &c.* (f) *Exceptis domibus eorum & Kaiis, ac libero paffagio in portu prædicto in batello qui dicitur verebote. Lib. Ecclef Chrifti Cant.* (g) *Pro* lx *libratis terræ in alio loco competenti, in Comitatu Kancia.* (h) Treatife of Cities and Boroughs, *Append.*
p. 10. D.

or Rights of receiving *Toll* for things bought and sold in Markets, and of *Wreck*, or Goods thrown over Board, when a Ship is over laden or cast away at Sea, did in all places belong to the Crown, and could not be injoyed but by special Grant or Privilege. I further add, That *lx. Libratæ* of Land, was so much Land as will afford every year lx. *Libras* or pounds Rent: Or else lx. full Plough-lands, (*a*) as *Sirmondus* explains it. I may further add, That the Prior of this Church, whilest he had the Customs of the Port of *Sandwich* was wont to receive two pence upon every Vessel of Wine coming into that Port. (*b*) *Rot. Claus. H. III. membr.* 17. N. B.] But let's to our Church Fabrick again.

The Cathe-dral fired a second time.

Which, it seems, by Fire, or otherwise, fell shortly to decay a second time. For of certain it was greatly ruinated, when *Lanfranc* came to the Chair ; (*c*) *Edmer* says, *that* Lanfranc, *at his first coming to* Canterbury, *found the Church of our Saviour reduced almost to nothing, by Fire and Dilapidations.* Indeed *Edmerus* elsewhere (*d*) saith expresly that the Church was burnt the third Year before *Lanfranc's* coming to the See. An Accident enough in it self, but for the loss of those ancient Privileges (certain Charters or Muniments) of the Church, which (as the same Author also there witnesseth) perished in that flame, much more deplorable. Of certain then, Fire brought this Fabrick to a second de-

Re-edified by Lanfranc.

solation before *Lanfranc's* time : And as certain it is, that his Care, Piety and Pity, raised both the Monastery and it in all its parts of new, and that in a no-vel and more magnificent kind and form of Structure than was formerly here used, which made it a Precedent and Pattern to succeeding Structures of this kind in the Kingdom. (*e*) *Endmer* again says, *That Religion was much advanced throughout all this Nation, and new Monasteries* (as is to be seen at this day) *were every where built.* Lanfranc *set the first Example of these Acts of Piety, who built* Christ-Church *in* Canterbury, *the Wall, which does encompass the Court, and all the Offices belonging to the Monastery, within the Wall thereof.* Indeed it is obser-ved (*f*), that before the *Normans* advent, most of our Monasteries and Church-Buildings were of Wood (all the Monasteries in my Realm, saith King *Ed-gar,* in his Charter to the Abby of *Malmesbury,* dated the Year of Christ, 974 (*g*), to the outward sight are nothing but worm-eaten and rotten Timber and Boards :) and that upon the *Norman* Conquest, such Timber-fabricks grew out of use, and gave place to Stone-buildings raised upon Arches, a form of Structure introduced by that Nation, furnished with Stone from *Cane* in *Nor-mandy.* " In the Year 1087, (*Stow's* words of the Cathedral at *London*) this " Church of St. *Paul* was burnt with Fire, and therewith the most part of " the City. *Mauricius,* then Bishop, began therefore the new Foundation " of a new Church of St. *Paul* ; a Work, that men (of that time) judged " would never have been finished, it was to them so wonderful for length " and breadth ; as also the same was builded upon Arches (or Vaults) of " Stone, for defence of Fire ; which was a manner of work before that time " unknown to the People of this Nation, and then brought in by the *French* ; " and the Stone was fetcht from *Cane* in *Normandy.* St. *Mary Bow*-Church in *London,* being built much about the same time and manner, that is, on Arches of Stone, was therefore called (saith the same Author) New *Mary* Church, or St. *Mary le Bow* ; as *Stratford*-bridge being the first builded with Arches of Stone, was called therefore *Stratford le Bow.* This doubtless is that new kind of Architecture, the Continuer of *Bede* (whose words *Malmesbury* (*h*) hath ta-ken up) intends, where speaking of the *Normans* In-come, he saith (*i*) You may observe every where, in Villages Churches, and in Cities and Villages Monasteries, erected with a new kind of Architecture. I have digressed, but return and proceed.

Lanfranc, you see, new built the Church, and that probably (as I conceive) after this new *French* form, and within the space of seven Years (saith *Edme-*

(*a*) Mr. *Somner's Glossar. in* X. *Scriptores.*   (*b*) *Philpot's Villare Cantianum.*   (*c*) *Hic er-go* Lanfrancus *cum* Cantuariam *primò venisset,* & *ecclesiam* Salvatoris, *quam regere susceperat, incendio at-que ruinis, pene nihili factam invenisset,* &c. *Hist. Novor. lib.* 1. *pag.* 7.   (*d*) *Ead. Hist. lib.* 1. *p.* 9.
(*e*) *Per totam terram illam religio aucta est,* & *ubique nova Monasteriorum ædificia, sicut hodie apparet, constructa ; quorum ædificiorum constructoribus ipse primus exemplum præbens, ecclesiam* Christi Cantuarien-*sem, cum omnibus officiis quæ infra murum ipsius Curiæ sunt cum ipso muro ædificavit. Pag.* 7.
(*f*) Stow, *Survey of* London, *pag.* 352. *ult. Edit.* Daniel. *Hist. in vita* Conquestoris.   (*g*) D H.
Spelman, *Concil. pag.* 488.   (*h*) *De gest. Reg. Aug. lib.* 3. *pag.* 102. Edit. Francof.
(*i*) *Videas ubique in villis ecclesias, in vicis* & *urbibus Monasteria novo ædificandi genere consurgere.*

rus)

rus) (*a*) He almoſt entirely compleated the Work, from the very Foundation thereof. Which, ſo by him perfected, probably he innovated the Name and Title of it ; dedicating the ſame to the Holy Trinity. For as until then it had been called (as you ſee before) (*b*) *The Church of our Bleſſed Saviour* : So in his time and from thenceforth it became called (as by *Doomſday*-Book appears), (*c*) *The Church of the Holy Trinity.* The Inſcription on the Church's firſt Seal (made no doubt ſince the Conqueſt, they not being in uſe in this Kingdom before (*d*)) ſhews as much ; which in alluſion (it ſeems) and reference to the Church's dedication, was this : (*e*) *God the Father, God the Son, God the Holy Ghoſt.* Name of the Cathedral altered.

Thus I am told, how truly, I make ſome doubt ; both becauſe, though converſant in the Church Records, I never as yet met with any ſuch Seal, and for that the Seal which was in uſe not long after the Conqueſt, namely, both in the time of *Anſelme* the Archbiſhop, (*Lanfranc*'s immediate Succeſſor) and *Arnulfe* the Prior ; *i. e.* about the beginning of the Eleventh Century, which I have often ſeen, hath no other Inſcription at all on it, but this (nor would the proportion of the Seal admit of a larger) (*f*) *The Seal of* Chriſt-Church. But to go on.

Next after *Lanfranc* ſucceeded *Anſelme*, as in his See, ſo in his Piety. For in his time, and chiefly by his care, coſt and providence, that Fabrick begun and perfected by his Predeceſſor, became much enlarged ; whereof *Edmerus* makes a double mention, to wit, firſt, *pag.* 35. and again, *pag.* 108. (*g*) *The Oratory or Quire, as far as from the great Tower to the Eaſt-end, was by the care of Archbiſhop* Anſelme, *enlarged,* ſays *Edmer.* The Monks (it ſeems by *Edmerus*) magnificently finiſhed this Work which *Anſelme* piouſly began ; the King (*Hen.* I.) affording it and them his Countenance and encouragement. For when ſome evil-minded Perſons maligning the Work, ſuggeſted to the King, that the Monks were mad, and prodigally waſted to ſuperfluous uſes, what might ſtand him much in ſtead in his Regal expences ; he anſwers them thus : (*h*) *What ? Do the Monks* (ſays the King) *ſpend their revenues on worldly things, on vain works, which are foreign, and contrary to their Profeſſion ? But if they lay them out for the glorious and magnificent enlarging of the Houſe of God ; Bleſſed be God, who both inſpired their minds to do ſuch works, and alſo beſtowed this Grace and Favour upon me, that in my days, the Church my Mother, ſhould rather be increaſed than decreaſed. Matthew Paris* records a dedication of the Church of *Canterbury,* in the year of Chriſt, 1114. Haply it was of that new piece, or new Work, as *Edmerus* calls it. This doubtleſs is the part meant by *Malmeſbury* (*i*), aſcribed to *Ernulfus* the then Prior of the Church, and of him ſaid to have been built in the place of a like part then demoliſhed ; whereof he hath theſe words. (*k*) He ſays, *That* Ernulph *pulled down the forepart of the Church which* Lanfranc *had built ; and rebuilt it with ſuch ſplendor, that the like was not to be ſeen in all* England, *in reſpect of the clear lights of the Glaſs-windows, the beauty and comelineſs of the marble Pavement, and the curious Paintings of the Roof.* Thus he.

[By the forepart of the Church, the Reader muſt underſtand the whole Quire, from the great Tower, now called *Bell-Harry-Steeple*, to the *Eaſt* End : All which was begun to be Rebuilt by *Ernulph*, and finiſhed by *Conrade* his Succeſſor in this Priory. N. B.]

Cathedral enlarged.

This Church thus new built, and thus alſo enlarged fell again ſome ſay, by a fire about the year 1130. But ſoon found ſuch as pitied her misfortune, and took commiſeration of her ruins : whereof Archbiſhop *Corboyl* is ſaid (*l*) to be the chief, who they ſay of his own Purſe ſet it up again, and then after a moſt ſolemn manner did dedicate the ſame, in the preſence of the King, the Queen, Cathedral again dedicated.

(*a*) *A fundamentis fermè totam perfectam reddidit. Hiſt. memorat. pag.* 8.   (*b*) *Eccleſia S. Salvatoris.*   (*c*) *Eccleſia Sanctæ Trinitatis.*   (*d*) *Cambd. Brit. In Eſſex, pag.* 444 *Engl. Edit.*
(*e*) *Deus Pater, Deus Filius, Deus Spiritus Sanctus.*   (*f*) *Sigillum Eccleſiæ Chriſti.*
(*g*) *Super hoc ipſum Oratorium, quantum à majore turri in orientem porrectum eſt, ipſo patre Anſelmo providente, diſponente auctum eſt.*   (*h*) *Quid in externas expenſas, in ſæcularia aliqua, in vana & ordini ſuo contraria opera, res ſuas Monachi ponunt ? At, ſi in augmentum & gloriam Domus Dei, eas expendant, benedicatur Deus, qui & illis hujuſmodi animum inſpiravit, & hanc mihi ſuo munere gratiam tribuit, ut meis diebus, mea Mater Eccleſia crementum potius capiat, quam detrimentum. Edmer. Hiſt. Nover. lib.* 5. *pag.* 109.   (*i*) *De Geſt. Pontif. lib* 1. *pag.* 234. *Edit. Francof.*   (*k*) *Cantiæ dejectam priorem partem Eccleſiæ quam Lanfrancus ædificaverat, adeo ſplendide erexit, ut nihil tale poſſit in Anglia videri, in vitrearum feneſtrarum luce, in marmorei pavimenti nitore, in diverſi-coloribus picturis, quæ mirantes oculos trahunt ad faſtigia lacunaris.*   (*l*) *Antiq. Brit. Harpsfield. Godwin in ejus vita.*

David

David King of *Scots*, most of the Bishops, and a great number of the Nobility of both Realms. [True it is that he solemnly performed the Rights of Dedication; that action is justly ascribed to him, but neither did he so reedify the Church, nor was there that occasion given for it (as the firing of it in his time) whereof my guides in the former edition, (the author of the *Antiq. Britan.* Mr. *Cambden,* and Bishop *Godwyn*) not without a clear mistake make mention. For the Church (saith *Gervas* a Monk of the place) was but only thrice burnt. First, for instance by the *Danes* in King *Ethelred's* days, *Ann.* viz. 1011. Secondly, at *Lanfranc's* coming to the See in the Conqueror's time. Thirdly, in the year 1174. Other than which three times the Author of the *Antiq. Brit.* relating when and how oft the Church was fired, mentions not. And besides both the same *Gervase* and *Thorn,* his neighbour Chronicler of St. *Augustin's,* making mention of the Dedication, say nothing of this man's repairing the Church, or of any fire then happening to occasion it. *Gervase* speaks of this Dedication and says, *Ann.* 1130 on the 4th day of *May,* the Dedication of this Church was celebrated with much pomp and solemnity. *W. S.*] Whereunto the King of *England* presently became a Benefactor, giving and granting, besides an Annuity of ten pounds in money, the Church (or Priory) of St. *Martin* in or near *Dover,* to this Church for ever *(a).* In and at which Dedication, the

Cathedral again named. Church's name was again changed, *(b)* from *the Church of the Holy Trinity* to *Christ-Church* Canterbury *Thorn.* (St. *Augustin's* Chronicler) records the thing, but under the year 1128.[*(c)* and says mistaking both the year and the month, that *on the 4th of* March 1128, *the Church of the Holy Trinity in* Canterbury *was Dedicated by Archbishop* William, *which afterwards was commonly called* Christ-Church. W. S.] And then also was the Church's Common Seal renewed, which in the fore-part had this Inscription about it, *(d) the Seal* of Christ-Church *at* Canterbury *the prime See* of Britain; and in the reverse, this about our Saviour's Picture, *(e) I am the way, the Truth and the Life.* This Seal continued till *Becket's* Martyrdom, and then was a third time changed, as you shall find hereafter.

About forty years after that, *viz.* In the year 1174 *(f),* I read of yet another combustion of this sacred edifice. At whose cost it recovered it self then, I find not; saving that the Pope's Bulls *(g)* shortly after provide that the offerings to the then newly murdered and canonized Archbishop, *Thomas Becket,* should go and be converted *(h) for the repairing of the Church* (one cause haply why it was called St. *Thomas* Church:) And that way (I believe) such store of Coin might come in, (the devotion of that age to St. *Thomas* inclining many to be forward and liberal Benefactors) that it cannot seem a thing improbable for the Church to have recovered by that means. [In the supplement concerning this Church, the Reader may expect a full account of the rebuilding of it, and at whose charge it was done; and another reason how it came to be called the Church of St. *Thomas,* than what Mr. *Somner* has now guessed at. *N. B.*]

The Monks now at length more nearly affected with the woful havock which these frequent fires had made of their Church-Fabrick, either occasioned or furthered by some neighbouring Edifices, carefully provide to remove that cause, and for that end, divers Houses belonging to St. *Augustin's,* being

Campanile of Christ-Church. built and situate near unto their *Campanile* or Steeple standing on the South-side of their Church-yard; after much suit, they prevailed at length with those their neighbours the Monks of St. *Augustin,* to exchange the houses with their ground about them for the like elsewhere. Let me inlarge this matter to you out of *Thorne* who records and reports it as followeth. *(i)* " In the year

(a) Harpsfield ubi supra.   *(b)* Ecclesia Sanctæ Trinitatis, Ecclesia Christi Cant.   *(c)* Anno Domini 1128 quarto nonas * Martii, fuit Ecclesia Sanctæ Trinitatis Cant. dedicata, à præfato Willielmo Archiepiscopo, quæ postmodum Ecclesia Christi Cantuariæ est vulgariter vocitata.   *(d)* Sigillum Ecclesiæ Christi Cantuariæ primæ Sedis Britanniæ.   *(e)* Ego sum via, veritas & vita   *(f)* Liber Ecclesiæ Cant. & antiq. Britan. pag. 291.   *(g)* In Archivis Ecclesiæ.   *(h)* In restaurationem Ecclesiæ.   *(i)* Anno Domini 1177. facta fuit quædam commutatio terrarum consualium inter Monasterium istud & Monasterium Sanctæ Trinitatis. Habebat enim istud Monasterium quasdam terras ex parte meridiana cœmiterii Sanctæ Trinitatis juxta Campanile eorum, quæ terra reddebant huic Monasterio singula annis xx s & xi d. & quia istæ terræ erant ipsi Ecclesiæ de Sancta Trinitate ita propinquæ & in casu ignis multum periculosæ. Ideo prædictus electus & conventus Sancti Augusti licet invite, precibus tamen Regis Henrici coacti mutaverunt prædictas terras cum quibusdam terris quæ fuerunt de Dominio Sanctæ Trinitatis diversis locis in Civitate jacentibus, quæ terræ reddebant singular' annue xxii: ii d. Hæc commutatio est confirmata sigillo Regis Henrici, & sigillis utriusque Monasterii, &c.

[*L Maii. N. B.]

" 1177,

" 1177, there was (faith he) an exchange of Lands made between the two Mo-
" nafteries of St. *Auguftin,* and of the *Holy Trinity.* The Monaftery of St. *Au-*
" *guftin* had certain Lands on the South part of the Church-yard of the Mo-
" naftery of the *Holy Trinity,* near their Steeple or great Clock-houfe ; which
" Lands paid xx. *s.* xi. *d.* yearly Rent to St. *Auguftin.* But in as much as thefe
" Houfes, being near the Church, were of great danger to it in cafe of Fire,
" therefore at the entreaty of King *Henry* II. an exchange was agreed upon
" for certain Lands in the City belonging to the Monaftery of the *Holy Trini-*
" *ty,* of the yearly Rent of xxii. *s.* xi. *d.* &c. Thus he, recording alfo the Compofition it felf, whereof my *Appendix* fhall give you a Copy. This exhange
(it feems) was made to good purpofe : for afterwards I find the Church free of all fires. **Numb XXVIII.** Once indeed fince, and that fhortly after this exchange, it was in
danger to be fired, but was preferved miraculoufly, if you will believe my Au-
thor (*Gervafe,* a Monk of the place about that time:) *(a)* From whom *Harpf-*
field makes this report of the matter ; " In the time of the Archbifhop *Richard*
" who immediately fucceeded *Thomas Becket* in the See of *Canterbury,* a Fire
" did break out in the City and burnt many Houfes : It drew towards *Chrift-*
" *Church.* The Monks were under great confternation. The danger feem'd to
" be greater than human aid could prevent. They betake themfelves to divine
" help, and particularly to the protection of St. *Owen* ; whofe Holy Relicks
" are with much affurance brought forth, and placed over-againft the Flames;
" the Succefs was wonderful: for the Flame, as if it had been driven back
" by a Divine Power, retreated and made no further progrefs. Thus he. And
fo far Hiftorically of the general Fabrick of the Church. Now I fhall defcend
to particulars, and fhew how feveral parts of it were fome built, fome repaired at feveral times, and by whom.

For new Buildings in the firft place. I read that Archbifhop *Sudbury,* by **Body of** whofe time the Nave (or body) of the Church (the *Aula ecclefiæ,* fo *Edmerus* **Chrift-Church** calls it) the *Auditorium,* as with the ancients I may ftile it, was fo decayed with **new built.** age that it could not, and fo far behind the upper part in Majefty of building,
as with his good liking it might not ftand any longer, took it down, with a
purpofe of his own Purfe to have built it of new after a more magnificent
manner ; but being cut off by the fury of thofe Rebels *(Wat Tiler* and his complices) in *Richard* II. time, was prevented. He dying, the Burthen of that
great work lay upon the Monks, or rather they confenting (as it feems) in a
common forwardnefs, willingly undertook it, and with the help of *Sudbury*'s
two next Succeffors *(Courtney* and *Arundel)* at length, brought the body, together with the Chapter-houfe and Cloifter to full perfection. *(b)Harpsfield*'s words
of this matter are ; " The Monks at vaft expenfes built the Nave of the Church
" which Archbifhop *Sudbury* had pull'd down, with a full intention of rebuild-
" ing it more magnificently, which he had done, if he had not been moft
" barbaroufly Murder'd by the Rebels. For their both Incouragement and In-
ablement to finifh which work begun, too chargeable for them to perfect without fome addition to their prefent Revenues ; after they had that way expen-
ded above 5000 Marks ; the Parfonages of *Godmersham* and *Weftwell* in *Kent,* at **Godmersham.** their Petition, were by Archbifhop *Arundell,* with both King and Pope's Li- **Weftwell.** cenfe, appropriated to them, as I have it from the Inftrument of that appropriation recorded in a Lieger of the Church, dated in the year 1397. The
Preface whereof is in the *Appendix,* Numb. XXIX.

Thomas Chillenden was Prior of the Church at this time. He, it feems, (as
beft able) of the Monks, was moft beneficial to thefe Works. The quoted
Inftrument fo infinuates and intimates ; and the Epitaph on his Tomb (whereof hereafter) verifies as much. Archbifhop *Courtney* (as I told you) was another Benefactor. I have it from his Will *(c)*, wherein he makes it his Petition

---

(a) *Conflagravit Civitas Cantuariæ, cumque jam pluribus ædibus confumptis, incendium ad Chrifti Eccle-*
fiam ferperet ; confternati monachi, cum res humanam opem fuperare videretur, ad divinum & divi Audoeni
patrocinium fe contulerunt. Sanctas itaque ejus reliquias igni, magna opis fiduciâ opponunt ; quæ nec fuit ina-
nis. Flamma enim divina quadam virtute repulfa, fe reflexit ac refiliit, nec ultra progreffa eft.

(b) *Inferiorem autem Ecclefiæ fuæ partem quam demolitus erat Simon Sudburienfis Archiepifcopus, magni-*
ficentius eam extruendi animo, quod & perfeciffet, nifi indigna illum cædes repentè è medio fuftuliffet, maxi-
mis monachi impenfis nobili ftructura exædificavunt. Hift. Ecclef. Angl. fæcul. 15. cap. 14 pag. 634.

(c) *In Archivis Ecclef. Cant.*

to the King; *(Richard* II.) *(a)* " That his Succeſſor might not demand or exact
" for dilapidations, more than is due, but might with a pious and juſt regard,
" conſider, in what State he found his Church and Manors, together with his
" Caſtle in *Saltwood*; and how afterwards, notwithſtanding an Earthquake, he
" repair'd them with vaſt and heavy expences, according to the utmoſt of his
" abilities, and the time wherein he had enjoyed the Archiepiſcopal Revenues;
" as the Prior of his Church, and many others of good reputation can witneſs.
" He gives alſo, by his Will, 200 *l.* or more, according to the diſcretion of his
" Executors, and as they ſhall be inform'd in the matter, to be laid out by them
" for a new Work or Building, of one ſide of the Cloiſter, to be carried on in a
" ſtrait line from the Gate of the Palace unto the Church. So his Will. The Table or Writing which was hang'd up at the head of his Tomb, taking its Account from the *Antiq. Britan.* by miſtake, informs us that this Gift was 1000 *l.*
Archbiſhop *Arundell* may not be forgotten, who queſtionleſs was not only an
Encourager, but a Benefactor alſo in his own particular to the Works I treat
of; though I doubt of his building that Steeple, which Archbiſhop *Parker,*
followed by Biſhop *Godwin* and ſome others, aſcribe unto him, for ſome Reaſons which when I come to ſurvey it, I ſhall propound.

Quire repair
ed.

And *Becket's*
Crown.

Hitherto of Parts new built : Now ſhortly of Parts repaired and beautified. I read *(b)* that in *Henry* the Prior's time, *viz.* in the Years 1304, and 1305,
the whole Quire was repaired, with three new Doors, and a new Pulpit or
aſcent unto it, as was likewiſe the Chapter-houſe with two new Gables; all
which coſt 839 *l.* 7 *s.* 8 *d.* I find alſo *(c),* that upon the beautifying of St. *Thomas's* Crown, that is, *Becket's* Crown, was expended in the ſame Prior's time,
to wit, in the Year, 1314. in Gold and Silver and precious Stones 115 *l.* 12 *s.*
So much for Reparations. And now have I done with the Story of the Fabrick. Only I may not omit what had almoſt ſlipt my memory, that Archbiſhop *Chicheley, Arundel's* immediate Succeſſor, built the Steeple called of Biſhop
*Godwin, Oxford-*tower, but vulgarly, *Dunſtan-*ſteeple, or the moſt part of it,
and alſo the Library *(d)*.

A Survey of the preſent Church, with the Monuments therein ; as alſo of the more
ancient Buildings within the Precinct both of it, and the Palace, with the Am-
bitus, or Precinct it ſelf.

3. Particular.

COming (in the next place) to the Survey whereof, I will begin *(e)* (with
that which deſerves to be firſt taken notice of) with the Church it ſelf,
that which (as *Eraſmus* hath it) *(f)* raiſeth it ſelf aloft with ſo great a Majeſty and Statelineſs, that it ſtriketh a ſenſible Impreſſion of Religion in their
minds that behold it afar off. Before our entrance whereinto, let me acquaint
you with what I have from the ſame *Eraſmus (g),* who obſerved it ; that over
head at the entrance of the South Porch of the Church, ſometime ſtood the
Statues cut in Stone of certain Armed men; thoſe, namely, which murdered Archbiſhop *Becket*; not in approbation of their fact, nor for any Honour intended them thereby, more than is given to *Judas, Pilate, Caiaphas,* or
the Band of Souldiers, whom (ſaith *Eraſmus)* you ſhall ſee elaborately engraven in gilded Altars. They are (ſaith he) ſet out to ſight for premonition,
that no Courtier afterward ſhould lay violent hands, either upon the Perſons
of Biſhops, or their Poſſeſſions.

Porch.

Body.

Now enter we the Body of the Church; a right noble Structure. *(h) And*
as ſoon as we are entred, a ſpacious and ſtately Fabrick preſents it ſelf to our view,
ſaith the ſame *Eraſmus.* This queſtionleſs is the identical Nave or Body ; of
whoſe Age and Authors you ſo lately heard. *(i)* There are two fair and great

---

(a) *Ne ſucceſſor meus pro reparationibus quicquam plus debito petat piè & juſtè habendo reſpectum in quo*
ſtatu Eccl. & maneria mea unà cum Caſtro meo Saltwood inveni, & qualiter ſubſequenter, non obſtante terræ-
motu, non ſine gravibus & ſumptuoſis expenſis. ſicut novit Prior meus & ſeniores & ſaniores Capituli, atque
valentiores totius Dioceſis, ipſa pro meo poſſe & tempore reparavi. 200 l. & plus juxta diſpoſitionem Execu-
torum meorum, & ſecundum informationem miniſtrand per eos pro nova facturâ ſive conſtructione unius panæ
clauſtri ab hoſtio Palatii uſque in Eccleſiam ſe erecto tramite extendentis.   (b) *Lib. Eccleſ. Cant.*
    (c) *Ubi ſupra.*   (d) *Author. Antiq. Brit. & Godwin in ejus vita.*   (e) *A digniori*
 (f) *Tanta majeſtate ſeſe erigit in cœlum, ut procul etiam intuentibus religionem incutiat. Peregrinatio*
Religionis ergo.   (g) *Ubi ſupra.*   (h) *Ingreſſis aperit ſeſe ſpatioſa quædam ædificii majeſtas.*
Ubi ſupra.   (i) *Turres ſunt ingentes duæ procul veluti ſalutantes advenas, miroque nolarum ænearum*
boatu longè latéque regionem vicinam perſonantes. Ubi ſupra.

Steeples, namely, at the Weſt end of the Church, furniſhed with very large
Bells, ſaith *Eraſmus.* Now that Steeple which you ſee at the Weſt-end and
South-ſide of the Church, is the *Oxford*-tower, or *Dunſtan*-Steeple I ſo lately *Dunſtan-*
ſpake of, and one of them. And the oppoſite one with the lofty Spire or Shaft *Steeple.*
covered with Lead is the other, and the ſame that is ſaid to be of Archbiſhop
Arundel's building, and at this day called by his name. But under correction, *Arundell-*
without warrant of truth, as I conceive, induced thereunto partly from the *Steeple.*
work of the Steeple, which I hold elder than *Arundel*'s time, by comparing
it with other pieces of that age, and partly by this Note in the Records of the
Church, ſeeming to me by the Character almoſt as ancient as the time of
Arundel. *(a) The Weight of the Five Bells in* Angel*-Steeple, newly given by the moſt
Reverend* Thomas Arundel, Anno 1408.

This Note, you ſee, calls it *Angel*, not *Arundel*-Steeple, as I ſuppoſe it would
have done, or at the leaſt have mentioned him the Founder, had he indeed
erected it. Beſides I meet with the *Angel*-Steeple in the Church-Records long
before *Arundel*'s time, *i. e.* in the days of *Henry* of *Eaſtry*, the Prior; and by   1317.
the ſame name this very Steeple I find to be called in divers dead mens Wills
(b) ſince *Arundel*'s time. Let me but add, that *Harpsfield* in the life of Archbiſhop *Arundel*, mentions not this Steeple amongſt the reſt of his Acts of Note,
and I proceed. [Concerning *Angel*-Steeple, Mr. *Somner* falls under a very
great miſtake. For the Steeple (which we now call *Bell-Harry* Steeple) was
formerly called the *Angel*-Steeple : And in this Steeple the Five Bells given by
Archbiſhop *Arundel*, were hanged. But afterward they were removed to the
great Steeple on the North-corner of the Weſt-end of the Church; whence
it has been called *Arundel*-Steeple. Of this I will undertake to give a juſt and
full Account in the Supplement. *N. B.*]

This Nave or Body of the Church *(c)* admits of all Comers, (ſaith *Eraſmus)*
but at the upper end, for the better ſecurity of the upper part of the Church,
where the Shrine was and other Treaſure, was of old parted off from the
Quire by certain Iron Grates or Bars; the Doors whereof for the ſame reaſon
doubtleſs, Archbiſhop *Winchelſey* by his Statutes *(d)*, commanded to be kept
always cloſe ſhut, unleſs in time of Divine Service, or at other times of neceſſary Ingreſs and Egreſs. Without offence to which Injunction let us enter.
At or near which place of entrance, ſometime ſtood a great Croſs, in the
head whereof was kept and incloſed that Golden Crown which (as is ſhewed
before) King *Knute* gave to the Church; and under it an Altar, which was
known by the name of *(e) The Altar of the Holy Croſs, between the Quire and
the Nave* ; and, *The Altar under the great Croſs of the Church.*

Next obſerve we the firſt Croſs-Iſles (Wings, ſome call them) of the Church.
thoſe (I mean) between the Nave and the Quire; which by the work, ſeem
of like age with the Body, ſaving that the North-Iſle (the goodly and glorious Window at the head whereof, a piece in its kind beyond compare, was
the Gift of *Edward* IV. as may be ſeen upon it) with the lofty Tower or Steeple in the midſt or meeting of the Croſier, by theſe Capital Letters *T. G. P.*
with the three Gold Stones, the Mitre alſo and Paſtoral Staff in them both,
and Archbiſhop *Warham*'s Coat of Arms beſide, in the roof of the latter (the
Steeple,) I conceive of ſomewhat a later building, and perfected, as in the
time, ſo chiefly at the coſt of Prior *Goldſtone*, in *Henry* VIII. days.

In this North-Iſle, between the Cloyſter-door and the Lady-Chapel, is a place
incloſed and ſet apart, called to this day the *Martyrdom.* Archbiſhop *Becket*   *Martyrdom.*
(as tradition hath it) being here or hard by (at or upon the third or fourth
griece or ſtep of the *Pulpitum*, or aſcent to the Presbytery or Quire, as
ſome will) murdered, martyred they call it; whence thoſe Verſes, on each
leaf of the door one, yet legible in part, importing, that *(f)* St. Thomas *was
martyred within this place.*

Here ſometime ſtood an Altar, by the Wall, where now Dr. *Chapman*'s Mo-

---

(a) *Pondus quinque campanarum in campanili* Angeli *de novo donatarum per Reverend. in Chriſto patrem
& D. D* Tho. Arundell Cantuar. *Archiepiſcopum Anno Dom.* 1408. *&c.*   (b) *In Regiſtris Con-
ſiſtorii & Officialitatis Cant.*   (c) *Omnes recipit.*   (d) *Liber M. Eccleſ Chriſti Cant.*
(e) *Altare ſanctæ Crucis inter chorum & navem, Altare ſub magna cruce Eccleſia. In archivis Eccleſ pred.*
(f) *Eſt ſacer intra locus, venerabilis, atque beatus,*
Praſul ubi ſanctus Thomas eſt Martyrizatus.

nument is set up, commonly called (a) *The Altar of the Martyrdom of St.* Thomas. Which together with the place *Erasmus* saw, and hath left it thus described. (b) " There is to be seen an Altar built of Wood, consecrated to the
" Blessed Virgin, small and remarkable on no other respect but as it is a Mo-
" nument of Antiquity, which upbraids the Luxury of these present times.
" At the foot of this Altar the Holy Martyr is said to have had his last Fare-
" well to the Blessed Virgin, at the point of death. Upon this Altar lies the
" piece of the Sword, which was broken off by striking at the head of this
" good Archbishop, and dashing out his Brains, that Death might seize upon
" him more speedily. We religiously kissed this piece of the Sword, as rusty
" as it was, out of love and veneration to the Martyr. From being the keeper of this Altar, *Roger* the Abbat of St. *Augustin*'s was chosen to that Abbacy
by the Monks there, in hope that he would bring with him some special Relicks (saith my Author (c)) of the Blessed Martyr; herein not deceived, for
(saith he) he conveyed to them a great part of *Thomas* his Blood that washed,
and a piece of his Crown that was pared off. A thing which they of *Christ-
Church* could not of a long time digest, nor would they suffer the other in quiet
with the purloined Relicks, until at length some amends was made them by
that composition made between the two Houses, passing over unto *Christ-Church*
(in exchange for other elsewhere) those houses and ground beside their *Campanile,* whereof you may read before : a Composition as *Thorn* comments on
it, (d) *very disadvantagious and incommodious to us of the Convent of St.* Augustin's.
But (e) I return from this Digression. This place (no doubt) was of high
esteem with our Ancestors, the walls whereof seem to have been hang'd, and
was a place pickt out for the solemnity of *Edward* I. espousals with his Queen
Margaret, whereof I read thus in the Records of the Church (f) *In the year*
1299. *On* September 9, Robert *Lord Archbishop of Canterbury celebrated the nuptial
Solemnities between our Sovereign Lord* Edward *King of* England *and* Margaret
Sister of the King of France, *in the entrance of the Church towards the Cloister near
the door of the Martyrdom of St.* Thomas.

Lady-chapel.   I pass hence to the Chapel contiguous, commonly called the Lady-Chapel, a
piece not old ; by the work it should be much what about the age of *Dunstan-*
steeple. *In Anno Domini* 1452. I find it called (g) *The New Chapel of the Blessed*
Mary.

I confess I read of the Lady-Chapel long before. Archbishop *Richard, Becket*'s immediate Successor, was buried in it. But that Chapel stood within the
old body of the Church, and was parcel of it. I have it from the Church records verified by the leaden Inscription and pontifical Relicks, to wit, his Cope,
Crosier, and Chalice lately found in digging Dr. *Anian*'s Grave by Sir *John
Boys* his Monument on the North side of the Body, toward the upper end.
That old Chapel was not heard of since the present body of the Church was
built.

St. *Michael*'s Chapel.   By the entry or *testudo,* under the grieces or steps (the *pulpitum* as wont to
be called) leading up to the Quire, from the body, I proceed and come to
St. *Michael*'s Chapel, standing on the other (the South) side of the Quire. A
Chapel indeed in name old. For Archbishop *Langton* in *Henry* III. days is
storied (h) to have been there intombed. But the work of the building of
the modern Chapel will not bear that age. I am therefore persuaded that the
old one was fain to be taken down, whilest the body and cross Isles of the
Church were in building, to give better way to that work, and that that being finished, this was new built as now it is.

Quire.   Ascend we now by the steps or *Pulpitum* to the Quire (Chancel or Presbytery.) (i) *And these steps are many,* saith *Erasmus :* which whole work of the

---

(a) *Altare Martyrii Sancti Thomæ.*   (b) *Illic ostenditur altare ligneum Divæ Virgini sacrum, pu-
sillum, nec ulla re visendum, nisi monumento vetustatis luxum hisce temporibus exprobrante. Illic vir pius dicitur extremum vale dixisse virgini, cum mors immineret. In ara est cuspis gladii, quo præfectus est vertex
optimi præsulis, ac cerebrum confusum, videlicet quo mors esset præsentior. Hujus ferri sacram rubiginem amore martyris religiose sumus exosculati. Peregrinatio religionis ergo.*   (c) *Thorn in vitis Abbat.
Sancti Augustini.*   (d) *Nobis multum inutilis & incommoda.*   (e) *In callem regredior.*
(f) *Anno Dom.* 1299 *Quinto idus Septembris, Dominus Robertus Cant. Archiepiscopus celebravit sponsalia
inter Dom. Edwardum Regem Angliæ & Margaretam sororem Regis Franciæ in ostio Ecclesiæ versus clau-
strum juxta hostium Martyrii Sancti Thomæ.*   (g) *Nova Capella beatæ Mariæ Antiq. Brit. in vita Stafford,* p. 289.   (h) *Antiq Brit. in ejus vita,* p. 149.   (i) *Ad hunc conscenditur multis gradibus.*

Quire, from end to end, I mean, from the Weſtern door thereof unto the Archiepiſcopal throne or marble Chair behind the high Altar, with the ſide-iſles, croſs-iſles and other buildings on both ſides the Quire (the Quire's curious Weſtern door-caſe only excepted, built, I take it, about the time that the body was) together with the under-croft (or vaults) to them (except the Princes Chapel there) are much of an age; there is that harmonious ſymmetry and agreement between the parts. But certainly of what age I cannot define; only confeſſing it far elder than the Nave; I dare conſtantly and confidently deny it to be elder than the *Norman* Conqueſt; becauſe of the building of it upon Arches, a form of Architecture though in uſe with and among the *Romans* long before, yet after their departure not uſed here in *England* till the *Normans* brought it over with them (as I told you) from *France*. So that (I ſay) elder than the Conqueſt this piece cannot be, and I dare not pronounce it, the roof of it at leaſt-wiſe to be ſo old, becauſe of the many combuſtions betiding the Fabrick ſince the Conqueſt. But by many inducements I am thoroughly perſwaded that it is (for the main) the upper part of the new Church which *Lanfranc* firſt built, whereof I have treated ſufficiently before. And ſo I have ſhortly done with the antiquity of this Fabrick, the Quire.

[Mr. *Somner* profeſſeth himſelf to be altogether at a loſs concerning the Age of the preſent Quire with the Undercroft and Iſles or Wings belonging to it. He writes here ſomewhat doubtfully: For he ſays, That the Quire was built about the ſame time that the Body was; and in the next Sentence ſays, That it is far elder than the Nave; and he concludes, that he was fully perſuaded, that it is (for the main) the ſame which *Lanfranc* built. But ſince Mr. *Somner* collected his Antiquities, *Gervas* being printed has given us a full light into this concern. The ſupplement will ſhew the Reader, that this preſent Quire was finiſhed about the year 1184, being built in the ſpace of Ten years. That the Body of the Church was above Thirty years in building, and finiſhed after the year 1401. And ſo the Quire is elder Siſter to the Nave of Church above 200 years N. B.]

Now a word or two of the Ornaments, and what elſe in it may worthily call for our ſpeculation. To begin with the Hangings ſetting forth the whole ſtory both of our Saviour's Life and Death. They were given, one part of them by Prior *Goldſtone*, and the other by *Richard Dering* the Church-Cellerar, in *Henry* VIII. days. Witneſs theſe ſeveral Memorials legible in the bordure of the Hangings. (*a*)

In the Church Records I meet with Inferior and Superior *chorus*; and one *Thomas Ingram* of *Canterbury*, by his will in the office gives (*b*) *To every Monk of the Superior Quire* xii. *d. to every Monk of the Inferior Quire* viii. *d.* [I find this diſtinction in another Regiſter of this Church, where the election of Archbiſhop *Winchelſea* is recorded. *The Supprior, Precentor, and one of the Penitentiaries were to take to them four other Brothers,* (*c*) *two from the right ſide of the Quire, and two from the left ſide of the Quire, that is to ſay, two of the upper Quire and two of the lower Quire.* The meaning ſeems to me to be plainly thus: One from the upper Stalls and one from the lower Stalls on each ſide of the Quire. The elder Monks being ſeated in the upper, the Younger in the lower Stalls. N. B.] Now as we ſee there are two rows of Stalls (an Upper and a Lower) on either ſide the Quire: ſo I conceive the Seniors and Superiors of the Monks uſed to ſit in the upper, as the Juniors or Inferiors in the lower row; and that thence ſprang the diſtinction of the ſuperior and inferior Chorus.

Above theſe Stalls on the South-ſide of the Quire ſtands the Archbiſhop's wooden Seat or Chair, ſometime richly guilt and otherwiſe well ſet forth, but now nothing ſpecious through age and late neglect. It is a cloſe ſeat made after the old faſhion of ſuch Stalls, called thence *Faldiſtoria* (*d*): Only in this they differ, that they were Moveable, this is Fixt.

A little higher up, on the other ſide of the Quire, between *Chichlie's*, and

Hangings.

1486.

(*a*) On the South-ſide, *Thomas Goldſtone hujus eccleſiæ Prior ſacraque Theologia Profeſſor me fieri fecit. Anno Dom. Milleſimo quingenteſimo undecimo.* On the North-ſide, *Richardus Dering hujus eccleſia Commonachus & Celerarius me fieri fecit. Anno Dom. Milleſimo quingenteſimo undecimo.* (*b*) *Cuilibet Monacho de Superiori choro eccleſiæ Chriſti Cant.* xii d. *& cuilibet Monacho de inferiori choro ejuſdem eccleſiæ* viii d. (*c*) *Duos de dextro Choro & duos de ſiniſtro ; viz. duos de ſuperiori Choro & duos de inferiori Choro. Reg. Eccleſ. Cant.* (*d*) *Gloſſar, D. H. Spelman, in hac wiſe.*

Bourgobier's Tombs was provision made heretofore for the storing and treasuring up of Saints Relicks. This Repository was shewed to *Erasmus*, who spends these words upon it. (a) *On the North-side (of the Presbytery) were kept close under Lock and Key, such precious Rarities as were not to be seen by every body : You would wonder, if I should tell you, what a number of Bones were brought forth, Skulls, Jaw-bones, Teeth, Hands, Fingers, whole Arms, all which out of devotion we kissed,* &c. Hence *Erasmus* then beheld, as we may now, the Altars, Table and Ornaments ; indeed (thanks to the piety of the times) very rich and becoming such days of blessed peace as our Church (by God's mercy) now enjoys, but not comparable surely to those that *Erasmus* saw, or else he much hyperbolifeth, where he faith : (b) *You would think the richest Monarchs more Beggars in comparison of the abundance of Silver and Gold, which did belong to the Furniture of this Altar.* [Mr. *Somner* liv'd to see the Altar despoil'd of all those Ornaments, which he commends as rich and becoming, and to see a new set of Furniture provided for it. I will here record what has been lately done in our days, that it may stand as a perpetual memorial of a Princely Benefaction. The most Illustrious Queen *Mary* II. of ever blessed Memory, who honour'd this Church with her Royal Presence, provided the Altar, as also the Archbishop's Throne, the stalls of the Dean and Vicedean, and the Pulpit, in this Church, with new and rich Furniture, such as became the piety and bounty of the best of Queens to give, and such as are now a fair Ornament to this Church. *N. B.*] This Altar was and is called the high Altar, more properly so, heretofore, then now, because it was the chief one in the whole Church, Christ's

Altars

Altar, and to distinguish it from the Saints Altars, whereof the Church had many, 25 in number, one in the midst of the Crosier between the Nave and the Quire, a second in the Martyrdom, a third in the Lady-chapel, a fourth in St. *Michael's* Chapel, two in either wing of the Quire, *viz.* in each semicircle there one, one in the Vestry, one in St. *Anselm's* Chapel on the other side of the Quire, three near unto the high Altar it self, whereof one was St. *Dunstan's,* a second St. *Elphege's,* a third (and that standing behind the high Altar) St. *Blase's,* two at least in *Becket's* Chapel, whereof one in the little side Chapel against *Henry* IV. Monument, and the other beyond the shrine, in the place called *Becket's* Crown, besides seven other in the undercroft, and two in the body of the Church which I had almost forgotten, whereof one was belonging to *Arundel's,* and the other to *Brenchlye's* Chantery there. One more there was, and that in the now *Dean's-*Chapel. [The Supplement will account for ten Altars, besides that in the *Dean's-*Chapel, more than Mr. *Somner* has nam'd. *N. B.*]

Becket's Chapel.

But leaving these things and the Quire too, let us now ascend. (c) *From behind the high Altar we go up as it were into another Church by several steps,* faith *Erasmus.* To this I proceed, the upper part of the Church (I mean) from the Grate between the Archiepiscopal Throne or marble Chair, by the Mosaick or Musaick-work (d), upwards, called (from the standing of his Shrine there) *Becket's* Chapel : which with the *vertex* of the work, called *Becket's* Crown (intended by *Erasmus,* where he faith, (e) *There in a certain Chapel is to be seen the whole Face of the Blessed Martyr set in Gold and adorn'd with many Jewels,* &c.) the either side-Isles, (except the Chapel on the North-side, and the Undercroft of it) I hold to be somewhat less ancient than the Quire and its Undercroft: The ocular and peeked or pointed form of the Arch, the round marble Pillars or Columns both above and below (to pass by other disagreements easily observable) showing a manifest discrepancy and difference one from the other. For truth is, about the place where the Quire ends and that Chapel begins (observe but the works above and underneath, and you will easily perceive it) the Church once ended, and extended no further, the Pillars and work coming in

---

(a) *Ad latus Septentrionale referuntur* [l. *referantur*] *arcana, dictu mirum, quantum ossium illinc prolatum est, calvaria, menta, dentes, manus, digiti, integra brachia, quibus omnibus adoratis fiximus oscula : nec erat futurus si is, nisi qui mihi tum comes erat ejus peregrinationis parum commodus, interpollasset ostentandi studium.* &c. Peregrin. Relig. ergo.   (b) *Biceres Midam & Crasium fuisse mendicos, si spectares vim auri atque argenti.* Erasm. ubi supra.   (c) *Post Altare summam rursus velut in novum templum ascenditur.*   (d) *Unde sic dist. unde* Pancirol. par. prior. tit. 23. & Martin. Lexic Philologic. verb. *Musivus.*   (e) *Illic in sacello quodam ostenditur tota facies optimi viri, inaurata multisque gemmis insignita,* &c. Peregrin. Relig. ergo.

and

and closing there. [All the work at the East end of the Church (except the Chapel of King *Henry* IV. is one entire building, of the same Age with the Quire, finished about the year 1184. as will appear in the Supplement. *N. B.*]

The certain age of this part neither can I find, but from great probability do conceive it to be that new work (whereof *Edmerus* speaks) begun and furthered by his Patron, Archbishop *Anselm*, but continued and consummated by *Ernulph* the Prior with the help of his Monks in *Henry* I. time. A work that (as I told you erewhile) was so envied of some about the King, and on the other side so much applauded and extolled by *William* the Monk of *Malmesbury*, who for the Windows, Pavement, and other Ornaments of it prefers it to any other in the whole Kingdom. *(a) The like*, says he, *was not to be seen in England, &c.* as before. Properties wherein it justly deserves the comparison. [The new work begun by *Anselm*, was not consummated by Prior *Ernulph*, but by his Successor *Conrade*. This was the whole Quire together with all the East end of the Church, which *Ann.* 1174. was burnt down to the ground, and within ten years was rebuilt, in the same beauty and stateliness, as is to be seen at this day. *N. B.*]

Some haply may here ask me, why *Becket*'s Crown, if it be a piece so ancient, is so imperfect on the top? For Answer unto them, I say, that time was, when that piece was to the mind of the first Founders compleat; being built not altogether so high at first, as now it is. The Monks (saith Tradition) at the time of the Dissolution, were in hand (in honour of *Becket*) to have advanc'd the Building to a higher pitch; but their fall prevented that's rise. So that whereas before it had a handsome compleat Battlement, it is now a great blemish to the Church, and an Eye-sore to Spectators, by the ragged and imperfect ruins of it. This is that *(b) Crown of St.* Thomas, in beautifying whereof the Church-Records tell me, and I have before told you 115 *l.* 12 *s.* was expended in *Henry* the Prior's time. — *Beckets Crown.*

Now retreating, let us take a view of the Vestry. A place, of the *Greeks* called *Diaconion*, and *Diaconicon*; but of the *Latins*, *Sacrarium*, *Secretarium*, and *Vestiarium*. This Vestry stands (like as Vestries generally do) on the Northside of the Quire. *(c)* The words which *Erasmus* spends upon it, are to this effect. *We are led into the Vestry. What an incredible number of rich embroidered Vestments of Silk and Velvet, was to be seen there? How many Candlesticks of Gold? There we saw the pastoral Staff of St.* Thomas. *It seem'd to be a Cane, cover'd over with a thin plate of Silver; very light, plain, and no longer than to reach from the ground to the girdle,* &c. — *Vestry.*

The Keeper or Curator of this place, was usually called *Sacrista*; we english it, the Sacristein or Sexten, and was one of the but three at first; afterwards four *Obedientiarii* or Officers (for so the word signifies, as *Obedientia (d)* doth an Office) of the Church; to one or other of which all the under Officers and Ministers within the Precinct, some few of the Prior's retinue excepted, did relate and appertain, *viz.* the Cellerar, the Sacrist, the Chamberlain, and the Treasurer. Within and under the Sexton's Office were these, *(e)* 1. The Keeper of the Waxhouse; being, I take it, the small dark Vault under the Steps leading up to *Becket*'s Chapel, &c. 2. The chief Bell-ringer. 3. The Watchman of the Church. 4. The Plummer of the Sacrist. 5. Two Clerks of St. *Mary*'s Altar. 6. Two Clerks of the Altars of the Tomb and Martyrdom. 7. Four under Bell-ringers. 8. The Glasier and his Boy. 9. The Door-keeper of the Quire. 10. The waiting Servant of the Shrine. 11. The Cleaner or Scourer of the Plate, and the Laundress of the Church. [I have called this last Officer, the *Aurifriga*, a Cleaner of the Church-Plate, being joined with the Church-Laundress, as that which imports his true Office, rather than an Embroiderer or Worker of Plate or Church-Vestments; as Mr. *Somner* would have it. *N. B.*] — *Sacrist.*

(a) *Nihil tale possit in Anglia videri, &c.*   (b) *Corona Sancti Thomæ.*   (c) *Post hæc ducimur in Sacrarium. Deas bone, quæ illic pompa vestium holosericarum, quæ vis candelabrorum aureorum! Ibidem vidimus pedum Divi Thomæ. Videbatur arundo lamina argentea obvestita, minimum erat ponderis, nihil operis, nec altius quam usque ad cingulum, &c. Peregrin. Relig. ergo.*   (d) *Cowel's Interpret. in hac voce.*   (e) 1. *Castos de Wexhousse.* 2 *Primus serviens ecclesiæ ad pulsandum.* 3. *Vigil ecclesiæ.* 4. *Plumbarius Sacrista.* 5. *Duo clerici Altaris beatæ Mariæ.* 6 *Duo clerici tumbæ & Martyrii.* 7 *Quatuor servientes ecclesiæ ad pulsandum.* 8. *Vitriarius & garcio ejus.* 9. *Ostiarius Chori.* 10. *Serviens feretri.* 11. *Aurifrig. & lotrix ecclesiæ. Lib. Eccles. Cant.*

For which laft, (the reft being of eafy underftanding) I conceive it was one that wrought the Church Veftments or Hangings, and the like, in Gold; but refer you to Sir *Henry Spelman*'s Gloffary, and *Martinius*'s Lexicon upon the word *Aurifrigium*, for fuller fatisfaction. Here, as feafonable, let me remember unto you, that *Gervafius Dorobernenfis*, the Monk of this place, for his good authority fo often cited of our late Hiftorians, was, in his time, dignified with this Office of the Sacrift here; a part whereof it was to deliver the Crofier to the new made Archbifhop, which Ceremony this man very folemnly performed to Archbifhop *Hubert* (a).

Treafury.

There is a Room next Wall to this, having had a door leading into it from hence, wherein partly, and partly in the Loft over this Veftry, the Church-Records are kept. The Treafury, we call it, but it was known to former times by the name either of *Armarium* or *Armariolum* (b), [i. e. the Armory. N. B.] and properly, fince it was the Church-Arcenal, yielding them weapons or Muniments wherewith to fecure unto the Monks their Poffeffions and Privileges; whence alfo the Curator thereof was called *Armarius*, [i. e. *Armourer*.]

Dean's Chapel.

Now a word or two of the Dean's Chapel, and my Survey of the Fabrick's upper part is at an end. This Chapel, with a Clofet to it newer than the Chapel, fell to the then Dean's fhare, upon the divifion of Houfes and Buildings, made anon after the change of the Foundation by *Henry* VIII. By what name it was formerly called, is a thing uncertain, or wherefore built. [It was the Prior's Chapel, built for the ufe of the Prior. N. B.] That divifion calls it only the Chapel next the *Dorter*. But obferving the Pictures of Pope *Alexander* III. and *Lewis* VII. of *France*, drawn on the Chapel-walls, the one oppofite to the other, towards the Eaft-end; obferving alfo *Becket*'s Picture (as I take it, conjecturing by the new white Glafs, put in place of his Coat of Arms, in the upper South-window, as the like was done generally throughout the Church where either this or his name was found:) and then confidering what a Patron Pope *Alexander* III. was to *Becket*; what a Friend King *Lewis* VII. was to him in his exile; and laftly, what a Benefactor, for his fake, to the Monks after his death, and that the Records of the Church have a Charter of *Edw*.II. of xx *l.* worth of Land to be purchafed for the fuftentation of Seven Chaplains, that fhould daily celebrate in the Chapel of St. *Thomas* the Martyr, near the Priory-gate, for the Souls of himfelf, his Anceftors, &c. Confidering laftly, that the Prior's ancient Gate, or the Gate of the Priory was, and is near this Chapel, being the fame which leadeth from the *Green*-Court into that which we now call the dark Entry, and fo to the door there now ftopped up, the Timber-frame whereof is yet hanging on the things, and anciently led into the Prior's Cellar, as that other hard by it into his Chamber. All thefe things (I fay) obferved and confidered, I am affured that this was St. *Thomas*'s Chapel, otherwife, *Anno* 16. *Edward* II. called (c) *The Chapel of the bleffed* Mary, *and the bleffed* Thomas *the Martyr, near the gate of the Priory*; our Lady pictured in many of the Windows, fharing (it feems) with him in the dedication.

Library.

Over this Chapel is the Church-Library; not the fame to the repair whereof Archbifhop *Hubert* gave the Church of *Halftow*, this being built (as erewhile I told you,) by Archbifhop *Chicheley*, and borrowed from the Chapel, or fuper-added to it; the juniority of the work, and the paffage to it, plainly intimate fo much. It was by the Founder and others once well ftored with Books, but in man's memory fhamefully robbed and fpoiled of them all; an act much prejudicial and very injurious both to Pofterity and the Commonwealth of Letters. The piety of the prefent Churchmen hath begun to replenifh it, and may it have (what it well deferves) many Benefactors, to the perfecting of the fair beginning; with which wifh I leave both it and the Chapel.

Windows.

And now I fhall defire you would take notice of the Windows, efpecially in the Church's upper part, which both for the Glafs and Iron-work thereof are well worthy your obfervation. This part of the Church was highly commended of *Malmsbury* (d) in his time, amongft other things, for this Ornament. (e) *No fuch thing could be feen elfewhere in* England, &c. faith he. And I think

---

(a) *Harpsfield Ecclef. Hift. facul.* 12. *pag.* 342.   (b) *Repertorium Munimentor. Ecclefia Cant.*
(c) *Capella beata Maria & beati Thoma martyris juxta portam Prioratus.* (d) *De geft Pontific.*
lib. 1. *pag.* 234. *Edit. Francofurt.*   (e) *Nihil tale poffit in Anglia videri, &c.*

his words hold true still. And I believe as much may be said of the Iron-work about them, apparently various in every Window. Besides, these Windows afford and offer to our view certain Verses containing a Parallel of the Old and New Testament. They are many, and therefore to avoid too great an Interruption here, you may find them in my *Appendix*, Numb. XXX. [Which I have compared with a fair Manuscript-Roll in Parchment, corrected the Print in many places, filled up several Gaps, and added some Verses that were omitted in the former Edition. *N. B.*]

Let me now lead you to the *Undercroft*. A place fit, and haply (as one cause) *Undercroft.* fitted to keep in memory the subterraneous Temples of the Primitives, in the times of Persecution. The West part whereof, being spacious and lightsome, for many Years hath been the Strangers Church: A Congregation for the most part of distressed Exiles, grown so great, and yet daily multiplying, that the *French* Church. place in short time is likely to prove a Hive too little to contain such a Swarm. So great an alteration is there since the time the first of the Tribe came hither, the number of them then consisting of but eighteen Families, or thereabouts; which with the Terms or Articles granted them at their humble suit by the then Mayor and Commonalty of the City, upon their first admittance, will appear unto you, if you peruse the (*a*) Instrument thereof in the *Appendix*, Numb. XXXI.

But enough of this. Return we to our *Undercroft*. Where under the South Cross Isle or Wing of the Quire, was and still is (though not so used now) Prince *Edward*'s Chapel. The Story whereof take here from the relation of Black Prince's its Estate given up to the Commissioners : These Emissaries sent to enquire Chapel. and examine the state of all Chanteries, *&c.* upon and according to the Stat. 37 *Hen.* 8. *cap.* 4. which tells, That the said Chantery was founded in *Christ-Church*, in a place called the *Undercroft*, in the Year of our Lord God 1363, by the aforenamed Prince *Edward*, who with License of his Father, King *Edw.* 3. purchased Lands (*b*), and made agreement with the Prior and Convent of *Christ-Church* for the Contentation and Stipend of two Chaplains : Ordaining Sir *John Steward*, and Sir *Nicholas de Lodington*, and their Successors for ever, to receive yearly of the said Prior and Convent, forty Marks above all Charges of Reparations or otherwise. Also the said Prince *Edward* gave to the said Chaplains and to their Successors for ever, a House being in St. *Alphage* Parish, of the Yearly Value of xx *s.* whereof 4 *d.* is yearly resolute to St. *Austins* ; the Reparation whereof to be kept always at the proper Cost of the said Prior and Convent of *Christ-Church*. Hence you may perceive the Founder, and time of Foundation of this Chapel. At or shortly after this Relation given up, the Chapel formerly with Grates and Bars parted off from the rest of the *Undercroft* growing out of use and deserted, was laid open to it, and sithence (I take it) the double way beaten and made through the Wall, for a Passage by that Chapel to the *French* Church there. I may not leave this Chapel before I have observed the Roof of it, a piece of newer and more curious Work than the rest of the Vaults about it, and yet the over-built Structure as old as any that stands within the neighbour Vaults of elder-fashioned Work. How this might be thus made, haply some will wonder. But their satisfaction is easy. For the elder Roof of the Chapel (as it might well be, without endangering the Church) was undoubtedly taken down ; and that the Chapel might in all parts the better correspond and suit with the dignity and degree of the Founder, was rebuilt in that neat quaint manner that now it is.

Leaving now this Chapel, come we to the next, commonly called the La- Lady-Chapel. dy *Undercroft*, an Edifice since the Dissolution and Reformation quite deserted also and despicable, but formerly so much celebrated, of such high esteem, and so very rich, that the sight of it debarred to the vulgar, was reserved for persons only of great Quality. *Erasmus*, who by especial favour (Archbishop *Warham* recommending him) was brought to the sight of it, describes it thus. (*c*) " There (saith he) the Virgin-mother hath an habitation, but somewhat dark, " inclosed with a double Sept or Rail of Iron for fear of Thieves. For in- " deed I never saw a thing more laden with Riches. Lights being brought,

(*a*) *Lib. Camera Civitatis Cant.*   (*b*) *Fawks-hall* Mannor by *London. Lib. Eccles Cant.* (*c*) *Peregrin Relig. ergo.*

" we saw a more than Royal spectacle. In beauty it far surpasseth that of
" *Walsingham.* This Chapel (as he adds) is not shewed but to Noblemen, and
" especial Friends, &c. The Chapel doubtless is ancient. For in the Church-
Records I read of (a) *The Altar of the Blessed* Mary *in the Undercroft,* [which
Undercroft when it was first built, was dedicated to the Blessed Virgin, and
had an Altar erected to her at that time, probably inclosed in a small Chapel.
N. B.] almost 400 years agoe, to wit, in the year 1242, and again in the year
1322. At what time the Altars in the Undercroft are recorded to be these :
St. *John* the Baptist, St. *Thomas* the Apostle, St. *Clement* the Pope, St. *Kathe-
rine* the Virgin, St. *Nicholas* the Bishop, St. *Mary Magdalen,* and St. *Mary* the
Virgin. [To these may be added the Altars of the *Holy Innocents,* St. *Audœnus,*
St. *Paulinus,* and St. *Augustinus,* which were also in the Undercroft. I find no Altar here to St. *Thomas* the Apostle, but there was the Altar of the Tomb of
St. *Thomas* the Martyr, at which before the translation of this Saint's Body to
the upper part of the Church, such rich Oblations were made, as it furnished
the Monks with the greatest part of the Money, which was expended in building the present Quire and all the East parts of the Church. Mr. *Somner* may
correct his own mistake of calling this the *Altar of St.* Thomas *the Apostle* :
For before the end of the next Paragraph, he makes mention of this *Altar of
the Tomb of the Blessed Martyr* Thomas. *N. B.*] If this word Altar amount not
to prove it a Chapel: *Capella* (I am sure) it is called in the foundation of the
Lady *Mohun's* Chantery, in the year 1397. long before Archbishop *Morton's*
days, who some say was the Founder of it. Which mistake in point of the
Chapel's Antiquity, thus corrected, let us proceed.

Becket's Tomb.   A few steps forward brings us to *Becket's* Tomb, the place (I mean) above
the Lady-Chapel, so called, and that from Archbishop *Becket's* first interment
there ; whose dead body the Assassinats giving out they would take and cast it
forth into the open Fields to be a prey for Beasts and Birds, or otherwise abuse
the Carkass, (b) the then Monks forthwith buried here, where afterwards it
rested until such time as *Stephen Langton* his Successor translated it in such solemn manner as you shall hear hereafter. In the mean time comes *Henry* II. with
bloody Feet to visit this place, and pray at his Tomb, in part of his Penance (c). Hither also came *Lewis* the seventh of *France,* and here offered his
(d) *Hundred Muyds of wine to be yearly given in Frank-Almoign for the use of the
Monastery for ever,* &c. This parcel of the Undercroft (a most goodly Vault
and rarely parallel'd, and a place heretofore until *Becket's* shrine and Saint-
ship's utter downfall and casheering, no doubt much set by, and celebrated)
fell to the share of Dr. *Bray* [now Dr. *Battely*] his predecessors upon the division of Houses and places of Accommodation for the Dean and Prebendaries,
whereof I have often told you. Which is all I have to say of it (unless I should
remember the Altar once standing there, called (e) *the Altar of the Tomb of the
Blessed Martyr* Thomas :) and periods my Survey of the Church's Fabrick,
both Cryptical and other, saving that in a word or two I must remember the
Cloister and Chapter-house.

Chapter-house   For the latter of which, questionless it is the same, which in Prior *Chillenden's* time (as whilome was said) was new-builded; you may find his name (as
a Benefactor) over the entrance, in the foot of the West-Window. This was
not only the place for Capitular meetings and treaties about Church Affairs, but
also for the exercise and execution of regular Discipline. Hence the discipline
here said to be inflicted on *Henry* II. for Archbishop *Becket's* Murder, whereof
our Stories tell (f).

Cloister.   As for the former (the Cloister, the keeping whereof, and so of the Refectory, the Dormitory and the Infirmary, very private, was cautiously provided for of Archbishop *Winchelsey* by his Statutes (g), especially excluding
Women thence) it likewise seems to be the same which was then new set up.
The South-pane or Quarter whereof, somewhat more beautified than the other
three, I take to be that which Archbishop *Courtney* (as we shewed before) took

---

(a) *Altare beatæ Mariæ in Cryptis.*   (b) *Antiq Brit. in ejus vita, pag.* 137. *Matth. Paris Hist.
Angl. pag.* 167. *Edit. London.*   (c) *Roger Hoveden Annal. par. poster. pag* 539 *Edit. Francofurt.*
(d) *Centum modios vini, per quandam cuppam auream in perpetuam eleemosynam annuatim in Castellaria
Pisciaci recipiendos ad opus Conventus Cantuariæ. Lib. Eccles. Cant.* 1179.   (e) *Altare Tumbæ
beati Thomæ martyris.*   (f) *Antiq. Brit. in ejus vita, pag.* 138.   (g) *Lib. MS. Eccl. Cant.*

order by his Will to be made, and hath his Arms set up about the entrance to it at the West-end. As for the many other Arms thick set about the Cloister, by the way, I suppose them to be theirs that were Benefactors in their time, either to the Church or Monastery, or both: whereof I persuade my self the number was not small, as may probably be argued from that one instance which Master *Cambden* gives of the new building of *Crowland* Abbey in *Lincolnshire*; whither I refer such as desire to know and learn, by what means such mighty huge and fair religious Houses and Buildings as these were raised in former times. And this shall suffice to have spoken of the Church.

Now to make my Survey compleat, I must another while play the *Mystagogus*, and shew you the Monuments, purposely reserving them till now, because being many, and some of them yielding length of discourse, they would have too much interrupted my Survey of the Fabrick, if I should have intermixt them with it. Here I intend not a recital of every Monument I meet with, but chiefly of the more ancient ones; those of latter times, being either fresh in memory, or more easily known by the Inscriptions and Epitaphs cut in the grave-stones, than those of elder times, either wanting Inscriptions (*a*) *at the first*, or else done in Brass, which for the most part is either with age defaced, or the Brass it self by wicked hands purloined. And not all of them neither will I set down in this place, purposing to mention the Archbishops and Priors Monuments in their several Catalogues. *Monuments.*

And so I begin with the first (I mean the lowermost) Monument in the body of the Church. Where is a very fair Grave-stone with much of the Brass yet remaining, and having almost all the Inscription or Epitaph still intire, saving (the principal) the interred parties name upon it. It begins thus: (*b*) *Here resteth* —— and there (the Brass being worn or rather torn away) breaks off. My diligence to enquire of the ancient retainers of the Church, whose Monument it was, could have no satisfaction. Yet at length one of them told me that the name was extant since his memory, which he said (as his memory served him) was either *Bobingham* or *Robingham*, or the like. This brought into my mind the name of *Bokingham*, which with *Bokingham* Chantery I had often read of in Records both of the Church and Consistory. From this hint therefore given, I proceeded in my search, and at length found (*c*) this story of one *John Bokyngham* or *Buckingham*, *viz.* That in *Richard* II. days he was keeper of the Privy Seal; afterwards Lord Bishop of *Lincoln*. From whence in the year of our Redemption 1397. Pope *Boniface* the IX*th* bearing him some grudge, translated him perforce unto *Lichfield*, a Bishoprick not half so good, which he refused to accept, and choosing rather a retired Monastick course of life, became a Monk of this Church, where he spent the rest of his days. Afterwards amongst the Church Records I met with the foundation of his Chantery (the Instrument or Charter thereof I mean) his Will likewise, in which he appoints to be Buried (*d*) *toward the lower end of the Nave of the Church*, &c. By this time (I suppose) you are satisfied with me whose Monument this is. In the Covenants between him and the then Prior and Convent for his Chantery, one Article required them with all convenient speed to build him a Chantery Chapel near unto his Sepulchre: but I find none he had. By his Will ((*e*) *among other things*) he gave to the fabrick of the high Altar (made it seems, about that time) xx*l*. His Monument thus restored I proceed. *Bishop Bokingham's Monument.*

Observing by the way, and that in the next place, one rare piece of Novelty; which because it hath been hitherto omitted, and is so worthy as I may not altogether balk or utterly pass it over in silence, I must afford a place here, and that not altogether improperly, since it is a Monument, not of the dead, I confess, but (which is much better) of the operative and exemplary Piety of the living Donor. Whosoever knows not my meaning, may know, that by the munificence of a late worthy Member of this Church, Dr. *Warner*, the now Right Reverend Lord Bishop of *Rochester*, the Church, this part of it at least, is newly much graced with (what before it never had, though much wanted) a fixed Font, and that such a one, as whether it be more curious or more costly I am not able, if worthy to judge; but both ways (I am sure) so *Font.*

(*a*) *Ab initio.* (*b*) *Hic jacet in requie* --- (*c*) *Godw.* Catal. of BB. in *Lincoln*; & *Harpsf. sæcul.* 14. *cap.* 25. (*d*) *In Navi ecclesia deorsum,* &*c.* (*e*) *Inter alia.*

excellent and exquisite, that the Author cannot but be famous for it, whilst the Church continues graced by it ; and the rather, because it is (I take it) the first thing of worth that by any private hand hath been offered to this Church of latter times.

[This fair Ornament of the Church had not been erected many Years, before the pious and honourable Benefactor, and Mr. *Somner* also saw it defaced and pull'd down by Sacrilegious hands in the time of the *Great Rebellion*. But as soon as the Church and State were delivered from those dismal Confusions, *Anno* 1660. the same generous and worthy Bishop *Warner* caused a new Font, more costly and beautiful than the former, to be set up at his own Charges. And let God for ever preserve both that and the Church from the outragious violence of Sacrilege and Rebellion.

The Survey of the rest of the Monuments, containing chiefly *Latin* Inscriptions, with some Additions, shall be transferr'd to the *Appendix*, where they may be view'd. Numb. XXXII. *N. B.*]

In St. *Michael*'s Chapel.

Margaret Duchefs of Clarence and her two Husbands.   Where (as *Wever* hath it) between her two Husbands (*John Beaufort*, Marquifs of *Dorfet*, [Earl of *Somerfet*. MS. *Ecclef. Cant. W. S.*] lying on her left fide, and *Thomas Plantagenet*, Duke of *Clarence*, on her right ;) *Margaret*, Daughter of *Thomas*, and Sifter, of one of the Heirs to *Edmund Holland*, Earls of *Kent* , lieth glorioufly intombed. Of her and them, you may be further informed, if you pleafe to confult *Wever*'s Monuments : For I haften.

Black Prince.   And am now come to *Becket*'s Chapel, where is offered to our view the fumptuous Monument of *Edward*, firnamed the Black Prince, (fo by-named, not of his colour, but of his dreaded Acts in Battel) with his Epitaph both in Profe and Verfe, in the *French* Tongue. It is large, and *Wever* hath taken it out already and *englifhed* it, wherefore that labour is faved. This was that Prince *Edward*, for whom, and by whom, in my Survey of the Church, I told you, the Chapel and Chantery was founded in the Undercroft.

Henry 4. and his fecond Wife.   Here alfo is the Tomb of *Henry* IV. King of *England*, (gracious in his time to the Monks of this Church, by his confirming to them the ancient Privileges and Prerogatives of the fame (a)) and of *Joan* his fecond Wife, Daughter of *Charles* V. King of *Navarre*. Of them both, as alfo of *Mary*, the fame *Henry*'s firft Wife, *Wever* hath many things, of him efpecially, both in Verfe and Profe ; amongft the reft his Will. In which (among other things) I note, that he willed to have a Chantery to confift of two Priefts, to fing and pray for his Soul in this Church, and in fuch place thereof and manner as fhould feem good to his Coufin the Archbifhop of *Canterbury*, (*Thomas Arundell*.) In all probability the little Chapel on the North-fide of his Monument, is the very Chapel which was built for that purpofe ; the Window-work whereof by Prior *Goldftone*'s name in the Foot of it, feems to be of his repairing.

Ifabel Countefs of Athol.   I leave this Chapel, and defcend to the *Undercroft*. Where are two Lady-Monuments ; the one of *Ifabel* Countefs of *Athol*, whereof let *Wever* further inform you.

Joan Lady Mohun.   The other of the Lady *Mohun* ; wherewith I will better acquaint you from the Charter or Inftrument of her Chantery, recorded in a Leiger of the Church. She lived in the days of *Richard* II. and writes her felf, (b) *Lady Dunfter*, fpringing (it feems) from that noble and mighty Houfe or Family of the *Mohun*'s of *Dunfter*-caftle in *Somerfetfhire*, which (as my Author (c) adds) flourifhed from the Conqueror's until *Richard* II. days. In the Indenture between her and the then Prior and Convent, for the Sum of 350 Marks Sterling, (and certain Utenfils, and Accoutrements convenient for her Chantery) with which money the Manor of *Selgrave* was purchafed and amortized to the Monks, with licence of the King in that behalf ; a perpetual Chantery is granted unto her, by the Prior and Convent, who covenant with her befide, that when fhe died her Corps fhould be laid in the Tomb, which fhe of her own coft had prepared, and caufed to be fet up near the Altar of our Lady, in the *Undercroft* : And being there fo intombed, fhould never be removed, nor the name of the Tomb ever altered, but be honourably kept ; and 5 *s. per an.*

(a) *Harpsfield, Saecul.* 15 *cap.* 14 *pag* 634. (b) *Domina de Doneſterr.* (c) *Cambd.*
Britan. in Somerfetfhire.

given to the Clerk that kept the Lady-Chapel, for the keeping clean of her Tomb, with many other Claufes inferted in the fame Indenture, which to the end the Chantery might not vanifh out of memory with their Succeffors the Monks, caufed to be enrolled and recorded in their Martyrology, that upon her Obit-day it might be annually recited. The Indenture is dated in the Year 1395, 19. *Richard* II. I will give you the very words of her Epitaph, becaufe *Wever* hath fet it down imperfectly. You may fee them in the Margin (*a*).

And fo I have done, as with hers, fo with the reft alfo of the Monuments mentionable in this place.

The Church it felf with her appendent, annexed and connexed Buildings thus throughly furveyed, my propofed method fends me to furvey next the other ancient Buildings within the Precinct of it and the Palace, &c. I begin with the Palace.

The Archbifhop's Palace.

AUgu*ftin* the Monk, and the firft Archbifhop of this See, and his Affoci- **Archbifhop's** ates, being kindly received of King *Ethelbert*, and admitted into the Ci- **Palace.** ty ; for their prefent accommodation were feated (as whilome was told you) firft at *Stablegate*, near unto this Palace, where prefently they began (faith venerable *Bede*) (*b*) *to follow the examples of the Apoftles, in their way of living.* By which and other means, at length converting the King to Chriftianity, and daily winning upon his favour ; the King fhortly after removing and withdrawing himfelf and his Court to *Reculver*, and there fetling, as his Succeffors in the *Kentifh* Kingdom, whilft it lafted, ever after did, (as fome report (*c*)) beftows upon his beloved *Auguftin* (for a perpetual Seat for him and his Succeffors) his own Royal Palace in the City, conceived to have ftood much hereabout. This Palace with the neighbouring Church, *Auguftin* afterward converted both into a Cathedral and Monaftery, yet (as I take it) not dividing his Dwelling, or fetting out his Habitation apart from the Monks ; but, as he was to them confider'd as Cathedral Canons, Bifhop ; and confider'd as Clauftral Monks, Abbat, or in place of Abbat ; and on the other fide, they to him confider'd as Bifhop, Cathedral Canons and Chapter ; and confidered as Abbat, a Convent of Clauftral Monks : So he and they, and both their Succeffors, intercommuning, as in Goods and Poffeffions, fo in one and the fame Habitation, of one entire Precinct ever after until (I take it) *Lanfranc's* days. Who innovating and altering the moft of our fafhions and former ufages in Church Affairs, and haply not digefting this amongft the reft, thought good (it's like) to change it. For no mention of any fuch Palace or like feveral Habitation for the Archbifhop, is to be found before his time. He indeed amongft his other Structures, built him a Court or Palace diftinct from the Monks (*d*), faith *Edmerus*, fpeaking of the fame Archbifhop. He it was that firft fhifted and fetled (in that manner that *Doomfday's* Survey found them) the Manors and Poffeffions between himfelf and the Monks ; fetting out to each of them and the Succeffors of them both, their diftinct and proper parts (*e*) ; and fo no marvel if he difcommoned himfelf and his Succeffors by a Palace, (*f*) by himfelf feparately, from the Monks ever after. *Lanfranc* then (I am perfuaded) firft furnifhed the See with a Palace here. Whereof I think little or no part is left to be now furveyed : Neither Hall, Chapel, or other whole piece about it (I exclude the Hall where the Archbifhop's Civil Court is holden, which I fhall fhew was but of late laid to the Parifh) being to my feeming of that Antiquity.

And no marvel : for this Houfe (faith *Lambard* (*g*)) by that time *Hubert* the Archbifhop had afpired to the See, was decayed, either with Age or Flame, or both. Who therefore (faith he) pulled down the moft part of it, and in place thereof laid the foundation of that great Hall and other the Offices that are now to be feen. But by reafon that himfelf wanted (prevented by death) and fome of his followers lacked Money to perform the work, it refted

(a) *Pour Dieu priez por l'ame Johane Burwafchs, que fut Dame de Mohun.* *Apoftolicam. Hift. Ecclef. lib.* 1. c. 26. (c) *Antiq. Brift. in vita Auguftini.* *vit & curiam fibi, &c. Hift. Novor. lib.* 1. *pag.* 8. (e) *Lib. Ecclef. Cant.* (g) *Peramb. of Kent. In Cant,*

(b) *Vitam imitari* (d) *Ædifica-* (f) *Per fe.*

unperfect

unperfect till the days of *Boniface*, who both substantially and beautifully finished the whole; and yet (as some think) *Stephen Langton* had accomplished the great Hall thereof before him. Thus *Lambard.* *Harpsfield* is express for *Langton*'s building of the Hall. (*a*) *He built*, saith he, *that famous Hall of the Palace*. For the rest, all or most of it is certainly much newer, as the Work plainly discovers: whereof the present Gate-house (I am told) was sometime used for the *Lollards*-Tower or Prison, and so called.

Great Hall. Thus my Survey of the Palace will shortly end, but that I may not let the Great Hall (a piece of goodly structure) pass without some little digression and enlargement of my discourse touching the same, it being famous for many solemnities and celebrious assemblies there. Amongst the rest, for that of King *Edward* I. his Wedding Feast kept there (*b*). As also for that great state and solemnity of Archbishop *Warham*'s Entertainment both of the Emperor with his Mother, and the King and Queen of *England*, at a Supper in the same Hall, and also of his own entertainment there at his first coming and inthronization into the See; whereof his Successor (Archbishop *Parker*) and others make mention. And lastly for the Entertainment there which the same Archbishop *Parker* gave the late Queen *Elizabeth*, and the *French* Monsieur, the Duke of *Rhetz*, and many of the *English* Nobility. So much for the Palace.

Church Precinct. I come now to the Church-precinct: which how it lies and where it goes at this day, is a thing easily traced and found out, as thus: From the partition Wall between the Palace and it, near the *Rush-market* to the Church Gate, and so directly upwards almost to *Burgate*, from thence by the Town-wall included to the Chancel-head of *Northgate*-Church, and from thence by the Almnary (or Mint-yard) Wall (crossing and taking in the way between the South-West corner of that Wall, and the opposite Palace Wall) to the Court-Gate, commonly called the Porters-Gate. Thus lies the modern precinct of the Church.

But time was when it lay otherwise, *Lanfranc* coming to the See; (*c*) *Built all the Offices within the walls of the Court, together with the Walls*, saith *Edmerus*. Archbishop *Theobald* in a Charter of his makes mention of the Walls that *encompassed the Church, the Court of the Archbishop's Palace, and the Court of the Monastery* (*d*). The Court and Church you see was sometime walled in; the Church-yard was the like. For by a Charter of *Henry* II. the Monks of the place had a way granted them, or rather restored, (*e*) about the Wall of the Church-yard, lately taken away in the time of War, (meaning, I take it, that which happened at the end of King *Stephen*'s Reign:) which the King chargeth *John* and *Hamon* the then *Præpositi* [or *Bailives*] of the City to deliver them (*f*). Some remains of this old Wall yet appear, as at Dr. *Casaubon*'s [now Dr. *Isham*'s N. B.] a little remanent of it, and a larger parcel and of good height by the Covent or Common-garden: whereby it appears that this Wall stood some pretty distance from the Wall of the City. The interposed Ground between which double Wall, not being then any parcel either of the Church demesnes or liberty, lay partly in *Northgate*, partly in *Burgate*-Ward. That (I am sure) between *Queningate* and *Burgate*, called *Queningate*-Lane, being in the Church-Records, before it came to the Monks, said to lye in *Bertha de Burgate*, as I conceive it thence probable, the rest to have lyen in *Northgate*-Ward. Besides, within the modern precinct, and that about the now Covent-Garden, lay the best part of St. *Michael*'s Parish, and of *Queningate* Parish between that and *Queningate*, within which St. *Austin*'s Abbey, and divers private men beside sometimes had Houses, Land and other Interest, as they had also lower down on the South-side of the now Church-yard. I will therefore (as pertinent) shew how in time the Church became possessed of the whole Precinct as now it is.

And first for the South-side of the Church-yard, I read thus. (*g*) *In the year of our*

(*a*) *Egregiam illam Palatii Cantuariensis ille aulam ædificavit. Ecclesiast. Hist. Sæcul.* 13. *cap.* 5. *p.* 434.
(*b*) *Stow*'s Annals, in *Ed.* 1.   (*c*) *Omnes Officinas, quæ infra murum Curiæ sunt, cum ipso muro ædificavit Histor Nov. l* 1 *p.* 7.   (*d*) *Si quis in prædicta Ecclesia, vel infra ambitum murorum Ecclesiam & curiam nostram & Monachorum cingentium, &c. Lib. Eccl. Cant.*   (*e*) *Circa murum Cœmiterii sui tempore guerræ nuper sublat.*   (*f*) *Lib. Eccles. prædict.*   (*g*) *Anno Domini* MIII. *Ethelredus Dux dedit Ecclesiæ Christi particulam terræ in Dorobernia quam sibi Rex Ethelredus dedit* XV *virgarum in longitudine, &* viii *virgarum in latitudine. Termini terræ sunt hii. In orientali parte terræ Regis In parte australi placea civitatis. In occidente terra Ecclesiæ Christi. In Aquilone cemiterium Christi. Lib. Eccles. memorata.*

Lord MIII. *Duke* Ethelred *gave to the Church of Chriſt a ſmall piece of Land in* Canterbury, *which King* Ethelred *gave him, containing* xv. *Rod in Length and* viii. *Rod in Bredth. It is thus bounded : On the Eaſt ſide lyes the Land of the King ; on the South, the place or ground of the City ; on the Weſt, the Land of* Chriſt-Church; *on the North,* Chriſt-Church-*yard.* This parcel of Land muſt needs lye on the South-ſide of the Church-yard, the North and South bounds argue it ſo plainly. *Henry* I. by his Charter confirms to *Hugh,* Abbat of St. *Auſtin's,* and to the Monks there. *(a) All thoſe Lands, which the Monks of* Chriſt-Church *gave them in exchange of Land, which they received of them for the enlarging their Church-yard, &c.*

St. *Auguſtin's* Abbey (as you may remember I told you) had ſometimes alſo divers Tenents, Tenements and Ground on the ſame quarter of the Church-yard, near and behind the *Campanile* or *Clocarium* of the Church, the ruined foundation whereof appearing now in the form of a little Mount lies incloſed in Mr. Archdeacon's Garden, now Mr. *Elſtobs.* Theſe Houſes and Lands in *Henry* II. time, and by his help, were obtained (upon exchange) of that neighbour Monaſtery, by the Monks of this Church, as by what I have ſaid hereof before, and by the compoſition made touching the ſame, copied in my *Appendix,* may further appear, as was before mentioned.

One *Gervaſius de Cornhill,* whom that Compoſition (as you ſhall ſee) makes mention of, had intereſt in divers Tenements near this *Campanile,* which the Church alſo about the ſame time, and for the ſame reaſons purchaſed of him, his Son *Reignald* and *Maud* his Wife, exchanging for them certain ground in *Friday-ſtreet,* London, which together with the former exchange were confirmed by ſeveral Charters of *Henry* II. to be ſeen in the Leigers of the Church. It ſeems by the premiſſes that this *Campanile* did terminate both the Church-ground and liberty at this time. But after this double exchange I ſuppoſe thoſe Houſes taken down, and the Ground there laid open unto the backſide of the row of Shops along *Burgate-ſtreet* (Shops I call them for ſuch they were built for, and not for Dwelling-houſes, becauſe, I take it, of Fires, which the neighbourhood of Dwelling-houſes might occaſion to the Church ; witneſs thoſe by the Steeple, which we ſee were therefore purpoſely gotten in and had away :) And the ſame ground being ſo diſhouſed and laid open, was made cemitery ground, and became part and parcel of the Church-yard, and ſo accounted. For the reaſon which the Prior and Convent render and ſhew to Archbiſhop *Winchelſey* in *Edw.* I. time, why they ought not to contribute to the Reparation of St. *Mary Magdalen's* Church in *Canterbury,* in reſpect of their Rents of thoſe Shops, was, that the ſame were *(b) within the bounds of the Cimitery of* Chriſt-Church, *&c.* Hitherto of the Church-ground there.

Now for the Ground between *Northgate* and *Queningate.* This parcel came firſt to the Church in *Henry* II. time, and of his Gift. For by his Charter extant in the Leigers of the Church, he gives to the Church, *(c) for the increaſe of the Almonry,* (as the words of it are) *the piece of ground between the Wall of the City, and the Wall that encloſeth the Court of the Prior and Convent, which lyes between* Northgate *and* Queningate ; *which piece of ground contains at the Eaſt end of it* xli. *foot in breadth, and at the Weſt end* xxiv. *foot in breadth, and in the middle of it* xvii. *foot ; and in length* lxxi. *perches.* In the Year 1305. the Monks are preſented, and charged by the Citizens to have ſtopped or made up the way between *Queningate* and *Northgate* ; a thing confeſſed on the Monks part, but defending themſelves by this Charter, they are acquitted *(d).* However for more ſurety (as I gueſs) *Henry* IV. afterwards by his Charter, grants them *(e) the way within the City-wall, which did formerly lead from* Northgate *unto* Queningate ; as the Church-Records inform me. And ſo much alſo for that parcel of the now Precinct.

For the reſt of it thereabout, namely at or near *Queningate,* and between it and *Burgate,* that is, the ground known of late days by the name of Convent-

---

(a) *Omnes illas terras quas Monachi* S. *Trinitatis eis dederunt pro excambio terræ quam ab eis receperunt ad amplifiandum cemiterium ſuum, &c.*   (b) *Infra limites Cemiterii Eccleſia Chriſti Cant. & de manſo Eccleſia, &c. Lib. Eccleſ. memorata.*   (c) *In augmentum elemoſinariæ ſuæ placeam illam inter murum Civitatis & murum qui claudit curiam Prioris & monachorum. quæ jacet inter Nergate & Queningate. Quæ quidem placea continet in fine ſuo verſus Orient.* xli *pedes in latitudine, & verſus Occiden.* xxiv *pedes ſimiliter in latitud. In medio ſui* xvii *pedes, & in longitudine* lxxi *perticas.*   (d) *Lib. Eccleſ. Cant.*   (e) *Viam infra murum Civitatis Cantuar. quæ ducere ſolebat de Northgate uſque Queningate.*

Garden.

Garden. I have seen (a) several Deeds, that shew how by parcels it became added to, and inclosed within the Church-Precinct. As first, the Church hath a Composition made by the Monks of the place, with their Neighbours of St. *Austin's*, and dated in the year 1287. wherein many Houses &c. within *Queningate*, are (in exchange for other) passed over to the Church. (b) The Deed runs thus: *Of the Lands and Tenements which the said Abbat and Convent had within* Queningate, *viz.* iii. s. viii. d. *of two Houses belonging to the Sacristy; and* viii. d. *of one void space, lying there from the Street to the Wall of* Christ-Church. *Also* iv. s. viii. d. *rent from a certain House of the Almonry, which the same* Aldhelm *held, together with a piece of Land there. Also* xi. s. *of three Houses of the Treasury there: Which Tenements* (mark this) *and Rents with the Appurtenances, remain to the said Prior and Chapter, and their Successors, free from all Rents and service in Fee*, &c. Afterwards, *i. e.* in the 41 *Edw.* III. I find the two Monasteries come to composition about certain other Houses and Land situate and lying about this place. The preamble of the Indenture thus states the matter. (c) *Whereas the said Prior and Convent did pretend to inclose for the inlargement of their garden, Messuages and Crofts, of which the said Abbat and Convent were wont particularly to receive the rent of* xv. s. *containing in length and breadth half an Acre, half a rod and the fourth part of a rod of Land,* &c. Thus you may perceive the Church-Precinct extending and spreading further and further. And this Composition gave scope for it. For after that preamble, it is yielded by the Abbat and Convent of St. *Austin's*, what lay in them, that the Prior and Convent of *Christ-Church* might at their pleasure inclose those Messuages and Ground.

After this, came yet another parcel of the Ground thereabouts to the Church. For I meet with a Deed or Charter of *Ralph Broughton* and *John Tent* Chaplains, made to the Church 16 *Rich.* II. (amongst other things) of one Messuage in the Parish of St. *Michael* in *Canterbury*, near *Queningate*, and of one Acre of Land in the same Parish near *Queningate-lane*: The House holding of the King in Burgage, and the Land of St. *Austin's* for x s. Rent *per Annum*.

Queningate-Lane.

By this time (I take it) the Church had gotten in all the Ground hereabouts, saving what lay between *Queningate* and *Burgate*, a slip called *Queningate*-lane. Now for that, I find that by an Act of Parliament, 1 *Rich.* III. (by which the Aldermanry of *Westgate* was granted to the City) the same parcel of Ground, together with the Postern and Bridge, was granted to the Church.

Aldermanry of Westgate.

But in case of eviction of the Aldermanry from the City, the slip of Ground and premises was to return to the City, a part of whose demesnes it was in Fee-ferm. And surely so it did; for in the 1 *Henry* VII. the same Aldermanry by a like Act of Parliament was restored to Sir *George Brown's* Heirs, who by the former Act were made incapable of it, for their Father's taking part with *Henry* VII. against *Richard* III. But yet at length after all this, by a composition between the Church and the City, made *Anno* 7 *Henry* VII. the Church becomes ever after quietly seized both of the same Ground and Wall, with the Towers, Postern, and Bridge.

Thus have I shewed you (as near as I think it may be found) the extent of the ancient Precinct, and how and when it became enlarged to that bigness that now it bears. And so much of the Precinct in general.

The Church-Gate.

Church Gate.

I Come now to the Survey of the particular ancient Buildings in and about the same, beginning with the Church-Gate. A very goodly, strong, and

---

(a) *In Archivis ejusd. Eccles.*   (b) *De terris & tenementis quæ dicti Abbas & Conventus habuerunt infra Queningate, viz.* iii s. viii d. *de duabus domibus Sacristiæ suæ, &* viii d. *de una vacua placea jacente à vico ibidem usque ad murum Ecclesiæ Christi præd. Item* iv s. viii d. *redditus de quadam domo elemosinariæ suæ quam ibidem Aldhelmus tenuit simul cum una pecia terræ quam similiter ille Aldhelmus tenuit ibidem. Item* xi s. *de tribus domibus Thesaurariæ suæ ibidem. Quæ tenementa & redditus cum pertinentiis remaneant dictis Priori & Capitulo & eorum successor. libera & quieta ab omni redditu & servitio in feodum & dominium & Jus Ecclesiæ suæ in perpetuum.*   (c) *Quod cum iisdem Prior & Conventus certa messuagia & tofta de quibus iidem Abbas & Conventus redditum* xv s *particulariter percipere consueverunt continentia in longitudine & latitudine dimidiam acram, dimid. rod. & quartam partem unius rod. terræ, & quæ de Nicolao Horne, Johanne Calward, Henrico atte Forstall & aliis in Queningate-lane separatim acquisiverunt, & partem inde calumpniarunt, & residuum eorund. Messuag. & Toftor. in augmentationem gardini ipsorum Prio. & Conv. ibidem includere prætendunt, &c.*

beautiful

beautiful Structure, and of excellent Artifice; built in the Year 1507. as appears by this now scarcely legible Inscription on the Gate's Front. *(a) This Work was built,* A. D. 1507. *Thomas Goldstone* the Junior, as I may call him, there being two *(*and he the latter*)* of that name, being then Prior, and *(*as he was famous for his piety that way *)* this Work's great Benefactor. A new Gate it is, and not the first *(*I take it*)* that was builded there, but succeeding a former standing where this doth. For that which was Alderman *Nicholson's* [and is now Alderman *Garling's*] Dwelling-house, is anciently, *i. e.* 41 *Henry* III. described to stand *(b) before the Gate of the Church of the* Holy Trinity: The most ancient Gate standing higher up, somewhat nearer *Burgate,* a good part whereof is yet remaining, but built upon, and converted to private use. This *(*I suppose*)* is that *(c) old Gate of the Cemitery* the old Records of *Christ-Church* so often mention, the opposition of it to that which is now Mr. *Fidge's,* and the other contiguous Houses to his, being Church-houses, serving to bound out and describe their situation in the ancient Rentals; calling them *(d) the great House against the old Gate of the Cemitery.* I have done with this Gate.

By which entring the Church-yard, and walking up towards the *Covent-Garden,* on the right hand, within the Cemitery-gate there *(*so called, I take it, because it had Cemitery-ground lying on either side of it, that within it being called *(e) the inward Cemitery)* I find yet standing the old School-house, now put to other use, but *(*I am assured*)* that which was the School-house, before the present School-house in the *Mint*-yard. The often-cited Division of Houses between the Dean and Prebends, appointing out Master-Archdeacon's now Prebend's House and Ground, bounds it out one way to the School Garden. There are that remember the Free-School kept there, and that by one Mr. *Twyne,* *(*sometime a Magistrate of the City*)* as they tell me. For it was a Free-School for the City chiefly, and so called, and sometime was of the liberty thereof, anciently wayed unto, and having a passage to it from some part of *Burgate-street,* *(*I take it*)* leading you to the old door of entrance which it had now made up at the South-end and West-side thereof, haply that which *Anno* 32 *Henry* III. is *(f)* called *the Lane which leads from Burgate-street toward the Sacrist's* House. It was a place of situation, for privacy and retiredness, well chosen *(g)*. What Antiquity the Free-School in this place carries with it, I am uncertain. Archbishop *Theodore,* the Seventh after *Augustin,* we read, erected at *Canterbury,* by licence of *Vitalianus* the Pope, a School or College, *(*a kind of Academical Foundation it was*)* wherein he placed Professors of all the liberal Sciences, which *(*saith my Author *(h))* was the very Pattern to that School, which *Sigebert* the King of *East-Angle* afterward builded, &c. But this School long since vanished. The *Danes* have so often wasted, and other Accidents and Casualties have so altered the face of the City, that it were much folly now to seek with hope to find out the place. *(i)* There are no foot-steps left so much as of the ruins thereof. Therefore no more of that School.

This we have in hand occurs to me *(k)* first in the year 1259. when as *Robertus was (l) Rector of the Church of the scholars of* Canterbury, his presence is taken to witness an appeal of the Prior and Convent in a cause of theirs then depending before the Official of *Canterbury.* A while after this I read that *Robert Winchelsey,* that in time came to be Archbishop of *Canterbury* in *Edward* I. time, was a Scholar here: at *Canterbury* they say *(m)*; and therefore I suppose here. In whose immediate Successor's time, there arose a great controversy between the Rector of this School and the Parson of S. *Martin* (who it seems by the right and custom of his Church held and kept a kind of petty Free-School there) about the rights and liberties of either School. The Records of the difference

Cemitery-Gate.

School-house.

(a) *Hoc opus constructum est Anno Dom. Millesimo Quingentesimo septimo.*   (b) *Ante portam Ecclesiæ Sancta Trinitatis. Charta in lib. Hosp. de Estbridge.*   (c) *Vetus porta cemiterii.*
(d) *Magna domus contra veterem portam cemiterii.*   (e) *Interius cemiterium.*   (f) *Venella quæ tendit de Burgate-street versus portam domus Sacrisiæ. Lib. Hosp. Pauperum Sacerdot. Cantuar.*
(g) *In deligendo loco certo auditorii civitatis electæ, adhuc danda opera, ut is quantum incommoditas civitatis patietur, sit salubris & separatus à tumultu transeuntium, maximè curruum seu plaustrorum, ne interpellentur docentes aut discentes, &c. Tholosanus Repub. lib. 18. cap 6 num. 1.*   (h) *Lambard's* Peramb. of *Kent,* in *Canterbury.*   (i) *Ipsæ periere ruinæ.*   (k) *MS. in Archivis Eccls. Cant.*
(l) *Rector Ecclesiæ Scholarium Civitatis Cantuar.*   (m) *Harpsfield Eccles. Hist. in ejus vita.*

registred in *Chrift-Church*, and faithfully extracted thence will beft report the matter with the circumftance, which therefore my *Appendix* fhall make publick, Numb. XXXIII.

Of this School the Archbifhop *(a)* the See being full, and the Church *(b)* the See being void, were Patrons. The Archbifhop's right will appear unto you from thofe Records. The Church's, I gather from this Note taken from other like Records. *(c) The Collation of the Mafterfhip of the Grammar Scholars by Ri-chard, Prior (of* Chrift-Church) *upon Mr.* John Bocton, *whom he invefted into that Office by delivering to him the Ferula and the Rod, the faid Mafter having firft made Oath that he would govern the School faithfully and diligently.* This was in the year 1374. at what time the See was void by Archbifhop *Wittlefey's* death. So much for the School.

Honors.

The next thing falling under my Survey are certain old Buildings called Ho-nors or the Honors ; in the apportionment of dwellings amongft the firft Dean and Prebends by that name divided and fhared between the predeceffors of Dr. *Jeffery,* and Dr. *Voffius,* now Dr. *Green,* and Dr. *Blomer* Prebends. With Sir *Henry Spelman,* and Dr. *Cowell's* help, I underftand the term ; but how to apply it, or how it may fuit with the prefent Buildings I know not : Unlefs in that the late Priory of *Chrift-Church* being a Barony, and the Prior there, in right of his dignity, one of the fpiritual Barons of the Parliament, thofe buildings (fometime the prime part of his feat) might fpecially appertain un-to him in right of the Barony, or be annexed to the Honor of the Barony, and thence take the name of Honors. Their name occurs not to me in any Record of the Church before this Divifion, elfe haply I could have faid more of it, and with more certainty. [I muft beg leave to put in my exceptions againft what Mr. *Somner* here writes. The Prior was a Lord Spiritual, as he was dignified with the Papal Licenfe or Grant, to wear a Miter, and to put on other Epifcopal Ornaments. But upon the Authority of Mr. *Selden* I muft deny, That the Priory was a Barony, or the Lord Prior was a Baron. I fhall offer fome further conjectures about thefe buildings, called the Honors, which I will referve for the Supplement. *N. B.*]

Fermary-Cha-pel.

A ftep or two further brings me to the ruins of that Building which in the Divifion is called the *Fermary-Chapel.*

Capgrave (d) tells of a Chapel which he calls St. *John's,* ftanding almoft contiguous to *Chrift-Church,* built by *Cuthbert* the Archbifhop, amongft other intents, for a place of burial for him and his Succeffors, and that he was there-in interred. Hence, and becaufe of the fuppofed Statue or Effigies of St. *John* [with the Infcription, *Ecce major me, &c.* that is, *Behold one greater than I am,* &c. *W. S.*] in part yet legible upon an open fcrowl in his hand (though in a cha-racter I dare fay lefs ancient than the *Norman* Conqueft:) and from the near fite of it to the great Church, fome are of opinion that this was that St. *John's* Chapel *Capgrave* fpeaks of. By their favour I think not. For Firft, granting for truth, that there fometimes was fuch a Chapel, and we have barely *Capgrave's* teftimony for it (fomewhat a weak ground to build upon;) yet I cannot imagine that fo much as is yet ftanding of this Chapel could furvive and ftand out fo many *Danifh* Inrodes, Devaftations and other combuftions as have beti-ded this place fince *Cuthbert's* days. Befides, *Capgrave* that tells of the beginning and foundation, withall ftraitway fhews the end and overthrow of that Cha-pel, where he fays. " But this Church of St. *John* many ages fince, together " with *Chrift-Church,* and the offices thereof exchanged her fubftance with the fire. Of the repair or reedifying whereof I never read. Some fuppofing this and that other part of ancient building that is below it Weft-ward, to have been one entire ftructure, and to have had dependance one upon the other, do conceive it to have been the Church of St. *Trinity* which Archbifhop *Lan-franc* built. Indeed the arched or embowed work of it inclines my belief that it was a building erected fince the Conqueft. But others will have it to be the remains of the old Church of St. *Saviour,* that was built and ftanding before the Conqueft ; that haply which *Agelnoth* the Archbifhop in King *Knute's* time,

---

(a) Sede plena.   *(b) Sede vacante.*   *(c) Collatio magifterii Scholarium grammaticalium Civitatis Cant. per Ricardum Priorem magiftro Johanni Bocton quem inveftivit per ferulæ & virgæ tradi-tionem, præftito per eum Juramento de fideliter & diligenter regendo.*   *(d) Quem refert Author Antiq. Brit. in vita Cutberti.*

after

after the former was deftroyed and burnt by the *Danes*, reedified. But by their favour, it was neither this, that, nor t'other.

[Mr. *Somner* has related thefe things fomewhat confufedly. A few lines will fet them in a clearer light. The Statue or Effigies is certainly of *John the Baptift.* The Label or Infcription, *Behold one greater than me*, do as plainly declare it, as if his name had been there at length. It is placed at the Eaft-end of the South Wall on the out-fide of the Infirmary-chapel: And the occafion hereof probably was, Becaufe the old Chapel of St. *John the Baptift* did either ftand in this place or elfe very near unto it, namely, between this place and the Eaft-end of the Cathedral, where now is the Garden allotted to the firft Prebend. If this Chappel of St. *John* did furvive the *Danifh* fury, and was repair'd or rebuilt by *Lanfranc*, yet it was certainly confumed by fire in *September* 1174, when the Quire, part of the Priory and all the Infirmary was confumed by Flames: And this Infirmary-Chapel on or near the place, where the Chapel of St. *John* had ftood, was built immediately after the Quire was finifhed, namely, juft after the year 1184; the Ruins of which Building is to be feen in the houfe affigned to the firft Prebend. The Church of the *Trinity*, built by *Lanfrane*, is no other than the Cathedral it felf, which he built and dedicated anew, not to *Chrift* but to the *Holy-Trinity*; and the Church of our Saviour reedified by Archbifhop *Agelnoth* was the Cathedral alfo, which after the *Danes* had deftroy'd it, he rebuilt and was called the Church (*S. Salvatoris*) of Chrift our Bleffed Saviour, which was the true old name of it. *N. B.*]

Truth is, as there is an upper and a lower part of this building, fo was each part a diftinct ftructure by it felf, and not one intire piece, the lower or Weftern part whereof was fometime a Hall, for the pulling down whereof there paffed a decree in Chapter *Anno* 1545, whence in the Divifion the very next year following it is called the late long Hall. And the upper or Eaftern part of the building was this very Fermary or Infirmary-Chapel. The fame Divifion calls it fo, and that in regard it did fometime appertain and was appropriate to thofe of the Infirmary or Infirmatory (the *Nofocomium* I may call it) of the Minfter fituate by it, confifting chiefly of an Hall or Refectory, for their common board or table (if able and fit to come to it, otherwife feeding in their Chambers) a Kitchen to drefs their neceffary Provifion in, a Dormitory or Dortor for their place of Sleep and repofe, diftributed into certain diftinct and feveral Chambers; of which that one might not difturb another, every of the infirm folk had one proper to himfelf. And a private Chapel for their Devotions, who either were fick and could not, or difeafed and might not accompany their brethren in their more publick and common Devotions in the Temple. Dr. *Langworth* a late predeceffor of Dr. *Blechynden* [now Dr. *Robinfon*] (as it is noted down in a Chapter-book) *anno* 1579, took down a crofs Wall between his houfe and Dr. *Lawfes* (a Predeceffor of Dr. *Brayes* [Mr. Archdeacon *Batteley's*]) at the Church's charge, and paved the way between them with the ftone. In all likelihood it was the Weftern-Wall of this Chapel, or the Wall which terminated the Chapel Weftward, a clear argument of the disjunction and feperation thereof from that other lower part of building. The Infirmary Hall or Refectory, which the Divifion calls the Table-hall, yet ftands perfect and intire, being the fame which is now Dr. *Blechynden's* Hall to his prebendal-houfe, built with other rooms (as I find) about the year 1342. For out of Treafurers Accompts of the Church, in that and the next year following, I have thefe Notes, *viz.* (*a*) *For a new Hall and one new Lodging, made a-new in the Infirmary* 96. l. 8. s. 2. d. *befides* 20 *Marks received of the Feretrarius for making a new Lodging. Alfo for new Lodgings in the Infirmary and Pentifes about the Hall there* 61. l. 1. s. 6. *Alfo for a new Pentife near the new Lodgings of the Infirmary* 6. l. 15. s. 4. d. ob.

This Infirmary (*b*) I read of in our Chronicles in King *John's* time. For the Monks of this Church quitting the Monaftery by command of the King forely offended at them, for their choice of *Stephen Langton* for their Archbifhop; 13 fick Monks which could not remove, were left behind (faith my Author (*c*))

Infirmary.

(a) *Pro nova aula & una Camera de novo factis infirmar.* 96 l. 8 s. 2 d. *prater* 20 *marcas receptas à Feretrario pro nova camera faciend. Item pro novis cameris infirmar. & pentifis circumaulan ibid.* 61 l. 1 s. 6 d. *Item pro novo pentifio juxta novas cameras infirmar.* 6 l. 15 s. 4 d. ob. (b) *Domus Infirmorum.* (c) *In Domo Infirmorum. Matth. Paris, pag.* 299.

in the Infirmary-house. The same had a Bath at or near the entrance of it, haply the Leaden Cistern yet remaining, of what use you may gather from the Decrees of *Lanfranc* in *Reyner*'s Book. Archbishop *Winchelsey*'s Statutes (a) also mention it, which have provided many things touching the place. Amongst the rest, that as a place of great secrecy, no secular shall be admitted into it to view or see it. And that the Prior of the Church should, if not twice, yet at least once a week personally visit and view the place, to see that there be nothing wanting to the sick there, nor ought else amiss, or if so, to see it reformed. It had a special Curator beside, who was called *Infirmarius*. But let us hence.

Dortor.

Of ancient buildings the next unto this is the Dortor, the common Dormitory for the Monks, a very old piece, as any now stands (I believe) within the precinct. Here the Monks (according to St. *Benet*'s rule) slept *vestiti*, i.e. in their Cloths, their regular habit, lying in the Wollen, and without any Sheet or Shirt. Would you know why? Partly (I take it) to further them in the way of Mortification of their Bodies, and partly for their more readiness to attend their *Nocturnes*, that is, their night Devotions, which in Imitation of the Primitives, they observed at certain of their Canonical Hours. To prevent disturbance this place (b) had two Vigils or Watchmen that guarded it every night; the one till midnight, the other till break of day. By Archbishop *Winchelsey*'s Statutes, no Woman or Stranger might by any means have access thither.

Near unto this Dortor, are the ruins of the Kitchen, Pantry, Larder, and other like Rooms or Offices built for the common use and service of the Convent in point of Food and repast, which was served in to them in their Common Hall or Refectory built contiguous to the Kitchen (the remains whereof shew it to have been a very goodly, large and curious piece of Structure) opening on the South-side with a fair door into the Cloister, before which door sometimes stood a double Cistern, partly (I take it) for the service of the Hall, and partly as a laver used at that Ceremony of washing the Hands and Feet of the Monks by the chief Prelate or Superintendent, by our Saviour's example towards his Disciples, commanded by St. *Benet*'s rule at certain times, especially at their Mandy, to be observed (c). This Hall they called the *Fratria*, in old *English* the *Fratery* (so the Division calls it) because it was the common place of resort and meeting for the Fraternity to their repast served into them from the contiguous Kitchin. Their ordinary fare and food here was Fish and Fruits, where they were not more commonly and constantly served in, then Flesh was rarely or never. Abstinence from which being, as to all sorts of Monks in general, so to these in particular expresly enjoyned, and strictly imposed, the common Refectory might upon no terms admit of or afford any. But were any of the Family sick, it was to be had for him in the Infirmary. The guests likewise in the *Cella Hospitum* (the guessing Chamber I may call it) were not denied it: And besides the Prior (to whose conscience and discretion in this behalf much was left) if he saw cause to refresh any one or more with flesh at his own Table in his private Chamber, he might call unto him thither now and then such as he thought fit. Thus and in these cases and places flesh might be at any time, and was many times eaten. But within the publick Refectory never, and that (as I conceive) because of the Rules violation in that behalf, which these specialties were so far from infringing, that like as exceptions do a general rule, they rather confirmed the same in the generality of it. For as in point either of the Office or other like agends in the Church, or of rest and repose in the Dortor, by observing the Rules (that is, the Rites and Customs) of the Monastery in those cases in the places proper thereunto, the Church and Dortor; by the generality of the Monks, the Rule in those cases was conceived and construed to be kept and fulfilled: So likewise by observing the Monastick Rules and Customs for food and repast (and particularly this of abstinence from Flesh) in the Refectory, the proper place of common refection to the whole Convent in general; the Rule in that case was by common intendment kept unviolated. And that it might be so; it was (no doubt) one main end of devising and erecting these common Refectories. For might

---

(a) *Lib. MS. Ecclesf. Cant.*   (b) *MS. memorat.*   (c) *Decreta Lanfranci & ceremoniale*
Benedictin.

the Monks have been allowed their particular Cells, and a *Præbenda* or portion set them out wherewith to find themselves, and provide them of their own Commons, as our Prebendaries now have, it might justly be feared, that the rule in this point of abstinence from flesh, would be either not at all, or nothing so well observed, as in the common and publick Refectory, where each one saw, what his Fellow ate. The consideration whereof probably moved *Wlfred* the Archbishop of this Church, 800 years ago and upwards, (when by his Codicil he allowed the then Monks of this place their proper Cells, or Houses) to provide that the having of them should not excuse nor hinder their resort to the Church, for Prayers and other like agends there, at their Canonical hours, from the common Refectory for their Board, nor from the common Dormitory for their Bed. As you shall find by the Charter it self (if you peruse it) in my *Appendix*, Numb. XXXIV. The *Latin* is much to blame, and the sense somewhat imperfect and incoherent; but I thought it not fit, nor my part to vary from it in the least Syllable.

Of this Hall and the provision for the same, and the ordering thereof, the chief care and oversight was intrusted to the Cellerar, one of the four great *Obedientiarii* (or Officers) of the Monastery, as I told you: The *Sacrista*, *Camerarius*, and *Thesaurarius*, being the other three. The Treasurer's Office was to collect and gather in the Rents and Revenues of the Monastery. The Chamberlains chiefly consisted in the care of *Vestitus* or Cloathing for the Monks; and therefore he had the Charge of the *Sartrinum* and *Sutrinum*, the Storehouses of that sort of Provision, as I guess by Officers and Retainers to them, such as these: (a) *The Master-Taylor. The Second Taylor. The Peltman. The Master Botcher, and his Boy. Three Servants in the Laundry*, &c. whence he was also called *Vestiarius*. It was the Sacrift's or Sexten's Office and Business to see the Church, the Temple kept (b) in all its Utensils whole and neat, and to have care of the sacred Vessels, the Vestments, Ornaments, Books and Utensils of the Church, and to dispose of and order both the place and manner of interring the dead, both Monks and others. And our Cellerar's Office regarded the (c) *Cibum Monachorum*, the provision of food for the Monks, and the ordering thereof; to which end he had the *Pistrinum* and the *Bracinum* (the Bakehouse, and the Brewhouse or Malthouse) under his charge. Accordingly, at the setling of the Church's Manors by Archbishop *Lanfranc*, some were assigned and allotted to the feeding, other to the cloathing of the Monks [and thence the one was called ꝼoꝺtꝼlanꝺ, the other ꞃcꞃuꝺlanꝺ, to say *Shrowdland. W. S.*] as you shall find by the distinction which is observed in the recital of those Manors in *Doomsday* Book, where some are said, and set down to appertain to the Monks (d) *for their food or table*, others (e) *for their cloathing*.

By the way, will you hear a learned man's opinion of this distinction of Monastick Offices, and assigning out unto them their peculiar Ferms and Revenues. (f) *Roverius* in his Illustrations of the History of St. *John's* Monastery, called *Reomans*; (pag. 649.) saith, " There is no doubt, but that the greatest " abuses and defects in respect of Discipline, and the greatest detriments in " respect of their Goods and Revenues, did arise to Monasteries from hence, " because the several Ferms and Profits belonging to the Monastery, were first " committed to the trust and management of the Domesticks, afterwards par- " ticularly assign'd and allotted to them, in manner of Prebendal Portions, " every Monk having his own proper Share appropriated to him. Hence the " profession of Poverty declin'd, and ceased; the Seeds of Covetousness were " sown, Charity apparently dwindled and came to nothing. The Wealth of " the Monastery was transferred to Kindred and Relations, and so admini- " stred food to licentiousness, and to all vices. This evil practice crept into

Cellerar.
Sacrift.
Chamberlain.
Treasurer.

(a) *Magister Cissor Secundus Cissor. Pelli-parius. Magister sutor & garcio ejus. Tres servientes in Lavendria, &c. Lib. Eccles. Cant.*   (b) *Sartum tectum.*   (c) *Or victum*   (d) *Ad cibum.*
(e) *Ad vestitum*   (f) *Non est dubium quin inde maxima fuerit & disciplinæ & rei familiaris in Monasteriis labes, quòd domesticis inprimis administris, ac subinde etiam Monachis singulis suæ attributæ fuerint sigillatim prædiorum aut proventuum Monasterii partes. Nam lapsum inde est paupertatis studium, jacta avaritiæ semina, charitas publicè imminuta, traductæ in affines & cognatos Monasteriorum facultates, licentiæ, ac vitiis suppeditata alimenta. Irrepsit verò hæc lues in Monasteria vulgò post annum millesimum. Ac licèt eatenus administrationes ejuscemodi obedientiæ dicerentur, quòd solo Abbatis & Capituli imperio, atque arbitrio quamdiu libitum esset gererentur; tamen haud multò postea Beneficiorum nomen, ac jus obtinuerunt, magnamque monasticis statutis, vitæque religiosæ puritati ac perfectioni perturbationem attulere.*

F f   " Mona-

" Monafteries, commonly, in the Eleventh Century. And although fuch ad-
" miniftrations of the Goods and Revenues of the Monaftery, be called *Obe-*
" *diences,* becaufe they are executed or performed by the fole Authority, and
" at the pleafure of the Abbat and Convent, by whom, and for as long time
" as they fhall think fit; yet afterwards thefe Adminiftrations became to have
" both the name and right of *Benefices,* and gave great difturbances to the
" Monaftical Inftitutions, and to the ftrictnefs, purity, and perfection of a
" Monaftical Life. Thus he.   And now I proceed.

The Cellerar no doubt was a great man in the College. Archbifhop *Win-chelfey's* Statutes (a) agreeably to *Lanfranc's* decrees; which fay, he ought to be (b) *the Father of the Monaftery,* exprefly call him fo. (c) And that he was a great man in his place, may appear by the large extent of his Charge. In the Lift of the Church's Family, taken in the Year 1322. I find all thofe Perfons forting to his Office, which are named in the *Appendix,* Numb. XXXV.

Cellerar's
Halimot.

Thefe (I take it) with thofe of the Bakehoufe, and Brewhoufe or Malt-houfe, were the Officers and Retainers, whereof the Cellerar's Halimot oc-curring to me in a very ancient Deed of this Church did confift; which, I fuppofe, was holden of him in his proper Hall, and thence took its name of Halimot, to fay, *Conventus aulæ.* The Office was indeed fo exceeding great and troublefome, that like as the Prior, for the fame reafon had his *Sub-Prior,* or *Prior clauftri;* the *Sacrift* or *Sexten,* for the like caufe his *Sub-facrifta;* fo had this our Cellerar his *Sub-Cellerarius* to affift him and bear a fhare with him (and furely need enough) in the managing of this burthenfome Office, and weigh-ty province.

I read that in the Abby of St. *Edmonds-bury,* (d) *a fair and ftately Apartment with large fields, were affigned to the Celerar's Office;* as my Author's own words are. So had our Cellerar here. For he had a large part of principal Houfing allotted him, all contiguous to the Convent-Hall and Kitchen, (the Sphere wherein he chiefly moved) namely his Hall and his Lodgings, as they were called. His Hall, that which is now the Archbifhop's, for the keeping of his tem-poral Courts. An ancient piece, and (I take it) a parcel of that Houfing *Ed-merus* (e) fpeaks of, which he faith Archbifhop *Lanfranc* upon the increafe of the number of his Monks, pulling down the former, too little for their ufe, fecondly built better and larger than the former: The *Dortor* and *North-hall,* being other part of it, as I conceive, all built upon brave arched Vaults of Stone. Into this (the Cellerar's) Hall, the prefent paffage lyes by the Palace Green or Court; whereas the ancient ordinary way to it was on the other fide the Hall, in at a fair door, over which is cut in the Stone-work the re-femblance of the Holy Ghoft, in the Dove's form defcending on our Saviour; and under his feet the Statue of an Archbifhop (haply the Founder) in his Pontificals. Between this Hall and the Court-gate, fometime lay a paffage by and through the long low Entry, in the Divifion called the *Pantife,* whereby ingrefs and regrefs, carriage and recarriage might be made to and from the Hall.

Cellerar's
Hall.

Cellerar's
Lodgings.

His Lodgings lay on the Weft-fide or Quarter of the Cloifter, into which it had a double Door, having in the Windows, the Name, Coat of Arms, and *Rebus* or Name-device of *Richard Dering* the Monk, one of them (f) that confpired with the Holy Maid of *Kent,* in *Henry* VIII. days, and faluted *Ti-burn* for his pains, who in his time was Cellerar to the Church. The fame *Hen-ry* VIII. afterward in his new erection and dotation of the Church, exprefly re-ferves to him and his Succeffors, both Hall and Lodgings, by the names of the Cellerar's Hall, and the Cellerar's Lodgings. But they are fince come to the See, and laid to the Palace, and paffages made to them from the fame.

Court-Gate.

I have done with them, and pafs from thence to the Court-gate, common-ly called the Porter's-gate, built (as I take it) by the old general Founder, Archbifhop *Lanfranc.* On the North-fide whereof ftands an ancient Stone-work pile, the North part whereof, *i. e.* from the ftairs or afcent North-ward, is now Dr. *Cafaubon's* Prebends Houfe: [Being the Houfe formerly affign'd to the Ninth Prebendary; but now by exchange, it is affign'd to the Auditor of

---

(a) *Lib. Ecclef Cant.*   (b) *Pater Monafterii.*   (c) *Item omnes Cuftodes Maneriorum,*
necnon omnes Obedientiarii excepto duntaxat Majore Cellerario, qui pater dicitur Monafterii, &c.
(d) *Illuftris ædium pars cum latifundiis ejus muneri defignata fuit. Spelman Gloffar, in Verb Cellerarius.*
(e) *Hift. Novor. lib. 1. pag. 7, & 8.*   (f) *Vid. Stat. 25 Hen. 8.*

the Dean and Chapter. *N. B.*] The name of which Building is now quite loft, ſaving that ſome call it *Hog-Hall* ; haply rather (as *Hogia, Hoga, Hogium* and saving that some call it Hog-Hall ; haply rather (as *Hogia, Hoga, Hogium* and Hog-Hall. *Hogum* is by Sir *Henry Spelman* (a) derived from the *German Hog*, ſignifying high or mounted) becauſe of the high and lofty ſite and poſture of it ; than, as ſome dream, from the dreſſing of Hogs ſometime in the *Undercroft* of it, a uſe for which it were abſurd to think it built. Others from the ſite of it, call it, and ſo do ſome of the Church-Records, *North-Hall*, and (b) *the great Hall near the Gate of the Court, toward the North*. I find it alſo in ſome of the Church-Records called *Oriall* ; but whether from the ſame Original with *Oriall*-College in *Oxford*, which name ſome conceive to be a corruption of *Aul-royal*, I leave to other men's judgments. But all this while we are without ſatisfaction for what uſe ſo ſtrong and goodly a Foundation as this is, ſtanding upon Vaults, and having to it a very graceful aſcent by Stone-ſteps, beſet on either ſide with ſmall Marble Columns, and other (arched) Stone-work was intended, or how uſed in former time. If I may ſpeak my opinion, I ſhall tell you (and I think rightly) what it was.

There was (you muſt know then) before the Diſſolution, (as by *St. Bennet's* Rule there ought to be) Hoſpitality kept, and Entertainment afforded and allowed both at bed and board unto ſuch Strangers (Travellers and Pilgrims eſpecially) as reſorting to the Monaſtery, ſhould crave it of the Monks ; and conſequently there was a place in the Monaſtery ſet apart for that purpoſe. This place of Receipt they called (c) *the Hall and Chamber for the Reception and Entertainment of Strangers*. Now I am perſuaded the preſent Building was that (d) *Hall and Chamber for Strangers*. I will give you my reaſons.

Firſt, it ſtood and ſtands moſt conveniently for the purpoſe, being by the Court-Gate, remote from the Monaſtery which ſtrangers were not to pry into. And Archbiſhop *Winchelſea* his Statutes (e) making mention of the place, ſeem to intimate the ſtanding of it within the Court (f) *Alſo the ſtrangers Hall and Parlor, and all other Offices and Houſes of the outward Court*, &c.

Secondly, the Cellerar had charge of it. Now the Pentice or Entry between the Court-Gate and his Hall, did (as it were) make them meet.

Thirdly, the preſent Building was not only a Hall, but divided (as appears by it) into an Hall and a Chamber (or Parlor) ſo to accommodate the intertained gueſt with both Bed and Board, and what do the ſame *Winchelſey's* Statutes call it but (g) *The ſtrangers Hall and Parlor ?* as you ſee before.

I muſt acknowledge to have received ſome light alſo in this matter from the following Story. A Keeper of Prince *Edward's* Ward-Robe (ſay the Records of the Church) in the great North-Hall of the Court, in the year 1304. kills another man within the precinct, and flies ſtreight way to the Chamber of the Hall, and though he were required by the Steward of the Church, refuſeth to come forth, or to ſuffer any to enter. Whereupon the Prince being conſulted, another Keeper is ſent down, and order given to have the Malefactor brought to his trial by a prefixed time. In the interim the Juſtices in a Seſſions holden (h) *before the gate of the Caſtle of* Canterbury, enquire of the Murder, and find it. Shortly after the Malefactor is brought before ſome Judges (i) *holding pleas of the Crown* in the Archbiſhop's Palace, where it being demanded of him how he would or could acquit himſelf, he anſwers that being a Clerk, he cannot (k) *anſwer without his Ordinary* : whereupon, being firſt found guilty of the Fact by the Jury, he is, as convicted, delivered over to the Ordinary, and ſent to the Archbiſhop's Gaol at *Maidſtone*. Thus goes the Story. Now I collect from hence that the Prince himſelf had been received here, and entertainment afforded to his Wardrobe after his departure ; a uſe ſuitable to the condition of the place in hand. By this time (I trow) you ſee enough to perſuade your belief of this building to have been the Strangers Hall and Chamber. And now knowing what it was I ſhall next acquaint you with what I further read concerning it in the Church Records.

The Hall had her proper and peculiar Steward ; who, under the Cellerar, was

---

(a) *Gloſſar.*   (b) *Magna aula juxta portam curiæ verſus Aquilonem.*   (c) *Aula & Camera Hoſpitum.*   (d) *Aula & Camera Hoſpitum.*   (e) *Lib. MS. Eccleſ. Cant.*   (f) *Item aula Hoſpitum & paralitorium & quæcunque officia ac domus exterioris curiæ, &c.* Say the ſame Stat.
   (g) *Aula Hoſpitum & Paralitorium*   (h) *Ante portam caſtri Cant.*   (i) *Regia placita tenentibus.*   (k) *Sine Ordinario ſuo reſpondere.*

to see to the accommodation of the guests with all neceffaries according to the Statutes and Customs of the Monastery. He was called (a) *the Steward of the Strangers Hall.* Here was entertainment to be had of Charity, for religious and secular Guests, and that (by the Statutes of Archbishop *Winchelfey*) for the space of at least a day and a night; Horse and Man. On the top or by the foot of the Stair-case of stone vaulted underneath, anciently hung a Gate, whereof (it seems) there was a constant keeper, who had his Chamber hard at hand. For in the year 1382. I find the Prior and Convent make a donation (b) *Of the Office of Keeper of the Inward Gate near the Strangers Hall to his Servant and Esquire with the Chamber belonging to the said Keeper, &c.* So much of this pile.

Steward's Court.

But by the way we must allow the Steward of the Liberties a part of this building for the keeping of his Courts, which have been holden here from good antiquity : witness these words extracted from a Charter of *Henry.* VI. (c) concerning the holding of a Court, he saith, *Know ye, that we considering that the Prior and Convent of the Church and their Predeceffors have been wont time out of mind, to hold a court at the North-hall within the precincts of the said Church or Priory, before their Bailiff for the time being, from three weeks to three weeks, which Court was called,* High Court, *and in the same Court to hold, hear, and determin Pleas,* &c. This Court (it seems) was first set up with the Archbishop' License many ages since (d) *the Archbishop granted them freely to hold their Court of their own Vaffals,* as *Roger Hovenden* hath it, speaking of Archbishop *Hubert, sub ann.* 1200, and recording there the agreement made between him and the Monks, first falling out about the Chapel at *Lambeth.* I have nothing more to observe of this Court, except the smallness of the room that it is kept in. The reason whereof may be this. The Dissolution diminishing the Revenues of the Church made the Churchmen (I suppose) to lessen their Court.

Almnery.

Hard by this place, in times past and until the Dissolution stood the Almnery or Elemosinary of the Church, being the place where the poor were daily fed with the remains of such fare as came from the Refectory and other Tables kept within the Monastery. (e) *Let all the Fragments and Relicks of Meat and Drink, left at the Tables of the Refectory, of the Prior's lodgings, of the Master (I suppose, Celerar), of the Infirmary, and of the Strangers Hall be gathered together into Dishes or Veffels fit for that purpose, and be carried all of them to the Almonry, and there be disposed of to no other use but of pure Alms only* : say the private Statutes of this Church made by Archbishop *Winchelfey.* Agreeable to that ordinance in the Provincial Constitutions (f). *That the full portion of Victuals should constantly be provided and set before the Monks in the Refectory, and whatfoever was left should be given wholly and intirely in Alms to the needy : And that no Abbat, Prior, or Almoner might dispense with this Rule.* The Monk that was intrusted with the care of this place was called (g) *Dean of the Almonry* or the Church-Almoner. King *Henry* II. by his Charter, gave unto the Monks, for and in augmentation of this their Almnery, the ground between *Northgate* and *Queningate* as is afore shewed. And Archbishop *Richard (Becket's* immediate Succeffor) appropriated to this Almnery (or, if you will, to the Monks (h) *to the use of the Almonry*) the Churches of *Monkton, Eastry, Mepham,* and *Eynesford.* Whereof *Harpsfield* thus (i) saith, speaking of that Archbishop. *He was much wanted by the Poor, for whom he well provided liberal and perpetual Alms by appropriating to the Almonry the Churches of* Monkton, Eastry, Mepham, *and* Eynsford. Afterwards (k) in the year 1319.

(a) *Senefcallus aulæ Hospitum.*   (b) *Custodiæ portæ interioris juxta aulam Hospitii servienti & armigero suo, cum camera dicti Custodis, &c.*   (c) *Sciatis quod nos considerantes quod Prior Eccl. & ejusd. loci conventus & prædeceffores sui usi sunt & consueverunt à tempore quo hominum memoria non existat habere tenere apud North hall, infra metas & septa ecclef. sive Prioratus prædicti coram Ballivo suo pro tempore existente de tribus septimanis, in tres septimanas quandam curiam vocatam* High-Court, *& in eadem Curia tenere, audire & terminare placita &c. In Archivis Ecclef. Cant.*   (d) *Conceffit autem eis Archiepifcopus gratis habere curiam suam de propriis hominibus eorum.*   (e) *Omnes etiam reliquiæ & fragmenta tam ciborum quam potuum Refectorii, cameræ Prioris, menfæ Magistri, Infirmitorii & etiam Aulæ hospitum in vafis ad id congruis colligantur, & ad elemosi:am plenè & integrè refferventur, in usus alios quam puram elemosinam nullatenus convertenda.*   (f) *Omnia autem victualia religiofis apponenda fine subtractione aliqua eis apponantur tam in conventu quam alibi ubi reficiuntur. Et de omnibus appositis totum refiduum fine diminutione aliqua cedat in elemofinam per Elemofinarium egentibus fimul erogandum. Ita quod nec Abbat nec Prior nec Elemofinarius possit contra hoc dispenfare. Cap. omnem de statu regular.*   (g) *Decanus Elemofinariæ & Elemofinarius Ecclefiæ*   (h) *Ad usum Elemofinariæ.*   (i) *Magnum tamen sui pauperibus quibus liberaliter perpetua elemofina profpexit, ad quem usum appropriavit ecclefias Monakenfem, Eftrienfem, Mephamenfem & Eynesfordenfem, defiderium reliquit. Hist. Ecclef. Secul.* 12.   (k) *Lib. Ecclef. Cant.*

11 *Edward* II. *Henricus de Eſtria* the then Prior of the Church, within the precinct of the ſame Almnery, erected a Chapel and founded a Chantery of ſix
Prieſts to pray, ſing and celebrate for the Souls of King *Edw.* I. *Edw.* II. Archbiſhop *Lanfranc* and *Winchelſey*, with the Founder himſelf and ſome others, confirmed by the King's Charter. Contiguous whereunto he built a Chamber for the
Prieſts, and afterwards, namely, in the year 1327. his Succeſſor, with conſent of
the Convent aſſigned and appropriated the Parſonage of *Weſtcliffe* by *Dover* to
the Almnery for ever, for the ſuſtentation of the Prieſts, and the maintenance
of the Chapel, and Chamber, &c. Which both are as yet ſtanding, but converted to the Free-School and houſing for the School-Maſter. This Almnery
was taken and pared from the Church at the Diſſolution, but reſtored by Queen
Mary, through her Couſin Cardinal *Poole's* means. In the Charter of which
reſtitution (*a*) mention is made of a Mint there, ſometimes kept by her Father
(*Henry* VIII.) from whence it took (as I told you formerly) and to this day retains the name of the Mint or Mint-yard. And thus I have done with the third
particular head of my Diſcourſe concerning the Church: and come in the
next place to (my fourth particular) the Catalogue of Benefactors.

A Catalogue of the principal Benefactors to the Church.

SOme, it is well known, have written whole Books of the Foundations,   4. Particular.
Gifts, Donations, and Endowments of Churches, Colleges, and the like.
Witneſs (amongſt the reſt) for the parts of *Germany* chiefly, the *Codex Donati-
onum*, written by *Miræus*. And all this to very good ends; namely, to preſerve
the honour and memory of ſuch pious and devout Benefactors, and to commend the worthy Example of their Zeal and Piety to the imitation both of
the preſent and future Ages, at home and abroad. And for the very ſame purpoſe have I pitched upon a Catalogue, containing the goodly Company of
pious Benefactors to the Church of *Canterbury*, with a brief Memorial of their
ſeveral Gifts, as I find them there upon the Record; and it is to be ſeen in
the *Appendix*, Numb. XXXVI.

The Record ends; much ſooner (I confeſs) than it ſhould. For a multitude
of Benefactors there were, both before and after this time that are here omitted. But (I take it) theſe were all or the moſt of the chief, and it would have
been an endleſs work to have mentioned all. In which regard, [and becauſe
the moſt of them are alienated and gone from the Church, *W. S.*] I hope it
will not be expected, that I ſhould perfect the Catalogue. I therefore leave it,
as I took it from the Regiſters of the Church.

And now am come to $\left\{\begin{array}{l} \text{1 Archbiſhops} \\ \text{2 Priors} \\ \text{3 Archdeacons} \end{array}\right\}$ of the Church.   5. Particular.
my Catalogue of the

Beginning with the Archbiſhops, let me ſet before you in the firſt place, a
few things very fit to be premiſed. *viz.*

    1. The Antiquity of Archbiſhops in general; and the Cauſe of their firſt
        Inſtitution.
    2. The Antiquity of our Archbiſhop in particular; with the number of
        Archbiſhops in *England* in former time, and at this day.

FOR the firſt, (the Antiquity of Archbiſhops, &c.) I ſhall not need to
take much pains to ſearch it out. For, truth is, the Antiquity both of the
Name and Office of an Archbiſhop, is already ſo fully laid down and proved
to my hand by the worthily admired Author of the *Defence of the Anſwer to the
Admonition*, and ſo vindicated and cleared from the Aſperſion of Antichriſtia-
niſm (wherewith ſome late turbulent Innovators have been pleaſed falſly to
ſtigmatize them) and that by his learned Pen, who fetcheth and deriveth them
(ſo venerable is their Antiquity) from before the time of the Goſpel's publick
embracing by any Prince, or in any Kingdom; and (if I miſtake him not)
the Office, though not the Name, from the Apoſtolick times: And Biſhop
Bilſon alſo, Biſhop *Downham*, and many others, as the learned well know,

---

(a) *In Archivis Eccleſ. præd.*

                                 have

have so laboured in this Argument, that if I shall further proceed in the observing of the Antiquity of Archbishops, I shall but as it were, (a) do the same thing over again. And therefore will it suffice that *remissive*, I refer the Reader to these mens Learned Labours, whom I have chosen to cite, because the vulgar, whose only information I here intend, can more easily both purchase and peruse them, their Works like themselves speaking *English*. The learned, I know, can further satisfy themselves in the point from *Bertherius*, in his *Pithanon*, and *Morinus* of late, in his *Ecclesiasticæ Exercitationes*; not to mention divers others. Of the former also, the *Defender* (I mean) *of the Answer to the Admonition*, he may see those men answered, who (relishing nothing but a *Presbyterian-Utopian Parity* in the Ministry) under pretence of zeal for the Reformation (as they term it) of disorders in the Church Government by Archbishops, *&c.* kick and carp at the same, and upon occasion, which unoffered, they take of the report of those, who to shew the Original of Archbishops in the Church, say, that they succeeded in the places of the *Archiflamines*, (certain Heathen High-Priests, or Arch-Priests, which had the oversight of the manners of the *Flamins*, Heathen Priests likewise, as Judges over them; of whom *Duarenus* (b), *Alexander ab Alexandro* (c), and our Countryman (d) *Fox* with others make mention) collect and conclude thus: " That the Mini- " stry of the Gospel was framed by example of Idolatrous and Heathenish " functions. Of my forecited Authors, the *Defender* (I say) *of the Answer to the Admonition*, chiefly takes these men to task. After what manner he encountreth their Arguments would be too prolix here to relate; and because his larger discourse is in my opinion well abridg'd and epitomized by Mr. *Mason*; I have chosen rather to present you with those words of his: (e) *But they are offended, that our Bishops and Archbishops may be said to have their Sees adapted to the number of the Flamins and Archflamins. But I beseech you, what inconvenience can arise from hence; if the worshippers of Idols being driven away, the worshippers of the true God be put in their place? For there are no places more fit for the erecting of Episcopal Sees in, than great and populous Cities. The Apostles themselves in the most Famous Cities, where there had been Flamins, Archflamins, or other like Presidents over the Rites of Religion, constituted Bishops*, &c. Thus far Mr. *Mason*.

Some learned men (I am not ignorant) there have been, and are, which will by no means yield, that the Sees of our Bishops and Archbishops were adapted to the number and places of the Flamins and Archflamins, arguing very stifly against it; by name Bishop *Godwin*, in his Treatise of the *Conversion of Britany*, preceding his Catalogue of Bishops; *fol.* 26. Sir *Henry Spelman*, in the first Book *Of the Councils*; *pag.* 13. and some others. But, put case it be granted that they were so, and let these Cavillers (which distasting our *Aristocracy*, (for such is our Church-Government (f)) and desirous, as it seemeth of an *Anarchy*, a Church like to *Pliny's Acephali*, all Body and no Head) be allowed their so much desired premises, yet still a *non sequitur* will attend on their conclusion. For were it (think they) a good Collection to say, that because there is now a Minister of the Gospel placed, where in the Pope's time there was a Massing Priest: *Ergo* the Ministry of the Gospel is framed by the Example of Massing Priests? If they cannot justly say so of Ministers, neither can they of Bishops and Archbishops. For the reason is the same in both. As much to this purpose, the said Author of the *Defence*, *&c.* hath it, *fol.* 321. Agreeable whereunto is that of Bishop *Hall*. (g) *Christianity* (saith he) *came in the room of Judaism; was it therefore derived from it?* I leave the judicious Reader to give the Answer.

And so enough of this, only pray we that *Anarchy* never get possession of our Stage, lest Confusion shut up the Scene. And that maugre the malice of all turbulent Innovators, our Church may still glory in this (the Commenda-

---

(a) *Actum agere.* (b) *Tract. de Beneficiis.* (c) *Genial. Dier.* (d) *Acts & Monum.* (e) *Sed id demum illos pessime habet quòd Episcopi nostri atque Archiepiscopi sedes suas ad Flaminum atque Archiflaminum Ethnicorum numerum aptatas habuisse dicantur. Verum quid obsecro inde nascetur incommodi, si pulsis Idolorum cultoribus, veri Dei adoratores succedunt? Neque enim ulli loci Episcopatibus erigendis aptiores quam maxima & frequentissimæ Civitates. Ipsi Apostoli in nobilissimis urbibus, in quibus fuerant aliquando Flamines & Archiflamines aut sacrorum Præsides eorum non dissimiles, Episcopos constituerunt. &c. De Ministeriis Anglican. lib 2. cap 3. pag. 79.* (f) *Downing's* Discourse, Conclus. 1. §. 6.
(g) Apology against *Brownists*, Sect. 46.

tion given by the late Learned *Isaac Casaubon*), that she *(a) keeps the mean between excess and defect.* And may continue to deserve that *Encomium* given her by divine *Herbert (b)* :

I joy , dear Mother, when I view	*Hath kiss'd so long her painted Shrines,*
Thy perfect Lineaments and Hiew,	*That even her face by kissing shines,*
Both sweet and bright.	*For her reward.*
Beauty in thee takes up her place,	*She in the Valley is so shy*
And dates her Letters from thy face,	*Of dressing, that her Hair doth lye*
When she doth write.	*About her ears.*
A fine aspect in fit aray,	*While she avoids her Neighbour's pride,*
Neither too mean, nor yet too gay,	*She wholly goes on th' other side,*
Shows who is best.	*And nothing wears.*
Outlandish Looks may not compare ;	*But, dearest Mother, (what those miss)*
For all they either painted are,	*The mean thy praise and glory is,*
Or else undrest.	*And long may be.*
She on the Hills, which wantonly	*Blessed be God, whose love it was,*
Allureth all in hope to be	*To double moat thee with his Grace,*
By her preferr'd,	*And none but thee.*

So much of the Antiquity of Archbishops.

The cause of their first Institution follows. And it was briefly this. As the whole *Hierarchie* was first invented and instituted *(c) that Unity and peace of that Divine and August City which we call the Church, might be the better preserv'd.* So *Duarenus*; who there proceeds to show the further utility of the Hierarchical Order: so consequently the final cause of ordaining an Archbishop (a principal member of that Hierarchical Body) was to promote and advance the Church's Peace. This the often alledged Author of the Defence, *&c.* well knowing, faith, that it is the chief and principal Office of an Archbishop, *To keep Unity in the Church, to compound Contentions, to redress Heresies, Schisms, Factions, &c.* as he gathereth out of St. *Cyprian,* as you may read, *Fol.* 355. And so I have done with my first Particular.

2.

AND come now to the other (*The Antiquity of our Archbishops in particular,* &c.) In the world (as I read in a *French* Author *(d)*, a Civilian, who hath noted it out of the *(e) The Provincial of all the Churches in the world,* a book so called, in which as he relateth all the Archbishopricks in the whole world with their Suffragans are particularly reckoned up) there are to the number of an hundred and thirty Archbishopricks. For the truth of this relation (because it is a thing not so easily proved as published) *(f)* I leave it to be believed upon the Credit of the Relator. But sure I am that we in this Kingdom acknowledge only two Archbishops to be in this our *English*-Orb at this day ; albeit in time past, namely from the conversion of King *Lucius* unto Christianity fourteen hundred years ago and upwards, unto the coming of *Augustin* (the Monk sent from *Rome*) into *England,* happening above one thousand years since, that is, for the space of about 400 years together, there were in this our Island, three Archbishops, to wit, of *London, York,* and *Caerleon.* To *Caerleon* the Churches of *Wales* were subject ; *York's* Province was *Scotland* and the North of *England* ; and lastly, *London* had Jurisdiction over the rest of the Kingdom *(g)*. In which three principal Cities of the Realm (as *Fox* and *Lambard* affirm) were before *Lucius* time, and in his reign also until his conversion, three Arch-flamins, who were by *Fugatius* or *Faganus,* and *Damianus* or *Dimianus* (Teachers or Preachers sent by *Eleutherius* then Bishop of *Rome* into this Island for the conversion of the King and People thereof) turned into Archbishops, about the year of our Redemption 180. Who, from and after that their plantation continued their Archiepiscopal seats there, until such time as *Augustin*

(a) *Inter vel excessu vel defectu peccantes mediam viam sequitur. Exercitationes.* (b) The Temple.
(c) *Ut Augusta illius ac divinæ Civitatis, quam ecclesiam vocamus, unitas ac tranquilitas melius conservetur. De sacr. Eccles. Minister. & Beneficiis, lib.* 1. cap. 9 (d) *Gualterus.* (e) *Provinciale omnium universi orbis Ecclesiarum.* (f) *Sit fides penes authorem.* (g) *Antiq Brit.* pag. 6. *Acts & Mon. tom.* 1. pag. 96. *Lamb. Peramb. pag.* 62. *Catal. of BB.* pag. 181.

came

came over and was entertained of *Ethelbert* the *Kentiſh* King, in the time of the *Saxon* Heptarchy. For at that time (according to that prediction of *Merlin* (*a*), *The Dignity of* London *ſhall grace* Canterbury) at the prayer of the Citizens of *Dorobernia* (as Mr. *Fox* (*b*) hath it) the Archbiſhoprick of *London* (whoſe Chair ſtood at St. *Peter's* in *Cornhill*) was by *Auguſtin* and *Ethelbert* tranſlated from thence to *Canterbury*. Other reaſons for the tranſlation of it are given by the Author of the *Antiquities of Britain* (*c*). You ſhall have his words. But *Auguſtin* (ſaith he) whether for *Ethelbert* the *Kentiſh* King, and his kind Hoſts ſake, whether becauſe *London* was not *Ethelbert's*, but *Sebert's* his Nephew, whether in charity or good will to the *Kentiſh*-men for their kind entertainment of him, or whether in regard that *Kent* was the prime and chief province of *Britany*, to the Dominion and Empire of whoſe King, the reſt of the Kings were ſubject, *&c.* But Maſter *Lambard* (*d*) ſaith flatly (if we may believe him) that *Auguſtin* by great injury ſpoiled *London* of this dignity of the Archbiſhop's Chair, beſtowing the ſame upon *Canterbury*. Indeed it appears, that Pope *Gregory* intending *London* for the Metropolitan Seat of *Auguſtin's* Archbiſhoprick, ſent him his Pall thither. But *Auguſtin* for many reaſons (wherein you ſee Authors are divided) placed the ſame at *Canterbury*. Whereof afterwards the Popes, *Boniface*, and *Honorius*, in their ſeveral Letters, the one to *Juſtus*, the other to *Honorius* ſucceſſors of *Auguſtin*, gave their expreſs approbations. The firſt thus: (*e*) *We confirm and command, That the Metropolitical See of all* Britain *be for ever hereafter in the City of* Canterbury : *And we make a perpetual and unchangeable Decree, That all Provinces of the Kingdom of* England *be for ever ſubject to the Metropolitical Church of that place.* The latter in theſe words, (*f*) *We therefore command all the Churches and Provinces of* England *to be ſubject to thy juriſdiction : And that the Metropolitical See and Archiepiſcopal Dignity, and the Primacy of all the Churches of* England *be fixed and remain in* Canterbury, *and never be transferred through any kind of evil perſuaſion by any one to any other place.* Which thing, for the honour of *Auſtin* it pleaſed the wiſdom of this Nation afterwards to eſtabliſh and confirm ; witneſs this paſſage in certain Letters of *Kenulphus* King of *Mercia* to Pope *Leo.* (*g*) *Becauſe* Auguſtin, *of Bleſſed Memory, who in the time of Pope* Gregory *preached the word of God to the* Engliſh *Nation, and preſided over the* Saxon *Churches, died in the ſame City, and his Body was buried in the Church which his ſucceſſor* Laurentius *Dedicated to St.* Peter, *the Prince of the Apoſtles. It ſeemed good to all the wiſe men of our Nation, That the Metropolitical Dignity ſhould be fixed in that City, where reſteth the Body of him, that planted the truth of the Chriſtian Faith in theſe parts.* But enough of this matter ; It is now time that I come to my Catalogue. Wherein I purpoſe, beſide their names, to repeat little of what others have written of the Archbiſhops, unleſs in a brief collection of their more memorable acts and places of Burial, adding what things of note I find omitted of others, with ſome pertinent obſervations.

Auguſtin. 1.

Anno Dom.
596.

Auguſtin (you ſee) was the firſt Archbiſhop of *Canterbury*. Whoſe whole Story is become ſo trite and vulgar that it needs no repetition. Wherefore let other men's copious Diſcourſe of him and his Acts excuſe my ſilence of either.

Lawrence. 2.

611.

Lawrence ſucceeded *Auſtin*, as it was appointed by *Auſtin* before his death, and ſat till 616, and then died.

Mellitus. 3.

619.

Mellitus ſucceeded him, and died in the year 624. Of the miraculous pre-

---

(a) *Dignitas Lonedoniæ adornabit Doroberniam.*   (b) *Tom* 1 *pag.* 108   (c) *Ubi ſupra.*
(d) *Ubi ſupra.*   (e) *Id ipſum præcipientes firmamus, ut in Dorobernia civitate ſemper in poſterum Metropolitanus totius Britanniæ locus habeatur ; omneſque provinciæ Regni Anglorum præfati loci Metropolitanæ eccleſiæ ſubjiciantur, immutilatâ & perpetua ſtabilitate decrevimus. Malmsh. de geſtis Pontif. lib.* 1. *pag.* 208.   (f) *Tuæ ergo juriſdictioni ſubjici præcipimus omnes Angliæ eccleſias & regiones ; & in civitate Dorobernia Metropolitanus locus & honor Archiepiſcopatus & caput omnium eccleſiarum Angliæ ſemper in poſterum ſervetur ; & à nulla perſona per aliquam malam ſuaſionem in alium locum mutetur Ibid Pag.* 209.   (g) *Nam quia beatæ recordationis Auguſtinus, qui verbum Dei (imperante beato Gregorio) Anglorum genti miniſtrabat, & glorioſiſſimè eccleſiis præfuit Saxoniæ, in eadem civitate diem obiit, & corpus illius in eccleſia beati Petri Apoſtolorum principis (quam ſucceſſor ejus Lawrentius ſacravit) conditum fuiſſet ; viſum eſt cunctis gentis noſtra ſapientibus, quatenus in illa civitate Metropolitanus honor haberetur, ubi corpus ejus pauſat, qui his partibus fidei veritatem inſeruit. Idem, de Geſtis Regum Anglor. l.* 1. *pag* 3.

fervation of our City from the fury of the Flame, by whofe Prayers and Prefence, you may read in *Bede's ecclef. Hift. lib. 2. c. 7.*

Juftus. 4.

Whom *Juftus* fucceeded, governed the See 10 years, and then died.

Honorius. 5.

Honorius fucceeded *Juftus.* This Archbifhop is famous for his divifion of the Kingdom into Parifhes. For I read, that about the year of our Redemption 636, this Man firft began to divide *England* into Parifhes: that fo (faith my Author (*a*)) he might appoint particular Minifters to particular Congregations. I read, that *Euariftus* the firft Bifhop of *Rome,* who fuffered Martyrdom under *Trajan* the Emperor, about the year 110, did the like in *Rome* (*b*). And that *Dionyfius,* that bleffed Martyr, Bifhop of *Rome circa ann.* 266 did attempt to do the like throughout the whole Chriftian world (*c*). I find no queftion made of any of thefe three divifions of Parifhes fave only of that of our *Honorius*; which Mr. *Selden* in his *Hiftory of Tithes* flatly denieth. His arguments you may find examined and anfwered by his Animadverfioner, to whom for brevity-fake I refer you, and come to the Hiftory of the Council of *Trent,* the Author whereof delivers his Opinion in the generality of the Point in hand thus. " The " divifion of Parifhes (faith he (*d*)) was firft made by the People, when a cer-" tain number of Inhabitants, having received the true Faith, built a Temple " for exercife of their Religion, hired a Prieft and did conftitute a Church, " which by the Neighbours was called a Parifh; and when the number was " increafed, if one Church and Prieft were not fufficient, thofe who were " moft remote did build another. In progrefs of time, for good order and " concord a cuftom began to have the Bifhop's confent alfo. Thus he. And fo I return to our Archbifhop who fate almoft 20 years, and died in the year 653.

Deuf-dedit, or Adeodatus. 6.

Him next fucceeded *Deuf-dedit,* or *Adeodatus.* He continued Archbifhop about fix years, and dying was buried (as all his predeceffors were) in the Church-Porch of St. *Auguftin's.*

Theodorus. 7.

Theodorus fucceeded him. Amongft his other defigns for the advancement of Learning, he founded the School at *Canterbury*; which I have on a former occafion mentioned: In his time and chiefly by his endeavours Learning fo flourifhed in this Ifland, that from a Nurfery [or as St. *Jerom* reads it, a nation of Tyrants. *W. S.*] it became a peculiar feminary of Philofophy (*e*). He continued Archbifhop two and twenty years, and dying *anno Dom.* 690. was buried within the Church of St. *Auftin's* Abbey, becaufe the Porch was full before, all his predeceffors (fix in number) being (as I told you) buried there. In memory of them all were compofed and ingraven in Marble certain Verfes, which *Wever* hath already publifhed both in *Latin* and *Englifh* (*f*).

Brithwald. 8.

Theodorus next fucceffor was *Brithwald,* fometime Abbat of *Reculver.* No Archbifhop continued fo long in this See as he, either before or fince his time. He fat 38 years and a half. Dying then, in the year 731, he was buried at St. *Auftin's* with his predeceffors. He held a Synod at *Cliff,* and another at a place then called *Bacanceld,* fince *Backchild* and now *Bapchild,* an obfcure village upon the rode near *Sittingbourn* in *Kene.*

Tatwyn. 9.

Tatwyn fucceeded him, and fat 3 years. Died in the year 734, and was buried at *Canterbury.*

Nothelmus. 10.

Nothelmus fucceeded *Tatwyn.* He was one of venerable *Bede's* Intelligencers for his Ecclefiaftical Story (*g*), and dying in the year 741, was buried alfo at *Canterbury.*

Cuthbert. 11.

Cuthbert was his Succeffor. This man was the firft that obtained Church-

---

(a) *Antiq. Brit. in ejus vita.* (b) *Pet. Greg. Tholof. de Benefic. cap.* 4 *num.* 5. (c) *Id. Tholof. ubi fupra.* (d) *Lib* 6. *pag.* 498. (e) *Malmfb. de Geftis Reg. lib.* 1. *pag.* 11. (f) *Ancient Fun. Mon. pag.* 248. (g) *Vide Prafat. Bede.*

yards for this Kingdom. For you muſt know, there was a Law amongſt the *Romans*, borrowed of the *Grecians*, and inſerted into their *Twelve Tables*, that none ſhould be buried or burned within any Town. (*a*). So that all were buried either in the fields, along the High-way ſide, (to put Paſſengers in mind of their mortality) upon the top or at the feet of Mountains. And this kind of interment, by general cuſtom, was uſed both of *Jews* and *Gentiles*; as you may find at large illuſtrated by *Wever* in his Monuments. Hence was it that *Auguſtin* the firſt of our Archbiſhops procured the ground, on part whereof he afterward erected his Abby, lying without the City, for a place of ſepulture for the Kings of *Kent*, himſelf, and all ſucceeding Archbiſhops of that See.

Cicero making mention of this Law, gives this reaſon for it. (*b*) *I ſuppoſe*, (ſaith he) *it was to prevent the danger of fire, or ſome other danger.* But (*c*) *Hoſpinian* out of *Durand*, *Ulpian*, and others, ſhews the reaſon of it more at large. It was a cuſtom (ſaith he) in times of old, that men and women were buried in their own private Houſes or Gardens; but afterwards, for the noiſome ſavour and contagious ſtink of the dead Carkaſſes ſo interred, it was inacted that all Burials ſhould be without Towns and Cities, in ſome convenient place appointed for that purpoſe. And however, that this Order was obſerved by the *Gentiles* upon this reaſon only, (*d*) *to prevent the infection of the air by the ſtink of dead Carkaſſes*, yet the true Chriſtians, and ſuch as by their lively Faith were adopted the Children of God, had a further myſtery in this their manner of interments: For by the Carriage and Burial of the dead Corps without their City-walls, they did publickly confirm and witneſs, that the Parties deceaſed were gone out of this world to be made free Denizens of another City, namely Heaven, there to remain with the bleſſed Saints in eternal Happineſs.

This Order or Cuſtom of Burial without Cities, continued amongſt the Chriſtians until the time of *Gregory* the Great; for as then the Monks, Friers, and Prieſts, (ſaith my foreſaid Author) began to offer Sacrifice for the Souls departed. So that for their more eaſe and greater profit, they procured firſt, that the places of ſepulture ſhould be adjoining unto their Churches; upon this reaſon, given by the ſaid *Gregory*. (*e*). Anciently (ſaith *Onuphrius Panvinius* (*f*)) the Bodies of the dead were buried only without the Cities, in Cœmiteries, or Sleeping-places, (as the word ſignifies) until the reſurrection. But perſecution being ended, and peace given to the Chriſtian Church, the manner grew in uſe to bury within Cities, at the entrance into their ſacred Temples, yea and afterwards in the very Churches themſelves. Now our Archbiſhop *Cuthbert* happening to be at *Rome*, and ſeeing of theſe Burials, obtained from the Pope a diſpenſation for the making of Cœmiteries or Church-yards within Towns or Cities throughout *England*.

By this time you may ſee when the old Cuſtom of burying without the City-walls ceaſed, and burying in Churches and Church-yards both here and elſewhere began, and may gueſs at the cauſe of the frequency of Burials in Churches in former times. A thing thus tartly reproved of *Balduinus* the Civilian. (*g*) Having ſpoken before of the prohibition of ſuch Burials, he ſaith, *Yet afterwards by the indulgence of Chriſtian Princes, it came to that paſs, that many ambitiouſly willed to be buried in the very Temples, and Chapels, and Coffins of the Saints; which ſuperſtition,* (ſhall I call it rather impudent ambition?) Gratian, Valentinian, *and* Theodoſius *endeavoured to ſuppreſs, by publiſhing this Reſcript: Let no man think, that the Seat of the Apoſtles or Martyrs is allowed to be uſed for the Burial-places of Men's Bodies*, &c. So he. But enough of this.

Now return we to our Archbiſhop, *Cuthbert*. Who, five years after his tranſlation to this See, to wit, *Anno* 747. by the Counſel of *Boniface* Biſhop of *Mentz*, called a Convocation at *Cliff* beſide *Rocheſter*, to reform the manifold

---

(a) *Hominem mortuum in urbe nè ſepelito neve urito.*   (b) *Credo vel propter ignem, vel periculum.*
(c) *Wever*, of Ancient Fun. Monum. *pag.* 7.   (d) *Scilicet ut in urbibus mundicies ſervaretur,*
& aër minus inficeretur, ex cadaverum putreſcentium fætore.   (e) *Cum gravia peccata non deprimunt tunc prodeſt mortuis ſi in eccleſiis ſepeliantur: quia eorum proximi quoties ad eadem ſacra loca veniunt ſuorumque ſepulturam aſpiciunt, recordantur & pro eis Domino preces fundunt.* 13. *Quæſt.* 2. *c.* 17
(f) *In lib. de Ritu ſepeliendi mortuos.*   (g) *Poſtea tamen Chriſtianorum Principum indulgentiâ res eò evaſit ut multi in ipſis etiam d-vorum templis atque ſacellis loculiſque ambitioſè ſepeliri vellent, quam ſuperſtitionem dicam an impudentem ambitionem Gratianus, Valentinianus & Theodoſius reprimere conati ſunt, edito hoc reſcripto. Nemo Apoſtolorum vel Martyrum-ſedem humanis (f. humandis) corporibus exiſtimet eſſe conceſſam, &c. Ad LL.* 12 *Tabularum.*

enormities wherewith the Church of *England* at that time was over-grown. The Conftitutions whereof you may read of elfewhere. He procured of *Eadbert* King of *Kent*, that the Bodies of all the Archbifhops deceafed, from thenceforth fhould not be buried at St. *Auguftin's*, (as heretofore) but at *Chrift-Church*. And dying, his Funerals were there folemnized accordingly.

Bregwyn. 12.

As alfo were the Funerals of his next Succeffor *Bregwyn*, who fat only three years, and died *Anno* 762.

Lambert. 13.

Lambert fucceeded *Bregwyn*. From Abbat of St. *Auftin's*, he was by the Monks of *Chrift-Church*, chofen for their Archbifhop, affuring themfelves, he would now be as earneft a Defender of their Liberties, as he had been heretofore an Oppugner in behalf of St. *Auftin's*, about the Burial of the Archbifhops; for which, being Abbat, he had contended with *Bregwyn* his Predeceffor: But their hopes failed them; for perceiving his end to approach, he took order to be buried in St. *Auftin's*, and was (faith my Author) very honorably interred in the Chapter-Houfe there. In his time, *Offa* King of *Mercia* erected a new Archbifhoprick at *Litchfield*, and obtained of the Pope authority for *Eadulfus*, Bifhop there, to govern the Diocefes of *Worcefter*, *Leicefter*, *Sidnacefter*, *Hereford*, *Helmham*, and *Dunwich*. So that *Canterbury* had left unto him for his Province, only thefe; *London*, *Winchefter*, *Rochefter*, and *Sherborne*. But

Athelard. 14.

Athelard, his Succeffor, prevailed with (*Offa's* Succeffor) *Kenulph*, and *Leo* 3. then Pope, to quafh this new Archbifhoprick, and to reduce all (*a*) into their former ftate. He fat 13 years, and then dying, was buried in *Chrift-Church*.

By his means King *Offa* became an efpecial Benefactor to this Church, as by his Charter appears; which, if it be authentick, and may be credited, (as I fee not why to queftion it) difcovers an error in the computation and accompt which the Current of our Hiftories and Chronologies do make of the beginning both of *Offa's* Reign, and this Archbifhop's Government. Wherefore, and becaufe it is otherwife remarkable, I have thought fit wholly to tranfcribe it, as you may find in my *Appendix*, Numb. XXXVII.

Wlfred. 15.

His Succeffor was *Wlfred*, who died in the year 830. In his time the Monks of his Church died all to Five (*b*).

Theologild or *Fleologild.* 16.

After *Wlfred*, *Theologild* or *Fleologild*, fometime Abbat of *Canterbury*, was Archbifhop for the fpace of three Months, and dying, was buried alfo in *Chrift-Church*. One named *Syred* fucceeded him, but being taken away before he had full poffeffion, is not reckoned amongft the Archbifhops.

Celnoth. 17.

Celnoth fucceeded and continued Archbifhop 38 years, died *Anno* 870, and was buried in *Chrift-Church*. He brought Clerks into his Church, in aid of thofe 5 Monks that furvived the Mortality before fpoken of in *Wlfred* (*c*).

Athelred. 18.

Athelred was Archbifhop after *Celnoth* 18 years, and died *Anno* 889, and was buried in the fame Church. He expelled thofe Clerks out of his Church, which his Predeceffor brought thither, and made up the number of his Monks again (*d*).

Plegmund. 19.

Plegmund fucceeded him, and fat Archbifhop 26 years, and dying *Anno* 915, was buried alfo in his own Church.

Athelm. 20.

Athelm fucceeded, and fat 9 years, died *Anno* 924, and was buried with his Predeceffors.

Wlfhelm. 21.

Wlfhelm fucceeded *Athelm*. He continued 10 years, and died *Anno* 934.

Odo. 22.

Odo firnamed *Severus* fucceeded him and fat 24 years. Dying then he was buried (fome fay) on the South-fide of the high Altar, in a Tomb built after

Anno Dom.
759.

764.

Archbifhoprick at Litchfield.

793.

807.

832.

832.

871.

889.

915.

924.

934.

(*a*) *In ftatu quo prius.*   (*b*) *Lib. Ecclef. Cantuar.*   (*c*) *Lib. fupradict.*   (*d*) *Lib. memorat.*

the

Odo's Tomb mistaken.

the form of a *Pyramis.* Bishop *Godwyn* in his Catalogue conceives it to be the Tomb of Touchstone (such are his words) standing in the Grate near the steps that lead up to St. *Thomas's* Chapel. And there indeed accordingly, shall you find a Table hanging, epitomizing the Story of his Life and Acts. Not without a great mistake doubtless. For first the modern Church is not the same that stood in *Odo's* days, or when he he died: that (I think) is made plain enough before. Secondly this Tomb is not built *Pyramis*-wise, or after the form of a *Pyramis.* Thirdly it is clear by Archbishop *Parker's* report, and by the words also of the same Bishop *Godwyn* in his foresaid Catalogue, that this was and is the Tomb of Archbishop *Sudbury,* who was slain by the Rebels in *Richard* II. time, whose body (they say) was intombed on the South-side of St. *Dunstan's* Altar (*Godwyn* adds) a little above the Tomb of Bishop *Stratford.* Now this is the next and only Tomb above *Stratford's,* and St. *Dunstan's* Altar (as shall appear unto you) stood hard by. But hereof no more, till I come to speak of Archbishop *Sudbury.*

Dunstan. 23.

Anno Dom. 961.

Dunstan succeeded *Odo,* sat 27 years, and then dying was buried in *Christ-Church,* that is (and so it must be understoood of all his predecessors said to be there buried) in the old Church, not in the modern. For his Piety and Miracles in his life time (so they say of him) he was (like his predecessor *Odo*) canonized a Saint after his death; and his Relicks were of such high account, even in those times, that (a) Archbishop *Lanfranc,* when he built the Church of new in the Conqueror's days, very solemnly translated his Corps from his first Sepulchre into his new Church, and thereof new intombed it (with the Pontificals, wherewith, according to the times, it was apparelled, and a plate of Lead bearing an Inscription to show upon enquiry whose Body it was) near unto the high Altar on the South-side. And from thenceforth the Tomb became called the Altar of St. *Dunstan,* and the steps leading to it the steps of St. *Dunstan's* Altar. Whoso observes the pavement on the South-side of the steps between *Stratford* and *Sudbury's* Monuments with the guilded work on the wall and pillar there, shall easily discern some such thing had thence, as questionless this Altar was at the purging of the Church of such things at or shortly after the Reformation.

Whilest it was standing there, such high estimation was had of this Saint and his Relicks, and so beneficial they became to the place that enjoyed them, by the Offerings to his Altar, that the Monks of *Glastonbury* (amongst whom he was brought up) in *Henry* VII. time, began to boast and give out that they had them in possession, being translated thither from *Canterbury* (as *Capgrave* in the life of *Dunstan* affirms) in the year 1012. Hereupon these Monks built him a Shrine (b); and by that and other means the stream of Benefit formerly running to *Christ-Church* became turned to *Glastonbury.* This at length so troubled the Archbishop of *Canterbury* and his Monks, that bethinking themselves of a speedy remedy, they resolve on a scrutiny to be made in his Tomb or Altar; by opening thereof to see whether really his Corps, his Relicks, were there inclosed or not. The Scrutiny is made, and the searchers find for the *Christ-Church* Monks. Whereupon *Warham* the then Archbishop forthwith directs and sends his Letters to the Abbat and Monks of *Glastonbury,* straightly charging them to desist from all further jactitation of their possession of St. *Dunstan's* Relicks, which Letters he was fain to iterate, before they would obey; so loth they were to forego their *Diana.* A Record of the scrutiny is kept *in Archivis ecclesiæ,* a true copy whereof you shall find in my *Appendix,* Numb. XXXVIII. It is a pretty relation and worth your reading.

Scrutiny in St. Dunstan's Tomb.

Æthelgar. 24.

938.

After *Dunstan* succeeded *Æthelgar,* who continued in the See only one year and three Months. Dying then he was buried in his own Church.

Siricius. 25.

989.

Him *Siricius* succeeded, sat four years, died *Anno* 993, and was buried at *Canterbury.*

Aluricius aliàs Alfricus. 26.

993.

Aluricius or *Alfricus* succeeded next, died 1006, and was buried first at *Abingdon,* but was afterward removed to *Canterbury.*

(a) *Harpsfield, Hist. Eccles. Angl. in ejus vita.*   (b) *Harpsfield, ubi supra.*

Elphege.

Elphege. 27.

Elphege fucceeded him, and fat fix years. He was moft barbaroufly Murder- *Anno Dom.*
ed by the *Danes* in the year 1011, at what time they both fpoiled the Church 1006.
and City, and tithed the Monks and other people therein, whereof our Chronicles are fo very full, that I forbear its further relation, only crave favour
to give you the defcription of it out of *Henry* of *Huntingdon* (*a*). Who thus fad-
ly tells. " *Anno undecimo, &c.* In the Eleventh year (faith he) when the *Danes*
" had done preying on the North-fide of *Thames*, they befieged *Canterbury* the
" Metropolis of *England*, and by treachery took it. For *Almar* whom before
" Archbifhop *Alfege* had refcued from death, betrayed the fame. Entring there-
" fore they took *Alfege* the Archbifhop, *Godwyn* the Bifhop, *Lefwyn* the Abbat,
" and *Alfword* the King's Provoft, the Clerks alfo with the Monks, the men
" with the women, and fo returned Conquerors to their Ships. But you might
" have feen an horrid fpectacle, the face of an ancient and moft beautiful City
" all brought to Afhes, the carcafes of the Citizens thick ftrawed in the ftreets,
" dying both Soil and River black with Blood, the weeping and howling of
" Women and Children which were to be led away Captive, the chieftain of
" Faith, and fountain of Doctrine of the *Englifh* hurried about in Fetters. Thus
he. Our Archbifhop *Elphege* being by thofe bloody Mifcreants thus bafely but-
chered, was buried firft in St. *Paul's* Church in *London*, afterward conveyed to
Canterbury by the command of King *Knute*, and interred in his own Church.
He was afterward made a Saint, and had an Altar proper to him ftanding oppofite to that of his predeceffor *Dunftan*, both near unto the high Altar that
now is, as is clear by thefe words in Archbifhop *Winchelfey's* Statutes. (*b*) Which
mentions the *High Altar and the two Altars neareft unto it, namely, of St.* Dunftan
and St. Elphege.

Living. 28.

Living fucceeded *Alphege*, and having been Archbifhop about 7 years died in 1013.
the year 1020.

Agelnoth. 29.

Agelnoth was his Succeffor. Who when he had fat Archbifhop 17 years and 1020.
upwards, in which interim of time he perfected the work of his Churches repair that had been deftroyed and burnt by the *Danes*, as formerly I have faid,
died *anno* 1038. I read that the Monaftery of *Reculver*, built by one *Baffa*, in *Reculver.*
the time of *Egbright* (the 7th King of *Kent* in fucceffion after *Hengift*) whereof
Brithwald that was afterward Archbifhop was (as we read) fometimes Abbat,
was in the year 949 given to *Chrift-Church* by King *Edred* (*c*). Notwithftanding which donation I find it ftill continued a Monaftery undiffolved unto this
Archbifhop's time, but the governor of it turned from an Abbat to a Dean,
as, with fome further difcovery of that Monaftery's then eftate and condition,
and fomewhat elfe alfo of Antiquaries obfervable, by a certain Charter of this
our Archbifhop concerning that Monaftery, to be found in my *Appendix,* will
appear, Numb. XXXIX.

Eadfin. 30.

Eadfin fucceeded *Agelnoth.* He continued Archbifhop almoft 11 years, and 1038.
died in the year 1050, was buried in his own Church, and after his death
made a Saint.

Robert. 31.

Robert firnamed *Gemiticenfis* fucceeded *Eadfin.* He died and was buried in the 1050.
Abbey of *Gemetica* where he was brought up, having been Archbifhop about the
fpace of 2 years, or fcarcely fo much.

Stigand. 32.

Stigand was his Succeffor. He was depofed by the Conqueror, whom (if 1052.
Spot, St. *Auftin's* Chronicler, fay true) with *Egelfine,* the then Abbat there, he
encountred as a ftout Champion for the *Kentifh* Liberties, whereof you may
read your fill elfwhere. He lies buried at *Winchefter,* dying 1069.

Lanfranc. 33.

Stigand being thus deprived, *Lanfranc* was confecrated Archbifhop. He cau- 1070.
fed the Sees of many Bifhops, that were before and until then in countrey-vil-

---

(a) *Hiftor. lib. 6.*   (b) *De redditibus verò magno altari & duobus altaribus vicinioribus, viz.*
fanctorum Dunftani & Elphegi, &c.   (c) *Lib. Ecclef. Cant.*

Bishop's See
the Note of a
City.

Cowell.

lages to be removed from thence into Cities, according to the Canon. *(a)*. So that a City with us *(Westminster* excepted*)* hath ever since been and yet is known by having in it a Bishop, and a Cathedral Church. *(b) The number of Cities and Episcopal Sees were the same in the account of our Ancestors,* saith Sir *Henry Spelman.* And not only here, but elsewhere also is this a note whereby to distinguish and discern a City from a Town or Village, as you may learn from the *Interpreter,* who for instance in this point, alledgeth that of *Cassaneus,* *(c)* where he averreth that within the territories of *France* are 104 Cities, and giveth this (saith he) for his reason, because there are within the same so many Bishopricks. But return we to our Archbishop.

Besides his new building of the Cathedral with the Monastery, and a Palace for himself and his Successors (whereof before*)* he built also the Priory of St. *Gregory's* without the *Northgate* of the City of *Canterbury,* and hard by it the Hospital called St. *John's,* as also that other of St. *Nicholas* at *Herbaldown* : all which he endowed with competent revenues, as hath been fully shewed already. And did many other good and pious Acts, whereof (as also of the former) you may find mention in the *Antiquit. Brit.* and the Catalogue of Bishops, in his life and elsewhere. He contended at *Windsor* with *Thomas Norman* Archbishop of *York* for the Primacy, and there, by Judgment before *Hugo* the Pope's Legate, recovered it from him. So that ever since the one (that is, he of *Canterbury*) is called *(d)* Primate of All *England* ; and the other *(e)* Primate of *England,* without any further addition. There happened afterward frequent Controversies between the succeeding Archbishops of both Provinces about the Primacy, and for the ones bearing up the Cross in the others Province : all which differences *Wever (f)* hath concatenated in a continued discourse, whither I refer you. This *Lanfranc* was the man that setled the Manors both of the See and the Priory, *i. e.* both of the Archbishop and the Monks in that manner as they are recorded in Doomsday-book, which for Antiquity-sake, and as a Monument which the curious that way haply may desire to see, my *Appendix* shall make publick. To the Prior and Monks of his Church, for their better future observance of St. *Benet's* rule and order, from which by the remisness and neglect of former times, he found in them a deviation, he prescribed in writing certain Ordinances, which intituled *(g) The Statutes of* Lanfranc *for the Order of the Benedictines,* you may find published in the latter end of *Reyners Apostolatus Benedictinorum.* This Archbishop having sat 19 years, and then dying was buried at *Canterbury* in his own Church. But his Monument is not now extant ; however *Wever* tells us he found his body to be interred there by a Table inscribed which hangs upon his Tomb. Erroniously. For there is neither Tomb nor Table of his there.

Title of *totius
Angliæ Primas.*

Archbishop
and Monks
Mannors.
Numb. XL.

Anselme. 34.

Anno Dom.
1093.

Anselme succeeded *Lanfranc,* who died in the 16 year of his Government, and was buried first at the head of his Predecessor *Lanfranc,* but afterward (saith *Malmesbury*) *(h) He had a more worthy Monument in the East part of the Church.* He was removed to the East end of his Church ; [and laid (I take it) in this Chapel, yet bearing his Name ; on the South-side of the High Altar. *W. S.*] Almost 400 years after his death, by the procurement of *John Merton* one of his Successors, he was canonized a Saint. For the finding of a light before whose Tomb, King *Stephen (i)* gave unto the Monks the Manor of *Berkesore* near *Shepey,* in *Kent.* He built (as I have already told you from *Thorn's* report*)* the Nunnery of St. *Sepulchre's* by *Canterbury.* The preceding Story of the Church's Fabrick will further inform you of his piety. Other things I pass over, as obvious enough elsewhere.

Ralph or Rodulph. 35.

1114.

Ralph or *Rodulph* succeeded *Anselme,* sat 8 years and then dyed ; to wit, *Anno* 1122, and was buried in the middle of the body of *Christ-Church* in *Canterbury, (k)* saith *Edmerus.* Howbeit (saith Bishop *Godwyn)* I see not any Monu-

---

(a) Distinct. lxxx *per totum.*   *(b) Plures igitur Civitates haud numerarunt nostri Majores, quam Episcopatus. Glossar. in verb Burgus.*   *(c) In Consuetud. Burgund. c.* 15   *(d) Totius Angliæ Primas.*   *(e) Angliæ Primas.*   *(f)* Of Ancient Funeral Monum. pag. 3. 5.   *(g) Decret. Lanfranci pro ordine sancti Benedicti.*   *(h) Dignius mausoleum in Orientali portica accepit. De Gest. Pontific. lib.* 1.   *(i). Lib Eccles. Cant.*   *(k) In medio aulæ majoris ecclesiæ decenter sepultus.*

ment or other Sign of his Sepulture there at all. But no marvel, becaufe the modern Nave or Body of the Church was built long fince this Archbifhop's time. His Burial-place was in the elder, the former body of the Church, which Archbifhop *Sudbury* (as I told you) took down, and was fithence rebuilt. Befides it is hard to find a Monument, much more an Epitaph fo ancient any Old Epitaphs where in *England*. That Age (it feems) was not very ambitious of either. The rare in *Eng-* ancient Cuftom was to put (*a*) a plate of Lead with the interred Party's name *land.* infcribed on it, into the Sepulchre with the Corps (*b*). So had Archbifhop *Dunftan*. So alfo *Richard, Becket's* immediate Succeffor. *Simon Iflip* (of the Archbifhops) is the firft that hath an Epitaph upon his Tomb, in the whole Church. About his time (I take it) they firft became common and frequent. Thefe things by the by. This our Archbifhop gave a Penny a day out of his Manor of *Liminge* in *Kent*, to *Herbaldown* Hofpital for ever ; which Gift his Succeffor *Theobald* renewed and confirmed (*c*).

William Corboyl. 36.

William Corboyl fucceeded *Ralph*, and died in the year 1136, having fat almoft *Ann. Dom.* 14 years, and lyeth buried in his own Church : The particular place I find not ; 1122. haply it was in the old body. He is famous for the new building of this Church, (whereof before) as alfo of St. *Martin's* by *Dover*. Of which pleafe you to hear Archdeacon *Harpsfield* fpeak. (*d*) He faith, fpeaking of St. *Martin's*, St. *Martin's* by " There were in that Chapel, anciently, fecular Canons, as they are called. *Dover*. " And whereas their Church ftood in the middle of that little, but populous " Town, and the Canons of that Church were carelefs in the performance of " the facred Offices, and wafted the Goods, and mifpent the profits of the " Church profufely, in luxury ; this Archbifhop *William* ferioufly confidering, " by what means a ftop might be put to this evil, built a new Church with- " out the Walls of the Town, with all Lodgings and Accommodations necef- " fary for men profeffing a Monaftical Life, &c. Out of this Monaftery, *Richard*, a Succeffor of this Archbifhop, was taken and chofen to the See.

Theobald. 37.

Theobald fucceeded *William*. He departed this life in the year 1160, when he 1138. had fat Archbifhop 22 years. He was the firft of the Catalogue that had the Title of (*e*) *Legate of the Apoftolical See*, conferred upon him, to wit, in the Title of *Apo-* year 1138. Which Title was retained until Archbifhop *Cranmer's* time. But *ftolica Sedis Le-* then the Pope's Authority finding its deferved ruin, in our clearer and better *gatus*. underftanding, a Decree paffed in the Synod, (*Anno* 1534.) that laying afide that Title, they fhould be ftyled, (I ufe now my Author's own words) *Primats* and *Metropolitans* of all *England* (*f*). This our Archbifhop perceiving his end to approach, made his Will, and gave all his Goods unto the poor ; and dying, was buried in his own Church, in the South-part of St. *Thomas's* Chapel, in a Marble Tomb joyning to the wall, (faith Bifhop *Godwyn*) and accordingly, there hangs a Table, lately made, of him and his Acts. But with what war- A miftake a- rant, give me leave to make queftion. The Table, I know, follows Bifhop bout *Theobald's* *Godwyn*. And fure I am, that none that have written his life befide *Godwyn* (be- Tomb. fore him I mean) have authorifed this report of his. The particular place of his Burial hath no mention amongft them, nor yet in his Will, which I have feen too. Befides this, another unlikelihood there is it fhould be *Theobald's*, and that is this : It hath no Infcription or Epitaph upon or about it ; whereas his had, and it was this, (as *Wever* fays) which is in the Margin. (*g*)

Now, if you will have my opinion where this Archbifhop was buried, I fhall tell you, that I think it was in the old body of the Church ; whofe de- molition and new erection, is the very caufe (as I conceive) we now mifs fo

---

(*a*) *Laminam plumbeam.*   (*b*) *Vide Mat.* Paris *ad Ann. Dom.* 1257. *pag.* 1258. *Lond. Ed.*
    (*c*) *Rotul. Hofp. de Herbald.*   (*d*) *Erant in eo facello antiquitus Canonici quos feculares appel-*
lant. Quorum ecclefia cum in medio oppidi, parvi illius quidem fed populofi confifteret, canonicique ecclefiæ
facra penfa perfunctorie obirent, illiufque bona per luftra, libidines & luxuriam profunderent & confumerent :
Guliel. diligenter meditatus fecum eft, qua potiffimum ratione huic malo occurreret. Ædificat itaque novam
extra muros oppidi ecclefiam, cum cæteris domibus ad habitationem monafticis viris accommodis, &c.
    (*e*) *Apoftolicæ Sedis Legatus.*   (*f*) Parker. *in vita* Cranmer.   (*g*) *Hic jacet Theo-*
baldus Cantuar. *Archiepifcopus, ob morum placabilitatem atque conftantiam,* Hen. 2 *valde gratiofus, affabi-*
lis, veridicus, prudens & amicus firmus, in omnes liberalis, & in pauperes munificus, qui fuæ tandem fe-
nectutis & languidæ vitæ pertæfus anteactam vitam morti perfolvit, Anno Dom. 1160 *cum* 22. *annis fediffet.*
Anima ejus requiefcat in pace. Amen.

many of thofe elder Monuments. [The Supplement will account for the Burial-places of almoſt all the Archbiſhops. *N. B.*]

Feverſham.   *Clarenbald* (a) the firſt Abbat of *Feverſham* (a village in the year 812. called the King's *little Town of* Feverſham (b); as it is in a Charter of *Kenulph*, King of *Mercia*, made to *Wulfred* the then Archbiſhop) received Benediction of this *Theobald*, (c) *in the preſence of Queen* Maud, *who founded and enriched that Monaſtery. Clarenbald* firſt having obtained his and his Fellows releaſe from the *Cluniacs*, to be clearly abſolved from ſubjection to that Order, being now to live under the rule of St. *Benet*, in *Feverſham* Abby : Whereof in *Chriſt-Church* a Record is kept to this effect, *viz.* that at *Clarenbald*'s benediction by Archbiſhop *Theobald*, were firſt read publickly, (d) *the Letters of Abſolution from ſubjection to the* Cluniacs. Thus the Record. Mr. *Cambden* then ((e) be it ſpoken with all due reſpect to him) is miſtaken, in ſaying, that King *Stephen* founded this Abby for the Monks of *Clugny*.

The ſame Records (being thus fairly occaſioned, let me note it by the way) furniſh me with a Catalogue of the names of divers Abbats as well of that place, as of ſeveral other Abbeys in the Dioceſe, that receiving benediction from the Archbiſhop, made profeſſion of obedience to him and his Church ; which I have thought not impertinent to inſert in the *Appendix*, Numb. XLI.

I paſs from *Theobald* and come to his Succeſſor.

Thomas Becket. 38.

Whoſe whole ſtory our Chronicles and Tradition withal have made ſo trite and vulgar, that leſt I be checked with a *Nil dictum quod, &c.* for ſaying nothing but what hath been ſaid before. I forbear to relate it, only I ſhall deſire to ſay ſomewhat of his Burial, Tranſlation and Shrine, and to ſhew what the Quarrel was he ſo ſtoutly (ſtubbornly I ſhould ſay) defended.

Being moſt barbarouſly Murdered, upon *Tueſday* the 28 of *December* 1170. his Body was buried firſt in the *Undercroft*. But the revolution of 50 years, hav-
Becket's Tran- ing brought about his Jubilee (to wit in the year 1220:) and being firſt matri-
ſlation. culated by the Pope a glorious Saint and Martyr ; his Body with great ſolemnity, was taken up and laid in a moſt ſumptuous Shrine at the Eaſt end of the Church, at the charge of *Stephen Langton* his Succeſſor, whereof I read as followeth. (f) " The day of his Tranſlation being come, an exceeding great " multitude of Rich and Poor being preſent, *Pandulphus* the Pope's Legate, the " Archbiſhops of *Canterbury* and *Rhemes*, and very many Biſhops and Abbats " with Earls and Barons (King *Henry* III. being preſent alſo) took the Coffin " upon their Shoulders, and honourably placed it, where now it ſtands.

His Fair.   The ſolemnity of this Tranſlation happened upon or about the *7th of July.* Hence (I take it) the occaſion and original of our (as we call it) *Becket*'s Fair at *Canterbury*, beginning to be holden annually on the *7th* of that month.

For, as Sir *Henry Spelman* (g) is of opinion, that Fairs began and came up by the flocking of Chriſtians to the place for the ſolemnizing of ſome Feſtival, ſuch either as the Feaſt of the Churches dedication or other the like; and ſaith it is eaſy to conjecture to what Saint the place hath been commended, by the Fair-day : So I am perſwaded that this Fair which we hold at *Canterbury* annually on the 7th of *July* (as that other on the *29th* of *December*) firſt came up as a means to gather the greater multitude thither for the celebration of the Anniverſary Solemnities of *Becket*'s Tranſlation, on the one, and his Paſſion
Fairs: (as they uſed to term it) on the other of thoſe days. And (for ſo my Author adds) as Fairs were greater, as the Church and Town were of more eſtimation: So however theſe our Fairs at *Canterbury* are now ſo ſmall as not at all conſiderable, yet aſſuredly time was when they were of greater requeſt, and might juſtly boaſt of great reſort as any elſewhere: the decay of them and of the

---

(a) *Lib. Ecclef. Chriſti Cant.*   (b) *In partibus ſuburbanis Regis oppidulo Fefreſham dicto.*
(c) *In præſentia Regina Matildis quæ prædictum monaſterium de Feverſham incepi, & terris aliiſque donis ditavit.*   (d) *Literæ abſolutoriæ Petri Abbatis Cluniacenſis, & B. Prioris S. Mariæ de Caritate, qua prædictos Clarenbaldum & Monachos qui ſecum venerant de Bermondeſeia ab omni ſubjectione & obedientia eccleſia Cluniacenſis abſolvebant, né vix eccleſia Cluniacenſis aliqâ ſubjectionis in eundem Clarenbald, ſive in ſucceſſores ejus vel aliqâ jura in Monaſterio de Fever. calumpniare poſſet in poſterum.*
(e) *Salva ejus Reverentiâ*   (f) *Adveniente igitur tranſlationis die, præſente maximâ multitudine tam divitum quam pauperum ; Pandulphus Apoſtolicæ ſedis Legatus, Cantuarienſis & Remenſis Archiepiſcopi, Epiſcopique atque Abbates quamplurimi cum Comitibus & Baronibus prædictam capſam, præſente Rege Henrico tertio, ſuper humeros ſuos ſuſceperunt, & in loco quo nunc honoratur cum omni gaudio collocaverunt.*   (g) *Gloſſar. in verb. Feria.*

                                         trading

trading of our City participating of both one cause, namely, the defacing of the Shrine we now treat of, and the demolishing of such religious Houses as were sometime standing in and about the City, the magazins of reputed holy Relicks, the incentives unto all sorts of people in those times for their frequent visitation of them. Whence that of Mr. *Lambard* (a). *To tell the truth* (saith he) *little had all these casualties of fire and flame been to the decay of this Town* (speaking before of the often firing of *Canterbury*) *had not the dissolution and final overthrow of the religious Houses also come upon it. For where Wealth is at command, how easily are buildings repaired? and where opinion of great holiness is, how soon are Cities and Towns advanced to great estimation and riches? And therefore no marvel if after Wealth withdrawn, and opinion of holiness removed, the places tumbled headlong to ruin and decay.* Thus he.

The so seasonable application of these observations will be plea good enough (I trust) for this digression. And in that hope I return to our Archbishop, or rather to his Shrine. Whereof let me first give you *Erasmus*, then *Stow*'s Description. (b) *Erasmus* saith that when this glorious Show was offered to view,

" They drew up with Cords a Chest or case of Wood, and then there were
" seen a Chest or Coffin of Gold, and inestimable Riches: Gold was the
" meanest thing that was there. It shone all over and sparkled and glittered
" with Jewels, which were very rare and precious and of an extraordinary
" size; some of them were bigger than a Goose's Egg. The Prior took a
" white Wand, and touched every Jewel, telling, what it was, the *French*
" name, the Value, and the Donor of it. For the chief of them were the gifts
" of Monarchs. Thus he. " It was built (saith *Stow* (c)) about a man's height
" all of Stone, then upward of Timber plain, within the which was a Chest
" of Iron, containing the Bones of *Thomas Becket*, Skull and all, with the
" Wound of his death, and the piece cut out of his Skull laid in the same
" Wound. The timber work of this Shrine on the outside was covered with
" plates of Gold, damasked and embossed with Wires of Gold, garnished with
" Broches, Images, Angels, Chains, pretious Stones, and great Orient Pearls,
" the spoil of which Shrine (in Gold and Jewels of an inestimable value)
" filled two great Chests, one of which six or eight strong men could do no
" more than convey out of the Church: all which was taken to the King's
" use, and the Bones of St. *Thomas* (by commandment of the Lord *Cromwell*)
" were then and there burned to Ashes, which was in *September*, the year
" 1538. *Henry* VIII 30.

This Shrine had a Clerk and other retainers that constantly gave their attendance upon it (d); and need enough in regard both of the Treasure that was about it and also of the continual Offerings thereunto by such as either of visitation or in pilgrimage made their approaches to it: Which Offerings amounted to a great value by the year, as I guess by the accompts thereof for certain years which I have seen, shewing that from about 200 *lib.* per annum which they arose unto about 300 years since; within a six or eight years following they were grown to be more than trebled. But (by the way) when the Accomptant comes to Christ's Altar (the high altar) that's dispatched with a blank or a *Nil:* (e) To the high Altar nothing. So much had that Shrine obscured this Altar. The less marvel that the Church dedicated to Christ, gave place (as it did) to the name of St. *Thomas*, and that the prints of their Devotion in the Marble Stones who crept and kneeled to his Shrine remain to this day; therein but royalists (as I may call them) or imitators of sovereign example, if we but consider with what reverence some of our Kings mention both him and his Shrine. *Whose pretious Body is gloriously enshrined in your Church* (f), are the words of King *Henry* VI. to the Monks of this place: (g) *In whose Metropolitical Church, the Body of St.* Thomas *the Martyr, towards whom we bear Singular Devotion lies honourably enshrin'd,* says King *Edw.* IV. in his Charter to our City.

(a) Perambulation of *Kent in Canterburie.*   (b) *Auream thecam theca contegit lignea, ea funibus sublata opes nudat inæstimabiles. Vilissima pars erat aurum, gemmis raris ac prægrandibus collucebant, nitebant ac fulgurabant omnia, quædam superabant ovis anserini magnitudinem. Prior candidâ virgâ demonstrabat contactu singulas gemmas, addens nomen Gallicum, pretium & authorem doni. Nam præcipuas Monarchæ dono miserant. Peregrinatio relig. ergô.*   (c) Annals in *Henry* VIII.   (d) *Liber compt. Ecclef. Chrifti Cant.*   (e) *Summo altari Nil.*   (f) *Cujus pretiosum corpus in Ecclefia veftra prædictâ gloriofe tumulatum extitit.*   (g) *In cujus Ecclefia Metropol. corpus B. Thomæ Martyris, ad quem devotionem gerimus specialem, honorificê feretratur.*

Becket's Jubilee.

It may not be omitted that this Saint's Jubilee was kept every fifty years from and after his death : becaufe fuch multitudes flocked to the City to folemnize the fame as is fcarce credible ; witnefs this Record kept of one happening in the year 1420, which I commend to your perufal, tranfcribed from a Book of the City Chamber, and added to the *Appendix*, Numb. XLII.

Becket our City's Patron.

Our City of *Canterbury*, (it feems) of old pitched upon this St. *Thomas* for its Patron and Tutelar Saint ; and therefore caufed thefe Verfes to be cut about the Ring of her old common Seal; (a) importing, that *Thomas*, who was murdered, was their Tutelar Saint. And, which is more, borrowed a part of the City-Arms, retained to this day (if I miftake not) from his Coat ; which is, three *Cornifh* Choughs proper. It is obfervable befide, that as by means of his fame, and the great account of his Martyrdom and Miracles, the name of *Chrift-Church* became changed to St. *Thomas's* Church ; fo the common Seal of the Church, from the new dedication thereof by Archbifhop *Corbeyl* until then ufed, upon his Martyrdom was changed, and on the one fide of it that reprefented, with thefe Verfes circumfcribed. (b) As in the Margin. This was the Church's third common Seal, and was not altered afterward, until the new Foundation by *Henry* VIII.

So much for this Archbifhop ; the Legend of whofe Miracles, were it utterly loft, might eafily (I think) be repaired from the Windows on each fide of the place where his Shrine fometime ftood, abounding altogether with the Story thereof.

I come now to his Quarrel ; which was, the Defence of the Clergy, and their Liberties, their exemption efpecially from fecular Judgment or Trial. The fhadow of which Privilege we ftill retain ; and call it *Clergy*. For your better underftanding whereof, and confequently of the quarrel *Becket* died in, my *Appendix*, Numb. XLIII. fhall treat unto you of thefe Five Particulars.

Clergy.

1. *The Nature and Quality of the Privilege, what it is, and whence it came.*
2. *The form and manner how it is put in practice.*
3. *The Antiquity thereof in this Land.*
4. *The Extent of it.*
5. *The declining of it by degrees, and reftrained condition thereof with us, at this day.*

I may not here forget our Archbifhop's foundation and erection of an ancient Spittle which we have at this day in our City, and is called *Eaftbridge* or *Kingsbridge* Hofpital ; whereof enough before in proper place.

To conclude ; the Monks (it feems) glorying and priding themfelves in nothing more than this of *Becket's* Martyrdom, (for fo they called his murther) or at leaftwife conceiving their Church in no one refpect fo famous and renowned as in that ; and not fatisfied with the refemblance or reprefentation of it in that their forenamed common Seal, nor knowing better how, either to perpetuate the memory of it, or to make it more generally known abroad than thus : At, or about what time that their common Seal was renewed, contriving another fpecial Seal, *ad caufas*, (that is, as I conceive, chiefly for matters concerning Jurifdiction, which, (c) in the vacancy of the Archiepifcopal See, devolved into their hands (did infculp it alfo in the fame. And now to diftinguifh this from that their more ufual and common Seal, they vary the Infcription on both fides of it ; that on the forepart, about the Ring (containing within it the figure of the Church, and *Becket's* Martyrdom) being this : (d) *The Seal of* Chrift-Church *in* Canterbury *ad caufas.* Whilft that on the reverfe, about the Ring (within which are three fmaller Rings or Circles, having in each of them an head or face like to the picture of our Saviour's) was this : (e) *God the Father, God the Son, God the Holy Ghoft.* An Infcription probably intended to help preferve the then decaying Memory of the Churches ancient name and dedication to the *Trinity*. This undoubtedly is that Seal, which fome, from ('tis like) the triple vifage, and that *Trinitarian* Infcription in the

A Seal ad caufas.

(a) *Ictibus immenfis Thomas qui corruit enfis,*
   Tutor ab off'nfis urbis fit Canturienfis.
(b) *Eft huic vita mori pro qua dum vixit amori*
   Mors erat & memori per mortem vivit honori.
(c) **Sede vacante.**   (d) *Sigillum Ecclefia Chrifti Cantuaria ad caufas.*   (e) *Deus Pater.*
Deus Filius. Deus Spiritus Sanctus.

reverfe,

reverse, have miftaken for our Cathedral's firft Seal; whereof before in my 1. Particular of the Church-Survey.

Richard. 39.

Richard firft a Monk of this Church, afterwards Prior of *Dover*, fucceeded *Becket*, and dying *Anno* 1183. his Body was honourably interred in *Chrift-Church*, in the then Lady-Chapel; not in that which now ftands, but in a more ancient one included within the old body of the Church; as is before fhewed more at large.

Anno Dom. 1171.

Baldwin. 40.

After *Richard* fucceeded *Baldwin*. He died in the Holy Land, whither he would needs attend the King, (*Richard* I.) when he had been Archbifhop even almoft feven Years, and was buried there. Between the Monks of *Canterbury* and him, there was great debate and ftrife, about the College which he firft intended and attempted to erect at *Hackington* by *Canterbury*, and afterwards at *Lambeth*, but was croffed in both, as you may find at large elfewhere. He firft laid *Wales* to the Province of *Canterbury*.

1184.

Reginald. 41.

Reginal Fitz-joceline fucceeded *Baldwin*, but died within fifteen days after his confirmation, and after his election forty nine.

1191.

Hubert Walter. 42.

Then fucceeded *Hubert Walter*. He it was that firft devifed our Affize of Bread, our Weights and Meafures of Wine, Oyl, Corn, &c. He compaffed the Tower of *London* with a ftrong Wall, and deep Mote, fo as the Water enclofed the fame quite round, which before that time could never be brought to pafs; and performed many other great works of ineftimable charge, fuch as his Ecclefiaftical Revenues alone could never have enabled him to do, had not other helps from his fecular Offices been adjoined. For at one time, befides that he was Archbifhop, and the Pope's Legate *à latere*, he was Lord Chancellor, Lord Chief Juftice, and High immediate Governor under King *Richard* I. of all his Dominions both in *Wales* and *England*. And having been Archbifhop almoft 12 years, died at his Manor of *Tenham*: And was buried *July* 13, 1205. in the South-wall of *Chrift-Church*, befide the Quire. His Tomb is there extant at this day, and is (I take it) one of the moft ancient ones that the Church vifibly affords. From the fituation whereof, let me give you this note, that the ancienteft Tombs in Churches are fo or alike fituate, namely, in or along by the Church-walls, For the honour of his Church, I may not omit his Crowning there of King *John* and Queen *Ifabel* his laft Wife, *Anno* 1201.

1193.

Ancient Tombs.

Stephen Langton. 43.

Stephen Langton fucceeded *Hubert*. He was made a Cardinal, and fat Archbifhop 22 years, and dying *July* 9. 1228, was buried in his own Church, in the Chapel of St. *Michael*; where you may find his Monument. The firft dividing of the Bible into Chapters, in fuch fort as we now account them, is afcribed to him, of fome (*a*), but denied of other (*b*). This man changed the Parifh Church of *Ulecombe*, now called *Ulcombe*, into a Collegiate Church. The *Ordination* whereof is extant in the Records of *Chrift-Church*, where I have feen it. The head of which Church or College was ftiled *Archipresbyter*, by which name one Sir *Benjamin*, in the vacancy of the See by Archbifhop *Peckham's* death, in the year 1293, prefents to the then Prior of *Chrift-Church* one Sir *John Elmeftone* a Prieft, with defire of his admiffion (*c*) to be one of the minor Canons of that Church, &c. as I have it from the fame Records.

In this Archbifhop's time five Marks *per annum* was holden a competency for a Vicars ftipend (at *Halftow*, anciently called *Halegeftow* fignifying the *Holy place*, a Vicarage being erected and indowed by Archbifhop *Hubert*, the Vicar's ftipend there was rated accordingly;) and thereupon that conftitution (*d*) *which is to be feen to that purpofe in the Provincial*, was agreed upon and made, for the eftablifhing of that rate as fufficient. Indeed five marks in thofe days was as much as ten [I may fay, twenty. *N. B.*] pounds in thefe. However, it feems it

1206.

Vicar's Stipend.

(*a*) *Parker & Godwin in ejus vita.*   (*b*) *Spelman Gloff verb. Heptaticus. Ulcombe.*
(*c*) *In minorem Canonicum Ecclefiæ prædictæ, juxta ordinationem bonæ memoriæ Domini Stephani quondam Cantuar. Archiepifcopi, &c.*   (*d*) *Quoniam autem de officio Vicarii, in Provinciali.*

was a great deal cheaper world in those days, and all saleable things were then of far less price than now, when four times five Marks of ours, nay four times [nay six or eight times, *N.B.*] five pounds of ours is now the ordinary, and yet (in respect to the chargeable state of these days) but reasonable and moderate stipend for a Curate [A Curate could then Board and be found with all necessary Provisions for Lodging and Diet at four Marks a year. *N. B.*]. Would you know the reason? It is then shortly this; The greater abundance of Money now, than heretofore. For (as Sir *Henry Savil* noteth upon *Tacitus*) the excessive abundance of things which consist meerly on the constitution of men; draweth necessarily those things which nature requireth, to an higher rate in the Market. (a) *When* Augustus *had taken* Alexandria, *the wealth of* Rome *did encrease in such an abundant measure that all things, which were set to Sale, were rated at a priee, double to what they were before, saith* Orosius. And so I leave this Archbishop.

Richard Wethershed. 44.

Anno Dom.
1229.

Richard Wethershed succeeded *Stephen Langton*: who enjoyed the Honour but a little while, to wit, two years or thereabouts, and died at St. *Gemma* in his return from *Rome*, where he was buried.

St. Edmund. 45.

1234.

St. *Edmund* succeeded him, who died *anno* 1242, eight years after his consecration, and was buried also in foreign parts. He married King *Henry* III. to Queen *Eleanor* at *Canterbury*, in the year 1236.

Boniface. 46.

1244.

Boniface succeeded St. *Edmund*. He died in *Savoy* (his own Countrey) in the year 1270, somewhat more than 26 years after his consecration. He performed two things not unworthy of memory; he payed the debt of 22 thousand Marks that he found his See indebted in. And built a good Hospital at *Maidstone*, called the new works, and indued it with revenues valued at the suppression at 159 *lib. 7 s. 10 d.* (*William Courtnay* his successor long after translated the same into a College of secular Priests.) Bishop *Godwyn* adds a third thing, at the belief whereof I somewhat stick; and that is, his perfecting and finishing that most stately Hall of the Lord Archbishop's Palace at *Canterbury*, with the Buildings adjoyning: unless it may be thus made good, to wit, by his paying the debt which his predecessors by building the same had run themselves into. And indeed in that sense he was wont to vaunt himself the builder of it, (b) saying, *My Predecessors built this Hall at great expences. They did well indeed: but they laid out no mony about this building, except what they borrowed: I seem indeed to be truly the builder of this Hall, because I paid their debts.*

Maidstone Hospital.

Robert Kilwardby. 47.

1272.
*Black-Friars,
London.*

Robert Kilwardby succeeded *Boniface*. He built the *Black-Friers* in *London*, being himself of that Order. Having been Archbishop about the space of six years he was made a Cardinal, and then resigning his Archbishoprick gat him into *Italy*, and died and was buried at *Viterbium*. Being yet Archbishop in the year 1277. By his kind and gentle persuasion he appeased the Citizens of *Canterbury* eagerly bent upon revenge in a very strange way to be taken of the Monks of *Christ-Church*, for refusing them their aid in that imposition of finding and setting forth twelve Horse-men to serve in the King's intended War against *Lewelyn* Prince of *Wales*, laid upon the City, whereof before in the Black-Friers I have spoken.

John Peckham. 48.

1278.
Wingham College.

John Peckham succeeded *Kilwardby*: and continued in the Chair 13 years, and almost and half. In which time he founded the collegiate Church at *Wingham* in *Kent* or rather changed the Parish-Church there into a Collegiate. The head of which College was called *Præpositus*, a Provost. The ordination of which Præpositure, together with this our Archbishop's Letters for the dividing of *Wingham* Church into four Parishes, dated *anno* 1282, are extant in the Records of *Christ-church*, where I have seen them, [and printed in the *Monasticum Anglic.* N. B.] Now *Wingham* it self (the mother Church) *Ash, Goodnestone,* and

---

(a) *Captâ ab Augusto Alexandriâ Roma in tantum opibus ejus crevit, ut duplo majora quam antehac rerum venalium pretia statuerentur.* (b). *Prædecessores mei istam aulam cum magnis expensis fecerunt, bene quidem fecerunt, sed expensas ad illam construendam nisi de pecunia mutua non invenerunt, videtur quidem mihi, quòd ego illam feci, quia illorum debita persolvi. Antiq. Brit. in ejus vita.*

Nonington (Chapels to it) were the four Parishes. *Overland* and *Richborough* were Chapels to *Ash*, and *Wimingswold* a Chapel to *Nonington*. This College of secular Canons (for such the founder placed in it) was valued at the time of the suppression at 84 *l.* of yearly Revenues (*a*) *Harpsfield's* words of this Foundation are to this effect : *The College of* Wingham *in* Kent *was first constituted by this Archbishop: but the continuation of it is owing to Archbishop* Robert *his Successor, who obtain'd of Pope* Gregory *leave to convert the parochial Church of* Wingham *to the use of the said College.* The City of *Canterbury* went to suit with this Archbishop about Limits and Liberties. Amongst other of his labours (as I have it from *Gavantus* his *Thesaurus sacrorum rituum*) he composed an Office for Trinity-Sunday, called (*b*) *the Office of the Holy Trinity*. It was received by the Church of *Rome*, and in use about the year 1290. but for the difficulty and obscurity of the Stile was sithence abrogated.

Leaving these things I come now to the place of this Archbishop's burial. He was buried (saith Bishop *Godwin*) in his own Church, but in what particular place I find not. Archbishop *Parker* (it seems) found it not neither, for he mentions it not. By a Record in the Church of the time of the death and place of the burial of this Archbishop which I have seen, it appears he was laid (*c*) *in the North-side near the place of the Martyrdom of St.* Thomas *the Martyr.* I fear the Author of the *Tables* hath done him some wrong in hanging Archbishop *Ufford's Table* upon that which (I take it) is rather *Peckham's* Tomb than his, that namely in the corner of the *Martyrdom* next unto *Warham*, which the *Table-*writer upon (it seems) Bishop *Godwyn's* conjecture, takes for granted to be *Ufford's* Tomb. But (as I conceive) the cost bestowed on that Monument (however the Archiepiscopal Effigies which it hath is framed of wood) being built somewhat *Pyramis*-like, and richly overlaid with Gold, which is not yet worn off, gainsays it to be *Ufford's*. For I read (*d*), that dying before he was fully Archbishop, having never received either his Pall or Consecration, and that in the time of that great plague which (as *Walsingham* reports) consumed nine parts of the men through *England* ; his Body without any Pomp or wonted Solemnity was carried to *Canterbury*, and there secretly buried by the North-wall, beside the Wall of *Thomas Becket*. But I pass to his Successor.

Peckham's Tomb.

Robert Winchelsey. 49.

Robert Winchelsey succeeded *Peckham.* In the Record of whose Inthronization, I find mention of three Sub-deacon Cardinals of the Church, which did assist the then Prior in that action. Such (it seems) the Church had at that time. Of the like sometimes in St. *Paul's* Church, *London*, Sir *Henry Spelman's Glossary* will inform you (*e*). But I come to the Archbishop, who kept possession of the Chair about the space of 19 years, and died in the year 1313. Much might be said of his admirable liberality, and charity to the poor, but hereof Archbishop *Parker*, and from him, Bishop *Godwyn* and others have said enough already. And I pass over his whole life, and come to his Burial-place, which is not now extant, by any Monument of him in the Church. But certain it is, he once had one there, and it stood (say those Authors) beside the Altar of St. *Gregory*, by the South-wall. This obscure description of the situation, at length I came to understand thus : First, I read in some Records of the Church a Gift (*f*) *to the Light of the Throne, which is over against the Image of our Saviour, against the Altars of St.* John *the Evangelist, and St.* Gregory. To shew me where these Altars stood, comes after to my sight the mention of (*g*) *the Altar of St.* John *the Evangelist in the South-cross Wing or Isle.* Which laid to the former, I perceive these Altars stood in the South-cross Isle of the Quire, the one under the one, the other under the other East-window thereof ; more assured of it by viewing the opposite Wall, where are tokens of something (most likely that Throne) once affixed to it, but now had away. By the South-wall then of this Cross-Isle, sometime stood this Archbishop's Tomb.

Anno Dom. 1294. Sub-Deacon-Cardinals at Christ-Church.

Winchelsey's Tomb.

(*a*) *Collegium in Cantia Wengamense ejus potissimum opera constitutum est, sed seminarium ejus beneficii à Roberto decessore ejus profectum est : Qui à Gregorio Pontifice impetrabat, ut liceret ecclesiam Parochialem Wengamensem in eum usum convertere.*　　(*b*) *Officium Sanctæ Trinitatis.*　　(*c*) *In parte Aquilonari, juxta locum Martyrii Beati Thomæ Martyris.*　　(*d*) *Antiq. Brit. in vita Ufford.*

(*e*) *In verbo Cardinalis.*　　(*f*) *Ad luminare troni qui est contra imaginem Salvatoris contra altaria Sanctorum Johannis Evangelistæ & Gregorii Papæ.*　　(*g*) *Altare Sancti Johannis Evangelistæ in Australi cruce.*

L l   About

About 13 years after his death, *Thomas* then Earl of *Lancaster*, implor'd his Canonization at the Pope's hands, but without success, for these reasons ; namely, saith the Pope in his Bull, " The Church of *Rome* is not wont to " proceed hastily in any Concern, especially in a Concern of so great mo- " ment as this is, without diligently searching into, and solemnly examining " the whole matter. Therefore, if it seem'd good to promote this business, it " must be solemnly proposed before the Cardinals in a Consistory, by solemn " Persons, specially deputed on the behalf of the Prelates, Clergy, and Peo- " ple of *England*, who should attest the life, merits, and miracles of that Arch- " bishop, and should subjoin also a supplication, that an Inquisition concern- " ing the truth and weight of their attestations, may be committed to fit Per- " sons ; and so according to the event of the Inquisition his Canonization " might be celebrated, or omitted. Hereupon his immediate Successor (*Wal- ter Reynalds*) and his Suffragans, *Anno* 1326. all joined in petition to the Pope for his Canonization, directing their Letters to him for that purpose under their several hands and Seals ; which it seems, were never sent, for the Ori- ginal is yet remaining in the Cathedral. (*a*) I my self have seen them, and look'd into them : And I do not read that he was ever canonized. Yet, for his Virtues, the common People would needs esteem him a Saint. And I find Treasurers of the Church give or make accompt divers years for Offerings to, or at his Tomb ; therefore it was afterwards pulled down. [The Suit in the Court of *Rome*, for the Canonization of this Archbishop, was not begun (as Mr. *Somner* seems to intimate) about 13 years after his death, but was begun soon after his death, and did not end until 13 years after his death ; at which time it ceased, without having obtain'd what was so much sought after. I can- not find the exact time when it began ; but I can trace the prosecution of it at least seven or eight years. For, whereas Archbishop *Winchelsey* died *Anno* 1313. *Thomas* Earl of *Lancaster* and *Leicester*, High Steward of *England*, sends his request to the Pope, that this Archbishop, for the sake of his holy and strict life, of his excellent merits, and glorious miracles done by him, might have the honour as he deserv'd, of being solemnly canoniz'd for a Saint. The Pope replies to these Letters, by his Bull, which is in the *Appendix*, that a thing of so great moment, as this was, ought not to be done in hast ; and that the process of the Suit must be ordered after this manner : That Persons of good credit should be appointed to inquire into this matter, here in *England* ; that these Persons should be especially deputed on the behalf of the Prelates, Clergy, and People of *England*, to attest the truth of this matter in the Court of *Rome* ; that to their Testimonials or Attestations they should subjoin a sup- plication to this effect, *viz.* That before the Cardinals in the Consistory, In- quisition might be made by fit Persons, concerning the life, merits, and mi- racles of this Archbishop, and that according to the event of the Inquisition, his Canonization might be celebrated, or else forborn. The Earl having recei- ved these directions from *Rome*, applied himself to Archbishop *Walter Reynolds*, and sends him, together with other Letters, this Bull of the Pope. Hereup- on, the Archbishop directs a Commission to *Stephen* Bishop of *London*, and *John* Bishop of *Chichester*, to make inquisition concerning the life, and mira- cles of the Archbishop his Predecessor. This Commission (wherein mention is made of the aforesaid Bull) is dated in *November*, 1319. Afterwards, the Earl writes concerning the same to the Prior and Convent of *Christ-Church* in *Canterbury*, dating his Letters, *April* 8. without making any mention of the year. The Prior and Convent return answer to the Earl by their Letters, da- ted 1321, *June* 19. Afterwards the Prior of *Christ-Church* writes again to the Earl concerning this matter. His Letter is dated *July* 8. 1322. The form of the abovenamed Commission, the Pope's Bull, and these three Letters in *French*, are to be seen in the (*b*) Registers of *Christ-Church*. The Earl did not live long after this time ; for he was dead before the end of the year 1326. When in the month of *March*, Archbishop *Walter* and the Suffragan Bishops of his Pro- vince, sent a Letter (in which mention is made of the death of the said Earl) to Pope *John* XXII. for the Canonization of this Archbishop (*c*) ; which is

---

(*a*) *Vidi inspexi.*   (*b*) *Reg. G. Part. II. fol. 227. Reg. K. Part. II. fol. 4.*   (*c*) *Angl. Sacr.*
Vol. 1. p. 174. &c.

also printed at large. So that from the first Commission granted by the Archbishop, to his last Testimonial Letter to the Pope, there are no less than seven years and four months, wherein this Suit was prosecuted and not brought to a final issue. And it is certain, that the Suit was begun at least some months before the date of the Archbishop's Commission above-named. 'Tis certain also, that his Holiness did never speak more infallibly, than when he declared, that nothing was done in hast in the Court of *Rome*, especially in a matter of so great a concern as this was, when the prolonging of the Suit brought many and vast Profits and Fees to that Court. *N. B.*] In the Records both of the Cathedral, and of the Hospital of *Herbaldown*, I have seen new Statutes of **His Statutes.** his making, namely, such as he made and gave to either, upon and after his Visitation of each place. It was he that first erected perpetual Vicarages in the Mother-Church of *Reculver*, and the Chapels to it, (*Hearne* and St. *Nicholas*) and endowed them ; as I find by an authentical Copy of the Ordination of those Vicarages which hath come unto my hands.

For the maintenance of the Churches Liberties, and Ecclesiastical Jurisdiction, **Prohibitions.** he mainly opposed Prohibitions grown frequent in his days, and caused the Clergies Grievances to be drawn into Articles: whereof see the *Antiquitates Britannicæ* in his life, *pag.* 211. See also *pag.* 215. in the life of his Successor *Reynolds* ; and if you would know what good courses have from time to time sithence been taken to restrain *Prohibitions*, see the same Author *p.* 216. in the life of the same *Reynolds*, *pag.* 286, in the life of *Stafford*, *pag.* 294 in the life of *Bourgchier*, in which last place you may find this worthy question properly, by my Reverend Author, subjoyned. (*a*) He saith, " Since therefore all the complaint
" of the Lay-Judges against the Bishop's-Court, even in those times, when
" the power of the Court of *Rome* did strike awe and terror into Kings themselves,
" was this only, that unless very many Causes were cut off (by Prohibitions)
" from the Ecclesiastical Court, they would be transferr'd by Appeals
" from being heard by the King, or from being pleaded in the King's Court,
" to be heard by the Pope and to be pleaded in the Court of *Rome*. What can
" they now say (on behalf of Prohibitions) when as the Prelates are better
" able, than the Lawyers themselves, to defend and maintain the Regal Authority,
" as more sacredly from the word of God, so much more skilfully by
" their own Jurisdiction ?

To return to our Archbishop. He married King *Edward* I. to his second Wife *Margaret* in his Church at *Canterbury*, whose nuptial Feast (saith *Stow*) was kept in the great Hall of his Palace.

Walter Reynolds. 50.

Walter Reynolds succeeded *Robert Winchelsey*, who when he had sat Archbishop 13 years and somewhat more, died and was buried in the South-wall of *Christ-Church* near the Quire, where his Tomb is as yet extant. At his inthronization (see the state of it in those days) *Bartholomew* Lord *Badlesmere* tendered himself to the Earl of *Glocester* chief Steward, to serve in the Office of Chamberlain to the Archbishop, for or in respect of) his Manor of *Hatfield* by *Charing* (*b*). Thus occasionally induced, let me set before you in this place the fees which by ancient Record in the Cathedral appear to have belonged to the Earl of *Glocester* in respect of his Office of Steward and Butler to the Archbishop of *Canterbury* on the day of his inthronization: and they were those, **Earl of Glocester.** which I have added to my *Appendix*, Numb. XLV.

See more of this (if you please) in Mr. *Lambard*'s Perambulation of *Kent* in *Tunbridge*. [Concerning these Claims of serving at the Inthronization-Feast, the Registers of this Church do abound. The supplement will make some Addition to what Mr. *Somner* has here offered. *N. B.*]

To return to our Archbishop. He gave unto his Covent (saith Bishop *Godwyn*) **Caldecote.** the Manor of *Caldcote*, and the Wood of *Thorlehot*. Now the Charters of **Thoreholt.** this gift I have seen in the Church Records, dated *Anno* 1326. In which the Archbishop gives to the Prior and Covent (*c*) our *Manor* as his words are, *of*

(*a*) *Cum itaque omnis Laicoram Judicum in Prælatos quærimonia, tum cum Romanæ Curiæ potestas etiam Regibus ipsis terrorem incussit ; sola hæc fuit, quod nisi pleraque causæ ab ecclesiastico foro amputentur, appellationibus à regia cognitione ad Papalem perferantur : quid nunc dicere possunt cum Prælati Regiam authoritatem & divino verbo sanctius, & sua jurisdictione multò peritius tueantur quam Causidici, &c.?*

(*b*) *Lib. Eccl. Cant.*   (*c*) *Manerium nostrum de Caldecotes juxta Cant. cum boseo nostro de Toreholt.*

Calde-

Caldecotes *with our Wood of* Thoreholt ; and that by confent of the King and Pope. In the Pope's Licenfe the fituation and value of the thing, together with the ufe which the Covent meant to make of it, and for which they begged it of the Archbifhop, is thus expreffed. (*a*) The Pope thus writes to the Archbifhop, "That the Manor of *Caldecote*, with the adjacent Lands belonging to it, " was of the value of Ten Pounds, and was in the poffeffion of the Archbi- " fhops of *Canterbury* for the ufe of their Table, and was fituated near *Canter-* " *bury*, and that the Monks of *Chrift-Church* did earneftly defire, That this Ma- " nor with the adjacent Lands might be granted to them, and appropriated for " ever to their ufe, in as much as it was a convenient place for the Monks to " retire unto, and to recreate themfelves at, when they had been let Blood, " or when they were wearied and tired with much Labour, becaufe it was at " no great diftance from their Monaftery, *&c.* In this paffage give me leave to take notice of two Things, to fhew what they mean and were. The firft is that of (*b*) *the diminution of Blood*, the other is the work or labour, what it was that the Monks employed themfelves about. For the former (*c*) (*the diminution of Blood*) it was (*d*)*the opening of a Vein to take away fome Blood*. And was ufed of the Monks partly (I fuppofe) to keep their Bodies under, and partly Phyfically and for their Health-fake, to evacuate corrupt and bad Humors contracted, fome may think, by their unwholfome Dyet, feeding moft what upon Fifh, and courfe Fare ; and true it is, by their Order they were to abftain from eating Flefh ; yet hear what *Polydor Virgil* faith of that matter. (*e*) He faith, *They alfo wholly abftain from Flefh, unlefs when they grow Sick. From whence thofe Monks, who now continually feed upon Flefh,* (mark now) *of whom there are vaft numbers in every Country, befides* Italy, *muft needs be alway Sick, unlefs they will impudently own, that they live contrary to the rules of their Profeffion.* So that I conceive they did thus evacuate not fo much for unwholefome as for full and high Feeding, and much Eafe withal, a courfe of life contrary to that of the Primitive Monks, who fared hardly, and not only lived by their Labour, but ufed it as a principal means of their Mortification (*f*).

[I can be eafily inclin'd to fubfcribe to Mr. *Somner*'s Opinion, that the occafions, which the Monks had of being let Blood, might frequently arife from fome Irregularity they had been guilty of, as by excefs of diet, particularly in drinking too much Wine, wherewith the Refectory was ordinarily plentifully furnifhed, befides what they had extraordinary allowed them on feveral particular Occafions, and what probably they fometimes gat at other places out of the Refectory. The Statutes and Ordinances of *Lanfranc* concerning the Rules to be obferv'd by the Benedictines, have one whole (*g*) Chapter or Decree concerning this Diminution of Blood ; where it is appointed that leave, muft be firft asked, but this leave was not to be granted at fome certain folemn Seafons (unlefs upon unavoidable neceffity) as when their abfence from officiating or affifting in the publick Service of their Church, was not to be difpenfed with. But Leave being granted, the Hour was to be notified to the Celerar of the Convent, thofe who were to have a Vein opened, were to come to the place appointed for that purpofe, where feveral Ceremonies and Formalities are ordered to be perform'd at that time and upon that occafion. Afterwards, they were to appear before the Prior and Chapter, and it being there openly faid, that fuch and fuch and fuch a Brother had Blood taken from him; the Monk was to ftand up (efpecially if a Vein in the Arm had been opened) and to fpeak for himfelf. Then it follows, (*h*) If he had been guilty of a fmall Offence, it

(*a*) *Cum tu inter alia menfa tua Archiepifcopalis Cant. bona, unum modicum receptaculum vocat. Caldecote juxta Civitatem Cant. fituat cum quadam terra eidem adjacen. valoris decem librarum vel circiter ad menfam eandem fpectan. obtinere nofcaris, quod utique receptaculum cum terra prædicta, iidem Prior & Capitulum ac dilecti filii monachi ecclefiæ tuæ Cantuarien. fanguine minuti, & ceteris laboribus fatigati ibidem interdum propter loci vicinitatem recreari valeant, multum afficiant per te fibi concedi, & in ufus eorum perpetuos affigxari, &c.*   (*b*) *Sanguinis minutio.*   (*c*) *Sanguinis minutio.*   (*d*) *Apertio venæ ad minuendum fanguinem. Reyneri Onomafticum.*   (*e*) *De Invent. Rer. lib. 7. cap. 2. Item à carnibus perpetuo fe abftinent, nifi cum ægrotare cæperint. Unde monachi qui hodie continenter carnibus vefcuntur, quorum numerus ubique gentium extra Italiam ingentiffimus eft, perpetuo ægrotent neceffe eft, nifi velint impudenter fateri fe contra fuas leges facere. Vide Eraf. Colloq. in Ichthyophagia. Fatetur, & defendit hoc Haius in Aftro inextincto, quæft 2. pag. 130 &c.*   (*f*) *Creccelius de Orig & Fund. Monaftic. Ord. cap. 1.*   (*g*) *Cap. 13 De fanguinis minutione.*   (*h*) *Si culpa levis, indulgeatur ei. Si autem talis fuerit, qua fine Corporali difciplina dimitti non debeat, in aliud tempus deferatur Ibid.*

should be forgiven. But if the Offence was such as could not be forgiven or passed over without bodily Punishment, the punishing of him should be deferred till another time; namely, till he had recovered better Health and Strength after the loss of Blood. This Chapter is somewhat Mystical, and perhaps designedly so, that the Reputation of the members of the Convent might be defended from being openly charged with Irregularities and foul Enormities. Such things were like the Rites of *Ceres*, religiously to be conceal'd. But it seems plain, that the want of having Blood taken away, was frequently occasion'd by Irregularity and Excess. I may further observe, That when the Lord High Steward with his Retinue, had according to his Office attended at an Inthronization-Feast of an Archbishop, it was one branch of his accustomed Right and Fee, which he claim'd, at his going away, to stop three days at one of the nearest Manors of the Archbishop *(a)* to diminish his Blood, that is, to have a Vein opened, or properly, to cool his Blood, which had been heated by high Feeding and Drinking at that Feast. *N. B.*]

As for the other point, their work or labour wherein they imployed themselves, and were occupied, it was of divers kinds. The *Ceremoniale Benedictinum* thus sets them forth *(b)The works, in which the Monks were to busy themselves, were such as these, to Write over Books, to mark them with Red, where they ought to be so marked, to prepare Parchments and other necessaries for binding of Books, and to bind Books and the like.* No longer to digress, this *Caldecote* Manor sometime lay partly in the old Park and there-away, about *Cockar-Barn*, as they now call it for *Caldcote-Barn*. [margin: Monks Employment.]

And now return we to our Archbishop. To the Nuns of *Davington* by *Feversham* which my Author thinks were *French*-women, he gave and prescribed Rules and Ordinances in the *French*-Tongue, for their more easy intellect. He amerced the President of St. *Bertins*, for leasing out, without his Privity, the fruits of *Chilham* Parsonage which belonged to the Priory of *Throuleigh*, a Cell to St. *Bertins*, and one of those that in the general suppression of Priors aliens by *Henry* V. was dissolved. And so much for this Archbishop, except I shall remember his appropriation of the Parsonages of *Farly* and *Sutton* to the Hospital at *Maidstone* of his Predecessor *Boniface*'s foundation, and his like appropriation of the Parsonage of *Waldershire* to *Langdon* Abbey, unto which about the same time King *Edward* I. gave the Parsonage of *Tong*. [margin: Harpsfield. Priors Aliens.]

Simon Mepham. 51.

Simon Mepham succeeded *Walter Reynolds*; and continued Archbishop Five years and somewhat more, and died *Anno* 1333, at *Mayfield* in *Sussex*. His Body was conveigh'd to *Canterbury*, and laid in a Tomb of black Marble, upon the North-side of St. *Anselm*'s Chapel; that so called at this day, for when he was buried there, it had another name. The Record of the place and manner, with the time of his Burial, kept in the Church, saith, he was laid in *(c)* St. Peter's *Chapel, on the South-side of the High Altar.* His Tomb is that, whereon, by error, Archbishop *Sudbury*'s Table now hangs. [His Coat is mistaken by Archbishop *Parker*, in his *Antiquities of Britain*, that which he there gives to a Successor of his name, *Simon Sudbury*, properly belonging to this Archbishop. *W. S.*] [margin: Anno Dom. 1327. St. Peter's Chapel. Mepham's Tomb mistaken.]

John Stratford. 52.

His Successor was *John Stratford*, who having sat Archbishop about 15.years, died, and was buried in a Tomb of Alabaster, on the South-side of the High Altar, beside the steps of St. *Dunstan*'s Altar: By the Table hanging whereon, you may easily find it. [margin: 1333.]

John Ufford or Offord. 53.

Him succeeded *John Ufford* or *Offord*. But he never received either his Pall or Consecration. Of his Burial, I have spoken before in *Peckham*. [margin: 1348.]

Thomas Bradwardin. 54.

Thomas Bradwardin succeeded, but within five weeks and four days after his Consecration, he died; so that he was never inthronized at all. He was buried in St. *Anselm*'s foresaid Chapel, by the South-wall. [margin: 1348.]

(a) *Ad minuendum Sanguinem.* (b) *Opera autem quibus se occupare debent, sunt hæc; videlicet, scribere libros, aut rubricare, vel ligare, pergamenum & alia necessaria præparare, & his similia, &c.*
(c) *Quædam capellâ sancti Petri nuncupata ex parte australi summi altaris.*

Simon

Simon Iſlip. 55.

Anno Dom.
1349.
Monkton.
Eaſtry.

Simon *Iſlip* was his next Succeſſor. Amongſt many other Acts of his Piety, he gave unto his Convent, to the uſe of their Elemoſinary, the Churches or Parſonages of *Monkton* and *Eaſtry* ; ſay the Writers of his life. Yet I find theſe very Churches, with others, formerly appropriated to them for that uſe ; to wit, by Archbiſhop *Richard,* *Becket's* immediate Succeſſor, as you may find before in my Survey of the *Almnery.* Both relations true. For the Church Muniments inform me, that theſe Parſonages were taken from the Church by Archbiſhop *Baldwin* ; that *Richard's* immediate Succeſſor, in and upon the quarrel that was between him and his Monks, (whereof before) and ſo they continued, at leaſt at the Archbiſhop's diſpoſe, until this *Simon Iſlip,* with the King's licenſe, did reſtore, reunite and annex them again unto the Church ; ſhortly after which Gift of his Vicars, perpetual were ordained and endowed to each Church ; Copies of the Ordination and Dotation of which Vicarages, I have ſeen in the Leigers of the Church, where they are fairly regiſtred.

Harpsfield.

But to our Archbiſhop again. With his conſent *Buckland* Parſonage was appropriated to the Priory of *Dover,* as was to *Bilſington* Priory, the Parſonage there. He died *Anno* 1366, after he had been Archbiſhop 16 years and upwards; and was ſometime buried under a fair Tomb of Marble, inlaid with braſs in the middle, and near the upper end of the Body of his Church ; ſithence removed and ſet between the two next Pillars on the North-ſide thereof. The

Great Mortality.
Note.

times were very mortal, by the raging of the Plague, when he came firſt to the See, as from *Walſingham,* is noted by *Harpsfield,* with this note of his upon it. (a) He ſaith, *When the fields lay untill'd, waſt, and deſerted, by reaſon of this Mortality of Men, and Cattel, and the Owners were diſappointed of receiving their accuſtomed Rents ; they were forced not only to remit ſomewhat of the uſual Penſion which was wont to be paid, but even to hire out unto Husbandmen their fields ready furniſhed with all manner of Husbandry-furniture. And if this Cuſtom is forborn to be obſerved by Lay-Landlords, who are more mindful of their concerns, yet it is continued even to our days, in the Farms belonging to Monaſteries, Biſhops and Colleges, to the great encouragement of Husbandmen.*

Simon Langham. 56.

1366.

Simon *Langham* ſucceeded *Iſlip.* Who ſat only two years, died *Anno* 1367. was firſt buried at *Avinion,* (where he died) in the Church of the *Carthuſians,* (whoſe Houſe he had founded) but afterwards at *Weſtminſter,* (where he had been firſt a Monk, afterward Prior, and laſtly Abbat) in a goodly Tomb of Alabaſter.

William Wittleſey. 57.

1368.

William Wittleſey ſucceeded *Langham,* who having continued in the See almoſt ſeven years, died in the year 1374, and was buried almoſt over againſt (his Uncle) *Simon Iſlip,* between two Pillars on the South-ſide of the Body of the Church, under a fair Marble Tomb inlaid with Braſs, as his Table will direct.

Simon Sudbury. 58.

1375.

Sudbury's
Tomb miſtaken.

Him next ſucceeded *Simon Sudbury.* Who being barbarouſly murthered by the Rebels in *Richard* II. days, *Anno Dom.* 1381. his Body after all ſtirs ended, was carried to *Canterbury,* and there honourably interred upon the South-ſide of the Altar of St. *Dunſtan,* the next above the Tomb of Archbiſhop *Stratford,* and is that (as in *Odo* I told you) whereon *Odo's* Table hangs ; even juſt over againſt the place (I take it) where his Predeceſſor St. *Elphege's* Altar-Tomb ſometime ſtood. That as there was but little or no difference between them, in the condition either of their Lives or Deaths, they being both Archbiſhops of the place, and both unworthily murthered (I might ſay martyred) by the outrage of the People, a Rabble of cruel Aſſaſſinats, of *Danes* the one, of Domeſticks the other ; little better than Devils incarnate both, ſo there might alſo be but little diſtance in their Sepulchres or Reſting-places after death. He built the *Weſtgate* of our City, together with the greateſt part of the Wall between it and the *Northgate,* commonly called by the name of the *Long-Wall.*

(a) *Cum verò propter hanc hominum animaliumque ceterorum peſtilentiam. agri paſſim inculti, vaſti, & deſerti jacerent, & poſſeſſores ſolitis redditibus deſtituerentur ; coacti ſunt non modo de ſolita penſione remittere, ſed etiam agros omni ruſtica facultate inſtructos colonis locare. Quod & ſi à laicis poſſeſſoribus, ad rem attentioribus obſervari fere deſitum eſt, in prædiis tamen cœnobiorum, Epiſcoporum & Collegiorum mos ille frequens, ad noſtra uſque tempora, maximo colonorum emolumento perduravit.*

A great

A great Work, (faith my Author) no lefs neceffary and profitable unto the *Leland.*
City, than coftly and chargeable unto the Builder. The Mayor and Aldermen once a year, ufed to come folemnly to his Tomb, to pray for his Soul,
in memory of this his good deed to their City. To remedy and remove which
piece of fuperftition, (I take it) his Epitaph (fome tokens whereof are yet
difcernable) was torn and taken from his Tomb at, or fince the Reformation.
Wever's Monuments hath a fragment of it, which is in the *Appendix*, Numb.
XLVI.

William Courtney. 59.

William Courtney fucceeded *Simon Sudbury*, and having fat Twelve years lack- *Anno Dom.*
ing one month, died *Anno* 1396. at *Maidftone*. Where he pulled down the old 1381.
work firft built by *Boniface* his Predeceffor for an Hofpital, and building it after a more ftately manner, tranflated it into a College of fecular Priefts, which *Maidftone* Col-
at the time of the fuppreffion was valued at 139 *l.* 7 *s.* 6 *d.* by the year. This lege.
Archbifhop lieth buried (faith Bifhop *Godwyn*) upon the South-fide of *Thomas
Becket*'s Shrine, at the feet of the Black Prince, in a goodly Tomb of Alabafter. But what fays *Wever*? *It was the cuftom of old,* (faith he) *and fo it is in
thefe days, for men of eminent Rank and Quality, to have Tombs erected in more places than one; for example and proof of my fpeech, I find here in this Church a Monument of Alabafter at the feet of the Black Prince, wherein both by tradition and writing, it is affirmed, that the Bones of* William Courtney, *(the Son of* Hugh Courtney, *the third of that Chriftian name, Earl of* Devonshire,) *Archbifhop of this
See, lies intombed. And I find another to the memory of the fame man, at* Maidftone
here in Kent, *wherein (becaufe of the Epitaph) I rather believe that his Body lyeth
buried.* Thus he. His place of Burial, appointed of him in his Will extant in *Contradiction*
Chrift-Church, was the Cathedral at *Exeter*, where he had fometime been a Pre- *about the*
bendary, and where he requefted the Bifhop of the place to bury him. After- *place of Court-*
wards, lying on his Death-bed, and having changed his mind in this point, *ney's burial.*
and holding his Body (as he then declared) unworthy of Burial in his Metropolitical or any other Cathedral or Collegiate Church, he wills it to be buried
in the Church-yard of his Collegiate Church at *Maidftone*, (a) *in the place defigned for* John Boteler, *his Efquire*; (as his own words are). Thus you fee, his
Will fends us to feek his Burial-place at *Exeter* : His After-declaration on his
Death-bed, to the Cemitery of his Collegiate Church at *Maidftone*. His Monument in that Church fays he lies there; and this in *Chrift-Church*, that he is
in none of the three, but here. And that I take to be the trueft. For I find in
a Leiger Book of *Chrift-Church*, that the King (*Richard* II.) happening to be
at *Canterbury* when he was to be buried, (upon the Monks fuit, 'tis like) over-
ruled the matter, and commanded his Body to be there interred.

This Archbifhop, upon the overture of an intended Invafion by the *French*, *Clergy armed*
directs his Letters to the then Commiffary of *Canterbury*, to arm the Clergy of *and rated.*
the City and Diocefe after thefe Rates and Proportions (b). A Benefice exceeding 100 Marks, to find a Man and two Archers; a Benefice exceeding
xl *l.* to find two Archers; a Benefice of xx *l.* one Archer; and for thofe under xx *l.* to find *Loricas*, Coats of Mail, and other fmaller Arms.

He had the Bailiffs of *Canterbury* in queftion, for medling in and with Ec- *Medling in*
clefiaftical matters, as the punifhment of *Adultery*, and the like; and made *Church mat-*
them to fubmit (c) *under the penalty of an Interdict laid upon the City.* He had the *ters by Laics*
Serjeants of the City alfo in *coram*, for bearing their Maces, and ufing their au- *punifhed.*
thority within the Precinct of his Church. But at the petition of the City they
were difmiffed; provided that for time to come they leave their Maces without the Outer-gate when they come to the Church, or within the Precinct.
He had the Bailiffs of *Romney* alfo in *coram*, for medling in Church-Bufinefs;
who obftinately rebelled, and fought, and thought to fecure themfelves by a
Prohibition, but were deceived; for the Archbifhop got it reverfed, and (faith
the Record) made that unadvifed Town fubmit. He obtained (d) of *Richard*
II. four Fairs for the Church at the four principal Feafts of peregrination in
the year, *viz.* one on the *Innocents* day, on *Whitfon*-Eve another, on the Eve
of *Becket*'s tranflation a third, and the fourth and laft on *Michaelmas*-Eve; to

---

(a) *In loco defignato Johanni Boteler, Armigero fuo.*   (b) *Ex Regiftro Courtney.*   (c) *Sub*
pana interdicti Civitatis.   (d) *Ex Lib. Ecclef. Cant.*

hold

hold for nine days next following every of them, and be kept within the fite of the Priory. [Over and befides which four Quarterly Fairs peculiar to the Church, the City had likewife its proper Fair, which by the Charter of *Henry* VI. was granted to it, to be annually holden on the fourth of *Auguft,* and the two next following days; but (I take it) is difcontinued and laid afide. *W. S.*]

Thomas Arundel. 60.

Anno Dom. **1396.**

A undel's Monument.

His Chantery.

Thomas Arundel next fucceeded after *Courtney.* Who fat one month above 17 years, and dyed *Anno* 1413. He lieth buried (as his Table will fhew) on the North-fide of the Body of *Chrift-Church,* where doubtlefs he fometime had a far better Monument than now remains of him. For his Will appoints out his Burial thus : (a) *in his Monument, built by him in his Chapel, in the Nave of the Church,* &c. But Chantery and Monument are both gone, a bare Grave-ftone levelled with the floor, with the Brafs all fhamefully torn away being only left ; whereas you may know there fometime ftood a Chapel (like to that, I fuppofe, of Bifhop *Kemp,* on the North-fide of the Body of *Paul's*) wherein both the Archbifhop lay fairly intombed, and his two Chanterifts did daily celebrate, which had for their Stipend x *l.* a-piece yearly, out of *Northfleet* Parfonage, and their Dwelling or Manfion ; which was built for them by himfelf, (b) *on the South-fide of the Church,* and contained in length 80, and in breadth 60 foot meafured. I fuppofe it yet ftanding, and to be one of thofe prefent Buildings on the South-fide of the Church-yard. The Chapel (as I learn from the report of the Chantery-Prieft thereof) was taken down, and fold away by *Hen.* VIII. his Commiffioners. This Archbifhop (c) confirmed the foundation of the Col-

Bredgare.

lege of *Bredgare,* to which the Parifh-Church there was in his time converted, by *Robert* then Parfon thereof. In the year 1413, what year this Archbifhop died, I find (d) him an Inhabitant in the Caftle of *Leeds* in *Kent,* which in a Decree or Sentence which he gave between his Monks, and the Convent of

Leeds Caftle.

St. *Gregory's* by *Canterbury,* dated at that place, the fame year, he calls his own Caftle. (e)

Henry Chicheley. 61.

1414.

Henry Chicheley fucceeded next after *Thomas Arundel.* He fat 29 years, and dying *Anno* 1443. was laid in a very fair Tomb built by him felf in his life-time, ftanding on the North-fide of the Presbytery. It is the Tomb which was lately repaired and beautified by the *All-Souls*-College men, whofe Founder he was. His Table will direct you to it. *Lindewood* dedicating his *Provincial* to this Archbifhop, ftyles him (f) *by the Grace of God, Archbifhop of* Canterbury. And no marvel, for 600 years before, his Predeceffor Archbifhop *Athelard* ufeth the ftyle, writing himfelf thus. (g) *I Æthilheard by the Grace of God Archbifhop of* Canterbury. The like (h) was ufual in the ftyles of other Archbifhops. And not only Archbifhops, Bifhops, and Dukes, in times paft ufed the fame in their Titles, but alfo Abbats, Priors, Earls, yea, the meaneft Magiftrates and Legates fometimes ; Earls efpecially which had *Jura Regalia,* and Mitred Abbats. But Kings in the mean feafon difdaining and difpleafed at it, and challenging it as the Symbol and Proof of their (fave under God) in-dependent Majefty, by little and little it became either wholly omitted, or elfe altered, as our Archbifhops into (i) *by divine providence,* or, *by divine permiffion.* Mr. *Selden* will inftruct you more at large in this matter, if you per-ufe the firft part of his *Titles of Honour,* cap. 7. §. 2. Unto whom let me add a pertinent difcourfe hereof. The Author of it, *Roverius,* in his *Illuftrations* upon the *Hiftory of St.* John's *Manaftery,* called *Reomaus, pag.* 618. his words at large are in the Margin (k).

(a) *In Monumento meo novo quod ad hoc licet indigniffimè conftrui & fieri feci in oratorio meo in navi fanctæ Cant Ecclefiæ, infra Cantariam meam perpetuam duorum Capellanorum ibidem ordinatam, &c.*

(b) *Ex auftrali parte Ecclefiæ*   (c) *Harpsfield*   (d) *Walfingham.*   (e) *Dat. in Caftello meo de Ledes.*   (f) *Dei Gratia, Cantuarien. Archiep.*   (g) *Ego Æthilheardus, Gratia Dei humilis fanctæ Dorobernenfis Ecclefiæ Archiepifcopus, &c.*   (h) *D. H spelman, Gloffar. in verb. Dei Gratia.*   (i) *Providentia Divina, Permiffione Divina*   (k) *Fecerant liberæ electiones, & Pontificia exemptiones, ut horum temporum Abbates (fpeaking of the Year 1192) fe Dei folius gratiâ conftitutos cenferent, atque inter dignitatis titulos hunc etiam annumerarent. Næ vero hoc primùm faculo natus eft hic fenfus, cum anno jam MXXX. Gandenfis Abbas S Bavonis fic fcriberet. Otgina Comitiffæ Othelboldus Gratia Dei Abbas, & annis plufquam centenis a tè Abbas S. Galli; Chrifti favente gratia Harmotus Abbas, & Chrifti difponente providentia, aut largiente clementia, Crimaldus Abba. Verum i., qui amantiores erant humilitatis religiofæ, non facile compertuitur hoc ufi fermone. Neque enim vel Clu-*

John

John Stafford. 62.

John Stafford succeeded. Sat almost nine years, and dying *Anno* 1452, was buried in the *Martyrdom*, under a flat Marble-stone inlaid with Brass.

John Kemp. 63.

John Kemp succeeded next. He continued not in the See above a year and a half. The Parish-Church of *Wy* in *Kent*, where he was born, he converted into a College, in which he placed secular Priests to attend divine Service, and to teach the Youth of their Parish. Their Governor was called a Prebendary. This College at the suppression was valued at 93 *l.* 2 *s.* by the year. It was surrendred *Anno* 36 *Henry* VIII. This Archbishop, with his two next Successors, were Cardinals.

Thomas Bourgchier. 64.

Thomas Bourgchier succeeded Cardinal *Kemp*; continued Archbishop 32 years, and dying *Anno* 1486. was buried upon the North-side of the High Altar, in a Marble Tomb. He gave to his Successor, by his Will, 2000 *l.* in recompense of dilapidations. He had a Chantery; the Revenues whereof were surrendred with the Priory to the King, (*Henry* VIII.)

John Morton. 65.

John Morton succeeded. Thirteen years he enjoyed the Archbishoprick, died the year 1500. He lieth buried in the Lady-Chappel of the *Undercroft*, under a Marble-stone. Howbeit a goodly Tomb is erected in memory of him, upon the South-side of the Chapel. [He was a Benefactor to the new Work, which we call *Bell-Harry*-Steeple, as by his devise in the Stone-work without, (which as Mr. *Cambden*, in his Remains, observes, usually was *Mor* upon a *Tun*) is evident enough. *W. S.*]

Henry Deane. 66.

Hnery Deane succeeded, who died *Anno* 1502. the second year after his Translation, and was buried in the *Martyrdom*.

William Warham. 67.

William Warham succeeded *Henry Deane*. The Pomp and State of whose Entertainment and Inthronization, you may read of at large elsewhere. He continued Archbishop 28 years, and died at St. *Stephen's* near *Canterbury*, in the House of *William Warham* his Kinsman, Archdeacon of *Canterbury*; and was laid in a little Chapel built by himself for the place of his Burial, upon the North-side of the *Martyrdom*, and hath there a reasonable fair Tomb; where he founded a Chapel, and a perpetual Chantery of one Priest, daily to say Mass for his Soul; but the dissolution of the Priory suppressed it, and seized the Revenues thereof to the King's use. *Erasmus* (upon whom this Archbishop bestowed the Parsonage of *Aldington* in *Kent*) so commends him for his Humanity, Learning, Integrity and Piety, that (as he concludes) (*a*) He was a most perfect and accomplished Prelate.

Thomas Cranmer. 68.

Thomas Cranmer succeeded, being consecrated Archbishop *Anno* 1533, and suffered most unworthy death at *Oxford*, *Anno* 1556. He was the man designed to succeed in the Chair by his Predecessor, who though he foresaw and foretold too that a *Thomas* should succeed him, who (as my Author saith, slan-

---

niacensis ullus, vel *Bernardus Claravallensis*, vel *Gofridus Vindocinensis*, vel *Lupus Ferrariensis* id sibi usquam tituli arrogarunt. Nam sive ea voce significetur Præfecturam Deo soli debitam, subditamve esse, sive Monasterio beneficium à Deo impertitum, quòd vir talis fuerit Præfectus, sive Abbati gratiam à Deo factam, quod sit Præfectus, non potest non aliquid continere sensus, quam humilitatem religiosam deceat. sublimioris, cum id de seipso Abbas profitetur, qui nec satis verè potest affirmare supremum sibi jus esse, vel sacrarum, vel temporalium rerum sui Monasterii, nec satis dimissè sua in Monasterium merita jactare, nec satis tutò Præfecturam; quæ gravissimum onus est pro divino favore habere. Itaque sapientissimi quique, & si aliis hunc titulum tribuunt, nunquam tamen sibi, dignum videlicet rati, ut de aliis sentiant, quod de se non ausint. Quamobrem suspicari licet has voces pluribus Abbatum chartis, actisque publicis non tam illorum quam pragmaticorum usu, ac instituto invectas, dum Abbates inducunt de seipsis eo loquentes modo, quo ipsi pragmatici sibi de illis sentiebant loquendum. Quanquam videri etiam possit has voces à Librariis in antiqua interdum scripta ex sui sæculi moribus intrusas. Vix enim ante secundam Regum Franciæ stirpem, aut Reges supremam potestatem rerum civilium, aut Episcopi rerum sacrarum his verbis expresserunt. Save & Episcopi, & Abbates aliqui invidiam titulo præclarè aliquando emollierunt, aut potius sunt interpretati, dum se permissione, aut concessione Dei Episcopos, vel Abbates dixere, &c.

(a) *Nullam absoluti præsulis dotem in eo desideres.* Peregrinatio Relig ergo.

dereth

Warham's evil presage of a Thomas. dereth I should say,) (*a*) *should more disgrace the Church, than* Thomas *the Martyr did honour it.* Yet to see, he pitches upon this Man (a *Thomas*) in his choice of a Successor. (*b*) The same Author saith, *that* Warham *had the same* Thomas *for his Successor, who first brought Heresy into this Church*; as he slanders our Religion.

Reginald Poole. 69.

Anno Dom. 1555.

Reginald Poole, otherwise and more vulgarly called Cardinal *Poole*, succeeded. Two years and almost eight months he continued Archbishop, and died even the same day that Queen *Mary* did. His Body was (and lies) intombed on the North-side of *Becket*'s Crown, where his Monument is extant. He was the last Archbishop that was buried in *Christ-Church*. Their Burials there have

Burial of the Archbishops in Christ-Church discontinued.

been ever since discontinued; a thing the whilst to some seeming very strange, that of all the Archbishops since the Reformation, not one hath chosen to be buried there, but all, as it were with one consent declined their own Cathedral, (the ancient and accustomed place of Archiepiscopal Sepulture) affecting rather an obscure Burial in some one private Parish-Church or other.

Matthew Parker. 70.

1559.

Matthew Parker succeeded Cardinal *Poole* in the Archbishoprick, held the same 15 years and 5 months, and deceased *Anno* 1575. Besides a multitude of pious Acts, he bestowed upon the reparation of his Palace at *Canterbury*, one Thousand four Hundred Pounds. He lies buried in the Chapel of *Lambeth-House*. Amongst other his Works, with the help no doubt of other able Antiquaries, he wrote the Lives of his Predecessors, the Archbishops of *Canterbury*; intituling his Book, *De Antiquitate Britannicæ Ecclesiæ, &c.* Whereof *Cuiacius* (having occasion to make mention of it) gives this commendation. (*c*) He saith, that *there are many excellent things in that Author. His Name is not known; his Book is to be had only in* England; *where it is sold at a dear rate.*

Edmund Grindal. 71.

1575.

Edmund Grindal succeeded, and sat seven years and almost a half, and died, and was buried at *Croydon*. He was a very grave man; and gave to our City 100 *l.* to be employed upon a Stock, to set the Poor on work.

John Whitgift. 72.

1583. Hosp. and School at Croydon.

John Whitgift succeeded, and continued Archbishop somewhat above 20 years. In which mean space, he built the Hospital and School at *Croydon*. After the finishing whereof (*d*), the *French* Leiger Ambassador, *Boys Sisi*, inquiring what Works the Archbishop had published, and receiving answer, that he had written only in defence of Church-Government; but it being incidently told him that he had founded an Hospital, and a School: (*e*) He presently says, *Truly an Hospital for the relieving of the Poor, and a School for the instructing of Youth, are the best Books which an Archbishop could write.* He lieth buried at *Croydon*.

Richard Bancroft. 73.

1604.

Richard Bancroft succeeded and sat 6 years, or thereabouts, died *Anno* 1610. A man of singular wisdom, and very zealous in defence both of Church-liberties and Discipline.

George Abbot. 74.

1611.

Guilford Hosp.

Conduit at Canterbury.

George Abbot succeeded, he sat Archbishop 22 years. In which space of time he bestowed great Sums of Money in building and endowing of an Hospital at *Guilford* in *Surrey*, the Town wherein he was born, and afterwards buried. He began also to shew himself a special Benefactor to our City; witness the goodly Conduit which he built for the common good and service of the same. A work as of great Charge to the Author, so of no less benefit to the City. He died in *July Anno Dom.* 1633.

William Laud. 75.

After whom succeeded the present Lord Archbishop, His Grace *William*

(*a*) *Per laxam & remissam vitæ licentioris indulgentiam populo concessam, perque prava dogmata, magis Cantuariensem, omnemque reliquam Angliæ Ecclesiam deformaret, quam eam olim Thomas Martyr suo martyrio amplificasset; admonuitque nepotem, ut si quis forte Thomas, eo vivo ea sede potiretur, ne ulla ratione in illius famulitium se ascribi pateretur, &c.* (*b*) *Waramus autem eum ipsum Thomam, de quo tam male ominabatur, quique primus ex omnibus Cantuariæ Episcopis hæresin in eam sedem invexit, successorem sibi sortitus est.* (*c*) *Sunt multa in eo auctore præclara, nomen ejus ignoratur, & liber tantum exstat in Anglia, unde accersitur, & accersitus est magno pretio. Ad cap. qua fronte de Appellationib.*

(*d*) Sir *George Paul,* in his Life. (*e*) *Profecto Hospitale ad sublevandum paupertatem, & Schola ad instruendum juventutem sunt optimi libri quos Archiepiscopus conscribere potuit.*

Laud, Primate of all *England*, and Metropolitan, One of the Lords of his Majesty's most Honourable Privy Council, and Chancellor of the University of *Oxford*. Of whom to speak, is not a task for my pen. I leave it to posterity hereafter, and to better abilities to set forth his constant Piety, great Wisdom, and spotless Justice. Howbeit, what all men take unto themselves a liberty to speak of him, I shall be bold to commemorate, namely those famous Works of his that so much praise him in the gate : As his Care, his Cost, his encouragement to the repair of what all men despaired as much to see repaired until he undertook it, as ever they did to see it finished (*a*), when *Mauritius* first began to build it, St. *Paul*'s Church in *London*. Another, that never to be forgotten Gift of his to the University-Library of *Oxford*, of an innumerable multitude of choice and rare Manuscripts ; with his great care and cost, gathered from all parts not only of this Kingdom, but also of the whole world. A third, the flourishing of the same University, by his means, in a twofold way ; one, in the Government of it, by his late new Statutes ; the other, in Buildings, at St. *John*'s first, at his own proper cost and charges ; and by his example and furtherance, in other Colleges; such Buildings all, and so goodly, as none did ever expect, and all do now admire to see raised.

Now that Providence, which by the means of a most pious and prudent King sent him unto us, grant we may long enjoy him, and afterwards translate him from the cares of the Church Militant here, to the joys of that Triumphant one above.

If any shall desire to see the ancient Form of our Archbishop's Inthronization, he may find it in my *Appendix*, Numb. XLVII. transcribed from a Record of that of Archbishop *Winchelsey*'s, kept in the Church, and (as it may be supposed by the general Title of it) intended for a Precedent in this kind. And so having done with the first part of my intended Catalogue, to wit, concerning the Archbishops of *Canterbury*, I proceed to the Second, *viz.* *Inthronization of the Archbishop of Canterbury, the Form of it.*

A Catalogue of the Priors of Christ-Church, *with a brief touch of the Contemporary Monks of Note.*

Until the Conqueror's time, I find no mention of any Prior of *Christ-Church*. *Henry*, brought hither by Archbishop *Lanfranc*, being the first I meet with. Aforetime (it seems) he that held the place was called *Decanus Ecclesiæ*. So it is intimated by Archbishop *Parker*, in the life of *Agelnoth* ; who tells also, that *Celnoth* the Archbishop, almost 200 years before, was first Dean of the Church. A *Saxon* Record of this Church makes mention of one *Æthelwine*, a Dean also in the same Archbishop's time ; and another Record tells of another, one *Godric* in Archbishop *Stigand*'s days, whom the Book of *Doomsday* makes mention of. Further than thus, I am not instructed in the names of those Deans; wherefore I must pass them over and come to the Priors.

Henry. 1.
Whereof (as I said) *Henry* was the first : Sometime Abbat of *Cane* in *Normandy* ; from thence brought hither by *Lanfranc*, and made Prior of this Church. Afterwards he became Abbat of *Battel* in *Sussex* (*b*), and so died. — *Anno Dom. 1080.*

Ernulphus or Arnulphus. 2.
Ernulphus or *Arnulphus*, first a Monk of the Church, afterwards became Prior, succeeding *Henry* ; then was preferred to the Abbatship of *Peterborough*, and lastly, had the Bishoprick of *Rochester* given him by his Predecessor in that See, *Ralph*, the Archbishop of *Canterbury*. You may read more of him in the Catalogue of Bishops in *Rochester*, and in *Fox*'s *Acts and Monuments* you shall find a Letter directed to him and others, about Priests Marriages. — *1104.*

Conradus. 3.
Conradus a Monk also of the place succeeded *Ernulphus*, made Prior, as his Predecessor by Archbishop *Anselm*. Of whom, and of *Henry* Predecessor to them both, *Edmerus* maketh this mention. (*c*) He saith, that *Anselm* put all the Affairs of the Monastery at the disposal of his own Friends ; constituting, after Prior — *1108.*

(a) *Stow. Godwin*   (b) *Reyner. Apost. Benedictin.*   (c) *Res Monachorum posuit in dispositione suorum, constituens eis in Priorem, post Henricum, Ernulphum, post Ernulphum, Conradum (ipsius loci Monachos) ad quorum nutum negotia ecclesiæ cuncta referrentur.*

Henry

Henry *was gone*, Ernulph *and* Conrade, *Monks of this Convent, to be succeſsively Priors, at whoſe command and pleaſure all the Buſineſſes of the Church ſhould be ordered and managed.* Which is all I read of him.

Gosfridus. 4.

Anno Dom.
1122.

The next Prior after *Conradus*, was *Gosfridus*; who (as I have it from the Continuer of *Florence* of *Worceſter*, in the year 1128.) at the Suit of *David* King of *Scots*, by the conſent of the Archbiſhop (*William Corboyl*) was choſen Abbat of the Monaſtery of *Dunfermelin*, in *Scotland*. My Author's own words are, (a) Gosfrid, *Prior of the Church of* Canterbury, *a man eminently Religious, at the requeſt of* David *King of the Scots, and with the conſent of Archbiſhop* William, *is elected Abbat of a place in* Scotland, *which is called* Dunfermelin. *And he received his Benediction from the Biſhop of the Church of St.* Andrew's. A Petition of the ſame King of the *Scots* to this purpoſe, is ſtill extant among the Records of this Cathedral, where I have ſeen and read it.

Elmerus or Ailmerus. 5.

1128.

Elmerus or *Ailmerus* ſucceeded *Gosfridus*. He was firſt alſo a Monk, afterwards Prior of *Chriſt-Church*, and continued Prior nine years, dying in the 1137. He was contemporary with *Edmerus* and *Alexander*, both famous Monks of the place, great Ornaments to the Church, and very dear both of them unto Archbiſhop *Anſelm*. This Prior wrote divers Treatiſes, mentioned of *Pitſeus*, who will further inform you both of him, and thoſe his Coætaneans. Here by the way to do *Balæus* right, let me note it once for all, that *Pitſeus* for theſe and many other like things which I ſhall have occaſion to cite him for, is but *Balæus* his Plagiary; yet I rather quote him than *Balæus* becauſe his Book is more common and eaſy to get.

Pitſeus, Baleus's Plagiary.

Jeremias. 6.

1137.

Jeremias (a Monk alſo of the place) ſucceeded *Elmerus* [by the vote and election of the Monks, the See being void. *W. S.*] Of whom I read in the Acts and Monuments, that Archbiſhop *Theobald* falling out with him for certain cauſes between them, for which the Archbiſhop taking ſtomach againſt him, would lay the Sentence of Interdiction againſt him. The Prior, to ſave himſelf made his appeal to Pope *Innocent*. The Archbiſhop provoked the more by that, depoſed him from the Priorſhip, and placed one *Walter* in his room. *Jeremias*, notwithſtanding, making his complaint and appeal to *Rome*, obtained Letters from the Pope to *Henry* Biſhop of *Wincheſter*, being the Pope's Legat; by the virtue whereof he, againſt the heart of the Archbiſhop, was reſtored, and *Walter* diſplaced. Nevertheleſs, the ſaid *Jeremy*, not willing there to continue with diſpleaſure of the Archbiſhop, ſhortly after, of his own accord, renounced his Priory, and *Walter* again was received in his ſtead. Thus Mr. *Fox*. Biſhop *Godwyn* in his Catalogue, in the life of Archbiſhop *Theobald*, writing of this matter, by miſtake affirms him to have been Prior of St. *Auguſtin*'s. That he is herein miſtaken you ſhall plainly perceive both by *Matthew Paris, pag.* 102. *London* Edition; and by Archbiſhop *Parker* in the life of *Theobald*, if you pleaſe to conſult them; of whom the latter tells, that this *Jeremy* had given him in conſideration of his ſurrender of the Priory, 100 Marks. Theſe things happened (you ſee) in the time of Pope *Innocent* II. who died *Anno* 1143. This Prior is mentioned by *Harpsfield*, in the ſtory of the new Work of *Dover*, by *Corboyl*.

Walterus. 7.

1143.

Walterus (as you ſee) was made his Succeſſor. I find him ſirnamed *Duruſdens*, in *Engliſh*, *Durdent* or *Hardtooth*. *Pitſeus*, in his *Appendix* to his Catalogue of *Engliſh-Writers*, mentions one of the name, this very Prior in all probability; and gives him a large Encomium, for his great Learning, eſpecially in Divinity, and mentions ſome of his Works. [*Anno* 1149. He was hence removed and preferred to the Biſhoprick of *Coventry*, whereunto he was elected by the Convent there. To whom, by the inſtitution of *Theobald* the Archbiſhop, with the advice of the Convent here, ſucceeded in the Priory a certain Chaplain of the Archbiſhop's, called *Walter Parvus*, or (as in the vulgar, *Petit*.

(a) *Vir Religionis eximiæ Cantuariæ Prior Gosfridus nomine, Rege Scotorum David petente, & Archiepiſcopo Gulielmo annuente, Abbas eligitur ad locum Scotiæ, qui Dunfermelin dicitur. Ordinatus eſt autem ab Epiſcopo Eccleſiæ S. Andreæ.*

Gerva's Dorobern. from whom I have collected thefe things, commends *Walter Durdent* for a moft Religious man, and of rare parts in Divinity (*a*).

Walterus parvus. 8.

Waterus (to diftinguifh him from his Predeceffor) firnamed *parvus*, fucceed- ed, whom [(befides the mention made of him in the ftory of the ftrife be- tween Archbifhop *Theobald*, and *Sylveſter* the 45th Abbat of St. *Auſtin's*, about his (the Abbat's) Confecration, oppofed of this Prior in the year 1151. re- corded in the Acts and Monuments. *Part* I. *pag.* 307.(*W. S.*] I know only by his name, and the time in which he lived.

Anno Dom. 1151.

Wibertus. 9.

And fo muft I fay of his next Succeffor, *Wibert*, faving that his Burial-place is lately come to my knowledge, by this Infcription in Brafs on a Grave-ſtone in the Chapter-houfe : (*b*) *Here lies* Wibert, *formerly Prior of this Church.* [I have learned fince from *Gervafe*, who calls him a man (*c*) *worthy to be commend- ed, and admirable in good Works* ; that his Predeceffor *Walter's* deprivation made way for his Succeffion, and that he was formerly the Sub-Prior ; and died *An- no* 1167. In a *MS.* Hiſtory, written in *French* by fome Monk of *Canterbury*, about *Edward* II. days, and now remaining with the Honourable Sir *Simon D' Ewes*, Kt. and Bar. is made honourable mention of this Prior in thefe words: (*d*) *This Year alſo* (1167.) *died* Wibert, *of good memory, Prior of the Mother- Church of* Canterbury, *on the Fifth of the Kalends of* October. The fame man caufed to be made the Conducts of Water in all the Offices, with the Court of the Priory. *W. S.*]

1160.

Odo. 10.

Odo fucceeded *Wibert*, and was Prior in Archbifhop *Becket's* days. After whofe death (faith Mr. *Fox* (*e*)) there was a great ſtir between the King (*Henry* II.) and this Prior about the choice of a new Archbifhop. *For the King* (faith my Author) *feeing the Realm fo oftentimes incumbred by thofe Popiſh Archbi- ſhops, and fearing leſt the Monks of* Canterbury *ſhould elect fuch another as would follow the ſteps of* Thomas Becket, *moſt humbly with cap in hand, and courteſie of knee, deſired* Odo *the Prior, that at his requeſt, and for contentation of his mind, fuch a one might be elected, whom he would appoint ;* (*appointing and naming a certain Biſhop, which was a good ſimple man, after the King's liking ;*) *but the Prior diſſem- blingly anſwering the King again, that he neither could nor would, without the conſent of the Convent, give promiſe to any man ; in fine, contrary to the King's fo humble requeſt, agreed to the election of another, which was the Prior of* Dover, *called* Ri- chard, *Anno* 1173. *who continued in that See eleven Years.* Thus *Fox.* His Con- vent and he (as the fame Author reports) fell out about his tranſlating the Re- liques of St. *Dunſtan.* This doubtlefs is the man whom *Pitſeus* mentions, and calls St. *Odo.* A man (faith he) of approved Virtue, and eminent Learn- ing. From Prior of this Church he was tranſlated and preferred to be Abbat of *Battel* ; faith the fame *Pitſeus.* One *Sampſon Dorobernenſis*, a man famous alfo for his Piety and Learning, was his equal in time, and Companion in place, being a Monk of this Church about the year 1170.

1170.

Benedictus. 11.

Benedictus fucceeded *Odo.* And in the year 1177. was a party to the compo- fition made between him and his Convent on the one fide, and the Abbat and Convent of St. *Auſtin's* on the other ; touching the Houfes and Ground on the South-fide of the Church-yard of *Chriſt-Church*, by the *Campanile* fometime ſtanding there, exchanged by St. *Auſtin's* with *Chriſt-Church* for otherlike elfe- where ; whereof before in my Survey of the Precinct. See more of him you may in *Pitſeus*, who faith, that from this Priory, he was tranſlated to the Ab- by of *Peterborough*, and therefore is known by the Sirname of *Petriburgenſis*, and died about the year 1200.

1177.

Herlewinus. 12.

Herlewinus fucceeded *Benedictus*, and was Prior in the days of Pope *Alexan- der* III. (who died 1181.) for I find him direct his Bulls to this Prior by name,

1180.

[(a) *Vir eximiæ Religionis, & in facris literis apprime eruditus.* Gerv. *Dorobern.* W. S.]
(b) *Hic jacet* Wibertus *quondam Prior hujus ecclefiæ.*   [(c) *Virum commendabilem, & in bonis operibus mirabilem.* Gerv. W. S.]   [(d) *Ceſt an auſi* (*fc. Anno* 1167) *moruſt de Bone memo- rie* Wibert le Priur, *&c. fol.* 134. *b.* W. S.]   (e) Acts and Monum. *Vol.* I *pag.* 307.

com-

commanding that the Offerings of the Church should be disposed of (*a*) for *the Repair of the Church,* &c. Extreme Age having indisposed him for Government, he gave over his place, and had to his Successor,

Alanus. 13.

Anno Dom.
1181. This *Alanus* (*Harpesfield* saith) was first a Canon of *Beneventum,* but *English*-born, afterward Sacrist or Sexton of this Church, then Prior, and lastly made Abbat of *Teuksbury.* He wrote much ; the particulars of whose labours you may find in *Pitseus.* Being Sexton he was very intimate with Archbishop *Becket.* But afterward, when he was Prior, he opposed himself against *Baldwin,* both in his election and in his proceedings afterwards ; by whose policy, because he could not win him to his side, under the pretence of his preferment, he at length procured his removal from this Priory to the Abbatship of *Teuksbury* ; where he lived till the year 1201, and then died. He was doubtless a strict and stout Prelate. For I read (*b*) that in the year 1181. when, in a Procession at *Christ-Church,* one Sir *Robert Martimer,* an excommunicate person for his contumacy, (*c*) *because he would not obey the Law, being questioned for a wrong done unto the Church of* Canterbury, *in taking from the Maner of* Diepham *a certain parcel of Land belonging to the Monks* ; intruded himself into the company : This Prior, *Alan,* espying of him there, informs the Archbishop, who was then present, of it, and that a second time, because the Archbishop would have connived at it ; the Archbishop's Servants dissuading the Prior because of the King's displeasure. At length, because the Prior saw the Archbishop would take no notice of it, he tells him that sith he would not use his authority without, he will use his own within the Church. And, accordingly, being entred the Church, and at Mass, the Prior requires the Convent to surcease, who obeyed ; and so the Excommunicate, to his shame, was by strong hand cast out of the Church ; and then they proceeded in their Devotions. You may see more of this Prior in the story of the Troubles happening between Archbishop *Baldwin* and the Monks of his Church, recorded in Acts and Monuments, *Vol.* I. *pag.* 308. [Of whom, and his immediate Predecessor *Herlewine, Gervas* writes thus : (*d*) " *Anno* 1179. *August* 6, *Herlewine,* Prior " of *Christ-Church,* resign'd his Priory in the third year of his being Prior ; for " he was grown old, dim-sighted, and could not see. On the same day he had " a Successor, Mr. *Alanus,* who, a few years before, was Canon of the " Church of *Beneventum* ; by birth he was an *Englishman,* and was five years " a Novice of the Convent of the Church of *Canterbury.* The Monks concei-" ved of him so great hopes of Integrity, and of a good Conversation, that " by the advice and consent of almost all the Convent, Archbishop *Richard* " was, as it were, forcibly compell'd to promote him to this Priory. *W. S.*]

Honorius. 14. *Roger Norris.* 15. *Osbertus.* 16.

1185. *Honorius* [a Chaplain of the Archbishop, and the Church-Celerar, *W. S.*] succeeded *Alanus* ; of whom, and of his next Successor *Roger Norris,* as also of *Osbertus* or *Osbernus* his next Successor, you may read in that story I last mentioned : Where it is said, that *Honorius* died [*Parker* saith,of the Plague) *W. S.*] at *Rome,* whither he was sent to oppose *Baldwin* in his Project for the College at *Hackington,* [was buried in the Cloister of the Church of *Lateran.* So *Gervas. W. S.*] And that *Roger* was made Prior in his stead, by *Baldwin,* who 1189. obtruded him upon the Monks ; whereupon in their Treaty for conditions of Peace and Composition, one Article was, that this Prior should be deposed. And accordingly he was so, and at the request of the Archbishop, promoted to be Abbat of *Eusham,* and with consent of the King and Convent, *Osbernus* 1190. designed and made Prior, who had before taken part with the Archbishop ; but continued not long in the place, for the Monks not pleased with him, after *Baldwin*'s death removed him again. About this time, one *William Stephens*

(a) *In restauratrouem Ecclesia, &c.*   (b) *Lib. Eccles. Christi Cant.*   (c) *Quia noluit juri parere, super injuria quam fecerat Cantuar. ecclesia de quadam pastura, quam abstulit manerio eorum quod dicitur Depekam.*   (d) *Herlewinus Prior Cantuar. Ecclesia resignavit Prioratum Anno Tertio sui Prioratus. Senuit enim & caligaverant oculi ejus & videre non poterat, cui successit eodem die Magister Alanus ante paucos annos Beneventana Ecclesia Canonicus, sed Natione Anglus, & Cantuariensis Ecclesia quinquennis fit novitius. De quo tanta spes probitatis & conversationis honesta habita est, ut ex consilio & consensu totius fere conventus Ricardo Archiepiscopo quodammodo vii inferretur, ut eum in Prioratum promoveret.* W. S.]

(or

(or *Gulielmus Stephanides*) a famous Monk, lead his life in this Monaſtery, of whom you may read a large *Encomium* in *Pitſeus.*

Gaufridus or *Galfridus.* 17.

Gaufridus or *Galfridus* ſucceeded *Osbert.* Letters or Bulls like to thoſe above-mentioned ſent by Pope *Alexander* to *Herlewin* his Predeceſſor, and as were alſo directed by Pope *Urban* III. to *Honorius* the Prior, I find inſcribed to this Prior by Pope *Innocent* III. I meet alſo with certain Letters of his and the Convent's, whereby, with conſent of *Hubert* the Archbiſhop, and at the Petition of Mr. *Firmin* then *Cuſtos* or Keeper of that Houſe, they take the Leprous Hoſpital of St. *Jacob's* near *Canterbury*, into their cuſtody and protection, as I have more at large made appear unto you in my Survey of that *quondam* Hoſpital. (*a*) In this man's time, the Controverſy between the Monks and the Suffragans of the Province, about the choice of the Archbiſhop, was decided by the Decree of Pope *Innocent* III. and the ſame Pope by another Decree and Letters to the Archbiſhop, diſcarded ſecular Clerks out of the Church and Monaſtery. Contemporary with this Prior, was the famous *Gervaſius Dorobernenſis*, a Monk of this Church, a great Hiſtorian and Antiquary, as *Pitſeus* will inform you ; as alſo of *Nigellus Wireker* another like Monk, and Chantor of the Church ; on whom my Author, from *Leland*, beſtows a moſt ample Commendation for his Piety and excellent Endowments.

Anno Dom. 1192.

St. *Jacob's.*

John Sittingbourn. 18.

John (from I ſuppoſe the place of his Birth) ſirnamed *Sittingbourn* ſucceeded, and was Prior in the time of the Church's troubles about the election of a new Archbiſhop to ſucceed *Hubert*, the Story whereof is obvious ; and was with his Monks, 64 in number, by King *John* on that occaſion ſent into baniſhment. Whoſe places he cauſed to be filled with certain Monks out of St. *Auſtin's* Abby. But the Storm at length being, after ſeven years baniſhment, blown over, they were called home, full reſtitution was made both to him and them every way, (*b*) and 1000 *l.* given them for recompence of all detriments, as our Stories witneſs, together with a Charter of Reſtitution, which becauſe our Stories have it not, I have thought good to annex and add as a Corollary to the Story ; and I find it to be of this Tenor, in the Leiger of the Church. It is in the *Appendix*, Numb. XLVIII.

1206.

Monks baniſhed.

This Prior afterwards, to wit, in the Vacancy by the death of *Richard* the great, was deſigned to the Archbiſhoprick by the free election of the Chapter, but going to *Rome* for confirmation, (*c*) tho the Cardinals deſigned for his examination gave teſtimony to the Pope of his fitneſs and ſufficiency ; yet the Pope perſuading him it was a Province (or Office) of too great care and difficulty for him to manage, being an Aged plain man, he humbly renounced the election, and craved licence to return home ; and St. *Edmund* afterward filled the Chair by the Pope's proviſion.

1234.

Rogerus de la Lee. 19.

Rogerus de la Lee ſucceeded *John Sittingbourn.* I find him and his Convent in the year 1242, enter into compoſition with the Abbat and Convent of St. *Auſtin's*, touching divers matters then in difference between them, eſpecially maritime Rights and Cuſtoms at *Minſtre* and *Sandwich* ; a Copy whereof you may find in my *Appendix*, Numb. LIII.

1234.

Nicholaus de Sandwico. 20.

Nicholas of *Sandwich* ſucceeded : But I find nothing of him more, unleſs that be (as it's like enough to be) his Epitaph or Inſcription, which I lately holp to diſcover, being in ſomewhat a ſtrange and unwonted Character, after the old faſhion, cut into the Stone at the foot of a Buttreſs, on the South-ſide of *Becket's* Chapel, a little within the Cœmitery-Gate, and, if read, runs as may be ſeen in the *Appendix*, Numb. XLIX.

1244.

That is as like to be either his Predeceſſor's or Succeſſor's Epitaph, which, on the contrary ſide of the Chapel, is in the like Character and manner, cut into the Wall, the briefeſt one ſhall ſee, being no more but (*d*) *Here lies* Roger.

Hard by which, on a Buttreſs, is a Sub-Prior's Epitaph, ſometime legible, but now obſcured for the moſt part by the Foundation of the little Chapel, put up between that and the next Buttreſs to it.

(a) *Reyner. Apoſtol Benedict. pag. 97, & 107.*   (b) *Matt. Paris, pag. 315. Lond. Edit.*
(c) *Fox* Acts and Mon. **Vol. 1.** pag. 356.   (d) *Hic requieſcit Rogerus.*

Rogerus de Sancto Elphego. 21.

Rogerus de S. Elpheg. was the next Prior. I find him a Benefactor to the Chapel, now the *Dean's*; for in several windows of it you may read (*a*) *Roger of St.* Elphege *gave this Window.* [The Book before cited in *Wibert*, speaks him Founder of the Chapel it self, in these words: (*b*) *This Year* (1262.) *died the Prior of* Canterbury, Roger *of St.* Elphege, *who founded and finish'd the fair Chapel of Stone between the Dorter of the Convent and the Infirmary; and after him succeeded in the same Office, by the Convent's election, Adam* of *Chillendene, a Monk of the self-same Church. W. S.*]

Adam Chillenden. 22.

Adam Chillenden is said to be the next Successor in the Priory. With the Abbat of St. *Austin's*, the Prior of St. *Gregory's*, and others, he was by the King's Writ, *Anno* 1269. 53 *Henry* III. declared quit and free from Tallage with the City, under this form, which I find in *Thorn*, and have transferr'd into the *Appendix*, Numb. L.

I have no more to say of this Prior, except I should mention his election to the Archbishoprick, the passages and effect whereof I had rather you should acquaint your self withal (gentle Reader) from the *Acts and Monuments, vol.*1. *pag.* 439. [The Manuscript before cited in *Wibert*, tells of his death, and who succeeded him thus: *The self-same Year* (1274.) *died the Prior of* Canterbury, Adam *of* Chillenden, *and him followed in that Office, by the Convent's election,* Thomas *of* Ringmere, *a Monk of the same Church, the* 13 *Kalends of* October, *on St.* Theodore's *day. W. S.*]

Thomas Ringemer. 23.

Thomas Ringemer succeeded. In his time, certain of the Monks of his Convent leaving the Monastery, dispersed and seated themselves abroad in the rural and Country-possessions of their House, and appropriating to themselves, and converting to their private use the fruits of the same, spent their days in worldly pleasures and delights, contrary to the Canons and Rules of Monastick Discipline. Whom this Prior, an honest and pious man, called home, and provided that for time to come, the Possessions of the Monastery should be commended to the care and managing of trusty Laicks, and not of the Monks. Herein he had to Friend the then Archbishop *John Peckham*, who took his part, and afforded him his help and furtherance in the business. Notwithstanding, he found the Monks very reluctant and averse to Reformation, who being impatient of an unwonted restraint, complotted to displace the one, (the Prior) and with their calumnious Aspersions sought the others infamy. Of certain

(saith my Author) this Archbishop, and *Robert* his next Successor, enacted many Decrees very useful and conducing to the Regulating of the Monks, and keeping them within the compass of Monastick discipline. And whereas (saith he) 30 of the due and ancient number of the Monks was decreased and wanting, the same *Robert* [restor'd *N. B.*] reduced them to their full number. But this *Thomas*, our Prior, betook himself to the *Cistertian* Discipline at *Beaulieu*, and afterward becoming more rigid to himself, turned *Anchoret*. *Peter Ikham* a *Kentishman*, and (as my Author thinks) a *Canterbury*-man born, a famous Historian and Antiquary, was contemporary with this Prior, of whom see more (if you please) in *Pitseus*.

Henricus de Eastry. 24.

Henricus de Eastry succeeded *Thomas Ringemer*, and continued Prior 37 years. A fair time, in which I find Record of many worthy Acts done both in and about the Church and Monastery, and also in their Demesnes abroad, which therefore, I may justly entitle to this Prior: Whereof, I may not forget the repair of the Quire and Chapter-house, which cost 839 *l.* 7 *s.* 8 *d.* and the (*c*) *New Steeple towards the North*, in the year 1317. a Steeple sometime standing on the North-side of the Church, sithence either with age decayed, or by some alterations or new Buildings defaced. He built also a new Grange at *Berton*, where, in his time, to wit, *Anno* 1302, I find the Church had a Gaol or Prison: For, (as the Story (*d*) goes) one of *Christ-Church Berton*, that year, killing another there, and being by the Church's Officers imprisoned in the

---

(a) *Rogerus de Sancto Elphego dedit hanc fenestram. de Canterbyre Roger de S. Elphege, &c. MS D'Eusian.* W. S]   [(b) *Cest ann* (1262.) *morust le Prior* (c) *Novum clocarium longum versus North.*   (d) *Lib. Eccles. Cant.*

Gaol there ; the Bailiffs of the City go to *Berton,* and by ſtrong hand take the Priſoner thence, and commit him to the Town Gaol. But after Treaty, and ſight of the Church-Charters of *Infangthef,* &c. they reſtore him, who at the next Aſſizes at *Maidſtone* was tried, convicted, condemned, and hanged at the Church-gallows at *Hollingborn.*

To return to our Prior. I find *(a)* that in his time the Church was plenti- **Vines.** fully furniſhed with Vines, as at *Colton, Berton,* St. *Martin's, Chertham, Brook,* and *Hollingbourn,* all Manors of the ſame. They had to all or moſt of their Manors, a domeſtick Chapel, to each of them almoſt, a new one of his ma- king, and a Bertary. The Total of the Charge of his 37 years work is record- ed to be 2184 *l.* 18 *s.* 8 *d.* In his time a Suit, or at leaſt a Complaint or Pre- ſentment was brought by the City againſt him and the Chapter, for building fourſcore Shops towards *Burgate* ; and for ſtopping up the way between *Que- ningate* and *Northgate.* But in the one, the latter, they defended themſelves by the Charter of *Henry* II. (whereof before :) And for the other, by the Jury it was found, that although they had made Shops opening to *Burgate,* yet up- on their own Soil, and without prejudice to the City, becauſe the Church did not demand nor had any ſtallage for them. In the Liſt of the Church's Fami- ly, in this Prior's time, a Notary makes one of the Company. The Prior *(*I **Notary.** take it) for the time being always had one, and uſed him (among other Em- ployments) chiefly as his *Amanuenſis* or Scribe, for the diſpatch of ſuch Buſi- neſs as was brought before him by delegation from the See of *Rome.* For, I find him petitioning the Pope for his authority to create Notaries ; as it is in a Leiger of the Church, and now in the *Appendix,* Numb. LI.

But the preſent Prior *Henry,* in the year 1306. makes it his ſuit to an *Imperi- al Count Palatine,* who by a Privilege annexed to his Dignity, hath power to make Notaries, to authoriſe him by Letters of deputation to create three. Whereunto he condeſcended : Whoſe Letters or Licenſe, together with the Inſtrument or Faculty of a Notaryſhip by virtue thereof granted, I purpoſe in my *Appendix,* Numb. LII. a. b. c. to tender to their peruſal who would know the Courſe of that Age in this point of creating Notaries. They even as little differ in tenor as in time, with thoſe of Mr. *Selden's* ſetting out in his *Titles of Honour,* Part 2. Cap. 1. §. 44. But (by the way) this way of creating Nota- ries is, ſo long ſince, diſuſed and left, and that originally for this reaſon, *viz.* *(b) Becauſe the Kingdom of* England *is abſolutely free from being ſubject to the Em- pire,* as it is in *Edward* II. Conſtitution or Writ, made for the future diſcarding that Courſe of creating Notaries, and directed and ſent to the Archbiſhop of *Canterbury,* and the Mayor of *London,* whereof you may read more at large in the ſame Author, both in the quoted place, and alſo *Part* 1. *c.* 2. §. 5. And indeed Notaries were ſcarce and rare in this Kingdom long before *Edward* II. time, as you may find by thoſe two Legatine Conſtitutions of *Otho* : *Cap. Quanto.* and *Cap. Quoniam Tabellionum,* in the Preface to each. And for that cauſe, and for Supply of that defect, it was thought requiſite for the credit of publick Inſtruments, to invent and have recourſe to *Authentick Seals.* Whence **Authentick** thoſe two Legatine Conſtitutions ; the one commanding them to be frequent- **Seals.** ly uſed, the other forbidding them to be at all miſuſed. Ever ſince which time, the publick Inſtruments of Biſhops and other Ordinaries have been juſtified, by ſuch Authentick Seals. And ſuch of them as going out under the Biſhop's Seal, (for, as one ſaith, *(c)* the Certificate of any Ordinary under a Biſhop is of no credit, nor will be received in the King's Courts) uſe hath been made of at the Common Law, for their Seal's ſake, have been of faith, and repu- ted Authentick. How true then their affirmation is, which ſay, that Eccleſia- **Courts of Re-** ſtical Courts are no Courts of Record, comes fitly here in place to be inqui- **cord.** red. Biſhops, I know for certain, (ſaith one) certifying *Baſtardy, Bigamy, Ex- communication,* the *Vacancy* or *Plenarty* of a Church, a *Marriage,* a *Divorce,* a *Spiritual Intruſion,* or whether a man be *profeſſed* in any Religion, with other ſuch like, are credited without further inquiry or controlement. Beſides, a Te- ſtament ſhewed under the Seal of the Ordinary, is not traverſable. Thus Dr. *Cowel,* in his *Interpreter,* in *Verb.* Record : Where he cites many Authorities for

---

(a) *Lib Ecclef. Cant.* (b) *Eo quod Regnum Angliæ ab omni ſubjectione imperiali ſit liberrimum.* (c) *Finch,* Of Law, *lib.* 4. *pag.* 138.

proof

proof hereof out of common Law, and Lawyers Books; whither I refer you, and return to our Prior. Who in the year 1285. entred into compofition with the then Abbat of St. *Auftin's*, touching a certain Key and Houfe built by him, or the preceding Prior, at *Fordwich*, to the great diftafte of the Abbat; whereof more hereafter in my *Appendix*, where I will give you the full relation of it from *Thorn.* Numb. LIV.

Priors Key at Fordwich.

In his time, namely, *Anno* 1296, the Priory was a while in great diftrefs, and worthily; for denying the King a Subfidy, by example of the Archbifhop (*Robert Winchelfey*) who made like denial of payment thereof. (*a*) " Whereby " (faith my Author) all their Temporalties were confifcated, and all that they " had within the Gates of the Church, were feiz'd upon; fo as they had no- " thing to live upon, but what their Neighbours of the next Monaftery fent " them, out of Charity. And this continued fo long, as Neceffity at laft com- " pelled the Prior and Convent to redeem their Goods and Poffeffions, *&c.*

I will conclude my Difcourfe of this Prior with what I find written by Archbifhop *Parker*, of him, and his ftout and faithful difcharge of his Duty in maintenance of fuch Rights, and putting into practice fuch power of Jurifdi- ction, as in the vacancy of the See (by *Walter Reynold's* death) devolved and appertained unto him and the Chapter. (*b*) He faith, " There was at that " time a Prior of the Church of *Canterbury*, *Henry* by name, one of great " Prudence and fingular Skill in the Rights of his Church; one that was dili- " gent in inquiring into the Privileges, and no lefs diligent and induftrious in " managing the Affairs of the Church. In a few Months time he exercifed " and renewed all manner of Jurifdiction which belong'd to the Prior and " Chapter during the vacancy of the Archiepifcopal Chair; which Jurifdi- " ction had been before intermitted, and not exercifed. He ftrictly inquired " concerning fuch Clergy as were prefented unto Ecclefiaftical Benefices, and " concerning the Rights of their Patrons. He granted Letters of Adminiftra- " tion of the Goods of Inteftate Perfons, receiv'd Appeals, took the *Probats* " of Wills, demanded Accounts of Executors and Adminiftrators, efpecially, " of the Wills of deceafed Bifhops, and of the Adminiftrations of their Goods. " In particular, he compell'd the Executors of the laft Will of Archbifhop " *John Peckham*, to give in their Accompts. Befides thefe things, he vifited, " received Procurations, celebrated a Synod, cited the Clergy to Parliament " by the King's Mandate, punifhed the contumacious, and thofe that were " difobedient againft his Jurifdiction, and collated to the Benefices of vacant " Sees. Befides thefe things, he claim'd, as the Rights of his Church of *Can-* " *terbury*, the Choral Copes, Rings, and Seals from every Suffragan Bifhop of " the Province of *Canterbury*, and he exercifed all manner of Archiepifcopal " Jurifdiction in every Inftance thereof; fo that he omitted no one particular " thereof, except in the Confecration of Bifhops, which, becaufe he could " not perform in his own Perfon, by his own Authority, he iffued forth his " Mandate and Injunction to the Bifhop of *London*, that he, together with the " reft of the Bifhops of the Province of *Canterbury*, being affembled in the

---

(*a*) *Unde omnia temporalia ejus confifcata funt, & quod horrendum eft, quicquid habebant Monachi ibidem infra portas fuæ ecclefiæ, feifita funt, ita quòd non haberent ad quod manus apponerent prò vitæ neceffariis, nifi quod vicini eorum Religiofi, & alii mittebant eis intuitu charitatis, & hoc tam diu duravit, donec Prior & Capitulum neceffitate compulfi redemptionem fecerunt, &c.* Reyner in Append. ad Apoftolat. Benedict. pag. 62.   (*b*) *Erat eo tempore Prior Cantuarienfis quidam Henricus, vir ut exiftimari convenit, mi- nus rerum ufu, quàm jure ipfo prudens, juriumque Cantuarien. Ecclefiæ vacante fede quòd ab anteceffioribus fuis neglecta videbantur, explorator fedulus atque fagax, tum in gerendis ecclefiæ rebus affiduus atque folers. Hic paucis menfibus omnem illam intermediam Jurifdictionem ante intermiffam plenè exercuit atque renova- vit. De Clericis ad ecclefiaftica beneficia præfentatis & patronorum Jure diligenter inquifivit, electiones con- firmavit, inteftatorum bona adminiftranda commifit, provocantium appellationes recepit, teftamenta actis in- finuavit, ab executoribus & adminiftratoribus rationes exegit, inter quos maximè Epifcoporum defunctorum teftamentorum executores, aut bonorum adminiftratores interpellavit. Ita ut Johannis Peckam (ut in ejus vita diximus) teftamentum exequentes ad rationes reddendas coegit. Ad hæc vifitavit, procurationes perce- pit, Synodum celebravit, Cleram ex mandato Regio ad Parliamentum citavit, contumaces & in fuam jurif- dictionem committentes pœnis coercuit, beneficia vacantium fedium contulit, ad hæc capas choreales, annulos & figilla à fingulis Cant. provinciæ Suffraganeis Cant. eccl. vendicavit, omniaque ad Archiepifcopalem Jurif- dictionem per fingulas fpecies tam exquifitè exercuit, ut nihil fuerit prætermiffum prater Epifcoporum confe- crationem, quam cum fua authoritate peragere non poterat, Epifcopo Londinenfi mandavit & injunxit, ut is fuffraganeis Cantuaria in Chrifti ecclefia die quodam ftatuto congregatis Menevenfem & Bangorenf. Epifcopos tunc electos & fua authoritate confirmatos confecraret. Quibus fic confecratis in teftimonium & fidem confecra- tionis literas conventus figillo figillatas dedit, &c.* Antiq. Britan. pag. 217.

" Church

" Church of *Canterbury*, upon a certain day appointed for that purpofe, fhould
" confecrate the Bifhops of St. *David's* and *Bangor*, then elect and confirm'd
" by his own Authority : And when they were thus confecrated, he gave
" them Teftimonial Letters of their Confecration, fealed with the Seal of the
" Convent, *&c.*

Richard Oxinden. 25.

Richard Oxinden fucceeded *Henry*. Who is the firft of all the Priors (except *Wibert*) that hath any Memorial of his Burial in the Church ; and that you fhall find to be in St. *Michael's* Chapel, upon a plate of Brafs faftned to and upon the Eaft-wall, bearing the Infcription which is in the *Appendix*, Numb. LV. a.   *Anno Dom.* 1322.

Johannes de Teneth (*Thanetenfis*, *Pitfeus* calls him) a man famous for his Piety and Learning, was a Monk of this place contemporary with this our Prior, and Chantor of the Church, (an Office of great account in thofe days) you may find him a Witnefs to *Henry* the preceding Prior's Letters, or Faculty of Notaryfhip, before mentioned.   Chantor.

Robert Hathbrand. 26.

Robert Hathbrand fucceeded *Richard Oxinden*, and having been Prior 32 years died, and was buried in the fame Chapel with his Predeceffor ; where he hath the like Memorial, infcribed, as in the *Appendix*, Numb. LV. b.   1338.

In his time the Monaftery being vifited with the Peftilence, then raging generally throughout the Kingdom, the whole Convent, almoft, died of it. *Appledore* Marfhes were inned in his time, to wit, *Anno* 1349. which coft the Church 350 *l.* (*a*).   *Appledore* Merfhes inned.

1370. Richard Gillingham. 27.
1376. Stephen Mongeham. 28.

Of thefe two, befides their Names, and Times in which they lived, as yet I find not what to fay.

John Finch. 29.

Of this Prior's Acts, or what he did living, I have feen no Monument, but that of him dead, you may find in the *Martyrdom* ; where he lies interred under this broken Epitaph, which is in the *Appendix*, Numb. LV. c.   1377.

I have feen a Bull of Pope *Urban* VI. to this Prior, (*b*) *of the Mitre, Tunic, Dalmatic, Gloves, and the Ring* ; [Epifcopal Enfigns, which were granted him and his Succeffors, to wear, by the Pope's Bull. N. B.] To thefe, the Paftoral Staff and Sandals were added, and granted to his Succeffor and the fucceeding Priors for ever ; to be ufed by them in the abfence only of the Archbifhop. From this time, (I take it) and becaufe thefe were Badges of Epifcopal Power and State, they and their Succeffors were (and are called) Lord-Priors. *Stephen Birchynton* was a Monk of this Church in thofe days. *Pitfeus* calls him *Stephen Brickington* ; and faith he wrote the Lives of the Archbifhops of *Canterbury*, all, until *Courtney* ; and a Catalogue of the Bifhops of *Ely*.   1378.   Lord Prior.

Thomas Chillenden. 30.

Thomas Chillenden (whom Archbifhop *Parker* by miftake calls *Henry Chillenden*, and fo doth Bifhop *Godwyn* from him) fucceeded *John Finch*. Concerning this worthy Prelate I have (as occafion was offered) fpoken much already in my Survey of the Church, unto which he was a matchlefs Benefactor, and deferves eternal memory for it ; wherefore, I will be fparing of much further difcourfe of him or his Acts. He was a man well beloved of Archbifhop *Courtney*, but more dear unto his Succeffor *Arundel*, (who made him his Commiffary of *Canterbury*) and lies hard befide him in the Nave or Body of the Church, a ftately Pile, and chiefly of his raifing ; as I have at large fhewed you before. And what faith his Epitaph ? See the *Apendix*, Numb. LV. d.   1390.   Body of *Chrift-Church* new built.

William Gillingham, a Monk of this Church, was Coætaneous with this Prior ; of whom you fhall find great commendation given by *Pitfeus*.

John Woodnesborough. 31.

John Woodnesborough fucceeded *Tho. Chillenden*. See this man's Courtefy to the City by what is taken from the Records of the Church, and added to the *Appendix*, Numb. LVI.   1411.

[I will give you in fhort the occafion of the lending this Aid to the City at

---

(*a*) *Lib. Ecclef. Cant.*   (*b*) *De mitra, tunica, dalmatica, cirothecis, cum annulo.*

this time. *Anno* 1415, which was the third year of the Reign of *Henry* V. The King had prepared an Army with a purpose to enter into *France* and to recover his Rights in that Kingdom. The *French* sent the Earl of *Vendoſm*, the Archbiſhop of *Bourges* and others in an Embaſſy to treat of Peace. They being attended with 350 Horſes, Landed at *Dover* and went to *Wincheſter* and *Southampton*, where the King then was. The Treaty was ſoon broke off, and the *French* were ordered to return home. Now to prevent all danger of a ſurprize in their return through *Canterbury*, the Bailives of this City ſet a watch and guard. To ſtrengthen this Guard the Prior of *Chriſt-Church* armed of their Servants and Vaſſals 16 Spearmen and 24 Bow-men ; and the Abbat of St. *Auguſtin* likewiſe lent them 9 Spearmen and 24 Bowmen , all well accoutred and furniſhed with compleat Arms ; which was indeed as much to the ſafety of thoſe Churches, as of the City it ſelf. *N. B.*]

This Man continued Prior about 17 years, and then dying was laid next above his predeceſſor *Chillenden*, in the body of the Church, with this Epitaph. See the *Appendix*, Numb. LV. *c.*

John Langdon a famous Monk of the place was contemporary with this *Prior*, of whom ſee further in *Pitſ*.

William Molaſh. 32.

Anno Dom. 1427. *Godwin.*

William Molaſh ſucceded *Woodnesb* : The Tower now called *Dunſtan*-Steeple, built for the moſt part by Archbiſhop *Chichely*, being finiſhed, this Prior in the year 1430, furniſhed it with a goodly Bell remaining there till this day, and known by the name of Bell *Duſtan*, as the Steeple is alſo from thence. The *Diameter* of that Bell at the loweſt brim (ſaith my Author) is two Yards and ſomewhat more. He alſo the year following beſtowed on the Church-Brewhouſe a great Cauldron of the Weight of Five thouſand four hundred and three quarters, as I find noted in a book of the *Church*.

John Salesbury. 33.

1437.

This *Prior* lyeth buried at the upper end of the body of the Church with this Epitaph. See the *Appendix*, Numb. LV. *f.*

John Elham. 34.

1440.

He lies next above his Predeceſſor *Woodnesborough*, under a fair ſtone with this *Epitaph*, which is in the *Appendix*, Numb. LV. *g.*

Thomas Goldſtone. 35.

1448.

This Man in behalf of himſelf and his Convent appealed to the then Commiſſary of *Canterbury*, for Juſtice againſt a certain foul mouthed abuſive Fellow, who (as he ſtands charged upon Record) *ann.* 1452, had called them *Whoreſons* and *farting Monks*. He lieth buried in the Lady-Chapel, but the Braſs is almoſt all torn from his Monument. *John Stone* a moſt pious Monk of the place was contemporary with this Prior, of whom ſee *Pitſ*.

1468. John Oxney. 36.
1471. William Petham. 37.
William Selling. 38.

1472.

Being a Monk of this Church, with leave of the Chapter he gat him over into *Italy*, ſtudied at *Bononie*, and became a great Scholar. Out of his affection to Antiquities he gathered together where ever he came in *Italy* all the ancient Authors, both *Greek* and *Latin*, he could get , and brought them over into *England* and to *Canterbury*. Not long after his return, by the common vote and ſuffrage of the Monks, he was choſen for their *Prior*. Shortly after his death

Harpsfield.

Priory fired.

by a fire which happened in the Monaſtery in the Night time by the careleſneſs of ſome drunken Servants, thoſe brave Books (which *Lambard* by error ſaith were brought over by a Monk of St. *Auſtin's*) amongſt which were *Tully's* Books *de Republica* ſo much deſired, and many other of great Price, were brought to Aſhes. *Henry* VII. taking notice of his worth, ſent him Embaſſador to the Pope. He died *ann.* 1494. and lieth buried in the *Martyrdom* with this Epitaph, which *Wever* hath curtail'd, but is now reſtored intire in the *Appendix*, Numb. LV. *h.*

Thomas Goldſtone. 39.

1495. *Harpsfield.*

Thomas Goldſtone ſucceeded *Selling*. He was a man alſo which had his Prince's Favour. For *Henry* VII. ſent him Embaſſador to *Charles* the *French* King. He is in nothing more famous than for his much building, and repairing of and about the Church, as (for inſtance) the new building of the Tower or Lantorn of the Steeple now commonly called *Bell-Harry-*Steeple, as alſo of the

Church-

Church-gate (ftately Piles both) and many other like pious Works, which are eafy of difcovery by the three Gold Stones, the two firft letters of his Name and Sirname, the *Miter* and *Paftoral*-Staff fet up in many places about the Church and Monaftery. He continued his government almoft 25 years, and dying *ann.* 1517 was laid by his immediate Predeceffor in the Martyrdom, with an Epitaph, (which *Wever* alfo hath curtail'd), in the *Appendix,* Numb. LV. *i.*

Thomas Goldwell. 40.

Thomas Goldwell fucceeded *Tho. Goldftone,* and was the laft Prior of the Church of *Canterbury,* governing the fame untill the year 1540, at what time this Priory was diffolved, and the Prior and Monks ejected and difplaced by *Henry* VIII. who, in lieu of them, placed a Dean and twelve Prebendaries. The names of the Deans it fhall not be amifs here to fet down.

Anno Dcm. 1517.

    1. *Nicholas Wotton,* Dr. of Law.
    2. *Thomas Godwyn,* Dr. of Divinity.
    3. *Richard Rogers,* Suffragran of *Dover.*
    4. *Thomas Nevill,* Dr. of Divinity.
    5. *Charles Fotherby,* Batchelor of Divinity.
    6. *John Boys,* Dr. of Divinity.
    7. *Ifaac Bargrave,* Dr. of Divinity

At the time of which new foundation of the Church by *Henry* VIII. the common Seal thereof was again changed and new made. [And whereas now for a long time together, the Church's ancient name (of *Chrift-Church*) had (*a*) actually given place to that upftart, adventitious, nick-name of St. *Thomas-Church* : *Becket's* Fame now falling with his Shrine, the Church (*b*) recovers and reaffumes her ancient Name and Cognizance, the which is fet forth in this new Seal, whereon not *Becket's* Murder as in the former, but our Saviour's Crucifixion is reprefented with this Infcription in the circumference on that fide thereof (*c*) ; *I am the Way, the Truth, and the Life, in the year of the Incarnation of Chrift,* 1540. whilft the new Founder is thus memoriz'd on the other (*d*). *The Seal of the Cathedral and Metropolitical Church of* Canterbury *newly erected by King* Henry *VIII.* W. S.] Which was the Church's fourth and laft common Seal, and continueth ftill in ufe, being not fo large as the former, which former was much larger than the next precedent, which was alfo far greater than the firft, which firft was much both of the fame fize and character with that leaden Seal to St. *Auguftin's* Bull or Charter lately fet out by Sir *Henry Spelman* in his Councils, *pag.* 122. And now having fo fit an occafion, it will not be thought impertinent, I hope, if I prefent you with the Infcriptions on the common Seals of that Abby. Whereof I find only two. The one, the fmaller of the two, a very old one, reprefenting on the one fide both the names and pourtraicts of the bleffed Apoftles *Peter* and *Paul,* with this Infcription in the Circumference. (*e*) *This Seal was made in the firft year of* Richard *King of* England. And on the other fide, the Effigies of an Archbifhop in his pontifical Habit (St. *Auguftin* probably meant by it) with this Infcription in the Circumference (*f*) *The Seal of the Church of St.* Auguftin *of* Canterbury *the Apoftle of the* Englifh. The other common Seal, the larger of the two, and of more curious work than the former, reprefenteth on the one fide a Church, and in the middeft of it, both the Name and Effigies of St. *Auftin,* together with the Abbies Arms (*g*) and fome other Embellifhments, with this Infcription in the Circumference, importing that *Auguftin* converted the *Englifh* Nation to Chriftianity (*h*). On the other fide, a Church alfo with the figures of both thofe Apoftles *Peter* and *Paul,* this with a Sword, the other with a Key in his hand, and underneath, (if I miftake not) the Chriftening or Bap-

The Cathedral's fourth and laft Seal.

St. *Auftin's* common Seals.

(*a*) *De facto.*   (*b*) (As it were *jure poftliminii.*)   (*c*) *Ego fum via, veritas, & vita. Anno incarnationis Chrifti,* 1540.   (*d*) *Sigill. Ecclefie Cathedr. & Metrop. x. Cant. noviter erecte per Regem Hen* 8   (*e*) † *Hoc figillum factum eft anno primo Henrici* [*Ricardi*] *Regis Anglorum.* (*f*) † *Sigill. ecclefie fancti Auguftini Cantuarie Anglorum Apoftoli.*   (*g*) Being a Crofs Argent in a Field Sable.
    (*h*) *Anglia quod domino fidei fociatur amore
    Hoc Auguftino debetur patris honore.*

        tizing

tizing of King *Ethelbert*, by *Auftin*, with this circumfcription in the Ring. *(a)* *The Seal of the Monaftery of the blessed Apoftles*, Peter *and* Paul, *the Companions of* Auguftin *the Apoftle of the* Englifh *at* Canterbury. But I will no longer digrefs.

For a Corollary to this Catalogue, I pray my Reader to take notice that this Prior, was a Lord-Prior, fometime a Spiritual Baron of the Parliament, *(b)* and the Priory whilft it had exiftence, poffeffed of great Revenues, being valued at the fuppreffion (but not to the worth) at 2489 *l.* 4 *s.* 9. *d.* The form of electing and inftalling this Prior, tranfcribed from the Church-Records, he may find in mine *Appendix*, Numb. LVII. And fo this Catalogue alfo being ended, I proceed to the third.

A Catalogue of the Archdeacons of Canterbury.

Original of the Archdeaconry.

FOR your better underftanding the Original of this Archdeaconry, take here, by way of Preface or Introduction to the enfuing Catalogue, the words of Archbifhop *Parker* touching the fame. *(c)* He fays, " Without the " Walls of the City of *Canterbury*, toward the Eaft-fide, is St. *Martin*'s Church, " which was once a Seat of a Bifhop, who was continually refident at his " own Houfe there, or at leaft in fome place within the Diocefe ; performing " in all things the Offices of a Bifhop in the abfence of the Archbifhop, " who, for the moft part, attended the King's Court. The Bifhop, even him- " felf being a Monk, received under obedience the Monks of *Chrift-Church*, " and celebrated in the Metropolitical Church the folemn Offices of Divine " Worfhip, which being finifhed, he return'd to his own place. He and the " Prior, who was then called Dean, of *Chrift-Church*, fat together in Synods, " both alike habited. And this cuftom continued even to the *Norman* times. " And the laft Bifhop of that See was *Godwyn*, who dying in the year 1065, " *Lanfranc* refufed to ordain a Bifhop of St. *Martin*'s Church, faying, that " there ought not to be two Bifhops in one City. Whereas in truth, this was " not a Bifhop within, but without the City. Therefore, inftead of a Bifhop, " he appointed a certain Clerk of his, to be Archdeacon ; of which thing he " repented before he died. Thus he. [Whereas Archbifhop *Parker* fays, *Godwyn* died *Anno* 1065, a *French* MS. Hiftory, written by fome Monk of *Canterbury* about *Edward* II. days, faith, he died in the year 1087. and indeed in the year 1065, *Lanfranc* was not Archbifhop, nor till divers years after. *W.S.*]

Let me further enlarge this matter unto you out of a Record of *Chrift-Church*, which is fomewhat more copious in the relation of it than the former, and is thus entituled : " A Remark, from what time there firft began to be an " Archdeacon of *Canterbury* ; and then follows, " That there was no Archdea- " con of *Canterbury* from *Auguftin*'s to *Lanfranc*'s time, by the fpace of ccclxii " years, but a Bifhop of St. *Martin*'s Church from *Theodore*'s time to *Lanfranc*'s " by the fpace of cccxlix years. But the laft Bifhop of St. *Martin*'s dying, " whilft *Lanfranc* was Archbifhop, *Lanfranc* would not ordain another Bifhop " of St. *Martin*'s, but transferr'd the whole Jurifdiction to *Valerius*, one of his " Clerks ; who was the firft that was entituled, *Archdeacon* of *Canterbury* ; to " whom he gave a fmall Houfe, near the Priory of St. *Gregory*, without the " *Northgate* of the faid City.

[I will here correct two miftakes, occafioned by the faulty Copy which Mr. *Somner* faw : From *Auguftin*'s to *Lanfranc*'s time, we muft compute not ccclxii years, but cccclxii : And from *Theodore*'s to *Lanfranc*'s time, not cccxlix, but cccxcix years ; as I find it in a Manufcript Copy of this Record, in the Arch-

---

(a) *Sigillum monafterii beatorum Apoftolorum Petri & Pauli fociorum Auguftini Anglorum Apoftoli Cantuar.* (b) *Selden's Titles of Honour.* (c) *Extra Civitatem Cantuariæ in parte orientali erat ecclefia fancti Martini, ubi fedes Epifcopi erat, qui domi, vel in Comitatu femper manebat, & vices Archiepifc. (qui Regis curiam frequentabat) per omnia gerebat. Monachos ecclefiæ Chrifti (ac ipfe Monachus) in obfequium accipiebat : folennitates in ecclefia Metropoli celebrabat, quibus peractis ad fua rediebat. Hic & Prior ecclefiæ Chrifti (quam Decanum vocabant) in Synodis pari ornatu confidebant. Atque hic mos ufque ad tempora Normannorum perduravit. ejufque Epifcopi præful extremus fuit Godwinus. Quo mortuo anno fcilicet 1065. Lanfrancus Epifcopum Ecclefiæ beati Martini fubftituere renuit, dicens quòd in una Civitate duo Epifcopi effe non deberent, cum revera in Civitate Epifc. non fuit, fed extra civitatem Is igitur loco Epifcopi quendam Clericum fuum Archidiaconum ordinavit, cujus rei ante mortem eum pænituit. Antiq. Britan. in vita Lanfranci.*

deacon's Black Book, from whence the whole Record fhall be transferr'd into the *Appendix* of the Supplement, entire and correct. *N. B.*]

By the premifes it feems clear, that *Lanfranc* erected the Archdeaconry (and inftituted the firft Archdeacon) of *Canterbury* ; yet I read, that *Almar* (or *Almarus*) the man fo much (and if guilty, worthily) condemned in our Stories for betraying the City of *Canterbury* (befieged by the *Danes*) into their hands, in the Reign of King *Ethelred, Anno* 1011, was Archdeacon of the Church of *Canterbury*, fo was, likewife afterwards, one *Haimo*, who, becaufe of the troubled ftate of his Country, infefted by the *Danes*, for a time forfook his Countrey, and got him over to *France*, where he kept until the times were more quiet and tolerable here at home, and then returning, was welcomed with this dignity. *Harpsfield* mentions both. But befide, long before either of thefe, I find in two *Saxon* Manufcripts in *Chrift-Church*, the one a Codicil or Libel, dated *Anno* 805, the other, the Record or Memorial of a Synod two years before, holden at *Clofeshoaf*, (*Cliff*, befide *Rochefter*) one *Wlfræd* to fubfcribe with the Archbifhop of *Canterbury*, and others of his Church, thus: (a) *Wlfræd Archdeacon.* The fame Records make mention of the names of other Archdeacons afterwards. As

	844.	*Beornoth.*
	853.	*Æthelweald.*
Anno Dom.	864.	*Ealftan.*
	866.	*Sigefreth.*
	Eod.	*Liaving.*
	890.	*Werbeald.*

Let me add, that in the year 1075. eleven years before *Godwyn's* time, (if we follow *Harpsfield's* account, which, queftionlefs, is the truer, for *Lanfranc* was not yet Archbifhop, when, *Parker* faith, *Godwyn* died) to the Inftrument or Record of the Council holden at *London*, (b) *concerning the Primacy of the Church of* Canterbury, &c. next unto the Archbifhops and Bifhops, is this Subfcription : (c) I *Anfchitillus, Archdeacon of the Holy Church of* Canterbury, *have fubfcribed.* How is it true then, that *Lanfranc* founded the Archdeaconry, and made the firft Archdeacon of *Canterbury*? I anfwer, and conceive for truth, that there was a fetled Archdeaconry before *Lanfranc's* days : But he that was Archdeacon of the Church, was withal Bifhop of St. *Martin's* ; that is, befide that of an Archdeacon, was endued with the Title, Power and Office of a Bifhop, or (as I take it rather) of a *Chorepifcopus*, whereby he might, and did (d) act in the ftead of the Archbifhop, or, become his Vicar or Deputy, and fupply his Abfence in many things ; wherein a bare Archdeacon, by his Office, by Law, cannot meddle. Now, *Lanfranc* finding the Cafe thus to ftand, and well knowing that *Chorepifcopi* (both in name and office) were abolifhed abroad, becaufe of their pride, ufurpation, and no very good ground of inftitution at firft, and (as his own reafon is) not liking to have two Bifhops to one City ; *Godwyn*, the Incumbent of that dignity, dying in his time, (as he was a man that much changed the face of things in our Church-Affairs) he changed the *Chorepifcopal* Archdeacon into a Simple Archdeacon, that is, ftript him of his *Chorepifcopal* Title and Power, reftraining the fucceeding Archdeacons power within the limits only of an Archdeacon's Office. (e) *And this is my opinion, which I have offered ; with free leave for any one that can, to propofe a better.* Now to my Catalogue.

Before *Lanfranc's* erection, or change rather, of the Archdeaconry, twelve are all the Bifhops or Archdeacons, whofe names I meet with. *viz.*

1. *Wlfred.*	7. *Werbeald.*
2. *Beornoth.*	8. *Almar.*
3. *Æthelweald.*	9. *Haimo.*
4. *Ealftan.*	10. *Edfin.*
5. *Sigefreth.*	11. *Anfchitillus.*
6. *Liaving.*	12. *Godwyn.*

Whereof the firft , (*Wlfred*) I take it, within few years after that his Sub-

---

(a) *Wifræd Archidiaconus.*   (b) *De primatu ecclefiæ Cantuar. & regulis ecclefiarum.*
(c) *Ego Anfchitillus fanctæ Dorobernenfis ecclefia Archidiaconus fubfcripfi.*   (d) *Vices gerere Archiepifc.*
(e) *Et ita mihi videtur, pace alterius meliùs me fentientis femper falva,*

ſcription, before remembred, became Archbiſhop of *Canterbury*. In the year 807. *Wlfred* being a Monk of *Chriſt-Church* in *Canterbury*, was made Archbiſhop of *Canterbury*, ſaith *Godwyn*. Likely to be this *Wlfred*. For he was always a Monk of *Chriſt-Church*, that was Biſhop of St. *Martin*'s. So *Parker*, as above.

Of the Six next I have nothing to ſay ; unleſs I ſhould note, that in ſubſcribing to a Charter of King *Ethelred*'s, *Beornoth*'s name is ſet before divers Dukes.

Of *Almar*, if you would know more, conſult the Story of the *Daniſh* Siege and ſurpriſal of our City, *Anno* 1011, related by *Roger Hoveden*, and others.

For *Haimo*, let *Balæus* and *Pitſeus* be your further Informers.

As for *Edſin*, I read in the Records of *Chriſt-Church*, that (*a*) *In the Year* 1035. *King* Kanute *gave to* Eadſin, *Biſhop of St. Martin's, which Church is placed without the City of* Canterbury, *on the Eaſt*, Apuldre, Palſtre, *and* Witricham, *for uſe of* Chriſt-Church *in* Canterbury. Whether this were the man, that in the year 1038. was made Archbiſhop of *Canterbury*, I am uncertain : Haply, it was. If ſo, the Catalogue of Biſhops will further inform you of him.

Of the other two, *Anſchitillus* and *Godwyn*, I have ſaid what I know.Wherefore I paſs now to *Lanfranc*'s firſt Archdeacon. Archbiſhop *Parker* names him not, nor yet Archdeacon *Harpsfield* ; but the Church-Record (as you may ſee before) doth, and calls him *Valerius* ; adding, that he was *Lanfranc*'s Clerk. How long this man held the place, I find not ; but he was the laſt of that (the Eleventh) Century.

[Mr. *Somner* has quoted the beginning of a Record, concerning the firſt Inſtitution of the Archdeaconry ; and in the following Catalogue of the Archdeacons, he cites ſeveral pieces thereof, as they occaſionally fall in his way. The ſame Record is to be ſeen whole and entire in the Archdeacon's *Black Book*. Inſtead of inſerting the ſeveral Fragments thereof, as they are placed in Mr. *Somner*, I will tranſcribe the whole Record in the *Appendix* to the Supplement, to which I will refer the Reader. Upon the credit of this Record, Mr. *Somner* has built all that he has written concerning the firſt Inſtitution of the Archdeaconry, which has led him into ſome miſtakes ; particularly, concerning the time, when upon the death of *Godwyn*, there ceaſed to be any more Biſhops of St. *Martin's*. For the Record ſays expreſly, that *Godwyn* died in *Lanfranc*'s time. Hence Mr. *Somner* rejects the Account of Archbiſhop *Parker*, who placeth the death of *Godwyn* in the year 1065, which was five years before *Lanfranc* came to this See. And in the year 1075 , when *Lanfranc* had been five years Archbiſhop, *Anſchitillus* was undoubtedly Archdeacon. So *Godwyn*, in Mr. *Somner's* Catalogue, is placed after *Anſchitillus* : And from a Manuſcript in *French*, *Godwyn* is ſuppoſed to dye *Anno* 1085. All this is mere miſtake. For *Godwyn* died *Anno* 1061, which was no leſs than nine years before *Lanfranc*'s time ; who refuſed to ordain any more Biſhops of that See, which we may call the Diſſolution of that See. Theſe things I ſhall diſcourſe upon more largely in my Supplement ; and offer ſome Reaſons to prove, that no Biſhop of St. *Martin*'s was Archdeacon of *Canterbury*, and that no Archdeacon of *Canterbury* was ever a Biſhop of St. *Martin*'s ; and I will further call the Truth of the whole Record in queſtion, and give ſome probable conjectures, that it is no better than a piece of Forgery, contriv'd by the Monks of *Chriſt-Church*, to ſerve their Ends. I will further undertake to derive the Antiquity of this Archdeaconry from a more honourable, as well as a more Ancient Original, than this Record does allow it to have had. *N. B.*]

Thoſe of the next Century, were the Nine next following.

1. *William.*	6. *Roger.*
2. *John.*	7. *Thomas Becket.*
3. *Aſcelinus.*	8. *Geffrey Ridell.*
4. *Helewiſus.*	9. *Herbert.*
5. *Walter.*	

Whereof *William* was the firſt. For in the year 1101. in the Enquiry whether *Maud*, Daughter of *Malcolme* King of Scots and *Margaret* his Queen, being to be Married to *Henry* I. were a Nun, or had taken on her the Veil and

---

(*a*) *Anno* 1035. *Kanutus Rex dedit Eadſino Epiſcopo Sancti Martini, quæ ecclesia ſita eſt extra Dorobernıam in Oriente, Apuldre, Palſtre & Witricham ad opus ecclesiæ Chriſti Dorobernıa, libere ſicut Adeſham.*

Vow of a Nun, or not, related by *Edmerus* (a), mention is made of one *William* Archdeacon of *Canterbury*, who together with *Humbald* the Archdeacon of *Sarum*,was fent by Archbifhop *Anfelme* to *Wilton* to enquire out the truth of the matter there, it being the place of her Education. He is again afterward, to wit, *anno* 1108. mentioned by the fame Author, *pag*. 96, as ufed and fent by *Anfelme*, on his behalf, to inveft and put into poffeffion of the Bifhoprick of *Rochefter*, *Ralfe*, *Gundulph's* next Succeffor, upon whom *Anfelme* had beftowed the fame. And that is all I read of him, faving a Letter of the fame *Anfelme* directed to him and others about *Priefts* Marriages, mentioned in the Acts and Monuments.

His next Succeffor (and he with whom *Harpsfield* begins his Catalogue) was one *John*, Nephew unto *Ralfe* the Archbifhop, who gave him this Archdeaconry with great and unwonted Solemnity, as *Edmerus* relates it, who faith that (b) " Archbifhop *Ralf* by the advice and at the requeft of thefe Bifhops, " *Richard* of *London*, *Roger* of *Salisbury*, *Herbert* of *Norwich*, *Ralf* of *Chichefter*, " *John* of *Bath*, and *Hervy* of *Ely*, and with the affent and approbation of the " Monks of *Canterbury*, gave the Archdeaconry of this Church to *John*, his " Nephew. Which Donation was made in the Chapter-houfe, the Convent of " Monks being prefent, a great multitude alfo both of the Clergy and Laity " being called together unto this very place for this purpofe. The faid *John* in " the prefence of them all took the Oath of Canonical Obedience to this " Church. In the year 1119, this man was fent by the Archbifhop to the Council then holden at *Remes*, there to withftand the Confecration of *Thurftan* the elect of *York* at the hands of the Pope, who had been rejected of *Ralph* the Archbifhop of *Canterbury*, for refufing to make profeffion of fubjection to his See. How he behaved himfelf in that Province, and what was the iffue thereof, I leave it to *Edmerus* (c), and the Catalogue of Bifhops to inform you. The fame man afterward, to wit, in the year 1125, fucceeded *Ernulph* in the Bifhoprick of *Rochefter*, which he injoyed till his death, which happened *anno* 1137.

Afcelinus or *Asketinus* fucceeded *John*, both firft in the Archdeaconry of *Canterbury* : and afterward (as I take it) in the Bifhoprick of *Rochefter*. For upon the death of *John*, *Afcelinus* (faith the Catalogue of Bifhops) fucceeded, and died *ann.* 1147. Likely to be this Archdeacon. [Here feems to be a miftake, eafy to be corrected. This Archdeacon is never called *Afcelinus* in any Writings that I have feen. Nor did he fucceed in the See of *Rochefter* *John*, who had been his Predeceffor in his Archdeaconry. For the Succeffion of Bifhops in that See about this time was thus : *John* Archdeacon of *Canterbury* was promoted to this Bifhoprick *ann.* 1125, and died *ann.* 1137. He was fucceeded by another, whofe name was *John* and who died *ann.* 1142. Upon his death, *Afceline* formerly *Sacrift* of *Chrift-Church*, and then Prior of *Dover*, but not Archdeacon of *Canterbury*, was conftituted Bifhop of *Rochefter* ; *viz. Anno* 1142, by which time *Asketine* had had two Succeffors in the Archdeaconry (d) N. B.]

Helewifus or *Helvinus* fucceeded. He was fent by Archbifhop *Corboyl* together with the Bifhops of St. *David's* and *Rochefter*, to put the Monks of *Dover* in poffeffion of their new Monaftery built for them by that Archbifhop, in the year 1134, which is all I read of him. *Harpsfield.*

Walter fucceeded him. He was afterward, to wit, in the year 1147, elected Bifhop of *Rochefter*, and was the firft that ever was made Bifhop there by the Monks Election (e). The Archbifhop of *Canterbury* was wont aforetime to nominate to this Bifhoprick whom pleafed him. *Theobald* the Archbifhop beftowed this privilege upon them, by whofe command they chofe this *Walter*, who was the Archbifhop's Brother, for their Bifhop. Which Bifhoprick he held 35 years, and died in the year 1182. [The venerable Compiler of the Antiquities of *Britain*, quoted by Mr. *Somner* in the Margin, fays, That *Theobald* **Bifhoprick of Rochefter made elective.**

(a) *Hift. Novorum lib* 3. *pag.* 57. (b) *Radulphus Archiepifc. confilio & petitione Epifcoporum, proximè fupra nominatorum dedit (concedentibus & approbantibus Monachis Cantuarienfibus) Archidiaconatum ipfius ecclefiæ Johanni nepoti fuo. Quæ donatio facta eft in Capitulo, præfente fratrum conventu, copiofa Clericorum ac Laicorum multitudine, pro hoc ipfo in medium adducta, facto prius, coram omnibus, ab eodem Johanne, tactis Evangeliis, facramento, quo fe fidelitatem ecclefiæ ipfi, per omnia & in omnibus exhibiturum, dum viveret, repromifit. Hift. memor. lib. 5 pag.* 114. (c) *Pag.* 125. (d) *Ang. Sacr.* P. I. *p.* 343. (e) *Antiq. Britan. in Theobald. Godwin. Catal. in Walter.*

R r Confe-

Confecrated this *Walter* Bifhop, being Elected by the Monks of *Roche-fter*, at the command of the Archbifhop. Bifhop *Godwyn* in his Treatife concerning the Bifhops of *England*, miftaking the meaning of the Author juft abovenam'd, tells us, That *Theobald* had transferred the nomination of a Bifhop of *Rochefter* to the Monks of *Rochefter*, which Privilege had from ancient time belong'd to the Archbifhop of *Canterbury*, but was now given away. Mr. *Somner* follows him in this miftake word for word. If the Chronicle of *Gervafe* had been printed at that time, this miftake might have been prevented. For he gives us a true Narrative of this thing, to this Effect. " There was " (fays he) a Cuftom, of moft ancient Date and obferv'd by the Holy Fa- " thers. Namely, That a Bifhop of *Rochefter* ought to be chofen in the Chapter- " houfe of the Church of *Canterbury*, by the Nomination of the Archbifhop " and by the Election of the Convent of the Church of *Rochefter*. After this " manner *Walter* the Brother of the Archbifhop was elected. Here was no beftowing any new Privilege upon thofe Monks; but the Archbifhop referv'd this Right to himself of naming whom he pleafed, to be elected Bifhop of that See. *N. B.*]

He was fucceeded in the Archdeaconry by *Roger*, firnamed (fays *Gervafe* Monk of *Canterbury*) *de ponte Epifcopi*, or of *Bifhop's-bridge*; preferred thereunto by *Theobald* the Archbifhop (as were his immediate Predeceffor and Succeffors:)

Lex talionis.

By whofe means he became afterwards Archbifhop of *York*. Read more of him (if you pleafe) in the Catalogue of Bifhops in *York* : where one thing is chiefly remarkable, *viz.* that whereas in his life time he had procured of Pope *Alexander* this privilege, that if any Clergyman died in his Province, and delivered not his Goods away by hand before his death, the Archbifhop fhould have the difpofition of them ; it pleafed God that the fame meafure he met unto other, he fhould be ferved withal himfelf. He left behind him (or had at leaftwife what time he fickned) 11000 *l.* in Silver, and 300 *l.* of Gold, befide an infinite deal of Plate, and fumptuous houfhold-ftuff. All this (though he had beftowed it to the ufe of the Poor and other good Purpofes) the King notwithftanding feized upon, and converted it to his own ufe, faying it was no reafon that his Will fhould ftand for good, that had difannulled the Teftaments of fo many other.

Godwin.

Being Archdeacon (as he was one that favoured not the Monks of his time) he proved very troublefome and offenfive to them of *Chrift-Church*, by intruding himfelf amongft them, and into their Chapters and Affemblies, as one of the Society. Being no Monk, but a Secular, the Monks could not brook his doings : but addreffing themfelves to the Archbifhop for remedy, they procured of him the Letters, which are remitted into the *Appendix*, Numb. LVIII.

Of this Archdeacon you may fee more in *Richard* Archbifhop of *Canterbury* in the Catalogue afore-cited.

Thomas Becket fucceeded *Roger*. But he that fo favoured him as to bring him to this Dignity, Archbifhop *Theobald*, prevailed fo far with the King for his further advancement, as that, after the acceffion of other preferments, at length *Theobald* dying, this man was felected by the King for his Succeffor. His Story is obvious, wherefore I will not repeat it, and the rather becaufe I have my felf delivered many things of him before in proper place.

Geffrey Ridell fucceeded *Becket* : and was as the 3 former, of *Theobald's* prefer-ring and putting in. He continued Archdeacon until Archbifhop *Becket's* time, whofe ftory mentions him as an Enemy to him and his proceedings, as taking part with the King in his quarrel with *Becket*, who therefore Excommunica-ted him, as you may read in *Roger Hoveden*, who will tell you more of this mat-ter. This Archdeacon afterward was confecrated Bifhop of *Ely*, to wit, *ann.*1174. The often-cited Catalogue in *Ely* will let you know more of him. [Mr. *Som-ner* falls into a great miftake in faying, That he was of *Theobald's* preferring and putting in : And that he continued Archdeacon until Archbifhop *Becket's* time : intimating that he was made Archdeacon, during the life of *Theobald* ; and that *Becket* had laid down his Archdeaconry for fome time, before he was made Archbifhop, thereby making room for *Geofry Ridel* : both which are evidently falfe. The fupplement will correct thefe miftakes. *N. B.*]

Matt. Paris.

Herbert fucceeded him, in the time of *Richard* the Archbifhop, *Becket's* im-mediate Succeffor. Who ('tis faid) made three Archdeacons to his Diocefs, which ufually had but one before. Their names were *Savaricus*, *Nicolaus*, and *Herebertus*. But this held not long, the three being in the fame Archbifhop's
time

time reduced to one again, namely this *Herbert*. To whom the Archbifhop made a perfonal Grant of *Jurifdiction* much like that whereabout the Archbifhop of *York* and the Archdeacon of *Richmond* differed about the fame time; for appeafing of which difference iffued out that Decretal Epiftle of *Innocent* III. *Cap.* I. the firft words whereof are *Cum veniffent. de Inftitutionibus*. Our prefent Archdeacons Grant, which for Antiquity-fake I will infert in the *Appendix*, Numb. LIX. [See alfo the Supplement concerning this Grant.]

Thus much of the Archdeacons of the Twelfth, I come now to them of the next Century, whofe Names and Order were as followeth:

1. *Robert.*	7. *Hugo de mortuo mari.*
2. *Hen. de Caftil.*	8. *Willielmus Middleton.*
3. *Hen. de Stanford.*	9. *Robertus de Gernemutha.*
4. *Simon Langton.*	10. *Richardus de Ferrings.*
5. *Stephan. de Vicenna.*	11. *Johannes de Langtona.*
6. *Stephan. de monte Luelli.*	

For the firft, *Robert*: I read that of Archdeacon of *Canterbury*, he was made Bifhop of *Salisbury*, fucceeding *Hubert* that was tranflated thence to *Canterbury*: in the year 1193. [Bifhop *Godwyn* writes, That *Herbert*, firnam'd the *Poor*, was confecrated Ann. 1194. Bifhop of *Sarum*; He feems to have been called by fome *Robert*, of whom I have nothing to fay, but that he was Archdeacon of *Canterbury*: So he makes thefe two to be one and the fame Perfon; but by what Authority he does it, I cannot conceive. Mr. *Somner* from this paffage runs himfelf into an error; faying, That *Robert* fucceeded in the See of *Sarum*, *Hubert* elected to the See of *Canterbury*. If they were two diftinct Archdeacons, it is certain, *Herbert* fucceeded *Hubert* in the See of *Sarum*; but whether the other was ever Bifhop of *Sarum*, is a matter of doubt. *N. B.*]

The fecond, *Henry de Caftilion*, fucceeded *Robert*, and was Archdeacon in *Hubert* the Archbifhop's time; as I find by divers of his Subfcriptions to Charters and other evidences of St. *Radigund*'s Abby by *Dover*, made by *Hubert* and others. In the year of our Lord 1202, this man being Archdeacon, there happened a great controverfy between King *John* and the Monks of St. *Auguftin*'s touching the right of the Patronage of the Church of *Feverfham*. They were *Feverfham.* fo ftiff and ftout on both fides in the carriage of the bufinefs, that through the Violence that was ufed by the one to out the other of Poffeffion, the Church's Prophanation enfued, whereupon this our Archdeacon challenging right to the cuftody of the Church during the vacancy thereof, interpofeth himfelf, excommunicates the *Monks* for holding the Church by force, overthrows the Altars as thereby profaned, and then interdicts the Church. The *Monks* ftraitway appeal to the *Pope*. He fends out his Commiffion for the full underftanding of the matter: But (faith *Lambard* (a)) the Monks (being now better advifed) took a fhorter way, and fending Prefents to the King, they both obtained at his hands reftitution of their Right, and alfo wan him to become their good Lord and Patron. Notwithftanding, the Archdeacon and they proceeded on in fuit at *Rome*, about the Cuftody and Fruits of their vacant Churches: this and *Milton* efpecially. In which Suit iffued out that Decretal Epiftle of *Innocent* III. beginning thus, *Bonæ memoriæ. de Appellatio.* directed to the Bifhop of *Rochefter* and *London*. I find alfo amongft the Records of *Chrift-Church* a long fcrowl of Witneffes depofitions taken as well on the one part as the other, but what was the iffue or final end of the controverfy I know not, but do guefs (by a like courfe afterward taken with a fucceeding Archdeacon upon this quarrel renewed) he had compofition given him by the Monks, and thereby fome fhare and part with them of the profits of their vacant Churches yielded to him for a Peace. The matter which they ftrove for, was in thofe days of moment and very confiderable, but the cafe is now alter'd by Statute (b), which gives the Succeffor the fruits in the vacancy, and fo hath cutt off fuch brabbles. I have nothing more to fay of this Archdeacon, but that you may find him a Witnefs to Queen *Alinor*'s Charter made to the Monks of *Chrift-Church*, acquitting them of the Cities Walling and Inditching in *Richard* I. time.

I come now to the third Archdeacon of this Century, which was *Henry de Stanford* or *Sauford*, (for I find him written either way, and *Harpsfield* writes

---

(a) Peramb. of *Kent*, in *Feverfham*.   (b) 28 H. 8. 11.

him *Stafford*) elected afterwards to the Bifhoprick of *Rochefter*, and confecrate *Anno* 1227. Being Archdeacon, he took a refignation of *Blean* Church, by the Title of (*a*) the Archbifhop's Vicar, which was Archbifhop *Langton*. He was Coexecutor with the Prior of *Chrift-Church*, of the Lady *Agnes Clifford*'s Will. See more of him in the Catalogue of Bifhops in *Rochefter* (*b*).

This Archdeacon being fo preferr'd; *Stephen Langton* who was then Archbifhop, having to his Brother one *Simon Langton*, (one that was not only out of means, but alfo out of favour both with the King and Pope; the latter by means of the former, giving him the repulfe for the Archbifhoprick of *York*;

Matt. Paris.

to which he was elected by the Chapter there) conferred the Archdeaconry upon him the year before he died. In favour of whom ((*c*) *Flefh and Blood revealing it*, faith a Record in *Chrift-Church*) he much amended the Archdeaconry. For with the confent and confirmation of the Chapter, he annexed

Tenham.
Hakynton.

and united to it, not only the Churches (or Parfonages) of *Tenham* and *Hackington*, but alfo the whole Jurifdiction over the Diocefe, with an exception only and refervation of fome Caufes and Churches. See the Record in the *Appendix* of the *Supplement*, concerning the firft Inftitution of this Archdeaconry. You may fee (if you pleafe) in my *Appendix* (*d*), the double Inftrument of the conveyance of both one and the other.

To compleat and make this Grant abfolute; Whereas *Baldwyn* and *Hubert* his Predeceffors, upon the controverfy between them and the Monks, about the Chapels of *Hakington* and *Lambhith*, upon difpleafure taken againft the Archdeacon (it is like) for oppofing them and their Project in behalf of the Monks, had exempted certain Churches: This *Stephen*, with the Monks confent, by a fpecial Charter reverfeth and revokes that exemption, and fubjects again the Churches to the Archdeacon's Jurifdiction, in fuch manner, as by the Tenor of the Charter copied in my *Appendix*, Numb. LXI. may, and will

Archidiaconal Jurifdiction enlarged.

appear. And then began the Archdeaconry to be enlarged, this Archdeacon being the firft that ever had a real or perpetual Grant made to him and his Succeffors of the Archidiaconal Jurifdiction, whofe Predeceffors never had other than a Perfonal, fuch as was that (before fet forth) made to *Herbert*, or the like.

Thefe things happening in *December*, *Anno Dom.* 1227. In the Month of *February* next following, the fame Archdeacon makes a double Charter to the Monks; whether in confideration of their paffing their confent to the uniting the two forefaid Churches of *Hakynton* and *Tenham* to the Archdeaconry, or wherefore elfe, to me appears not; by the one, conveying to them, with confent of his Brother the Archbifhop, (*e*) *all the Tithes of* Eylwarton, *great and*

Tithery of Telverton.

fmall, lying within the Precincts of the Chapelry of Stone, *in the Parifh of* Tenham; which, at this day, pafs by and under the name of Dominical or Demefne Tithes, *i. e.* Tithes of the Demefnes of that Manor, which is now called *Yelverton*. By the other, becoming ingaged for himfelf and his Succeffors, that nothing fhould be done in the Church or Chapel of *Hackynton*, then there built, or to be built, to the prejudice of the Church of *Canterbury*; a thing which the late ftir between Archbifhop *Baldwyn* and the Monks made them fearful of, and therefore cautious, wary, and careful to prevent; and the rather, becaufe the Archdeacon had now feated himfelf there. For, whereas

Archdeacon's Houfe.

from *Lanfranc*'s until his time, the Archdeacon's dwelling was near St. *Gregory*'s, (*f*) hard by the Court there; it was in this *Simon*'s time removed, and the place given to the Monks of *Chrift-Church*, (haply in confideration of their confent to the Archbifhop's forenoted *Indultums* or Grants made to this Archdeacon) who kept it, as to the propriety of it at leaftwife, until the 25 *Edward* III. and was the fame (I take it) which they then exchanged with the Canons of the place, for other the like of theirs: In the Deed whereof, I find it thus defcribed, *viz.* (*g*) *Their place with the appurtenances, lying between the Court of St.* Gregory's *toward the South, the Lane of* Baggeb, *toward the North, the Garden of* Forgehagh *toward the Eaft, and the Garden formerly of* John

---

(*a*) *Vices gerens Domini Stephani Cantuarienfis. Lib. Hofp. de Eftbridge.*   (*b*) *Ibid. m.*
(*c*) *Carne & fanguine revelante.*   (*d*) Numb LX. *a, b.*   (*e*) *Omnes decimas de Eylwarton majores & minores fitas infra limites parochiæ de Stanes Capella de Tenham.*   (*f*) *Record. Ecclef. Cant.*   (*g*) *Placiam fuam cum pertinen. jacen. inter Curiam S. Gregorii verfus South, venellam de Baggeb verf. North, ortum de Forgehagh verf. Eaft, & ortum quondam Johannis le Gerdeler verfus Weft.*

the Girdler toward the West. The Archdeacon then removing thence, he setled and seated himself (as I said) at *Hakynton*, where his usual residence continued, until that, of late days, the Mansion-house was alienated. Of late days, I say, for I read, that not only Archbishop *Arundel*, in *Henry* V. time dyed at the Archdeacon of *Canterbury* his Mansion-house at *Hakynton*, but that of late in *Henry* VIII. days, Archbishop *Warham* did likewise. But now it is gone, and the Archdeacon, (*a*) *as* Archdeacon, left houseless.

I return to our present Archdeacon, *Simon*, who in the vacancy of the See by Archbishop *Edmund*'s death, withstood *Peter Lumbard* the Monks Official for that time of the vacancy, challenging to himself in right of his Archdeaconry, all the Jurisdiction both Provincial and Diocesan. But at length, after some altercations (*b*) on both parts, all contentions between the Chapter and him in that behalf, were friendly ended by a personal composition, a Copy whereof (that you may see the then state of this Archdeaconry) I purpose in my *Appendix*, Numb. LXII. to set forth. This man, before he was Archdeacon, took part (against King *John*) with *Lewis* the *French* Dauphin, who made him his Chancellor; for whose establishment here he was very active, as you may find more at large in *Matthew Paris*, and others. The Pope, by his Letters, consulted with this *Simon* about *Ralph Nevill*, the Bishop of *Chichester*, and Chancellor of *England*; whom the Monks of *Christ-Church*, to gratify the King who much respected him, had (as the *Canonists* phrase it) postulated for their Archbishop, in the vacancy by the death of *Richard* the Great, whose relation of the man so wrought the Pope against him, that he was put by it, and *Edmund* promoted to the place. Shortly, this Archdeacon founded the Hospital of Poor Priests in *Canterbury*, whereof enough already in proper place, and died about the year 1248, having been Archdeacon 21 years; upon whom *Matthew Paris* bestows this Epitaph. (*c*) " In this year died " *Simon de Langtune*, Brother of *Stephen* Archbishop of *Canterbury*, of famous " Memory, Archdeacon of *Canterbury*. Do not wonder, if he caused distur- " bances in his own Church of *Canterbury*, since he disturb'd both Kingdoms " of *France* and *England*. [We must remember this Character was given him by a Monk. *N. B.*] See more, if you please, of this man in *Pitseus*. *(margin: Matt. Paris.)* *(margin: 1248.)*

Stephanus de Vicenna succeeded *Simon Langton*. So the process of the Suit between his Successor *Richard de Ferrings* and the Chapter, about Title of Jurisdiction, in the vacancy of the See, informs me, which gives a Catalogue of the Archdeacons, and the order of their Succession, from *Simon Langton* down to that *Richard*. He held the place till his death, which, by the computation of that process, was about 10 years. [This computation of 10 years to *Stephen de Vicenna*, will admit of an alteration; for in the Year 1252, the Supplement will add *Othobone* to the Catalogue of Archdeacons. *N. B.*]

But I am persuaded, that one *Stephanus de monte Luelli* ought to have a share with him, of that time allotted to him for his incumbency in that dignity; which that process, omitting this *Stephen*, reckons between the former *Stephen* and *Hugh Mortimer*. For in the year 1257. in the time of Archbishop *Boniface*, I find in a Leiger of St. *Radigund*'s Abby by *Dover*, the subscription of this *Stephanus de monte Luelli*, by the express Title of Archdeacon of *Canterbury*, as (with others) a witness to some Instruments or Charters, made to that Abby by what time, I find that *Hugh Mortimer* was the Archbishop's Official. To whom I pass.

This *Hugh Mortimer* was first (as I said) Official of *Canterbury*. (*d*) " *Boni-* " *face* being Archbishop elect, and taking Ship to go for *Rome*, commanded " the Woods belonging to his Archbishoprick to be cut down and sold, and " certain Taxes and Impositions to be levied upon the Lands; and constitu- " ted Mr. *Hugh Mortimer*, a Native of the Province of *Poictou*, his Official, *(margin: 1245.)*

(*a*) *Quatenus.*   (*b*) *Hinc inde.*   (*c*) *Sub eodem quoque annali curriculo, obiit Magister Simon de Langetuna, frater præclaræ memoriæ Stephani Cantuariensis Archiepiscopi, Ecclesiæ Cantuariensis Archidiaconus. Qui si Ecclesiæ suæ, videlicet Cantuariensis, persecutor & perturbator fuisset, non est mirandum, quin imò Regnum Francorum, Regnum & Anglorum, quandoque cùm ex multiplici bello vexaretur, sicut sufficienter in loco suo prædictum est, movit, commovit & perturbavit, &c.*   (*d*) *Electus Cantuar. naves ascensurus jussit nemora Archiepiscopatus abscidi & vendi, & quasdam tallias & collectas in terris suis fieri, & constituit quendam suum Officialem natione Pictaviensem, Magistrum Hugonem de Mortimer, qui diligenter mandata sua exequebatur. Florileg.*

" who diligently executed his Commands. He continued Official very long, it seems. For in the Year 1270, I find a decision of his (as Official) of a controversy, wherein the Monks of *Horton* Priory in *Kent*, were interessed, recorded in the Leiger of that House. It seems he was also Chancellor or Vicar-General to the Archbishop. For in the Year 1258, he sends his (*a*) *Mandat of Induction* to the Archdeacon's Official, for the inducting of the Abbat of St. *Radegund* into the Parsonage of *Alcham*, in the Form which is in the *Appendix*, Numb. LXIII.

Afterwards, to wit, about the year 1271, he became Archdeacon, which place he held about 14 years. [Archbishop *Boniface* died 1270. (*b*) At which time *Hugh Mortimer* was in possession of the Archdeaconry, and had been so (as is most probable) ten years before the death of that Archbishop. Upon this Supposition, we may rightly compute the years of his being Archdeacon to have been 14 years; otherwise if he was constituted Archdeacon about the year 1271, he cannot be allowed to have enjoyed that Dignity above 4 or 5 years. *N. B.*] In which time, to wit, in the vacancy of the Archbishoprick by the death of *Boniface*, I find him (*c*) play the *Diocesan*, in appropriating (*d*) by Authority as Ordinary to the *Hospital of Poor Priests* in *Canterbury*, the Parish Church of St. *Margaret* in *Canterbury*, with consent of the Patron, the Abbat of St. *Austin's*. [The like Authority he made use of in consenting to the appropriation of the Church of *Preston* to the Abby of St. *Augustin*, which he ratified, as far as the Power or Faculty of the *Ordinary* is required (*e*). *N. B.*] His challenging of this and the like Power in the time of the Vacancy, begat a quarrel between him and the Monks of *Christ-Church*, the like to that between his Predecessor *Simon Langton* and them, both in the nature and end of it. [See the Record concerning the first Institution of this Archdeaconry in the *Appendix* to the Supplement. *N. B.*] This composition is much like that which you shall find copied in my *Appendix*, made to *Simon Langton*.

William Middleton succeeded *Hugh Mortimer*, and held the place 2 years and upwards. And in the year 1278, was removed thence to the Bishoprick of *Norwich*. Where, in the Catalogue of Bishops you may read somewhat more of him.

Robertus de Gernemutha (or of *Yarmouth*) whom *Fox* calls *Gernemine*, succeeded *William Middleton*, and like his Predecessor continued Archdeacon upward of two years. This man renewed the old quarrel for Jurisdiction in the Vacancy, twice set on foot before, as you may see in *Simon* and *Hugo*; appealing the Monks to the Pope about it. During the dependance of which Appeal in the Court of *Rome*, this Archdeacon died. This Suit happened in the vacancy by *Kilwardby's* remove or translation. See the Record in the *Appendix* to the Supplement.

Ricardus de Ferrings succeeded in the Archdeaconry and held it fifteen years, until he was removed thence to the Archbishoprick of *Dublin* in *Ireland* vacant by the death of one *Ottoninus* (so *Parker* from *Matt.* of *Westminster*) and conferred on him by the *Provision* of Pope *Boniface* VIII. but he died by the way in his return from *Rome*; where, being Archdeacon, he revived the Suit then dormant by the death of his Predecessor, which Suit was hotly prosecuted for a while, but to little purpose. See the *Appendix* to the Supplement.

John Langton (or *Johannes de Langtona*) succeeded *Richard* in the year 1299. which thing came thus to pass (*f*). This *John*, being Chancellor of *England*, first constituted *ann.* 1293, and a second time *ann.* 1307, was by a part of the Convent of *Ely* chosen for their Bishop, and he endeavoured mainly to have his election confirmed: but being disappointed of that Bishoprick, the Pope, *Boniface* VIII. (to whom from the Archbishop who had disannulled his election he appeal'd, but in vain) preferring another to that Bishoprick, in way of recompense of his labour and cost, made him Archdeacon of *Canterbury* in the place of his Predecessor *Ferrings*. This *John* afterwards, to wit, in the year 1305, was made Bishop of *Chichester*, being consecrated by Archbishop *Winchelsey* on the 10th *Kal.* of *Octob.* the same year (*g*). *Harpsfield* reports, that between him

(*a*) *Mandatum ad inducendum.*   (*b*) *Somner.*   (*c*) *Liber Hosp. Pauper. Sacerd. Cant.*
(*d*) *Authoritate ordinaria.*   (*e*) *In quantum ordinariæ facultatis requirit potestas. Thorn.*
(*f*) *Godwin*, Catal. of BB. in *Ely.*   (*g*) *Anno* 1305, 10 *Kal. Octob. Robertus Winchelsey Archiep. consecravit in Ecclesia Cant. Dom. Johannem de Langtone Archidiaconum Cant. in Episcopum Cicestrensem*

and both the Archbishop and Monks arose certain controversies about (the old quarrel) *Jurisdiction* in the Sees vacancy. But I suppose he mistakes him in this for his predecessor *Ferrings.* See more of him in the Catalogue of Bishops in *Ely* and *Chichester,* as also in *Harpsfield, Century* 13.

Thus have I briefly run over the 11 Archdeacons of this 13*th Century.* A greater number (if you mark) than *Harpsfield* reckons upon: who of these names only *Simon, Henry, William, Richard* and *John.* He adds *Robert Winchelsey,* but errioniously. Indeed he was Archdeacon of *Essex,* but of *Canterbury* never that I can find. Now let us on to those of the next *Century.* viz.

1. *Simon de Feversham.*	9. *Petrus Rogerius.*
2. *Bernardus de Eyci.*	10. *Henricus Wakefield.*
3. *Gutterdus Labredus.*	11. *Willielmus.*
4. *Simon Convenius.*	12. *Audomarus de Rupy.*
5. *Johannes Brutonius.*	13. *Willielmus Packington.*
6. *Raymundus.*	14. *Adam de Mottrum.*
7. *Hugo de Engolisma.*	15. *Ricardus Clifford.*
8. *Robert Stratford.*	

Harpsfield begins this *Century* with *Bernardus,* ranking him next Successor to *John Langton.* But I find one between them, namely, *Simon de Feversham*: to whom Archbishop *Winchelsey* gave the Archdeaconry vacant by *Langton's* remove to the Bishoprick of *Chichester.* For the last cited Record goes on thus. (*a*) *And the same day he gave to Mr.* Simon *of* Feversham *the Archdeaconry of* Canterbury. Which is all I read of him, saving the testimony given him by *Pitseus* (*b*).

Of *Bernard,* I read that in the year 1313, when the See of *Canterbury* was void by Archbishop *Winchelsey's* death, this man was Archdeacon, and that he suffered the *Chapters* then *Official* quietly to hold and exercise all manner of Jurisdiction belonging to the See. The Record is in the Supplement to the *Appendix.*

For the next three, I find they did successively hold the Archdeaconry in the time of *Walter Reynolds* the Archbishop, and that is all: saving that the Records of the *Cathedral* have a Bull of Pope *John* xxii. thus intituled (*c*) *A Bull to recall the Collation of the Archdeaconry of* Canterbury *made to* John de Bruiton *by the Archbishop, and that it should be conferred upon* Raymond, *of St.* Mary *in* Cosmeden *Deacon Cardinal.* From which *Raymund* I pass unto (I take it) his next Successor,

Hugo de Engolisma. Both in the year 1327, and 1330. I have seen Records (*d*) that stile him Archdeacon of *Canterbury,* adding that one *Petrus de Matre* was his *Proctor* and *Vicar general.* To him *Nicholas Trivet* dedicated his History.

Robert Stratford (I take it) succeeded next. For I find him Archdeacon in his brother *John Stratford* the Archbishop's time. He was Chancellor of *England* first constituted 11 *Edward* III. and again afterwards 14 *ejusd.* How this came to pass you may learn in the Catalogue of Bishops in *Chichester,* to the which Bishoprick he was preferred, succeeding therein his Predecessor in the Archdeaconry, *John Langton.* I have seen (*e*) a Plea of his, consisting of many Articles, and containing in the first place an enumeration or particular of all the Rights and Privileges of his Archdeaconry; after which follows a suggestion of certain grievances offered to him and it by the then *Commissary of Canterbury* put up against him to his brother the Archbishop, with what success I know not, for I cannot find the issue.

Petrus Rogerius sanctæ Mariæ novæ Diaconus Cardinalis, in the year 1356, was Archdeacon of *Canterbury* (*f*), and *Stratford's* next Successor (I take it:) whose absence was supplyed by one *Hugo Pelegrinus,* who thus writes himself. (*g*) Hugh Pelegrin *Treasurer of* Lichfield, *Nuncio of the Apostolical See to* England, *Vicar General in Spirituals to the Reverend Father in Christ* Peter Rogerius *Archdeacon of* Canterbury, *Cardinal Deacon of the Holy Church of* Rome.

(a) *Et eodem die dedit Magistro Simoni de Feversham Anchidiaconatum Cantuar.* (b) *De illust. Angl. Scriptor. ætate* 14. *pag.* 505. (c) *Bulla revocationis collationis Archidiaconatus Cant. fact. magistro Johanni de Bruiton per Archiepisc. ut conferatur Raymundo sanctæ Mariæ in Cosmedin Diac. Card. per Johannem Papam.* (d) *Lib. Hosp. Pauper. sacerd.* (e) *In Archivis Consistorii Cant.* (f) *Lib. Hosp. Pauper. sacerd.* (g) *Hugo Pelegrinus Thesaurarius Lickfield Apostolica sedis in Anglia Nuntius Reverendi Patris in Christo Domini Petri Rogerii sanctæ Mariæ novæ Diaconi Cardinalis Archidiaconi Cantuar. Vicarius in spiritualibus generalis.*

In the Vacancy of the See by the death of *William Wittlefey, ann.* 1374, one *Henry* of *Wakefield* was made Archdeacon by the then Prior and Convent of *Chrift-Church* (*a*), who fwore them Canonical Obedience (*b*) during the Vacancy.

In the year 1379. 2 *Richard* II. *Fox* (*c*) mentioneth two Archdeacons of *Canterbury.*

Thus the one.

Lord William *of the Holy Church of* Rome *Cardinal, a ftranger, doth hold the Archdeaconry of* Canterbury, *and is not refident, the true value of all the yearly Fruits, Rents, and Profits, is worth feven hundred Florens.* [He was Archdeacon before *Henry* of *Wakefield*. N. B.]

Thus the other.

Lord Audomar de Rupy *is Archdeacon of* Canterbury, *to the which Archdeacon belong the Church of* Lymin *within the fame Diocefs, worth by year after taxation of the tenth* XX *l. The Church of* Tenham *worth by year after the faid taxation,* Cxxx *l.* vi *s.* viii *d. The Church of* Hakington *near* Canterbury *, worth by year twenty Marks. The Church of St.* Clement *in* Sandwich, *worth by year after the taxation aforefaid, eight Marks. The Church of St.* Mary *in* Sandwich, *worth by year eight Pounds, of the which the faid Archdeacon receiveth only fix Marks. The Profits of all which premiffes Sr.* William Latimer *Knight hath received, together with the Profits arifing out of the Jurifdiction of the Archdeaconry, worth by year* XX *l.*

Afterwards, to wit, in the year 1381, one *William* of *Packington*, or (as *Pitfeus* writes him) *Pachenton*, had the Archdeaconry conferred upon him by the then Prior and Convent (*d*) in the vacancy by *Sudbury's* death: his Proctor making and taking the accuftomed Oath of Obedience to the Prior and Convent; and that he will not attempt any thing to the Prejudice of the Church of *Canterbury*, and will faithfully execute fuch mandates as he fhould receive from the Prior and Chapter. *Pitfeus* will further acquaint you with this man, and his great worth, and good parts, if you confult him.

In Archbifhop *Courtney's* time (*Sudbury's* next Succeffor) one *Adam de Mottrum* was Archdeacon, and withall the Archbifhop's Chancellor, as I find by *Courtney's* Will extant in *Chrift-Church*, wherein he is a Legatary.

He was fucceeded by *Richard Clifford*, who was Archdeacon in Archbifhop *Arundel's* days. *Harpsfield* (*e*) tells of a Controverfy that happened to arife between the Archbifhop and him about matter of Jurifdiction, but it was compounded (*f*). The compofition is extant (for I have feen both Prototype and Copy) in the Church Records. The Lieger of the Confiftory hath alfo a Tranfcript of it. He was afterward confecrated Bifhop of *Worcefter*, to wit, *ann.* 1401, and tranflated thence to *London ann.* 1407. See more of him there in Bifhop *Godwyn's* Catalogue who fpeaks very honourably of him. I find his Name and Picture drawn and fet up in the Weft-Window of the Chapter-houfe of *Chrift-Church*, as in likelihood, a Benefactor to the work, it being new built in his time, as you may find elfewhere.

For that was the way by which the religious men ufed to exprefs their thankfulnefs to their Benefactors, namely, by reprefenting their Effigies, and fetting up their Names, their Coats alfo that had any, in fome part of that building, which by their Bounty they had help to advance; fometimes adding withal their gift and largefs, what and how much it was: as for inftance in that particular, in the Cloifter, hard by the door of the Chapter-houfe, about the Shield of a Coat reprefenting the Effigies of a Monk in his Habit, one that about the fame time with this Archdeacon, was a Benefactor to that work, I read as followeth, (*g*) That, John Shepene, *with the help of his friends gave* 100 l. *to the building of the Cloifter*, &c.

I have done with the Archdeacons of this fourteenth *Century*, and come now to them of the next, by name,

---

(a) *Lib. Ecclef Cant.*   (b) *Vacatione durante.*   (c) Acts and Mon. *Par.* 1. *pag.* 562. *Ex bundello brevium Regis de Anno* 2 *Rich.* 2 *par* 1.   (d) *Lib. Ecclef. Cant.*   (e) *Hift. Ecclef. Angl. Sæcul.* 15 *cap.* 14 *pag.* 634   (f) *Ricardo controverfia quædam, de exercenda Jurifdictione, cum Arundellio interceffit, quæ certa tranfactione, mutuo ipforum confenfu compofita eft.*

(g) *Frater Johannis Schepene, cum adjutorio amicorum fuorum contribuit ad fabricam clauftri C. lib. cujus anima propitietur Deus. Amen.*

1. *Robertus* (*a*) *Hall.*
2. *Johannes Wakering.*
3. (*b*) *Thomas Rumnoth.*
4. *Willielmus Chichley.*
5. *Prosper de Columna.*

6. *Thomas Chichley.*
7. *Thomas Wittembourne.*
8. *Johannes Bourgchier.*
9. *Hugo Pentwin.*

The first of these ((*c*) *Hall*) was (as *Harpsfield* says) Archbishop *Arundel's* Vicar General.

The second, *Wakering*, was Keeper of the Privy Seal (saith Sir *Henry Spelman*) to *Henry* IV. (*d*) Secretary, saith *Harpsfield*; and in the year 1416 he was Elected and Consecrated Bishop of *Norwich*. *Godwyn* writes very honourably of him, as you may see in his Catalogue in *Norwich*.

The third, *Rumnoth* (*e*), questioned and called before him *John* Bishop of St. *Assaph*, as not legally holding his Bishoprick, being never inducted or put into possession by his Predecessor *Robert*, as the manner was, and of right he should have been, it being one of the Rights of the Archdeacon to induct all Bishops of the Province into the possession of their Sees.

The fourth, *William Chichley* (*f*), being Archbishop *Chichley's* near Kinsman, was by him made Archdeacon, what time he was with the King in the *French* expedition. This *William* being a Notary of the Apostolick See, and dying in the Court of *Rome*, Pope *Martin* V. bestowed the Archdeaconry upon his Nephew *Prosper de Columna*, a Boy under fourteen years of age, and richly provided for before by the Pope his Uncle, but not to the content of the Pope's avaritious Mind; who so prevailed with the King, that his Nephew being an alien, and so incapable of the dignity by the Laws of the Realm, he was by Royal indulgence indenized and made capable of the same, but so as the Pope should by his Bull, (*g*) in express words, give way to the Patron freely to confer it afterward, as it should fall void, and that this indulgence should not be drawn into example. This Archdeacon after a few years was made a Cardinal.

The sixth, *Thomas Chichley*, had the Archdeaconry afterward conferred upon him by the same Archbishop *Henry Chichley*, his near Kinsman also. In an Exemplification of his (which I have seen) belonging to St. *John's* Hospital without *Northgate*, I find him style himself thus: (*h*) Thomas Chichley, *Doctor of the Canon Law, Archdeacon of* Canterbury, *and Prothonotary of the Lord the Pope.* In the year 1463, he was Provost of *Wingham* College in *Kent* (*i*).

The seventh and ninth I know only by their names. For as yet I find nothing at all written of them.

The eighth, *John Bourgchier*, was (I take it) Brother or near Kinsman to the Archbishop *Thomas Bourgchier*. He died in the year 1495, and was buried in the Lady-Chapel of *Christ-Church*, where you may find his Monument. I have transcribed the Inscription or Epitaph upon it before in the Survey of the Church Monuments. The Windows of this Chapel where he lies are very full of the *Bourgchier's* Arms.

Thus much very briefly of the Archdeacons of the fifteenth *Century*. I come now to those of the next, by name.

1. *William Warham.*
2. *Edmund Cranmer.*
3. *Nicholas Harpsfield.*
4. *Edmund Guest.*

5. *Edmund Freake.*
6. *William Redman.*
7. *Charles Fotherby.*

The first, *William Warham*, was Archbishop *Warham's* Kinsman, in whose House (*k*) then situate at *Hakintgon*, the Archbishop died. He was withal *Provost* of *Wingham*. For the cause (it's like) of his Conscience, by *Cession*, as the *Canonists* phrase it, he left both it, and the Archdeaconry, and by the privity and consent of the then Archbishop (*Thomas Cranmer*) had a Stipend or Pension of 60 *l. per ann.* allowed him during his life, out of the Archdeaconry, and 20 *l. per ann.* out of his Prepositure of *Wingham* (*l*),

By his Successor in both, *Edmund Cranmer*, Archbishop *Cranmer's* Brother,

---

(*a*) [*L. Hallum.* N. B.] (*b*) [*L. Henry.* N. B.] (*c*) [*L. Hallum.* N. B.]
(*d*) *Regi ab archivis sive scriniis.* (*e*) *Harpsfield ubi supra.* (*f*) *Idem Harpsf. ubi sup.*
(*g*) *Conceptis verbis.* (*h*) *Thomas Chicheley, decretorum Doctor, Archidiaconus Cant. & Domini Papæ Prothonotarius.* (*i*) *Liber testam. penes registr. Domini Archid. Cant.* (*k*) *Antiq. Brit. in ejus vita.* (*l*) *Ex Registro Cranmeri.*

who

who continued Archdeacon afterward until Queen *Mary*'s days, and was then deprived of it, his Prebend alſo, and Parſonage of *Ickham,* which were all taken from him in the year 1554, for being a Married Clerk, and the firſt given to *Nicholas Harpsfield* Doctor of Law, the ſecond to *Robert Collens* Batchelor of Law and Commiſſary of *Canterbury,* and the third to one *Robert Marſh* (*a*).

Concerning *Harpsfield, Fox,* a Proteſtant, and *Pitſeus,* a Papiſt, give their ſeveral Cenſures : but clearly (*b*) contrary, and ſo full (I fear) of partiality, and by their reflexion upon the cauſe of Religion, ſo prejudicate, that I leave it to the moderate to give a temper to them both, not deſirous to interpoſe my judgment, but wiſhing only he may be cenſured with truth and indifferency. He was withal a Prebendary of *Canterbury* whom Doctor *Moulin,* after many other, doth ſucceed. Being a Priſoner, he wrote the *Eccleſiaſtical Story* of England, and other Books, whereof ſee a Catalogue in *Pitſeus.*

Harpsfield in the beginning of Queen *Elizabeth*'s Reign, being deprived, *Edmund Gueſt* ſucceeded in the Archdeaconry, and ſhortly after, to wit, *Ann.* 1559. was conſecrate Biſhop of *Rocheſter,* and tranſlated thence to *Salisbury Anno* 1571. Where you may ſee more of him in the Catalogue of Biſhops.

His next Succeſſor was *Edmund Freake,* both in the Archdeaconry, and alſo in the Biſhoprick of *Rocheſter,* with which latter he held the Archdeaconry in *Commendam,* until he was afterward removed to *Norwich,* and from thence to *Worceſter.* The fore-cited Catalogue will tell you more of him.

William Redman ſucceeded in the Archdeaconry, but in the year 1594, was removed to the Biſhoprick of *Norwich.* Conſult the often cited Catalogue in *Norwich,* if you would know more of him.

Charles Fotherby upon *Redman*'s remove to *Norwich* was made Archdeacon, and afterwards *Dean of Canterbury*: both which with other Spiritual Livings beſides, he held till his death, which happened *Anno Domini* 1616. He lyeth buried in the Lady-Chapel in *Chriſt-Church*; and, *Bourgchier* excepted, who lies buried in the ſame Chapel, is the only Archdeacon of *Canterbury,* that by any Monument or Record appears to have been buried in *Chriſt-Church.* He was (you ſee) the laſt of that *Century*; as the modern Archdeacon, the reverend Dr. *Kingſley,* is the firſt of the next, and makes the 59*th* Archdeacon. But (*c*) I forbear. And here let me cloſe this diſcourſe of the Archdeacons with a touch of that *Prærogative* anciently belonging to them, of putting the *Suffragan-Biſhops* after their conſecration or tranſlation to a Biſhoprick, in poſſeſſion of the ſame, (which we vulgarly call *induction* or *inſtallation*) together with ſuch Rights and Fees as were uſally paid unto the Archdeacon in reſpect thereof. Their private Leiger called (from the ſable Cover) the black Book, ſets forth the matter at large; but affecting brevity, I have choſen rather to repreſent it in Archdeacon *Harpsfield*'s more compendious way. He writes to this effect, (*d*)" That the Archdea-
" con of *Canterbury* has this prerogative to inſtall or inthronize all Biſhops,
" namely, within the Province of *Canterbury.* And he uſually went in Perſon
" to perform this Solemnity: At which time he received as his Fee, the Bi-
" ſhop's Horſe and Furniture and twenty Pieces of Gold. It was the cuſtom
" alſo for the Biſhop at the Table in Dinner-time to drink to the Archdeacon
" in a Cup of Silver, ſometimes gilt, and the Archdeacon received the Cup
" as his Fee. But of late years, the Archdeacon has not gone in perſon to in-
" thronize Biſhops, but has committed the tranſacting of that Solemnity to
" others by Mandatory Letters, and has received no other Fee, beſides the
" twenty Pieces of Gold. Thus he. And ſo both this Catalogue, and my whole task for the Cathedral is abſolved. [What Mr. *Sommer* contriv'd to relate in a moſt compendious way, The Supplement will preſent to the Reader more fully, not only in this particular, but alſo in the whole Hiſtory of the Archdeaconry and Archdeacons. *N. B.*]

(a) *Lib. Eccleſ. Cant.*　　　(b) *Ex diametro*　　　(c) *Manum de tabella.*　　　(d) *Eſt quidem Cantuarienſis ceterorum in Anglia Archaiaconorum anteſignanus, habetque & hoc etiam ſaculo habuit id prærogativa, ut deſignatos & inuteatos Epiſcopos, quaſi in præſenti rerum omnium poſſeſſione conſtituat. Ad quam poſſeſſionem tradendam, ſolebat ipſe proficiſci ad Epiſcopum in poſſeſſione locandum. Quibus temporibus equum Epiſcopi, & penulum ad ſuos uſus; & viginti præterea aureos* * *ad ſumptus accipiebat. Moris præterea erat, ut ex argenteo aut deaurato quodam poculo Epiſcopus et in menſa præbiberet, acceptumque poculum ad Archidiaconi commodum cederet. Poſterioribus, & noſtris præſertim temporibus, Archidiaconi poſſeſſionem hanc tradendi provinciam aliis per literas mandantes, ipſi non proficiſcebantur, viginti illos aureos ſolummodò ſibi decerpentes. Hiſtor. Eccleſ. Sæcul. 13. pag. 450.*

' 10 *marcas,*
f.ith *Parker.*
Antiq. Britan.
p g. 28.

Parochial Churches.

I Come in the next place, according to my method, to speak of the Parochial Churches in and about the City. Give me leave, before I treat of them in several, (as I mean to do) to premise a few things touching them in general. It is but of a very few of them, that I know or have found the certain either Time or Author of their Foundation. But as I shall shew you, that some of them have been erected since the Conquest; so I conceive (and am verily persuaded) none of them (except St. *Martin's*) do much, if at all, exceed the same in Age, and that for many inducements. One, that before it our Churches were generally built and made of Wood; and it is a thing noted of the *Normans*, that upon their In-come they builded their Churches of Stone (*a*). Another is, that the Saints, whose names some of our Churches do carry, will not bear any much greater age; as St. *Alphege*, St. *Dunstan*, St. *Edmund* the King and Martyr. A third Reason I have, and I take it from a Deed or Charter (*b*) of *Cænulph* King of *Mercia*, and *Cuthred* his Brother, King of *Kent*, made to the Abbess and her Nuns of *Liminge*, and dated *Anno Dom.* 804. granting them a certain parcel of Land in our City, appertaining (saith the Charter or *Landboc*) to a Church situate in the West part of the same, built in honour of St. *Mary*. Now no such Church is, or since the Conquest (that I ever found) was standing in that part of our City. Whence I infer, that the face and condition of our City hath suffered an utter change since those days; and because we read that the *Danes* made havock both of People and Place in King *Ethelred*'s days, slaying the most part of the one, and burning and spoiling all the other, (not sparing the Cathedral it self) I think we may justly charge upon that all-wasting deluge the utter subversion of such Churches as then were in our City, and consequently may not imagine any of our modern Churches (except as is before excepted) so ancient as to precede, but contrariwise to succeed and follow the same. The Deed or Charter, because it may give content to some sort of Readers, and indeed Historically glanceth at the misery that our Country suffered by the frequent invasion of the *Danes*, as I conceive of it, from the end for which this Land was given by it to the Nuns, (being (*c*) *for a refuge in time of distress*) I will subjoin in the *Appendix*, Numb. LXIV.

Now of all the present Churches in and about our City, I find only two that were not of the Patronage of some Abby, or other Religious House, in or near-neighbouring to the City; and they were St. *Martin* without, and St. *Alphege* within the Walls of the City, both appertaining to the See of *Canterbury*. Of St. *Martin*, I have spoken enough already, on a former occasion. Leaving that then, I will make to (the other) St. *Aelphege*; where I meet with the following Monuments. *Appendix*, Numb. LXV.

In the Chancel. *John Piers*, born at *Maidstone*, and Rector of St. *Elphege*. *John Parmenter*, Rector of this Church, *Anno* 1501. This *John* was Commissary of *Canterbury*, in his time, and Parson of *Adisham* in *Kent*. *Robert Provest*, Parson of St. *Elphege*. *John Lovelych*, who was, in his time, Register of the Archbishop's Consistory at *Canterbury*. *Richard Stuppeny*, who was, in his time, a Proctor of *Canterbury*.

In the South Chancel. *Henry Gosborn.*

This worthy Patriot, by his Will (*d*), gave Twenty Marks (a large Legacy in those days) towards the repairing of the City-walls, at such places as the Abbat of St. *Augustins*, and the Mayor of the City should assign. It appears by and upon his Monument, that he had two Wives, and by them twenty five Children, whereof ten were Sons. *Robert Gosborn*, his Brother lieth hard beside him.   In the same Chancel. *Richard Engham.*

In the Body. *John Caxton*, and his two Wives, *Joan* and *Isabel*. *John Colfol*. *Nicholas Reve*.

On the second Pillar from the West end,

Thomas Prude (*e*). With his Coat of Arms engraven (as the rest) in Brass. He lived in *Edward* IV. days, and by his Will (*f*) appoints to be buried

---

(a) *Stow. Daniel.*   (b) *In Archivis Eccles. Cant.*   (c) *Ad necessitatis refugium.*
(d) *In Regist. Consistor. Cant.*
    (e) *Gaude Prude Thoma*
        Per quem fit ista columpna.
(f) *In Registro memorato.*

by *Christ-Church* Porch, and therein gives as much as will build a Pillar in this Church, and five Marks to *Christ-Church* Works, *Anno* 1468.

In the West Window. *Edmund Staplegate*, and *Elinor* his Wife.

This man, who took his name from his place of Habitation, which was *Staplegate* in this Parish, was in his time, namely in *Edward* III. days, divers times one of the Bayliffs of our City. Of whom see more in *Staplegate*.

In the West Wall, without. *Agnes Halk.*

Having now done with St. *Alphege*, let us on and survey the rest. Whereof three, to wit, St. *George*, St. *Mary Bredman*, and St. *Peter*, anciently were, as they still are, of the patronage of *Christ-Church*, as were likewise whilst they stood, two other, *viz.* St. *Michael* of *Burgate*, and St. *Mary* of *Queningate*: all which Five, together with St. *Sepulchres*, were confirmed to it by Bulls of Pope *Alexander* III. and divers succeeding Popes, and every one of them anciently paid (*a*) to it a several annual Pension, as St. *George* 5 *s*. St. *Mary Bredman* 6 *d*. St. *Peter* 6 *s*. 8 *d*. St. *Michael* 2 *s*. and St. *Sepulchres* 12 *d*. But let us on to the rest; whereof Six, *viz.* St. *Mary Magdalen*, St. *Andrew*, St. *Mary Castle*, St. *Mildred*, *All-Saints*, and St. *Paul* belonged to St. *Austin*'s; and whilst it stood, also St. *John*'s, and sometime St. *Margaret*'s. Three, *viz.* St. *Dunstan*, *Holy Cross* of *Westgate*, and St. *Mary* of *Northgate*, to St. *Gregory*'s. One, *viz.* St. *Mary Bredin*, and whilst it stood, St. *Edmund of Ridingate*, to the Nuns of St. *Sepulchres*; and One also, to wit, St. *Margaret*, to the Hospital of *Poor Priests*, of later time, as formerly to St. *Austin*'s. I will begin with those belonging to the Cathedral: And of them first with St. *George*'s. In the Chancel whereof, you may read upon a Grave-stone the Epitaph of *John Lovel.*

[He gave a Silver Saltsellar to the Refectory of *Christ-Church*. W. S.]

Which one is the only Monument of any Antiquity that I find there. I pass therefore hence to St. *Mary Bredman*. Sirnamed (I take it) to distinguish it from other *Maries* in and about the City ; and so sirnamed, I conceive, and so have said before, because of the Bread-market kept beside it, as it is (we see) to this day. It was (as I have elsewhere also noted) anciently in *Latin* called *Ecclesia S. Mariæ Piscariorum*, and in *English*, St. *Mary Fishmans-Church*, from a Fish-market thereby. But yet more anciently and before all this *Ecclesia S. Mariæ de Andresgate* (*b*), from that place hard by it where the 4 ways meet at St. *Andrews-Church*, of old called *Andresgate*, to say *Andrews-gate*. Whence the Inn, now the Checquer, an house from great Antiquity belonging to *Christ-Church*, in the elder Rentals thereof stands described to be situate by *Andresgate*. But enter we the Church, and we shall there find some ancient Monuments, as

In the Chancel. *Thomas Alcock* Rector of this Church. 1500. *Robert Richmond* Rector of this Church. 1524. In the Body. *William Megg.*

St. *Peter*. Whence *Weaver* hath taken these Monuments of, *Thomas Ickham* and *Joan* his Wife. *William Ickham.* *William Septvans.*

He mentioneth another ; of one *John Biggs* but imperfectly. I balk his, and set it out of new : from the Windows. See the *Appendix.*

In the next Window. *William Bygg* and *Joan* his Wife.

This *William Bigg* was he (I take it) that with *John Coppyn* of *Whitstable*, built our Market-Cross at the *Bulstake*: and gave x *l*. towards the new building of St. *George*'s-gate, whereof before.

In the Chancel. *John Colley* Rector of this Church. This man (it seems) built the *Chancel-Window*, for in the foot thereof is or lately was legible, (*c*) *By* John Collay *who was Parson here.*

In the Body. *John Syre.*

As a thing worthy a Monument, a *Memorandum* at least, let me acquaint you that *ann.* 25 *Edward* III. the Parsonage house of this Church was given to *Thomas* the then Rector, by one *Richard Langdon* of *Canterbury*, with Licence of the King (*d*).

St. *Michael* of *Burgate* and her Chapel St. *Mary* of *Queningate* are both down and gone : and so far from yielding any Monument of others, that they rather stand in need of one for themselves, left they be quite forgotten, both name and place.

Having done with the Churches, by right of Patronage, belonging to

---

(*a*) *Lib. Eccles. Cant.*　　(*b*) *Lib. Eccles. Cant.*　　(*c*) *Per Jehan Collay qui estoit Person icy.*
(*d*) *Lib. Eccles. Cant.*

Christ-

Chrift-Church, let us proceed to thofe of St. *Auftin's*. Out of all which the Abbey anciently had and received certain annual Penfions (a), to wit, out of St. *Mildred's* 10 s. St. *Mary Caftle* 12 d. St. *John* 6 d. St. *Margaret* 3 s. *All Saints* 12 d. St. *Andrew* 12 d. St. *Mary Magdalen* 12 d. and St. *Paul* 3 s. Which together with the like in other Churches of their patronage in the Diocefs, *Robert* the Abbat and his *Covent*, ann. dom. 1242, in confideration of a valuable recompenfe another way did releafe and relinquifh.

St. *Mary Magdalen*.

Joan Hach. Chriftopher Alcock. Sibell Orchard.

One *Richard Wekys* of this Parifh, a Butcher, in the year 1471, by his Will (b) was a great Benefactor to this Church, as if you fearch the Office you may find by his Will there. The Steeple of this Church was new built in the year 1503, towards which at that time (as I find by his Will (c)) one Sir *Harry Ramfey* of St. *George* gave fix Seams of Lime. Concerning the ftopping up the Chancel-Window of this Church, I find that in the year 1511, a Prefentment of the matter was made to Archbifhop *Warham* in a Vifitation of his, in thefe words: *viz. That* John Fifh *hath joyned his houfe to the Church by a dormant to the hurt of the Church, and the light of the Church is ftopped by it.* Fifh being called into queftion for it, compounds with the Church-Wardens, who the year following judicially appear and acknowledge it (d).

At a Vifitation holden *Anno* 1560. it was by the fworn Officers of this Church prefented as followeth, *viz. That there doth belong to the Parfonage houfe a piece of Ground called* Maudelen croft, *which is and hath been wrongfully detained by Mr.* Hyde *Auditor of* Chrift-Church, *to the great impoverifhing of the faid Parfonage* (e). By other Records (f) I find this ground to lye in the Parifh of St. *Martin*, that it was *Northward* bounded with the Street, and *Southward* with certain Lands of St. *Auftin's*; and that the Parfon of this Church paid for it 4 s. per *ann.* to the Hofpital of St. *Jacob*, I find in a *Chantery*-book.

St. *Andrew*.

Edward Bolney, whom you fhall find in the Catalogue of our Mayors; and *Stephen White*.

In the Windows. *William Mellrofe*, and *John Fanting*.

Thefe, haply, were Benefactors to this Church about the fame time that one *Thomas Petyt*, of this Parifh, was; who in the year 1498. by his Will (g), gave five Marks to the making of a new Steeple, and a new Roof to this Church; like as did one *John Swan* (h), another Parifhioner there at the fame time, and an Alderman, and fometime Mayor of the City, *viz.* lxvi s. viii d. (i) *toward the work of a new Roof and Steeple there, when it fhall happen to be new made*; as his Will expreffeth it. It was prefented to Archbifhop *Warham*, at his Vifitation holden *Anno* 1511. (k) *That fome Tithes and Oblations, due to the faid Church by reafon of fome Sheds,* (I fuppofe) *or fmall Stalls belonging to the Fifhmarket, lying within the fame Parifh, were withheld by the Mayor and Commonalty of the City.* But the Chamberlain of the City appearing, and, in the Town's behalf, denying the Prefentment to be true, it doth not appear that the matter proceeded any further (l). Here was fometime a Chantery for *William Butler*.

St. *Mary Caftle*.

So firnamed for diftinction fake, from the other *Maries* of the City. This Church hath lyen long defolate; and the Chancel only (to the repair whereof, one *Roger Ridley*, *Anno* 1470. by his Will, gave 4 l.) is left ftanding of it. Time was, it was as abfolute a Parifh Church as any about the City, and in time of Popery, no doubt, for its Tutelar Saints fake, fared well and flourifhed, the change of the Times, in that point, being very probably a main caufe of the Church's decay and defolation. For Offerings, Altarages, and the like Profits, whereof the Living did mainly confift, and whereby the Incumbent confequently chiefly fubfift, being (as the Reformation would) withdrawn, there was not otherwife a competency for him to fubfift by, which

---

(a) *Thorn in vitis Abbat. S. Auguftini.* (b) *In Regift. Confift. Cant.* (c) *In Regift. Dom. Archid Cant.* (d) *Ex Regiftro Warham.* (e) *In Archivis Conf. Cant.* (f) *Lib. Cameræ Civitatis.* (g) *In Regift. Dom. Archid Cant.* (h) *In eod. Regift.* (i) *Factura novæ teftudinis & campanilis ibidem, cum contigerit de novo fieri.* (k) *Quod Major & Communitas Civitatis Cantuar. fubtrahunt decimas & oblationes ratione opellarum fori pifcarii in dicta parochia fcit. debitas ecclefiæ fupradict.* (l) *Ex Regiftro Warham.*

U u   made

made it be deserted. St. *Austin's* Abby, before the diffolution, having the patronage both of it and St. *John's*, another Parifh Church not far diftant from
it, now, in a manner, forgotten; this latter, with the confent of the Patron,
was by the Prior and Covent of *Chrift-Church*, in a vacancy, *Anno* 1349. united to the former *(a)*. Both which united Churches and Parifhes, fince their
defolation, tacitly devolved to St. *Mildred's*, and have been reckoned of that
Parifh, until now very lately this of St. *Mary Caftle* is begun to be divorced
again from it, by having a particular Incumbent prefented and inducted into
it. A word or two more of St. *John's*, and I leave them both. It feems, the
Parifh was of fmall extent, and fo the Living was according, poor and mean.
For Records do call it, *(b) The Church of St.* John, *called the Poor.* The Church
ftood much about the upper end of that Lane leading from *Caftleftreet*, which
at this day, we call the *Back-*lane; but was from thence anciently called
St. *John's* Lane *(c)*. It being come into private hands, is (they fay) and hath
been of a long time prophaned into a Malt-houfe, or the like. St. *Lawrence's*
Book makes mention of fome portions of Tithes belonging to this Church,
thus. *(d) Alfo the faid Hofpital receives all the Tithes of 4 Acres of Land in Market-field; and the Rector of St.* John *in Canterbury, receiveth of two Acres 8
Sheafes, and of two other Acres feven Sheafes, in all one Copp. And the faid Hofpital receiveth two parts of the Tithes of Six Acres of Land, lying at Stoneftreet, toward the South, and a narrow way toward the North. And the Rector of St.* John's
in Canterbury, *receiveth a third part of the Tithes.* One *Henry Plaiee* was found
dead in *Canterbury*, by a fall from a Ladder, as he was in tyling St. *John's*
Church in *Canterbury*, fay the Crown-Rolls.

Anno 5 Ed. 3.

The Parifhes of St. *Andrew*, St. *Mary Magdalen*, and for a while, St. *Paul*,
which, before the Diffolution, buried at St. *Auguftin's*, fince the Churchyard
there was withdrawn, in lieu thereof, I take it, (this St. *Mary Caftle* Church
being of that Abby's patronage) had this Churchyard affigned them for the
Burial of their dead there; a privilege wherein St. *Mary Bredman's* Parifh did,
and doth (but by what right, that being of the patronage of *Chrift-Church*, I
know not) communicate with the reft, but all, or fome part of the benefit
arifing by the Burials there, went to the Poor of *Mayner's* Spittle, who in refpect thereof, anciently kept it in repair, and for default thereof, *Anno* 1560,
were prefented from St. *Andrews (e)*. Since which time the cafe is altered, each
Parifh keeping their part of the enclofure.

St. Mildred.

This Church, and a great part of the City (as *Stow* hath it in his Summa-
ry) was burnt in the year 1246.

In the Windows. *Richard Atwood*: In a very ancient Character.

A Family of this name anciently dwelt in this Parifh, being houfed in *Stour-
ftreet*, where one *Thomas Atwood*, that lived in *Henry* VIII. days, dwelt, and
(being four feveral times Mayor of the City) kept his Mayoralty. The fame
man, here built the South-fide Chancel or Chapel, for a peculiar place of Sepulture for himfelf and his Family; divers of whom lye there interred, under fair Grave-ftones, fometimes inlaid with Brafs; all not worn but fhamefully torn away, even Founders and all: Who yet hath a remembrance left of
him in the Glafs. See the *Appendix.*

Thomas Wood, and *Margaret* his Wife.

In the Windows. *John Boold. John Mawny. Robert Bennet. John Boys.
John Pocot.*

One *John Stulp* (it feems) as a Benefactor, had a great hand in making divers new Pews in this Church, as appears by his name upon them.

At this place, *Lambard (f)* faith there was, long fince, an Abby. (St.*Mildred's*, faith he, *in the South-fide of the City, long fince,* (but not lately) *an Abby.*)
But furely he is miftaken, and that hence, as I conceive. In the Siege, Surprizal, and Sacking of our City by the *Danes*, in the days of King *Ethelred*,

---

(a) *Lib. Ecclef. Cant.*   (b) *Ecclefia sancti Johannis dicti pauperis. Lib. memoratus.*
(c) *Rental. vet. Ecclef Cant.*   (d) *Item prædict. Hofpitale percipit totam decimam de 4 acris terræ in Marketfield, & Rector sancti Johannis Cantuar. percipit de 2 acris, 8 garb. & de aliis 2 acris, 7 garb.
in toto 1 copp. Item prædict. Hofp. percipit duas partes decimæ de 6 acris terræ capit. ad Stoneftreet verf.
South & parvam femitam verf. North. Et Rector sancti Johannis Cant. percipit tertiam partem decimæ.*
(e) *Ex Archivis Conf. Cant.*   (f) Peramb. of *Kent*, in *Cant.*

amongft other Perfonages of note that are ftoried to have been led Captive by them, one *Lefwine* (whom fome call *Leofrune*) the Abbefs of St. *Mildred's*, is named for one. Now this happening to be done at *Canterbury*, and fhe ftyled an Abbefs, and that of St. *Mildred Canterbury*, as in *Harpsfield*; Mr. *Lambard*, it feems, finding in *Canterbury* a Parifh Church of that name, fuppofed it had fometimes been that Abby, whereof *Lefwine* or *Leofrune*, in the *Danes* time, was Abbefs; whereas, indeed, fhe was Abbefs of St. *Mildred's* Minfter in the Ifle of *Thanet*, and the laft Abbefs of the fame. So *Thorn*; and from him, *Reyner (a)*, will both tell you.

All-Saints.

This Church affords no ancient Monument with an Infcription or Epitaph. Yet I find fome men of good note buried there. Amongft the reft, one *Roger Brent*, fometime an Alderman, and thrice Mayor of *Canterbury*, who, by his Will *(b)*, dated *Anno* 1486. gave unto the City his Meffuage, called *Stone-Hall*, in this Parifh, the Houfe (I take it) wherein Mr. *Delme* lately dwelt. *Roger Brent.*

This Church's Cœmitery was acquired and laid to it but of late days, as it were. For in *Henry* III. days, and (long after that) in *Edward* III. days too, it was in private hands, as I find by feveral Deeds of thofe times, and did anciently belong to *Eftbridge* Hofpital, in part at leaft *(c)*.

St. Paul.

In the Chancel-Windows foot is this remembrance of Mr. *Hamon Doge*, in an ancient Character or Letter. *Magifter Hamo Doge.* He was a man of note in his time, lived in *Henry* III. Reign, was the Archdeacon of *Canterbury* his Official *(d)*, and the laft Parfon of this Church. For which *Thorn* is my Author, who faith, That *(e)* in the year 1268. the Ordination of the Vicarage of St. *Paul's* was made by Mr. *Hugh Mortimer* with the affent of R. Lord Abbat and Mr. *Hamon Doge*, the laft Rector there. Fifteen years he had and held the Aldermanry of *Weftgate*, and then paffed it over to the Abby of St. *Auftin's*, who infeoffed one *Nicholas Doge* with it *(f)*. The fame *Hamon* founded the Chantery in this Parifh, whereof I have formerly informed you. *Hamon Doge.*

In other of the Windows. *Richard Wavere*, *John Stace* and *Conftance* his Wife. *John Gale* and *Chriftiana* his Wife. *George Windbourn* and *Katherine* his Wife. *Richard Bern* and *Joan* his Wife. *Thomas Pollard*.

Againft a Pillar. *Edmund Hovynden*.

By the South-wall. *John Twyne*.

Of thefe *Richard Berne*, by his Will *(g)* dated *ann*. 1461. full of pious and charitable Legacies, gave x *l*. towards the repair of this Church at that time in great want thereof. *(h)* He faith, Item, *I bequeath to the Church of St.* Paul's *for the repair of the fame in fuch places, as there is moft need, the fum of Ten pounds to be delivered by my Executors Weekly in fuch Portions as fhall be expended about the faid reparations week by week.*

Becaufe of fome ancient and late differences between the City and St *Auftin's*, touching the extent of the Cities Franchife or Liberty hereaway, to help clear the doubt, my *Appendix* fhall give you a Copy of an ancient compofition, whereby this difference was in part compofed between them. And there alfo you may find a Copy of the ordination of this Church's Vicarage. Numb. LXVII. Numb. LXVI.

And now having done with the Churches in and about our City of St. *Auftin's* patronage, I come to thofe next belonging to St. *Gregory's*, viz. *Northgate*, *Weftgate* and St. *Dunftans*.

St. Mary Northgate.

Geofry Holman and *Walter Garrade*.

Upon a Plate fet in the North-wall. *Ralf Brown*.

For the time that this man lived in, fee my Catalogue of the Mayors.

Archbifhop *Stratford* in the year 1346. with confent of the Prior and Con-

---

(a) *Apoftolatus Benedictinorum, Tract. 1. Sect. 1. pag. 62.*   (b) *In Regift. Conf. Cant.*

(c) *Lib. Hofp. de Eftbridge*   (d) *Lib. S. Rad-gundis.*   (e) *Anno quo fupra* (viz. 1268.) *ordinatio vicariæ fancti Pauli facta fuit per magiftrum Hugonem de mortuo mari per affenfum Domini R. Abbatis, & magiftri Hamonis Doge ultimi Rectoris ibidem.*   (f) *Ex Archivis Turris London.* 4 & 9 Edw. 1   (g) *In Regift. D. Archid. Cant.*   (h) *Item lego Ecclefiæ Sancti Pauli pro reparatione operum ejufdem Ecclefiæ locis maximè indigentibus x lib. deliberandas per executores meos feptimatim ficut denarii prædicti expendi poffint in operibus prædictis.*

vent

vent of St. *Gregory*'s, Patrons of this Church, erecting a Vicarage here, endowed the fame in fuch manner, as by the *ordination or compofition* thereof extant in my *Appendix* fhall be fully fhewed. Numb. LXVIII.

Holy Crofs of Wefgate.

[This Church (that I mean which now ftands) was firft erected in this place in *Richard* II. time; formerly the Church that was, ftood over the Town gate, both which being decaied by Age, were by Archbifhop *Sudbury* demolifhed, and eftfoon rebuilt, but a-part, the Church being placed no longer over the gate, but hard befide it under the Wall, where now it is. Touching the demolifhing and the new erecting thereof from the Lieger-book of St. *Gregory*'s, I have extracted and tranfcrib'd a certain Record not unworthy the perufal, which the Reader may find in the *Appendix.* Numb. LXXIII. *W. S.*].

Stephen Matthew, William Hall, Robert Colt, William Colkin, John and *Robert Nailor,* &c. You may find *John Nailor* in the Catalogue of Mayors.

The Monument of *William Charnel* firft Chantery Prieft of *Ihefus,* reduceth to my memory (what I have often met withal) the *Fraternity of Ihefus maffe* (as they called it) kept of old in this Church. For your better underftanding whereof, you may pleafe to know that (*a*) in our Forefathers days there was a Prieft named *Jefus Maffe-Prieft* maintained within the faid Church by the Brothers of the faid Brotherhood with the help and devotion of the Parifhioners there, which bought and purchafed divers Lands and Tenements to maintain the fame, that is to fay, one Meffuage and 66 Acres of Land and Merfh lying in *Afh,* 6 Tenements in this Parifh, 4 little Tenements in St. *Dunftan*'s, and 2 in *Harbledowne,* at the valuation of them by *Henry* VIII. Commiffioners for vifiting of *Chanteries* and the like, found worth together 11 *l.* 7 *s.* 8 *d.* per annum. Out of this the Prieft had for his Stipend or Wages by the year with the charges of Wax and Wine 7 *l.* And the Parifh Clerk for ringing to the faid Mafs at 6 of the Clock in the Morning, and for helping to fing the Mafs had yearly 6 *s.* 8 *d.* The names of fuch as were admitted to be of the *Fraternity* were entred in a Bead-roll, and like as thofe that of old had their names entred in the *Diptycks,* were fpecially and particularly mentioned and recommended to our Saviour's Mercy by the Prieft at Mafs. In *Edward* VI. time, this and all fuch *Fraternities* were diffolved.

As a caufe or token at leaft of this Church's name of *Holy Crofs,* there was fometime over the Porch or Entrance into the Church a *Crucifix* or reprefentation of our Saviour's Crucifixion. *Richard Marley*'s Will (*b*) tells me fo, who therein appoints to be buried in this Church-yard before the Crucifix of our Lord, as nigh the coming in of the North-door there as conveniently can be. And wills his Executors to fee gilt well and workmanly the Crucifix of our Lord with the *Mary* and *John* ftanding upon the Porch of the faid North-door; as his Will hath it, dated 1521. The Crucifix is gone, and the King's Arms fet up in place of it.

The Vicarage of this Church was erected and endowed by the fame Archbifhop that *Northgate*-Vicarage was. If the ordination thereof come to my hands, I fhall impart it to you in my *Appendix.*

St. *Dunftan.*

In a fide Chapel or Chancel here belonging to the *Ropers* [founded by *John Roper. Pat.* 4. *H.* 4. N. B.] (and (*c*) wherein anciently two Chaplains were of that Family maintained to Sing [at the Altar of St. *Nicholas.* N. B.] for the Souls of fuch of the Family as were dead and for the profperity of their Heirs living, and had given and allowed to each of them 8 *l. per annum* for their Salary or Wages, befide a little Tenement, next the manfion place of the *Ropers,* for their habitation) you may find the Monuments of *Edmund Roper, John Roper* and *Jane* his Wife, *William Roper* and *Margaret* his Wife. [Of the Family of the *Ropers* fee *Philpots Villare Cantianum.* p. 95. N. B.]

There are other Monuments of the *Ropers,* but out of my furvey, being not of any Antiquity.

On the Northfide, and Weft-end of this Church, is a little forlorn Chapel, founded (*d*) by one *Henry* (firnamed) *of* Canterbury, the Kings Chaplain

---

(a) Chantery Book.   (b) *In Regift. Conf. Cant.*   (c) Chantery Book
(d) *Lib. Hofp. Pauperum Sacerdot. Cant.*

(as he writes himſelf) in the year 1330. and dedicated to the *Holy Trinity*, together with a perpetual Chantery committed to the care and over-ſight of the Hoſpital of *Poor-Prieſts* in *Canterbury*, who being to reap the Profit, were to find the Chaplain and undergo all burthens.

Archbiſhop *Reynolds*, in the year 1322, erected and endowed the *Vicarage* here. For the firſt ordination whereof and its augmentation afterwards ſee my *Appendix*, Numb. LXX. And now let us paſs to the Churches ſometime appertaining to the Nunnery. *viz.* St. *Mary Bredin*, and (whileſt it was in being) St. *Edmund* of *Ridingate*.

St. *Mary Bredin.*

John Hales ; *Humphrey Hales* alſo, and *James Hales*, others of the Family lye beſide him. Their ſeat was the *Dungeon*, a Manor continuing to the Succeſſion to this day. More anciently it was the *Chiches* ; of which Family one of the firſt, and moſt famous was *Thomas Chich*, that lived in *Henry* III. days: whoſe Name Effigies and Coat, being Argent, 3 Lions Rampant, azure ; you ſhall find ſet up in the Weſt-Window, as the Coat alſo is in Stone in one Corner of the Chancel of this Church.

William the Son of *Hamon*, the Son of *Vitalis* one of them which came in with the Conqueror, built this Church, as his father *Hamon* did that whither we are going *(a)*.

St. *Edmund* of *Ridingate.*

A Church ſo quite deſolate, as the place is no where to be found. And therefore, and becauſe I have made it the ſubject of my Survey on a former occaſion, I will ſpare all further diſcourſe of it in this place, and come to St. *Margaret*, a Church ſometime, by right of Patronage, belonging to St. *Auſtin*, but in the year 1271, given to the Hoſpital of *Poor-Prieſts*, as I have at large ſet forth in my Survey of that Spittle.

St. *Margaret.*

In the Chancel. *John Winter* gave a Lamp to burn continually before the High Altar in this Church, about which he takes Order by his Will : therein giving the Rent of two Tenements at *Yren-Croſs* in the ſaid Pariſh, of the yearly value of 16 *s.* to maintain the ſaid Light, as alſo to acquit the Church-yard of this Church from the yearly Rent of 3 *s.* payable to the Prior and Convent of *Chriſt-Church* in *Canterbury*, as his Will runs : whoſe words I have propoſed becauſe they give occaſion of ſome further pertinent diſcourſe : as firſt about our Church-yard which it ſeems was anciently in whole or in part *Chriſt-Church* Land, and indeed I have in the Records there met with an ancient Deed, that bounding out an houſe out of which was given to the Monks a Rent, lays it Eaſtward to St. *Margaret*'s Church : *Chriſt-Church* afterwards parting with her Intereſt, was (it ſeems) conſidered with 3 *s.* a year for it. Another thing is the *Iron-Croſs* there ſpoken of. Some that would ſpeak or write it ſhort called it *Tierne-Crouch*, or *Tierne-Croſs*. It ſtood and that within memory of man, at the meeting of the four-ſtreets in this Pariſh, whereof one leads to the Caſtle, another to *Bridewel* Hoſpital, a third to *Ridingate*, and the laſt up the City to the Cathedral. It gave name to the whole Quadrangle there, and the Houſes thereaway are in ancient Deeds *(b)* deſcribed to be ſituate *apud Tierne*, or *apud Tierne-Crouch*. So is that corner Houſe there ſtone-built moſt-what, out of which iſſueth a certain yearly Rent to *Chriſt-Church (c)*. So where you ſee the two Houſes of this *John Winter*'s gift, being thoſe very two which of late Alderman *Watſon* (who purchaſed them from the Crown to which they eſcheated of old becauſe given to Superſtitious uſes) by his Will freely gave unto the City to the uſe of Poor people. But let us on.

margin: Tierne Croſs.

Leonard Cotton, (I have remembred him before in *Maynard*'s Spittle) *Thomas Fort*, *John Hosbrand* and his two Wives, *Joans* both ; and *Richard Prat*, (whom you ſhall find in the Catalogue of Mayors) and his Wife *Alice*.

Here are no other ancient Monuments now extant. Some more have been, but the Braſs is gone. Haply amongſt thoſe, one was for *John Broker* of this Pariſh, in his time an Alderman, and twice Mayor of our City ; who, by his Will *(d)* dated *Anno* 1521, appoints to lie before St. *John*'s Altar. To under-

margin: John Broker.

(a) *Lib. Hoſp. S. Lawrentii.* (b) *Lib. Hoſp. Paup. Sacerd.* (c) *Rental. Eccleſ. Cant.*
(d) *In Regiſt. Conf. Cant.*

ſtand him, I muſt tell you, that as this Church hath a double, or either ſide Iſle and Chancel, ſo the one, *i. e.* the South-Chancel or Chapel was dedicate to St. *John*, and the other to our Lady ; each of which had its proper Altar now removed, the Official's Court taking up the place of our Lady's, a Tribunal Seat firſt erected and ſetled there in the year of our Lord 1560 (*a*). I have the rather made mention of this *John Broker*, becauſe of his Liberality to the City ; to the Mayor and Commonalty whereof, and their Succeſſors for ever, he gave two Houſes, the one in St. *Mary Caſtle* Pariſh, the other at the *Waterlock* in this Pariſh. For which, excuſe me, if I think him memorable.

On the North-ſide of this Church our City hath her Fiſh-market, and long hath had, of my knowledge from good Record, about 100 years ; but anciently all, or ſome part of the Ground was the Parſon's of this Church. (*b*) As ſaith a Deed in the Leiger of Poor Prieſts Hoſpital, as ancient as about the firſt of *Henry* III. Reign: *That* Alexander *of* Glocefter *gave to God, and the Church of St.* Margaret, *and to* John Rector *of the ſame Church, and to his Succeſſors, a certain piece of Land near the ſaid Church, on the North-ſide, before the houſe of* John Turre, *between the Highway or Street and a Lane, before a houſe which formerly belonged to* John Pikenot, *and reaches toward the Bakehouſe of* Durand *the Vintner, &c.* I fall not upon this, any way intending to diſturb the quiet of our City's Title to this piece of Ground, nor ſo much regarding the thing given, as its Bounds, and of them chiefly what it calls (*c*) *the Lane before a houſe, which formerly belong'd to* John Pikenot. Here, then, fixing a while, let me tell you firſt, that this *venella* was a Lane , which ſometime led by the backſide of the now Fiſh-market ſtraight on till you come into the *High-ſtreet*, opening into the ſame, much-what over againſt the now Checquer-gate. And was then called *Pikenot*-alley, you may ſee from whence, namely from one *Pikenot* in his time a man of note, living or dwelling by it : It being a very common practice with our Anceſtors to call their Lanes by their Names, who were known, and Eminent men, and either dwelt in them or at one end of them. Hence (to begin with that) *Canterbury-Lane* took name firſt from a Family of *Canterburies* ſometime dwelling in or near the ſame. The name of a Lane hard by it in that Pariſh which we call *Shepeſhanklane*, but ſhould call *Sepeſonklane*, had a like original, namely, from one of that Name an inhabitant there. A Lane in St. *Peters* Pariſh over againſt the Church called of old *Pocoekſlane* took name from the like occaſion. So did alſo that Lane in St. *Margaret*'s which we at this day call *Hawkeſlane*, but was anciently known by the name of *Willards-lane*. As likewiſe did a Lane ſometime in St. *Mildred's*-Pariſh, now loſt, opening at the one end into *Stour-ſtreet*, at the other againſt the Chapel-Churchyard, to this day remembred by the name of *Ballock-lane*. For the ſame cauſe was that Lane in St. *Andrew's*-Pariſh which we call *Angell-lane*, anciently called *Sunwinſlane*, afterward *Salcockſlane*, after that *Clements-lane*. Hence laſtly, another Lane ſometime in St. *Peter's*-Pariſh, now loſt, opening againſt the Black-Friers gate there, was called *Cokins-lane* : and whether the Lane late, at the one end opening into the middle of *Caſtle-ſtreet*, and into *Stour-ſtreet* at the other, in St. *Mildred's* Pariſh, by name (as uſually called) *Ware-lane*, which the late Mr. *Thomas Cranmer* bought of the City, did take it names from hence or not, from one *Ware*, I mean, that had his habitation by it, though it be uncertain, yet is it not unlikely that it did. But enough of theſe things. One word more of the *Fiſh-market*. Certain old Verſes made in commendation of ſome Cities of this Kingdom ſingular in affording ſome one commodity or other, commend of *Canterbury* for her Fiſh, wherewith indeed, by reaſon of the Seas vicinity, as *Malmsbury* hath long ſince obſerved,her Market is ſo well ſupplied, as none that know the place will think the Poet flattered her. The Verſes are in the Margin (*d*).

Pikenot-Alley.

Canterbury-lane

Sepeſonk lane.

Pocoeks lane.

Willards-lane.

Ballock lane.

Sunwines-lane.
Salcocks-lane.
Clements-lane.

Cokyns-lane.

Ware-lane.

(a) *Lib. act. penes Regiſt. Domini Cant.*   (b) *Sciant, &c. quòd ego Rogerus filius Henrici de Northamtona & Chriſtiana filia Andreæ Flandrenſis conceſſimus & confirmavimus illam donationem & conceſſionem quam Alexander de Glovernia fecit Deo & eccleſia beatæ Margaretæ & Johanni Rectori ejuſdem Eccleſiæ ac ſucceſſoribus ſuis de quadam terra juxta prædictam eccleſiam ex parte Boreali ante domum Johannis Turre inter regiam ſtratam & venellam ante domum quæ fuit quondam Johannis Pikenot & extenditur verſus piſtrinum Durandi vinetarii, &c.*   (c) *Venella ante domum quæ fuit quondam Johannis Pikenot.*
(d) *Teſtis eſt London ratibus. Wintonia Baccho.*
Herefordeque Grege. Worceſtria Fruge redundans.
Batha Lacu. Sarumque Feris. Cantvaria Piſce, &c.

Having

Having now done with the Churches, a word or two of their Endowments Tithes how
in general, I mean in Tithes. The custom and manner of Payment whereof paid in *Canter-*
at this day, whether predial or personal is not in kind, but by and according *bury.*
to the Rents of Houses, *viz.* after the rate of x *d.* in the Noble, quarterly
payable. This I say is the present general custom of Tithing throughout our
City, one Parish (St. *Andrew*) only excepted, where, but why I know not,
the custom is to pay somewhat more, *viz.* x *d. ob.* in the Noble. How long
this custom hath been in force with us I find not, but by Records in the Archbishop's Registry to be found Copied in my *Appendix*, it will appear that an- Numb. LXXI.
ciently our Clergy of this City were at like pass for their Tithes and Offerings with their Brethren the Clergy of *London*; and did partake with them of
their Custom, which, how long afterwards it did continue, or when, or
wherefore it ceased and was changed and abated into the present manner of
Tithing; and whether or no, personal Tithes were then paid beside (as *Lin-* Personal
wood's opinion is, they ought to be, this being, according to him, a predial Tithes.
Tithe) I no where find. But I persuade my self, that personal Tithes were
likewise paid, and that because, that almost every Testator, as well of City,
as Country, gave satisfaction more or less by his Will to the Parish Priest, for
his Tithes forgotten or negligently paid; which, I conceive, could not easily
happen in this certain kind of payment. Yet I rather than otherwise suppose
these privy personal Tithes seldom or never drawn from the Parishioner by any
legal compulsory way, or by any course taken for their recovery in *foro exteri-*
ori, as it is called, but by other means in those times as prevalent; one, the
calling the Parishioner to accompt for them in *foro conscientiæ*, that in Court
of Conscience, at the time of confession and shrift (one cause haply of their
name of privy Tithes) another, the much affrighting danger to incur the Privy Tithes.
greater curse pronounced, and (which confirms me much in my persuasion of
the usual payment of them) in every Parish Church in Town and Country,
until the Reformation, four times in the year declared against all With-hold-
ers of such Tithes, as elsewhere may be found (*a*): The cause, haply, that
every man was so careful not to die in the Priests debt for them. Hitherto,
and enough, of the Churches, both Cathedral and Parochial, in and about
our City.

Ecclesiastical Government of the City.

HAving now run through the Description of the whole City, with all
Parts and Members of the same, let us, in the next place, take notice
of the Policy, whether Spiritual or Temporal, whereby the same is governed, beginning with the Spiritual or Ecclesiastical.

According to the *Aristocratical* Form of Church Government, used in this
Realm (*b*), our City, in (*c*) *Spirituals*, is subject to the Ordinary of the place,
which is the Archbishop of *Canterbury*, for the time being, immediately; but
mediately, and under him in a subordinate way, partly to the Archdeacon,
partly to the Commissary; and in (*d*) *some things* to the Dean Rural of the
place. Of the Archbishops and Archdeacons, elsewhere enough; somewhat
I have thought fit to speak in this place of the remaining other two. And first
of the Commissary, a Subordinate Officer anciently relating and retaining to
the See of *Canterbury*. But before I fall upon his Original, give me leave to
premise a few things touching our Ecclesiastical Judges in general, and their
Consistorial Form of Judicature, which (by the consent of our Learned Antiquaries) began under the *Norman* Conqueror, it being of a different condition aforetime. For until then, (*e*) the Bishop, and the Aldermen were the
absolute Judges to determine all Businesses in every Shire, and the Bishops in
many cases, shared in the Benefit of Mulcts with the King. But the Conqueror confined the Clergy within the Province of their own Ecclesiastical Jurisdiction, to deal only in Business concerning Rule of Souls, according to the
Canons and Laws Episcopal. Further, and better to illustrate this matter, well
worthy your knowledge, (Courteous Reader) I must let you know, that it

---

(a) Relicks of *Rome, fol* 243.   (b) *Downing's* Discourse, *Concl.4.* 1. §. 6.   (c) *Spiri-*
tualibus.   (d) *Quibusdam.*   (e) *Daniel, Hist. in Will.* 1.

was the Law of King *Edgar*, (a *Saxon*) (*a*) *In every County, twice every year, let there be a Court held; at which, let the Bishop of that Diocese, and the Alderman be present, and let one of them teach the people the divine, the other the human Laws.* A Law by King *Canutus* the *Dane*, reinforced thus: (*b*) *Thrice in a Year, let there be a Burgemote; that is, a City-Court; and a Shiremote, that is, a County-Court, twice; unless there be need of it oftner. And let the Bishop, and Alderman be present, and let them teach the Law of God, and secular Right, each of them according to his Function.* Hence that of Mr. *Selden*, speaking of the Jurisdiction that belonged to the *Saxon* *Ealdormen*, or Earls: *The Scyregemot* (saith he (*c*)) *which was a Court kept twice every Year, as the Sheriffs Turn is at this day, was held by the Bishop of the Diocese, and the Ealdormen (in Shires that had Ealdormen) and by the Bishops and Sheriffs, in such as were committed to the Sheriff that were immediate to the King. And so both the Ecclesiastical and Temporal Laws were together given in charge to the Country.* Thus he. Hence also that of Sir *Henry Spelman*, speaking of the *Saxon* Count or Earl. (*d*) He says, *He presided in the County-Court, not alone by himself, but join'd with the Bishop, that the one might dictate the divine, the other the human Law, and that the one might give help and counsel to the other; especially, that the Bishop might aid and advise the Earl. For he had a right often to animadvert upon the Earl, and to check him when he err'd. For this reason both of them had the same Territory and Limits of Jurisdiction.* As also, hence that of him in another place. (*e*) He says, *The* Thani (the same which sithence are called Barons) *were present, to wit, in the Hundred-Court,* (which was kept and held once a month) *and the Ecclesiastical Judges, with the Clergy of that division, were present also. For in the Hundred as well as in the County, were exercised together all Causes belonging both to the Ecclesiastical and to the Secular Court, until* William *the* Conqueror, *the Jurisdiction Ecclesiastical and Secular being made distinct, did separate the one from the other.* In *English* even the same with that of Mr. *Selden* in another place than any of those out of him above-cited. *In the* Saxon-*times* (saith he (*f*)) *all Jurisdictions of ecclesiastical Causes was exercised joyntly by the Bishop of the Diocess, and the Sheriff or Alderman of the Shiregemot, or Hundred or County Court, where they both sate; the one to give God's Right, the other for Pupulds Right, that is, the one to judge according to the Laws of the Kingdom, the other to direct according to Divinity. But at the* Norman *Conquest, this kind of holding Ecclesiastical Pleas in the Hundred or County Court was taken away.* Thus he. The Law or Edict ordaining or commanding this separation of the two Courts you may find elsewhere (*g*); with the repetition whereof, because it hath at several times been Published, and for brevity sake, I will not trouble you. In those days one way and manner of trial and determination of Causes was by a kind of *Decisory Oath* of the party. As it is observed by the forenamed Learned Knight (*h*). The same observation hath Mr. *Lambard* in his *Perambulation. In Eareth.* An example whereof they severally set forth. I my self have met with the like amongst the Records of our Cathedral, of the year 844. containing in it (if you will pardon the barbarous false *Latin*, the fault of that Ages ignorance) many observable passages, which you shall find in my *Appendix*, Numb. LXXII. But let me go on where I left. Since that Edict of the Conqueror, as I find by searching and turning over ancient Monuments, *Ecclesiastical Jurisdiction* was a while exercised chiefly and for the most part, for Clergy-men's Causes, especially in Synods or Chapters, the Bishop using in

---

(*a*) *Ex omni comitatu bis quotannis Conventus agitur, cui quidem illius Diæcesis Episcopus & Senator interjunto, quorum alter Jura divina, humana alter populum edoceto. Jan. Angl. lib. 2. pag.* 130. *Fox Acts & Mon. vol.* 1. *pag.* 1017.   (*b*) *Habeatur ter in Anno Burgesmotus (i. e Civitatis Conventus) & Shiremotus (i. e. pagi vel comitatus Conventus) bis, nisi sæpius opus sit ; & intersit Episcopus & Aldermannus, & doceant ibi Dei rectum & sæculi, uterque scilicet pro suo munere. Spelman, Glossar. in verbo Aldermannus. Fox ubi supra.*   (*c*) Titles of Honour, *par.* 2. *cap.* 5. §. 5   (*d*) *Præsidebat autem foro comitatus non solus, sed adjunctus Episcopo: hic ut jus divinum, ille ut humanum diceret, alterque alteri auxilio esset & consilio : præsertim Episcopus Comiti, nam in hunc illi animadvertere sæpe licuit, & errantem cohibere. Idem igitur utrique territorium, & jurisdictionis terminus. Gloss. in verb. Comes.*
(*e*) *Aderant scilicet Hundredo Thani ipsique Judices ecclesiastici, cum partis illius Clero. In hundredo enim non minus quam in comitatu una tunc agebantur, quæ ad forum pertinent ecclesiasticum, & quæ ad seculare, donec Gulielmus Conquestor divisis Jurisdictionibus, hanc ab illa separavit. Gloss. in verbis Gemotum & Hundred.*   (*f*) Hist. of Tithes, *cap.* 14 § 1. *Vid* Fox Acts and Monum. *vol.* 1. *pag* 193.   (*g*) *Jan. Angl. lib.* 2 *pag.* 76. Hist. of Tithes, *cap.* 14. § 1.   (*h*) *Adja autem, id est, jusjurandum sive sacramentum, appellabant Saxones nostri, litium illud dirimendi genus, quo ex consacramentalium (uti vocant) assertione, de litigatis cognoscebant & judicabant, &c. Concil. Tom.* 1. *pag.* 336.

Person

Person to preside over the one, as the Archdeacon over the other. Afterward upon the revival of the Civil, and promulgation of the *Canon-law*, sufficiently repleat with Light and directions for deciding of Doubts, and determination of Causes without need either of Synods or Chapters, they began by little and little to decline, or at least not to be of such ordinary use for the hearing and ending of Causes, such especially as were only Civil, and not Criminal, as before ; and then as a more easiy and speedy way of dispatch the Consistorial form of Judicature which we now retain, exercised by *Officials,Chancellors, Commissaries*, and the like Ecclesiastical Judges, came into request, of whom, in this Nation, until about Pope *Alexander* III. days, no mention at all, in any Record with us extant at this day is (I take it) to be found. I deny not the Antiquity of *Ecclesiecdici*, or Church-Lawyers. I would not be so mistaken. For I grant (as behoves me) an existence of them many hundreds of Years before, whereof the late learned Sir *Thomas Ridley* in his view of the Civil and Ecclesiastical Law (*a*), worthily vindicating their challenged Antiquity, hath made very satisfactory Proof. Whom in their Office I conceive not much unlike (if not the same that were) the *Periodeutai* mentioned by *Justinian* in his Constitution (*b*). Of whom see *Gothofred*'s Notes there : as also *Cujacius* there, and upon the Title of the *Pandect* (*c*), and *Justellus*, in his Notes upon the *Codex canonum Ecclesiæ universæ, pag.* 216. who all agree that these *Periodeutai* were certain (*d*) Visitors, that, as Vicars of the Bishop, went in circuit from one Parish to another, visiting all places within the Bishop's Jurisdiction, and had no proper Seat of their own. And I grant that such Church-Lawyers were ever after of use, as Assistants (or Assessors) to Bishops, for their help and direction in debating and deciding Controversies according to the forms and formalities of Law (hence our Archbishop had his (*e*) *Auditors of Causes*:) but came not, I conceive, to that perfection of Authority, here in *England* at least, untill about the time I told you.

Synods then thus (as I said) declining, and their Authority being transferred upon *Officials* and the like ; our *Commissariship* of *Canterbury* did not presently take beginning, but the Archbishop's Official partly, and partly the Archdeacon did for a time use and exercise the Jurisdiction throughout the City and Diocess, whilest as yet there was no *Commissary* at *Canterbury*. Afterwards the increase of Causes in the Arches Court at *London* requiring the Officials constant residence and attendance there, who before (like the *Periodeutai*) was ambulatory, and followed the Archbishop, leaving the Dean of the Arches to dispatch Causes there as his Deputy in his absence ; and complaint being made (*f*) (and it, as one amongst many other grievances by some propounded and put up) to Archbishop *Peckham*, to wit, the *non-Residence* of the Official, he was by a Statute (*g*) of Archbishop *Winchelsey*, *Peckam*'s next Successor, enjoyned to residence ; and about the same time, and upon that occasion (as I conceive) and the Archbishop's more constant residence at *Lambhith*, a *Commissariship* was established in and for the City and Diocess of *Canterbury*, and a perpetual or setled *Commissary* appointed to attend the same : the first (I take it) that by *Patent* or *Commission* held the place, being one Mr. *Martin*, in his time Parson of *Ickham* in *Kent*, and his Patent or Commission runs, as may be seen in the *Appendix*, Numb. LXXIV.

I shall spare recital of the succeeding *Commissaries* Names, and their Patents or Commissions, not because I want instruction to do either, but for brevity sake.

For which cause, though I might instance in many particular favours which several Archbishops graciously inclined to the advancement of their Episcopal *Consistory*, have been pleased to grant unto their *Commissaries*, rendring it a Court of good credit, yet I forbear the mention of them all : and the rather because being mostly upon Record in the Registry, they are already publick, and obvious to all men's Scrutiny. But yet one thing which antedates those Records, and concerns the Court, at least is not impertinent to our present discourse of the original thereof, I crave leave to particularize, and it is this,

Ecclesiecdici.

Periodeutai.

Commissary of Canterbury his original.

(*a*) Pag. 104.   (*b*) *Omnem.* 42. *de Episc. & Cler.*   (*c*) *De excus. tutor. lib.* 6 § 1.
(*d*) *Circuitores sive visitatores qui veluti Episcoporum vicarii Regiones Civitatibus subjectas visitant ac circumeunt, nullamque propriam sedem habent.*   (*e*) *Auditores Causarum.*   (*f*) Ex Lib. *Eccles. Christi Cant.*   (*g*) MS. penes mem.

     viz.

viz. A course taken upon and anon after the erection of the Commissarship, for the inlargement and bettering of the same, by the Archbishops revoking and calling the Jurisdiction, which divers Rectors or Parsons of exempt Churches within the Diocess exercised, from and out of their *quasi* possession (*Jura etenim incorporalia non possidentur, sed quasi possidentur* (a)) and conferring or transferring it upon the *Commissary*, whereof I find the Record in *Christ-Church*, transferr'd now into the *Appendix*, Numb. LXXV.

Now only a word or two to shew how it came to pass that the Records of the *Consistory* fall so much short of the original of the Court, as indeed they do, beginning not until about the year 1396, above 100 years after the erection of the *Commissarship*, and then leaving the *Commissary*, I shall proceed to speak somewhat of the *Dean.*

The cause I cannot impute to the injury of Time consuming the Records, because Records of greater Antiquity are daily seen, and frequently and generally extant. As I cannot impute it to that, so neither will I ascribe it to the sloth or negligence of the Registers in times past, which I cannot, in Charity presume upon no better warrant than Conjecture; although the meaness of their places and the moveablenefs of the Court in those and latter times would readily help to support that surmise. To these Causes (I say) I will not attribute the cause of our Courts disability to produce the Records of those elder times. Because (after a hint received from some well versed in Antiquity) spending some time about perusing our Chronicles which make mention of the rebellious Insurrection made by *Wat Tyler* and *Jack Straw,* happening in the reign of *Richard* II. and in the year of our Lord 1381. by and upon this perusal of the story, I found that they and their complices bare an especial hatred and spite to Lawyers, insomuch that not only they wasted and consumed with fire the Lawyers Houses then situate near *Temple-Bar, London*; but also being at *Canterbury,* and having received kind welcome and entertainment of the Town's-men there (all the People being of their assent) upon their departure, taking their way to *Rochester*, they sent their People to the Villages about, and in their going they beat down and robbed the houses of *Advocates* and *Procurers* of the King's Court and of the Archbishop, bearing him much malice for imprisoning their Priest, *John Ball,* a seditious Malecontent and hypocritical Preacher. What should kindle in them this fire of envy to Lawyers,is easily apprehended if the drift of this their seditious rising be but considered. For (like the *Stoicks* of old, whose hearts were set upon a *Community*; whence that of *Seneca. Homines quietissime viverent si hæc duo Pronomina de medio tollerentur, meum & tuum*) a *Parity* and *Community* was the thing projected, and the effecting of a *Plebeian Liberty* their aim, whereunto they well knew (as who knows it not) that Laws and Lawyers were notorious enemies and obstacles: in as much as *meum* and *tuum* cannot stand with *Community,* for

Si teneant omnes omnia, nemo suum.

Therefore saith one, speaking of this *Ball,* he persuaded or counselled them to kill and murder (amongst others) all Lawyers, Justicers, and all manner of Judges, Magistrates and Men in Authority, *&c.* Herewithal, what Writings or Records soever they could fasten on where they came (as another obstacle to their projects thriving, which they were to remove) they concluded to set on fire. Hence was it that at *Cambridge,* the rabble of them there, breaking up the Chests and forcing the places where the Records of the University were kept, without regard had, or difference made of any Writings, whether *Charters, Bulls, Letters Patents, Statutes* or other Monuments whatsoever, in the Market place, some, other elsewhere they committed to the Flame. Now to bring this home to my present purpose, which is to shew what is become of our Records of the *Consistory* of *Canterbury* before those now extant. Having by this Story found how Lawyers and Law-Records were maliced by these allwasting Rebels, and considering (by comparing of the times) that our Registry takes its beginning not till awhile some few years after this Rebellion, (it not being able presently to gather breath again) and that it was and is the Archbishop's Registry whom they maliced even to the death: I cannot but persuade my self, and in my opinion more than conjectural it is, that those

Froissard.

(a) *L. 3. §. qui usufructus. F. de vi & vi ar. & Inst. de Interdict. in princ.*

elder

elder Records and their *Registry* bare a share with the rest of the Records and Lawyers Houses which suffered the violence of those Rebels.

I pass now from our *Commissary* with an hearty wish that the following Distichon (which *George Sandys* (*a*) tells me is set over the court of Justice at *Zant*) may be ever verifi'd of this *Consistory.*

> *Hic locus odit, amat, punit, conservat, honorat,*
> *Nequitiam, pacem, crimina, jura, probos.*

Thus Englished.

> *This place doth hate, love, punish, keep, requite,*
> *Voluptuous riot, peace, crimes, laws, th'upright.*

Having done with the *Commissary*, it remains that I speak somewhat of the Dean, an ecclesiastical Officer set to over-see a certain number of Parishes, amongst which are those of our City, and a necessary Member in the Ecclesiastical or spiritual Government of the same. We call him a *Rural Dean.* Dean of Canterbury.

Now Rural Deans (to speak of them first in the general) are the same with *Archipresbyteri vicani* or *rurales*, and their names are often confounded, but more frequently occurreth the name of *Archipresbyter*, and is more used amongst the *Canonists*, than that of *Decanus.* Wherefore I am minded to expound this of *Dean* by that of *Arch-priest* (an Ecclesiastical Degree, by the order of the *Decretals* following next unto an Archdeacon, and following rather than preceeding, because that albeit the *Arch-priest* be, than the *Arch-deacon* (if he be but a *Deacon* and not a *Priest*) *major ordine*, yet is the Archdeacon than the *Arch-priest major dignitate* (*b*).

Of *Arch-priests* there is a double kind. *Duarenus* shall bring you acquainted with them. *Sunt autem* (saith he (*c*)) *Archipresbyterorum duo genera, quorum urbani quidam dicuntur, alii vicani. Urbani dicuntur qui in urbe & in majori ecclesia officio suo funguntur. Cum enim Episcopus propter absentiam forte, vel occupationes suas non possit omnia Episcopi munia, vel solus, vel una cum presbyteris obire, sed curas suas cum eis partiri necesse habeat : utilius visum est ex presbyteris unum cæteris præponere, qui ea quæ ad presbyterorum officium pertinent, partim ipse exequatur, partim aliis facienda præscribat, quàm omnibus simul presbyteris id committere, ne contentio aliqua inter ipsos ex communione administrationis oriretur. Et Archipresbyteri vicani nullam in urbe potestatem, nullum ministerium habent, sed in majoribus celebrioribusque pagis constituuntur. Ac singulis, præter ecclesiæ propriæ curationem, certarum ecclesiarum, certorumque presbyterorum, qui videlicet per minores titulos habitant, inspectio observatioque committitur, &c.* Thus he ; who in the next Chapter to that above cited proceeds to shew and set forth the original of these *Arch-priests* or *Deans-rural*, and how they first sprang up, and is persuaded (as he tells us) that upon the abolishing and antiquating of the *Chorepiscopi*, these *Deans* or *Arch-priests* succeeded in their stead. Wherein Sir *Henry Spelman* concurring with him in opinion, delivers the same very succinctly thus. *Chorepiscoporum munus* (saith he (*d*)) *cum nomine sensim antiquatum abolevit (nec pridem) ecclesia : subinductis verò in eorum vicem (qui Episcopis liberiùs cedunt, & humiliori jure contenti sunt) Archipresbyteris, alias Decanis ruralibus, & Plebanis.* So have you both the definition and original of *Rural Deans.*

To speak now more purposedly of their use and office in this Kingdom especially. *Decani rurales* (saith *Lindwood* (*e*)) *sunt Decani temporales, ad aliquod ministerium sub Episcopo vel Archidiacono constituti, &c.* From this place in *Lindwood*, Dr. *Cowell* tells us, that Deans rural are certain persons that have certain Jurisdiction Ecclesiastical, over other Ministers and Parishes near adjoining, assigned unto them by the Bishop and Archdeacon, being placed and displaced by them (*f*). Would you know upon what ground, and for what intent first instituted ? Briefly this ; the assistance of the Bishop, or Archdeacon, or both. *Cum enim* (saith one (*g*)) *ad presbyteros rure degentes extendere se continuò non posset Episcoporum, aut Archidiaconorum vigilantia, collocati fuere per intervalla, in quibusdam quasi excubiis Presbyterorum aliqui Decani, vel Archipresbyteri vocitati, ut cæterorum Presbyterorum, ac plebis moribus, vice Episcopi aut Archidiaconi invigilarent.* Their Jurisdiction, for ought that I can find, is not so certain, nor

---

(a) *Relation. lib.* 1. *pag.* 6   (b) *Gl. in c.* 1. *de Offic. Archipresb. verb. subesse.*   (c) *De sacr. Eccles. Minist. & Benefic. lib.* 1. *c.* 8.   (d) *Glossar. in verb. Chorepiscopus.*   (e) *De Constitut. cap.* 1. *verb. Decanos Rurales.*   (f) *Interpret. in verb. Dean.*   (g) *Rover. Illust. Histor. Monast. S. Joann. Reomaens. p.* 629.

particularly laid down any where, as it can be said to be, of this or that form, or to be thus or thus bounded out. And therefore, as they are generally amotive, and removeable *ad nutum constituentis,* so is it arbitrary to the Superior that ordains them, I suppose, with decency and order, what charge or business they shall undergo. Yet these particulars of their Office I meet with. First, that by custom warranted by Law (*a*) many of them have a kind of Jurisdiction to visit their Deanry, and to enquire of Crimes and Defamations happening in the same, especially by the Clergy, and to take cognizance thereof; correcting, for the smaller offences, by themselves, and for the rest, referring them to the Superior, the Bishop, namely, or Archdeacon, at the next Synod, Chapter, or Visitation, reporting unto them what they find; (like as did the *Irenarchæ* and *Apparitores,* of old, their *Notoria* to the Magistrate) whence they are termed *Testes Synodales* (*b*). But are, by Law, flatly forbidden not only to take to ferm Episcopal Jurisdiction (*c*), but also to meddle in arduous or weighty Causes, such as Matrimony, and the like (*d*), as being by common intendment, not qualified with Skill enough to handle them: And those of *Canterbury* Diocese, by an ancient injunction of the Archdeacon, were forbidden *Probat* of Wills. Moreover, I find, that these rural Deans had each of them their Seal, and were appointed so to have by the Legatine Constitution of *Otho. Quoniam Tabellionum,* which will have it authentical: And such Seal to have only cut and graved in it the name of Office, *sine nomine proprio,* saith the Gloss; because upon the expiration of their Office, it was presently to be resigned and surrendred up into the hands of him from whom they derived their Office, (so runs the Constitution.) The use which they made of these Seals, was this, among other. Citations being often, at least, in Causes of moment, and against the Clergy of their Deanry, directed, committed, and intrusted to their execution, they (as a part of their Office) either executed the same themselves, or else they caused them to be executed by their Apparitors, Servants, Beadles or Messengers, (for such they had as well as the Bishop himself, or other Ordinaries had theirs) and then returned the same Citations, together with a Certificate of the manner and form of their execution thereof, under their Seal. These things will appear to any that shall have recourse to the places quoted in the Margin (*e*). Those particularly of *Canterbury* Diocese, were Receivers of the *Peter-pence* or *Romescot,* in their several Deanries, had many times purgations committed by the Commissary to their dispatch, for the ease and benefit of the Subject, and their wisdom and fidelity was intrusted for taking of them; a thing warranted (if not required) by the Provincial Constitution. *Item licet de purgatio. Canon.* Besides, they were Pœnitentiaries, and Confessors for the Clergy of their several Deanries. They convocated the Clergy to Visitations, and to the choice of Clerks of the Convocation. Upon the vacancy of any Church in their Deanry, it was usual with them of old to have the custody of it; that is, to collect the fruits, and get the cure supplied, in the name and stead of the Archdeacon, during the Church's Widow-hood or vacancy; and to that end, the Dean had the Church-door Key delivered him, which, upon his induction of the new Incumbent, to put him in possession of the Church, he used to deliver him, according to the manner of giving corporal possession, in those elder times observed, springing, haply from those Laws in the *Digests. l. qua ratione. §. 9. Item si quis. D. de acquir. rer. dom. l. clavibus. 74. de contra. empt.*

These and many other things, brought them in such profit, as that some of them were unwilling to depose their Office, and deliver up their Seal (*f*). The choice and ordination of them, is not hitherto quite worn out of use amongst us, but their Office in any of the premises, is either quite obsolete, or at least, much diminished. Hence that of Sir *Henry Spelman: Ruralium Decanorum genus* (saith he (*g*)) *hinc ab Episcopo, illinc ab Archidiacono, vel exhaustum omnino est, vel pristino splendore denudatum.* The Authors and Projectors of the intended *Reformation of the Laws Ecclesiastical,* of this Realm, meant to endue them

---

(*a*) *Vide Sum. Sylvestr. in verb. Archypresbyter.*   (*b*) *Lindwood ubi supra.*   (*c*) *Cap. quoniam. Ne prælati vices suas, &c.*   (*d*) *In Const. Othon. c. cum non solum. de Judiciis.*

(*e*) *Const. Otho. Tanto calliditatis, c. excussis, &c. quidam ruralium de Judic. &c. Item contra. de censib. in Provinciali.*   (*f*) *Jo. de Atho. in Const. quoniam tabellionum. Verb. & sine molestia.*

(*g*) *Gloss. in Verb. Decani.*

with no mean power, as is plainly seen by the Fifth Chapter of the Title, *De ecclesia & ministris ejus, illorumque officiis ;* running thus :

De Archipresbyteris, sive Decanis ruralibus. Cap. 5.

DEcanatus quilibet Archipresbyterum rusticanum habeat, vel ab Episcopo, vel ecclesiæ Ordinario præficiendum. Munus autem ejus erit annuum. Hic tanquam in specula presbyteris, diaconis, gardianis, & ædituis, ut singuli quæ ad eorum munus attinent præstent, perpetuò invigilabit. De Idololatris, & hæreticis, de Symoniacis, de lenonibus & meretricibus, de adulteris & fornicatoribus, de his qui duas uxores simul habent atque maritos duos, de magis & veneficis, de calumniatoribus & blasphemis, de Sodomiticis & ebriosis, de ultimarum voluntatum corruptelis & perjuriis, de injunctionum aut nostrarum aut Episcopi violatoribus, inquirat. Et vocandi ad se, examinandi horum scelerum suspectos authoritatem habeat. Omnem accusationis ortum sive per famam publicam, sive deferentium testimonio probatum, vel suspectum, Episcopo aut ejus loci ordinario infra decem dies in scriptis prodet. Qui autem venire ad eum recusaverit, per apparitorem vocatus tanquam contumax Episcopi voluntatem omnibus ejus Decanatus ecclesiis, sibi per literas significatam, quanta poterit celeritate subinde exponi curabit : alioqui subibit supplicium contemptus. Officii sui sexto quolibet mense Episcopum aut loci ordinarium certiorem faciet, quot infra ejus decanatum conciones eo temporis spatio fuerint habitæ.

By this intended Constitution, you see much of the pristine Authority of rural Deans was meant to be annexed to them and their Office. But this, as the rest of those Laws, never came in force. So that of the quality, use, and office of our rural Deans, all the face that surviveth, or can be gathered from any express Law or Constitution made touching them, since the Reformation, is represented and exhibited unto us by part of an *English* Canon, made and published in *Anno Dom.* 1571, running thus : *When the Visitation is finished, the Archdeacon shall signify unto the Bishop, whom he hath found in every Deanry, so furnished with Learning and Judgment, that they may be thought worthy to instruct the people in Sermons, and to rule and govern others. Of these, the Bishop may choose some, whom he will have rural Deans (a).* Hitherto, and enough, of rural Deans in general ; only let me tell you, that I suppose they were more in request when Ecclesiastical Courts were moveable, and kept from Deanry to Deanry, (for which, see the Constitution *Excussis. De Judiciis in Provincial.*) and when rural Chapters, whereof there were four more principal in the Year, each Quarter one, were in use, (for which, see the Constitution *Quia Incontinentiæ. De Constitutio. in text. & glos. in verb. capitulis ruralibus.*) which rural Chapters are not hitherto so exsolete and disused, but that our Archdeacon of *Canterbury* every year holdeth one, namely, about *Michaelmas*, annually, throughout the whole Archdeaconry ; which he therefore calleth *Generale*. Than which one, though now he do not, yet did he formerly hold more, as is probable, because by the old Composition made between the Archbishop and him, his Apparitors are in express words assigned him, *pro capitulis celebrandis*, and for no other purpose.

Now a word or two of our particular Dean, to whom I find that former times have had recourse for his assistance in many things. The Treasurer of *Christ-Church* (b), in the year 1257, being unpaid divers Rents due by the Church Tenents in *Canterbury*, hires the Dean's Cryer for 12 d. at four several times, to denounce or publish throughout the City, all such retainers of Rents excommunicated ; and makes it parcel of his demands in his Accompt for that year, *viz. Preconi Decani Cantuar. 12 d. ut denuntiaret detentores reddituum excommunicatos per totam Civitatem, &c.* His Seal being authentical, he had a hand in many Exemplifications ; in some joining with other, in other, alone by himself. Of which, I have seen of each sort not a few. Wherein, especially in those of the elder sort, he writes and styles himself, *Decanus Christianitatis Cant.* For the same cause, I suppose, that our Spiritual Courts were and are to this day, called *Curiæ Christianitatis (Courts Christian)* originally so called (as Mr. *Selden (c)* notes upon the term frequent with *Eadmerus*, and other Writers of that age, using it to denote Episcopal Authority and Jurisdiction) because

1396ᵗ

(a) This under the Title of *Archdeacons.* (b) *Lib. ejusd. Ecclesia.* (c) *In Notis ad* *Eadmerum, pag.* 208, & 209.

in the primitive age of the Church, and in the Edicts of ancient Emperors, Bishops were specially and chiefly understood by the general name of Christians. *Generali Christianorum nomine* (saith he) *in edictis Imperatorum veterum Episcopos speciatim designari volunt Jurisconsulti nonnulli, ad l. 11. Christianos. C. de Episcopali audientia. Hinc apud nos Fora sacra quibus jure nempe communi subnixis aut Episcopi præsunt, aut ii qui eo nomine Episcopos, utpote quos provocare licet, suspiciunt, Curiæ Christianitatis etiamnum vocitantur. Primo Christianitatis vocabulum, legem Christianam seu venerationem Christianam & Christianum cultum generatim sonabat, uti videre est in C. tit. de Apostolatis. l. 4. & C. Theodos. tit. de spectaculis l. 5. C. Eod. tit. de Decurionibus. l. 112. C. Eod. tit. de Judæis, Cælicolis l. 19. alibi item. Sed postea Functio atque Jurisdictio illa quæ in gerenda Christianæ religionis seu Christianitatis aut politiæ Ecclesiasticæ cura potissimum exercentur, Christianitas etiam signanter dicta sunt; atque inde sacra Fora, Fora Christianitatis vocitata.* Thus he. And hitherto of the Ecclesiastical Government of the City. I proceed to the Temporal. But, by the way, let me refer you for further understanding of that style or title of *Decanus Christianitatis,* and of the quality, antiquity, and use of rural Deans to *Roverius* his *Illustrations* upon the History of St. *John's* Monastery, called *Reomans. pag.* 628, 629.

Curiæ Christianitatis.

Temporal Government.

HOW our City was governed *in temporalibus,* before the time of the Bailiffs, is somewhat obscure. Yet, questionless, it always had a special and distinct Magistrate to preside over it, whom I find styled, either, the Præfect, the Portreeve, or the Provost; names, differing more in sound, than in sense and signification. For the first of which, in the year 780. in certain Charters of *Christ-Church,* bearing date at *Canterbury,* mention is made of one (a) Aldhune *Præfect of this City,* as in one, (b) *the King's Præfect in* Canterbury, as in another of them, who having purchased *Burne,* consisting of four Ploughlands, of his Master, the *Kentish* King *Egbert,* for two thousand Shillings, gave it all to the Monks of that Church, *ad mensam;* that is, for their maintenance in food or dyet. For the second, Portreve or Portgreve, in the year 956. to a Deed of the Sale of a parcel of Land in *Canterbury,* to one *Ethelstane,* by two Knights, *Ethelsi* and *Wlfsi,* is the Subscription (amongst other Witnesses) of one *Hlothewig Portgerefa,* on this wise, viz. After King *Edgar,* Queen *Eadgive,* and some others, it follows: ✠ Eᵹo hloðpɩᵹ poɲtᵹeɲeꝼa. ꝺɲe hɩoɲeð ᴛo xpeꞇꞇꞇpꞇcean. ꝺɲe hɩoɲeð ᴛo ꝼꞇe Aᵹuꝛꞇɩne. ꝺða ðɲeo ᵹeꝼenꝛꞇpaꞛ ɩnnan buꞛh-ꞛapa uᴛan buꞛhꞛapa mɩccle ᵹemɩꞇꞇan. By the way, these ᵹeꝼeɲꞇpaꞛ here mentioned as Witnesses in the last place, and which I meet with in two other like Charters of *Christ-Church,* about the same age, were (I take it) of the nature of those Fraternities, Gilds or Gilscips, which Mr. *Lambard,* in his explication of *Saxon* words, *in verb. Contubernalis,* and more at large Sir *Hen. Spelman,* in his *Glossary, in verb. Geldum,* severally expound. I proceed. In the *Danish* Massacre here, under King *Ethelred,* happening *Anno* 1011. *Alfword* (as *Huntington*) *Elfrig* (as *Hoveden*) *Alfred* (as *Thorn* calls him,) *Præpositus Regis* (the City-Governor, I take it) was one of the Personages of Quality then taken Prisoners. Afterwards *Doomsday* Book records the name of another like *Præpositus, Brumannus* by name, in these words. *Quidam Præpositus, Brumannus nomine,* (c) *T. R. E. cepit consuetudines de extraneis mercatoribus in terra S. Trinitatis, & S. Augustini, qui postea* (d) *T. R. W. ante Archiepiscopum Lanfrancum & Episcopum Bajocen. recognovit se injuste accepisse &c.* (as it is before in the Record, taken from *Doomsday* Book, in the *Appendix,* Numb. I.) Thus before the Conquest.

In succeeding times, it seems, the City was the Archbishop's, especially *Lanfranc's,* and his immediate Successor *Anselm's,* the former holding it, as it were, in Fee-ferm, the latter freely, *ex solido,* in the nature of what the *Lumbards* call an *Alodium.* Hence that of Mr. *Lambard* (e): *The Bishops* (saith he) *were never absolute owners thereof, till the time of King* William Rufus, *who* (as the Annals of St. Augustin *say*) *Dedit civitatem Cantuariæ Anselmo ex solido, quam Lanfrancus tenuerat ex beneficio.* Hence also that of *Eadmerus* (f), who then lived. *Præcepit*

Præfect.
Portreeve.
Provost.

(a) *Aldhune hujus Civitatis Præfectus.*   (b) *Regis Præfectus in Dorobernia*   (c) *Id est, Tempore Regis Edwardi.*   (d) *Id est, Tempore Regis W—i Imi.*   (e) **Peramb** of *Kent,* in *Cant.*   (f) *Hist. Novor. lib.* 1. *pag.* 18.

itaque Rex, ut fine dilatione ac diminutione inveftiretur de omnibus, ad Archiepifcopa-tum pertinentibus intus & extra, atque ut civitas Cantuaria quam Lanfrancus fuo tempore in beneficio à Rege tenebat, & Abathia S. Albani quam non folum Lanfrancus, fed & anteceffores ejus habuiffe nofcuntur in alodium ecclefiæ Chrifti Cantuarienfis, pro redemptione animæ fuæ, perpetuo jure, tranfirent. Neverthelefs, the City ftill had a Portreve to fuperintend and rule over it. For, in the fame Archbifhop *Anfelm*'s time, one *Calveal*, by the name and title of *Portgreva*, is mentioned as a Witnefs to an exchange of Houfes, between the Church and the City ; the Deed whereof, for the old *Englifh* fake, and becaufe withal a good evidence of that age's plainnefs and fimplicity, as much (it feems) affecting the *Imperatorian Brevity*, as ours abhors it (an age truly then in which men were never more extraordinarily cautious, and yet never more ordinarily couzened) it fhall not be amifs here, *verbatim* to infert.

Ðir beoð þa gehþonre betpux ðan hipeðe æt xpercincean. ꞇ þan cnihtan on Cantþapebepig oþ cepmannegilðe. ðe heap on ceapmannegilðe let þam hipeðe to hanðe viii hagan piðiman Buphgate mið race ꞇ rocne rpa hi hit relue hærðen anð re hipeðe let heom to hanðe þæn to gæner nigan hagen tþegen pið utan Reaðingaten. on þam anen rit ælfric. ꞇ on pam oðþam Bpuman. Ða reoran rinðan pið innan Nipingate. ðærpeon pittað ðipoþð Cutrent ꞇ Bphtpit ꞇ Golðpine ꞇ hepe poþð. ꞇ pillelm ꞇ pulrgeue ꞇ Ælrpine mið race ꞇ rocne. rpa re hipeðe hic hærðe. Ðæpto ir gepitnerre Anrelme ænceb. ꞇ re hipeð æt xpercincean. ꞇ Calueal pontgeneþa ꞇ ða ylðirta men oþ þam heape. Ðir to gerputelian re hipeð hærð an gepþit ꞇ re heape an oðep. Which in our modern *Englifh* may be thus rendred.

This is the Exchange between the Family or Convent at Chrift-Church, *and the Knights or men (Burgeffes) at* Canterbury, *of the Society of Merchants. The Society of Merchants give up (or put over) into the hands of the Family eight houfes within* Burgate, *with (the Liberties of* Sace *and* Socne, *as they themfelves enjoy them. And the Family give up (or put over) into their hands, on the other fide, nine houfes ; two without* Readingate. *In one of them dwelleth* Ælfric, *and* Bruman *in the other. The (other) feven within* Newingate. *In them dwell* Siward Cutfert, *and* Brihtric , *and* Goldwine, *and* Hereword, *and* Willelm, *and* Wulfgeve, *and* Alfwine, *with (the Liberties of)* Sace *and* Socne, *as the Family enjoys them. Thereunto is Witnefs* Anfelm *Archbifhop, and the Family at* Chrift-Church, *and* Calveal Portreve, *and the chiefeft men of the Society. To fhew (or manifeft) this, the Family hath one writing (or part) and the Society another.*

Not long after, the fingle was changed into a double Portreeve, Bailiff, or *Provoft* ; yet not elective by the vote and fuffrage of the Citizens until *Henry* III. time, (*a*), who in the eighteenth year of his Reign, by his Charter granting the Town to the Citizens in Fee-Ferm , infranchifed them with Licenfe and Power yearly to chufe them Bailiffs of their own. From and after which time, the City continued a Bailiff-Town, that is, was governed by Bailiffs, untill the change thereof into a Mayoralty by *Henry* VI. in the 26th Year of his Reign, in which eftate it now ftands. My paft endeavours cannot as yet furnifh me with a compleat Nomenclature of all the Bailiffs : If my future fhall, I fhall willingly impart them.

Bayliffs of Canterbury.

Mayors.

[In fearching into the Regifters and Charters, now in the Archives of the Church of *Canterbury*, I found feveral Bailiffs of the City Witneffes to feveral of the faid Charters ; from fo many of them as were dated, I have inferted this following, though imperfect Catalogue of Bailiffs.

Ann. 1215. *Johannes Dodikere, Galfridus de Stureia. Præpofiti.*
1218. *Johannes Turte, Willielmus Wilard. Præpofiti.*
1221. *Arnoldus Binnewith, Carolus Mercerius. Ballivi.*
1222. *Johannes Turte, Thomas Speciarius.*
1230. *Nigellus Calibot, Johannes Dedikere.*
1232. *Nigellus Calibot, Maynerus le Rich.*
1234. *Hubertus Mercerius, Willielmus Samuel.*
1235.
1236. } *Nigellus Calibot, Johannes Dodikere.*
1237.

(a) See the *Appendix*, Numb. VI.

Ann. 1240.

Ann. 1240. *Codinus Speciarius, Nicolas de Herford.*
1242. *Nigellus Calibot, Galfridus de Stureya.*
1243.
1244. } *Johannes Dodikere, Galfridus de Stureya.*
1247. *Willielmus Samuel, Maynerus Dives.*
1248.
1249. } *Johannes Dodikere, Robertus Polre.*
1250. *Robertus Polre, Willielmus Cockin.*
1255. *Thomas Chiche, Johannes Dodiker.*
1257. *Gregorius Palmiger, Robertus Polre.*
1258. *Johannes Digges, Robertus Polre.*
1260.
1261. } *Thomas Chiche, Daniel Filius Huberti.*
1262. *Thomas Chiche, Simon Payable.*
1265. *Thomas Chiche, Robertus Polre.*
1266.
1267. } *Robertus Polre, Willielmus Cockin.*
1269. *Robertus Polre, Thomas Chiche.*
1270.
1271. } *Thomas Chiche, Simon Payable.*
1272.
1273. *Johannes Digges, Daniel Filius Huberti.*
1274. *Willielmus de Aula, Petrus Durant.*
1275. *Daniel Filius Huberti, Stephanus Chiche.*
1276. *Radulphus Fanceys.*
1277. *Simon Payable, Petrus Durant.*
1281. *Thomas Chiche, Johannes de Standune.*
1282.
1283. } *Willielmus de Orlaston Miles, Custos Civitatis.*
1285. *Robertus Clericus.*
1290. *Edmundus de Tyrne, Rogerus de Leycestre.*
1296. *Reginaldus Hurel.*
1313. *Simon Bartolomew, Johannes de Bishop's-gate.*
1314. *Henry Daniel, Adam Bill.*
1323. *Thomas Chiche, Thomas Polre.*
1325. *Edmundus de Tyrne, Rogerus de Leicestre.*
1327. *Willielmus Chilham,* who committed a Riot against the Monks. See *Stow's* Annals, p. 228.
1335. *Alexander Andrew, Hugo Wadour.*
1344. *Edmundus de Stablegate, Johannes de Sheldwich.*
1350. *Thomas Evererd, Nicolas Horn.*
1351. *Willielmus French, Johannes Chiche.*
1352. *Johannes Chiche, Johannes de Sheldwich,*
1353. *Henricus Daniel, Adam Bell.*
1358. *Edmundus Cokyn, Stephanus de Sellinge.*
1359. *Edwardus Cokyn, Stephanus Taverner.*
1360. *Richard de Chelesfield, Robertus de Sancto Martino.*
1363. *Nicolas Atte Crouch, Hugo Hosier.*
1373. *Henricus Palude, Johannes Balsham.*
1374. *Willielmus de Salisbury, Willielmus de Walschip.*
1375. *Nicolaus de Baa, Willielmus Cornwaille.*
1382. *Willielmus Cornwaille, Edmundus Horn.*
1383. *Richardus Bartelot, Thomas Ickham.*
1384. *Henricus Garnate, Johannes Somerton.*
1391. *Edmundus Horn, Robertus Bennet.*
1392. *Willielmus Elys, Robertus Bennet.*
1394. *Willielmus Elys, Robertus Benner.*
1395. *Edmundus Horn, Robertus Bennet.*
1396. *Willielmus Elys, Thomas Ickham.*
1397. *Stephanus Selling, Johannes Heronhill.*
1398. *Henricus Lyncolle, Stephanus Taverner.*
1402. *Robertus Coupre, Johannes Privy.*
1409. *Thomas Ickham, Thomas Lance.*

Ann. 1410. *Edmundus Horn, Johannes Sheldwick.*

1414.
1415. } *Willielmus Lance, Willielmus Mason.*

1425. *Willielmus Bilsington, Richardus Cateler.* Thefe committed a horrible Riot in the Church (*a*).

1448. *Johannes Lynde, Gilbertus German.* This *John Lynde* was the firft Mayor of the City.

Thus I have given rather a Specimen than a Catalogue of the Bailiffs; and I fuppofe, it is as much as any one can defire to know of them. Several of the Gaps in this Lift may be filled up with the Names which are inferted; for moft of them were feveral times Elected Bailiffs. *N. B.*]

But of the Mayors this, fo near as I can, is a true Lift or Catalogue according to their feveral Succeffions.

[A Catalogue of the Mayors of the City of *Canterbury.* In which the Figure before the Name contains the number of Mayors; the Figure after the Name, how often any one has born that Office. Then follows the date of the Year of their Mayoralty; together with fome fhort remarks concerning fome of them. *N. B.*]

1. **J**Ohn Lynde. 1. *A.D.* 1449.
He lyeth Buried in *Weftgate*-Church. If you look back you may find his Monument or Epitaph there.

2. *William Bennet.* 1. *A. D.* 1450.
He was divers times before, one of the Bailiffs of the City, unto which at his death he became a Benefactor. For by his Will (*b*) he gave unto the City his Tenements befide *Jury-lane* in St. *Mary Bredman*'s Parifh. Thofe two Stone Houfes (I take it) they are, the one the *Tigre*, the other the *White-Horfe* ftanding by that Lane, very ancient both, and known to belong unto the City at this day. He gave alfo to the Wardens of St. *Andrew*'s Church in *Canterbury* where he was a Parifhioner, 4 *s.* 4 *d. per annum*, to keep and maintain the Clock there, for ever. His other good Deeds have their deferved mention elfewhere.

3. *Gervafe Clifton.* 1. *A. D.* 1451.
4. *Roger Ridly.* 1. *A. D.* 1452.
He gave by his Will (*c*) five Marks to the paving of the *Bulftake*, and as much to the new building of S. *George's-gate*, and 4 *l.* alfo towards repairing of the Chancel of St. *Mary Caftell* Church in *Canterbury.*

5. *John Mulling.* 1. *A. D.* 1453.
6. *John Mulling.* 2. *A. D.* 1454.
7. *John Winter.* 1. *A. D.* 1455.
He lies buried in St. *Margaret*'s Church. where if you look you fhall find by his Epitaph what were his works of Piety. He was in his former days one of the Bailiffs of the City, *viz. ann.* 25 Henry VI. the very laft

year of the Bailiffs government thereof.

8. *William Bonnington.* 1. *A.D.* 1456.
9. *Richard Pratt.* 1. *A. D.* 1457.
What he was, may be further known by his Epitaph formerly taken and fet forth in St. *Margaret*'s Church, where he lies interred.

10. *Philip Belknap.* 1. *A. D.* 1458.
He dwelt (they fay) at the *Mote*, but died within the year, and *William Bold* fupplyed the place.

11. *Roger Ridly.* 2. *A. D.* 1459.
12. *William Bigg.* 1. *A. D.* 1460.
He it was that with one *John Coppyn* of *Whitftable* built our prefent Market-Crofs at the *Bulftake*, as the Infcription upon it will fhew you. By his Will (*d*) he gave 10 *l.* towards the work of St. *George's-gate*. He was a Benefactor alfo to the window-work of St. *Peter*'s Church, as is before remembred.

13. *John Freningham* Efq; 1. *A. D.* 1461.
His Will (*e*) fhews him to be a man of much Piety. For thereby he gave twenty Nobles to St. *Mary Magdalen*'s Church, 20 *l.* to *Chrift-Church*, 20 Nobles to the Prior of *Chrift-Church* for overfeeing his Will, 20 *l.* to the repairing of St. *Michael*'s-Gate, or Paving of the *Bulftake*, and 20 Nobles to the amending of foul ways in and near *Canterbury.*

This year the City was made a County *per fe*, and that upon thefe (very valuable Confiderations. *Nos* (faith the King, *Edward* IV.) *Civitatem noftram prædict. unam de antiquiffimis An-*

Canterbury one of the ancienteft Cities of England.

(*a*) *Regift. R.*   (*b*) *In Regift. Dom. Archid. Cant.*   (*c*) *In Regift. Dom. Archid. Cant.*
(*d*) *In eod. Regift.*   (*e*) *In eod. Regift.*

gliæ Civitatibus existentem in loco ejusdem regni eminentiori in prospectu omnium tam in idem regnum peregrinantium, vel aliter à partibus exteris venientium, quam per idem transeuntium sitam existere considerantes, sedemque ejusdem Regni Metropolem in eadem existere, in cujus ecclesia Metropolitica corpus beati Thomæ Martyris, ad quem devotionem gerimus specialem honorificè feretratur, necnon ossa carissimi consanguinei nostri ac prænobilis principis Edvardi nuper principis Walliæ, requiescunt **Citizens commended.** *humata. Insuperque fidelitates & obsequia laudabilia, ac probitatem, industriam & strenuitatem Majorum & Civium Civitatis nostræ prædict. quibus se nobis inclitæque recordationis atque memoriæ progenitoribus nostris Regibus Angliæ hucusque gratos in omnibus & paratos exhibuerunt, & precipuè fidelitates & obsequia laudabilia nobis jam nuper per Cives Civitatis prædict. ad sumptus, custas, expensas, labores, pericula, & gravamina Majorum & Civium nostrorum prædict. plura & non modica exhibita meritò contemplantes &c.* As it is in the Charter. The very same year, 16 *l.* 13 *s.* 4 *d.* part of the 60 *lib. per annum*, until then, paid as Fee-ferm to the King by the City, was first abated, and, by the King's Charter, for ever after remitted to the City. The Reasons and Inducements were these. *Quia nos* (saith the same *Edward*) *ex gravi & lamentabili querela, eorundem nunc Majoris & Civium nostrorum Civitatis prædictæ accipientes quòd eadem Civitas nostra ac inhabitantes eandem in tantam paupertatem tam ob grandem & onerosam solutionem prædictæ firmæ sive feodi firmæ ejusdem civitatis* lx *l. nobis & progenitoribus nostris solut. ac grandes & onerosas custas & expensas suas in resistentia inimicorum nostrorum Regnum nostrum Angliæ in partibus ejusdem Regni eidem Civitati vicinis quampluries invadere nitentium quàm ob alia onera eidem Civitati necessariò incumbentia ac paucitatem inhabitantium ibidem in tantum depauperantur & vastantur, quòd ipsos inhabitantes Civitatem illam necessario oportebit, quod absit, omnino relinquere desolatam, nisi eis per nos in hac parte gratiosius succurratur, &c.* as it is in the same Charter.

14. *Thomas Foster.* 1. *A. D.* 1462.
15. *William Sellow.* 1. *A. D.* 1463.
16. *Hamon Beal.* 1. *A. D.* 1464.

He was a Benefactor to St. *Pancrace* Chapel; as may be seen before, and beside gave 40 *s.* to the Friers Minors, or Gray-Friers in *Canterbury.* Where,

by his Will (*a*), he appoints to have his Body interred, (*in medio navis ecclesiæ fratrum minorum*, such are his own words) and to have a Tomb of three foot high, at his Executor's Charges, set over him and *Isabel* his Wife, *Anno* 1492.

17. *John Harndell alias Hearnhill.* 1. *A. D.* 1465.
18. *William Bigg.* 2. *A. D.* 1466.
19. *John Freningham* Esq. 2. *A. D.* 1467.
20. *Roger Ridley.* 3. *A. D.* 1468.
21. *Nicholas Faunt.* 1. *A. D.* 1469.

He was hanged (as tradition gives) at the Bulstake in *Canterbury*, for aiding Bastard *Falconbridge*; and the Liberties of the City were seized into the King's hands, so that the City was without a Mayor for some good space.

22. *Roger Brent*, Esq. 1. *A.D.* 1470.
23. *Roger Brent*, Esq. 2. *A.D.* 1471.

See more of him in *All-Saints* Church.

24. *John Bygg*, Esq. 1. *A. D.* 1472.
25. *John Bygg*, Esq. 2. *A. D.* 1473.
26. *John Bygg*, Esq. 3. *A. D.* 1474.

See further of him in St. *Peter's* Church; to the Window-work whereof he was a Benefactor, as there is to be seen.

27. *John Whiteloke.* 1. *A. D.* 1475.
28. *Roger Brent.* 3. *A. D.* 1476.
29. *Thomas Atwood*, Esq. 1. *A. D.* 1477.

See more of him in St. *Mildred's.*

30. *Hamon Beale.* 2. *A. D.* 1478.
31. *Tho. Atwood*, Esq. 2. *A.D.* 1479.
32. *Tho. Atwood*, Esq. 3. *A. D.* 1480.
33. *Richard Carpinter.* 1. *A. D.* 1481.
34. *Nicholas Sheldwich*, Esq. 1. *A.D.* 1482.
35. *Nicholas Sheldwich*, Esq. 2. *A.D.* 1483.
36. *William Sellow.* 2. *A. D.* 1484.
37. *John Whiteloke.* 2. *A. D.* 1485.
38. *Tho. Atwood*, Esq. 4. *A.D.* 1486.
39. *Stephen Barret.* 1. *A. D.* 1487.
40. *John Ingram.* 1. *A. D.* 1488.
41. *John Crispe.* 1. *A. D.* 1489.
42. *John Carlile.* 1. *A. D.* 1490.
43. *John Swan.* 1. *A. D.* 1491.

See more of him in St. *Andrews.*

44. *Thomas Propchant.* 1. *A.D.* 1492.
45. *Edward Bolney.* 1. *A. D.* 1493.
46. *Edward Bolney.* 2. *A. D.* 1494.

See more of him in St. *Andrews.*

47. *Tho Atwood*, Esq. 5. *A. D.* 1495.
48. *Stephen Barret.* 2. *A. D.* 1496.

(*a*) *In Registro prædict,*

49. *Henry*

49. *Henry Gosborn.* 1. *A. D.* 1497.

This Year, being 13 *Henry* VII. by his Charter, called *Nova Ordinatio* (*inter alia*) the number of Aldermen, till then but Six, was increased to Twelve, and the number of the Common Council abated from Thirty Six to Twenty Four; both which continue to this day.

See concerning him in St. *Elphege's* Church.

50. *Thomas Sayer.* 1. *A. D.* 1498.
51. *John Plumpton.* 1. *A. D.* 1499.
52. *Thomas Atwood,* Son of *Thomas Atwood.* 1. *A. D.* 1500.
53. *John Huet.* 1. *A. D.* 1501.
54. *Henry Gosborn.* 2. *A. D.* 1502.
55. *Thomas Sayer.* 2. *A. D.* 1503.
56. *Thomas Atwood.* 2. *A. D.* 1504.
57. *William Cramp.* 1. *A. D.* 1505.
58. *Henry Gosborn.* 3. *A. D.* 1506.
59. *Ralph Brown.* 1. *A. D.* 1507.

See concerning him in *Northgate* Church.

60. *John Nayler.* 1. *A. D.* 1508.
61. *William Cramp.* 2. *A. D.* 1509.
62. *John Huet.* 2. *A. D.* 1510.

He died in the time of his Mayoralty, and *Ralph Brown* supplied.

63. *Roger Clark.* 1. *A. D.* 1511.

By his Will (*a*) he appoints to be buried between the Church-gate and the Church-door of St. *Peter* in *Canterbury, Anno* 1542. It seems then one of the Altar-tombs there at this day, was erected for him.

64. *Thomas Atwood.* 3. *A. D.* 1512.
65. *John Broker.* 1. *A. D.* 1513.

See concerning him before in St. *Margaret's* Church.

66. *Thomas Wainflet.* 1. *A. D.* 1514.

He died, and *John Foukes* served out the Year.

67. *John Nayler.* 2. *A. D.* 1515.

See concerning him before, in *Westgate* Church.

68. *Henry Gosborn.* 4. *A. D.* 1516.
69. *Thomas Foukes.* 2. *A. D.* 1517.
70. *William Rutland.* 1. *A. D.* 1518.
71. *John Broker.* 2. *A. D.* 1519.
72. *John Briggs.* 1. *A. D.* 1520.

One of the name *Anno* 36 *Edw.* III. gave unto the City a parcel of Land, called *le Gravelpet,* in *Winchepefield,* in *parochia* S. *Mariæ de Caftro, inter quandam femitam ducentem de Wincheape ad Dodindale verfus South, &c.* as the Deed or Charter expresseth it (*b*).

73. *Roger Clarke.* 2. *A. D.* 1521.
74. *William Note* or *Nutt.* 1. *A.D.* 1522.

75. *Thomas Beale,* Son of *Hamon Beal.* 1. *A. D.* 1523.
76. *John Briggs.* 2. *A. D.* 1524.
77. *John Alcock.* 1. *A. D.* 1525.

He willed his Body to be buried by his Wife, in St. *Pancrace's* Chapel at St. *Auguftin's,* and gave Twenty Nobles for the buying in of vii *l.* x. *s.* parcel of the City's Feeferm, which was yearly paid (fo runs his Will) unto the Heirs of Mr. *John Lucas.*

78. *Roger Clarke.* 3. *A. D.* 1526.
79. *Jacob Whitlaffe.* 1. *A. D.* 1527.
80. *William Rutland.* 2. *A. D.* 1528.
81. *Robert Lewis.* 1. *A. D.* 1529.
82. *Thomas Atwood.* 4. *A. D.* 1530.
83. *John Alcocke.* 2. *A. D.* 1531.
84. *Thomas Beale.* 2. *A. D.* 1532.
85. *William Note* or *Nut.* 2. *A. D.* 1533.
86. *John Bridges.* 3. *A. D.* 1534.
87. *John Alcocke.* 3. *A. D.* 1535.
88. *Robert Lewes.* 2. *A. D.* 1536.
89. *Roger Clarke.* 4. *A. D.* 1537.
90. *John Starke.* 1. *A. D.* 1538.
91. *Thomas Beale.* 3. *A. D.* 1539.
92. *Robert Lewes.* 3. *A. D.* 1540.
93. *William Coppin.* 1. *A. D.* 1541.
94. *Thomas Gower.* 1. *A. D.* 1542.
95. *John Freeman.* 1. *A. D.* 1543.
96. *John Alcocke,* Son of *John.* 1. *A. D.* 1544.
97. *John French.* 1. *A. D.* 1545.
98. *Thomas Batherst.* 1. *A. D.* 1546.
99. *George Webb.* 1. *A. D.* 1547.
100. *George Rand. A. D.* 1548.
101. *John Freeman.* 2. *A. D.* 1549.
102. *Robert Lewes.* 4. *A. D.* 1550.
103. *William Coppin.* 2. *A. D.* 1551.
104. *George Webb.* 2. *A. D.* 1552.
105. *John Twyne.* 1. *A. D.* 1553.

See concerning him before in S. *Paul's.*

106. *Thomas French.* 2. *A. D.* 1554.
107. *Edward Carpenter.* 1. *A. D.* 1555.
108. *John Fuller.* 1. *A. D.* 1556.
109. *George May.* 1. *A. D.* 1557.
110. *Stephen Seare.* 1. *A. D.* 1558.
111. *John Fuller.* 2. *A. D.* 1559.
112. *Henry Alday.* 1. *A. D.* 1560.
113. *Richard Furner.* 1. *A. D.* 1561.
114. *Richard Raylton.* 1. *A. D.* 1562.
115. *Thomas Percy.* 1. *A. D.* 1563.
116. *Thomas Giles.* 1. *A. D.* 1564.
117. *George May.* 2. *A. D.* 1565.
118. *William Fisher.* 1. *A. D.* 1566.
119. *James Netherfole.* 1. *A. D.* 1567.
120. *Peter Kelsham.* 1. *A. D.* 1568.
121. *John Seamark.* 1. *A. D.* 1569.
122. *James Drayton.* 1. *A. D.* 1570.

(a) *In Regiftro præd.*   (b) *Lib. Teftam. pertinen. ad cameram Civitatis.*

123. *Anthony*

123. *Anthony Webb*, Son of *George Webb.* 1. A. D. 1571.

124. *James Netherſole.* 2. A. D. 1572.

He was, for Forgery, diſplaced, and *William Fiſher* choſen in his room, who ſerved out the year.

125. *Simon Broom.* 1. A. D. 1573.

126. *John Roſe.* 1. A. D. 1574.

See concerning him before where I have ſpoken of our River.

127. *Peter. Kelſham.* 2. A. D. 1575.

128. *Simon Broome.* 2. A. D. 1576.

129. *Thomas Limitary.* 1. A.D. 1577.

130. *Clement Baſſocke.* 1. A.D. 1578.

131. *James Netherſole.* 3. A.D. 1579.

132. *Leonard Cotton.* 1. A. D. 1580.

See concerning him before both in the Hoſpital called *Maynard*'s Spittle, and in St. *Margaret*'s Church.

133. *Richard Gaunt.* 1. A. D. 1581.

134. *John Nutt.* 1. A. D. 1582.

135. *John Roſe.* 2. A. D. 1583.

136. *Ralfe Bawden.* 1. A. D. 1584.

137. *John Eaſday.* 1. A. D. 1585.

See concerning him before where I treat of our City-Wall.

138. *Gilbert Penny.* 1. A. D. 1586.

139. *Simon Broome.* 3. A. D. 1587.

140. *Adrian Nicholle.* 1. A. D. 1588.

A fatal year to the *May-pole* at *Dungel-hill*, as of us corruptly called.

141. *Bartholomew Broome.* 1. A. D. 1589.

142. *Edward Netherſole*, Son of *James.* 1. A. D. 1590.

143. *Chriſtopher Leeds.* 1. A. D. 1591.

144. *Marke Berry.* 1. A. D. 1592.

145. *Thomas Long.* 1. A. D. 1593.

A great Plague this year.

146. *William Amy.* 1. A. D. 1594.

147. *Thomas Hovenden.* 1. A.D. 1595.

148. *James Fringeham.* 1. A. D. 1596.

149. *William Clarke.* 1. A. D. 1597.

150. *Charles Whetenhall.* 1. A.D. 1598.

151. *Robert Wynne.* 1. A. D. 1599.

152. *Warham Jemmet.* 1. A.D. 1600.

153. *Simon Broome.* 4. A. D. 1601.

154. *Richard Gaunt.* 2. A. D. 1602.

155. *Ralf Bawden.* 2. A. D. 1603.

156. *Edward Netherſole.* 2. A.D. 1604

157. *Mark Berry.* 2. A. D. 1605.

158. *Thomas Hovenden.* 2. A.D. 1606.

159. *Thomas Paramor.* 1. A. D. 1607.

He obtained the Sword for the City, not without great expence to the ſame.

160. *William Watmer.* 1. A.D. 1608.

161. *George Clagget.* 1. A. D. 1609.

162. *Thomas Hawks* 1. A. D. 1610.

163. *Joſeph Colfe.* 1. A. D. 1611.

164. *Thomas Fetherſtone.* 1. A.D. 1612.

165. *George Elven.* 1. A. D. 1613.

166. *John Pierce.* 1. A. D. 1614.

167. *John Watſon.* 1. A. D. 1615.

168. *Marke Berry.* 3. A. D. 1616.

169. *Thomas Hovenden.* 3. A. D. 1617,

170. *Avery Sabin.* 1. A. D. 1618.

171. *Henry Vanner.* 1. A. D. 1619.

172. *Ralfe Hawkins.* 1. A. D. 1620.

173. *John Hunt.* 1. A. D. 1621.

174. *George Clagget.* 2. A. D. 1622.

175. *Richard Lockly.* 1. A. D. 1623.

176. *James Maſter* 1. A. D. 1624.

177. *William Whiting.* 1. A. D. 1625.

178. *John Stanley.* 1. A. D. 1626.

179. *John Fuſſer.* 1. A. D. 1627.

180. *John Roberts.* 1. A. D. 1628.

181. *William Watmer.* 2. A. D. 1629.

182. *Avery Sabin.* 2. A. D. 1630.

183. *John Meryam.* 1. A. D. 1631.

184. *George Clagget.* 3. A. D. 1632.

185. *John Lade.* 1. A. D. 1633.

186. *Walter Southwell.* 1. A. D. 1634.

187. *James Nicholſon.* 1. A. D. 1635.

188. *William Bridge.* 1. A. D. 1636.

189. *John Terry.* 1. A. D. 1637.

190. *James Maſter.* 2. A. D. 1638.

191. *John Stanley.* 2. A. D. 1639.

[192. *Daniel Maſterſon.* 1. A. D. 1640.

193. *Olive Carter.* 1. A. D. 1641.

194. *John Watſon.* 1. A. D. 1642.

He died in his Mayoralty and *Daniel Maſterſon* by Election in *Burghmote* ſupplied his place.

195. *John Lade.* 2. A. D. 1643.

196. *John Pollen.* 1. A. D. 1644.

197. *Avery Sabine.* 3. A. D. 1645.

198. *Paul Petit.* 1. A. D. 1646.

199. *William Bridge* 2. A. D. 1647.

200. *Michael Page.* 1. A. D. 1648.

201. *William Reve.* 1. A. D. 1649.

202. *William Whiting.* 1. A. D. 1650.

203. *Thomas Treſſer.* 1. A. D. 1651.

204. *John Lee.* 1. A. D. 1652.

205. *William Stanly.* 1. A. D. 1653.

206. *Henry Knight.* 1. A. D. 1654.

207. *Henry Twyman.* 1. A. D. 1655.

208. *Richard May.* 1. A. D. 1656.

209. *Zachariah Lee.* 1. A. D. 1657.

210. *Thomas Ockman.* 1. A. D. 1658.

211. *Squire Beverton.* 1. A. D. 1659.

212. *William Turner.* 1. A. D. 1660.

213. *George Milles.* 1. A. D. 1661.

214. *Henry Twyman.* 2. A. D. 1662.

215. *William Stanley.* 2. A. D. 1663.

216. *Avery Hills.* 1. A. D. 1664.

217. *Thomas Ockman.* 2. A. D. 1665.

218. *Leonard Brown.* 1. A. D. 1666.

219. *John Sympſon.* 1. A. D. 1667.

220. *Francis Mapleſden.* 1. A.D. 1668.

221. *Nicolas Burges.* 1. A. D. 1669.

222. *Thomas Elwin.* 1 A. D. 1670.

223. *Thomas Fidge.* 1. A.D. 1671.

224. *William Gillam.* 1. A. D. 1672.

225. *Thomas Knowler.* 1. A. D. 1673.

226. *Thomas Enfield.* 1. A. D. 1674.

227. *John Lot.* 1. A. D. 1675.

228. *John*

228. *John Stanly.* 1. *A. D.* 1676.
229. *John Muns.* 1. *A. D.* 1677.
Both thefe two laft nam'd died in their Mayoralty.
230. *Nicolas Nicolfon.* 1. *A. D.* 1678.
231. *Thomas Dunkin.* 1. *A. D.* 1679.
232. *John Garlin.* 1. *A. D.* 1680.
233. *Jacob Wraith.* 1. *A. D.* 1681.
234. *William Gilbert.* 1. *A. D.* 1682.
235. *Squire Beverton.* 1. *A. D.* 1683.
236. Sir *William Rook.* 1. *A. D.* 1684. He was then High Sheriff of *Kent.*
237. Sir *William Honywood.* 1. *A. D.* 1685.
238. *Thomas Knowler.* 2. *A. D.* 1686.
239. *Henry Lee,* Efq; 1. *A. D.* 1687. This year the Charter of this City was furrendred, or rather taken away by the will and pleafure of King *James* II. And the Corporation was new modelled, and fuch Perfons were put into the Government of the City, as King *James* could beft confide in, that they would be aiding to him in promoting his defigns, namely, of taking away the Teft, and of bringing in Popery and Arbitrary Power. Hereupon Mr. *John Kingsford* was conftitu-ted Mayor by the King in the new Charter, as a moft trufty and faithful Servant; and he fo well approv'd himfelf to his Royal Mafter, that he was at the King's nomination continued in this Magiftracy the next year alfo.

240. *John Kingsford.* 1. *A. D.* 1688. Upon the happy Landing of the Prince of *Orange,* the old Charter was reftored to the City again : And Mr. *Henry Gibbs* was regularly elected Mayor for the remaining part of this year.

241. *Francis Jeffry.* 1. *A. D.* 1689.
242. *Henry Waddel.* 1. *A. D.* 1690.
243. *John Bean.* 1. *A. D.* 1691.
244. *Nicolas Nicholfon.* 2. *A.D.*1692.
245. *Matthias Gray.* 1. *A. D.* 1693.
246. *John Brickenden.* 1. *A. D.* 1694.
247. *John Garlin.* 2. *A. D.* 1695.
248. *Henry Waddel.* 2. *A. D.* 1696.
249. *Squire Beverton.* 2. *A. D.* 1697.
250. *Joseph Webb.* 1. *A. D.* 1698.
251. *Francis Jeffry.* 2. *A. D.* 1699.
252. *Matthias Gray.* 2. *A. D.* 1700.
253. *John Bean.* 2. *A. D.* 1701.
254. *Anthony Oughton. A. D.* 1702.
N. B.]

Hitherto of the Temporal Government of our City, the concluding Chapter of the prefent Difcourfe or Survey thereof.

B b b   *C H A R-*

CHARTHAM NEWS:

OR,

A Brief Relation of some Strange Bones there lately digged up, in some Grounds of Mr. *John Somner's* of *Canterbury*.

To the READER.

Kind Reader,

THE *Author of this short Discourse, even whilst he was upon it, and had scarce read it over himself, was seized upon, first by sickness, then death, the common Fate of all men. If therefore, there be any thing amiss or imperfect in it, it would be great unkindness to impute it to him, who, by such unavoidable necessity, was prevented the benefit of a Review; and no less unkindness, perchance, though more tolerable, to blame him, who, as out of a due respect to the Author; so, out of a desire to gratify them, (not a few probably) who may desire to satisfy their Curiosities, or improve their Knowledge, in such things; hath published it. Farewel.*

ALtho it may, and perhaps must be granted, that *Miracles* (strictly understood) are long since ceased: Yet in the latitude of the notion, comprehending all things uncouth and strange, (*miranda*, as well as *miracula*; wonders, as well as miracles) they are not so: but do, more or less, somewhere or other, daily exert and shew themselves. *Dies Diem docet.* New days make new discoveries; especially to such as are in any measure curious, (shall I say) or ingenious and inquisitive; as few enough amongst us here in *England* are, unless acted and animated by some profit or advantage to themselves by the discovery; how considerable and remarkable soever it may be otherwise. 'Tis true, *New Lights* are now-a-days much cried up: but as in matters (mostly) of Religion; so (if you mark it) by whom? But such, as not so much for Conscience, as for lucre sake, broach and intrude them upon a credulous giddy sort of people, whose applause they first catch, and then their purses. But leaving these spiritual Mountebanks, and their counterfeit ware, *New Lights* only in pretence; I shall here acquaint you with a piece of New Light indeed, but of another kind, presented and held forth upon no account or aim at all of profit or advantage to the publisher; (but if he mistakes not) of good use and profit (in point of knowledge) unto others, (learned *Antiquaries* and *Naturalists*, as I suppose) of more skill, insight, and judgment, (if they please to employ them on this occasion) in things so rare and extraordinary, than he can, doth, or would be thought to pretend unto. Well, to the matter of fact then.

Mr. *John Somner*, in the Month of *September*, 1668. sinking a Well at a new House of his in *Chartham*, a Village about three Miles from *Canterbury*, towards *Ashford*, on a shelving Ground or Bank-side, within twelve rods of the River, running from thence to *Canterbury*, and so to *Sandwich* Haven; and digging for that purpose about seventeen foot deep, through gravelly and chalky ground, and two foot into the Springs; there met with, took and turned up a parcel of strange and monstrous Bones, some whole, some broken, together with four Teeth, perfect and sound, but in a manner petrified, and turned into Stone; weighing (each Tooth) something above half a pound, and almost as big (some of them) as a Man's fist. Cheek-teeth, or Grinders, as to the form, they are all, not much unlike, but for the bigness, the Grinders of a Man. And whereas I said, *almost as big, some of them, as a Man's fist*; it brings to my remembrance what I have read in *Ludovicus Vives*, of such a Tooth, but a little bigger; (*dens molaris pugno major*; he saith: that is, *a*

Cheek

Cheek Tooth, bigger than a fist) which was shewed to him for one of St. *Christo-pher*'s Teeth, and was kept in a Church that bare his name: Which whether he believed or not, I know not; but contradict it he doth not, I'm sure; neither he, nor his learned Companion, whom he doth name there. Just such another Tooth, *of the bigness,* he saith, *of an ordinary fist,* was seen by *Acosta,* (a very creditable Author) in the *Indies,* digged out of the ground in one of their Houses there, with many other Bones; which, put together, represented a Man, of a formidable, or as he speaketh, *deformed bigness,* or, *greatness*; as he judged of it. And so must we have judged of these Teeth, and of the Body to which they belonged, had not other Bones been found with them, which could not be Man's Bones. Some that have seen them, by the Teeth, and some other circumstances, are of opinion, that they are the Bones of an *Hippopotamus,* or *Equus Fluvialis*; that is, a *River-horse*; for a *Sea-horse,* as commonly understood and exhibited, is a fictitious thing. Yet *Pliny* makes *Hippopotamum* (*mari, terræ, amni communem*) to belong to *Sea,* Land, and *Rivers.* But what are the differences and properties of each kind, I leave to others to enquire. The Earth or Mould about them, and in which they all lay, being like a Sea-earth, or Fulling-earth, not a Stone in it, unless you dig three foot deeper, and then it rises a perfect gravel.

So have you the Story; an Account, if you please, of what was found, where, when, and upon what occasion. For more publick satisfaction, and to facilitate the discovery, at least, to help such who are minded to employ their skill in guessing and judging of the Creature, whose remains these are, what it was for kind; we have by, and with the help of an able Limner, adventured on a Scheme or Figure, of several of the Teeth and Bones, with their respective dimensions of breadth, length, and thickness.

No man, we conceive, not willing to be censured of rashness, will be very forward to divine, much less to define or determine, what the Creature was; and, doubtless, dubious enough it is, whether of the twain, the Sea or the Land may more rightly lay claim unto it. But leaving all others to the freedom of their own judgments and conjectures; if he may have the same liberty from them for his, who, as he knows the place, with the Country about it, hath taken a large time of consideration of all particulars and circumstances fit to be duly and deliberately weighed and observed in the case; he would adventure to conjecture it to be some Marine, or Sea-bred Creature, to which the Land can of right lay no claim. But admitting that (supposing it, I mean, a Sea-bred Creature) how then (will some say) should it possibly come there? *Piscis in arido?* and at such a depth under ground too? I answer, first, with as little wonder as a Land-creature should, which who with reason can imagine to have ever had at first so deep a burial? Next, I say, the Mould, Soil or Earth, wherein it lay, was altogether miry, like to that *cænum* (*oase,* some call it) on many parts of the Sea-coast, both in *England,* and abroad. But how possibly (will it be said) a Sea-creature, when found at so remote a distance from the Sea? For solution (if it may be) of this, and the like incidental doubts, and removing all rubs out of the way of this conjecture; our future discourse, and further progress in this Argument, shall branch it self out into these four following Queries.

1. Whether the situation and condition, face and figure of the place, may possibly admit of the Sea's once insinuating it self thither?

2. Whether (that possibility being granted, or evinced) the Sea did ever actually insinuate it self so far as to this place, and when?

3. How in probability, and when this Valley or Level, being once Sea-Land, should come to be so quite deserted and forsaken of the Sea, as it is at this day; the Sea not approaching by so many, a dozen Miles, or more?

4. By what means, the Sea once having its play there, this Creature comes to lodge, and be found so deep in the ground, and under such a shelving Bank.

1. As for the first, (the place's capacity and aptitude for the Sea's influx, or insinuation) such as know the situation, withal cannot but know, and must agree it to be so. As for Strangers, and such as are unacquainted with the place, for perfecting information in what either the common Maps, or a particular Scheme and Draught of the Level, herewith intended, may chance to be defective in; they may please to know, that the place (the *locus loci*) we
are

are upon, is a part of that wide, fair, and fruitful Level, or Valley, extending it self not lefs than twenty Miles in length, between a continued feries and range of Hills, Downs, or high Grounds, lying at a pretty diftance each from other all the way ; beginning at the Eaft *Kentifh* Shore, and ftretching it felf, Weft-ward, by *Sandwich, Fordwich, Canterbury, Chartham, Chilham, Godmerfham, Wy, Afhford,* fometime in a direct, fometime in a winding courfe, as far at length, as to that famous fpacious Level of *Romney*-Marfh, and is wafhed and watered all along, at leaft from about *Afhford,* by a fweet and pleafant River running through the midft of it, as far as to *Sandwich,* and there by the Creek or Haven, emptying it felf into the Sea : nothing at all of obftruction, by the interpofition of Hills, or high Grounds, hindring, or controlling the Sea's free play and paffage for fo many miles together. The place then, with the parts, the tract above and below it, from the condition or conftitution of it, is plainly not unapt or uncapable of the Sea's infinuation and influence.

If any fhall object, *Canterbury*'s being in the way, as an obftruction or bar ; they are eafily enough anfwered. For although that City feemeth, and indeed is, at this day, for the moft part fomewhat elevated above the pitch of the reft of the Valley or Level, we are upon ; yet not fo much as to defend it felf many times from floods and over-flowings in the lower, and moft depreffed parts of it, even by the Springs it ftands upon, to her great damage and annoyance : towards the helping whereof, by the care and providence of former Ages, it is very certain, and by digging Wells, Vaults, Cellars, and the like, daily experimented, that the moft part of the City, not excepting the very Heart and Centre of it, is made and raifed Ground ; the tokens of Foundations upon Foundations, to a very confiderable depth, daily appearing, and the ground (as at *Amfterdam, Venice,* and elfewhere) for fupporting Superftructures, in feveral places often ftuck and ftuff'd with Piles of Wood, or long Poles and Stakes forced into the ground, as Wells and Cellar-diggers have inform'd me. Nay, and as if, where about now the Bull-ftake Market-place is kept, the River had fometime had its Courfe or Current, Pits and other like Tanners Utenfils, have, not many years fince, been met withal in digging for Cellars thereabouts. To this let me add, that my very next Neighbour in *Caftle-ftreet,* within thefe thirty Years, finking a Cellar, did a good depth (*five or fix foot deep*) light upon, and was put to fome ftop and ftand in his work, by a ftrong and well couched arched piece of *Roman* Tile or Brick, which he was fain to take, or break, afunder, and remove, before he could proceed. Hereof I was an Eye-witnefs, and (for curiofity fake) took one of the Bricks or Tiles to my felf, which, with fome other like *Roman* remains, (fome found in that which is my own Garden) I keep by me to this day. However then, *Canterbury* may now feem to ftand in the *Æftuary*'s way ; yet time was when in probability it did not ; when, I mean, the place, the Soil which now the City occupies, as the reft of the whole Valley both above and below it, was of too low a pitch to be an obftacle to it.

2. As to the fecond enquiry, (Whether, probably, the Sea did ever actually infinuate it felf fo far as to this place, and when) the anfwer is nothing fo eafie : Record of it we have none. The beft and eldeft account we have now of the Condition, Site, and Conftitution of thefe our Eaftern Parts and Tract, we owe to *Julius Cæfar,* and the *Romans* after him : from whom (alas) we have not the leaft fpark of light to fuch a difcovery ; rather indeed the contrary ; both the Sea-coaft, and In-land parts, by his, and their relation, bearing in a manner one and the fame Face and Figure then, as now. However, that the Level we are upon was fometime an *Æftuary,* or Arm of the Sea, feveral *Criteria,* or tokens are not wanting. For example ; befides what may be argued and inferr'd from this parcel of ftrange Teeth and Bones now under confideration, much (as I conceive) there is of probability for it, refulting from our River's name of *Stour,* more anciently not feldom both called and written, *Æftur, Æfture,* &c. which I doubt not to proceed and come from the Latin *Æftuarium,* and, in procefs of time, to have been corrupted and contracted into *Sture* and *Stour* ; giving name in part to *Stourmouth,* a place (a Parifh) about fix Miles Eaftward from *Canterbury* ; fo called from the River's difemboguing there into the Sea, or Salt-water flowing up thither : As alfo giving name to that Mannor of the Archbifhop's, at this day and for fome

Ages

Ages paſt, called *Weſtgate-Court,* at *Canterbury* ; but more anciently, as in the Conqueror's time, *(*witneſs *Doomſday* Book*)* called the Mannor of *Eſture* and *Eſtureſate,* from its ſituation by the *Sture* or *Stour.* From which occaſion, doubt-leſs, the late Lord *Finch*'s Seat in —— about five or ſix Miles nearer to the Spring-head, at this day vulgarly miſcalled *Eaſt-Steward,* is, of old, ſometime called *Eſture,* ſometime *Et-ſture.* From *Saxon* Monuments and Records, I could eaſily trace the name up to a very high date, by many examples.

But to leave that, and proceed to other *Criteria* ; as by the Teeth and Bones now under conſideration, we have an Inſtance on that ſide of the Valley for the probability of the Sea's *quondam* occupation of it ; ſo I ſhall give you here another no leſs remarkable from the other, or oppoſite ſide of it. By credible relation and aſſurance, then, you may know, that a place called *Weſtbere,* an obſcure Village about three Miles from *Canterbury,* Eaſtward, lying under the Brow of the Hill ſtretching out by *Upſtreet,* as far as to the Weſt-end of *Sarr-wall,* by which you make your entrance into *Thanet* ; upon the like occaſion to that here at *Chartham,* (the digging, or ſinking of a Well) at a very great depth, ſtore of Oyſters, and other-like Shells, together with an Iron Anchor, firm and unimpaired, were found and turned up in our time. The like I have been told of an Anchor in our days, digged up at *Broomdown,* on the ſame ſide of the Level ſomewhat above *Canterbury,* Weſtward. And although I can at preſent inſtance only in theſe few on either ſide the Valley ; yet haply, up-on enquiry, other might be found for confirming our conjecture. And I ſhall deſire and hope, that every ingenuous perſon will ſo far oblige and encourage me, as upon this overture to help me in this reſearch and ſcrutiny, by impart-ing to me, what either of his own knowledge, or credible relation from others, may conduce towards ſo noble a diſcovery.

3. Mean time let us entertain our ſelves with our third Query, and ſee if haply ſomewhat may not thence reſult adminicular, and ſuppletory to what may be defective and wanting in the former. Our third Query now is ; how in probability, and when, this Valley or Level, being once Sea-land, ſhould come to be ſo quite deſerted, and forſaken of the Sea, as it is at this day, the Sea not approaching it by ſo many, a dozen Miles, or more ? In anſwer whereof, I muſt needs ſay and grant, that in caſe this Level were once Sea, an *Æſtuary,* I mean, or Arm of it ; ſo very long it was ago, as we may not reaſonably think, that *Canterbury* (whether as a City, or never ſo mean a *Pa-gus,* or Village) was then *in rerum natura,* or a place inhabited ; which hap-ly it may have been ; if not as long as *Julius Cæſar*'s days, yet undoubtedly not long after. For an account we have of it (as of ſome other places in *Kent)* in the *Romans* time, both from *Ptolomy* the Geographer, *Antoninus*'s *Itinerary,* and elſewhere. Now (as was hinted e'rewhile) elder Records either of *Kent,* or of *Britain,* that we may confide in as Authentick, we have none that I know of before the *Romans* time : no written credible evidences to help us in this ſcrutiny. We muſt therefore either ſit us down, and reſt contented to throw off all further enquiry, or elſe caſt about for information as we can. Such as are for this latter, will tell you, that the world (all know) is very aged, many thouſand years old, and that many and manifold are the altera-tions, changes and mutations, which time hath made in ſeveral parts and quar-ters of the world, to the notice and diſcovery whereof, no written Record, or unwritten Tradition, at this day, can reach or direct us : Tradition it ſelf (longer liv'd many times than any written evidence) failing us for age. Of ſuch a nature, they conceive, may this of the *Æſtuary* be ; ſo very ancient, as time hath quite worn out the memory of it, withdrawn all light from us, that might conduct us in the ſcrutiny, and left us as men in the dark, without either *vola* or *veſtigium,* to ſtumble out our way, and rome and ramble at un-certainties. Such a one, haply, ſhall he be thought, that adventuring to conje-cture at the reaſon and occaſion of the Sea's receſs here, with an abſolute va-lediction to the place of its wonted reſort, ſhall pitch upon the Seas breaking, burſting and cleaving aſunder that *Iſthmus,* or Neck of Land, between *Gaul* and *Britain,* rendring the latter of the ſame Continent with the former ; ſuch things ('tis certain) hath hapned elſewhere. Thus (ſaith *Seneca*) hath the Sea rent *Spain* from the Continent of *Africk.* Thus, (as he adds) by *Deucalion*'s Flood, was *Sicily* cut from *Italy.* More inſtances of this kind may be found in Mr. *Cambden*'s *Cantium,* and elſewhere. And although there be no certain evi-

dence

dence of such an accident here, from ancient either Historians or Geographers, yet is the thing so strongly and rationally argued, by him especially, as by *Verstegan* also, *Twine*, and others before him; and the conjecture back'd with such plenty and probable *Criteria*, by the former, that what others may think, I know not; but were I of the Jury, I should more than incline to concur with them who find for the *Isthmus*. Especially, when to the plenty of Arguments, mustered up by Mr. *Cambden*, I shall have contributed this one, by him and the rest omitted; which is, that by a received, constant Tradition, *Romney-Marsh*, that large and spacious Level, containing (saith Mr. *Cambden*) 14 Miles in length, and 8 in breadth, was sometime Sea-land, lying wholly under Salt water, and is therefore of some, not improperly called the Sea's Gift; which having, when time was, forsaken it, and withdrawn his wonted influence from it; the place thereupon become, and continues firm Land. And if I may guess at the time and occasion of both that, and our *Canterbury* Level's recovery and riddance from Sea, I shall (for my part, with submission to better judgments) be apt to pitch upon that of the Sea's breaking through, and, in time, working and washing away that *Isthmus* between Us and *France*. And then, whereas beforetime *Romney* Level (which had, and hath its *Stours* too, or *Æstuaria*, as well as ours) and this other, not improbably (no high Lands, as we see, interposing for impeding their conjunction) were but one and the same Level, and lay under the Sea's and Salt waters tyranny; now both the one and the other (the Sea having so much play and elbow room, than formerly, by cleaving asunder the *Isthmus*) were rescued from it, and of an *Æstuary*, became such a rich and noble Valley or Level, as is second to none (I take it) in *England*.

I am resolved to keep home, and conceive my self no further concerned than in our own Level. But if from hence any other shall take an hint to consider of the *Netherlands* or *Low Countries*, and enquire whether those in whole, or in part, may not have risen out of, and conjecturally assigned for our *Kentish* Low-lands; I shall not at all wonder at it, thinking it (for my part) a task not unworthy a learned, judicious, sober undertaker: And were I as much concerned, and as well instructed there, as here, I should not know how to purge my self of negligence, if I did not undertake it with the first.

4. To come at length to the fourth and last of our Queries; By what means, the Sea once having its play there, (at *Chartham*) this Creature comes to lie and be found so deep in the ground, and under such a shelving Bank? My Answer is, That supposing this with the rest of the Level or Valley once occupied by the Sea or Salt water, that being a Creature which by fluxes and refluxes always is in motion, and thereby in time beating upon, and working it self into the Bank or rising-ground there, might at length so far undermine, eat into, and loosen it, as to fetch down so much Mould or Earth upon, or over the place, as to lodge the Creature at so great a depth. Or else perhaps, the continual agitation of the Water might, in time, force, drive up, and cast over it, that great quantity of Ouse, Earth, and other matter, under which it lay. By the way, it is observed, that the nature of the Soil, here and there, is such; so loose, supple, rotten and sandy, that meerly of it self, it is apt to sink and fall in; as was lately experienced by a Saw-pit, digg'd hard by, which after a little time, by the Earth's giving way on each side of it, fell in, and fill'd up it self.

Thus have you (gentle Readers) our *Chartham News*, or Discoveries, with the Circumstances; and the use my little skill will serve me to make of them, in point either of History or Geography. *Arcana* they are; but whether *tanti*; whether, I mean, grateful, or useful to the Publick, is left to the judicious Antiquaries, Naturalists, &c. who are desired to take the matter where the Historian hath left it. It hath been the Finder's care and good will, as to preserve, so to expose and communicate what he hath found: and if at length, to this of the parts, and by them a full discovery of the whole, by the Skill and Dexterity of the Learned, in the School, and secrets of Nature, may be added, for the benefit of the Commonwealth of Learning; both the Finder and Relator will think their time and pains very well both bestowed and recompenced.

Reflections upon Chartham News.

MR. *J. Luffkin* (*a*) gives an Account of divers Bones of an extraordinary Bigness, found lately deep under Ground in a Gravel-pit, not far from *Harwich* in *Essex*: He supposeth them to be the Bones of an Elephant, not of an *Hippotamus*, or other Marine Animal, as Mr. *Somner* doth conjecture those Bones to have been, which were found at *Chartham*. Mr. *Luffkin* in his Letter says, That Claudius *landed at* Rutupiæ *near* Sandwich, *whether* Richborough *or* Stoner, *it matters not*. And that, *His nearest Passage to the* Thames, *whither he was going, was indisputably through this Down of* Chartham.

We who live at or near *Canterbury*, have the advantage of being well acquainted with these Roads, both Ancient and Modern. The *Roman* Way from *Rutupiæ*, which beyond dispute was *Richborough*, to *London*, was through *Durovernum* to *Durolevum*, and so forward, as we are directed by the Tables of the *Itinerary. Chartham*-Downs lying about Three Miles or more Southward of *Canterbury*, cannot be the nearest Passage from *Richborough* either to *London* or the *Thames*: Nor have I ever seen any Footsteps upon Record, that the *Romans*, contrary to their usual Practice, did occasionally decline from the strait Road, to pass through these Downs in their Way to *London*.

Mr. *Somner* makes way for his supposed Sea-horse to come into these Parts, by suggesting that the River which now runs from *Ashford* through *Chartham* and *Canterbury* to *Sandwich*, was in former Times an *Æstuary*. In this Conjecture he is seconded by the Learned Dr. *Wallis*, &c. (*b*). And there appears no reason why we should not subscribe to the same Opinion. For the more easy granting of an *Æstuary* to have been here, we may reasonably conclude that this whole Valley is much raised, partly by the Slime, Mud, Sand, and the like, which the Tide left behind and lodged here, when it withdrew it self by degrees, and partly by Earth from the adjacent Hills, which Rains, especially hasty Showers, did wash down in the long Tract of Time, (namely, several Hundred Years,) since the *Æstuary* hath ceased to flow. And the particular Place or Ground whereon the City is built, may be somewhat elevated above the pitch of the Valley or Level that is on either side of it, *North* or *South*, by the Care and Industry of the Inhabitants in former Ages, according to Mr. *Somner*. The Nature of the Soil, upon the digging of Wells and Cellars at this day, near the Course of the present River, does abundantly confirm this Observation.

I will add Three fresh Instances to those which Mr. *Somner* has given us concerning the digging of Vaults or Wells in this City. While they were digging a Cellar in St. *Margaret's* Parish, they met with a strong piece of Stone-work, about Five Foot under Ground: It was indented and so firm, that it resisted very strong Blows of the Workmens Tools. In sinking a Well in *Lamb-Lane*, as it is called, within about Two Rods and a half of the Current of the River, the Labourers were stopt at about 15 Foot deep, by a Piece of Timber that lay cross the place, until it was sawn asunder. It appeared by the Mortices that were in it, to have been the Groundsell of some old Building. They continued to dig deeper, till they came to a Spring arising from a Gravelly or Stony Soil: And the Water seems to be Mineral, so far as Gall or Oak-Leaves will give a Proof thereof. I had my Information from the chief Workman who cut the foresaid Piece of Timber asunder in the Well. Upon the digging of a Cellar on the West-side of the Gate going into *Christ-Church*, near the Market-place, about Ten Foot under Ground, a Well was discovered not many Years since, which is about Twelve Foot deep, with a Curb to it.

(*a*) *Philosoph. Transact. Numb.* 274.   (*b*) *See Philosoph. Transactions for the Year* 1701.

Mr. *Som-*

Mr. *Somner* mentions some Pits, discovered not many Years since, about the place where the Market is now kept; and intimates from thence, as if the River had some time had its Current thereabouts: It seems probable that these were *Roman* Cisterns. In fine, he that would search for the *Roman* Antiquities of this City, must seek for them, so far as he can, *in Cantuariâ subterranea*, that is, under Ground.

We are inform'd by the Philosophical Transactions, That Two of the Teeth mentioned in this Treatise, are in the Repository at *Gresham* College; I can further certify, That another of them is in the Possession of Mr. Alderman *Grey* at *Canterbury*, and the Fourth of them is in the Library of *Christ-Church*, or at least a Tooth very like to one of them; which was reposited there, together with several other Rarities, by the Reverend Dr. *Bargrave*.

A POSTSCRIPT.

July 30. 1703.

SInce the abovesaid Reflections or Observations have been sent to the Press, there have been made some fresh Discoveries of Subterranean *Roman* Works in this City. As in digging a Cellar in the Parish of St. *Elphage*, the Workmen came to an Old Foundation of *Roman* Bricks, so strongly cemented, that they could not break it without much difficulty. It was Indent-wise, broad four Foot and four Inches, deep about four Foot, and about 8 Foot under Ground. Several of the Bricks were taken up whole. They were 17 Inches and a half long, and 11 Inches and three quarters of an Inch Broad; hereof I was an Eye-witness. I have been also informed, That a little within St. *George's*-Gate, where a new House is now Building, in digging the Cellar, the Workmen came to an Arch, firm and solid, which they broke to pieces: And that in a Garden near adjoyning, there was found a Pavement of broad free-stone several Foot under Ground: In *Mercery Lane*, in digging a Cellar, an Oven with Wood-coals in it, and Wood by it, was found, about 7 Foot under Ground, with two large broad Stones not far from it, lying one upon another, and in the middle of the upper Stone a Mortice-hole. In *Lamb Lane*, in a Well just by the River-side there are two Stones, laid there in former Ages by Art, so firm and heavy, as they could not be removed. The Workmen from the bigness and shape of them, call them Tomb-stones. And I am told of a *Roman* Pavement, of *Mosaick* Work, (whereof I have some of the little square Stones by me) discovered in digging a Cellar in St. *Margaret's* Parish. These Instances do confirm, That the *Roman* Antiquities of this City are to be searched for from 6 to 9 Foot under Ground; and that by future Searches and Enquiries Time may produce a fuller Knowledge of these Matters.

F I N I S.

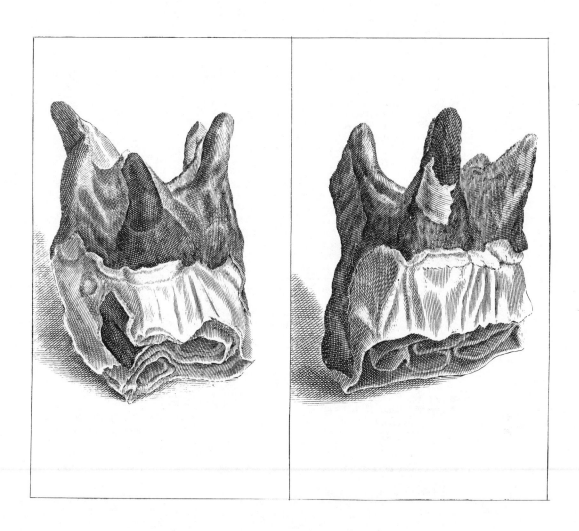

Fossil teeth found at Chartham, Canterbury, 1668

AN

Account of the Chantries, Free-Chappels Fraternities, &c. within, and near the City of Canterbury, *as they were returned into the late Court of Augmentations, by Commiſſioners appointed to ſurvey the ſame, by Virtue of a Commiſſion dated the Fourteenth Day of* February, *in the Second Year of the Reign of King* Edw. *the* VIth. *taken from the Original Survey.*

The Pariſhe of the Holy Croſs at Weſtgate in the Citie of Canturburye.

A Salarye of one Preyſte called *Jeſus Maſſe* Preiſte : within the ſame Pariſhe Churche of *Weſtegate*, Founded by whom it is not knowen, which Prieſte hath been accuſtomed to ſay Maſſe, and to help to mayntene Dyvyne Service within the ſame Church, and was removeable at the pleaſure of the Pariſheners there. The yerelye value of the Landes and Tenements thereunto apperteyninge by the yeare, xi *l*. ix *s*. viij *d*. whereof in Rents reſolut. XLiij *s*. viij *d*. *ob*. Rewards as well to the Clerke there as to thoverſeers of the ſaid Land, xxj *s*. iiij *d*. The Charges of one yerely Obit iij *s*. iiij *d*. And ſo remaneth clere, viij *l*. xix *d*. *ob*..... There hath been a Preiſte accuſtomed to ſerve in Forme aforeſaid, tyme oute of memorye of Man, untyll the Feaſte of Sainte *John Baptiſte, Anno primo Regis nunc* Edw. VI. ſyn's which Feaſte there hath bene no ſuch Preiſte maynteyned— The ſame Salarye is no Pariſhe Churche nor yet hath any Pariſhe Churche therunto appropriate, and therefore there is no Vicar there aledye endowed other then the Vicar of the Pariſhe Churche, nor yt is not requiſite to endowe a new Vicar. And there is CCXL Houſling People within the ſame Pariſh .. There hath not been any Gramar Scole kepte or Preacher maynttened by the ſame Salary, howbeit thiſſues and proffitts of the ſame Lands and Tenements by the ſpace of one yere laſt paſt have bene diſtributed to the pore People of the ſame Pariſh— There hath not been any Sale of Landes or Tenements, Spoyle or Waſte of Woods, or Gift of Goodes belonginge to the ſame Salarie. As concerning Goods Ornaments or Jeweſs, there is none.

Obit Landes given by the laſte and ſeverall Willes of *John Delphes* and *John Boll* for that their ſeverall *Obitts* ſhulde be yerelye kepte within the ſaid Pariſh Churche of *Weſtgate* for ever .... The yerelye value of the ſame Land ... xxxij *s*. whereof in Money diſtributed to the Poore: x *s*. Reparations of the Churche: viij *s*. And ſo remaneth clere: xiiij *s*....... Lampe Land there gyven by *William Harnehill* by his laſte Will for the findinge of one Lampe to burne contynually before the Sacramente within the ſame Churche for ever ... The yerelye value of the ſame Lande is: x *s*: ...... The Fraternitie called *Jeſus Brotherhed*, Founded by whom it is not knowne, within the ſame Pariſhe Church :... The yerely value of the Lande therunto appertaining is : x *s*: .... *Memorand*. There were divers Men and Women of their Devotions did geve unto the ſame Brothered in Money ſome iiij *d*. and other ſome viij *d*. yerely, for the whiche they were named Brothers and Syſters, which Money was as well beſtow'd upon the Lights in the ſame Church, as alſo upon one Maſſe and Dirige for the Brothers and Syſters departed. But there is not any other Landes or Tenements belonging to the ſame Brotherhed.

The Pariſh of Mary Magdalen in Canturbury.

Lands given by *Edmond Brandon* by his Laſt Will to thentent one Preiſt ſhuld ſay Maſſe of *Jeſu* Weekly within the ſaid Pariſhe Churche of *Mary Magdalene* for ever ... The yerely value of the ſame Land : x *s* whereof in Rent reſolute: vi *d*. And ſo remaneth clere.. ix *s*. vi *d*........ Light Rent given by *John Brande* by his Dede for the mayntinance of a Light as well to burne Nightlye before the Body of Chriſte as alſo at the Celebration of Divine Service within the ſaid Pariſhe Church for ever ... The ſame Rent is by the yere : viij *s*.

The Pariſh of Saynt George within the Cytie of Canturbury.

Obite Landes geven by the laſt and ſeveral Wills of *Edward Parlegate*, *Thomas Rayley*, and *John Williamſon*, as well for th'obſervation of their Obitts as for the ſuſtentation of one Lampe within the ſame Church for ever ... The yerelye value of the ſame Lands .. lxxvi *s*. viij *d*.... whereof in Rents reſolute... viijs *s*. i *d*. *ob* .. diſtributed to the Poore x *s*. Reparation of the Church xxij *s*. xi *d*. *ob* .. And ſo remaneth clere xxxv *s*. vij *d*.

Obite Rente geven by *Thomas Cadbury* to th'entent that one Obyte ſhulde be kepte within the Pariſh Church there for ever .. The ſame Rent is by the yere v *s*.

Obite

Obite Lands given by the laſte and ſeveral Wills of *Robert Bone*, *John Swanne* and *Edmond Mynot*, for that their ſeveral Obitts ſhulde be yerelye kepte within the ſaid Pariſh Churche for ever. The yerelye value of the ſame Land .. xxxvj *s*. . . whereof in Rents reſolute v *s*. xi *d*. diſtribution to the Poor: ij *s*. vj *d*, And ſo remaneth clere xxvij *s*. vij *d*.

Obite Rente given by *William Bennet* for one Obyt to be kepte within the ſame Churche for ever . . . The ſame Rent is by the yere: x *s*. . . . Lampe Land geven by *William Bennet* to th'entent one Lampe ſhulde be found within the ſame Churche for ever . . . The yerelye value of the ſame Land .. x *s*. . . . Churche Rente there geven by whom it is not knowne . . . The ſame Rente is by the yere .. i *d*.

Obite Lands geven by *William Bygge* by his laſt Will for one Obyt to be kept and a Lampe to be mayntened within the ſame Churche for ever— The yerelye value of the ſame Landes, xiiij *s*. iiij *d*. wherof in Rente reſolute xvj *d*. diſtribution to the Poor ij *s*. ix *d*. And ſo remaneth clere .. x *s*. iij *d*. . . . Light Lande gyven and bequeathed by *Thomas Ikham* by his laſt Will as well for the mayntenance of ij Tapers before the Sacramente in the ſame Churche as alſo to be employed in other works of Charitie for ever . . . . The yerely value of the ſame Lande xxiij *s*. iiij *d*. whereof in Rente reſolute ij *s*. And ſo remaneth clere xxj *s*. iiij *d*.

Obite Landes within the ſame Pariſh gyven and bequeth'd by divers Perſons for that one yerelye Obyt ſhulde be kepte there for ever . . . . The yerelye value of the ſame Landes . . xxiij. *s*. iiij *d*. . . . whereof in diſtribucion to the Pore xij *d*. Rente reſolute xxj *d*. . . And ſo remaneth clere .. xx *s*. vij *d*.

A Salarie or Stipend within the ſaid Pariſh Church of *All-Saynts* contynued and mayntened by the diſcretion and at the pleaſure of the Executors of *Thomas Beal* and *Alis* his Wyff . . . The yerelye Stipend of the ſame Salarie is perceived at the Hands of the ſaid Executor, whiche is by the yere . . . vj *l*. xiij *s*. iiij *d*. *William Thomſon* is Stypendarie Preiſt there of the age of xl yeares, indifferently lerned, and hath Pention of c *s*. at the Kings Majeſties Hands for term of his Lyff . . . . The ſaid Article for Indowment or not Indowment reqnyreth not any anſweare herein. And there is Ciiij Houſlyng People within the ſaid Pariſh . . . . Any Gramar Scole kept, Preacher mayneteyned, or pore People releved, there is none. Lands or Woods to be made Sale or Waſt of, there is none . . . Goods there is none.

Obite Lands gyven by *Thomas Fryer* by his laſt Will for an yerelye Obyt to be kept within the ſaid Church for ever . . . The yerelye value of the ſame Land is .. xiij *s*. iiij *d*. whereof diſtributed to the Pore .. ij *s*. viij *d*. And ſo remaneth clere x *s*. viij *d*. . . . . . Obite Rent gyven by *John Coleman* by his laſt Will for an Obyt to be kepte in the ſaid Church by the ſpace of xx yeres beginning the laſt Day of *January Anno Dom.* MDXXXVI . . . The ſaid Rente is by the yere .. x *s*. . . . . whereof diſtributed to the Poor: ij *s*. iiij *d*. And ſo remaneth clere: vij *s*. viij *d*.

Lampe Landes gyven and bequethed by the laſt Will and Teſtament of *John Winter* and *Johan* his Wife for and to the mayntenance of a Lamp within the Pariſh church there for ever .. The yerelye value of the ſame Landes is. xii *s*. whereof in Rent reſolute: x *d*. And ſo remaneth clere ·· xj *s*. ij *d*.

Obite Landes gyven and bequethed to the ſame Church by the Teſtament and laſte Will of *Jamys Aſe* for one Obyt yerelye to be kept there for ever . . . The yerelye value of the ſame Landes is .. iiij *s*. whereof in Rent reſolute: viij *d*. . . And ſo remaneth clere: iij *s*. iiij *d*.

A Meſuage appertaynynge to the late chauntric called Prynce *Edwards* Chauntrye within the Cathedral Church in *Canterbury* ſcytuat and being within the ſaid Pariſhe of Saynt *Alphege* . . . The yerelye value of the ſame Meſuage. xx *s*. . . . whereof in rent reſolute iiij *d*. And ſo remaneth clere xix *s*. viij *d*. . . . . . Lands geven by *Iſabell Fowle* by her laſt Will, as well to th'entent that a Preyſt ſhulde celebrate Maſſe within the ſaid Churche from the 3d week in Lent untill the morrow after Eſter daye, as alſo that one torche ſhulde be bought yerelye to ſerve the Highe Aulter for ever . . . The yerelye value of the ſame Land: xij *s*. . . . . Lampe rent gyven and aſſigned by *John Sellowe* for the mayntenance of one Lampe to burne yerely before the Image of Saint *John Evangeliſt* within the ſame Church for ever . . . . The ſame rente is by the yere . . . vj *d*.

The Sallarye or Stipende of ij Prieſts within the ſame Churche called Mr. *Ropers* Chauntrie Prieſts or Chaplyns, founded by the Aunceſtors of the ſame Mr. *Roper*, to the intent to ſerve and celebrate at the Aulter of Saint *Nicholas* there. The yearly ſtipend is xvj *l*.

Thomas Freeman and *Thomas Ward* be nowe Chauntrye Prieſts or Chaplens there, either of them being of the age of xl yeares, of honeſt qualities and well lernyd And the

ſaid

said *Thomas Freeman* is nowe refident, and the other liveth in another place; howebeit he hath been refident within five years laft paft.

To the Article whether there be any Vicar alredie .... endowed, or what neceffitie theɹe is newely to endow one, it requireth no anfwear herein; for that the fame Salarie is neither a Parifh Church nor yet any Parifh Church thereunto appropriate. And there is clxxiiij: houfling People within the fame Parifh.

There is not any Gramar Scole kepte, Preacher mayntayned, or pore People relevid by the fame Sallarie.

Lands or Woods to be made Sale or waft of there is none.
Goods there is none.

Obite Landes there given and affigned by *John Delves* by his laft Will, as well for one obyt to be kept yerelye within the faid Parifhe Church, as alfo to be delte and diftributed amonges pore People for ever ... The yereɩye value of the fame Land: vij *s.* whereof diftributed to the Pore: ij *s.* And fo remaneth clere: v *s.*
Light rent within the fame Parifhe, given by whom it is not knowen ... The fame rent is yerelye: ij *s.* x *d.* ob.

The Chauntrie of our Bleffed Lady the Virgyn within the Hofpitall of the Kings bridge in *Canturbury,* was founded by one *Jamys* of *Bourne* to th'entent and purpofe that one Priefte fhulde celebrate divyne wirhin the faid Hofpitall, and to praye for the Soule of one *Ifabelle* fometyme Queen of *England,* and for the Soule of the faid Founder and all Chriftian Soules for ever ... The yerelye value of the Lands Tenements and Annuityes thereunto apperrayning x *l.* xj *s.* viij *d.* whereof in Rents refolute vj *d.* .... perpetual tenthes. xx *s.* viij *d.* .... And fo remaneth clere .. ix *l.* x *s.* vj *d.*

Nicholas Champion Clerke is Incumbent or Chauntrie Preift there, of the age xl yeares, of honeft learning qualities and converfation, and hath nothing whereon to live over and befides the Revenues of the faid Chauntrie.

The fame Chauntrie is no Parifhe Churche nor any Parifhe Churche thereunto appropriate; wherefore it ɩequyrith no new Endowment of a Vicar there.
There hath not been any Gramar Scole kepte, Preacher mayntened, or pore People relived by the faid Chauntrie.
There hath not been any Sale of Lands or Tenements, fpoyle or wafte of Woods, or gift of Goods belonging to the fame Chauntrie.
Goodes or Juells there none.

The Chauntrie within the Parifh Church of Saint *Nicholas* in *Harbaldon* was Founded by *William* fome time Archbifhop of *Canterbury,* to th'entent that a Preift, being one in number of the Brothers of the Hofpital there, fhulde celebrate Divine Service, minifter the Sacraments, and take Cure of the faid Brothers of the faid Hofpitall for ever ... The yerelye value of the Lands and Poffeffions apperteynynge to the fame Chauntrie: viij *l.* xiij *s.* iiij *d.* whereof in Rente refolute: iiij *s,* viij *d.* ob: perpetual tenth: xvij *s.* iiij *d.* .... And fo remaneth clere to the Chauntrie Prieft there ... vij *l.* xj *s.* iij *d.* ob.

George Higges is now Incumbent and Chauntrie Preift there, of the age of li years, indifferently learned, and of honeft converfation and qualities, and hath not any other Living befides the fame Chauntrie.
There is not any Vicar there alredie endowed, and it is requifɩte one Preift or Minifter to ferve there, for there be xvij Houflyng People within the forefaid Hofpitall.
There is not any Gramar Scole kepte, Preacher maintayned, or poor People releved by the faid Chauntrie.
There hath not been any Sale of Landes or Tenements, fpoyle or wafte of Woodes, or gifte of Goodes belonging to the faid Chauntrie.
Goodes there is none.

The Names of the Commiffioners appointed by King *Edward* the Sixth for this purpofe were.

Raffe Vane,		*Henry Crifp,*		*Chriftofer Nevifon,*	
Anthony Aucher,		*Thomas Spilman,*		*William Hide,*	
Walter Hendle,	Knts.	*Paule Sidnor,*	Efqs;	and	Gent.
and		and		*John Lendall,*	
James Hales,		*Thomas Watton.*			

APPENDIX.

A Transcript out of Domes-day Book.

CHENTH.

IN civitate *Cantuaria* habuit Rex *Edwardus* L. & I. burgenses reddentes gablum & alios cc. & xij. super quos habebat sacam & socam. & iij. molend. de xl. sol. Modo Burgenſ. gablum reddentes sunt **xix.** * De **xxxij**ᵒᵇᵘˢ aliis qui fuerunt, sunt vastati **xj.** in fossato civitatis, & Archiepiscopus habet ex eis **vij.** Et Abbas Sancti Augustini alios **xiiij.** pro excambio castelli. & adhuc sunt cc. & xij. burgenſ. super quos habet Rex sacam & socam & iij. molend. reddunt c. & viij. sol. & thelonium redd. lxviij sol. Ibi viij. acræ prati quæ solebant esse legatorum Regis mo. reddt de censu. xv. sol. & mille acræ silvæ infructuosæ de qua exeunt xxiiij sol. Inter totum † *T. R. E.* valuit lj. lib. & tantundem quando Hamo vicecom. recept. & mo. l. lib. appreciat. Tamen qui tenet reddit xxx lib. arsas & pensatas, & xxiiij. lib. ad numerum super hæc omnia habet Vicecom. c. & x sol.

* De aliis qni fuerunt xxxii. obierunt. & adhuc, &c. Dr. *Brady's History of English Burghs.*

† Id est Tempore Regis Edwardi.

Duas domos duorum Burgensium unam foris aliam intra civitatem quidam Monachus ecclesiæ *Cantuar.* abstulit. Hæ erant positæ in Regis calle.

Burgenses habuer. xlv mansur. extra civitatem de quibus ipsi habebant gablum & consuetudinem. Rex autem habet sacam & socam. Ipsi quoque Burgenses habebant de Rege **xxxiij** acr. ‖ terræ in gildam suam. Has domus & hanc terram tenet *Rannulfus de Columbeis.* Habet etiam quater **xx** acr. terræ super hæc. Quas tenebant Burgenses in alodia de Rege. tenent quoque **v** acr. terræ quæ justè pertinent uni ecclesiæ. De his omnibus revocat isdem *Rannulfus* ad protectorem episcopum Baiocensem.

‖ Alit prati Brady

Radulfus de Curbespine habet **iiij** mansur. in civitate quas tenuit quædam concubina Heraldi. de quibus est saca & soca Regis. Sed usque nunc non habuit.

Isdem *Radulfus* ten' alias **xj.** mansuras de episcopo *Baioc.* in ipsa civitate quæ fuer. Sbern Biga. & reddunt xj sol. & xi den. & i. obolum.

Per totam civitatem *Cantuariæ* habet Rex sacam & socam excepta terra ecclesiæ S. Trin. & S. *Augustini.* Eddevæ *Reginæ.* & *Alnod' Cild.* & *Esber Bigà.* & *Siret de Cilleham.*

Concordatum est de rectis callibus quæ habent per civitatem introitum & exitum quicunque in illis forisfecerit Regi emendabit. Similiter de callibus rectis extra civitatem usque ad unam leugam, & iij perticas & iij pedes. Si quis ergò infra has publicas vias intus civitatem vel extra foderit, vel palum fixerit; sequitur illum Præpositus Regis ubicunque abierit & emendam accipiet ad opus Regis.

Archiepiscopus calumniatur forisfacturam in viis extra civitatem ex utraque parte ubi terra sua est. Quidam præpositus Brumannus nomine *T. R. E.* cepit consuetud. de extraneis mercator. in terra S. Trinit. & S. *Augustini,* Qui post ea temp. *R. W.* ante Archiepiscopum *Lanfranc.* & Episcopum *Baioc.* recognovit se injustè accepisse. Et sacramento facto juravit quòd ipsæ ecclesiæ suas consuetud. quietas habuer. *R. E.* tempore Et exinde utræque ecclesiæ in sua terra habuer. consuetud. suas judicio Baronum Regis qui placitum tenuer.

Carta **Alianor.** *Reginæ quòd homines noſtri non tenentur facere foſſat. vel murum circa Civitatem* **Cantuariensem.**

A Dei gratia humilis *Angliæ* Regina, omnibus Christi fidelibus ad quos literæ præsentes pervenerint, salutem in vero salutari. Audito quòd karissimus filius noster Rex Angliæ *Richardus* detentus est ab Imperatore Romano, vovimus ad memoriam beati & gloriosi martyris *Thomæ,* ut liberationem Domini Regis filii nostri possemus ejus intervenientibus meritis & precibus obtinere. Cum autem *ob terræ turbationem Cantuariæ* Civitas fossatis & muris & aliis propugnaculis muniretur, omnésq; ad hoc compellerentur; quidam homines Prioris & Conventus ecclesiæ *Cant.* non de jure, non de consuetudine, sed ad nostrarum precum instantiam ibidem operati sunt. Nos itaque diligentius attendentes libertates & immunitates ad præfatam ecclesiam & ejus homines ubicunque fuerint pertinentes, monachis ejusdem ecclesiæ concessimus & promisimus, quòd operatio illa quam urgens necessitas & nostra intervenio inducebat, eis vel hominibus eorum in posterum non noceret, eorumque cartis & libertatibus, quæ illis à multis Regibus confirmatæ sunt, præjudicium

*A

cium

cium non afferret. In hujus rei teſtimonium præſentes literas ſigillo noſtro fecimus communiri. Teſt. *H.* Archidiac' ejuſdem eccleſiæ, & magiſtro *P. Bleſſ. Bathon.* Archid. apud *London.*

Numb. III. OMnibus ad quos præſens ſcriptum pervenerit, *Hubertus de Burgo* Juſtitiarius Domini Regis, ſalutem in Domino. Noveritis quòd ad magnam petitionem meam & civium Civitatis *Cant.* Monachi eccleſiæ Chriſti *Cant.* vendiderunt civibus *Cant.* de boſco ſuo ad faciendum Cleias ad defenſionem Civitatis *Cant.* Et quia conſtabat nobis plenè per cartas Domini *Johannis* Regis noſtri, & anteceſſorum ſuorum quod prædicti Monachi ad munitionem prædict. Civitatis non tenentur, nè prædicta venditio poſſit in poſterum prædictis Monachis vel eccleſiæ *Cant.* præjudicare, literis præſentibus cum ſigilli noſtri appoſitione jus & libertates dictorum Monachorum & *Cant.* eccleſiæ proteſtamur ſuper prædict' venditione. Val'.

Numb. IV. *Menſuratio murorum circa Civitatem Cant' per* Thomam Ickham *honorablem Civem Civitatis prædict' fact. Ann. Reg. Hen. tertio.*

PRimo á parva porta de Quyningate uſque ad Burgate xxxviij. perticat, & porta de Burgate continet unam.

Item, à dicta porta de Burgate uſque ad Newingate xxxvij. perticat, & porta de Newingate continet unam.

Item, à dicta porta de Newingate uſque ad Ridingate xlviij. perticat, & porta de Ridingate continet unam.

Item, à dicta porta de Ridingate uſque ad Worgate lxxxiij. perticat, & porta de Worgate continet unam.

Item, à porta de Worgate uſque ad aquam quæ eſt à retro S. Mildredæ, lxj. perticat, & riparia ibidem continet, iiij. perticat.

Item, à riparia uſque ad Weſtgate, cxviij. perticat, & dimid', & porta de Weſtgate continet unam.

Item, a porta de Weſtgate uſque ad finem muri qui vocatur Long-wall continet', lix. perticat, & quartam partem perticat.

Item, aqua quæ vocatur Stower ab illo muro uſque ad murum qui vocatur Waterlocke continet, xviij. perticat, & dimid.

Item, & murus ab illo loco uſque ad Northgate continet, xl. perticat, & porta de Northgate continet unam.

Item, à porta de Northgate uſque ad Quyningate continet lxix. perticat, quæ eſt verſus Prior' eccleſiæ Chriſti Cant.

         Summa totalis DLXXXII.   perticat, & quarta pars perticat.

Numb. V. APud manerium de *Newington* fuerunt quondam Moniales quæ tenuerunt manerium illud integrè, ſcilicet id quod Dominus Abbas S. *Auguſtini* tenet, & id quod hæredes Domini G. *de Lucy* tenent, & id quod hæredes B. *de Ripariis* tenent, præter id quod Richardus de Lucy adquiſivit de Brunell de Middleton, & tunc defendebat' illud manerium pro uno ſullingo terræ verſus Regem apud Middleton. Poſtea contingebat quod Prioriſſa ejuſdem Monaſterii ſtrangulata fuit de conventu ſuo nocte in lecto ſuo, & poſtea tracta ad puteum quod vocatur Nonnepet: quo comperto, cepit Dominus Rex manerium illud in manum ſuam, & tenuit illud in cuſtodia ſua, cæteris monialibus uſque Scapeiam inde amotis. Poſtea Henricus Rex Pater ſubſtituit quoſdam canonicos ſeculares, & dedit illis illud manerium integrum cum xxviij. penſis caſei de manerio de Middelton. Subſequenti verò tempore unus occiſus fuit inter eos, de qua morte quatuor fuerunt culpabiles, & duo reliqui culpabiles non inventi, per licentiam Domini Regis portionem ſuam dederunt ſancto Auguſtino, quinque partibus remanentibus in manu Regis uſque dedit illas partes Domino Richardo de Lucy Iuſtitiario ſuo. Unde Abbas S. Auguſtini tenuit prædictas duas partes quoſque per concambium, ut ſupradictum eſt, unà cum xj ſol. v^d annui redditus in hamleto de Thetham fuit ſibi ſatisfactum, qui quidem Hamlet poſtea devenit in manus Abbatis de Feverſham, ex dono prædicti Richardi de Lucy, qui Abbas de prædicto redditu eccleſiæ beati Auguſtini reſpondet in præſenti. Alia quædam ſcripta tradunt illos præbendarios tempore Regis Willielmi conqueſtoris ſic deliquiſſe, per quorum delictum omnia ſua ibidem in manu Regis fuerunt forisfacta, qui quidem Dominus Willielm' Rex duas partes ſæpe nominatas dedit Abbati S. Auguſtini. Quæ verò iſtarum opinionum ſit verior, in effectu ad eligendum relinquo optioni legentis. *Thorn in vitis Abbatum S. Aguſtini.*

Records extracted from the Tower of London, *touching the Liberties of* Numb. VI.
Canterbury. *viz.*

Ex bundello recordorum & brevium Regis, de anno decimo nono Regni Regis Ricardi fecundi.

Rcardus Dei gratia Rex Angliæ & Franciæ & Dominus Hiberniæ Thes' & Camerar' fuis falutem. Volentes certis de caufis certiorari quæ & cujufmodi libertates civibus Cantuar. apud Cantuar. coram Johanne de Berewyk & fociis fuis Jufticiar' itinerantibus in comitatu Kanciæ Anno Domini Edwardi filii Regis Henrici quondam regis Angliæ vicefimo primo allocatæ fuerunt, necnon quæ & cujufmodi libertates eifdem civibus allocatæ fuerunt coram Henrico de Stanton & fociis fuis Jufticiar' Domini Regis Edwardi proavi noftri itinerantibus apud Cant. Anno regni fui fexto in recordo & proceffu coram eifdem Jufticiar' habitis de morte Alexandri Carectarii Prioris ecclefiæ Chrifti Cantuar. infra Prioratum ejufdem Prioris ut dicitur interfecti, vobis mandamus quod fcrutatis rotulis prædictorum Jufticiar. de annis prædictis in Thefaur' noftra fub cuftodia veftra exiftentibus nos de eo quod inde inveneritis in Cancellar' noftra fub figillo fcaccarii noftri diftincte & aperte fine dilatione reddatis certiores, hoc breve nobis remittentes. Tefte meipfo apud Weftm' quarto decimo die Novembris, anno regni noftri decimo nono.   Scarle.

Placita coronæ coram I. de Berewyk, Thoma de Normanville, Willielmo de Bereford, Johanne de Lythegreynes & Hugone de Kane Jufticiar' itinerantibus apud Cantuar. in Comitatu Kanciæ à die Pafchæ in quidecim dies anno regni regis Edwardi fillii Regis Henrici vicefimo primo.

De feriantiis dicunt quod Willielmus de Lynftede Rector ecclefiæ de Stureye tenet Alderman' de Weftgate in capite de Domino Rege per feriantiam unius efperuarii fori quæ **Weftgate.** valet per annum decem marcas, nefciunt quo waranto. Et fimiliter Johannes filius Johannis de Handlo tenet Aldr' de Redingate Cant. in Capite de Domino Rege quæ valet per **Redingate.** annum duos folid', nihil inde faciendo Domino Regi per annum nefciunt quo waranto. Et fimiliter Edmundus de Tyerne tenet Alder de' Worthgate quæ valet per annum duos folid' **Worthgate.** in capite de Domino Rege, nihil inde faciendo eidem Domino Regi per Annum, nefciunt quo waranto. Et fimiliter Thomas Chicch tenet Aldr' de Burgate quæ valet quadraginta denar' per annm. Et Stephanus Chicche tenet Alder' de Northgate quæ valet duos folidos **Burgate.** per annum. Et Johannes de Holt tenet Aldermann' de Newingate quæ valet per annum duos **Northgate.** folidos nihil inde faciendo Domino Regi per annum, nefciunt quo waranto. Ideo præ- **Newingate.** ceptum vicecomiti quod venire faciat eos, &c. Poftea prædictus Stephanus Chicche & alii excepto magiftro Willielmo de Lynftede veniunt & dicunt quod prædictæ Aldermanriæ fpectantes funt & annexæ ad firmam Civitatis prædictæ, viz. fexaginta libr' quas folvunt Domino Regi pro prædicta Civitate per annum. Et Jur' iftius civitatis hoc idem teftantur. Ideo remaneant quoufque & Poftea venit prædictus mag' Willielmus ac Lynftede & dicit quod ipfe tenet prædictam feriantiam de quodam Willielmo de Godftede, reddendo eidem Willielmo inde per annum centum folid. fine quo ipfe non poteft inde refpondere, &c. Ideo præceptum eft Vicecom' quod venire faciat eundem Willielmum, &c. Et prædictus mag' Willielmus ponit loco fuo Phm' de Intebergh' clericum. Poftea Willielmus de Godftede per attornatum fuum venit & dicit quod ipfe tenet eandem feriantiam de communitate civitatis prædictæ reddendo inde per annum quadraginta denar' ad firmam civitatis & hoc à tempore quo non extat memoria. Et Jur' hoc idem teftantur. Ideo prædicti mag' Willielmus de Lyndeftede & Willielmus de Godftede inde fine dine, falvo jure Domini Regis, &c. De libertatibus dicunt quod cives Cantuar' tenent eandem civitatem de Domino Rege reddendo inde per annum ad fcaccarium Domini Regis fexaginta libras. In qua quidem civitate prædicti cives clamant habére return' brevium, emendas affifæ panis & cervifiæ, Pillor', Tumbrell', & furcas nefciunt quo waranto. Ideo præceptum eft vicecom' quod venire faciat prædictos eives. Poftea prædicti cives veniunt & dicunt quod Dominus Henricus Rex pater Domini Regis nunc conceffit eis & carta fua confirmavit quod ipfi & heredes fui habeant & teneant de eodem Henrico Rege & heredibus fuis imperpetuum prædictam Civitatem Cantuar. ad firmam pro fexaginta libris fterlingorum fingulis annis folven' per manum fuam viz. ad Sccm' Pafche triginta libr', & ad Sccm' fancti Michaelis triginta libr' per cartam fuam quam proferunt & quæ hoc idem teftatur. Et quoad return' brevium & alias prædictas libertates dicunt, quod idem Dominus Henricus Rex conceffit eis quod ipfi & eorum heredes imperpetuum habeant return' brevium Regis prædictam civitatem & libertatem ejufdem civitatis tangen' tam infra fuburbium quam infra Civitatem prædictam. Et quoad prædictas libertates, viz. tenere placita coronæ habere mercatum, feriam, furcas & Weyf' in civitate prædicta, dicunt quod Dominus Henricus Rex pater Domini Regis nunc conceffit eis omnes libertates & liberas confuetudines quas habuerunt tempore Henrici Regis avi ipfius Henrici Regis patris Domini Regis nunc, quando meliores & liberiores eas habuerunt. Et dicunt quod cives prædicti & anteceffores fui prædictis libertatibus à tempore prædicti Henrici Regis proavi Domini Regis nunc plene

ne uſi ſunt. Et Johannes de Mulford qui ſequitur pro Rege petit judicium pro Domino Rege de ſicut prædicti cives nullam ſpeciale warantum oſtendunt à Domino Rege vel ab aliquo anteceſſore ſuo de libertatibus prædictis niſi tantum quod Dominus Henricus Rex pater Domini Regis nunc conceſſit eis omnes libertates & liberas conſuetudines quas habuerunt rempore Henrici Regis proavi Domini Regis nunc, quæ quidem libertates non ſpecificantur in prædicta carta, ſi prædictas libertates, viz. emendas aſſiſe panis & Serviſie, pillòr' tumbrell', furcas & Weyf' clamare poſſunt per eandem cartam. Poſtea inquiſitum eſt per Jur' iſtius civitatis ſi prædictæ libertates annexæ fuerunt prædictæ civitati tempore quo prædictus Dominus Henricus Rex dimiſit prædictis civibus prædictam civitatem ad feodi firmam dicunt quod ſic. Ideo remaneant ſalvo jure Domini Regis, &c.

Borgha ſancti Martini.

Quædam Avicia de Lymeberneſtere de London inventa fuit occiſa in Borgha ſancti Martini, neſcitur quis eam occidit. Primus inventor & quatuor vicini veniunt & non maletr'. Et prædicta Borgha ſancti Martini in qua iſta felonia facta fuit ab ultimo itinere hic uſque nunc ſubtraxit ſe à civitate iſta cum qua ſolebat eſſe reſpondens in itinere Juſtic. de omnibus ad coronam Domini Regis pertinentibus. Et ſimiliter compertum eſt per rotulos I. de Reygate & ſociorum ſuorum Juſticiar. ultimo itinerantium hic quod præſentatum fuit coram eiſdem Juſticiar' quod tenentes iſtius Borghæ ſancti Martini & de la Fyſpole ſolebant

F/ſhepole.

Portmotum.

facere ſectam ad hundredum Domini Regis de Burgate, de tribus ſeptimanis in tres ſeptimanas, & ad Portmotum civitatis, & quod ſubtraxerunt ſe ad dampnum Domini Regis duorum ſolidorum per annum per quendam Johannem de Tonford tunc ballivum Archiepiſcopi Cantuar. Et idem Johannes modò venit & dicit quod prædicta Borgha nunquam ſubtracta fuit per ipſum. Et prædicta Borgha ſancti Martini venit & quoad hoc quod ſolebant reſpondere & intendere cum hominibus iſtius civitatis ad præſentandum quæ ad coronam pertinent, bene cogn. quod ipſi in aliis itineribus reſpondere ſolebant cum hominibus iſtius Civitatis. Et quod ipſi nunquam præmuniti fuerunt nec ſunt ad aliquid præſentandum cum eis. Et quod ipſi ſemper parati fuerunt ad præſentandum cum eis ſi præmuniti fuiſſent. Et Jur. iſtius Civitatis præſentes ſunt & non poſſunt oſtendere nec verificare quod unquam præmuniverunt prædict. borgham ad aliquid præſentand. cum eis. Set omnino prædictam feloniam infra præcinctum iſtius Civitatis factam concelaverunt. Ideo ad judicium de eiſdem duodecim Jur. Et prædicta borgha de cetero ſit intendens & reſpondens cum prædictis civibus de hiis quæ ad coronam pertinent. Et quod Coron' Civitatis de cetero fac. officium coronatoris in prædicta Borgha. Et eadem borgha ſancti Martini quoad prædictam ſectam dicit quod nunquam conſueverunt facere ſectam ad hundredum de Burgate nec ad Portmotum Civitatis prædictæ tantum bis in Anno ad arma monſtranda. Et de hoc ponit ſe ſuper patriam. Et Jur. iſtius Civitatis ſimul cum militibus ad hoc electis dicunt ſuper ſacramentum ſuum quod omnes reſidentes & commorantes in eadem Borgha debent venire quater per annum ad hundredum de Burgate ad ſummonitionem Ballivorum Civitatis ad præſentandum ea quæ ad viſum franci-plegii pertinent. Et ſimiliter venire debent ad Portmotum iſtius civitatis quociens cives prædicti corniare fecerint commune cornu Civitatis prædictæ, & dicunt quod predicta ſecta ſubtracta eſt per octodecim annos elapſos ad dampnum Domini Regis duodecim denar. per annum. Ideo conſideratum eſt quod prædicta Borgha de cetero faciet prædictas ſectas, & quod diſtr. deceterò ad prædictam ſectam fac. Et quod Dominus Rex recuperet arreragia ſua de eadem borgha viz. octodecim ſold. Et prædicta borgha in miſericordia. Et quoad tenentes de Fyſpole dicunt quod ipſi fac. ſectam ſicut facere conſuerunt. Et quod nichil eſt à retro domino Regi Ideo remaneant, &c. Et quoad Johannem de Tonford dicunt quod ipſe non fecit prædictam ſubtractionem, nec per ipſum facta fuit.

Plita' coronæ de Com. Kanciæ coram Henrico de Stanton, Willielmo de Ormeſby, Henrico Spigurnel, Iohanne de Mutford & Willielmo de Goldington Iuſticiar. Domini Regis itinerantibus apud Cantuar. in octabis Nativitatis ſancti Iohannis Baptiſtæ, anno Regni regis Edwardi filii regis Edwardi ſexto.

Adam le Corour occidit Alex' Carectarium Prioris eccleſiæ Chriſti Cantuar. infra Prioratum ejuſdem Prioris. Et ſtatim poſt captus fuit & coram Iuſticiariis ad diverſas tranſgreſſiones, &c. tanquam clericus convictus liberatus fuit Archiepiſcopo Cant. & adhuc eſt in priſona de Maydenſtan, nulla habuit catalla nec fuit in warda quia extraneus primus inventor & duo vicini veniunt & non maleter. Et Alex. atte Amerye & Thomas Biane duo vicini non veniant & nec maletr. Et Alex. fuit attach' per Thomam Beane & Galfrm' Coupere. Ideo in miſericordia. Et prædictus Thomas fuit attach' per Williel' Sellinghale & Richardum de Wykham. Ideo in miſericordia. Poſtea compertum eſt per rotulos Coron' Civitatis Cantuar. & teſtatum quod Iohannes Andrew tunc coronator, &c. venit in craſtino circa horam primam poſt feloniam prædictam factam, & voluit vidiſſe corpus & feciſſe officium Coronatoris, & Willielmus de Derby tenens locum Richardi de Wylmynton tunc Seneſcalli prædicti Prioratus, & Thomas Percy cuſtos portæ prædicti Prioris non permiſerunt ipſum Coronatorem intrare. Et poſtea prædictus Prior miſit pro coronatoribus forinſecis, viz. Henrico de Woghope, Willielmo Baroun qui obierunt & Johanne de Aldeloſe

Barbecan.

Coronatore ſuperſtite qui ceperunt Inquiſitionem de morte prædicta apud le Barbecan extra Caſtrum Cantuar. in præſentiis Warreſe' de Valoign' & Johannis de Bourne tunc Cuſtodum pacis, &c. Et præceptum eſt vicecom' quod venire faciat prædictum Priorem, &c. Poſtea venit prædictus Prior & dicit quod Prioratus ejus eſt locus exemptus à Civitate Cantuar. & ab ejus libertate. Dicit etiam quod prædictus Cotonator per ipſum impeditus non

fuit

fuit; nec prædicti Coronatores forinseci per ipsum fuerunt mandati. Et hoc petit quod inquir. Et Jur. Civitatis simul cum militibus ad hoc e'ectis dicunt super sacramentum suum quod Richardus de Wylmynton qui obiit tunc Senescallus ejusdem Prioris non permisit dictum Johannem Andrew Coronatorem intrare dictum Prioratum pro officio suo faciendo set claudere fecit portas ejusdem Prioratus ita quod intrare non potuit, set dicunt quod hoc fecit nesciente Priore. Dicunt etiam quod idem Richardus misit pro prædictis Coronatoribus forinsecis qui ibidem venerunt, & prædictum mortuum viderunt. Et dicunt quod idem mortuus postea sepultus fuit per quosdam graciones qui prius erant socii ipsius mortui quorum nomina ignorant. Et quod prædicti Coronatores ceperunt inquisitionem prædictam de prædicto mortuo apud le Barbacane, ut prædictum est. Et Jur. quesiti qui Coronatores solebant facere officium Coronatoris in prædicto Prioratu temporibus retroactis, dicunt quod semper ante illud tempus Coronatores Civitatis Cantuar. illud fecerunt. Quesiti etiam si prædicti Coronatores forinseci venissent ibidem per mandatum Prioris, dicunt quod non, set per prædictum Richardum de Wylmynton ignorante prædicto Priore. Ideo idem Prior inde quietus. Postea venit prædictus Willielmus de Derby & non potest dedicere quin impedivit prædictum Coronatorem Cantuar. Nec quin claudere fecit portas prædicti Prioratus, per quod idem Coronator officium suum de prædicto mortuo ibidem facere non potuit. Ideo ipse custoditur: Et præceptum est vicecom' quod capiat prædict' Thomam Percy, &c. Postea venit prædictus Willielmus de Derby & fecit finem pro prædicta transgressione per quinque marcas, per pl' Johannis de Iseld, & Thomæ Dod de Faveretham. Postea venit prædictus Thomas, & non potest dedicere quin fecit prædictam transgressionem. Ideo ipse custoditur. Postea venit & finem fecit per quadraginta denar. per plm' Richardi de Haddelegh.

M^d. quod iste tenor exemplificatus est sub eo qui sequitur tenor. Richardus dei gratia Rex Angliæ & Franciæ & Dominus Hiberniæ. Omnibus ad quos præsentes literæ pervenerint salutem. Inspeximus quandam certificationem nobis in Cancellaria nostra per Thes. & Camerar. nostros de mandato nostro missam in hec verba. Placita Coronæ &c. de verbo in verbum usque in finem. & tunc sic. Nos autem certificationem prædictam ad requisitionem dilectorum nobis Ballivorum Civitatis nostræ Cant. tenore præsentium duximus exemplificandam. In cujus, &c. Teste Rege apud West' quintodecimo die   Anno

King Stephen's Grant of the Mill call'd King's-Mill to the Church of St. Augustine.

Numb. VII. a.

STephanus Rex Angliæ Archiepisc. Episc. Abbatibus, &c. salutem. Sciatis quod pro salute animæ meæ, &c. dedi & concessi Deo & Ecclesiæ S. Augustini Molendinum quod habui infra Civitatem Cantuar. juxta Eastbrigge, & totum cursum aquæ illius Molendini in restaurationem vadimonii centum marcarum quas ego pro necessitate mea ab eadem ecclesia cepi, præsentibus Baronibus meis; quare volo & firmiter præcipio, quod præfata ecclesia S. Aug. teneat & habeat prædict' molendinum cum omnibus eid' pertinentibus ad servitium altaris illius ecclesiæ, ita bene & in pace liberè & quietè & honorificè sicut ego aut aliquis Rex prædecessorum meorum melius liberius & quietius tenuit, &c.

Numb. VII. b.

ET nota quòd istud Molendinum per Clarembaldum superius nominatum, cum aliis rebus & possessionibus per eum nequiter distractis Domino Regi Henrico & successoribus suis alienatum, & ad opus suæ Civitatis rehabitum. Iste tamen Hen. Rex ad recompensationem hujus injuriæ isti Monasterio multas libertates scribitur concessisse, &c.

Numb. VII. c.

COncessit idem Rex Henricus istis temporibus Civitatem suam Cantuar. civibus ejusdem, sub gubernaculo duorum Ballivorum regendam, ad feodi firmam lx. librar. ad errarium suum annuatim solvend. cum omnibus consuetudinibus ad eand. Civitat. pertinent' cum molendino de Eastbrigge, vel aliter Kingsmill dictum. Et hîc nota quòd præd' Molendinum per Stephanum Regem ecclesiæ beati Aug. ut dict' est extitit datum, per Clarembaldum intrusorem Henrico Regi tum Anglorum alienatum, & à successoribus Regibus ad opus Civitatis injuriose detentum, & per istum Hen. præd' Civibus unà cum Burgo in forma prædicta resignatum.

Numb. VII. d.

QUI requisitus an fuerat Firmarius dicti molendini, dixit quòd non, sed fatetur ipsum fore servientem Majorum Civitatis Cantuar. per eos ibid. deputatum. Item requisitus, fatetur quòd omnes pistores villæ totum bladum pro albo pane faciend. debent molere sine tollo, vel receptione aliqua in blado vel alio modo. Item oneratur, & fatetur, quòd de farina bladi pistorum pro pane nigro, debent solvere pro mulctura tollum. Item omnes alii ibid.

Numb. VII. e.

MOlendinum de Abbotteftnelle quod ipsemet proprio labore adquisivit, ad Sacristiam deputavit, hac interposita conditione, ut tota annona Curiæ sancti Aug. ibidem liberè absque thelonio molatur, decimam prædict. molendini elemosinariæ Sancti Aug. solvatur, residuum quoque profectus illius molendini in usus sacristiæ convertatur.

* B

The

Numb.
VIII. a.

The Charters of King Ethelbert and Arch-bishop Augustin, concerning the Foundation and Endowment of a Monastical Church Dedicated to St. Peter and St. Paul and afterward to S. Augustin also.

Char. 2.

IN nomine Domini nostri Jesu Christi : omnem hominem qui secundum Deum vivit, & remunerari à Deo sperat, & optat, oportet ut piis precibus consensum hilariter ex animo præbeat ; quoniam certum est, tantò faciliùs ea, quæ ipse à Deo poposcerit, consequi posse: quantò & ipse libentiùs Deo aliquid concesserit. Quocirca ego Ethelbertus Rex Cantiæ,

Donatio suus Abbatiæ.

cum consensu venerabilis Archiepiscopi Augustini ac Principum meorum, dono & concedo Deo in honorem sancti Petri aliquam partem terræ Juris mei, quæ jacet in oriente civitatis Doroberniæ, ita duntaxat ut Monasterium ibi construatur, & res quæ infra memorantur in potestate Abbatis sint qui ibi fuerit ordinatus. Igitur adjuro & præcipio in nomine Dei omnipotentis, qui est omnium rerum Judex Justus, ut præfata terra subscripta donatione sempitrenaliter sit confirmata, ita ut nec mihi nec alicui successorum meorum Regum aut Principum, sive cujuslibet conditionis dignitatibus & ecclesiasticis gradibus de ea aliquid

Imprecatio.

fraudare liceat. Si quis verò de hac donatione nostra aliquid minuere, aut irritum facere temptaverit : Sit in præsente separatus à sancta communione corporis & sanguinis Christi :

Metæ Abbatæ.

& in die judicii ob meritum malitiæ suæ á consortio sanctorum omnium segregatus. Circumcincta est hæc terra his terminis, in Oriente ecclesia sancti Martini, in meridie via de Burgate, in Occidente & Aquilone Droutingstreet. Datum in civitate Doroberniæ, anno ab incarnatione Christi 605. indict 6. † . Ego Ethelbertus Rex Cantiæ sana mente integroque consilio donationem meam signo crucis propria manu roboravi confirmavique. Ego Augustinus gratia Dei Archiepiscopus testis consentiens libenter subscripsi. Edbaldus. Hamigisilus. Augemundus Referendarius. Hocca. Tangil. Pinca. Geddy.

Numb.
VIII. b.
Char. 2.
Reyner. Apost.
Bened. p. 49.
Thorn. Col.
1761.
Donatio.

IN nomine Domini nostri Jesu Christi. Notum sit omnibus tam præsentibus quam posteris quòd ego Ethelbertus Dei gratia Rex Anglorum per Evangelicum genitorem meum Augustinum de Idolotatra factus Christicola tradidi Deo per ipsum antistitem aliquam partem terræ juris mei sub orientali muro Civitatis Doroberniæ, ubi scilicet per eundem in Christo institutorem Monasterium in honorem principum Apostolorum Petri & Pauli condidi; & cum ipsa terra, & cum omnibus, quæ ad ipsum Monasterium pertinent, perpetua libertate donavi, adeo ut nec mihi, nec alicui successorum meorum Regum, nec ulli unquam potestati sive sæculari quicquam inde liceat usurpare;

Imprecatio.

sed in ipsius Abbatis sint omnia libera ditione. Si quis verò de hac donatione nostra aliquid imminuere aut irritum facere tentaverit, authoritate Dei & B. Papæ Gregorii, nostrique Apostoli Augustini simul & nostra imprecatione sit hic segregatus ab omni sancta ecclesiæ communione, & in die judicii ab omni electorum societate. Circumcingitur hæc

Termini.

terra his terminis : In Oriente ecclesia S. Martini, & inde ad Orientem hy Sibbendowne, & sic ad Aquilonem be Wykingesmerk, iterumque ad Orientem & ad Austrum be Burgaweremarka, & sic ad Austrum & Occidentem be Kingesmearke, iterum ad Aquilonem & Occidentem be Kingesmerke, ad occidentem to Rederchepe, & ita ad Aquilonem to Droutingstreet. Actum est hoc in Civitate Doroberniæ Anno ab incarnatione

Subscriptiones.

Christi. 605. indictione octava. † . Ego Ethelbertus Rex Anglorum hanc donationem meam signo sanctæ crucis propria manu confirmavi. † . Ego Augustinus gratia Dei Archiepiscopus libentur subscripsi. † . Edbaldus Regis filius favi. † . Ego Hamigisilus Dux laudavi' † . Ego Hocca comes consensi. † . Ego Augemundus Referendarius approbavi. † . Ego Graphio comes benedixi. † . Ego Tangifilus Regis Optimas confirmavi. † . Ego Pinca consensi. † . Ego Gedde corroboravi.

Numb.
VIII. c.

Char. 3.
Leyn. Apostol.
Benodict. p. 49.
Thorn.Col. 1762

REX Anglorum Ethelbertus misericordia Dei omnipotentis Catholicus omnibus suæ gentis fidelibus & adventum gloriæ magni Dei & salvatoris nostri Jesu Christi beata spe expectantibus, salutem vitæque æternæ beatitudinem largiente summi Regis clementia. Ego Ethelbertus in solio paterno confirmatus, paceque divinitus concessa eo jam per decem quinquennia sceptrigera potestate potitus, per venerabiles sacræ fidei Doctores spiritus sancti gratia irradiatus, ab errore falsorum Deorum ad unius veri Dei cultum toto corde conversus, ne ingratus beneficiorum appaream illi, qui de sua è cœlis sancta sede nobis in regione umbræ mortis sedentibus lux veritatis emicuit, inter alias quas fabricavi ecclesias,

* Papæ. Thorn.

monitu & hortatu beatissimi * patris Gregorii & sancti patris nostri Augustini Episcopi, beatissimo Apostolorum Principi Petro, & Doctori gentium Paulo monasterium à funda-

† Studui. Thorn.

mentis construxi, illudque terris, variisque possessionum donariis decorare † statui, inibi monachos Deum timentes aggregari feci : & cum consilio ejusdem Reverendissimi Archipræsulis Augustini, ex suo sancto sanctorum collegio venerabilem virum secum ab Apostolica sede directum Petrum monachum elegi, eisque ut ecclesiasticus ordo exposcit, Abbatem præposui. Hoc igitur Monasterium, ad provectum debiti culminis promovere desiderans, suarumque possessionum terminis dilatare gestiens, sana mente, integroque consilio, cum Eadbaldi filii mei, aliorumque nobilium optimatum meorum consensu, ob redemptionem animæ meæ, & spem retributionis æternæ, obtuli ei etiam villam nomine Sturiag alio no-

Sturiag.
Chistelet.

mine dictam Chistelet, cum omnibus redditibus ei jure competentibus, cum mancipiis,

sylvis

fylvis cultis vel incultis, pratis, pafcuis, paludibus, fluminibus & contiguis ei maritimis terminis eam ex una parte cingentibus, omniaque mobilia vel immobilia in ufus fratrum fub regulari tramite & monaftica religione inibi Deo fervientium, miffarium etiam argenteum, fceptrum aureum, item fellam cum fræno auro & gemmis ornatam, fpeculum argenteum, armiganfa oloferica, camifiam ornatam, quæ mihi de Domino Gregorio fedis Apoftolicæ directa fuerat: Quæ omnia fupradicto monafterio gratanter obtuli. Quod etiam monafterium ipfe fervus Dei Auguftinus fanctorum Apoftolorum ac martyrum reliquiis, variifque ecclefiafticis ornamentis ab Apoftolica fede fibi tranfmiffis copiofe ditavit, fefeque in eo, & Locus fepuluræ Reg. & Archie-pifc. cunctos fucceffores fuos ex Authoritate Apoftolica fepeliri præcepit, fcriptura dicente, non effe civitatem mortuorum fed vivorum; ubi & mihi & fuccefforibus meis fepulturam providi, fperans me quandoque ab ipfo Apoftolici ordinis principe, cui Dominus poteftatem ligandi atque folvendi dedit, & claves regni cœlorum tradidit, à peccatorum nexibus folvi, & in æternam beatitudinis januam introduci. Quod monafterium nullus Epifcoporum, Immunitas mo-nafterii. nullus fuccefforum meorum regum in aliquo lædere aut inquietare præfumat: Nullam omnino fubjectionem fibi ufurpare audeat: fed Abbas ipfe qui fuerit ordinatus, intus & foris, cum confilio fratrum fecundum timorem Dei libere eum regat & ordinet: ita ut in die Domini dulcem illam piiffimi redemptoris noftri vocem mereatur audire, dicentis, *Euge ferve bone*, &c. Hanc donationem meam in nomine patris & filii & fpiritus fancti largitate divina, ut mihi tribuatur peccatorum remiffio per omnia cum confilio reverentiffimi patris Auguftini condidi, idque ad fcribendum Augemundum presbyterum ordinavi. De his igi- Interminatio. tur omnibus, quæ hic fcripta funt, fi quis aliquid minuere præfumpferit, fciat fe æquiffimo judici Deo, & beatiffimis Apoftolis Petro & Paulo rationem effe rediturum. Confirmata eft hæc donatio, præfentibus, Reverentiffimo patre Auguftino Doroberniæ ecclefiæ Archie- Teftes. pifcopo primo, Mellito quoque & Jufto Londonienfis & Roffenfis ecclefiæ præfulibus, Eadbaldo filio meo, Hamigiflo, &c. & aliis pluribus diverfarum dignitatum perfonis. Actum fane 45. Anno regni noftri, Anno Domini 605.

Privilegium Sti. Auguftini *huic cœnobio fuo conceffum.*

Numb.
VIII. d.
Char. 4
Reyn. Apoftol.
Benedictin. p. 51.
Thorn Col. 1763.

AVguftinus Epifcopus Dorobernie fedis famulus, quem fuperna infpirante clementia beatiffimus Papa Gregorius Anglicæ genti Deo acquirendæ legatarium mifit, ac miniftrum, omnibus fuccefforibus fuis Epifcopis, cunctifque Angliæ Regibus, cum fuis pofteris, atque omnibus Dei fidelibus, in fide & gratia falutem & pacem. Patet omnibus quòd Deo amabilis Rex Ethelbertus primus Anglorum regum Chrifti regno fanatus noftra inftantia, & fua prodiga benevolentia inter cæteras ecclefias quas fecit & Epifcopia, monafterium extra Metropolim fuam Doroberniam, in honorem principum Apoftolorum Petri & Pauli regaliter Doroberniam Regis Metropo-lim vocat. condidit, & regalibus opibus amplifque poffeffionibus * ditavit, magnificavit, perpetua liber- * Dicatavit. tate & omni jure regio cum omnibus rebus & judiciis intus & foris illi pertinentibus muni- Thron. vit, fuoque regio previlegio, & fuperni judicii imprecatione, atque Apoftolica fanctiffimi papæ Gregorii interminatione excommunicatioria contra omnem injuriam confirmavit. Ego quoque ejufdem libertatis adjutor & patrocinator omnes fucceffores meos Archiepifcopos, omnefque ecclefiafticas vel fæculares poteftates per Dominum Jefum Chriftum & Apoftolorum ejus reverentiam obteftor, Atque Apoftolica memorati Patris noftri Papæ Gregorii interminatione interdico, ne quifquam unquam ullam poteftatem aut dominatum aut imperium in hoc dominicum vel Apoftolicum monafterium, vel terras vel ecclefias ad illud pertinentes ufurpare præfumat, nec ulla prorfus fubjugationis, aut fervitutis, aut tributi conditione, vel in magno vel in minimo, Dei miniftros inquietet aut opprimat. Abbatem a fuis Abbatis electio frarribus electum in eodem monafterio, non ad fui famulatum, fed ad dominicum mi- & conditio. nifterium ordinet: nec fibi hunc obedire, fed Deo fuadeat; nec verò fibi fubjectum, fed fratrem, fed confortem, fed collegam in comminiftrum in opus Dominicum eum reputet. Non ibi miffas, quafi ad fuæ ditionis altare, nec ordinationes, vel benedictiones, ufurpativè, fine Abbatis vel fratrum petitione exerceat: nullum fibi jus confuetudinarium vel in viliffima re exigat, quatenus pacis concordia unum fint in domino uterque, nec quifquam quod abfit dominandi diffidio in judicium incidat Diaboli, qui fuperba tyrannide corruit de Celo. Reges gentium (inquit Dominus) dominantur eorum, vos autem non fic; cumque ab alienigenis, non a filiis accipiantur tributa, fic ipfe Dominus concludit, ergo liberi funt filii: qua ergo irreverentia patres ecclefiarum in filio Regni Dei fibi vendicant dominationem? maximè autem in hanc ecclefiam fanctorum thefaurariam, in ejus materno utero tot Pontificum Doroberniæ, Regumque ac principum corpora fperamus alma refovenda Pontifices & Re- fepultura requie, ex authoritate fcilicet Apoftolica, & hinc ad æternam gloriam refufcitan- ges hic fepelien-di. da. Tales fupremi Judicis amicos fi quis offendere non metuens hujus privilegii ftatuta violaverit, vel violatorem imitando vim fuam tenuerit, fciat fe Apoftolico B. Petri gladio Confirmatio. per fuum vicarium Gregorium puniendum, nifi emendaverit. Hæc igitur omnia, ut hic funt fcripta, Apoftolica ipfius Inftitutoris noftri Gregorii comprobatione & authoritate fervanda fancimus, fuoque ore confirmamus, præfente gloriofo rege Ethelberto, cum filio fuo Eadbaldo, & collaudante cum ipfo, & omnibus Optimatibus regiis atque ultrò volentibus reverendiffimis fratribus noftris à fancta Romana ecclefia huc mecum, vel ad me in Evangelium Domini deftinatis, fcilicet Lawrentio, quem nobis Deo favente, fuccefforem conftituimus, & Mellito Londoniarum Epifcopo, & Jufto Roffenfi Epifcopo, & Petro venerabili ejufdem monafterii principum Apoftolorum Abbate primo cum cæteris in Domino adjuto-
ribus

ribus meis ; obnixè poftulantibus, fimulque in eos, qui hæc fideliter fervaverint, benedictionem ; aut in impœnitentes, quod * volumus, tranfgreffores damnationem exercentibus.

*Nolumus
Thorn.

The Privilege of the Abbot of S. Auguftin, to Mint Money.

**Numb.
VIII. e.**

MEmorandum, quòd ifte Silvefter Abbas & multi prædeceffores ejus Abbates habuerunt
Cuneum monetæ in Civitate Cant. ficut per inquifitionem factam per Arnoldum
Ferre, Wulfinum Mercere & alios qui jurati dixerunt quòd quidam Abbas S. Aug. Silvefter nomine habuit in Civitate Cant. unum cuneum monetæ & Eluredus Porre cuftodivit
cuneum illud ex parte illius Abbatis, & quando ille Abbas obiit feifita fuit Abbatia in manu Domini Regis unà cum prædicto cuneo recuperavit feifinam. Et fuit ifta inquifitio
facta temporibus Hen. fecundi Regis, & Regis Richardi filii ejufdem.

**Numb.
VIII. f.**

CUm Dani Cantuariam ferro undique & flamma vaftantes fævirent, quidam illorum fa-
crilegi, non caufa orandi, fed deprædandi malitia monafterium iftud ultrò introierunt:
moxque unus eorum ad malum proclivior, ad fepulchrum Apoftoli noftri Auguftini (ubi
tunc jacebat tumulatus) improbè acceffit, palliumque, quo illud pretiofum Auguftini mau-
folæum operiebatur, furtim rapuit, atque fub axilla fua illum abfcondit : fed divina ultrix
miferatio raptorem mox rapuit, palliumque illud fub axilla furis abfconditum, connativum
cutis axillis furis Inhæfit ; nec unguibus nec ulla violentia aut arte deponi poterat, donec
reatum fuum coram fancto prædicto, & loci fratribus, veniam pofcendo de commiffis, fur
ipfe prodiderat. Quæ ultrio ira cæterorum Danorum multitudinem terruit, ut hujus Monafterii non folùm fieri timerent invafores, fed magis ejus præcipui forent defenfores.

**Numb.
IX. a.**

[*The Licence of the Prior of* Chrift-Church *granted to* Stephen de Wyke, *to
Celebrate Divine Service in his Chappel at* Wyke.

Ex Archiv. in
Ecclef. Chrifti
Cant.

RIchardus permiffione divina Prior Ecclefiæ Chrifti de Cantuar' dilecto fibi in Chrifto Domino Stephano de Wyke Capellano Salutem, &c. Ut in Capella tua apud Wyke decenter ornata in Parochia S. Martini juxta Cantuar' & jurifdictionis Ecclefiæ Noftræ immediatæ, miffas celebrare poffis, ac tibi & tuis ydoneis, abfque parochial. juris, quoad oblationes & parochialia jura hujus Ecclefiæ, præjuditio canonice facere celebrari devotioni
tuæ (fede Cantuar' vacante) autoritate Noftra & capituli, qua fungimur in hac parte,
tenore prefentium licentiam in Domino concedimus fpecialem. In cujus rei Teftimonium,
&c. dat. A. D. 1333. N. B.]

**Numb.
IX. b.**

Foundation of Lukedale Chantery.

SCiant præfentes & futuri ad quos præfens fcriptum pervenerit quod ego Rogerus Dei
gratia Abbas Sancti Auguftini Cantuarien. & Conventus ejufdem loci conceffimus Re-

Reginaldus de
Cornhelle.
Curia de Lnke-
nale.

ginaldo de Cornhelle & heredibus fuis habere cantariam fuam in capellâ fua quæ conftructa eft intra fepta Curiæ fuæ de Lukedale faciendam per Capellanum fuum commenfalem
in propriis expenfis, falvo in omnibus Jure matricis ecclefiæ de Littlebourne, ità quod præfatus Reginaldus vel heredes fui nullis futuris temporibus onerabunt perfonam vel facerdo-
tem prædictæ ecclefiæ de Littlebourne occafione cantariæ in jam dicta capella facienda.
Reddet igitur tam prædictus Reginaldus quam heredes fui integrè & plenariè decimationes
omnium terrarum quas habent in eadem parochia tam magnas quam minimas matrici ec-

Molendinum de
Bremlinge.

clefiæ de Littlebourne. Præterea dabunt decimas duarum partium molendini de Bremlinge & tertiæ partis fi eam recuperare potuerint, & decimas feni tantilli prati quod ibi habent & duos folidos annuos fuper altare matricis ecclefiæ de Littlebourne, reddend. per manum Willielmi de Stocting vel heredum fuorum in duobus terminis, fcilicet in media
quadragefima 12d. & in fefto fancti Michaelis 12d. Vifitabunt etiam matricem ecclefiam
cum oblationibus fuis in quatuor annuis feftivitatibus, Natalis fcilicet Domini, Purificationis,
Pafchæ, & feftivitate fancti Vincentii, cum in partibus illis fuerint, ut parochiani fæpedictæ ecclefiæ de Littlebourne. Sacerdos etiam qui pro tempore in fæpenominatâ capellâ
miniftrabit fidelitatem faciet perfonæ fæpedictæ matricis ecclefiæ, quod in nullo defrau-
dabit eam in decimis magnis five minimis, nec in prædictis oblationibus, confeffionibus five
teftamentis, fponfalibus, five purificationibus, vel tricennalibus, vel in aliquibus ad Jus
ecclefiæ de Littlebourne pertinentibus. Veniens itaque fæpeuominatus Reginaldus in Capitulum noftrum facramentum præftitit pro fe & heredibus fuis, fe & heredes fuos in omnibus
& per omnia hæc fupradicta fideliter obfervaturos. Hiis teftibus, &c.

**Numb.
IX. c.**

The Foundation of Doge's Chantery in St. Paul's Church.

ANno Dom. 1264. Magifter Hamo Doge fuæ noviffimæ memor ordinavit Cantariam pro
anima fua, parentum fuorum, & pro anima Domini Rogeri de Ciceftria Abbatis Sti Auguftini, & pro animabus Succefforum fuorum, & pro conventu eiufdem loci, & benefactoribus fuis, & eorum fuccefforibus, de toto capitali Mefuagio cum omnibus ad idem pertinentibus

nentibus in Nova ſtrata in parochia ſancti Pauli ſit. cum quinquaginta & ſeptem acris terræ & quatuor lib. ſex ſolid. & novem den. annui redditus. Habend' & tenend' omnia prædictá, ſcilicet in terris, redditibus, meſſuagiis, viis, planis, paſturis, releviis, curiis, ſectis, eſcaetis, wardis, maritagiis & omnibus aliis libertatibus. Et ordinavit in prædicta Cantaria duos Capellanos in perpetuum, & unus celebret in prædicto Meſuagio in libera Cantaria, & alius ad altare St. Johannis Baptiſtæ in Eccleſia St. Pauli Cant. niſi infirmitate ve aliqua neceſſitate rationabili fuerint præpediti. In creatione verò cujuſſibet novi Capellani & perpetui ad prædictam Cantariam admiſſi idem Capellanus ſolvet Abbati & Conventui St. Auguſtini Cant. xiij. ſol. iiij. den. nomine relevii pro omnibus terris & tenementis quæ de ipſis tenuerit. Jus verò conferendi, inſtituendi, in corporalem poſſeſſionem inducendi & inductum tuendi Abbati & Conventui & eorum ſucceſſoribus dedit & confirmavit, &c.

The Charter of the Endowment of the Hoſpital of St. Lawrence.

NOtum ſit omnibus Dei fidelibus tam præſentibus quam poſteris, quòd ego ſecundus Hugo Dei gratia Abbas ſancti Auguſtini ejuſdemque loci conventus pro redemptione animarum noſtrarum, prædeceſſorum noſtrorum atque ſucceſſorum conceſſimus ac dedimus in elemoſinam novem acras terræ de dominio noſtro precio quondam adquiſitas, ad faciendum Hoſpitale in illis novem acris ſupra memoratis juxta viam quæ à Canterburia ducit ad Dover, in dextra parte viæ. Contulimus etiam illi loco ad ſuſtentationem infirmorum aut pauperum decimam totius annonæ de tota terra illa quam habemus in dominio in dextra parte viæ, & omnem decimam frumenti & piſarum totius terræ quæ adjacet ad Langeport de dominio noſtro in ſiniſtra parte viæ. Quicunque igitur pro amore Dei benefecerint infirmis illic habitantibus, & locum illum manutenuerint, benedictionem Dei habeant, & gratiam ſimul & commune beneficium loci noſtri.

The Grant of Dodingdale Tythes to the Hoſpital of St. Lawrence.

ITem prædictum Hoſpitale percipit totam decimam de 300 Acris terræ & ultra Johannis Chich, de quibus 50 jacent apud Havefeld, & reſiduum jacet juxta curiam ſuam, & in Mellefield juxta Sanctum Lawrentium. Et idem Johannes percipiet de prædict. Hoſp. in autumpno pro famulis ſuis quinque panes frumenti & 2 Lagenas & dimid. cerviſiæ, & dimid' caſeum quatuor denarior. Idem etiam percipiet unum par cirocecarum ferinarum pro ſeipſo & unam libram ceræ in candelis, & pro famulis ſuis percipiet tria paria cirocecarum.

RIchardus de Marci omnibus ſuis hominibus Francigenis & Anglicis tam preſentibus quam futuris, Salutem. Sciatis me conceſſiſſe & dediſſe decimas terræ meæ de Dodingdale Hoſpitali Sancti Lawrentii quod eſt juxta Cant. in perpetuam Elemoſinam, pro ſalute animarum prædeceſſorum meorum, & mei, & uxoris meæ, & meorum infantium: Quare volo & præcipio quatenus prædictum Hoſpitale decimas præd' habeat & poſſideat bene & in pace & liberè. Præcipioque ex parte Dei & ex parte mea ut fratres & ſorores prædicti Hoſpitalis habeant decimas illas nominatim ad lineum pannum emendum in feſto Sancti Johannis Baptiſtæ, quia credo quòd tunc mei & meorum memores erunt.

Charters of Protection and Endowment of the Hoſpital of St. James.

OMnibus Chriſti fidelibus ad quos præſens ſcriptum pervenerit G. Prior & Conventus Eccleſiæ Chriſti Cant. in Domino ſalutem. Sciatis quod intuitu caritatis & pietatis, de conſenſu & voluntate Domini Noſtri H. Archiepiſcopi & ad petitionem magiſtri Firmini cuſtodis domus ſancti Jacobi extra Cant. recepimus in cuſtodiam & protectionem noſtram prædict. Domum Sancti Jacobi extra Cant. ſitam. Et tenebimus in eadem domò ſemper tres ſacerdotes hic per nos inſtituend. Qui erint profeſſi in eadem prædicta domo in forma & habitu religionis. Quorum unus cotidie celebrabit miſſam de beata virgine, alius cantabit requiem pro benefactoribus ejuſdem domus, tertius dicet commune ſervitium, & iſti tres ſacerdotes habebunt unum clericum. Et erint in prædicta domo ſemper xxv mulieres leproſæ per nos inſtituendæ. De eccleſia de Bradegate & aliis redditibus & terris & ſubſtantiis & elemoſinis & obventionibus ejuſdem domus providebimus tam ſacerdotibus illis quam leproſis prædict' neceſſaria. Et ut hæc ſupradicta firma & inconcuſſa permaneant impoſterum preſenti carta noſtra & ſigilli noſtri appoſitione roboravimus: ſalva dignitate Domini Archiepiſcopi. His teſtibus Gilberto Roffenſi Epiſc. H. Cant. Archidiac' Rogero Abbate ſancti Auguſt. Algaro Abbate de Faverſham, &c.

HEnricus Dei gratia Rex Angliæ & Dux Normanniæ & Aquitanniæ & Comes Andegav' Archiepiſcopis, Epiſc, Abbatibus, Prioribus & Comitibus, Baronibus, Juſticiariis, Vicar. Miniſtris & omnibus fidelibus ſuis Angl' Salutem. Sciatis me dediſſe in liberam & perpetuam elemoſinam & preſenti carta mea confirmaſſe leproſis mulieribus Hoſpitalis ſancti I. apud Cant. eccleſiam de Bradegate cum omnibus pertinentiis ſuis. Ita quòd

Mr. Firminus libere omnia teneat & possideat tota vita sua, & post decessum ejus libera remaneant prædictis mulieribus leprosis. Quare volo & firmiter precipio quòd eadem leprosæ mulieres eandem ecclesiam habeant & teneant in libera & perpetua elemosina sicut predeterminatum est, benè & in pace, liberè & quietè, integrè & plenariè & honorificè cum omnibus pertinentiis suis & libertatibus & liberis consuetudinibus suis. Hiis testibus, &c.

Burton Laxar's *Hospital in* Leicestershire,

Numb.
XIII.

UNiversis sanctæ matris ecclesiæ filiis ad quos præsentes literæ pervenerint, Frater Willielmus Sutton Magister de Burton sanc' Lazari ordinis Jerlm' in Anglia & ejusdem loci confratres, salutem ac utriusque hominis incrementum. Quùm quanto magis spiritualia dona erogantur, tanto ut credimus potentiora æternæ salutis præmia consequantur. Igitur veræ dilectionis ultræ innotescimus per præsentes qd' sanctæ Romanæ ecclesiæ Pontifices ex eorum plenitudine potestatis nobis gratiosè indulserunt ut omnibus qui de facultatibus & bonis suis eisdem à Deo collatis subvenerint, seu ad benefaciendum nobis alios exortati fuerint, vel in nostram fraternitatem extiterint assumpti toties quotiès unum annum de injuncta eis pœnitentia misericorditer relaxarunt, & ad plenam participationem omnium missarum matutinarum & aliarum orationum & devotionum in singulis ecclesiis nostri ordinis per orbem Dei offerendarum admittunt, ac singulis annis die Veneris majoris ebdomadæ proprio Curato plenam concedunt potestatem eisdem absolvendi ab omnibus peccatis & criminibus nisi talibus super quibus sedes Apostolica sit meritò consulenda. Vota igitur abstinentiæ & peregrinationis quæcunque commutandi in alia pia subsidia & dona caritativa domui sive Hospitali nostro de Borton sancti Lazari Jer'lm' eroganda, Votis ad terram sanctam & ad limina beatorum Apostolorum Petri & Pauli & voto castitatis in vita duntaxat exceptis : In articulo verò mortis omnium peccatorum suorum plenam remissionem. Personis autem ecclesiasticis in nostram fraternitatem assumptis qui propter notam irregularitatis sententiam à canone vel homine contractam ad Sed. Apostolicam pro absolutionis beneficio deberent accedere, ut id à proprio Curato valeant recipere misericorditer concesserunt. Ac etiam ab eodem Curato proprio de horarum canonicarum aut servitii divini omissione pro recompenso plenam remissionem accipere valeant. Insuper si ecclesiæ ad quas pertinent qui in nostram fraternitatem sunt assumpti ab officiis & servitio divino fuerint interdict ipsosque mori contigerint eisdem sepultura ecclesiastica non negetur nisi vinculo excommunicationis majoris nominatim fuerint innodati. Nos igitur Magistri & Confratres Hospitalis prædict' auctoritate Apostolica vigoréque privilegiorum in nostram fraternitatem sanctam Johannem Dyg & Johannam consortem devotè recipientes nostrorum privilegiorum, indulgentiarum & aliorum pietatis operum participes in omnibus facimus per præsentes sigillo nostræ fraternitatis signat'. Dat' apud Borton Sancti Lazari prædict' in domo nostra Capitulari, Anno Dom. Millesimo cccc° octogesimo quarto.

Thus Endorsed.

AUctoritate Domini nostri Jesu Christi & ex spirituali gratia mihi concessa à sanctissimo Domino nostro Papa. Ego absolvo te ab omnibus peccatis tuis quæ contra Deum & teipsum fecisti, necnon ab omnibus sententiis, interdictis & suspensionibus concedo tibi plenam remissionem si in hac infirmitate decesseris & in mortis articulo existas, alioquin ex misericordia Dei salva sit tibi gratia donec fueris in mortis articulo constitutus, *Amen.*

The Foundation of Herbaldowne-*Chantery.*

Numb.
XIV.

THomas permissione divina Cant. Archiepisc. totius Angliæ Primas & Apostolicæ sedis Legatus. Dilectis in Christo filiis Priori & Priorissæ ac fratribus & sororibus Hospitalis nostri de Herbaldowne. Salutem, gratiam & benedictionem. Scrutato registro bonæ memoriæ Domini Willielmi Wittlesey prædecessoris nostri dotationem sive ordinationem perpetuæ cantariæ in Hospitali nostro prædicto, reperimus in eodem, tenorem qui sequitur continentem. Universis sanctæ matris ecclesiæ filiis presentes literas inspecturis. Willielmus permissione divina Cant. Archiepisc. totius Angliæ Primas & Apostolicæ sedis legatus. Salutem in Domino sempiternam. Cum Custos quilibet Hospitalis nostri de Eastbrigge in Cantuaria qui pro tempore fuerit suis sumptibus & expensis invenire teneatur sacerdotem idoneum qui jugiter divina celebret coram pauperibus alterius Hospitalis nostri de Herbaldowne in ecclesia sancti Nicholai ibidem, & eorum confessiones audiat, eisque diebus & noctibus prout oportebit ecclesiastica ministret Sacramenta. Sitque in præsenti & erit verisimiliter in futurum plurimum difficile stipendiarios reperire idoneos sacerdotes, qui inter dictos pauperes taliter conversari voluerint, præsertim cum ipsorum pauperum nonnulli lepra sint infecti, ac pro infectis hujusmodi ipsum Hospitale principaliter sit fundatum, nisi forsan mansionem ab eis separatam habuerint & vicinam, cantariamque non mobilem sed perpetuam obtineant ac ad victum eorundem Capellanorum dotatam competenter.

Hospitale pro Leprosis principaliter fundatum

Nos præmissa debito considerationis intuitu pensantes, curæque animarum dictorum pauperum
rum

rum & hofp. prædict, utilitati providere volentes, quandam perpetuam Cantariam unius Capellani ut præmittitur divina apud Herbaldowne celebraturi fundamus, dotamus, & ut fubfcribitur ordinamus. Habebit fiquidem facerdos hujufmodi ipfius cantariæ perpetuus in partem dotis ejufdem unam manfionem fufficientem & honeftam ædificatam ex oppofito portæ dicti Hofpitalis de Herbaldowne cum prædiis & gardinis adjacentibus, & quodam columbari ibidem jam conferend. dicto Hofp. de Eaftbrigge per Dominum Willielmum Attewelle Capellanum de Regis licentia jam obtenta ut inter benefactores habeatur utriuf- Claveringe que Hofpitalis fapradicti, necnon quandam aream præfato hofpitali noftro de Herbaldowne contiguam vocat' Claveringe * : habebit etiam facerdos iftius Cantariæ de fratribus & fo- * Where, before, roribus hofp. de Herbaldowne duas marcas de claro per equales portiones annuatim in per- speaking of this petuum. Reputabitur infuper & erit facerdos ipfe abfque noftro aut fuccefforum noftrorum Hofp. Ifaid the Chantery Prieft novo onere unus de numero pauperum in eodem hofp. noftro de Herbaldowne requifito dwelt over againft propter ipfius converfationem, celebrationes & orationes quas quafi continuè faciet coram the Hofp. I find eis & inter eos, tantum percipiens & taliter ficut eorum unus incedens fi voluerit veftitus I was miftaken. pro reverentia fui ordinis ut facerdos fecularis. Habebit infuper quinque marcas liberi & For the Accompt of the Chanteries fecuri redditus in denariis tempore Domini Thomæ Eltone jam cuftodis dicti noftri hofp. de indowment , gi- Eaftbrigge eid' hofp. adquifito apud Herne quas folvent quidam Thomas de Court here- ven to the Com- des & affignati ejus pro terris & tenementis dimiffis eis per factum in hac parte fufficiens de miffioners about the times of the folvendo, ac etiam duas marcas cum dimid. annuatim de cuftode quocunque ipfius hofp. fuppreffion, faith, noftri de Eaftbrigge pro tempore eidem Capellano perfolvend. ad quatuor anni terminos he had his dwel- ufualiter principales quas cuftos ipfe cum ulteriori fumma annis fingulis de certis terris red- ling here, at ditibus & pafturis libere habere poterit quas dictus Dominus Thomas cuftos etiam fuæ Clavering. cuftodiæ tempore adquifivit de Domino Thoma de Ros milite apud Hothe. Super quibus Dominus Tho- terris & pafturis, libere diftringere facerdos ipfe valeat pro omni tempore ipfarum duarum mas de Ros. marcarum & dimidiæ poft unumquemque terminum fupradictum per menfem, fi poftea in folutione ejufdem fit ceffatum. Et fic dos ipfius Cantariæ undecim marcas cum dimidia vel circiter verifimiliter inpofterum valebit annuatim. Ad ipfam autem Cantariam quotiens eam vacare contigerit, Cuftos dicti Hofp. de Eaftbrigge qui pro tempore fuerit facerdotes idoneos qui in ea refidere voluerint, & quotidie coram ipfis pauperibus, ceffante impedi- mento legitimo juxta Canonum exigentiam celebrare divina, aut per alium facere celebrari & animarum curam gerere eorundem ut eft dictum, ad quæ omnia & fingula facerdotes hujufmodi teneri volumus & arctari nobis & fuccefforibus noftris præfentabit, Ad fumptus autem reparationis domorum præfatæ manfionis & colum- baris ac exhibitionem panis, vini, luminariorum honeftorum pro celebrationibus miffarum prædictarum neceffariorum tenebitur facerdos ipfe ratione prædictæ do- tis fuæ. Si autem facerdos idoneus haberi non poterit qui ipfam cantariam habere velit, & ad celebrationes & curam prædict. ac alia prædicta onera arctari noluerit ut eft dictum, extunc Cuftos memorati Hofp. de Eaftbrigge qui pro tempore fuerit poffeffiones dictæ do- tis fuperius defcriptas ingrediatur & teneat, ac de dictis celebrationibus & cura difponat ficuti prius tenebatur & prout melius videbitur fibi expedire. In quorum omnium teftimo- nium has literas noftras fieri fecimus patentes figillo noftro confignatas. Dat' apud Croy- done iiij°. Non. Feb. Anno Domini Mccclxxj°. & noftræ tranflationis quarto. Nos igitur Thomas permiffione divina Cant. Archiepifcopus, totius Angliæ Primas & Apofto- licæ fedis Legatus prædictus, prædictam dotationem five ordinationem ratam habentes pa- riter & acceptam fimiliter approbando & quantum in nobis eft confirmantes : Vobis Con' & divi' firmiter injungendo mandamus quatenus Dominum Johannem Bray Capellanum prædictæ Cantariæ modernum tantum unum de numero pauperum in Hofpitali prædicto admittatis tantum & taliter ficut alicui alteri pauperi ejufdem in quibufcunque pecu- niarum fummis feu aliis vitæ neceffariis effectualiter miniftrantes. Dat. in Palatio noftro Cantuar. xviij°. die menfis Maii. Anno Dom. Mcccciij°. & noftræ tranflationis Anno fexto.

The Charter of King Henry to the Hofpital of Herbaldown.

Numb. XIV. b.

HEn. Rex Angliæ Archiepifcopo Cantuar. & Vicecomiti & omnibus Baronibus, & Mi- niftris & fidelibus fuis de Chent Francis & Anglis Salutem. Sciatis me dediffe & con- ceffiffe pro Dei amore & anima Patris & Matris meæ & Matildis Regine & Willielmi Filii mei & pro Redemptione peccatorum meorum, in acremento Hofpitalis de bofco de Blen x. perticatas terræ ad exfartandum & excolendum undique circa Hofpitale : Et volo & firmi- ter præcipio ut habitantes in loco illo habeant meam firmam pacem, ne aliquis eis inju- riam vel contumeliam faciat. T. Willielmo Elemofinario Capellano meo & Pagano filio Johannis & Gaufrido filio Pagani & Pagano Peur. apud Odeftoc.

The

Numb.
XIV.

The Articles between the Prior of St. Gregories *of* Canterbury *and the Convent of the same Church on the one party, and the Major and Communalty of the City of Cant. of the other party, by the mediation of* Thomas, *Prior of* Christ-Church *of* Cant. John Hales *one of the Barons of the Exchequer of our Soveraign Lord the King,* Christopher Hales *General Attorney of our said Soveraigne Lord the King, and* Thomas Wood *Esquire, by the consent of the most Reverend Father in God* William *Lord Archbishop of* Canterbury.

FIrst it is agreed and determined that the said Monastery as it is enclosed at this present date with the new Houses and Tenantaries which beene built next adjoyning unto the said Monastery, as well on and by the South-part of the said Church-gate, as on and by the North-part of the Court-gate of the said Church, be fully and entirely to all intents of and within the Liberties and Franchises of the said Citie of *Cant.* And that the Tenants inhabiting in the same Tenements shall at all times doe and owe their Obedience unto the Major of the said City, and to the Aldermen and other Officers of the said City and of the Ward of North-gate for the time being, and shall be contributory to every Charge within the same City in like wise as all the other Inhabitants of the same City be, and shall be. And that the said Mayor and Aldermen of the said City and Ward and their Successors shall execute their Office within the said Monastery as they should doe in any other pars of the said City, except in the Causes and Articles following.

Item, It is agreed for the quietnesse of the said Prior and Covent and their Successors that no Person shall be Arrested by his Body within the said Monastery for any personal Action to be attempted by way of Plaint before the Mayor of the said City, but in Forme following, that is to say, If any Plaint be entred and affirmed against the said Prior or his Successors or any Person inhabiting or abiding within the said Monastery in such manner that the Process and Execution according to the same Plaint cannot be had and done upon the said Prior, his Successors, or any such foresaid Person there inhabiting or abiding within the said Monastery, that then if the said Prior, his Successors or other Person inhabiting or abiding within the said Monastery, having knowledge by the said Mayor or by any of his Officers thereof by monition to be given by the time of two Days before the time prefixed for the appearance, he at the time of that monition being within the said Monastery or elsewhere within the liberties of the same City: If then the said Prior, the next Court-day after the said summons or knowledge so given put in pledges of right according to the custom of the said City to answer to the said plaints so taken and affirmed, that then no manner of arrest nor attachment of any of the said Bodies shall not be put in execution within the said Monastery against the said Prior his Successors or any such person inhabiting or abiding within the same. And it is condescended agreed and determined by this composition that every such monition or warning hereafter to be given against the Priors or any other person spirituall or temporall inhabiting or resident within the same Monastry shall be good and effectuall to be given to the party to be sued or to any religious Man of the same Monastery then being a Priest.

Item, it is agreed that all the manuell and necessary servants of the said Prior and Covent that hereafter shall be inhabiting within any of the said tenantries shall not hereafter be impanelled, summoned, amerced ne distryned for any mercements for any manner of Jury that shal be sued between party and party.

Numb.
XV.

A Codicil (or Charter) of Kenulf *King of* Mercia, *of the Gift of certain Land in* Canterbury *(at a place now called* Binney) *to* Wlfred *the Archbishop.*

✠ IN nomine sancti Salvatoris Dei & Domini nostri Jesu Christi regnante ac gubernante eodem Domino Jesu simulque spiritu sancto gubernacula in imis & in arduis disponendo ubique regit. Licet sermo sapientium consiliumque prudentium stabilis permaneat, tamen ob incertitudine temporalium rerum divinis numinibus muniendo perscrutandos pro ignotis & incertis eventis stabilienda roborandaque in Deo vivo & vero sunt. Quapropter ego Coenulfus gratia Dei Rex Merciorum viro venerando in Christi charitate summo pontificalis apice decorato Wlfredo Archiep. dabo & concedo aliquem partem terræ juris mei quæ mihi largitor omnium bonorum Deus donare dignatus est pro intimo caritatis affectu, ut Apost' ait, hilarem enim datorem diligit Deus; Et hoc est in loco qui dicitur binnan ea circiter xxx. jugera inter duos rivos gremiales Fluminis quod dicitur Stur. Et hæc terra libera permaneat in perpetuam possessionem ecclesiæ Christi. Quod si quisque huic largitioni cantradixerit, contradicat ei Deus & deneget ingressum cœlestis vitæ. Actum est hoc Aº. Dominicæ incar. Dccc. xiiijº. Indict. vjª. his testibus consentientibus atque confirman. Quorum nomina nota sunt·

Binnan ea.

✠ Ego

✠ Ego Coenuulf gratia Dei Rex Mercio-   ✠ Ego Wlfhard æpſc' conſ. & ſub.

rum hanc donationis confirmationem ſigno   ✠ Signum manus Eadberhti ducis.

crucis Chriſti rob.   ✠ Signum manus Ealhheardi Ducis.

✠ Ego Wlfred arc' æps' conſ. & ſub.   ✠ Signum manus Ceolwlſi Ducis.

✠ Ego Denebyrht æpſc' conſ. & ſub.

A Compoſition between Chriſt-Church *and the Friers.*

Numb. XVI.

NOtum ſit omnibus præſentibus & futuris quòd in feſto Natalis beati Johannis Bapti-ſtæ Anno Dom. Mccxciiijº. Regni verò Regis Edwardi xxijº. Ita convenit inter Pri-orem & Conventum eccleſiæ Chriſti Cant. ex parte una, & Gardianum & Conventum fra-trum minorum Cant. ex altera, viz. quod cum diverſa tenementa continerentur infra ambi-tum ipſorum fratrum de feodo prædict' Prioris & Conventus, viz. tenementum quod quondam fuit Samuelis Tinctoris pro quo debebatur eis annuatim vij*d.* quad. Item pro tenemento quondam Beringeri in With pr. quo xij*d.* Item pro tenemento ejuſdem in Ottemed. pro quo v*d.* Item pro tenemento quondam Seronæ de Boctone pro quo vj*d.* Item pro redditu Wiber-ti quondam Prioris eccleſiæ Chriſti præd. juxta Ottewell, pro quo xij*d.* Item pro tenemen-to Stephani filii Lewini Samuel pro quo xviij*d.* Præfati Prior & Conventus remiſerunt & quietum clamaverunt in perpetuum prædictis fratribus & eorum Succeſſoribus omnia ar-reragia ſibi debit' de tenementis præd. intuitu caritatis. Ita viz. qd' iidem fratres & eorum Succeſſores de cetero per ſuos procuratores fideliter ſolvi facient annuatim prædict. Priori & Con. in Theſauraria ſua iijs. annui redditus pro omnibus tenementis prædict. viz. medi-um ad Paſcha & aliud medium ad feſtum Sancti Michaelis pro omnibus ſerviciis & ſecu-laribus demandis ad ipſos Prior. & Con. de eiſdem tenementis ſpectan. & ſi contingat præ-fat. procuratores poſt viginti dies poſtquam ſuper hoc præmuniti fuerint in ſolutione prædicti annui redditus deficere, bene licebit præd. Prior. & Conventui & eorum miniſtris diſtringere omnia tenementa præd. pro arreragiis quæ à retrò fuerint de annuo redditu ſupradict. In cujus Rei teſtimonium Sigillum eccleſiæ Chriſti præd. & ſigillum commune fratrum prædict. huic ſcripto Chirographato alternatim ſunt appenſa. Acta ſunt hæc apud Cantuar. die & anno ſupradictis.

The Ordination of Arch-biſhop Stratford *concerning* Eaſtbridge *Hoſpital.*

Numb. XVII.

JOhannes permiſſione divina Cantuar. Archiepiſcopus totius Angliæ Primas & Apoſtolicæ ſedis Legatus. Dilecto in Chriſto filio Domino Rogero de Rondes presbytero magiſtro Hoſpitalis pauperum de Eſtbreg in Civitate Cantuar. patronatus noſtri Salutem, gratiam & benedictionem. Et ſi votivus noſter invaleſcat affectus, decus & commoda locorum ad miſerabilium perſonarum & pauperum receptionem & ſuſtentationem divinique cultus augmentum providè deputatorum nobis potiſſimè ſubditorum, quatenus poſſumus procu-rare: tamen conſervatio & relevamen neceſſarium Hoſpitalis de Eſtbreg prædict' per bea-tum & glorioſum martyrem Thomam olim Cant. Archiepiſc. prædeceſſorem noſtrum fun-dati antiquitùs & dotati, ob ipſius martyris qui ſuis veneratoribus opem porrigit, hono- Fundator quis. rem præcipuum præ cæteris locis hujuſmodi inſident nobis cordi. Sane tua petitio nuper nobis exhibita continebat quòd idem Hoſpitale per beatum martyrem antedictum, pro pau-perum peregrinorum Cantuar. confluentium receptione nocturnâ, & ſuſtentatione aliquali ab olim, & pro jam incumbentibus eidem oneribus dotatum exiliter per ipſius Hoſpitalis in-curiam magiſtrorum, qui ejus proſtrarunt nemora, eaque & alia jura poſſeſſiones & bona ipſius tam mobilia quam immobilia modis alienare variis temerè preſumpſerunt, ad ſupre-mam egeſtatis inopiam eſt deductum ac æris alieni immoderatè per ipſos fatuéque contracti plurimis oneribus, ad quorum ſolutionem bona dicti Hoſpitalis abſque remedio & auxilio extrinſeco his diebus non ſufficiunt, primitus manifeſtè in ſuis etiam domibus olim ſuffici-enter conſtructis deformitates evidentes in tantum patitur & ruinam, quòd niſi ejuſdem Hoſpitalis provideatur indigentiæ aliunde, illud nedum peregrinos hujuſmodi ad ipſum poſt glorioſum triumphum & canonizationem dicti ſancti plus ſolito confluentium, admittere non valebit, ſet deſolationis tantis ſubiciet obprobriis quòd vix aliquis aut nullus idoneus invenietur, qui recipere velit hujuſmodi regimen Hoſpitalis. Quapropter nobis humiliter ſupplicaſti, ut ad relevamen omnium præmiſſorum, & pro ſuſtentatione pauperum peregri-norum illuc copioſe indies confluentium pleniori, eccleſiam parochialem beati Nicholai de Herbaldowne noſtræ Dioc. cujus ad dictum Hoſpitale jus ſpectare dinoſcitur patronatus Eccleſia parochi-eidem tibi ſucceſſoribuſque tuis ipſius Hoſp. magiſtris ex cauſis præmiſſis in proprios uſus alis. Sancti Ni-in perpetuum concedere, annectere, & unire vellemus. Nos ſiquidem Hoſp. prædict. quod cholai de Herbal-nuper viſitavimus defectum notorium quem patitur intuentes tam circa divina obſequia downe. quam alia caritatis opera inibi exercenda ſub formâ competenti & indubia ſicut convenit mimè ordininati, ipſiuſque indigentiis evidentibus paterno compatientes affectu, tuis etiam juſtis in ea parte ſupplicationibus inclinati, ſuper cauſis ſuperius expreſſatis, ac veritate ipſarum, vocatis ad hoc omnibus evocandis de Jure, per viros fide dignos in forma juris juratos, & ſingillatim examinat. ſufficientem præmiſſorum notitiam optinentes, authoritate noſtra, inquiſitione juxta exigentiam juris facta, demum ſuper religioſis viris cum his filiis noſtris Priore & Capitulo noſtræ Cantuar. eccleſiæ in ipſius Capitulo tractatum diligentem habuimus & ſolempnem prout requiritur in conceſſionibus hujuſmodi perpetuis & alienationibus Eccleſiarum de jure. Et quia dictas cauſas & per te nobis in hac parte ſuggeſta omnia & ſingula invenimus eſſe vera legitimeque probata, necnon juſta & ſufficientia fore ad appropriationem dictæ eccleſiæ faciend. cum urgens neceſſitas ac evidens notorie ſubſit utilitas in hac parte, præfatam eccleſiam beati Nicholai de Herbaldowne, interveniente in ea parte quorum intereſt conſenſu, cum Priore & Capitulo noſtris prædictis, tractatu ut eſt dictum ſuper his ſolempni & diligenti præhabito, ac de ipſorum conſenſu, concurrentibuſque omnibus & ſingulis qua in præmiſſis & ea tangen. requirebantur de jure, prædictiſque ex cauſis, authoritate noſtra ordinaria, Hoſpitali prædicto tibique & tuis ſucceſſoribus magiſtris ejuſdem miniſtraturis in eo, appropriamus, annectimus & unimus, ipſiuſque eccleſiæ fructus, redditúſque & proventus in dicti Hoſpitalis uſus proprios & tuos ac Succeſſorum tuorum magiſtrorum ejuſdem & peregrinorum pauperum ad illud confluentium, juxta modum inferius annotatum concedimus in perpetuum convertendos, ſalvo idoneo ſacerdoti dictæ ſervituro eccleſiæ in divinis qui & animarum curam exercebit in ea, tuo ſucceſſorumque tuorum magiſtrorum ibidem arbitrio deputando & amovendo, propter exilitatem eccleſiæ antedictæ ad perpetui vicarii ſuſtentationem & onerum relevamen hujuſm' minime ſufficientis, pro ſuis victualibus & ſuſtentatione de ipſius eccleſiæ fructibus redditibus, & proventibus congrua portione; alia ſiquidem onera eidem eccleſiæ incumbentia per magiſtrum Hoſpitalis prædicti volumus ſupportari. Ceterúm quia ſuper modum divina celebrandi officia in Hoſp. prædicto, & caritatis opera cæteraque peragenda inibi exercendi clara, ſufficiens & indubia ordinatio minime reperitur, licet quædam obſervantiæ in his & præcipue in proviſione pauperum uſitatæ in eo nobis fuerunt intimatæ. Nos ad perpetuam rei memoriam ſuper his certos modum & formam in Hoſp. prædict' in perpetuum obſervandos edere ſeu conſtituere duximus, &

taliter ordinamus, viz. quód in ipſo Hoſp. per nos & ſucceſſores noſtros Archiepiſc. Cant. ponatur ſeu præficiatur Magiſter, qui tempore quo ponetur ſeu præficietur eidem, ſit in ſacerdotali ordine conſtitutus, cui per Nos & ſucceſſores noſtros hujuſmodi dicti Hoſp. regimen committatur, prout canonicis convenit inſtitutis. Magiſtrum etiam quemlib' hujuſmodi cum ipſum Hoſp. primo adeptus fuerit infra menſem ſequentem prox. de ipſius Hoſp. bonis ſingulis ſingillatim & ſpecifice Inventarium plenum conficere, ipſiuſque copiam infra menſem eundem Priori noſtræ Cant. eccl' qui erit pro tempore tradere, ac eidem vel Suppriori ejuſdem dicto prioratu vacante, ſeu alteri ad hoc deputando per ipſorum arbitrium, ſuo caſu, in ipſo Prioratu, vice Cant. Archiep. & authoritate præſentium annis ſingulis inter Sancti Michaelis & omnium Sanctorum feſta de adminiſtratione ſua reddere plenam & diſtinctam volumus rationem. Ordinamus inſuper qd' magiſter ipſe qui erit pro tempore unum alium ad ſe habeat continue ſecum in Hoſp. præd' idoneum Capellanum ſecularem ponend' & amovend' prout eidem magiſtro videbitur expedire. Quodque magiſter & Capellanus hujuſm' in Hoſp. præd' matutinas & ceteras horas canonicas ad invicem, legitimo impedimento ceſſante, ſecundum uſum Sar. eccl' pſallere vel convenienter dicere & devote ac divina, viz. unus eorum miſſam de die, alius vero diebus dominicis, de ſancto Nicholao, diebus Martis de beato Thoma Martyre antedicto, diebus Jovis de beata Virgine Catherina, cæteris vero diebus ebdomadatim miſſam pro defunctis & pro benefactoribus Hoſpitalis prædicti teneantur diebus ſingulis celebrare, ac orum quilibet orationem, Rege queſum' Domine famulum tuum Pontificem noſtrum, & cætera pro nobis quam diu agimus in hac vita, & poſt ſolutum noſtræ carnis debitum, orationem. Deus qui inter Apoſtolicos ſacerdotes, diebus ad hoc aptis competen' dicere, necnon in Canone miſſæ pro nobis ſpecialiter orare, noſtrique habere memoriam ſpecificam in celebrandis ſuis miſſis ſingulis in perpetuum ſit aſtrictus. Ordinam' preterea quod ad dicti magiſtri diſpoſitionem & curam ſolicitam, fructus, redditus & proventus dictique totius Hoſp. regimen, quamdiu magiſter ibidem fuerit cum moderamine pertineant infraſcripto. viz. quód magiſtro & Capellano hujuſm' celebraturis & miniſtraturis pro tempore in Hoſpitali prædicto ſingulis communibus diebus de uno ferculo duplicato, in dominicis vero diebus & feſtis duplicibus ac ſolempnibus cum hujuſmodi ferculo de una pitantia non minus ſumptuoſa deſerviatur in menſa. Inhibemus inſuper & interdicimus ne commune ſigillum in Hoſp. prædicto habeatur à modo vel exiſtat. Peregrini ſiquidem valetudinarii pauperes quos arripit infirmitas in ſuæ peregrinationis itinere non leproſi in Hoſp. ſuſcipiantur eodem, & in fata decedentes ibidem, in Cimiterio noſtræ Cantuar. eccleſiæ ſepeliantur in loco ad hoc antiquitus aſſigna-

to. Sani autem peregrini pauperes accedentes ibidem per noctem unam recipiantur duntaxat: in quorum tam valetudinar. quam ſanor. peregrinor. hujuſmodi uſus ad ipſorum vitæ ſubſidium diebus ſingulis ad quatuor denarior. eſtimationem de bonis Hoſp. prædict. volumus & ordinamus expendi. Peregrinos valetudinarios pauperes illuc confluentes cum ſanis tam ac moram quam ad vitæ ſubſidium in eſtimatione prædicta percipienda ſanis volumus anteferri. Quod ſi dierum aliquo in uſus prædict. peregrinorum hujuſmodi de bonis Hoſp. ipſius propterea quia nullos vel paucos peregrinantes hujuſmodi contigerit declinare ad eſtimationem non expendat. eandem; ordinamus & volumus quód diebus aliis ſeu temporibus copioſoris adventus peregrinorum præd' ibidem, quod minus diebus præced' eſt expenſum, in ampliori receptione ſubſidiorumque vitæ neceſſarior. & miniſtratione pauperum peregrinorum hujuſmodi juxta modum ſuperius annotatum ſuppleatur tali cum affectu quód in uſu tam pio & laudabili de bonis Hoſp. præd' ad ſummam iiij*d.* pro numero ſingulor' dier' in anno diſcretione prævia integraliter & fideliter erogetur. In hoſp' etiam præd' 12. lectos competentes ordinamus debere inperpetuum conſiſtere ad

uſum

uſum confluentium pauperum peregrinorum ibidem, ac mulierem aliquam honeſtæ vitæ, quæ quadraginta annorum etatem exceſſerit miniſterio peregrinorum hujuſmodi tam in lectis quam vitæ neceſſariis ut præmittitur miniſtrandis eſſe volumus intendentem, cui mulieri de bonis Hoſpitalis prædicti miniſtretur in ſingulis vitæ ſuæ Neceſſariis competenter. Et ad ordinationem præſentem in ſingulis ſuis articulis prout eſt poſſibile fideliter obſervand. & quatenus in eo eſt facere fieri obſervari, necnon de corrodiis, penſionibus, poſſeſſionibus, nemoribus aut bonis immobilibus ſeu juribus ipſius Hoſpitalis non vendendis, concedendis in perpetuum, vel ad tempus donandis, vel alio quovis alienationis titulo non alienand. nobis aut ſucceſſoribus noſtris Archiepiſcopis Cantuar. inconſultis, & non conſentientibus ad hoc expreſſe, per quoſcunque magiſtros Hoſp. prædict. quibus ejus regimen committetur impoſterum præſtari volumus & ordinamus in commiſſionibus ſingulis de ipſo faciendis eiſdem corporale ad ſancta Dei Evangelia Juramentum, Commiſſionem autem Hoſp. prædicti ſi facta fuerit alteri quam in ſacerdotio conſtituto, vel prædicto non exacto vel præſtito Juramento fore volumus ipſo facto irritam & inanem. Reſervata nobis & ſucceſſoribus noſtris Archiepiſc, Cantuar. hujuſmodi ordinationi noſtræ addendi, detrahendi, eamque mutandi & corrigendi prout expedire videbitur plenaria poteſtate. Acta & dat' in Capitulo dictæ noſtræ Cantuar. Eccleſiæ xxiij°. die menſis Septemb. Anno Domini MCCCXLII. & noſtræ tranſlationis nono.

Foundation of the Vicarage of Coſmus-Bleane.

Numb. XVIII.

UNiverſis ſancti matris Eccleſiæ filiis præſentes literas inſpecturis Simon permiſſione divina Cant. Archiepiſcopus totius Angliæ Primas & Apoſtolicæ ſedis Legatus Salutem in Domino. Quia tam ex fama publica quam ex inquiſitione ex officio noſtro in hac parte capta evidenter comperimus eccleſiam parochialem ſanctorum Coſmæ & Damiani in la Bleen noſtræ Dioc. Hoſpitali noſtro ſancti Thomæ Martyris de Eſtbrigge in Civitate Cantuar. ab antiquo fuiſſe & eſſe appropriatam, unitam pariter & annexam, per unum milliare & amplius ab ipſis Civitate & Hoſpitali notorie diſtantem, ſacerdotemque qui curæ animarum parochianorum eccleſiæ prædictæ hactenus intendebat ſeu intendere ſolebat in dicto Hoſp. per dies & noctes quaſi continuò fuiſſe commorantem, cum alibi pro ſacerdote hujuſmodi hoſpitium ſive habitatio minimè extiterat ordinat', quodque vix in eccleſia præfata ſingulis ebdomadis ſacerdos prædictus propter dictorum locorum diſtantiam per dies duos miſſam celebravit, ac parochiani eccleſiæ nonnulli infirmati ſacerdotem hujuſmodi diebus & noctibus inquirendo in loco ut præmittitur ſæpe diſtanti quam plurimum fuerant fatigati, & ſæpius in infirmitatibus ſubitis proper præfati ſecerdotis abſentiam multiplicem neque confeſſi neque communicati lamentabiliter deceſſerunt, ac alii infirmitatibus hujuſmodi remanſerunt periculoſe & multipliciter deſolati. Nos itaque præmiſſa pericula mentis noſtræ intuitu debite ponderantes, eiſque quantum cum Deo poterimus ex noſtri officii debito mederi cupientes, de voluntate & aſſenſu Dilecti nobis in Chriſto Domini Thomæ Newe de Wolton cuſtodis ſive magiſtri Hoſp antedicti, intervenientibus etiam authoritate & aſſenſu dilectorum filiorum Prioris & Capituli eccleſiæ noſtræ Chriſti Cant. de conſilio Juriſperitorum nobis aſſiſtentium, volentes dei cultum, animarumque profectum parochianorum eccleſiæ prædictæ, Domino diſponente, ſalubriter augmentare, ſtatuimus, ordinamus & diſponimus, ut de cetero ſit in dicta eccleſia perpetuus Vicarius habens infra ejuſdem parochiam manſionem quam præfatus Dominus Thomas Newe Cuſtos erexit pro eodem. Habebit etiam idem Vicarius decimas ac oblationes ſubſcriptas ad valorem annuum decem librarum & ultra ut communiter creditur ſe extendentes, pro victu ſuo & oneribus infraſcriptis ſupportandis, ejus quoque Vicarii præſentatio in vacationibus ipſius Vicariæ ſingulis ad Cuſtodem ipſius Hoſp. inperpetuum pertinebit. Habebit etiam ipſe Vicarius in partem ſummæ prædictæ pro dote ſua omnes decimas prædiales apud Natyngdon dicto Hoſp. debitas ab antiquo, quæ quinque marcas aut circiter de claro valebunt annuatim, nec non omnes decimas prædiales per totam parochiam dictæ eccleſiæ ſanctor. Coſmæ & Damiani præterquam de terris & prædiis dominicalibus omnibus & ſingulis prædicti Hoſp. jam cultis & colendis infra parochiam antedictam & preter omnimodas decimas prædiales & alias quaſcunque provenient' ex terris ſubſcriptis & animalibus in eiſdem depaſcendis & eorum ſetuum ſuper terras hujuſmodi emittend. quæ terræ ſic exceptæ ſunt & jacent ex auſtrali parte cujuſdam curſus aquæ currentis in ipſa parochia quæ vocatur Viſchmannysbourne in quadam valle infra dictam parochiam inter eccleſiam prædictam ſanctor. Coſmæ & Damiani in le Bleen & Curiam dicti Hoſp. apud le Hothe dictæ noſtræ Dioc. ſcituat. Ita quod Vicarius ille de decimis prædialibus nec aliis cujuſcunque generis fuerint ex illa parte auſtrali dicti curſus aquæ infra parochiam prædict. qualitercunque provenien. nihil penitus vendicare poterit vel debebit. Habebit inſuper dictus Vicarius in complementum ſummæ decem librarum prædictarum omnes decimas vitulorum, agnorum, aucarum, lini, lanæ, lactis, lacticinii, caſei, fœni, herbagii, ſilvæ ceduæ, aliarumque rerum omnium decimabilium infra dictam parochiam, decimis de terris & prædiis dominicalibus & poſſeſſionibus quibuſcunque prove. nientibus ac de animalibus dicti Hoſp. & ipſorum fœtibus in ipſa parochia ubicunque depaſcendis & emittendis, cujuſcunque generis fuerint, decimis quoque animalium hominum aliorum quorumcunque ſuper ipſas terras dominicales & ſuper terras aliorum ex parte auſtrali

Cauſæ fundationis.

Dotatio Vicariæ.

Decimæ apud Natingdon.

Fiſhmannesbourne.

ftrali curfus aquæ prædiđ' fœtus emittentium, & ex quibus ipfe Vicarius nihil omnino percipiet duntaxat exceptis. Habebit itaque onnes oblationes in diđa parochiali ecclefia
fanđor. Cofmæ & Damiani & ejus parochia extra Curiam diđi Hofp. apud la Hoth ubicunque faciendas & quia tanta commoda ipfe Vicarius infra diđam parochiam quafi Rector
loci optinebit, fubfcripta onera de emolumentis & proficuis prædiđis diđus Vicarius qui fuerit pro tempore futuris temporibus fupportabit, viz. Cancellum diđæ ecclefiæ fanđorum

(margin) Onora Vicaaii.

Cofmæ & Damiani conftruet & reparabit fuis fumptibus & expenfis quotiens & quando o-
portebit. Et volumus quod fi in ea parte per Cuftodem præfati hofp. debite monitus infra tempus congruum per ipfum Cuftodem limitandum reparationes & conftrucđiones hujufmodi fieri non fecerit competenter, licebit extunc eidem Cuftodi qui pro tempore fuerit de
diđis oblationibus & decimis partem rationabilem & non exceffivam liberè capere & levare,
cum qua reparationes aut conftrucđiones ipfas poterit fieri facere competenter, & fi fic partem rationabilem ceperit & levaverit ipfe Cuftos, vicarius ille pro reparationibus aut con-
ftrucđionibus tunc neceffariis excufatus habeatur penitus ne fraus aut malitia locum habeat
in hac parte. Suftentabit etiam Vicarius hujufmodi qui ibidem pro tempore fuerit fuis fumptibus competentem manfionem pro ipfo vicario in diđa parochia jam conftrucđam. Ora-
buntque finguli qui ibidem erint Vicarii in fingulis fuis miffis pro noftra falute dum vixeri-
mus, & pro anima noftra cum ab hac luce migraverimus, ac pro falute Domini Thomæ
Newe dum vixerit, & pro ejus anima cum ab hac luce migraverit, necnon pro anima bonæ
memoriæ Domini Simonis de Iflep dudum Cant. Archiepifc. prædecefforis noftri, quia cum
ejus bonis in majori parte ipfa manfio ut accepimus erecđa extitit & conftrucđa, & pro a-

(margin) Dominus Thomas de Ros. & Beatrix ejus uxor. Dominus Euftacius de Dapf-checourt & uxor. * L. Daprich, court.

nimabus Domini Thomæ de Ros qui multas poffeffiones dedit diđo hofpitali in partem dotis uniuf Cantariæ perpetuæ pro falute animæ fuæ & Beatricis confortis fuæ
ac etiam Domini Euftacii de * Dapfchecourt & confortis ejus, de quorum bonis multa pietatis opera fađa funt in diđo Hofp. fanđi Thomæ martyris. Inveniet in fuper diđus Vicarius qui fuerit pro tempore vinum & panem ac luminar' in præfata ecclefia pro celebrantibus
neceffaria, & fuis fumptibus ea exhiberi faciet competenter, & fubibit omnia alia onera
prædiđæ ecclefiæ impofterum imponenda quæ ad decimas folvendas taxata non exiftunt eaque agnofcat debite & perfolvat. Artabitur etiam ad refidentiam continuam infra parochiam præfatæ ecclefiæ faciendam, ficut ad refidentiam continuam alii ecclefiarum Vicarii per
conftitutionem funt artati. Obedietque cuftodi præfati hofp. qui fuerit pro tempore in licitis & honeftis. Refervamus infuper nobis & Succefforibus noftris Archiepifc. Cant. poteftatem corrigendi, augmentandi & diminuendi noftram ordinationem prædiđam quotiens
nobis vel eis videbitur expediens & opportunum. In cujus Rei teftimonium figillum noftrum
fecimus hiis apponi. Dat' apud Otteforde tertio Non. Augufti Anno Domini Millefimo
CCC ᵐᵒ. feptuagefimo quinto, & noftræ tranflationis anno primo.

The Foundation of Eaftbridge *Chantery.*

(margin) Numb. XIX.

(margin) Caufæ fundatio-nis. † le. Unam.

SAnđæ matris Ecclefiæ filiis univerfis ad quos præfentes literæ pervenerint Simon permiffione divina Cantuar. Archiepifcopus &c. falutem in Domino fempiternam. Quia per
infpecđionem cujufdam patentis literæ bonæ memoriæ Domini Simonis de Iflep nuper Cant.
Archiepifc. prædecefforis noftri ejus figillo confignatæ comperimus evidenter quod ipfe ex
certis caufis † una perpetuam cantariam in Hofpitali noftro apud Eftbrig' in Civitate Cant. ad
honorem Dei cultufque divini, & pro falute animarum quorundam benefacđorum ipfius
Hofp. & omnium fidelium defuncđorum devotè & legitimè ordinavit, ejufque Cantariæ fa-
cerdotem qui fuerit pro tempore annuatim percipere voluit ad certos anni terminos in ordinatione eadem expreffos de cuftode ejufdem Hofpitalis in perpetuum decem marcas ex valore antiquarum & novarum poffeffionum eidem Hofpitali adquifitarum capiendas & etiam
perfolvendas, prout in diđa ordinationis litera plenius expreffatur. Sacerdotem quoque ipfius Cantariæ per literas ordinationis prædiđas artavit ad refidentiam continuam in diđa
Civitate aut ejus fuburbio faciendam, ita quod fe ab ipfis Civitate aut fuburbio per fpati-
um unius diei minimè abfentaret nifi de Cuftodis diđi Hofp. aut tenentis ejus locum licentia
fpeciali petita pariter & obtenta, quam ex caufis licitis neceffariis & honeftis dare poterit diđus Cuftos aut locum ejus tenens quotiens ubi & quamdiu fibi videbitur expedire, dum
tamen idem capellanus in abfentia fua hujufmodi per alium capellanum idoneum faciat divina
celebrari, quodque pauperibus & peregrinis ad ipfum Hofp. confluentibus & in ipfo infirmi-
tatis facramenta & facramentalia quæ fi præfens fuerit in eodem per fe vel per alium miniftrabit & debite faciat miniftrari. Volumus itaque & etiam ordinamus quod facerdos ipfius

(margin) Manfio Canta-riftæ.

Cantariæ qui eft & erit inpofterum manfionem habeat infra fepta diđi Hofp. inter Infirma-
riam & magnam portam ejufdem Hofp. jam ei affignatam, cum una camera fupra ipfam
portam ædificata, fuis fumptibus continuè in ftatu debito confervandam. Verum poft ipfam ordinationem Dominus nofter excellentiffimus Dominus Edwardus Rex Angliæ &
Franciæ illuftris qui nunc eft quoddam meffuagium fuum in Civitate Cant. fitum, la
Chaunge vulgariter nuncupatum, in magna parte tempore donationis ejufdem infrafcrip'
collapfum ex pia donatione fua Domino Thomæ Newe de Wolton nunc magiftro prædiđi Hofp. ad terminum vitæ fuæ donavit, ita quod poft mortem fuam ipfum meffuagium
Succefforibus * ipfius magiftris, viz. Hofp. prædiđi remaneret in perpetuum, in auxilium

(margin) * L. Suis. † L. Celebraturi

fuftentationis unius capellani perpetui † divina celebranti in Hofp. prædiđo, pro falubri ftatu
ipfius Domini Regis dum vixit, & anima cariffimæ matris fuæ Ifabellæ defunđæ, & anima
ipfius Domini Regis cum ab hac luce migraverit, anima etiam Domini Johannis at Lee
qui

qui in parte dotavit dictam Cantariam, ac animabus omnium fidelium defunctorum, prout in carta dicti Domini nostri Regis plenè vidimus contineri. Ac per inquisitionem & informationem fidedignorum accepimus quod dictum messuagium per præfatum Dominum nostrum Regem collatum ut præmittitur, per executores dicti prædecessoris nostri & cum bonis ejus caritativè est taliter reparatum & constructum quod verus valor ejus in certo redditu ad septem marcas ascendit, & in futurum ascendet annuatim ut speratur. Quodque difficile sit in presenti honestum reperire sacerdotem, qui pro salario decem marcarum ad tam continuam residentiam & cotidianas celebrationes voluerit ut præmittitur onerari. Devotionemque dicti Domini nostri Regis quoad augmentum dictæ dotis hactenus frustratum esse comperimus : Ordinamus & statuimus addendo ordinationi prædicti prædecessoris *Augmentatio* noftri, de consensu dicti Domini Thomæ custodis præfati Hosp. & executores prædecessoris nostri prædicti quod dos dictæ Cantariæ decem marcarum per quinque marcas & dimidiam de septem marcis redditus messuagii five tenementi prædicti per Dominum Regem dati ut premittitur percipiendas per sacerdotem prædictum qui fuerit pro tempore equis portionibus, ad quatuor anni terminos, ad quos dictæ decem marcæ in ordinatione dicti prædecessoris nostri sunt solvendæ augmentetur, & eandem Cantariam cum dictis quinque marcis & dimidia tenore presentium augmentamus, cum potestate per dictum Capellanum distringendi in dicto messuagio seu tenemento vocat' la Chaunge per Dominum nostrum Regem dato ut præfertur, quotiens per aliquem terminorum prædict' in ordinatione prædicta contentorum pars debita ipsius redditus quinque marcarum & dimidiæ in parte vel in toto per dies quindecim eidem capellano non fuerit persoluta. Et quia præsentatio Cantariæ de *Cantaria de* Bourne Hospitali prædicti unitæ prout in ordinatione primæ Cantariæ prædictæ per Præde- *Bourne.* cessorem nostrum facta plenius continetur, ad Bartholomeum de Bourne seu ejus heredes aut assignatos ante unionem prædictam pertinebat : statuimus, ordinamus, & propterea declaramus quod præsentatio dictæ Cantariæ cum vacaverit, nobis seu successoribus nostris, aut sede ecclesiæ Cant. vacante, Priori & Capitulo ejusdem ecclesiæ facienda, ad præfatum Bartholomæum, heredes aut assignatos suos, collatioque ejusdem ad nos & Successores nostros cum eam vacare contigerit alternis vicibus pertinebunt, & quod collatio dictæ Cantariæ in prima vocati' ejusdem ad nos vel Successores nostros pertineat, quia assignatus dicti Bartholomei ad ipsam Cantariam tunc vacantem Capellanum præsentavit eandem occupantem in præsenti. Jurabit quilibet Capellanus ejusdem Cantariæ in admissione sua seu collatione sibi facienda, ordinationis dictæ Cantariæ & singula contenta in eisdem fideliter observare, alioquin ejus admissio, collatio & institutio nullius penitus sint momenti. In quorum omnium testimonium sigillum nostrum fecimus hiis apponi. Dat' apud Wingham xv. Kalen. Novembris. Anno Domini Mccclxxv°. & translationis nostræ anno primo.

Inſtruments concerning the Change.

Numb. XX. a.

QUandam placeam terræ cum domibus superedificatis muris & aliis pertinentiis suis quæ pars fuit tenementi vocat' la Chaunge jacen' in Civitate Cant. in parochia omnium Sanctorum, simul cum quodam introitu ducente ab alto vico ex parte South per magnum hostium dictæ placeæ usque ad eandem placeam, inter tenementum heredum Willielmi Child versus East, & tenem' Prioris & Conventus ecclesiæ Christi Cant. versus West, & tenem' Edmundi Horne versus North, & tenementum prædicti Thomæ de Wolton quod pars est tenementi vocat' la Chaunge versus South.

Numb. XX. b.

QUandam placeam quæ pars est tenementi quod la Chaunge vocabatur, & quod Dominus noster Rex qui nunc est mihi dedit ad terminum vitæ meæ & meis successoribus in perpetuum ad augmentum dotis Hospitalis memorati, in qua quidem placea unum cellarium, duo solaria & una domus intermedia ad instar aulæ cum quadam pecia gardini jacen' ad finem dicti cellarii, quæ omnia conjunctim jacent & situantur in dicta Civitate in parochia omnium Sanctorum inter unam partem dicti tenementi vocat' la Chaunge quam modo tenet Magister Thomas Mason ex dimissione mea versus North, & aliam partem ejusdem tenementi de la Chaunge quam etiam idem Mr Thomas tenet ex traditione mea, & quasdam choppas dicti Hospitalis versus West, & tenementum heredum Willielmi Child versus East, & Regiam stratam versus South. Tres etiam choppas præfati Hosp. cum una parva placea jacen' per longum inter ipsas choppas, & ten' dicti Magistri Thomæ quod etiam habet ex dimissione mea ex parte North, & introitum quendam antiquum in ipsum tenementum de la Chaunge ex parte East, & Regiam stratam versus South, cum uno muro lapideo qui est ad finem ipsarum placeæ & schopparum, a tenemento dicti Magistri Thomæ linealiter extenso usque ad hostium dicti introitus ex parte sinistra ingredientium per illud.

The Arch-biſhop's Mandate concerning the Auguſtine *Friers.*

Numb. XXI.

WAlterus permissione divina &c. Dilecto filio Commissario nostro Cant. salutem, gratiam & benedictionem. Licet universaliter tam jura civilia quam canonica prohibeant ne quis absque pontificali authoritate Oratorii domum de novo construere præsumat,

ac

ac fedes Apoftolica per multa privilegia fpecialiter indulferit & exprefsè, ne quis in fundo ecclefiæ Cant. præter authoritatem Cantuar. Archiepifcopi & capituli, ecclefiam, capellam vel oratorium de novo edificare moliatur. Fratres tamen heremitarum fancti Augustini hac die dominica in fefto Natalis beatæ Mariæ Virginis in quadam domo Civitatis Cant. in fundo ecclefiæ Cant. abfque licentia & affenfu noftro & Capituli noftri, oratorium feu eccle-fiam de novo erexerunt, & pulfata campana miffarum folempnia publicè celebrare & obla-tiones, ecclefiæ parochiali debitas temere recipere ut afferitur præfumpfer'. Quocirca vobis firmiter injungendo mandamus quatenus per viros fide dignos hujus rei plenam noticiam ha-bentes diligentem faciatis inquifitionem. Et fi per inquifitionem prædict' fuggefta invene-ritis veritate fulciri, tunc ipfum locum in quo prædicti fratres fic ut præmittitur temere celebrarunt, & adhuc ut dicitur celebrant, vice & authoritate noftra ecclefiaftico fuppona-tis interdicto. Citantes nichilominus nominatim illos fratres quos in prædicto loco per dictam inquifitionem convinceritis celebraffe, ac ipfos fratres ibidem commorantes, fi qui fint, quòd compareant coram nobis die legitimo per vos ftatuendo ubicunque in Civitate Dioc. feu Provinc. noftræ Cant. tunc fuerimus de hujufmodi injuria & contemptu nobis & ecclefiæ noftræ Cant. per eofdem illatis refponfuri, ulteriufque facturi & recepturi quod canonicis convenit inftitutis. De die verò receptionis præfentium, & quid feceritis in præ-miffis nos dictis die & loco certificetis per literas veftras patentes harum feriem continentes. Dat' apud Tenham 18. Kal. Octob. Anno Domini Mcccxxv°.

Numb.
XXII.

The Grant of Sir John Fineux to the Auguftine Friers.

UNiverfis fanctæ matris eccefiæ filiis præfentes literas vifuris feu audituris Willielmus Mallaham Prior Conventus domus fratrum heremitarum divi Augustini ordinis in Civitate Cantuar. fit' & fundat' ac ejufdem loci fratres, falutem & finceram in Domino ca-ritatem. Cum in officiis caritatis illis primo loco teneamur obnoxii à quibus nos beneficia recepiffe cognofcimus, nec magnum immo digniffimum fore arbitremur ut illos fpiritua-libus reficiamus epulis qui nos temporalibus dotaverunt : & Dominus Johannes Fyneux miles Dominique Henrici Regis feptimi necnon & octavi capitalis Jufticiarius ad placita coram eifdem Regibus tenend' vir utique prudentiffimus, genere infignis, Juftitia præclarus, pietate refertus, humanitate fplendidus & caritate fecundus, ex ejus munificentia & boni-tate circa ecclefiæ noftræ, refectorii, dormitorii noftri, murorum noftrorum reparationem & refectionem quadraginta librarum fummam ampliufque largiffimè expofuerit. Hinc eft quod Nos Willielmus Prior antedictus & ejufd' domus fratres hujus digniffimi viri carita-tem fecundam advertentes pro hujufm' ejus largitione fua piiffima unanimi confenfu & af-fenfu, conceffimus, donavimus ac præfentis donationis noftræ fcripto roboravimus & pro perpetuo confirmavimus prout per præfentes confirmamus eidem Johanni Fyneux heredibus & fucceff oribus fuis unum Capellanum ex fratribus noftris quotidie & imperpetuum apud al-tare in honore beatæ Mariæ Virginis vocat' in Capella beatæ Mariæ edificata de vifitatione ejus, miffam quæ vocabitur miffa beatæ Mariæ inter horam feptimam & octavam celebra-turum. Et quòd idem Capellanus pro tempore celebraturus quotidie poft offeratorium, & ante manuum lotionem ad cornu Altaris converfus alta voce recitabit in quadam tabula no-mina infrà fcripta ut fequitur. Oretur divina clementia pro animabus Domini Johannis Fyneux militis & Elifabeth confortis fuæ, Henrici Regis ejus nomine feptimi, Johannis Morton Cardinalis quondam Archiepifcopi Cantuar. Willielmi Apuldorfeld & Mildredæ confortis fuæ, ac pro animabus omnium fidelium defunctorum. Et ut hæc donatio & con-ceffio noftra firmiter & perpetuò obfervetur : Nos Willielmus Prior præfatus & hujus ejufdem loci Conventus hanc donationem & conceffionem noftram non folum figilli noftri communis & Capitularis appofitione fed & manuum noftrarum fubfcriptione confirmavimus, & per præfentes confirmamus. Dat' in domo noftra Capitulari prædictæ domus noftræ apud Cantuar. vicefimo octavo die menfis Novembris Anno Domini Milefimo quingen-tefimo vicefimo fecundo.

Et ego frater Willielmus Wederhall Doctor in Theologia & Provincialis ejufdem ordinis fratrum heremitarum omnia & fingula prædicta condignè & falubriter percontentus fuiffe conceffa & condonata, pro confirmatione omnium & fingulorum, fic ut præfertur per Pri-orem & confratres prædictos concefforum & condonatorum ad fpecialem rogatum & re-quifitionem præfatorum Prioris & Conventus, præfcriptis conceffioni & condonationi figil-lum meum quo ad talia negotia utor appofui. Dat' quoad figillationem hujus confirma-tionis noftræ vicefimo die Decembris Anno Dom. fupra dicto.

Numb.
XXIII.

The Grant of Stodmerfh Church to the Hofpital of Poor Priefts.

OMnibus Sanctæ matris, &c. R. Dei Gratia, &c. Ad Univerfitatis veftræ noticiam vo-lumus pervenire, nos divinæ pietatis intuitu ad inftantiam viri venerabilis & amici no-ftri kariffimi Magiftri Simonis de L. Archidiac. Cant. Ecclefiam Sanctæ Mariæ de Stodm. quæ ad noftram pertinuit donationem perpetuè conceffiffe & dediffe Hofpitali pauperum Sacerdotum quod fitum eft in parochia de Sancta Margareta in Cant. ad fuftentationem eorundem cum proventibus quatuor acrarum fingulis annis de Dominio noftro de Stodmarfh
antiquo

antiquo more de gratia noftra fpeciali percipiendum hoc adjecto, quòd in dicta parochia nullas terras vel redditus de noftris tenentibus, dicti Sacerdotes vel eorum procuratores ement vel aliquo titulo fibi appropriabunt nifi de noftro vel Succefforum noftrorum licentia fpeciali, nec decimas aliquas de Dominio noftro de Stodm. requirent in futuro. Quandò autem dictam eis fecimus donationem Syndicus dicti Hofpitalis de voluntate Archidiaconi memorati, nomine dictorum Sacerdotum & Hofpitalis fupradicti nobis & ecclefiæ noftræ Sacramentum præftitit fidelitatis, & hoc idem facient omnes Succeffores fui. Dictus autem Procurator vel aliquis Sacerdos Hofpitalis fupradicti omni anno fuper majus altare in eccle- fia noftra in die S. Auguftin' unum cereum unius libræ in fignum recognitionis præmif- forum, &c.

The Grant of S. Margarets Church to the fame Hofpital.

Numb. XXIV.

ANno Domini Millefimo Cclxxj°. data fuit ecclefia Sanctæ Margaretæ Cant. Hofpitali pauperum Sacerdotum ibidem in liberam & perpetuam elem' ab abbate R. quæ fuit ante noftri patronatus. Et non licebit Syndico vel Sacerdoti Hofp. præd' aliquas terras redditus vel tenementa in dicta parochia fanctæ Margaretæ de tenentibus noftris emere, vel aliquo titulo fibi appropriare fine licentia abb. & Con. fpeciali. Syndicus autem præd' Hofp. qui pro tempore fuerit in recognitionem Juris noftri præd' facramentum nobis præ- ftabit fidelitatis in Capitulo cum ad hoc fuerit requifitus. Pulfatio vero in eadem ecclefia fiet contra Dominum Abbatem quotiens eum per illam ecclefiam tranfire contigerit.

VIcefimo feptimo Julii 1554. D'nus admifit Hugonem Barret presbyterum ad Hofpitale pauperum facerdotum Civitatis Cant. necnon & Rectoriam five ecclefiam parochialem divæ Margaretæ ejufdem Civitatis dicto Hofpitali appropriat. per mortem naturalem Ni- colai Langdon ultimi Incumbentis ejufdem vacan'. Ad quam five quod per venerabilem virum magiftrum Nicolaum Harpesfield legum doctorem Archidiaconum Cant. dict. Hofp. & ecclefiæ verum & indubitatum ut dicitur patronum D'no præfentatus extitit. Ipfumque Præpofitum Magiftrum five Rectorem inftituit & inveftivit canonice in & de eifdem cum fuis juribus & pertinentiis univerfis, curamque & regimen animarum, &c. fibi in Domino commifit, Juribus capitularibus, &c. & ecclefiæ Metropol' Chrifti Cantuar. dignitate & honore in omnibus femper falvis, ac præftito Juramento per Jacobum Canceler procurato- rem fupradicti Hugonis Barret in hac parte legitimè conftitutum de obfervand' ftatutis & ordinationibus dicti Hofpitalis juxta fundationem ejufdem, ac etiam de canonica obedientia, &c. Scriptum fuit Archidiacono Cant. feu ejus Officiali pro ipfius inductione, &c.

Numb. XXIV. b.

The Grant of Poor Priefts Hofpital with the Lands and Appertinances to it, by the late Queen, to the City.

Numb. XXV. a.

ELizabetha Dei gratia Angliæ, Franciæ & Hiberniæ Regina fidei defenfor &c. Omnibus ad quos præfentes literæ pervenerint Salutem. Cum Blafius Winter clericus Magifter hofpitalis pauperum Sacerdotum in Comitatu Civitatis Cantuar. necnon Ed. Freake Roffen' Epifcopus Archidiaconus Cantuarien. verus & indubitatus Patronus dicti Hofpitalis in Jure Archidiaconatus prædicti & Mattheus Cant. Archiepifcopus totius Angliæ Primas & Metropolitanus Ordinarius ejufdem Hofpitalis per fcriptum fuum gerens datum quarto de- cimo die Maii anno Regni noftri decimo feptimo ob diverfas caufas eofdem moventes in prædicto fcripto mentionat' & expreffas, dederunt, concefferunt & confirmaverunt nobis he- redibus & fuccefforibus noftris in perpetuum totum Hofpitale pauperum Sacerdotum infra Civitatem Cant. prædictam, & advocationem ejufdem Hofp. necnon omnia & fingula do- mos, ædificia, ftructuras, gardin', pomar', terras arabil'. glebas, tenementa, prata, pa- fturas, marifcos, bofcos, fubbofcos, redditus, reverfiones, fervitia, portiones, penfiones, annuales redditus, decimas bladorum, granorum & feni, advocationem & advocati- ones ecclefiæ & ecclefiarum, vicariæ & vicariarum quarumcunque & reverfio- nem & reverfiones omnium & fingulorum præmifforum, ac omnia & fingula proficua, franches', emolumenta & hereditamenta quæcunque dicto Hofp. fpectan- tia & pertinentia, vel ut pars, parcella vel membrum ejufdem hofp. nunc vel antehac ac- cept', ufitat, cognit' feu reputat', tam infra Civitatem prædictam quam infra Comitatum Kanc. Habend' nobis, heredibus & Succefforibus noftris ad folum opus & ufum noftrum heredum & Succefforum noftrorum in perpetuum, ea tamen intentione & fiducia quod nos, heredes & Succeffores noftri ad humilem fupplicationem & petitionem Majoris & Com- munitatis dictæ Civitatis noftræ Cantuar. totum dictum Hofp. & omnia & fingula alia præmiffa cum fuis pertinentiis præfatis Majori & Communitati & Succefforibus fuis per li- teras noftras patentes fub magno figillo noftro Angliæ debito modo fiend' & figilland' dare & concedere dignaremur Tenend. prædictum Hofp. & omnia & fingula cætera præmiffa cum pertinen' de nobis & Succefforibus noftris ut de manerio noftro de Eaft-Greenwich in dicto comitatu noftro Kanc' in libero facagio per fidelitatem tantum & non in capite, prout per prædictum fcriptum nobis heredibus & Succefforibus noftris per prædictos Magiftrum, Epifcopum, & Archiepifcopum inde confectum & figillatum, quod quidem fcriptum Deca-

Surfum redditio Hofpit.

nus

nus & Capitulum ecclefiæ Cathedralis & Metropoliticæ Chrifti Cant. per eorum fcriptum
fub eorum communi figillo figillatum gerens dat' decimo fexto die Maii anno regni noftri
fupradicto confirmaverunt, & in omnibus ratificaverunt & approbaverunt, quod quidem
fcriptum———— & irrotulat' in Curia Cancellariæ noftræ prout per eadem manifeftè liquet & apparet. Ratione cujus nos modò feifiti fumus de toto prædicto Hofp. ac de
omnibus & fingulis præmiffis fupradictis cum fuis pertinentiis in Dominico noftro ut de feodo ut in Jure coronæ noftræ ad intentionem & fiduciam prædict' in nobis repofit. Sciatis
igitur quod nos tam ad humilem petitionem dictorum Majoris & Communitatis quam in
performando & perimplendo intentionem & fiduciam prædict' in nobis repofit' per prædict.
Magiftrum, Epifcopum & Archiepifc. comfirmat' per prædict' Decanum & Capitulum in
fcript' prædict' ut præfertur expref' & mentionat', de gratia noftra fpeciali, ac ex certa
fcientiâ & mero motu noftris dedimus, conceffimus & confirmavimus, ac per prefentes, pro
nobis, heredibus & Succefforibus noftris damus, concedimus & confirmamus præfatis Majori & communitati & fuccefforibus fuis in perpetuum totum prædictum hofpitale pauperum
Sacerdotum, & advocationem ejufdem, necnon omnia & fingula domos, edificia, ftructuras, gardina, pomaria, terras arabiles & pafturas, terras glebales, tenementa, prata, pafcua,
pafturas, marifcos, bofcos, fubbofcos, redditus, fervitia, portiones, penfiones, annuales redditus, decimas bladorum, granorum & feni, advocationem & advocationes ecclefiæ & ecclefiarum, Vicariæ & vicariarum quarumcunque & reverfionem & reverfiones omnium &
fingulorum præmifforum, ac omnia & fingula proficua, libertates, franches', emolumen-
tâ & hereditamenta quæcunque dicto Hofp. fpectantia, pertinentia, vel ut pars, parcella
vel membrum ejufdem Hofp. nunc vel antehac accept', ufitat', cognit' feu reputat'————
nobis, heredibus & Succefforibus noftris per prædictum fcriptum fuperius recitarum ut præfertur dat' & concef', tam infra Civitatem prædictam quam infra Comitatum Kanc.
habend. tenend. & gaudend. prædictum Hofp. necnon omnia & fingula præmiffa cum omnibus & fingulis fuis pertinentiis præfatis Majori & Communitati & Succefforibus fuis in perpetuum, Tenend. de nobis heredibus & Succefforibus noftris ut de manerio noftro de Eaft
Greenwich in dicto Comitatu noftro Kanc' in libero & communi focagio per fidelitatem
tantum & non in Capite. Et ulterius de ampliori gratia noftra dedimus & conceffimus ac
per præfentes damus & concedimus præfatis Majori & Communitati omnia exitus, redditus, reventiones & proficua prædicti Hofpitalis & ceterorum omnium & fingulorum præmifforum per præfentes concefforum cum pertinent' à dicto quartodecimo die Maii ultimò
præteriti hucufque provenien' five crefcen' Habend. eifdem Majori & Communitati ex
dono noftro abfque computo feu aliquo alio, proinde nobis heredibus vel fuccefforibus
noftris quoquo modo reddend' vel faciend. Et ulterius volumus & per præfentes
concedimus præfatis Majori & Communitati & fuccefforibus fuis quod nos heredes &
Succeffores noftri in perpetuum annuatim & de tempore in tempus exonerabimus, ac-
quietabimus & indempnes confervabimus tam eofdem Majorem & Communitatem &
fucceffores fuos quam totum predictum hofpitale & cætera præmiffa, cum omnibus & fingulis fuis pertinen. fuperius per præfentes præconceffa de omnibus & omnimodis corrodiis,
reddittibus, feodis, annuitatibus & denariorum fummis ac oneribus quibufcunque per nos
antehac quoquo modo factis feu conceffis de præmiffis præconceffis, feu de eifdem aliquo
modo exeun' feu folvend. vel fuperinde onerat' feu onerand. præterquam de fervitiis per præfentes nobis heredibus & fuccefforibus noftris refervatis. Et ulterius
volumus ac per præfentes pro nobis, heredibus ac Succefforibus noftris concedimus præfatis Majori & Communitati & Succefforibus fuis quod hæ literæ noftræ patentes & irrotulament' earundem erunt firmæ, validæ, bonæ, fufficientes & efficaces in leges erga nos, heredes & fucceffores noftros tam in omnibus curiis noftris quam alibi infra regnum noftrum
Angliæ abfque aliquibus confirmationibus licentiis vel tolerationibus de nobis, heredibus
vel fuccefforibus noftris inpofterum per prædictos Maiorem & Communitatem vel fucceffores fuos procurand. vel obtinen. non obftan' male nominand. vel malè recitand. vel
non recitand. prædicta Hofp. domos, ædificia, ftructuras, gardina, pomaria, terras arabiles & pafturas, terras glebales, tenementa, prata, pafcua, pafturas, marifcos, bofcos,
fubbofcos, redditus, reverfiones, fervitia, decimas bladorum, granorum & feni, advocationes, penfiones, portiones, ac cætera omnia & fingula præmiffa vel alicujus inde parcellæ, aut non obftan' male recitan' vel non recitand. aliquarum dimiff. feu conceff. præmifforum feu alicujus inde parcellæ de recordo five non de recordo exiften', vel non obftan'
aliquibus aliis defectibus in non nominando alicujus villæ, hamletti, parochiæ aut Com' in
quibus præmiffa vel aliqua inde parcella jacent vel exiftunt, aut in non nominando vel male
nominando præmifforum five alicujus inde parcellæ in natura, genere, fpecie, feu qualitate
fua. Volentes etiam & per præfentes firmiter injungendo præcipientes tam Thefaurar. Camerar. Cancellar. & Baronibus curiæ fcaccarii noftri prædicti quam omnibus receptoribus,
auditoribus & aliis officiariis & miniftris noftris, heredum & fuccefforum noftrorum quibufcunque pro tempore exiften' quod ipfi & eorum quilibet fuper folam demonftrationem
harum literarum noftrarum paten' vel irrotulament' earund' abfque aliquo alio brevi feu
warranto à nobis heredibus vel fuccefforibus noftris quoquo modo impetran' feu profequen'
plenam, integram, debitamque allocationem & exonerationem manifeftam de omnibus &
omnimodis————corrodiis, redditibus, feodis, annuitatibus, denariorum fummis & oneribus, quibufcunque de præmiffis exeun' feu folvend. vel fuperinde onerat' feu oneran' præfatis Majori & Communitati & fuccefforibus fuis facient & de tempore in tempus fieri caufa-
bunt.

Conceffio ejufd.
Civitati.

bunt. Et hæ literæ noſtræ patentes & irrotulament' earundem erunt annuatim & de tempore in tempus tam dict' Theſaurar. Camerar. & Baronibus dictæ curiæ ſcaccarii noſtri, quam omnibus, receptoribus, auditoribus, & aliis officiariis & miniſtris noſtris heredum & ſucceſſorum noſtrorum quibuſcunque pro tempore exiſtentibus ſufficiens warrantum & exoneratio in hac parte. Volumus * & jam & per præſentes concedimus præfatis Majori & Communitati, quod ipſi habeant has literas noſtras patentes ſub magno ſigillo noſtro *Angliæ debiro modo fact' & ſigillat' abſque fine ſeu feodo magno vel parvo nobis in hanaperio noſtro ſeu alibi ad uſum noſtrum proinde quoquo modo reddend. ſolvend. vel faciend. eo quod expreſſa mentio de vero valore annuo aut de aliquo alio valore vel certitudine præmiſſorum ſeu eorum alicujus, aut de aliquibus aliis donis ſive conceſſionibus per nos vel alios progenitores noſtros præfatis Majori & Communitati antehac in præſentibus minimê facta exiſtit aut aliquo actu, ſtatuto, ordinatione, ſive proviſione, aut aliqua alia re, cauſa, vel materia quacunqne in aliquo non obſtante. In cujus Rei teſtimonium has literas noſtras fieri fecimus patentes. Teſte meipſa apud Weſtm' quinto die Julii, anno regni noſtri decimo ſeptimo.

Per breve de privato ſigillo & de dat. prædict.
Authoritate Parliamenti.   Lutley.

*L. etiam.

The Indorſement.

IN the Yeare of our Lord God 1575. and in the ſeventeenth Yeare of Queen Elizabeth within written, this bountiful and worthy Gift by our ſaid Soveraign Lady Queen Eliz. to the Major and Communalty of the City of Canterb. of the Hoſp. within mentioned, and the Lands and Tenements to the ſame, to the uſe of the Poore, was of the Charge of the Citizens by Seſſe to fifty Pounds and more procured and obtained by John Roſe then Major of the ſaid City and Richard Gaunt then Sheriſe of the ſame Suters and Soliciters in and about the procuring thereof of the proper Money and Charge of the ſaid John Roſe firſt disburſed till the full accompliſhment and obteining the ſame, after he again was payed the ſame as it was Collected and Gathered.

It is likewiſe Indorſed upon theſe Letters Patents, That the Lands and the whole Revenues thereof were intended by her Majeſty to be to the uſe of the Poor of Canterb.

Compoſition between the Parſon of St. Margaret and the Hoſpital of Poor Prieſts.

Numb. XXV. b.

HEc eſt compoſitio facta inter Rectorem eccleſiæ ſanctæ Margaretæ Cantuar. & Hoſpitale pauperum ſacerdotum, quod Capellanus qui in Capella pauperum ſacerdotum Cantuariæ quæ infra limites parochiæ ſanctæ Margaretæ eſt conſtituta pro tempore miniſtrabit, inſpectis ſacroſanctis jurabit, quod nullas oblationes, nullas decimas, nullas obventiones ad eccleſiam beatæ Margaretæ Jure parochiali pertinentes, in prajudicium ipſius eccleſiæ ex certa ſcientia recipiet, & ſi forte receperit ignoranter, eas cum omni integritate Rectori ipſius eccleſiæ reſtituet. Omnes vero ſervientes in dicto Hoſpitali ſive mares ſive feminæ à Rectore dictæ eccleſiæ ſanctæ Margaretæ ſacramenta ſpiritualia recipient ſicut parochiani, & in feſtivitatibus in quibus oblatio debetur eccleſiis, ad prædictam eccleſiam venient ſicut alii parochiani facturi. Idem etiam tam in laicis quam in clericis peregrinis ſi in dicto Hoſpitali moram faciant undecunque ſint obſervabitur: Ita quod ſi aliquem ex talibus perſonis peregrinis in dicto Hoſpitali infirmari contigerit, ſpiritualia à prædicto Rectore recipiet, & eccleſiam ſanctæ Margaretæ ſi ipſum in dicto Hoſp. mori contigerit, pro ſua reſpiciet facultate. Capellani verò & clerici degentes ibidem ab eo qui in ſpiritualibus à Rectore eccleſiæ beatæ Margaretæ cum ſacramento ut dictum eis præficitur prædicta recipiant ſacramenta & liberam habebunt poteſtatem ubi voluerint eligendi ſepulturam. Habebunt etiam poteſtatem ſine calumpnia recipiendi annalia ſive tricennialia ex devotione fidelium qui non ſunt parochiani eccleſiæ ſanctæ Margaretæ, vel etiamſi ſint parochiani, dum tamen non procurent hoc fieri in præjudicium matricis eccleſiæ; quod ſi fuerit ab eis procuratum, & ſuper hoc convinci potuerint, plena reſtituent quicquid taliter perceperunt. Inſuper pro orto quem habeant in Binnewitht unam libram cymini ſolvent annuatim pro decimis prædicto Rectori, & in feſto ſanctæ Margaretæ, ſuper altare ipſius eccleſiæ matricis in ſignum Juris parochialis pro loco in quo habitant duos cereos trium librarum offerri faciant vel decem & octo denarios. Si verò contigerit quod aliquis ſeparatim ab eis domum in Binewith ſitam inhabitaverit, erit parochianus ſanctæ Margaretæ ſicut antea fuit. Item de tenemento Domini Abbatis & conventus ſancti Auguſtini nullum ſibi tenementum perquirent niſi de eorum voluntate, & ſi aliqd' tenementum alterius Domini in prædicta parochia quocunque titulo perquiſierint, ſalvum erit matrici eccleſiæ jus quod in eo prius habuerat. Item ſi forte aliquo tempore in prædicto Hoſp. Capellanus non præfuerit, ſed laicus procurator : idem ad conſimile ſacramentum tactis ſacroſanctis ſe aſtringet ſcilicet ad obſervationem præmiſſorum. In diebus verò dominicis & aliis feſtivitatibus in quibus ex conſuetudine oblationes fiunt generales in eccleſiis, non celebrabunt miſſam in dicto Hoſp' donec Evangelium jn eccleſia beatæ Margaretæ ſit perlectum ſive miſſa conſummata,

Jura Rectoris.

Jura Capellanorum.

Hortus in Binnewiht.

Tempus miſſæ celebrandæ in Hoſpitali.

* F

niſi

nisi de licentia hoc fiat ecclesiæ memoratæ Rectoris, & his diebus parochianos sanctæ Margaretæ non admittent nisi cum missa in ecclesia sanctæ Margaretæ fuerit expleta. Campanas verò in prædicto loco non habebunt. Et si qua partium prædictarum contra formam hic scriptam) venire præsumpserit, unam marcam nomine pœnæ totiens solvet Abbati sancti Augustini & Archidiacono Cantuariæ vel cui viderint secundum Dominum libere conferendam, quotiens contravenerit, compositione nihilominus firmum robur optinente. In cujus Rei testimonium tam Abbas sancti Augustini quam Archidiaconus Cantuar. huic compositioni sigilla sua apponi fecerunt.

Campanæ Hospitali prohibitæ.

Pœna Trausgressioris.

Numb. XXVI.

An Act of Parliament for Paving the Streets.

EDwardus Dei gratia Rex Angliæ & Franciæ & Dominus Hiberniæ Omnibus ad quos præsentes literæ pervenerint salutem. Inspeximus quandam petitionem nobis in Parliamento nostro apud Westm' sexto decimo die Januarii ultimo præterito summonit' & tento per Communitatis Regni nostri Angliæ in eodem Parliamento existen', ex parte Majoris & Communitatis Civitatis Cantuar. exhibitam in hæc verba. To the right Wise and Discreet Commons in this present Parliament assembled. Shewne unto your Wisdoms the Major and Communalty of the City of *Canterbury,* Forasmuch as the same City is one of the eldest Cities of this Realme, and therein is the principal See of the Spiritual Estate of the same Realme, and which City also is most in sight of all Strangers of the Parts beyond the Sea resorting into this said Realme and departing out of the same, aud because of the glorious Saints that there lie shrined is greatly named throughout Christiandome unto which City also is great repair of much of the People of this Realme as well of Estates as other in way of Pilgrimage to visite the said Saints. And it is so that the same City is oftentimes full fowle, noyous, and uneasie to all the Inhabitants of the same, as to all other Persons resorting thereunto, whereof oftentimes is spoken much disworship in divers places as well beyond the Sea as on this side the Sea, which cannot be remedied in any wise but if the said City might be Paved, whereunto the more partie of the Inhabitants of the same Citie having Burgeses Houses or Tenements in the same be well willed and agreeable, so that there might Authority be had to compell other such Persons as have Burgeses, Houses, Lands or Tenements therein to be contributary to doe the same. Please it therefore your Wisdoms the Premisses considered, and that the Major and Communalty have no Lands nor Tenements, nor other yearely Revenues in common whereof they may make or sustain any such Payment, to pray the King our Soveraign Lord that he by the advise and assent of the Lords Spirituall and Temporall of this his Realme in this present Parliament assembled, and by the Authority of the same Parliament to Ordain, Establish and Enact that all and every Person and Persons being seised of Meses or Tenements within or adjoyning to the principal Streat of the said City which beginneth at the Gate called *Westgate* sett in the West-part of the said City and extendeth from thence Eastward unto a Gate called *Newingate* sett in the East-part of the said City, and in or adjoyning to another Streat of the said City which beginneth at a place called *Burgate* sett in the East-part of the same City, and extendeth from thence West-ward unto a place of the same City called the *Bulstake* where the other Market of the same City is usually kept, or in or adjoyning to another Streat extending West-ward from the same place called the *Bulstake* unto the Gate of the House of the *Black-friers* of the same City or in or adjoyning to another street of the same City extending from the same place called the *Bulstake* Southward unto the Church of St. *Andrew* in the same City, and from the Church Southward unto another place of the same City being in the Parish of St. *Margrett* in the said City called the *Iron-Crosse,* into which Streats and Places commonly is more resort aswell of Strangers as of other than to any other Streat or Place within the said City ; by reasonable premunition to the same Person or Persons, or to the Inhabitants or Occupiers of the same Burgeses, Meses or Tenements by the Major, Sheriffe and Chamberlyns of the same City for the time being, or by two of them, or by any of their Ministers or Servants to be made, as often- times as shall need or reasonably require hereafter make or do to be made, repair or do to be repaired sufficient and sufficiently Pavement before all and every the said Burgeses, Meses or Tenements sett lying or adjoyning in or to any of the said Streats or Places, immediately from the said Burgeses, Meses or Tenements, and every parcel thereof unto the middest of the Street afore them and every of them, and unto such place or places of the streat afore them and every of them as shall be thought fit to the Maior, Aldermen, Sheriffe, Burgesses and Chamberlyns of the same City for the time being or to the more part of them in number the Canell place afore the said Burgeses, Meses, or Tenants or afore any of them to be made. And if any Person or Persons having any Burgeses, Meses or Tenements sett lying or adjoyning in or to any of the said Streats or Places above rehearsed after such premunition to them or to any of them made, make not or do to be made, repaire nor do to be repaired the said Canell or such Pavements sufficiently after the manner and forme above rehearsed within six Monthes next after such premunition to them or to any of them to be made : Then the Mayor, Sheriff and the Chamberlyns of the said City for the time being, or two of them have full Power and Authority to make or do to be made, repair or do to be repaired as the cause and time of necessity

Canterbury one of the eldest Cities of England.

Westgate.
Newingate.
Burgate.

Bullstake.

Black-Friersgate.

The Iron-Cross.

cessity

cessity shall require, the said Pavement sufficiently in forme afore-said before the said Burgeses, Meses and Tenements and every of them which shall happen not to be made or repaired sufficiently in the manner afore-reherfed within other six Months after the said first six Monthes next ensuing. And that it shall be lawful to the said Mayor, Sheriff and Chamberlyns of the said City for the time being and to every of them to take sufficient distress within every place of the said City of the Goods and Chattells of such Person or Persons as shall happen hereafter to be found in default of making or repairing of such Pavement, or of the Goods and Chattels of the Inhabitants or Occupiers of the same Burgeses, Meses or Tenements afore which such default shall happen to be found, to the value of such reasonable Costs and Expenses as shall happen to be due to the said Mayor, Sheriffe or Chamberlyns of the said City for the time being, or any of them in making or repairing of the said Pavement, and the said distress to do Praise by the Oaths of fower, three or two honest Persons of the same City, and it sell, and the Money thereof coming retaine to him or them that shall happen to make or do to be made, or repair or do to be repaired the said Pavement for the Costs or Expences by them or any of them donne in making or repairing of the same Pavement. And the surplusage of the Money coming of the said Goods or Cattels so sold; if any be over the said Costs and Expences, be delivered to him or them that were Owners of the said Goods and Chattells so taken and praised afore the time of the said taking. And also that every Person and Persons having any Rent in Fee-simple, Fee-tayle, terme of Life, or terme of Years, so the terme exceed ten Years going out of any of the said Burgeses, Meses or Tenements, sett lying or adjoyning in or to the said Streats or places or in or to any of them be contributors and contributory, chargeable and charged by dewe premunition to them and every of them in manner and forme afore rehearsed.

Cætera desunt.

SAnctus Ethelbertus Rex Anglorum qui suscepit Christianitatem à beato Augustino misso à beato Gregorio Papa Anno Domini Dxcvi[to]. in ecclesia Christi Cant. dedit eidem Augustino & Successoribus suis Palatium Regium & sedem perpetuam in Civitate Doroberniæ quæ nunc dicitur Cantuar. cum ecclesia veteri quæ ab antiquo tempore Romanorum ibidem fuerat fabricata, quam ipsemet Augustinus S. Salvatoris nomine dedicavit post consecrationem suam Arelatensis factam. Statuit etiam idem Rex authoritate S. R. E. ut in Ecclesia Cantuar. ordinem Monasticum Monachi in perpetuum observarent, ne primorum viz. prædicatio Monachorum à memoria deleretur, sed semper recens in mentibus succedentium perseveraret, &c.

Numb.
XXVII. a.

AEthelbertus Rex, anno Regni sui xxxv. ad fidem Christi per sanctum Augustinum conversus statim palatium suum eidem Augustino & Successoribus suis infra Civitatem Doroberniam perpetuè dedit, ut ibi sedem Metropolitanam in evum haberent : Quam beatus Gregorius primam totius Regni esse decrevit & confirmavit, ut sicut prima fuit fidem suscipiendo, prima esset in dignitate. Hoc donum fecit Rex Anno Domini Dxcvij.

•Numb.
XXVII. b.

FUndatio Ecclesiæ Christi Cantuariæ ab antiquis temporibus jacta fuit per Lucium Britannorum Regem, Christi primum Professorem : Quo quidem tempore Romani incolebant Britanniam, cum eisdem Britonibus Romano Imperio tunc subjectis. Sed Institutio Monasticæ vitæ in eadem Ecclesia Christi Cantuariæ fuit a tempore Beati Augustini Prothodoctoris Angliæ, sicut ait Beda in libro primo Ecclef. Hist. gentis Anglorum. c. 33. *Beatus* (inquit) *Augustinus, ubi in civitate Regia scilicet Dorobernia, Quæ nunc dicitur Cantuaria, sedem Episcopalem accepit, recuperavit in eâ, regio fultus adminiculo, Ecclesiam quam inibi antiquorum Romanorum fidelium opere factam fuisse dedicerat, & eam in nomine Sancti Salvatoris Dei & Domini nostri Jesu Christi sacravit atque ibidem habitationem statuit, & cunctis successoribus suis.* Ad cujus habitationis mansionem & monasterii inibi similiter constructionem instituit. Nam Rex Ethelbertus dedit ei palatium suum cum tota civitate (Dorobernensi) ubi ipse Augustinus cum Monachis suis conversabatur, viventes omnes simul iu communi, exemplo sanctorum Christi Discipulorum, sicut B. Gregorius ipse B. Augustino Scripsit. W. S.]

Numb.
XXVII. c.

Composition between Christ-Church *and* St. Augustine's, *about Lands lying by the* Campanile *of* Christ-Church.

Numb.
XXVIII.

RIchardus Dei gratia Cantuar. Archiepiscopus totius Angliæ Primas & Apostolicæ sedis Legatus Universis sanctæ matris ecclesiæ filiis ad quos præsentes literæ pervenerint eternam in Domino Salutem. Ad omnium volumus noticiam pervenire qualiter dilecti filii nostri Benedictus Prior & Conventus ecclesiæ Christi Cantuar. cum Rogero electo monasterii sancti Augustini & Conventu ejusdem loci quasdam terras suas pro quibusdam terris ad idem monasterium pertinentibus commutaverunt. Præfatus siquidem Electus & Conventus sancti Augustini quasdam terras habuerunt ex parte meridiana cimiterii nostri juxta Campanile nostrum in Cantuar. scillicet terras Gervasii de Cornhelle unde solebant habere annuatim v[s]. & x[d]. terram Willielmi Furbatoris unde habebant ii[s]. terram Willielmi filii Ricardi unde
ha bebant

habebant viij s. de quibus reddedant ad firmam Domini Regis annuatim xx d. unde monachi nostri eos acquietabant erga Regem, terram etiam Baldwini presbiteri & Davidis de Chert fratris ejus unde habebant ij s. terram Philippi Parmentarii unde habebant xx d. terram quæ fuit Everwaker unde habebant xvij d. Terram quæ fuit Mudekyn & Sedegos quæ reddebat eis xx d. Summa quorum reddituum est xx s. & x d. & terram in qua quædam Capella construćta fuerat. Quoniam vero hæ prædićtæ terræ nobis & ecclesiæ nostræ periculosæ fuerunt propter crebra incendia : Idcirco prædićtus Rogerus Elećtus & Conventus prænominati Monasterii ad preces Domini nostri Henrici Regis Angliæ & nostras concesserunt & dederunt & assignaverunt in escambium nobis & ecclesiæ nostræ has terras liberas & quietas ab omni questione & querela, salvo quidem jure illorum qui prænominatas terras de Monasterio sanćti Augustini tenebant. Nos autem pro jam dićtis rerris concessimus dedimus & assignavimus in concambium eidem Elećto & Conventui ad elećtionem ipsorum quasdam de terris nostris liberas & quietas ab omni questione & querela, salvo quidem jure illorum qui terras illas de nobis tenere solebant, scilicet terram Roberti filii Richardi Flatbold, &c. ut in compositione plenius poterit apparere : *as* Thorne *cuts it off, and that because (as he adds)* Ubi situantur non invenitur scriptum. Summa quorum reddituum est xxij s. ij d. Cumque volumus hanc commutationem & escambium hinc inde sic de utriusque partis consensu factum firmiter & inviolabiliter observari ipsam commutationem præsentis scripti nostri patrocinio confirmamus & sigilli nostri munimine roboramus. Faćta est autem hæc commutatio anno Incarnationis Dominicæ Millesimo Centesimo septuagesimo septimo, Regnante illustrissimo Anglorum Rege Henrico secundo.

Causa finalis. hujus compositionis.

Numb. XXIX.

The Preface *to the* Grant *of the* Appropriation *of the* Churches *of* Godmersham *and* Westwell *in* Kent, *to the* Convent *of* Christ-Church *in* Canterbury.

COnsiderantes expensas graves & sumptuosas quas circa construćtionem & reparationem ejusdem ecclesiæ urgente necessitate sudistis & inevitabiliter successivis temporibus, prout futura per præterita præcaventes animi compassione sentimus, vos refundere oportebit, ut præsidium vobis & ecclesiæ vestræ quod cum Deo possumus procuremus, ne forte tam laudabile & necessarium opus inceptum, moderni (quod absit) subtraćtione Prioris, vel aliàs ex adversæ fortunæ insultu perfectum diutinè non consequatur effećtum, aut alicujus temeritatis incursus sanćtorum diminuat numerum monachorum, aut robur vestræ sacræ religionis infringat ; hinc est quod exhibita nobis pro parte vestrâ petitio continebat, quod cum bonæ memoriæ Dominus Simon de Sudburia quondam Archiepiscopus Cant. prædecessor noster navem præfatæ nostræ ecclesiæ prosterni fecerat funditus, & suis sumptibus demoliri, causa ipsam erigendi de novo prout proposuit & ferventer optavit, si non per Dei emulos fuisset inauditâ per prius populi furoris audaciâ decollatus. Vosque Prior & Capitulum circa construćtionem navis prædićtæ, & alia necessaria opera ejusdem ecclesiæ nostræ de communibus bonis vestris ultra quinque millia marcarum laudabiliter expenderitis, ut gaudium operum exempla cunćtorum oculis manifestant, quodque incepta opera & alia inibi de necessitate fienda prostrati claustri vestri & capitularis Domus vestræ pensatâ imminente ruinâ, cum sex millibus marcarum perfici nequeant, & reparari decenter, attentâ Hospitalitate Dominorum & aliorum diversorum Regnorum apud vos indies confluentium, quam declinare non poteritis cum honore, &c.

Numb. XXX.

Fenestræ in superiori parte ecclesiæ Christi Cant. *incipientes a parte septentrionali.*

Fenestra prima.

1. MOses cum Rubo.   In Medio.   Angelus cum Maria.
   Rubus non consumitur, tua nec comburitur in carne virginitas.
2. Gedeon cum vellere & conca.   Vellus cœlesti rore maduit, dum puellæ venter intumuit.
3. Misericordia & veritas.   In medio Maria & Elizabeth.

   Plaude puer puero, virgo vetulæ, quia vero
   Obviat hic pietas: veteri dat lex nova metas.

4. Justitia & Pax.

   Applaudit Regi previsor gratia legi.
   Oscula Justitiæ dat pax ; cognata Mariæ.

5. Nabugodonosor & lapis cum statua.   Puer in præsepio.

   Ut Regi visus lapis est de monte recisus
   Sic gravis absque viro virgo parit ordine miro.

6 In medio Maria.
7 Mofes cùm virga.   In medio.   Angelus & Paftores.

    Ut contra morem dedit arida virgula florem
    Sic virgo puerum, verfo parit ordine rerum.

8 David. Gaudebunt campi & omnia quæ in eis funt.
9 Abacuc. Operuit cœlos gloria ejus, &c.

Feneſtra Secunda.

1 IN medio tres Reges equitantes.   Balaam.   Orietur ſtella ex Jacob, & exurget
  homo de Ifrael.   Ifaia & Jeremia. Ambulabunt gentes in lumine tuo &c.
2 In medio. Herodes & Magi.   Chriſtus & Gentes.
    Qui fequuntur me non ambulabunt in tenebris.
    Stella Magos duxit, & eos ab Herode reduxit
    Sic Sathanam gentes fugiunt, te Chriſte fequentes.
3 Pharaoli & Mofes, cum populo exiens ab Egipto.
    Exit ab erumpha populus ducente columpnâ
    Stella Magos duxit. Lux Chriſtus utrifque reluxit.

4 In medio. Maria cum puero. Magi & Paſtores. Jofeph & fratres fui cum Egiptiis.

    Ad te longinquos Jofeph trahis atque propinquos.
    Sic Deus in cunis Judæos gentibus unis.
5 Rex Solomon, & Regina Saba.
    Hiis donis donat Regina domum Solomonis.
    Sic Reges Domino dant munera tres, tria, trino.

6 Admoniti funt Magi ne herodem adeant : Propheta & Rex Jeroboam immolans.

    Ut via mutetur redeundo Propheta monetur
    Sic tres egerunt qui Chriſto dona tulerunt.
7 Subverfio Sodomæ & Loth fugiens.
    Ut Loth falvetur ne refpiciat prohibetur.
    Sic vitant revehi per Herodis regna Sabei.

8 Oblatio pueri in templo: & Symeon. Melchifedech offerens panem & vinum pro Abraham.

    Sacrum quod cernis facris fuit umbra modernis.
    Umbra fugit. Quare? quia Chriſtus fiſtitur aræ.
9 Oblatio Samuel.
    Natura geminum triplex oblatio trinum
    Significat Dominum Samuel puer, amphora vinum.
10 Fuga Domini in Egiptum. Fuga David & Doech.
    Hunc Saul infeſtat : Saul Herodis typus extat.
    Iſte typus Chriſti, cujus fuga confonat iſti.
11 Elias Iefabel & Achab.
    Ut trucis infidias Iefabel declinat Elias
    Sic Deus Herodem, terrore remotus eodem.

12 Occifio Innocentum. Occifio facerdotum Domini fub Saule.

    Non cecidit David, pro quo Saul hos jugulavit
    Sic non eſt cæfus cùm cæfis transfuga Iefus.
13 Occifio Tribus Benjamin in Gabaon.
    Ecce Rachel nati fratrum gladiis jugulati
    His funt fignati pueri fub Herode necati.

Feneſtra Tertia.

1 JEfus fedet in medio Doctorum. Mofes & Iethro cum populo.

    Sic Mofes audit Iethro vir fanctus obaudit
    Gentiles verbis humiles funt forma fuperbis.
2 Daniel in medio feniorum.
    Mirantur pueri feniores voce doceri
    Sic refponfa Dei fenfum ſtupent Pharifei.

* G

3 Baptizatur Dominus. Noah in archa.
   Fluxu cuncta vago submergens prima vorago
   Omnia purgavit : Baptisma significavit.
4 Submersio Pharaonis & transitus populi.
   Unda maris rubri spatio divisa salubri
   Quæ mentem mundam facit à vitio notat undam.
5 Temptatio gulæ & vanæ gloriæ. Eva capiens fructum.
   Qui temptat Iesum movet Evam mortis ad esum
   Eva gulæ cedit, sed non ita Iesus obedit.
6 Eva comedit.
   Victor es hic Sathana : movet Evam gloria vana
   Sed quo vicisti te vicit gratia Christi.
7 Tentatio cupiditatis. Adam & Eva comedunt. David & Goliah.
   Quo Sathan hos subicit Sathanam sapientia vicit
   Ut Goliam David, Sathanam Christus superavit.

Fenestra Quarta.

1 VOcatio Nathanael jacentis sub ficu. Adam & Eva cum foliis. Populus sub lege.
 Vidit in hiis Christus sub ficu Nathanaelem.
 Lex tegit hanc plebem, quasi ficus Nathanaelem

2 Christus mutavit aquam in vinum. Sex hydriæ. Sex ætates mundi. Sex ætates hominum.
 Hydria metretas capiens est quælibet ætas,
 Primum signorum Deus hic prodendo suorum.
 Lympha dat historiam, vinum notat allegoriam
 In vinum morum convertit aquam vitiorum.

3 Piscatores Apostolorum. S. Petrus cum Eccles. de Jud. Paulus cum ecclesia de gentibus.
 Verbum rete ratis Petri domus hæc pietatis
 Pisces Judæi, qui rete ferant Pharisei
 Illa secunda ratis, domus hæc est plena beatis
 Retia scismaticus, & quivis scindit iniquus.

4 In medio Jesus legit in Synagoga. Esdras legit legem populo. S. Gregor. ordinans lectores.
 Quod promulgavit Moses, legem reparavit
 Esdras amissam ; Christus renovavit omissam.
 Quod Christus legit, quasi pro lectoribus egit.
 Exemplo cujus sacer est gradus ordinis hujus.

5 Sermo Domini in monte. Doctores Ecclesiæ. Moses suscepit legem.
 Hii montem scandunt Scripturæ dum sacra pandunt.
 Christus sublimis docet hos sed vulgus in ymis
 Ex hinc inde datur in monte quod inde notatur
 Christum novisse debemus utramque dedisse.

6 Christus descendens de monte mundat leprosum. Paulus baptizat populum. Heliseus. Naaman & Iordanis.
 Carne Deus tectus quasi vallis ad ima provectus
 Mundat leprosum genus humanum vitiosum :
 Quem lavat ecce Deus quem mundat & hic Heliseus
 Est genus humanum Christi babtismate sanum.

Fenestra Quinta.

1 IEsus ejicit Demonium. Angelus ligavit Demonium.
 Imperat immundis Deus hic equis furibundis
 Hiis virtus Christi dominatur ut Angelus istin.

2 Maria unxit pedes Christi. Drusiana vestit & pascit egenos.
 Curam languenti, victum qui præbet egenti
 Seque reum plangit, Christi vestigia tangit.
 Illa quod ungendo facit hæc sua distribuendo
 Dum quod de pleno superest largitur egeno.

3 Marta & Maria cum Jesu. Petrus in navi Iohannes legit.
 Equoris unda ferit hunc ; ille silentia querit ;
 Sic requies orat dum mundi cura laborat.

4 Leah & Rachel cum Jacob.
 Lyah gerit curam carnis ; Rachelque figuram
 Mentis, cura gravis est hæc, est altera suavis.

5 Jesus & Apostoli colligunt spicas. Mola fumus & Apostoli facientes panes.
 Quod terit alterna Mola lex vetus atque moderna
 Passio, crux * Christi fermentans cibus iste.

* L. Christe tua Sermo tuus.

Petrus & Paulus cum populis.
 Arguit iste reos, humiles alit hic Phariseos
 Sic apice tritæ panis sunt verbaque vitæ.

6 Jefus cum Samaritana Synagoga & Mofes cum quinque libris. Ecclefia de gentibus ad * Johannem.

> Potum quefifti fidei cum Chrifte fitifti
> * Equa viri cui fex Synagoga librique fui fex?
> delicta notat hydria fonte relicta
> Ad te de gente Deus Ecclefia veniente.

* l. Æqua.
* l. Jefum.

7 Samaritana adduxit populum ad Jefum. Rebecca dat potum fervo Abraham. Jacob obviat Rachaeli.

> Fons fervus minans pecus hydria virgo propinans
> Lex Chrifto gentes mulierque fide redolentes.
> Jacob laffatus Rachel obvia grex adaquatus
> Sunt Deus & turbæ mulier quas duxit ab urbe.

Feneftra Sexta.

1 JEfus loquens cum Apoftolis. Gentes audiunt. Pharifei contemnunt.

> Sollicitæ gentes ftant verba Dei fitientes
> Hæc funt verba Dei quæ contemnant Pharifei.

2 Seminator & volucres. Pharifei recedentes à Jefu. Pharifei tentantes Jefum.

> Semen rore carens expers rationis & arens
> Hii funt qui credunt, temptantes ficque recedunt.
> Semen fermo Dei, via lex fecus hanc Pharifei
> Et tu Chrifti fator, verbum Patris infidiator.

3 Semen cecidit inter fpinas. Divites hujus mundi cum pecunia.

> Ifti fpinofi locupletes deliciofi
> Nil fructus referunt quoniam terreftria querunt.

4 Semen cecidit in terram bonam. Job. Daniel. Noah.

> Verba * prius feruit Deus his fructus fibi crevit
> In tellure bonâ, triplex fua cuique corona.

* l. Pa...

5 Jefus & mulier commifcens fata tria. Tres filii Noæ cum Ecclefia. Virgines. Continentes. Conjugati.

> Parte, Noæ nati, mihi quifque fua dominati.
> Una fides natis ex his tribus eft Deitatis.
> Perfonæ trinæ tria funt fata mifta farinæ
> Fermentata fata tria tres fructus operata.

6 Pifcatores. Hinc pifces boni, inde mali. Ifti invitam æternam.

> Hii qui jactantur in levam qui reprobantur
> Pars * funt à Domino maledicta cremanda camino
> Vafe refervantur pifces quibus affimulantur
> Hii quos addixit vitæ Deus & benedixit.

l. Eft.

7 Meffores. Seges reponitur in horreum. Zizania in ignem. Jufti in vitam æternam. Reprobi in ignem æternam.

> Cum fudore fata mefforis in horrea lata
> Sunt hic vexati fed Chrifto glorificati.
> Hic cremat ex meffe quod inutile judicat effe
> Sic pravos digne punit judex Deus igne.

8 De quinque panibus & duobus pifcibus fatiavit multa millia hominum. Dominus Sacerdos, & Rex.

> Hii panes legem, pifces dantem facra Regem
> Signant quaffatos à plebe nec adnihilatos.

Synagoga cum Mofe & libris. Ecclefia cum Johanne.

> Quæ populos faturant panes pifcefque figurant
> Quod Teftamenta duo nobis dant alimenta.

[Rex fecit nuptias filio & mifit fervos.

> Rex Pater ad natum regem fponfæ fociatum:
> Præcipit afciri populum renuuntque venire:

Excufant fe quidem per villam.

> Quos vexat cura caro. Quinque boum juga rura
> Nuncius excufans: hic ortans, ille recufans.

Petrus docens fed fequuntur Moyen & Synagogam.

> Sunt afcire volens Deus hunc, hic credere nolens
> Petrus docens iftumque ftudens Judæa fuifti.

Johannes predicat intente audientibus.

> Vox invitantis caufæ tres diffimulantis.
> Sponfam Sponfus amat: vox horam previa clamat.

Yfaias prædicat audientibus tribus.

> Ecclefiam Chrifti junctam tibi prædicat ifte.
> His invitata gens eft ad edenda parata.

Quidam fequuntur Regem, quidam fugiunt.

> Hic (Regis) factum confirmat Apoftolus actum.
> Credit & accedit, cito Gens Judæa recedit.

Contemplatur Rex comedentes. Refurgunt mortui.

> Ad menfam tandem cito plebs fedet omnis eandem.
> Sic omnis eadem vox hora cogit eadem.

Dominus dicit electis venite Benedicti.

> Rex plebem pavit fpretis quos ante vocavit
> Chriftus fe dignos reficit rejicitque malignos.

Invenitur & ejicitur non ve-⎱ Dives & extrusus servus tenebrisque reclusus;
stitus veste nuptiali.   ⎰ Quem condemnavit rex ejecit cruciavit.

Ananias & Saphiras moriuntur a Petro. Dominus ejecit vendentes à templo. N. B.]

Fenestra Septima.

1 CUravit Jesus filiam vi-⎫ Natam cum curat matris prece ; matre figurat
duæ. Ecclesia de gen-⎪ Christo credentes primos, nataque sequentes.
tibus cum Jesu. Petrus orat ⎬
& animalia dimittuntur in ⎪ Fide viventes signant animalia gentes ;
linthea.   ⎭ Quos mundat sacri submersio trina lavacri.

2 Curavit Jesus hominem ad ⎫ Lex tibi piscina concordat sunt quia quina
piscinam. Moses cum quin-⎪ Ostia piscinæ, seu partes lex tibi quinæ.
que libris. Baptizat Do-⎬ Sanat ut ægrotum piscinæ motio lotum
minus.   ⎭ Sic cruce signatos mundat baptisma renatos.

3 Transfiguratio Domini. ⎫ Spes transformati capitis, spes vivificati
Angeli vestiunt mortuos ⎪ Claret in indutis membris à morte solutis.
resurgentes. Angeli ad-⎬ Cum transformares te Christe, quid insinuares
ducunt justos ad Deum. ⎭ Veste decorati declarant clarificati.

4 Petrus piscatur & invenit ⎫ Hunc ascendentem mox mortis adesse videntem.
staterem. Dominus ascendit ⎬ Tempora ; te Christe piscis prænunciat iste.
in Hier. Dominus cruci-⎪ Ludibrium turbæ Deus est ejectus ab urbe.
figitur. ⎭

5 Statuit Jesus parvulum in ⎫ Hoc informantur exemplo qui monachantur
medio Discipulorum. Mo-⎪ Ne dedignentur peregrinis si famulentur.
nachi lavant pedes paupe-⎬
rum. Reges inclinantur do-⎪ Sic incurvati pueris sunt assimulati
ctrinæ Petri & Pauli. ⎭ Reges cum gente Paulo Petroque docente.

6 Pastor reportat ovem. Chri-⎫
stus pendet in cruce. Chri-⎬   Sine versu.
stus spoliat infernum. ⎭

Fenestra Octava.

1 DOminus remittit debita ⎱ Ut prece submissa sunt huic commissa remissa
servo poscenti.   ⎰ Parcet poscenti seu parcit Deus egenti.

Petrus & Paulus absolvunt pœ-⎫
nitentem , & Dominus sibi ⎪ Cur plus ignoscit Dominus minus ille poposcit
credentes. Servus percutit ⎬ Conservum servus populus te Paule protervus
conservum. Paulus lapi-⎪ Regi conservo repetenti debita servo
datur. Stephanus lapida-⎪ Assimulare Deus Martyr nequam Pharisæus.
tur. ⎭

Tradidit eum tortoribus. ⎫
Mittuntur impii in ig-⎬ Cæditur affligens, captivatur crucifigens
nem. Judæi perimun-⎪ Hunc punit Dominus flagris, hos igne caminus.
tur. ⎭

Fenestra Nona.

HOmo quidam descende-⎫
bat de Hier. in Ierico & ⎬ Perforat hasta latus, occidit ad mala natus.
incidit in latrones. ⎭

    ⎫ Ex Adæ costa prodiit formata virago.
    ⎪ Ex Christi latere processit sancta propago.
Creatur Adam. Formatur Eva, ⎪ Fructum decerpens mulier suadens mala serpens
comedunt fructum, ejiciun-⎬ Immemor authoris vir perdit culmen honoris
tur de Paradiso. ⎪ Virgultum. fructus. mulier. vir. vipera. luctus
    ⎪ Plantatur. rapitur. dat, gustat. fallit. initur.
    ⎪ Pœna reos tangit, vir sudet, fœmina plangit.
    ⎭ Pectore portatur serpens, tellure cibatur.

Sacerdos & Levita vident vulneratum & pertranfeunt.

> Vulneribus plenum neuter miferatus egenum.

Mofes & Aaron cum Pharaone. Scribitur tau. Educitur populus. Adorat vitulum. Datur lex. Elevatur Serpens.

> Pro populo Moyfes coram Pharaone laborat:
> Exaugetque preces, fignorum luce coronat.
> Cui color eft rubeus ficcum mare tranfit Hebræus
> Angelico ductu patet in medio via fluctu.
> In ligno ferpens pofitum notat in cruce Chriftum
> Qui videt hunc vivit, vivet qui credit in iftum.
> Cernens quod fpeciem Deitatis dum teret aurum
> Frangit fcripta tenens Moyfes in pulvere taurum.

Samaritanus ducit vulneratum in ftabulum cum jumento. Ancilla accufat Petrum. Dominus crucifigitur. fepelitur. Refurgit. Loquitur Angelus ad Mariam.

> Qui caput eft noftrum capitur: qui regibus oftrum
> Prebet, nudatur: qui folvit vincla ligatur.
> In figno pendens. In ligno brachia tendens.
> In figno lignum feparafti Chrifte malignum
> Chriftum lege rei, livor condemnat Hebræi
> Carne flagellatum, rapit, attrahit ante Pilatum
> Solem juftitiæ tres, orto fole, Mariæ
> Quærunt lugentes, ex ejus morte trementes.

Feneftra Decima.

SUfcitat Jefus puellam in Domo. Abigael occurrit David & mutat propofitum. Conftantinus jacens & matres cum pueris..

> Quæ jacet in cella furgens de morte puella
> Signat peccatum meditantis corde creatum
> Rex David arma gerit, dum Nabal perdere quærit
> Obviat Abigael mulier David, arma refrenat.
> Et nebulam vultus hilari fermone ferenat.
> Rex foboles Helenæ, Romanæ rector habenæ
> Vult mundare cutem quærendo cruce falutem.
> Nec fcelus exercet, flet, humet, dictata coercet.

Dominus fufcitat puerum extra portam. Rex Solomon adorat Idola & deflet peccatum. Pœnitentia Theophili.

> Qui jacet in morte puer extra limina portæ
> De foris abftractum peccati denotat actum.
> Errat fœmineo Solomon deceptus amore:
> Errorem redimit mens fancto tacta dolore.
> Dum lacrimando gemit Theophilus acta redemit
> Invenies veniam dulcem rogando Mariam.

Dominus fufcitat Lazarum. Angelus alloquitur Ionam fub hedera ante Ninevem. Pœnitentia Mariæ Egiptiacæ.

> Mens mala mors intus; malus actus mors foris: ufus
> Tumba, puella, puer, Lazarus ifta notant.
> Pingitur hic Nineve jam pene peracta perire
> Vefte fidus Zofimas nudam tegit Mariam.

Mittit Dominus duos Difcipul. propter afinam & Pullum. Sp. fanctus in fpecie columbæ inter Deum & hominem.

> Imperat adduci pullum cum matre Magifter
> Paruit huic operæ fuccinctus uterque minifter.
> Signacius fimplex quod fit dilectio duplex
> Ala Deum dextra fratrem docet ala finiftra.

Jefus ftans inter Petrum & Paulum.

> Genti quæ fervit petris Petrum, petra mittit.
> Efcas divinas Judæis Paule propinas.

Adducunt difcipuli Afinum & Pullum. Petrus adducit ecclefiam de Judæis. Paulus adducit ecclefiam de gentib.

> Quæ duo folvuntur duo funt animalia bruta
> Ducitur ad Chriftum pullus materque foluta.
> De populo fufco Petri fermone corufco
> Extrahit ecclefiam veram referando Sophiam
> Sic radio fidei cæci radiantur Hebræi
> Per Pauli verba fructum fterilis dedit herba
> Dum plebs gentilis per eum fit mente fidelis
> Gentilis populus venit ad Chriftum quafi pullus.

Occurrunt pueri Domino fedenti fuper Afinam.

> Veftibus ornari patitur Salvator afellam
> Qui fuper aftra fedet, nec habet frenum neque fellam.

Ifaias dicit. Ecce Rex tuus fedens fuper afinam.

> Qui fedet in cœlo ferri dignatur afello.

David ex ore infantum &c.

> Sancti fanctorum laus ore fonat puerorum.

Fenestra Undecima.

IN medio cœna Domini David gestans se in manibus suis. Manna fluit populo de cœlo.
  { Quid manibus David se gestans significavit
  Te manibus gestans das Christe tuis manifestans
  Manna fluit saturans populum de plebe figurans
  De mensâ Jesum dare se cœnantibus esum.

Lavat Jesus pedes Apostolorum.
Abraham Angelorum Laban camelorum.
  { Obsequio lavacri notat hospes in hospite sacri
  Quos mundas sacro mundasti Christe lavacro.
  Cum Laban hos curat, typice te Christe figurat
  Cura camelorum mandatum Discipulorum.

Proditio Jesu.
Venditio Joseph. Joab osculatur Abner & occidit.
  { Fraus Judæ Christum, fraus fratrum vendidit istum
  Hii Iudæ, Christi Joseph tu forma fuisti.
  Fœdera dum fingit Joab in funera stringit
  Ferrum, Judaicum præsignans fœdus iniquum.

Vapulatio Jesu. Job percussus ulcere. Helizeus & pueri irridentes.
  { Christi testatur plagas Job dum cruciatur
  Ut sum Judeæ, jocus pueris Helisee.

Fenestra Duodecima.

CHristus portat crucem. Isaac ligna. Mulier colligit duo ligna.
  { Ligna puer gestat, crucis typum manifestat.
  Fert crucis in signum duplex muliercula lignum.

Christus suspenditur de ligno. Serpens æneus elevatur in columpna: Vacca rufa comburitur.
  { Mors est exanguis dum cernitur æreus anguis
  Sic Deus in ligno nos salvat ab hoste maligno
  Ut Moyses jussit vitulam rufam rogus ussit
  Sic tua Christe caro crucis igne crematur amaro.

Dominus deponitur de ligno. Abel occiditur. Heliseus expandit se super puerum.
  { Nos à morte Deus revocavit & hunc Heliseus.
  Signat Abel Christi pia funera funere tristi.

Moses scribit Thau in frontibus in porta de sanguine agni. Dominus in sepulcto. Samson dormit cum amica sua. Jonas in ventre ceti.
  { Frontibus infixum Thau præcinuit crucifixum
  Ut Samson typice causa dormivit amicæ.
  Ecclesiæ causa Christi caro marmore clausa.
  Dum jacet absorptus Jonas Sol triplicat ortus
  Sic Deus arctatur tumulo triduoque moratur.

Dominus ligans Diabolum. Spoliavit infernum. David eripuit Oves. & Samson tulit portas.
  { Salvat ovem David; sic Christum significavit.
  Est Samson fortis qui rupit vincula mortis.
  Instar Samsonis, frangit Deus ossa Leonis.
  Dum Sathanam stravit, Christus Regulum jugulavit.

Surgit Dominus de sepulcro. Jonas ejicitur de pisce. David emissus per fenestram.
  { Redditur ut salvus, quem ceti clauserat alvus:
  Sic redit illesus, à mortis carcere Jesus.
  Hinc abit illesus David: sic invidia Jesus
  Agmina conturbat, ut victa morte resurgat.

Angelus alloquitur Mariam ad Sepulcrum. Joseph extrahitur è carcere. Et Leo suscitat filium.
  { Ad vitam Christum Deus ut leo suscitat istum.
  Te signat Christe Joseph; te mors; locus iste.

[Sanctus Gregorius dat aquam manibus pauperum, & apparuit ei Dominus.
  { Hospes abest: ubi sit stupet hic, cur, quove resistet.
  Membra prius quasi me suscepisti sed heri me.

Gregorius dictat. Petrus scribit. Solitarius cum cato.
  { Pluris habes catum, quàm Presul Pontificatum.
  Quæ liber includit signata columba recludit.

Hostia

Hostia mutatur in formam } Id panis velat, digiti quod forma revelat.
digiti. } Velans forma redit, cum plebs abscondita credit.

Gregorius trahitur & papa ef- } Quem nomen, vultus, lux, vita, scientia, cultus
ficitur. } Approbat extractus latebris fit papa coactus. W. S.]

To these verses in the Windowes let me adde foure other legible of late on the Wall in the North Ile of the Quire *, in the foote almost of the painted peece there, and do containe a briefe dialogue betweene Saint* Anselm *sometime Archbishop here, and an Heretike, about the Virgin-conception of our blessed Lady, written (it there appeares)* Anno Domini 1477.

Hæreticus.

Nunquam natura mutavit sic sua jura ;
Ut virgo pareret, ni virginitate careret.

Anselmus.

Lumine solari nescit vitrum violari ;
Nec vitrum sole, nec virgo puerpera prole.

The Articles granted to the French Strangers by the Mayor and Aldermen of the Citty.

Numb. XXXI.

Dignissimis Dominis Domino Maiori & fratribus Consiliariis urbis Cantuariensis Salutem.

Supplicant humilimè extranei vestra libertate admissi in ista urbe Cantuariensi quat' velitis sequentes articulos illis concedere.

Prior Articulus.

1. Quia religionis amore (quam libera conscientia tenere percupiunt) patriam & propria bona reliquerunt, orant sibi liberum exercitium suæ religionis permitti in hac urbe, quod ut fiat commodius sibi assignari templum & locum in quo poterint sepelire mortuos suos.

Secundus Articulus.

2. Et ne sub eorum umbra & titulo religionis profani & male morati homines sese in hanc urbem intromittant per quos tota societas male audiret apud cives vestros ; supplicant nemini liberam mansionem in hac urbe permitti, nisi prius suæ probitatis sufficiens testimonium vobis dederit.

Tertius Articulus.

3. Et ne Iuventus inculta maneat, requirunt permissionem dari præceptori quem secum adduxerunt instruendi Iuvenes, tum eos quos secum adduxerunt, tum eos qui volunt linguam Gallicam discere.

Quartus Articulus.

4. Artes ad quas exercendas sunt vocati, & in quibus laborare cupit tota societas sub vestro favore & protectione sunt Florence, Serges, Bombasin, D. of Ascot Serges, &c. of Orleance, Frotz, Silkwever, Mouquade, Mauntes, Bages, &c. Stofe Mouquades.

Nomina supplicantium sunt.

Hector Hamon Minister verbi Dei.
Vincentius Primont Institutor Iuventutis.
Egidius Cousin Magister operum, & conductor totius congregationis in opere.

Michael Cousin.	Johannes de la Forterye.
Jacobus Querin.	Noel Lestene.
Petrus du Bose.	Nicolaus Dubuisson.

Antonius

Antonius du Verdier.
Philippus de Neuz.
Robertus Jovelin.
Johannes le Pelu.

Petrus Defportes.
Jacobus Boudet.
Tres viduæ.

Numb.
XXXII.

Infcriptions upon Monuments &c.

In the Body or Nave of the Church fome what higher up, then Buckenham's *Tomb, upon the graveftone of one* Sᵗ William Septvans, *I reade as followeth.*

Sr. William Sept-
vans Knight.

Icy gift Gulian Septvans chevalier qui moruft le dernier jour D'auft, l'An de Grace M. cccc. vij. de quele alme Deux eit pite & mercy Amen.

This Sᵗ Wᵐ. (*faith* Wever) *ferved in the wars of France under* Ed. 3. Milton *by* Canterb.

* In Regift. Con-
fiftor. Cant·
Manumiffion.

(*I take it, and as I gather by his Will* *) *was his feat. In and by which his Will, it is remar-kable that he gave Manumiffion to divers of his flaves and Natives.*

Hard by the former.

Sr.William Sept-
vans Knight and
Elifabeth his
wife.

Sub hoc marmore jacent corpora Willielmi Septvans militis, qui obiit quarto die menfis Martii Anno Dom. 1448. & Elifabethæ uxoris ejus filiæ Johannis Peche militis, quæ obiit 28. Martii. fequen' quorum animabus propitietur Deus.

Sum quod eris, volui quod vis, credens quafi credis
    Vivere fortè diu, mox ruo morte fpecu.
Ceffi quo nefcis, nec quomodo, quando fequeris,
    Hinc fimul in cœlis ut fimus quoque preceris.

This family of the Septvans, *or de feptem vannis, a long time together flourifhed in thefe parts. Molond in* Afh *was a feat of theirs, where in one of the windowes, this motto or impref-fe, properly, pertinently and moft fignificantly alluding to their coat, is found.* Diffipabo inimi-cos Regis mei ut paleam. *Many of the family lie inter'd in* Afh-church. *And of the name one, a Knight Templar he was as it feems by the croffe-legged pofture of his effigies on the grave-ftone, hath a monument in the Chancell of* Chartham *Church. He was one I fuppofe of the* Septvans of Milton, *anciently a Chapell to* Chartham. In callem regredior.

Not farre hence.

Odmar Heng-
ham.

Hic jacet Odomarus Hengham armiger qui obiit 4. April. Anno Dom. 1411.

On the South-fide of the Body.

Sir John Guil-
ford.

Hic jacet expectans mifericordiam Dei, pernobilis vir Johannes Guilford miles, unūs Con-filiarior. illuftriffimi Regis Hen. 7. qui quidem Johannes obiit 19. die Menfis Jul. 8. Hen. 7. Anno 1493. Cujus animæ propitietur altiffimus. Jefu Filius Dei miferere mihi.

Of him and his familie Wever *hath many things.*
On the fame fide.

Sir William
Brenchley knight
and Joane his
wife.

Hic jacent Willielmus Bruchelle (five Brenchley) miles quondam Juftitiarius Domini Re-gis de comnuni banco, qui obiit in Holborne in Suburb. London xx. Maii 1446. & Joanna uxor ejus quæ obiit 1453. Aug. 8. *He had a Chantery and Chantery-Chapell, the revenues whereof the Diffolution feized on and fwept away. The Chapell is that (I take it) hard by his monument, which is now called Deane* Nevells *Chapell, from his buriall there, and his coft in re-pairing it, whileft he lived for that purpofe, after it had lien long defolate.*

There alfo.

*Edmund Haute.
In Reg. Confift.
Cant·

Here lieth Edmund Haute *Efquire* ————— 1408. *By his Will *, he gave ten pounds* operi ec-clefiæ Chrifti Cant.

On the North-fide of the Body.

Sir Thomas Fog-
ge Knight and
Joane his wife.

Thomas Fogge jacet hic, jacet hic fua fponfa Johanna,
Sint celo cives per te Deus hos & Ofanna ;
Regni protector Francos Britones fuperavit
Nobilium Rector ficuti Leo Caftra predavit
Et quoque militiam fic pro patria peramavit
Ad fummam patriam Deus hunc ab agone vocavit.

* In Regiftro
prædicto.

Reade more of him, and others of his name and family, if you pleafe you may in Wever. *I finde ten marks given by him in his Will, * ad opus ecclefiæ Chrifti Cant. Anno 1407. It is re-*
                                                            corded

corded *in the Obituary of this Church that* St Thomas Fogge *gave* 20 *l. Sterling towards the new Chapter-House, and his Wife gave* 20. *to each Monk in the Convent, that she was descended from the Royal Blood of the Kings of* England, *being Daughter of* St Stephen de Valence, *who was descended from* William *de* Valence * *Earle of* Penbroke, *half Brother by the Mother to King* Henry III. *She dyed* 8. *July* 1425. N. B.]   * Brooks Catalogue.

There.

Sub isto marmore requiescit corpus magistri Ricardi Willeford, quondam Capellani Cantariæ de Arundell, cujus animæ &c. Obiit 1520.

There also.

Hic jacet Robertus Clifford armiger, frater recolandæ memoriæ Domini Richardi Clif- Robert Clifford. ford Episcopi Londoniarum, qui obiit ix. die mensis Martii, Anno Dom. 1422. Cujus &c.

There also.

Hic jacet Dominus Willielmus Arundell miles Justiciarius Domini Regis.   Sir William Arundell Knight.

In the same Body are also the monuments of Prebendary Milles, *of one* Thomas Hoo *the younger of* Cant. 1407. *of* William Lovelace *Serjeant at Law, and high Steward of the liberties of* Christ-Church, *and of* Anne *his first Wife* 1576. *of* Dobs *an Alderman of* Cant. 1580. *of the Lady* Crook *Wife of* St Gerard Crook *Knight* 1579. *as also of divers other, but mostly obscure and mean personages, which I think not mention-worthy. Wherefore I leave the Nave, and step to the Martyrdome. Where I reade upon one of the grave-stones,*

Hic jacet Johannes Fyneux miles, & Elizabetha uxor ejus filia —— Paston —— *the* Sir John Fyneux *rest gone. To supply which defect, I desire you to look back to the* Augustine-Friers, *where you* Knight and Elizabeth his Wife. *shall finde that he was Lord chief Justice of the Kings bench, both under* Hen. 7. *and* Hen. 8. *and an especiall benefactor to that Covent.*

In the Lady-Chapell.

Hic jacet sub hoc marmore expectans misericordiam Dei, venerabilis vir Magister Jo- Archd. Bourg- hannes Bourchier Archidiaconus Cantuariensis, qui quidem Johannes migravit ad chier. Dominum sexto die mensis Novemb. 1425. Cujus &c.

Concerning the School at Canterbury.   Numb. XXXIII.

ACta & processus super statu scolar: ecclesiæ sancti Martini juxta Cant. coram mro Ex Regist. Eccl. Roberto de Mallingg generali Commissario Cant. primò viva voce, & post per spe- Cant. cialem commissionem Domini W. Archiepiscopi Anno Domini 1321. inter magistrum Radulphum de Waltham Rectorem scolarum Civitatis Cant. & mrum Robertum de Henney Rectorem ecclesiæ sancti Martini juxta Cant.

Commissio.

WAlterus permissione divina Cantuar. Archiepiscopus totius Angliæ Primas dilecto filio Commissario nostro Cantuar. Salutem, gratiam & benedictionem. Cum nuper tibi præcepimus viva voce ut in negotio tangente mrum Radulphum rectorem scolar' grammaticalium Civitatis nostræ Cantuar. & magistrum Robertum, Rectorem ecclesiæ sancti Martini juxta Cant. ac ejusdem loci Rectorem scolarum, ex officio, authoritate nostra procederes, & inquisita veritate idem negotium debito fine terminares, dictum negotium de quo miramur adhuc coram te pendet indecisum. Quocirca tibi committimus & mandamus quatenus ulterius in dicto negotio authoritate prædicta procedas, & finem sententiando, previa ratione, celeritate qua poteris, imponere non omittas. Dat' Cantuariæ tertio Non. Januarii Anno Domini Millesimo trecentesimo vicesimo primo.

Inquisitio.

DOminus Richardus Rector Ecclesiæ de Monketon. Dominus Galfridus Vicar. Ecclesiæ de Chyleham. Dominus Stephanus de Wyks. Dominus Nich. Capellanus sancti Sepulchri. Dominus Theob. Vicar. Ecclesiæ S. Pauli. Dominus Simon Rector Ecclesiæ S. Mariæ de Castro. Dominus Thomas Rector Ecclesiæ S. Petri. Dominus Johannes Rector

I

Ecclesiæ

Ecclefiæ omnium Sanctorum. Dominus Johannes Rector Ecclefiæ S. Mich. Magister Robertus de Honynton· Alexander de Elemofinaria. Johannes le Taillour. Simon at Fermcrye. Johannes de Stablegate. Johannes de Strode. Robertus de fancto Martino.

Jurati dicunt quod non debent effe plures grammatici in Schola fancti Martini nifi xiij. & hoc fe dicunt fcire ex relatu bonorum & fide dignorum ab antiquo & dicunt quod femper confuevit Rector Scholarum Cant. Scholas fancti Martini per fe vel fuos propter numerum fcholar. vifitare. Dicunt etiam quod quando hoftiarius vel fubmonitor fcolar. Cant. propter numerum fcolarium fcolas fancti Martini vifitavit, fcholares fancti Martini abfconderunt fe ufque ad numerum xiij. & hoc fe dicunt fcire ex relatu fidedignorum ab antiquo. De aliis fcholaribus in fcholis fancti Martini alphabetum, pfalterium & cantum addifcentibus non eft certus numerus limitatus, ut dicunt.

Sententia Diffinitiva.

IN Dei nomine Amen. Cum nuper inter m^rum Radulphum, Rectorem fcolarum Civitatis Cant. ad collationem venerabilis patris Domini W. Dei Gratia Cant. Archiepifc. tot'us Angliæ Primatis fpectantium, & m^rum Robertum de Henny, Rectorem Ecclefiæ Sancti Martini juxta Cant. & ejufdem loci fcolar. Rectorem ad dictam Ecclefiam fancti Martini de patronatu ejufdem exiftentem pertinentium, fuper eo quod idem Magifter Radulphus prætendebat dictum m^uum fcolarum S. Martini habere deberet in fcolis fuis xiij. fcolares in gramatica erudiendos duntaxat. Idemque magift' fcolarum S. Martini omnes indiftincte ad fcolas fuas confluentes in præjudicium fcolarum Civitatis prædictæ & contra confuetudinem admittere, & in fuis fcolis tenere & docere in grammatica præfumpfit, orta fuiffet materia quæftionis ; tandem dictus venerabilis pater utriufque loci Patronus & Diocefanus, nobis Commiffario fuo Cant. generali tam vivæ vocis oraculo, quam fubfequenter literatorie hujufmodi queftionem feu negotium per viam inquifitionis ex officio commifit fine debito terminandum. Nos igitur Commiffarius prædictus magiftros utriufque fcolarum prædict. & Rectorem Ecclefiæ S. Martini prædidict. coram nobis fecimus evocari, & fuper d.cto negotio viros fidedignos clericos fpecialiter juratos inquiri fecimus diligenter. Qua inquifitione facta puplicata & dictis magiftris & Rectori copia decreta, nihil dicto contra inquifitionem vel probato, fed ad audiendum pronuntiationem noftram die eifdem præfixo. Quia Nos Commiffarius antedictus invenimus quod magifter Scolarum S. Martini xiij fcolares d ntaxat in gramatica per ipfum fcolarum magiftrum quicunque fuerit docendos habere & tenere ac docere debet ex confuetudine ab antiquo, illam confuetudinem, authoritate, nobis in hac parte commiffa decernimus obfervandam. Inhibentes magiftro fcolarum S. Martini ne plures fcolares ultra numerum prædict. in fuis fcolis in gramatica docendos admittat de cetero, nec confuetudinem prædictam infringere præfumat quoquo modo.

Ab ifta fententia prædictus Magifter Robertus appellavit ad fedem Apoftolicam, & pro tuitione Curiæ Cant. Unde Officialis Cur. Cant. inhibuit Commiffario, &c.

OFficialis Curiæ Cantuar. difcreto viro magiftro Roberto de Mallingg Commiffario Cantuar. generali Salutem in autore falutis. Ex parte m^ri Roberti de Henney Rectoris Ecclefiæ fancti Martini Cant. nobis extitit intimatum, quod cum ipfe ac præceffores feu prædeceffores fui Rectores in Ecclefia prædicta omnes & finguli, temporibus fuis, à tempore cujus contrarii memoria hominum non exiftit fuerint, & adhuc fit idem magifter Robertus de Henney nomine fuo & Ecclefiæ fuæ præd' in poffeffione vel quafi Juris habendi fcolas grammaticales in dicta Ecclefia S. Martini feu infra fepta ejufdem, magiftrofque ad informandum & inftruendum in arte gramatticali quofcunque illuc ea de caufa accedentes ibi præficiendi feu deputandi, & eos libere admittendi, informandi & inftruendi in arte gram' prædicta. Ex parte m^i Roberti de Henney in poffeffione vel quafi Juris hujufmodi ut præmittitur exiftentis, ac metuentis ex quibufdam caufis probabilibus & verefimilibus conjecturis grave fibi & Ecclefiæ fuæ prædictæ circa præmiffa præjudicium poffe generari in futurum, ne quis circa præmiffa vel eorum aliquid quicquam in ipfius vel Ecclefiæ fuæ prædictæ præjudicium attemptaret feu faceret aliqualiter adtemptari, ad fedem Apoftolicam, & pro tuitione Curiæ Cant. extitit ut afferitur palam & publice ac legitime provocatum. Set vos ad inftantiam feu procurationem cujufdam Radulfi magiftrum fcolarum Cant. fe prætendentis, provocatione prædicta quæ vos verefimiliter non latebat non obftante, poft & contra eam, prædictum m^rum Robertum de Henney quo minus poffeffione fua hujufmodi libere gaudere potuit, contra juftitiam moleftatis, inquietaftis ac multipliciter perturbaftis, ac tredecim fcolares duntaxat in dictis fcolis Ecclefiæ fancti Martini & non plures admitti debere minus veracirer pretendentes, cuidam magiftro Johanni le Bucwell m^ro fcolarum hujufmodi per dictum m^rum

Rober-

Robertum de Henney præfecto seu deputato, ne ultra 13. scolares hujusmodi inibi admitteret seu haberet inhibuistis minus juste in ipsius mri Roberti de Henney & Ecclesiæ suæ prædictæ præjudicium, dampnum non modicum & gravamen. Unde ex parte ejusdem mri Roberti sentientis se & Ecclesiam suam prædictam ex hiis & eorum quolibet per vos indebitè prægravari, ad dictas sedem & Curiam extitit ut asseritur legitimè appellatum. Quare vobis inhibemus, & per vos omnibus & singulis quibus jus exigit inhiberi volumus & mandamus ut pendente in Curia Cant. hujusmodi tuitoriæ appellationis negotio quicquam hac occasione in dictæ partis appellantis præjudicium attemptetis vel attemptent, faciatis aut faciant aliqualiter attemptari, quo minus liberam habeat appellationis suæ prosecutionem prout justum fuerit. Citetis etiam seu citari faciatis peremptorie dictum Radulfum partem ut præmittitur appellatam quod compareat coram nobis vel nostro Commissario in Ecclesia beatæ Mariæ de Aldermarichurche London sexto die Juridico post festum sancti Martini yemalis in dicto tuitoriæ appellationis negotio processurum, facturum & recepturum quod justitia suadebit. De die vero receptionis præsentium, & quod in præmissis feceritis nos vel nostrum Commissarium dictis die & loco certificetis per literas vestras patentes harum seriem continentes. Dat. London' xij. Kalen. Novemb. Anno Domini 1323.

Sed quia pars appellans appellationem suam præfatæ Curiæ Cantuar. suggestam, sufficienter prout debuit non probavit, pars appellata dimissa fuit ab examine dictæ Curiæ Cant. per literam subscriptam.

THomas de * Themnstr' Curiæ Cantuar. examinator generalis Domini Officialis ejusdem Curiæ in ipsius & Domini Decani Ecclesiæ beatæ Mariæ de Arcubus London Cammissarii sui generalis absentiâ Commissarius, discreto viro magistro Coberto de Mallingg Commissario Cant. generali Salutem in authore Salutis. Cum nos intuitoriæ appellationis negotio quod in dicta Curia vertebatur, inter mrum Robertum de Henney Rectorem Ecclesiæ S. Martini partem ut suggeritur appellantem ex parte una, & Mrum Radulfum mrum scolarum Cant. partem appellatam ex altera legitimè procedentes, dictam partem appellatam eo quod pars appellans prædictam appellationem suam præfatæ Curiæ in hac parte suggestam prout debuit, non probavit, ab examine dictæ Curiæ duxerimus dimittendum. Tenore præsentium vobis intimamus quod inhibitione quacunque sub dat' London' xij. Kal. No. Anno Domini Millesimo trecentesimo vicesimo tertio à Curia Cant. in hac parte impetrata, & vobis directa non obstante, libere poteritis exequi quod est vestrum, Dat' London xiijtio. Kalen. Aprilis Anno Domini supradicto.

* Chereminst'. Reg. Cant.

A Grant made by Archbishop Wlfred to the family at Christ-Church permitting them to enjoy certain houses which themselves had built (it seemes) upon the reedifying of the Monastery.

Numb. XXXIV.

IN nomine sanctæ Salvatoris Dei & Domini nostri Jesu Christi Anno ab incarnatione ejusdem Dei & redemptoris mundi D. CCC. xiij. Indict. iij. præsidente Christi gratia Archipontifice Wlfredo Metropolitano sedem Ecclesiæ Christi quæ sita est in Dorovernia civitate Anno iiij. Episcopatus ejusdem Archiepiscopi divina ac fraterna pietate ductus amore Deo auxiliante renovando & restaurando pro honore & amore Dei sanctum monasterium Dorovernensis Ecclesiæ reædificando refici auxiliantibus ejusdem Ecclesiæ Presbiteris & Diaconibus cunctoque Clero Domino Deo servientium simul. Ego Wlfredus misericordia Dei Archisacerdos pro intimo cordis affectu dabo & concedo familia Christi habere & perfruere domos quas suu proprio labore construxerunt jure perpetuo hereditatis munificentia illis viventibus seu decedentibus cuicunque relinquere vel donare voluerint unusquisque liberam habeant facultatem in eodem monasterio donandi sed nec alicui foras extra congregationi. Ita etiam in Christi caritate obsecrans præcipio omnibus successoribus meis hanc prædictam donationem inconcusse & inviolatam salva ratione servandam sine fine semper in evum: hac tamen conditione ut Deo humiliores & gratiores omnium beneficiorum Dei semper existant, seduloque frequentatione canonicis horis Ecclesiam Christi visitent orantes ac deprecantes pro seipsis propriis piaculis & pro aliorum remissione peccatorum misericordiam Domini implorent. Necnon domum refectionis & dormitorium communiter frequentent juxta regulam monasterialis disciplinæ vitæ observant. Ut in omnibus honorificetur Deus & vita nostra & bona conversatio nobis nostrisque proficiat in bonum. Si quis illorum per audaciam suæ malæ voluntatis hanc prædictam constitutionem inritam habere & in oblivionem deducere, & congregare Convivias ad vescendum & bibendum seu etiam dormiendum in propriis cellulis sciat se quisquis ille sit reatum se esse propriæ domi & in potestate Archiepiscopi ad habendum & cuicunque ei placuerit donandum. l' manentem itaque hanc kartulam in sua nihilominus firmitate. Ego Wlfred gratia Dei Archiepisc' signo sanctæ crucis Christi confirmans subscripsi.

✠ Ego

✠ Ego Wernoth pr' Ab' con' & subscripsi.   ✠ Ego Diornoth pr' con' & sub'.
✠ Ego Wulfheard pr' con' & sub'.   ✠ Ego Guthmund pr' con' & sub'.
✠ Ego Heamund pr' con' & sub'.   ✠ Ego Cuthberht pr' con' & sub'.
✠ Ego Oswulf pr' con' & sub'.   ✠ Ego Coenhere Dia. con' & sub'.
✠ Ego Ceolstan pr' con' & sub.   ✠ Ego Brunheard Dia. con' & sub'.
✠ Ego. Tudda pr' con' & sub'.   ✠ Ego Hæhferth præposi' con' & sub.

Numb. XXXV.

A Catalogue of the Officers under the Cellarer.

Seneſcallus Libertatum.	Salſarius qui eſt Oſtiarius.
Clericus ſen' Libertatum.	Coquinæ, & garcio ejus.
Seneſcallus aulæ hoſpitum.	Focarius coquinæ.
Janitor portæ exterior. Curiæ.	Portarius.
Janitor portæ cimiterii.	Partitor coquinæ.
Panetar. in Celar.	Tractor vini & cerviſiæ.
Garcio ejus.	Qui eſt Cupparius.
Hoſtiarius Clauſtri.	Garcio ejus.
Garcio ejus.	Armiger Celerarii.
Panetarius aulæ.	Stabularius Celerarii.
Vigil Curiæ.	Carectarius Celerarii.
Scutellarius aulæ.	Et duo garciones ejus.
Potagiarius.	Coltonarius interior.
Scutellarius refectorii.	Coltonarius exterior.
Garcio ejus.	Venator, & garcio ejus.
Lardarius qui eſt jus coquus.	Janitor portæ aulæ.
Conventus & garcio ejus.	Garcio ejus.
Secundus cocus conventus.	Cuſtos prati Celerarii.
Cocus aulæ & garcio ejus.	Gayolarius.

Numb. XXXVI.

*Donationes Maneriorum & Eccleſiarum Eccleſiæ Chriſti Cantuarien. & no-
mina donantium, unà cum privilegiis & libertat' eid. Eccleſ. con-
ceſsis.*

Palatium regium in Cantuar.

ETHELBERTUS Rex, Anno regni ſui xxxv. ad fidem Chriſti per ſanct. Auguſtinum con-
verſus, ſtatim Palatium ſuum eidem Auguſtino & ſucceſſoribus ſuis infra Civitatem
Doroberniam perpetuè dedit, ut ibi ſedem Metropolitanam in ævum haberent *, quam beatus Gregorius primam totius regni eſſe decrevit & confirmavit, ut ſicut prima fuit fidem ſuſ-
cipiendo, prima eſſet in dignitate. Hoc donum fecit rex Anno Domini, Dxcvii.

* In quo fundata eſt Eccleſia Cantuarien. & in nomine ſancti Salvatoris dedicata. As in another Mſ.of the Church Adeſham.

Ethelbaldus filius Ethelberti dedit monachis ejuſdem Eccleſiæ manerium de Adeſham ad
cibum, Anno Domini Dcxvi. cum campis, ſilvis, paſcuis & omnibus aliis ad villam illam rite pertinentibus, liber, ab omnibus ſecularibus ſervitiis, & fiſcali tributo, exceptis iſtis tribus
conſuetudinibus, expeditione, Pontis Arciſve conſtructione. i. communi labore de quo nullus excipiebatur.

Pageham.

Anno Domini Dclxxx. Cedwalla Rex dedit Wilfrico Archiepiſcopo Pageham , cum appendiciis ejus. ſcil. Slindon, Scrippaneg, Ceretun, Bucgrenora, Beorgamſtede, Chriſmeham-
me, Mundanham aquilonare & aliud Mundanham.

Geddinge. Wodetone.

Anno Domini Dclxxxvij. Cedwella Rex cum conjuge ſua Keneldritha dedit Theodoro
Archiepiſcopo & familiæ Eccleſiæ Chriſti in Dorobernia, Geddinge & Wodetone, liberè ſicut
Adeſham.

Nunhelmeſtun.

Anno Domini Dclxxxxiij. Withredus Rex Cantiæ dedit terram quatuor aratrorum pro
amore Dei & Brithwaldi Archiepiſcopi, Eccleſiæ beatæ Mariæ quæ ſita eſt apud Liminge ,
quæ terra vocatur Nunhelmeſtun, L. S. A. *.

* i. Libere ſicut Adeſham. Piſcaria de Lamhethe.

Anno Domini Dccxlj. Eadbriht Rex dedit Eccleſiæ Chriſti in Dorobernia capturam piſ-
cium in Lamhethe, & alia quædam Eccleſiæ de Liminge, tempore Cuthberti Archiepiſcopi,
L. S. A.

Anno Domini Dccxlvij. Eadbertus Rex Kanciæ dedit Eccleſiæ de Reculure, tempore
Bregwini Archiepiſcopi tributum unius navis in villa de Fordwic.

Hlyden.

Anno Domini Dcclxxiiij. Offa Rex, Janiberto Archiepiſcopo rogante, dedit monachis Eccleſiæ Chriſti Doberniæ Hlyden juxta Sandwicum, L. S. A.

Hlyden.

Eodem Anno Offa Rex totius Angliæ dedit Janiberto Archiepiſcopo ad Eccleſiam Chriſti
Dorober. terram trium aratrorum, quam Cantiani Anglice dicunt thre ſwollinges in occidentali parte regionis quæ dicitur Merſware, ubi nominatur illa terra data Hlyden. Et ſi-
gnatum eſt hoc ſcriptum ſignis prædict. Regis & Archiepiſcopi, & ſimiliter Kinedrithæ reginæ, trium Epiſcoporum, quinque Abbatum, Edbaldi Ducis & xi. Principum.

Bramling.

Wullafus dedit Bramling Monachis Eccleſiæ Chriſti Cantuar. qui illud habuit ex dono
Edwlfi Regis idem donum confirmantis, ut ſcriptum ſuum inde teſtatur.

Anno

Anno Domini Dcclxxxiiij. Eadmundus Rex Kanciæ dedit Hwatrede * Abbati de Recu- `Sheldwich.`
lure, & ejus familiæ ibidem degenti Scheldwihc, scil. terram xij. aratrorum. L. S. A. `* Wihtrede forte·`

Anno Domini Dccxc. Offa Rex Anglorum Anno regni sui xxxviij. ad instigationem A-
thelardi Archiepiscopi, dedit Ecclesiæ sancti Salvatoris in Dorobernia xc. tributaria terræ
bipartita in duobus locis, lx. in loco qui dicitur Linganhæse & Geddingas, circa rivulum `Lingahæse. Ged-`
qui dicitur Fisces burna, & xxx. in aquilonali ripa fluminis Tamis, ubi appellatur Twican- `dinges. Twican-`
ham. lx. ad emendationem Ecclesiæ Salvatoris, & xxx ad indumentum fratrum qui Deo `ham.`
serviunt in illa sancta Ecclesia.

Anno Domini Dccxcj. Offa Rex dedit Ecclesiæ Christi Doroberniæ, Otteford, & terram `Otteford. Ye-`
quindecim aratrorum in provincia Canciæ nomine Yecham, ad cibum monachorum. Per- `cham. Rokinge.`
hamstede, Rokinge & in saltu qui dicitur Andred pascua porcorum in his locis. Dunma- `Sandherst, Bo-`
lingdene, Sandherst, Swihelmigdene. Et in silvis qui dicuntur Bocholte & Blean Heanhric. `cholt.Blean.& al.`
Et aliud inter torrentem nomine Nortburnan & Aghne treon, & pastuum unius gregis juxta
Theningden, & quinquaginta porcorum binnan Smede.

Eodem Anno. Cenulfus Rex, rogatu Athelardi Archiepiscopi Doroberniæ dedit vicario
munere terram duodecim aratrorum ubi dicitur Tenham, ad Metropolem Salvatoris Ecclesiam in Dorobernia. Hanc munificentiam maxime fecit Rex quia idem Archiepiscopus gratia recompensationis terram xij aratrorum dedit in loco ubi dicitur Creges emilina.

Anno Domini Dccxcix. Cenewlfus Rex , Archiepiscopo Athelardo rogante, Ecclesiæ `Cherring.`
Christi in Dorobernia reddidit terras quas Offa Rex abstulerat Janiberto Archiepiscopo scil. `Chert. Burne`
Cherring. Selebertes Chert ad vestimentum monachorum. Brumgland & Burne. `& al.`
`Terra in Cant.`

Anno Domini Dccciiij. Cenulfus Rex & Rex Cuthredus dederunt Ecclesiæ de Liminge,
ubi jacet corpus beatæ Eadburgæ sex mansuras in civitate Doroberniæ, rogatu Athelardi
Archiepiscopi. `Burne.`

Anno Domini Dcccv. Athelardus Archiep. dedit vel potius restituit monachis Ecclesiæ Dorobern. villam dictam Burne, ad victum monachorum, scil. terram quatuor aratrorum,
quam terram prius homo bonus, nomine Aldhun, qui in hac regali villa hujus civitatis
Præfectus fuit, prædictis monachis contulit ad victum, sed rapacitate Offæ Regis de eadem `* Libere sicut A-`
terra privata est eadem Ecclesia. L. S. A. *. `delham.`

Eod. Anno Cuthredus Rex Canciæ, cum licentia Cenulfi Regis Merciæ, tempore Wlfredi
Archiep. dedit Ecclesiæ Christi Cant. terram duorum aratrorum, quæ dicitur Bocholte & Kin- `Bocholt.`
gescualand, L. S. A.

Eod. Anno Cenulfus Rex dedit Wlfredo Archiepiscopo, ad opus Ecclesiæ Christi in Do- `Bixle.`
robernia terram x aratrorum scil. Bixle. L. S. A.

Anno Domini Dcccix. Cenulfus Rex Canciæ dedit Wlfredo Archiepisc. Doroberniæ, & `Bereham.`
monachis Ecclesiæ Christi, terram septem Aratrorum, quæ dicitur Beroham. L. S. A.

Anno Domini Dcccxj. Wlfredus Archiepisc. emit à Cenulfo Rege has terras, ad opus Eccle- `Gravene. Elme-`
siæ Christi in Dorobernia, scil. Gravenea. Cassingburnan. Ealmestede. Suuithunigland juxta `sted. & al.`
Gravene, & Appingland. L. S. A.

Anno Domini eod. Wlfredus Archiepisc. Doroberniæ concambium fecit cum conventu suo `Eastria pro`
de villa de Eastria pro Burne. `Burne·`

Anno Domini Dcccxiiij. Cenulfus Rex dedit Wlfredo Archiepiscopo, & monachis in Ec- `Binne.`
clesia Christi Doroberniæ circiter xxx jugera inter duos gremiales rivos fluminis quod dicitur Stour, & vocatur terra illa Binne. L. S. A.

Lyfchild dedit Middeltone Wlfredo Archiepiscopo, & monachis Ecclesiæ Cant. & postea `Meltone.`
scil. Anno Dom. Dcccxxij. Cenulfus Rex Merciorum idem donum confirmavit, ab omni seculari gravitate liberum, & fiscali tributo.

Anno Domini Dcccxxij. Cenulfus Rex dedit Wlfredo Archiepisc. Coppanstan. Gretamarsc. `Shaldeford.`
& Shaldeford. L. S. M. *. `* i. Libere sicut`
`Meltone.`

Eod. Anno Beornulfus Rex Merciorum dedit Ecclesiæ Christi Godmersham, ad victum `Godmersham.`
& vestitum monachorum, rogante Wlfredo Archiep. L. S. A.

Eod. Anno Wlfredus Archiep. Doroberniæ concilium celebravit in loco præclaro qui di- `Harghes Ged-`
citur Clovesho, presente Beornulpho Rege Merciorum, super libertate Ecclesiæ, ubi idem Ar- `ding. Cumbe,`
chiepiscopus recuperavit quasdam terras Ecclesiæ Christi Doroberniæ ablatis, scil. Harghes, `& al.`
Herefordingland, Wambelean, Gedding & Cumbe.

Anno Domini Dcccxxiij. Cenulfus Rex dedit Wlfredo Archiep. quondam terram infra `Terra in Cant.&`
mœnia urbis Doroberniæ, scil. lx pedum in longitud. & xxx pedum in latitud. partem etiam `extra.`
extra civitatem ab aquilone Civitatis xxx jugera, xxv in arido campo & v agros prati.

Lifstanus dedit Southcherch monachis Ecclesiæ Christi Cant. & postea Celulfus Rex Mer- `Southcherch·`
ciorum dedit eisdem, & idem donum confirmavit.

Anno Dom. Dcccxxiiij. Wlfredus Archiepiscopus dedit Monachis Ecclesiæ Christi Doro- `Eghethorne &`
bern. Eghethorne & Langedone pro commutatione de Bereham. `Langdone pro`
`Bereham.`

Item idem dedit eisdem villam quæ dicitur Eastur-Waldington in occidentali plaga Ec- `Terra in Cant.`
clesiæ Christi, infra mœnia urbis Doroberniæ, intra ripam fluminis Stoure.

Item idem dedit eisdem terram quæ vocatur Folquingland in regione Estriæ. Ruriculum `Byri.`
quoque unius aratri in loco qui vocatur Byri.

Anno Domini Dcccxxviij. Wiglaf Rex Merciorum dedit Ecclesiæ Christi Dorobern, & `Brotewelle.`
Wlfredo Archiep. ejusd. Ecclesiæ Brotewelle in Middx. L. S. A.

Anno Domini Dcccxxx. Werhardus Presbyter præpotens in Anglia, de præcepto Archie· `Harghes, Otte-`
piscopi dedit Monachis Ecclesiæ Christi Dorobern. terras prius ablatas, scil. Harghes Ciiij. `ford. & alia.`

hydas. Otteford C. hydas. Graveneyam xxxij hydas. Burnan xliiij. hydas. Sefwalun x. hydas. Bereham xxxvj hydas &c.

Ebbeney & alia. Anno Domini Dcccxxxij. Rex Athulfus inſtinctu Ceolnothi Archiepiſc. dedit Ebbeneyam, Deſerthefia, Miſtanham, Langebornam, Blakebornhamme, Plegimunhamme, Ofnehamme, & ſilvam quæ vocatur Oſtrynden, & villam juxta civitatem Doroberniæ quæ vocatur Bertun, ad quam pertinent quinque jugera & duo prata apud Scertingan, & aliud apud Tanintun, omnia L. S. A. *

* i. libere ſicut Adelham.

Loſe. Ethelwfus Rex dedit Loſe Suete viduæ & filiæ ejus, & illæ dederunt Monachis Eccleſiæ Chriſti Cantuar. & eſt de veſtitu eorum.

Anno Domini Dcccxxxv. Cinnewarra Abbatiſſa dedit Humberto Duci terram juris ſui, nomine * Wircefmuth, ea conditione ut omni anno det Eccleſiæ Chriſti in Dorobernia pro gablo, plumbum trecentorum ſolidorum ad opus ejufdem Eccleſiæ Archiepiſcopo Ceolnotho, & ſucceſſoribus ſuis in perpetuum.

* Wirefmuth.

Hadleghe. Eod’ Anno Hadleghe in Suthfolca data fuit per Elſledam ſciente & conſentiente Ethelredo Rege.

Mallings. Anno Domini Dcccxxxviij. Ecgbertus & Athelwlfus Rex filius ejus dederunt Eccleſiæ Chriſti in Dorobernia Mallings in Suthſexan, quod viz. manerium prius eidem Eccleſiæ dedit Baldredus Rex, ſed quia non fuit de conſenſu magnatum regni, donum id non potuit valere. Et ideo iſto anno in concilio apud Kingſtone celebrato ab Archiepiſc. Doroberniæ Ceolnotho reſtauratum eſt Eccleſiæ antedictæ. L. S. A.

Chert. Anno Domini Dcccxxxix. Ceolnothus Archiepiſcopus propria pecunia ſua emit Chert à quodam principe vocato Halethe concedente Rege Athelwlfo, & eandem villam Eccleſiæ Chriſti monachis dedit. L. S. A.

* Ethelwlf. Mſ. Eccl. Cant. Anno Domini Dcccxxxix. * Athulfus Rex dedit Ceolnotho Archiepiſcopo terram unius manſionis quæ dicitur Eaſtreaſta Delham, ſcil. vij jugera, quæ viz. terra adjacet Eccleſiæ S. Mariæ de Liming. L. S. A.

Chertham. Anno Domini Dccclxxj. Elfredus Dux dedit Ethelredo Archiepiſcopo Doroberniæ, & Monachis ejuſdem Eccleſiæ villam de Chertham, ad veſtitum Monachor. ut patet per chartam ſuam inde confectam, quam potius Codicellum dicimus.

Anno Domini Dcccxcv. Wefinghwerhs juxta flumen quod dicitur Romeneya datum fuit per Plegmundum Archiepiſcopum Eccleſiæ Chriſti.

* Another Mſ. calls Ethered-ſhith. [Heth. F.Writh. Vide Lamb. Per-ambul. Cant. p 442. Folkſtane. Anno Domini Dcccxlix. * Heth dat’ fuit per Elfredum Regem Plegmundo Archiepiſcopo, & ſucceſſoribus ſuis ad opus Eccleſiæ & Monachorum.

Anno Domini Dccccxxiij. Wlfelmus Archiepiſcopus agros comparavit ab incolis qui nominantur Waldland & Wlfrethingland, juxta locum qui dicitur Rethercheap, extra portas Doroberniæ.

Anno Domini Dccccxxvij. Athelſtanus Rex, pro anima patris ſui Edwardi & honore Wlfelmi Archiſacerdotis Doroberniæ, dedit Folkſtane ſitam ſuper mare, ubi quondam fuit

* i. Libere ſicut Adelham. Monaſterium & Abbatia ſanctarum virginum, ubi etiam ſepulta eſt S. Eanſwitha, qui locus à Paganis deſtructus fuit. L. S. A *.

Hamme. Anno Domini Dccccxxxiiij. Eylfleda dedit Hamme Eccleſiæ Chriſti Cant.

Terra à meridie Doroberniæ. * Jugera, as in another Mſ. Anno Domini Dcccc xxxix. Winhelmus dedit Wlfelmo Archiep. Dorober xj. agros * à meridie Doroberniæ. Et eſt terra illa circumdata his terminis. Ab oriente Adredſland, ab aquilone Kingſland, à meridie publica ſtrata, & ab occidente Brihtelmeſland. Factum fuit donum iſtud in præſentia Athelſtani Regis.

Mepeham. Anno Domini Dccccxl. Eadulfus Dux per conceſſionem Regis Athelſtani, præſente Wlfelmo Archiep. dedit Mepeham. L. S. M.

Preſtantun Wing-ham & al. Anno Domini Dccccxlj. Preſtantun. Wingham. Wolecumbe, Swerdlingan, Boſington & Graveney reſtitut. Eccleſiæ per Eadmundum Regem, & Eadredum fratrem ejus, & Edwinum filium ejuſdem Edmundi.

Terrings. Athelſtan Rex dedit villam de Terrings ſitam ſuper mare in Suthſexan, Eccleſiæ Chriſti in Dorob. L. S. A.

Perhamſtede. Anno Domini Dccccxliiij. Eardulfus Rex Cantiæ dedit Heahberthæ Abbati de Racul. & ejus familiæ, ſcil. Monachis conſiſtentibus in illo loco vocato Raculfre, & etiam unius aratri in loco qui nominatur Perhamſtede.

Pecchinges. Anno Domini Dccccxlvii. Pecchings dat’ Eccleſiæ per Wlfricum, preſente & conſentiente Rege Edredo, matreque ejus Regina Eadgiva, Odoneque Archiepiſcopo Doroberniæ, Wlſtano Archiepiſcopo Eborac. & aliis multis nobilibus. L. S. A.

Monaſterium Raculfenſe. Anno Domini Dccccxlix. Edredus Rex preſente Odone Archiepiſcopo Eadgiva regina matre ipſius Edredi dedit Eccleſiæ Chriſti in Dorobernia Monaſterium Raculfenſe bis denis ſemiſque eſtimatum caſſatis interiuſque exteriuſque cum omnibus pertinen’ ſive litorum ſive camporum, agrorum, ſaltuumve. L. S. A.

Iccham. Anno Dom. Dcccclviij. Villa de Iccham data fuit per Athelwardum, præſente Odone Archiepiſcopo.

Meapham & alia. Anno Domini Dcccclxj. Ediva regina, alio nomine dicta Edgiva, ſcil. mater Eadmundi & Eadredi Regum dedit Mepeham, Coulings, Oſterland, Leanham, Pecham, Farnleghe Monketone, & Aldintone, huic Eccleſiæ.

Anno Dom. Dcccclxiij. Dunſtanus, de conſenſu regis Edgari dedit huic Eccleſ. Fenegg’ vij aratrorum, quod Anglicè dicitur vij hides emptorum de Ingelram Optimato ejuſdem regis.

Anno Domini Dcccclxiiij. Ethelſtanus, conſentiente & concedente Archiepiſc. Dunſtano dedit

dedit Ecclefiæ Sanctæ Mariæ de Liminges, ubi fepulta eft fancta Eadburga terram unius ju- Ulcham.
geri quæ Vleham nominatur.

Anno Domini Dcccclxxix. Egelredus Rex dedit Ecclefiæ in Dorobernia Sandwich, ad ve- Sandwich.Eftrey?
ftitum Monachorum, & Eftreyam ad cibum Monachor. L. S. A.

Anno Domini Dccccxcj. Afchwinus Dorfetenfis Epifcopus reddidit Ecclefiæ Chrifti Alfrico Risbergh.
Archiepifcopo Risbergh.

Anno Domini Dccccxcvij. Elfgiva regina dedit huic Ecclefiæ Newinton & Brotewelle in Newington &
regione de Oxinaford, & calicem aureum cum patena aurea, in quo funt xiij. marcæ de pu- Brotewell, & al.
ro auro, & duo dorfalia de pallio, & duas capas de pallio cum taffellis auro paratis. L.S.A.*. Adefham.
Anno Domini Dccccclxxx *. Athelftanus filius Ethelredi, de confenfu & licentia ejus dedit * Mxv. as in a
Ecclefiæ Doroberniæ Holingburnan, ad cibum Monachorum, quam villam emit à patre nother Mf.
fuo. L. S. A.   Holingbourne.

Edmundus Rex filius Edivæ Reginæ dedit Prefton *, & Eylwartone Monachis Ecclefiæ * i. Copton. Pre-
Chrifti Cantuar. & eft de victu eorum.   fton & Eylwar-
                                                                                            ton. Läling. Il-
† Anno Domini Dccccxlj. Dux Brithnotus iturus ad bellum contra paganos, dedit Laling, legh. Hadlegh.
Illegh, Hadlegh, confentiente Rege Ethelredo, prefente Sirico Archiep. Dorober.   † l. 991.

Anno Domini Miij. Ethelredus Dux dedit Ecclefiæ Chrifti particulam terræ in Dorober- Terra in Cant. &
nia, quam fibi Rex Ethelredus dedit, xv. virgarum in longitud. & viij. virgarum in lati- extra.
tud. & vj. agros extra murum. Termini terræ infra murum funt hii. In orientali parte
terra Regis, in parte auftrali placca civitatis. In occidente terra Ecclefiæ Chrifti. In aquilone cœmiterium Chrifti.

Anno Domini Mvj. Ethelredus Rex confirmavit omnes donationes terrarum quæ datæ funt Confirmatio Do-
Ecclefiæ Chrifti in Dorobernia, & fuper hoc fcriptum fuum dedit Elfrico Archiep. cum pif- nationum & Li-
cationibus, venationibus, aucupationibus, & aliis omnibus libertatibus, exceptis illis tribus in bertatum.
Adefham, figno ipfius confirmatum, una cum xxxj. fignis optimatum fuorum.

Eod' anno Ethelric & Leofwina, annuente rege Athelredo, dederunt Bocking & Merfey Bocking & Mer-
ad victum Monachorum.   fey.

Anno Domini Mx. Elfegus Archiepifcopus adauxit Ecclefiæ Chrifti Cantuar. quandam Werehorne &
terram, nomine Werehorne, Fremingham & Wodetone, & eft de veftitu Monachorum. alia.
L.S.M. *.   * 1. Libere ficut
Anno Domini Mxviij. Mefteham & Cheyham, duæ villæ in regione Surreyæ dat per E- Milton.
thelftanum, qui & Livingus.   Merfteltam. &
                                                                                            Cheyham.
Eod. anno Knuht Rex dedit Livingo Archiepifcopo, ad opus Ecclefiæ, filvam Hefeleherft.
L. S. A.

A. D. Mxxiij. Kanutus Rex dedit Ecclefiæ Chrifti in Dorobernia portum de Sandwico Portus Sandwici.
cum corona fua aurea, quæ adhuc fervatur in capite crucis majoris in navi ejufdem Ecclefiæ.
Portum illum dedit Monachis cum thelonio ejufdem villæ, wrecco maris & omnibus aliis confuetudinibus ad portum illum pertinentibus.

Anno Domini Mxxxij. Apuldre, Orpintone, Palftre, & Wihttrifcheham dat' ecclefiæ per
Edfinum presbyterum *, confentientibus Canuto Rege, & Elfgiva, Regina fua.   * Epifcopum S.
Anno Domini Mxxxvj. Theored. confentiente & concedente Knuto, dedit Horfleghe, ad Martini qnæ Ec-
opus & victum Monachorum. L. S. A.   clefia fita eft
                                                                                            extra Civitatem
Memorandum quòd idem Rex Kanute, confirmavit privilegia prædecefforum fuorum le- Doroberniæ in
galia in libertatem Monafteriorum infra Kanciam pofitorum.   Oriente. as ano-
                                                                                            ther Mf. hath It
Eod. anno. Hethe & Saltwode data Ecclefiæ per unum de principibus Angliæ, nomine Apuldre & alia.
Haldene.   Horfleghe.
                                                                                            Heth & Salt-
Eod. anno. Godmerfham data fuit Ecclefiæ per Egelnothum Archiepifcopum.   wode.
Anno Domini Mxxxviij. Knuthus Rex reddidit Ecclefiæ Chrifti in Dorobernia villam de Godmerfham.
Folkftane, quam olim Rex Athelftanus filius regis Edwardi eidem Ecclefiæ dedit, ea condi- Folkftane.
tione hanc donationem fecit Knutus, ut nunquam alienaretur eadem villa per Archiepifco-
pum fine licentia Regis & Monachorum.

Wlftanus, cognomento Wildepreoft, annuente Domino fuo Hardeknuto, dedit huic Ec- Thurrock.
clefiæ Thurrock.

Anno Domini Mxliiij. Egelricus Bigge dedit huic Ecclef. Chert. Stouting & Meletune. Chert. Stouting.
Anno Domini Mxlvj. Wlfgith relicta Elfwine, & Godwinus, confentiente fancto Edwar- Meletune.
do Rege dederunt Ecclefiæ Chrifti in Dorobernia, Stiftede & Coggefhale in Effex, ad vi- Stiftede. Gogge-
ctum Monachorum. L. S. A.   fhale.

Anno Domini Mli. Villæ de Chertham & Walworth conceffæ & confirmatæ fuerunt per Chertham &
fanctum Edwardum, cum maneriis jam habitis, & multis libertatibus conceffis. Prædictam Waleworth.
villam Walworth Edmundus Rex dedit cuidam joculatori fuo nomine Hitardo. Tempore
tandem Regis Edwardi idem Hitardus volens limina Apoftolorum Romæ vifitare venit ad
ecclefiam Chrifti in Dorobernia, & per confenfum & conceffionem Regis Edwardi dedit eandem villam eidem Ecclefiæ Chrifti, chartam quoque ejufdem terræ pofuit fuper altare
Chrifti &c.

Siwardus & Matildis uxor ejus dederunt Merfham Monachis Ecclefiæ Chrifti Cantuar. Merfham.
Sancto Edwardo Rege anno Domini Mlj. per fcriptum fuum idem donum confirmante, &
eft de cibo eorum.

Eodem anno. Sake. Sokne & aliæ libertates conceffæ & confirmatæ per fanctum Ed- Libertates.
wardum.

Carta ejufdem de libera Warenna.

Anno

Meſſuagium &
Eccleſia in Civi-
tate London·

Anno Domini Mliij. Brihtmerus civis London dedit Eccleſiæ Cantuar. meſſuagium ſuum apud Gerſcherche, & de licentia & conſenſu Stigandi Archiepiſcopi & Godrici Decani dedit eidem Eccleſiam omnium Sanctorum, teſtimonio Lieſſtani Portreve & aliorum.

Haltone.

Willielmus Rex conqueſtor reddidit manerium de Haltone in comitatu Bock. Monachis Eccleſiæ Chriſti Cantuar. antiquis & modernis temporibus à jure ipſius Eccleſia ablatum, & multa alia ut in martilagio * continetur. Et plenius ſcriptum ſuum inde confectum teſtatur. Pro Deo & ſalute animæ ſuæ gratis hoc fecit, & ſine ullo pretio.

* Ita Mſ.

Anno Domini Mlxxv. Conqueſtor confirmavit donum fratris ſui Odonis Epiſcopi Bai-

Domus in Sand-
wico.

cenſis, & Comitis Canciæ de domibus in Sandwico datis Eccleſiæ &c.

Carta Regis Wmi Conquſtoris ut Monachi Cantuar. omnes terras ſuas liberè teneant.
Similis Carta Regis Hen. 1. & 2.

Anno Domini Mlxxiij. Conqueſtor confirmavit Lanfranco Archiepiſc. omnes conſuetudi-nes in Eccleſia de Newenton anteceſſorem ejus, & in Eccleſia ſancti Martini de Doffris, & in Scapeia.

Charta ejuſdem de eadem in omnibus Dominicis Eccleſiæ Chriſti Cantuar.
Charta ejuſdem Anglicè & Latinè de libertatibus Eccleſiæ Chriſti Cant. conceſſis.
Charta ejuſd' de libertatibus quas S. Edw. conceſſit eid' Eccleſiæ,
Charta Regis Henrici primi de eiſdem.
Charta Regis Richardi de eiſdem.

Broke.

Karlemannus levita dedit Broke Eccleſiæ Chriſti Cantuar. & poſtea Hen. Rex Imus idem manerium per chartam ſuam eidem Eccleſiæ contulit, & Hen. Rex IIdus per chartam ſuam idem manerium confirmavit.

Slindone.

Anno Domini Mcvj. Rex Hen. I. rogatus ab Anſelmo Archiep. reddidit Eccleſiæ Chriſti Cant. villam quæ vocatur Slindone in Suthſex.
Carta Regis Hen. I. Hen. III. & Richardi de Geld & Danegeld.

Medietas Altaris

Anſelmus Archiepiſcopus Cantuar. reddidit monachis Eccleſiæ ſuæ medietatem altaris Chri-ſti, quam in manu ſua habebat poſt mortem prædeceſſoris ſui Lanfranci Archiepiſcopi, qui eis aliam medietatem, cognita veritate quòd ad illos pertineret, in vita ſua reddiderat. Si-

Stiſtede.

militer & manerium de Stiſtede eis reddidit idem Anſelmus, eò quòd ad eos pertinere ſcitur.

Eccleſia Sancti
Martini Dovor.

Anno Domini Mcxxx. Henricus Rex primus dedit Eccleſiam ſancti Martini Dover mo-nachis Eccleſiæ Chriſti Cantuar. in dedicatione ejuſdem Eccleſiæ Cant. cum omnibus perti-nen. & provenien. tam in terra quam in mari, ut inde charta teſtatur.

Reculver octo
libr.

Anno eodem Wmus Archiep. dedit octo libras annui redditus de manerio ſuo de Reculvere, monachis Eccleſiæ Chriſti Cant. in dotem ipſius Eccleſiæ Cant. in perpetuum & hoc tem-pore Regis Hen. I. quòd donum S. Edmundus Archiepiſc. poſtea confirmavit.

Diepham.

Anno Domini Mcxlvj. Henricus de Rya ſeiſivit Eccleſiam Chriſti Cant. de manerio de Diepham per quendam cultellum ſuper altari Chriſti, preſentibus Teobaldo Archiepiſcopo, Waltero Priore aliiſque multis, & acceptus fuit in fraternitatem à prædictis Archiepiſc. & Prio. Anno ſupradicto. Quam donationem Hen. Rex 2. confirmavit.

Berkeſore.

Manerium de Berkeſore datum per Stephanum Regem, ad inveniendum lumen ante cap-ſam beati Anſelmi Archiepiſcopi.

Berkeſore.
Leiſdone &c.

Henricus Rex 2dus dedit & confirmavit Deo, beato Thomæ, & Eccleſiæ S. Trinitatis Cantuar. xv libratas redditus in Berkeſor, & in Hokis aiſſe, & Riſſendona, & xxv libratas redditus in Leiſdona, & ita libere &c. ſicut ego &c.

Doccombe.

Wmus Tracy dedit Doccombe tempore Regis Hen. II. idem donum confirmantis.
Carta Regis Hen. II. de via circa murum Cemiterii noſtri.

Hollingbourne.

Carta ejuſdem de terra noſtra ſuper montes de Hollingborne.
Carta ejuſdem de libertatibus noſtris liberè tenendis.
Carta Regis Stephani de eiſdem.

Boſcus de Blean.

Anno Domini Mcxcix. Richardus Rex primus, anno regni ſui primo, dedit Boſcum de Blean, monachis Eccleſiæ Chriſti Cant. per unum par cirotecarum, ſalvo tamen uno ſum-mario quem pater ejuſdem regis conceſſit Eccleſiæ & Canonicis S. Gregorii in eodem boſco.

Tenementa in
Cant.
Terſtane & alia
pro Sandwico.

Duæ cartæ Alienoræ reginæ de xiij tenementis in Judaiſmo Cantuar.
Carta ejuſdem de maneriis de Terſtane & Weſtfarlegh, cum advocationibus Eccleſiarum de Weſtclive & Weſterham pro portu de Sandwice, quam donationem Edwardus Rex pri-mus per cartam ſuam confirmavit.

Caldecote.
Torholte.

Anno Domini Mcccxxvj. Dominus Walterus Rynold Archiepiſc. de licentia ſpeciali Ed. Regis 3. dedit monachis Eccleſiæ Chriſti Cant. manerium de Caldecote juxta Cantuar. cum boſco de Torholte, & cum omnibus & ſingulis libertatibus, &c.

Bovyton.

Anno R. R. Ed. 3. xxvij. Richardus Bovyton, de licentia ſpeciali ejuſdem regis dedit manerium ſuum de Bovyton, cum omnibus pertinen. in villa de Bocking in Com. Eſſex, Priori & Conventui Eccleſiæ Chriſti Cant.

Fawkſhall.

Dominus Edus Princeps filius Regis Ed. 3. dedit monachis Eccleſiæ Cant. manerium de Fawkeſhall, eodem rege Edwardo idem donum confirmante, ad ſuſtentationem duorum Ca-pellanorum in eadem Eccleſia celebratur.

Borle pro Sand-
wico.

Edwardus 3. Anno Regni ſui xxxviij. dedit in eſcambium Prio. & Conventui Eccleſiæ Chriſti Cant. manerium de Borle in Comitatu Eſſex, pro conſuetudinibus & redditibus una cum omnibus juribus &c. quæ iidem P. & C. habuer' vel habere aliquo modo potue-runt.

runt in villa & portu de Sandwico, cum aliis redditibus in insula de scapeia, ut in carta, &c.

Carta Regis Hen. 4. ne furagium capiatur ubicunque in Comitatu Canciæ ad equos sustentandos in Castello Dovor.

Item carta ejusdem Regis, de via infra murum Civitatis Cant. quæ ducere solebat de Northgate usque Queningate.

Ecclesiæ appropriatæ Ecclesiæ Christi Cantuar.

HUbertus Archiepiscopus dedit Ecclesiam de Halstow, ad officum Præcentoris, pro reparatione librorum Ecclesiæ Christi Cantuar. & postea Bonifacius Archiepiscopus eandem Ecclesiam per sigillum suum confirmavit. — Halstowe.

Stephanus Archiepiscopus dedit Ecclesiam de Freningham, & per sigillum suum confirmavit, ad opus Elemosinariæ Ecclesiæ Christi Cantuar. Anno Domini Mccxxv. [Mense Novemb.] — Freningham.

Sanctus Edmundus Archiepiscopus dedit Ecclesiam de Fairfield Ecclesiæ Christi Cant. & per sigillum suum confirmavit Anno Pontificat. sui quarto. — Fairfield.

Gregorius Papa ix. de assensu Episcopi Norwicen. & Capituli ejusdem Ecclesiæ, confirmavit Ecclesiam de Deipham ad opus Ecclesiæ Christi Cantuar. ut patet per bullam suam inde confectam, Anno Pontificat. sui prim. — Deipham.

Idem Papa appropriavit Ecclesiam de Sesaltre monachis Ecclesiæ Christi Cantuar. in sustentationem eorum, ut patet per bullam &c. Anno Pontificatus sui xmo. — Sesaltre.

Edwardus Rex 2dus Anno Regni sui xixno appropriavit Ecclesiam de Esshe in Comitatu Suffolc. ad novam capellam Elemosinariæ Ecclesiæ Christi Cantuar. — Esshe.

Simon Islep Archiepiscopus, de speciali confirmatione Regis Edwardi 3tii. Anno ejusdem regis xxxixno. fecit appropriari Ecclesias de Monketon & Eastry monachis Ecclesiæ Christi Cantuar. — Monketon. Eastry.

Idem Archiepisc. de speciali confirmatione & licentia ejusdem Regis, Anno Regni sui xlvjo. fecit appropriari Ecclesiam de Pageham in augmentationem scolarium studentium Oxoniæ in Collegio Ecclesiæ Christi Cantuar. — Pageham.

Willielmus Courtney Archiepisc. de speciali licentia Regis Ricardi secundi, Anno regni sui nono, fecit appropriari Ecclesiam de Mepeham monachis Ecclesiæ Christi Cantuar. — Mepeham.

Anno Domini Mccccxcvij. Dom. Thomas Arundell Cantuar. Archiepisc. de licentia speciali Regis Ricardi II. fecit appropriari Ecclesiam de Godmersham monachis Ecclesiæ Christi Cant. ad fabricam Ecclesiæ Christi prædictæ. — Godmersham.

Anno Domini Mcccc. Idem Archiepiscopus, de licentia speciali regis Hen. IV. regni vero sui Anno 2. fecit appropriari Ecclesiam de Westwell monachis Ecclesiæ Christi Cantuar. ad habendum vocationem Ecclesiæ de Aldermancherche London, ad opus Ecclesiæ Christi prædictæ. — Westwell.

De Ecclesiis de Westerham & Westclyve vide cum mareriis de Westfarlegh & Terstane, ut supra patet. — Westerham. Westclyve.

King Offa's Charter of the **donation** *of certaine Lands to Christ-Church.*

EGo Offa Rex Anglorum Dccxc. Anno Dominicæ incarnationis, nostri autem regni Dei gratiâ concessi xxxviij. cogitans de salute animæ meæ, & de statu regionis Merciorum perveni ad Lundoniam Civitatem cum venerabilis viri Aethelheardi Archiepiscopi, & locutus sum cum eo quid pro salute animæ meæ, & totius gentis Mercior. Deo omnipotenti darem. Inter hæc postulavit à me venerabilis Archiepiscopus Aethelheard ut darem tibi aliquod supplementum ad Ecclesiam sancti Salvatoris in urbe Doroberniæ ; dicens cum omnibus Episcopis nostræ regionis esse inonestum non ditari matrem Ecclesiarum à filiabus & filiis suis regibus quos fonte baptismatis regeneravit. Ego vero * concessi petitioni illius & omnium Episcoporum nostrorum, & dedi illi xc. tributaria terræ bipertita in duobus locis. lx. in loco qui dicitur ou Linga hæse & Geddingas circa rivulum qui dicitur Fisces burna, & xxx. in aquilonali ripa fluminis Tamis, ubi appellatur Twicanham, ut habeat lx. ad emendationem Ecclesiæ sancti Salvatoris. xxx verò in Twicanhamme ad indumentum fratrum qui serviunt Deo in illa sancta Ecclesia. Hanc elemosinam humilis & devotus ego Offa Rex Anglorum pro pignore Christianæ fidei totius gentis nostræ offero Deo omnipotenti, ad suam sanctam Ecclesiam, ut mei memoria & meæ carissimæ gentis ibi celebretur & Deo commendetur. Erat autem in conventu nostro celeberrimus dies Pentecostes, & conventus famulorum Dei quorum nomina scripta sunt hic. Aethelheard Archiep. Ceolwulf Episc. Unwona Episc. Hathored Episc. Ceolmund Episc. Ealhheard Episc. Elfhun Episc. Cyneberht Episc. Dunferth Episc. Wermund Episc. Weohthun Episc. Omnes isti una mecum clamaverunt ad Dominum in die sancto in ecclesia sancti Pauli. Spiritus Domini qui hodie replevit orbem terrarum, & omnia continet, & scientiam habet vocis *all' & omnes sancti Dei Apostoli qui ab illo spiritu repleti sunt, tribuat * benedictionem sempiternam consentientibus & defendentibus hanc largitatem, & condemnet & excommunicet & in hoc sæculo & in futuro eum qui auferat vel minimam partem hujus doni ab Ecclesia sancti Salvatoris quæ sita est in urbe Cantewariorum. Et respondit omnis

Tempus.
Donatio.

* l. consensi. Ms.
Eccl. Cant.

Donum.

Solemnis.
Ap ⎱ precatio.
Im ⎰
* Alleluya. Ms.
* Ita Ms.

Testes.

L   chorus

chorus, Amen. Ad confirmandum verò hoc largitatis donum in testes aderant & subscripserunt & confirmaverunt donum Salvatori nostro.

Ego Offa Rex Merciorum cum benedictione omnium Episcoporum impono signum sanctæ ✠ ad confirmationem hujus doni, mihi donanti ad redemptionem. Et minuenti ad æternam condempnationem, & sine ullo remedio in inferno ad æternæ pœnæ cruciatum.

✠ Ego Ecgferth Rex consensi & subscripsi, & promisi hoc donum semper firmare & augere.

✠ Ego Aethelheard Archiepiscopus signum sanctæ crucis impono. Et in nomine sancti Salvatoris conscribo.

✠ Ego Colwulf *Episf. Conf.*	✠ Brorda *Princ.*
✠ Ego Unwona *Episf. Conf.*	✠ Bynna *Princ.*
✠ Ego Hathored *Episc.*	✠ Esne *Princ.*
✠ Ego Ceolmund *Episc.*	✠ Heardbriht *Princ.*
✠ Ego Ealheard *Episc.*	✠ Ethelmund *Princ.*
✠ Ego Elfhun *Episc.*	✠ Eadgar *Princ.*
✠ Ego Cyneberht *Episc.*	✠ Wigga *Princ.*
✠ Ego Deneferth *Episc.*	✠ Cydda *Princ.*
✠ Ego Wermund *Episc.*	✠ Cudberht *Princ.*
✠ Ego Ealhmund *Abb.*	✠ Ceolmund *Princ.*
✠ Ego Utel *Abb.*	✠ Vbba *Princ.*
✠ Ego Fothred *Abb.*	✠ Eobing *Princ.*

Numb.
XXXVIII.

Scrutinie in Dunstans Tombe.

Scrutinium factum circa feretrum beatissimi Patris Dunstani *Archiepiscopi, ex mandato Reverendissimi Patris ac* Dⁿⁱ *Domini* Willielmi Warham *Cantuar. Archiepisc. & Domini* Thomæ Goldston *sacræ paginæ Professoris, ejusdemque Ecclesiæ Prioris dignissimi Anno Domini* 1508. *die* 22. *Aprilis.*

Vicesimo die Aprilis Anno Domini 1508. quo die tunc accidebat cœna Domini, ex mandato ipsius Domini Archiepisc. & Prioris, deputati sunt tres vel quatuor de confratribus ad ejusmodi opus aptiores & ferventiores, ut in vespere, postquam fores Ecclesiæ essent clausæ, ne laici hujusmodi negotio adessent, ad scrutinium faciendum circa feretrum sancti Dunstani, ut ipsi explorarent qua via faciliori possent ejus sacræ reliquiæ videri : ea ratione ut omni ambiguitate & scrupulo semotis, oculata fide rei veritas probaretur. Hii quidem fratres in ipsa noctis tempestate non tam diligenter quam prudenter ad id quidem perduxerunt opus, ut antelucanum oculis perspicere potuerunt arcam quandam plumbeam ubi sacræ ejus reliquiæ recondebantur. Quæ quidem arca deposita fuit & immersa * in opere lapideo feretri ex parte australi summi altaris scituati. Ea siquidem arca intus erat lignea exterius, interiusque plumbo undique cooperta & clavis omni in loco affixa, adeo ut inter clavum & clavum non erat spatium relictum latitudinis humanæ palmæ. Erat quoque hæc arca longitudinis juxta longitudinem operis lapidei ipsius feretri, viz septem pedum, latitudinis autem circiter pedis cum dimidio. Eratque in omni sua parte ferreis ligamentis circumducta tutissimis adeo ut vix possit discerni via possibilis illam aperiendi. Confisi tamen in divino auxilio & sancti Patroni suffragio, instituit Dominus Archiepisc. cum Priore ut quidam confratres in sequenti nocte, laicis semotis, iterum opus aggrederentur. Quod & factum est. Sex enim de confratribus per Priorem ad hoc deputati una cum ope aliorum, quos convocarunt, ingenti sudore hanc arcam quæ est maximi ponderis fecerunt supra opus lapideum sublevari. Id cum fecissent, tandem cum magna difficultate satagentes anteriorem patrem arcæ aperierunt quod profecto facere nequivissent nisi partem asseris quo in superiori parte arca claudebatur, effringerent. Eo sane confracto licuit videre interius ab uno fine arcæ usque in alium finem. Ibi verò patebat aspectui cista quædam plumbea : quæ quidem cista facta est non ex plano plumbo, sed arte quadam pulcherrime fabricata & plicata. Ea vero aperta, reperta est etiam & alia cista plumbea quasi tabefacta : quæ putatur esse illa in qua ossa sancti Dunstani cum primum sepeliebantur, recondebantur. Intra has duas cistas plumbeas cum aperirentur primò reperta est quædam parva lamina plumbi jacens supra pectus corporis. In qua quidem lamina continebatur hæc scriptura. *Hic requiescit sanctus Dunstanus Archiepiscopus.* Et scribitur hic titulus literis Romanis. Deinde repertus est pannus quidam lineus nitidus valde atque integer superpositus corpori sancti Dunstani. Quo sublevato, apparuit illud sanctissimum organum Spiritus Sancti indutum pontificalibus vetustate pro magna

*Situs Feretri.
* l. immissa.*

Quid repertum.

parte

parte confumptis. Porro apparuit ibidem tefta capitis quæ & tangebatur & ofculabatur tam à Domino Archiepifcopo qui valdè mane in craftino fequenti viz. in vigilia Pafchæ aderat, quam à Priore ceterifque quamplurimis de conventu monachorum. Cujus quidem teftæ partem à reliquo divifam Dominus Archiepifcopus tradidit Priori ea ratione ut decenter adornaretur, ut inter reliquias Ecclefiæ veneranda reponeretur. Denique videbantur & alia offa diverfa tam de brachiis quam de coftis, ac etiam nonnullæ maffæ de carne ejufdem patroni noftri. Quæ revera omnia odore redolebant fuaviffimo. Ad iftud non tam jocundum quam defideratiffimum fpectaculum affuere prope omnes de conventu. Ad hoc etiam invitati funt Teftes. per Dominum Archiepifcopum hi Capellani de familia fua, viz. Prior Dovoriæ Epifcopus Suffraganeus ejus, nomine Johannes Thornton Doctor Sacræ Theologiæ. Mr. Cuthbertus Tunftall, Doctor legum, Cancellarius ejufdem Domini Archiepifcopi. Mr. Thomas Wellys, Doctor Theologiæ, Mr. Robertus Wekys. Mr. Andreas in artibus Mag. Magifter, Johannes Pers Bacalarius in legibus. Hi verò vocati funt ad videndum & teftimonium perhibendum eorum quæ fuperius fcripta funt. Erant interea ad id ipfum advocati per Dominum Archiepifcopum tres Notarii Publici, puta Mr. Johannes Baret fcriba actorum prærogativæ Ecclefiæ Cant. Mr. Johannes Colman fcriba Confiftorii Cant. & Mr. Willielmus Potkyn fcriba Jurifdictionis immediatæ. Eos notarios Dominus Archiepifcopus requifivit ut fingulis quæ fuperius fcripta funt de fcrutinio facto circa reliquias fancti Dunftani diligenter per eos infpectis & confideratis, inftrumentum publicum de eifdem conficerent, idque complere fuper depofitione teftium prædictorum polliciti funt. Hæc cum peracta fuiffent, tunc ad mandatum Domini Archiepifcopi arca fuperius dicta iterum claufa eft firmiffimis tam opere ligneo quam plumbeo clavis quamplurimis affixa tutiffimis. Idque factum eft in prædicta vigilia Pafchæ. Nec fores Ecclefiæ antea aperiebantur, quam confratres noftri id operis expleviffent.

A Grant or Demife of part of the demeafnes of Reculver Monaftery made by Archbifhop Agelnoth *to two of his Minifters.*

IN nomine Domini noftri Jefu Chrifti. Ego Aegelnothus peccator, Servus fervorum Dei, & minifter Ecclefiæ Chrifti, Anglorum quoque licet indignus Archiepifcopus. Notum volo effe omnibus noftræ mortalitatis Scccefforibus, quod quandam terram dominicam fanctæ Mariæ Raculfenfis Monafterii, L. fcilicet agros in præftariam annuo duobus miniftris meis, Alfwoldo & Aedredo, ex confenfu fratris noftri Givehardi Decani ejufdem Ecclefiæ Givehardus Defanctæ matris Dei, ut illam terram habeant non longius quam ipfi placuerit Decano, vel canus. ejus Succeffori. Quamdiu vero eam tenuerint, fingulis annis dent in ipfo monafterio Deo famulantibus rectam decimam frugum & omnium pecorum quæ in ipfa terra nutriunt, & pro cenfu L. denarios, & de fubjectis pafcuis j. penfam cafeorum & fi quid fracturæ contigerit. Ubi verò eidem fratri noftro Decano vel ejus fucceffori vifum fuerit ut illam terram poffint fructificare dominicatui fuo, recedant ab ea, abfque querela & contradictione, quia Dominica eft fanctæ Mariæ, nec eam fibi vel pofteris fuis ullo modo poffint defendere. Quod fi præfumpferint, & ipfi & fautores fui iram Dei & excommunicationem omnium Dei fidelium incurrant, & legem patriæ Domino fuo folvant. Hujus præftariæ traditionis teftes funt fratres ejufdem Monafterii, & quidam milites mei qui fubter funt ordinatè defcripti.

Ego Givehardus fubfcripfi.   Ego Frefnotus ^{mon'} fubannotavi.

Ego Tancrad' ^{mon'} recognovi.   Ego Milo ^{mon'} affignavi.   Ego Siward ^{miles} conteftificavi.

Ego Godric ^{miles} teftis fui.   Ego Wlfi. ^{miles}   Ego Wlfige. ^{miles}   Ego Radwine. ^{miles}

Ego Ordnoth. ^{miles}   Ego Alfric. ^{miles. hog.}   Ego Ofward. ^{miles.}   Ego Aelfhelm. ^{miles.}

Ego Lefsona. ^{Miles.}   Ego Aelfric. ^{miles. quatm'}   Ego Sibriht. ^{miles.}   Ego Aelwine. ^{miles.}

     Ego Haimericus presbyter jubente Domino Agelnotho Archiepifcopo hanc cartulam confcripfi die Nativitatis fancti Johannis Baptiftæ.

The

The Kentish-manors, in the Conquerors time, belonging both to the Archbishop and Monkes of Canterbury, *and recorded in the Booke of Doomsday.*

De maneriis Archiepiscopatus.

De Stursæte.

* Id est Tempore Ed. Regis.

STursæte est manerium Archiepiscopi, & in * T. E. R. se defendebat pro vij. sullinges, & nunc similiter, & est appretiatum hoc quod est in dominio xl. lib. & nunc habet Archiep. xx. & v. burgenses, qui reddunt x. sol. de gablo, & ex his supradictis vij. sullin' habet Godefridus dapifer unum sulline de Archiepiscopo Tenitune, & est appretiatum C. sol.

Adhuc autem & Vitalis habet inde unum jugum terræ de Archiep. & est appretiatum xxᶜ. Hamo vero tenet inde similiter dimidium sulling' quod tenuit Alric. Bigge a' pore Archiepiscopi in T. E. R. & est appretiatum Cᶜ.

Rodbertus de Hardes tenet inde unum jugum terræ ex isdem sull' & est appretiatum xxxᶜ. & ex his vij. sullin' habet Archiep. unum sull' apud sanctum Martinum ; & de eodem sullino habet Radulfus Camerarius in feodo medietatem de Archiepiscopo & valet iiijˡ. & * dominium valet vijˡ.

ˠ l. Dominicum.

Et in Canterberia sunt vij. burgenses, qui reddunt huic manerio vijᶜ, & iiij. denarios de gablo.

Et inibi sunt iterum xxx. & ij. mansuræ & unum molendinum quæ tenent clerici sancti Gregorii ad eorum ecclesiam. Ibique manent xij. burgenses qui reddunt eis xxxvᶜ. & molendinum reddit vᶜ.

Adhuc etiam tenet Aegelwardus iiij. juga in Natinduna unde reddidit T. E. R. & adhuc reddit altari sanctæ Trinitatis xijᶜ. & est appretiatum xlᶜ.

Albold vero tenet de supradictis sull' unum jugum Wic, & est de terra monachorum sanctæ Trinitatis, quod est appretiatum xxxᶜ.

Hic finitur hundredus de Stursæte.

In Fordwic habet Archiepiscopus vij. mansuras terræ quæ modo non faciunt servitium ad mare ut in T. E. R.

De Wingeham.

Wingeham est proprium manerium Archiepiscopi & in T. E. R. se defendebat pro xlˡ sull' & nunc pro xxx. & v. & valet Cˡ. hoc quod Archiepiscopus habet inde.

Et ex isdem sull' habet Willielmus de Archis unum sull' Fleotes ab Archiepiscopo in feodo & valet vjˡ.

Et Vitalis habet j. sull' & valet xlvᶜ.

Wibertus & Arnoldus habent iij. sull' qʼ valent xijˡ.

Et Heringod habet inde j. sull' decem agros minus & valet xlᶜ.

Et Godefridus Archibalistarius habet inde j. sull' & dimid' & valet Cˢ.

De Burne.

Burnes est proprium manerium Archiep. & in T. E. R. se defendebat pro vj. sull' & nunc similiter, & est appretiatum xxxˡ. & est in Hundret de Berham.

De Petham.

Peteham est proprium manerium Archiep. & in T. E. R. se defendebat pro vij. sull', & nunc similiter, & est appretiatum xxl.

Et ex istis sull' habet Godefridus Dapifer dimid. sull' quod pertinet ad vestimenta monachorum, id est Suurtling.

Et Nigellus habet unum sull' & unum jugum terræ quæ est appretiata xls.

Hoc est in hundredo de Peteham.

De Aldintune.

In hundredo de Bilicholt habet Archiepiscopus unum manerium, Aldintune, & in T.E.R. se defendebat pro xxj. sull', & nunc pro xx. & valet Cl. & xij.

Et ex his habet Will' de Archis unum manerium stutinges quod Aelfere tenuit de Archiep. & tunc defendebat se pro j. sull' & dimid' & nunc pro uno, & valet x l.

Item ex supradictis sull' de Aldintune habet Archiep. dimid. jugum & dimid. virgam in Limines & valet xijl. & tam' qui tenet reddit xvl. de firma.

In Rumene sunt xxv. burgenses qui pertinent ad Aldintune·

De

De Limminge.

In Limwarlethe in hundret de Noniberge habet Archiepifc. in fuo dominio unum manerium Limminges quod T. E. R. fe defendebat pro vij. full' & nunc fimiliter.
Rodbertus filius Watfonis habet ex his ij. full' in feodo.
Et Rodbertus de Hardes dimid. full'.
Et Osbertus Pasfora dimidium jugum.
Et in marefco de Rumene jacet unum full' Aelmefland, de elemofina monachorum fanctæ Trinitatis, & non eft de fupradictis full'.
Et de ifto full' habet Will' Folet unum jugum, id eft, Sturtune.
Et de eodem full' habet fupradictus Rodbertus tria juga. i. Ordgarefwice, & Caffetvifle & Eadruneland.

De Raculf.

Raculf eft manerium Archiepifcopi & in T. E. R. fe defendebat pro viij. full' & eft appretiatum xl. & ij lib. & v. fol. tres minutes minus.

De Northewode.

Nordewode eft manerium Archiepifcopi & in T. E. R. fe defendebat pro xiij. full', & nunc fimiliter, & eft appretiatum L l. v s.
Et ex iis full' habet Vitalis de Canturberie unum full' & unum jugum, & in Tanet full' & dimid. & etiam in Macebroc habet xj. agros & di' full' ab Archiepifcopo. Et Ezilamerth & tota hæc terra eft appretiata xiiij l. & v s. & vj d. Hæc maneria habet Archiepifc. in hundret de ipfo Raculf.

De Boctune.

Boctuna eft manerium Archiepifcopi & in T. E. R. fe defendebat pro v. full' & di' & nunc fimiliter, & fuit appretiatum in T. E. R. x l. Et Archiepifcopus habet inde C s. & iv. & iij. denarios de gablo. Nunc autem valet xx l. Sed tamen reddit xx. & v. lib. de firma. & Archiepifcopus habet fuum gablum ficut prius.
Ricardus Conftabularius habet inde unum manerium Gravenai in feodo ab Archiepifcopo quod in T. E. R. fe defendebat pro uno full', & nunc fimiliter & valet vj l. Hanc terram habet Archiepifc. in Hundret de Boctune.

De Tæneham.

Teneham eft manerium Archiepifcopi & in T. E. R. fe defendebat pro v. full' & dimid. & nunc fimiliter, & eft appretiatum L l.
Dimidium full' terræ tenet Godefridus de Melling in fcapai ab Archiepifcopo quod valet iiij l. & tn' reddit C s.
Ofwardus vero tenuit hoc idem full' ab Archiepifcopo Cantuarberiæ in T. E. R. Hanc prædictam terram habet Archiepifcopus in Hundret de Tenham.

De Cerringes.

Cerringis eft proprium manerium Archiepifcopi & in T. E. R. fe defendebat pro viij. full', & nunc pro vij. quia Archiepifc. habet aliud ad fuam propriam carrucam, & valebat in T. E. R. xx l. & habet inde Archiep. iiij l. & vij s. de * glabo. Nunc vero valet xxx l. * l. Gabl. fed tn' reddit xl l. de firma. Et Archiep. habet inde gablum ficut prius.

De Plukele.

In eodem Hundredo & in Left de Wiwarleth habet Archiepifcopus unum manerium Plukelai in dominio quod in T. E. R. fe defendebat pro uno full' & nunc fimiliter & valet xv l. & tam' reddit xx l. de firma. Hæc maneria habet Archiepifcopus in Hundret de Calchela.

De Geldingeham.

Gelingham eft proprium manerium Archiepifcopi, & in T. E. R. fe defendebat pro vj. full' & eft apretiatum hoc quod Archiepifc. habet inde in dominio x. & viij. lib. & hoc quod Anfcetillus de Ros & Rodbertus Brutinus habent xl s. Et tamen reddit Archiepifcopo de firma xx. & v. lib. & xviij s. Hoc manerium eft in hundredo de Cettaham.

De Meideftane.

Mæideftane eft proprium manerium Archiepifcopi & in T. E. R. fe defendebat pro x. full'. Et ex iis tenet Radulfus unum full' quod eft apretiatum l s. Et Willielmus frater

* M   Epifco.

Epiſcopi Gundulfi ij. ſull', & ſunt apretiat' x l. Et Anſcetillus de Ros unum ſull' quod eſt apretiatum lx s. Et duo homines habent inde j. ſull', qui reddunt altari ſanctæ Trinitatis xvj s. & tamen valet illud ſull' xx s. Hoc manerium habet hundret in ſeipſo.

De Nordſlita.

Nordſlita eſt manerium Archiepiſcopi, & in T. E. R. ſe defendebat pro vj. ſull' & nunc pro v. & eſt apretiatum xx. & vij. lib. Sed tamen ille qui tenet reddit inde de firma xxx. & vij l. Et infra leugam de Tonebrig eſt inde tantum quod eſt apretiatum xxx s. Hoc manerium & Meppaham jacent in hundredo de Tollentr'.

De Bixle.

Bixle eſt manerium Archiepiſcopi & in T. E. R. ſe defendebat pro iij. ſull' & nunc pro ij. & eſt apretiatum xx l. & reddit xxx l. & viij s. & eſt in hundredo de Ealmeſtrou, & in dimidio Led de Sutune iiij. ſull'.

De Earhede.

Earhede eſt manerium Archiepiſcopi, & in T. E. R. ſe defendebat pro iiij. ſull' & nunc ſimiliter. Et Oſuvardus tenuit illud ab Archiep. in T. E. R. & eſt apretiatum xvj l. & tam' reddit xxj l. Hoc manerium habet Archiep. in hundredo de Litelet j. ſull. & dimid.

De Bradeſtede.

Bradeſtede tenuit Wlnodcild ab Archiep. T. E. R. Et nunc tenet illud Haimo ab iſto Lanfranco Archiepiſc. & tunc defendebat ſe pro uno ſull' & dimid. & nunc ſimiliter, & eſt apretiatum xvij l. Iſtud manerium eſt in hundredo de Hoſtreham.

De Otteford.

Otteford eſt manerium Archiep. & in T. E. R. ſe defendebat pro viij. ſull' & nunc pro totidem. Et eſt apretiatum lx l. Et hoc quod Haima inde tenet eſt apretiatum lx s. & x. & hoc quod Rodbertus interpres, & Goſfridus de Ros inde tenet viij l. & x s. Et hoc quod Ricardus de Tonebrig inde tenet x l. & xxiiij. porcos.

De Sunderherſce.

Sunderherſce eſt manerium Archiepiſc. quod Godwinus tenuit T. E. R. injuſte & Archiepiſcopus iſte Lanfrancus explacitavit illud contra Epiſcopum Bajocenſem juſte per conceſſum Regis, & in T. E. R. ſe defendebat pro uno ſull' & dimid. & nunc ſimiliter. Et eſt apretiatum xviij l. & tam' qui tenet illud reddit inde xx. & iiij. lib. & unum equitem de firma Archiepiſcopo. Hæc maneria ſunt in hundredo de Codeſede.

De Wroteham.

Wroteham eſt manerium Archiepiſcopi & in T. E. R. ſe defendebat pro viij. ſull' & eſt apretiatum xx. & iiij. lib. & tam' ille qui tenet reddit inde de firma xxx. & v. lib. Et de iis prædict. viij. ſull' tenet Will' Diſpenſator j. ſull' quod eſt apretiatum iij l. Et Goſfridus de Ros aliud quod eſt apretiatum iij l. Et Faremanus unum ſull' & dimid. & eſt apretiat' C s. Et hoc quod Ricardus habet xv l. Hic finit hundredus de Wroteham.

De Mellingetes.

Mellingettes eſt manerium Archiep. & in T. E. R. ſe defendebat pro ij. ſull' & nunc ſimiliter, & eſt apretiatum ix l. & tam' reddit de firma Archiepiſcopo xv l. Hoc manerium habet Archiepiſcopus in hundredo de Lavercefeld.

De Derente.

Dairente eſt manerium Archiepiſcopi, pro ij. ſull' ſe defendebat in T. E. R. & nunc ſimiliter. Et eſt apretiatum xv l. Et x. s. habet Inde Ricardus infra Caſtellum ſuum, & tam' Archiepiſcopus habet in firma ſua xviij l.

De Einesforde.

Einesford eſt manerium Archiepiſcopi, & in T. E. R. ſe defendebat pro vj. ſull', & nunc ſimiliter, & nunc tenet Radulfus filius Hoſpaci ab Archiepiſcopo, & eſt apretiatum xx l. Et ex eo habet Ricardus de Tonobrig tantum quod eſt apretiatum iij l.

De

De Hulecumbe.

Hulecumbe tenuit Aelferus in T. E. R. de Archiepifcopo, & defendebat fe pro ij. full' & dimid. & nunc tenet Comes de Oˢ de Archiepifcopo, & defendit fe pro ij. full', & eft apretiarum xj *l.*

Archiepifcopus habet iiij. præbendas ad Nuventune, & funt apretiatæ vi *l.*

Tota fumma Clxxx. & vij full' & dimid.

Incipiunt maneria Monachorum in Kent.

* NOrdunda eft manerium monachorum Sanctæ Trinitatis, & eft de cibo eorum, & eft de hundredo de Cantuarberia, & in T. E. R. fe defendebat pro uno full'. & ei fubjacent C. Burgenfes iij. minus qui reddunt viij *l.* & vj *d.* de gablo, & eft apretiarum **x.** & vij. lib. Hoc manerium eft de Hundret de Cantuar.   * Nordwda.

De Eaftrege.

Eaftrege eft manerium manachorum, & de cibo eorum, & in T. E. R. fe defendebat pro vij. full' & nunc fimiliter. Et in alia parte eft dimid. full' & unum ioc'. & v. æceres. Gedinges, & valet xxx. & vij. lib. & x *s.* & iij *d.* inter totum.

De Tilemanneftune.

Willielmus Folet tenet j. manerium Tilefmanneftune ab Archiepifcopo, & hoc eft de terra monachorum, & in T. E. R. fe defendebat pro j. full', & nunc facit fimiliter, & valet xxx *s.*

Ifte idem Will' habet de prædicta terra dimid. full' ab Archiepifc. in Fenglefham, quod tenuit Lenenot in T. E. R. ab Archiepifc. & valet xx *s.*

Ifte idem Will' habet adhuc ab eod. Archiepifc. & de prædicta terra monachorum Stepenberga quod fe defendebat T. E. R. pro dimid' full', & nunc facit fimiliter. Et Godwinus tenuit illud in tem. E. R. ab Archiepifc. Aedzi & valet xxx *s.*

Bocland fe defendit pro j. jugo.

Hic finit Hundret de Eftrege.

De Sandwic.

Sandwic eft manerium fanctæ Trinitatis, & de veftitu Monachorum, & eft Leth & Hundredus in feipfo, & reddit Regi fervitium in mare ficut Dovera ; qualitate fcilicet non quantitate & homines illius villæ antequam Rex eis dedit fuas confuetudines reddebant xv *l.* quando Archiepifcopus recuperavit reddebat xl *l.* & xl. milia de alecibus. Et in præterito anno reddidit L *l.* & allecia ficut prius. Et in ifto anno debet reddere lx. & x. lib. & allecia ficut prius. In T. E. R. erant ibidem Ccc. & vij. manfuræ. Nunc autem lx. & xvj. plus.

De Muneketune.

Munechetun eft manerium monachorum & de cibo eorum, & in T. E. R. fe defendebat pro x. & viij. & eft apretiarum xl *l.* Hoc prædictum manerium eft in Hundredo de Tenet.

De Eadefham.

Edefham eft ma nerium monachorum fanctæ Trinitatis & de cibo eorum & in T. E. R. fe defendebat pro xvij. full' & nunc fimiliter, & de gablo reddit xvj *l.* & xvj *s.* & iiij *d.* & valet xxx. *l.* de firma & C *s.* de gerfuma.

Et ex iis full' habet Rodbertus filius Watfonis ij. id eft, Egedorn qui valent vij *l.* & tamen qui tenet reddit inde viij *l.*

Et Rogerius tenet ex his j. full' ad Beraham q' valet iiij *l.* Hoc manerium habet hundret in feipfo & in Læd eft de æftraie.

De Iecham.

Iecham eft manerium monachorum & de cibo eorum. & in T. E. R. fe defendebat pro iiij. full'. & nunc fimiliter, & eft apretiarum xxx. & ij. lib. Et hoc quod Will' de Hedefham habet inde viz. j. full' ad Rocinges valet vij *l.* Hoc manerium eft in Hundret de Dunahamford.

De

De Sæsaltre.

Sæsealtre eſt Burgus monachorum & de cibo, & proprie de coquina eorum. Et Blittære tenet illud de monachis. Ibique eſt terra duarum carrucarum & eſt apretiatum C s. Hoc manerium in nullo Hundret eſt.

De Certeham.

Certaham eſt manerium monachorum & de veſtitu eorum & in T. E. R. ſe defendebat pro iiij. ſull', & nunc ſimiliter, & eſt appretiatum xx. & v. lib. & tamen reddit xxx l.

Godmereſham.

Godmæreſham eſt manerium monachorum & de veſtitu eorum & in T. E. R. ſe defendebat pro viij. ſull' & eſt apretiatum xx l. ſed tamen reddit xxx. Hic finitur Hundretus de Feleberga.

De Cert.

Cert eſt manerium monachorum, & de veſtitu eorum & in T. E. R. ſe defendebat pro iij. ſull' & nunc ſimiliter & eſt apretiatum xx l. Iſtum Cert eſt hundret.

De Litlecert.

Litelcert iterum eſt manerium monachorum & de cibo eorum quod in T. E. R. ſe defendebat pro iij ſull', & nunc pro ij. & dimid. & valet viij l.
Et ex iis habet Will' fil' Hermenfridi dimid. ſull', iſt eſt, Pette, ab Archiepiſcopo in feodo, & reddit inde altari ſanctæ Trinitatis xxv d. pro omnibus conſuetudinibus & valet xl s.

De Apeldre.

In Letd de Limware jacet hundret de Blacetune, in quo Rodbertus de Rumene tenet ad firmam j. manerium Apeldre, & eſt de cibo monachorum S. Trinitatis & in T. E. R. ſe defendebat pro ij. ſull' & nunc pro j. & valet xij l. Sed tamen reddit xvj l. xvj s. & vij d.

De Welle.

Wælle vo eſt manerium monachorum ſanctæ Trinitatis, & eſt de cibo eorum, & in T. E. R. ſe defendebat pro vij ſull' & nunc pro v. & valet xxiiij l. & iiij d. & tamen reddit xj l. de firma. Hoc manerium & Litlecert ſunt in hundret de Calehele.

Holingeburne.

Holingburne eſt manerium monachor. & de cibo eorum, & in T. E. R. ſe defendebat pro vj. ſull' & nunc ſimiliter.
Et de iſto manerio tenet Eps' Baiocenſis dimid. ſull' ab Archiepiſc. per gablum, & poſtquam Eps' habuit hoc dimid. ſull' nunquam reddit inde ſcottum. Et eſt appretiatum inter totum hoc manerium xxx l.

De Boctune.

Ratel tenuit Boctune de Archiepiſcopo Cantuarberiæ & defendebat ſe in T. E. R. pro dimid. ſull', & iſtud dimid. ſull' eſt & fuit de vj. ſull' de Holingeburne. Nunc autem tenet illud Radulfus filius Toroldi ab Archiepiſc. & eſt apretiatum xl s. Hæc maneria ſunt in hundret de Haihorna.

De Merſeham.

Merſeham eſt manerium S. Trinitatis & de cibo eorum, quod T. E. R. ſe defendebat pro vj. ſull', & quando Archiepiſcopus eum recepit pro v. & dimid. & modo pro iij. & Hugo de Mundford habet ex iis unius medietatem & valet xviij l. Hoc manerium jacet in Limwarled in hundret de Langebrige.

De Aelmeſland.

Rodbertus filius Watſonis tenet de Priore Cantuarberiæ Aelmeſland ad firmam, & præcepto ejuſdem Prioris reddit firmam ſecreſtano ejuſdem eccleſiæ.

De

De Werehorne.

In Limwarled & in hundret de Hamme habent monachi S. Trinitatis de vestitu eorum j. manerium Werehorne j. sull', & est apretiatum lx s.

De Broke.

In I æd de Wiworlæd & est hundret in quo tenet Rodbertus de Rumene j. manerium Broc ad firmam de cibo monachorum, & pro j. sull' defendebat se, & nunc pro dimidio, & valet iiij l.

De Langeport.

Idem Rodbertus habet in Langport de terra monachorum j. sull' & dimid. de Archie-pisc. quod idem Archiepisc. diratiocinavit contra Epm' Baiocensem. Et Godwinus Comes tenuit illud, ibique pertinebant & pertinent xx. & j. burgenses, de quibus Rex in mare habet servitium, ideoque quieti sunt per totam Angliam, exceptis tribus forisfacturis quæ habet Rodbertus de Rumene. Adhuc vero pertinet ibi j. jugum terræ, & hæc omnia va-lent xvj l.

De Niwendenne.

In Limwarlæd & hundred de Selebrichtindæne habet Archiepiscopus de terra monacho-rum j. manerium Niwendene in Dominio quod in T. E. R. tenuit Leofric de præterito Archiepiscopo, & pro j. sull' se defendeba & subjacebat Saltwude. Nunc est apretiatum viij l. & x s. garsumæ.

De Berewicke.

In Limwarlæd in Hundred de Strate habet Will' de Edesham de terra monachorum j. ma-nerium de Archiepiscopo Berewic quod tenuit Godricus Decanus & pro dimid' sull' se de-fendebat & nunc similiter, & est apretiatum xj l.

De Hede & Saltwde.

In Limwarlæd in Hundred de Hede habet Hugo de Munford de terra monachorum j. ma-nerium Saltwode de Archiepiscopo, & comes Godwinus tenuit illud & tunc se defendebat pro vij. sull' & nunc sunt v. & tam' non scottent nisi pro iij. & in Burgo de Hede sunt cc. & xxv. burgenses qui pertinent huic manerio, de quibus non habet Hugo nisi iij. forisfacta, & est apretiatum xxviij l. & vj s. & iiij d.

De Prestteune.[1]

Prestetune est manerium monachorum & est de victu eorum, & in T. E. R. se defende-bat pro j. sull' & nunc similiter, & est apretiatum xv l. Hoc manerium est in Hundred de Feversham.

De Liveland.

Liveland est terra manachorum, quam Ricardus Constabularius tenet in feodo ab Ar-chiepiscopo, & Decanus Cantuarberiæ habuit & tenuit eandem terram & in T. E. R. se defendebat pro j. sull' & nunc similiter, & valet xx s. Hæc maneria habent monachi in Hundred de Feversham.

De Leanham.

Lenham est manerium monachorum quod Godefridus de Mellinges tenet ab Archiepis-copo in feodo & in T. E. R. se defendebat pro ij. sull' & nunc similiter, & valet viij l. & tam' reddit xij l. & x s. de firma.

De Fearnlege.

Fernlege est manerium monachorum, & est de cibo eorum, & in T. E. R. se defendebat pro vj. sull' & est appretiatum xxij l. Et hoc quod Abel monachus inde tenet per jussum Archiepiscopi est apretiatum vj l. Et hoc quod Ricardus inde habet infra leugam suam iiij l. & de istis vj. sull' tenet Godefridus dapifer dimid. sull' quod est apretiatum ix l. Hoc manerium habent monachi in Hundred de Mædestane.

* N   De

De Pecham.

Pecham eſt manerium S. Trinitatis de cibo monachorum & in T. E. R. ſimiliter ſuit, & ſe defendebat pro vj. ſull' & ex iſtis habet nunc Ricardus de Tunebrige ij. ſull' & j. jugum. Et ex iſtis ij. ſull' & joco iſto nunquam ſcottavit Ricardus poſtquam habuit ea. Et in T. E. R. fuit hoc manerium apretiatum xij l. & nunc viij l. Et præfata pars Ricardi valet iiij. l.

Et in Stotingeberga quod tenuit Edricus de E. R. eſt dimid. ſull' unde ipſe Edricus dabat Scottum ad Pecham ſpontanee, non quod pertineret ad ſanctam Trinitatem, nec ad monachos. Hoc manerium eſt de Hundred de Litelfeld.

De Meapeham.

Mepaham eſt manerium monachorum, & de cibo eorum, & in T. E. R. ſe defendebat pro x. ſull' & eſt apretiatum xxvj l. & infra leugam Ricardi habetur tantum quod eſt a-
* Toltetrui. pretiatum xviij s. & viij d. Hoc manerium habent monachi in Hundred de Toltetem. *

De Cliva.

Cliva eſt manerium monachorum & de veſtitu eorum & in T. E. R. ſe defendebat pro ij. ſull' & dimid. & eſt apretiatum xvj l. Hoc manerium eſt in Hundred de Scamele.

De Orpintune.

Orpintuna eſt manerium monachorum & de veſtitu eorum & in T. E. R. ſe defendebat pro iij. ſull' & nunc pro ij. ſull' & dimid. & eſt apretiatum xxv l. & tamen reddit de firma xx. & viij. lib.

Et in hoc eodem manerio tenet Malgerus ab Archiepiſcopo iij. juga terræ quæ quidem li-ber homo tenuit in T. E. R. & hæc tria juga non ſcottabant cum hoc manerio & ſunt de explacitatione quam fecit Archiepiſcopus contra Epm' Baiocenſem per conceſſum Regis. Et illa iij. juga ſunt appretiata L s. & ex iis eiſdem ſull' habet Dirmannus dimid. ſull' ad Keſtane.

De Sændlinge.

Elfgat tenuit Sændlinge ab Archiepiſcopo T. E. R. & nunc tenet Hugo nepos Herberti ab Epiſcopo Baiocen. & defendebat ſe in T. E. R. pro j. ſull' & dimid. & nunc ſimiliter, & eſt
* Aelmſtria. appretiatum viij l. Hæc maneria ſunt de Hundred * Aelmeſtrin & ſunt in medio Led de Sudthune.

De Freningeham.

Freningeham eſt manerium monachorum & de veſtitu eorum quod Anſgodus Rubitonien-fis tenet ab Archiepiſcopo, & tn' reddit firmam monachis & in T. E. R. ſe defeudebat pro j. ſull' & nunc ſimiliter, & eſt appretiatum xj l. Hoc manerium eſt in Hundred de Clacſtane.

De Gravenea.

Gravene eſt manerium monachorum & de veſtitu eorum quod Richardus Conſtabularius tenet in feodo ab Archiepiſcopo, & tamen reddit firmam monachis, & pro j. ſull' ſe defendit, & jacet in Hundred de Boctune.

De Hloſe.

Hloſe eſt manerium monachorum & de veſtitu eorum & pro j. ſull' ſe defendit quod Abel monachus tenet & firmam monachis reddit. Hoc ſull' jacet in vj. ſull' de Fernlege.

De Surlinge.

In Surlinge eſt dimid. ſull' & pertinet ad veſtitum monachorum quod Godefridus Dapi-fer tenet & firmam reddit.

De Huntindune.

Huntindune eſt manerium monachorum & de veſtitu eorum & defendit ſe pro dimid. ſull' quod Godefridus Dapifer tenet & firmam reddit. Iſtud dimid. ſull' eſt de vj. ſull' de Fernlege.

De

De Burriceſtune.

Burgericeſtune tenent Wlfricus & Cole & eſt ibi dimid. ſull' & reddunt inde C s. altari
S. Trinitatis. Hoc dimid. ſull' eſt de x. ſull' de Meideſtane.

Tota ſumma Cxxx. & iij. ſull' & dimid.

Profeſſiones.

Feverſham.		Boxley.	
Clarenbaldi primi Abbatis, Theobaldo.	Lamberti.	Theobaldo.	
Guerrici. Richardo.	Thomæ.		
Algari.	Johannis.		
Petri.	Willielmi.		
Petri. Bonifacio.	Dioniſii.		
Johannis.	Walteri.		
Petri de Herdeſlo.	Simonis.		
Oſwardi.	Roberti.	Bonifacio.	
Clementis.	Gilberti.		

Sᵗ Radegund.		Langdun.		Combwell.	
Hugonis.	Huberto.	Richardi.	Huberto.	Johannis.	
Henrici.		Johannis.			
Richardi.		Roberti.			
Johannis.		Willielm.			
Henrici.		Willielm.	Huberto.		
Willielmi.		Rogeri.	Bonifacio.		
Roberti.	Waltero.				

De anno Jubileo apud Cant.

MEmorand quòd anno ab incarnatione Domini 1420. & anno Regni illuſtriſſimi Regis
& Principis Hen. 5. à conqueſtu Angliæ octavo, tempore Willielmi Bennet & Wᵐⁱ
Ickham tunc Balivorum Cant. Henrici Chichele tunc Archiepiſcopi Sedis Cant. & Johannis
Woodnesberwe ad tunc Prioris Eccleſiæ Chriſti Cant. die Dominica in feſto tranſlationis
ſancti Thomæ Martyris extitit apud Cant. annus Jubilæus in Eccleſia Chriſti Cant. qui tunc
extiterat ſextus annus Jubilaus à tranſlatione prædicti Thomæ Martyris glorioſi. Cujus
quidem Jubilei ſolemnizatio incepit ad horam duodecimam in vigilia dicti feſti, & conti-
nuavit per 15. dies continuos proximò & immediatè ſequentes; quo tempore idem Rex &
Princeps illuſtriſſimus fuit in francia cum ſuo honorabili exercitu ad obſidion' villæ Millon'
quæ diſtat à Civitate Pariſienſi triginta milliaria. Qui quidem verò Ballivi prælibati uni-
verſa iter præceperunt civibus Civitatis illius ſufficientiam domorum ad herbigandum & ad
hoſpitandum populum ad tunc pro ſalute animarum ſuarum adipiſcenda venturum, divina
gratia ſuffragante, tam infra Civitatem prædictam, quam infra ſuburbia Civitatis ejuſdem
habentibus, quòd eſſent parati in lectis & aliis populo prædicto neceſſariis: Ac etiam præceperunt univerſis vitellariis dictæ Civitatis, viz. Tabernariis, Pandoxatoribus, Piſtoribus, Car-
nificibus, Piſcinariis, Cocis & hoſpitatoribus quòd ordinarent contra tempus prædictum victualia populo prædicto tunc ſuffectura, qui quidem populus ut æſtimabatur ad tunc attin-
gebant ad numerum Centum millium hominum & mulierum tam Angliginentium quam alie-
niginentium exterorum viz. Hibernicorum, Wallicorum, Scotticorum, Francorum, Normannorum, Garniſientium, & Gerniſientium, ad eandem Civitatem, pro gratia prædicta
habenda ad tunc affluentium, pace verò & tranquillitate inter populum prædict' opitulatione
Dei omnipotentis ſuæque glorioſiſſimæ genetricis Dei Mariæ, precibus quoque glorioſi Martyris Thomæ ſociorumque ejus ſanctorum Curiæ celeſtis, veniendo, morando & redeundo,
toto tempore Jubilarii illius habitis & optentis. Qui quidem vitellarii ordinarunt victualia pro
populo prædicto copioſa, ita quòd lagena vini rubii de Vaſconia tunc vendebatur ad octo denarios, & lagena vini albi ad ſex denarios, & duo panes levati vendebantur ad unum denarium, & omnia alia victualia, Domino diſponente, de bono foro extiterunt ; per quæ Civitas prædicta & totus Comitatus Kanciæ exinde per totam Angliam favente altiſſimo magnum & diutinum revera obtinuerunt honorem.

Thomas Chirch fecit & ſcripſit, & ad hoc per plenam Curiam de Burgemoto, tam per
Ballivos, Aldermannos, xij Juratos, cum xxxvj hominibus in numero conſueto, ſpecialiter
requiſitus fuerat, & in forma prædicta redegit in ſcriptis.

A Diſcourſe

Numb. XLIII. *A Difcourfe of the Priviledge commonly called Clergy, branched into the five following Particulars, viz.*

> 1. *The nature and qualitie of the priviledge, what it is, and whence it came.* 2. *The forme and manner how it is put in practice.* 3. *The Antiquity thereof in this Land.* 4. *The extent of it to lay men, and the caufe thereof.* 5. *The declining of it by degrees, and reftrained condition thereof with us at this day.*

1. Particular.

TO begin with the firft. The better to know the nature and quality of this priviledge, liberty, immunity, exemption (call it which you pleafe) I muft let you know, that by the Canon-low (for I will looke no higher) every Clergie man hath a certaine Franchefe granted him, knowne by the terme of *Privilegium Clericale*, the which as a chaine, confifteth and is made of many links. One, and that the chiefe, whereof is this. *That*

* c. Si diligenti. De foro comp. & Lindw. in Provinciali de offic. Ord. e. a. verb. clericali privilegio.

he may not be called to fecular judgement *. That is, that he may not be convented nor brought into queftion for any matter by or before a temporall Judge. Within the compaffe and extent of the which priviledge, the Canons and Canonifts bring as well civill as criminall caufes, fo exempting Clerkes from the fecular power in the one as well as the other. And by the way, if Dr. *Ridley*, from whom I have it, be not deceived, this I may fafely fay, that many titles of the Canon-law, fuch as thofe *of buying and felling, of leafing, letting and taking to ferme, of morgaging and pledging, of giving by Deed of gift, of detecting of collufion, and coufenage, of murder, of theft, and receiving of theeves, and fuch like*, although they are known notorioufly to belong to the conufance of the Common-law at this day, yet with the matters whereof they treate, were anciently in practice and allowed in Bifhops Courts, in this Land, amongft Clerks. My Author, in my Judgement, fpeakes probably, but his reafons are many and large his difcourfe, and therefore (for brevity fake) I referre you over

* View of the Civill and Ecclefiafticall Law. pag. 103.

to his Booke *. In cafe this once were fo, yet time hath worne it quite out of ufe, a thing both at home and abroad notorious; for *Covarruvias* a late *Civilian* of *Spaine* can fay, that, as in *France*, in reall actions, fo alfo in *England*, in reall, mixt and perfonall actions, by cuftome here ufed, Clerks are convented and compelled to anfwer before the fecular Judge *.

* Covarr. Pract. quæft. c. 31. Tom. 2. p. 497. num. 5.

A courfe (as he noteth) that much withdrawes them from their calling, and fuch an one as is not knowne to take place in *Spaine*. *Ad rem redeo.* The Clergy of this Kingdome bearing themfelves too much upon this priviledge, heretofore dared, and in other parts to this Day are not afraid, to act and commit many foule and hainous crimes: the truth of which affertion will eafily appeare by the Story both of the *Venetian Controverfie*, and of Archbifhop *Becket*, who may be rightly faid, like a ftout Champion, to have ftood in defence and maintenance of this ecclefiafticall liberty (amongft the reft) *ufque ad aras*: This being one of the articles, (as himfelfe in his Epiftle to Pope *Alex.* 3. reports) for which he and the King were at mutuall defiance *viz. That Clerks and religious men might be taken from the*

* Fox. Acts and Monum. Tom. 1. pag. 282.

Church to fecular judgement * The Confequence of this priviledge being fo bad, and withall the peremptorineffe of the men of the Church in claiming it as due and derived to them *Jure divino* (for fo they here fometimes did, and in other parts yet doe think of it) have provoked many to argue and debate the cafe *pro & contra*. Amongft which (befides the controverfie betweene Pope *Paul*. 5. and the *Venetians* about it; and another like difference happening in *France* between the Prelates and the Lord *Peters* many yeares agone, reported in

* Cov. in Digeft. tit. de Judic. ea ult. pag. 166.

the *Acts* and *Monuments vol.* 1. *pag.* 462. and fo forward) *Duarenus* * a famous *Civilian* of *France*, and *Covarruvias* * (whom I named afore) an eminent Lawyer of *Spaine*, and a Bifhop, both, as to the Papifts, without exception, being fuch themfelves, have fcanned and

* Ubi fupra.

difcuffed the point, both of which conclude, that this priviledge defcendeth not *de Jure divino*. Which being fo, inquire we next what pofitive law there is to uphold it; The Bafes then and props whereon it refts, have their chiefe foundation laid in many chapters of that queftion 11. Q. 1. and in C. at *fi clerici. c. clerici.* and *c. qualiter. de Judic. c. Nullus. c. fi diligenti* and *c. fignificafti de foro competenti*, and in many other places of the Conon-law mentioned of *Covarruvias. ubi fupra.* Through the countenance and warrant of which Canons, and in imitation of them (as I fuppofe) the *Conftitutions* extant in the *Provincial. c.* 1. *de foro competen.* and *c.* 1. *de Pœnis.* and other the like unto them were agreed upon and made with us. Taking thefe and the like Canons for their warrant, the Ordinaries heretofore with us in *England* were wont to addreffe themfelves to the fecular Magiftrates, and of them to require and claime fuch Clerks (called convict before, and attaint after judgement) as they detained, and went about to bring or had brought to a triall, for any criminall matter, fuch as felony and the like. And if deniall or refufall were made of their delivery, then to proceed to the coertion of the Judge by the cenfures of the Church, untill he fhould actually

* Cap. 1. de foro competenti in Provinciali.

deliver up the Clerke *. But if they were delivered upon their demand, then they tooke them and the matter to their hearing. Who if Clerks in holy orders, and able canonically to purge themfelves of the objected crime (I fay, canonically, becaufe vulgar purgation was

and

and is forbidden by the Canon-law[h]) then were they acquitted. If they failed in such their purgation, then were they degraded, or else sent to doe perpetuall penance in some *Monastery*. But if no Clerkes, but meere laymen, then were they dismissed in case of such purgation, but if they were not able to purge themselves, then were they perpetually imprisoned (the punishment for an attainted Clerke, without any allowance of purgation at all[i].) Which things shall more largely be made appeare unto you out of the Statutes and Canons to be cited in the ensuing discourse. Of the further nature of Clergie, see *S. Hen. Finch* his *Booke Of Law. lib.* 4. *pag.* 462. For I have tarried long enough on that point. Yet before I pass to the next, be pleased that I set before you the forme of a *Proclamation* used to be sent out and published before purgation, as I met it in an old manuscript booke in my keeping, intituled

b Tit. 15. de purgatione canonica & vulgari.

i The ætiology of this see in the Reformatio. legum ecclesiastic. de Purgatione. cap. 4

Litera proclamatoria seu citatoria quorum interest.

W. Permissione divina Conventualis ecclesiæ Westm' Abbas humilis discreto viro Decano de B. salutem & mutuum in Domino charitatis affectum. Instat apud nos W. de A. clericus super crimine homicidii per ipsum (ut imponitur) in villa de B. perpetrati, in Curia laicali coram non suo judice, de facto dampnatus, nobisque adjudicandus secundum libertates ecclesiasticas liberatus, & carceri nostro, prout moris est, vinculis mancipatus, ut sibi ob ecclesiasticæ libertatis honorem, paternæ solicitudinis officio assistentes, ipsius clerici purgationem super imposito sibi crimine canonicè recipere dignaremur. Volentes igitur dicto clerico in sua justa petitione, quatenus cum justitia poterimus nostri officii debitum impartiri, ceterisque quorum interest, plenam & celerem exhibere justitiam in hac parte: discretionem vestram sub mutuæ vicissitudinis obtentu requirimus & rogamus in juris subsidium, quatenus tribus diebus dominicis proximis post receptionem præsentium, in ecclesiis de B. & C. & aliis convicinis publicè & solempniter denuntietis seu denuntiari faciatis, si qui dictum clericum super facinore memorato accusare, seu aliter procedere voluerint, contra eundem, seu reclamare quominus ipsius purgationem in forma juris admittere, & ad ejus liberationem procedere non debeamus, coram nobis vel Commissario nostro compareant in ecclesiæ nostra Conventuali Westm' proximo die Juridico post festum O. S. propositura & ostensuri in forma canonica, causas siquas habeant quare dictam purgationem ejusdem W. super dicto crimine (ut præmittitur) diffamati in forma juris admittere, & ad ejus liberationem procedere non debeamus, ac etiam audituri & facturi in præmissis quod juris fuerit, & consonum rationi, alioquin in dicto negotio procedetur quatenus de jure poterit & debebit, eorum absentiâ non obstante qualiter autem, &c.

To this place belongs the Writ called *Terris, bonis & catallis rehabendis post purgationem.* For which see the *Interpreter, in Litera. T.* I leave it to the learned to informe and satisfie themselves in this first *Particular* by many learned treatises written on this subject, especially of late by occasion of the *Venetian Controversie.* And so I passe to the second *Particular,* namely the *forme how this Priviledge is put in practice,* that is, the *Formalities* used at and about the demanding and allowing of *Clergie* here in *England.* But these are so common to be seene at every *Assises* and *Sessions,* and so obvious in many mens writings, that I shall not need to make their recital take up any part of my discourse. I leave them therefore, and invite you to my next *Particular.*

2. Particular.

The *Antiquity of this Priviledge here in England.* As concerning which I finde that *Matthew Paris* makes mention of it in the dayes of *Hen.* 2. in these words. *Quod de cætero clericus non trahatur ante Judicem secularem personaliter pro aliquo crimine vel transgressione, nisi pro forestâ & laico feodo, unde Regi vel alii Domino seculari laicum debetur servitium*[k]. The Antiquity of this priviledge also shewes it selfe by many of the provinciall *Constitutions,* for example, by *c. Item statuimus,* and *c. si aliqui. de Pœnis.* as likewise by *c. contingit de Judiciis,* all made by *Boniface* Archbishop of *Canterbury An. Dom.* 1261. and other the like. And indeed the Antiquity of it is plainely seene in *Beckets* dayes. For albeit the King and his Ministers opposed and resisted it, yet then, if not sooner, it began to take roote here in *England.* And however by his *Customs* or *Articles of Clerendon,* the Kings purpose was to put it downe, and take it away, yet, in part of his penance for the death of the Archbishop, these Articles that originally were the occasion of the murder were by himselfe revoked[l], So as it may be said to have prevailed at that time, as it were, *in contradictorio judicio.* And not only so but afterward, by degrees, through the means of succeeding Archbishops (*Stephen Langton* especially, and *Boniface,* stout Prelates both) backed by the *Pope* and his *Canons,* it did take place so farre, as that, not onely after the publication of *Magna Charta,* it was ever construed and conceived to be a Church-liberty[m], but also sithence, beside the participation that it had with the rest of the Church-liberties in generall in their allowance by the often iterated confirmation of that *Grand-Charter,* it became at length established by many particular Acts of Parliament, as first of all by that of the 3. *Ed.* 1. *c.* 2. following within little more then twenty yeares after the making of the great Charter. The next whereunto (from which we may argue the allowance of it) is that of the 4. *Ed.* 1. *c.* 5. Thirdly it obtained expresse confirmation by the Stat. of *Articuli Cleri.* 9. *Ed.* 2. *c.* 15. & 16. But my purpose being onely in this place to shew

3. Particular.

k Matth. Paris. in Hen. 2.

l Antiquitat. Britan. in vita Thomæ Becket.

m Vide Stat. 4. H. 4. c. 3.

*O

the

the *Antiquitie* of this priviledge, and not to make any larger Catalogue of the Acts of Parliament that have *de tempore in tempus* confirmed it to the Church, then may serve to prove the same to have once, and that how long since, beene in it numbers absolute here in this land, therefore enough of this.

4. *Particular.* Come we now to the extent of this Priviledge. Touching which I must needs say that the Canon-law (as all know) affords it onely to Clerkes in orders. Secondly, that, for ought that I can finde, there is not any Statute of this land that *ex professo* hath granted or extended it to laymen, onely the Stat. 4. *Hen.* 7. *c.* 13. and some other since imply it. How is it then that heretofore and at this day laymen lay hold of, and have the benefit of this priviledge? Surely, by Custome, which as *Harpsfield* [n] writing of *Hen.* 7. witnesses, first set footing here in those dayes. *Quin & hoc* (saith he) *his temporibus in Anglia obtinuit, ut si quis legere potuisset, & si nullo sacro ordini foret initiatus, pari potiretur privilegio.* Now how this Custome came up I freely confesse I am to learne, and one would wonder how lay-men should come to share with Clerkes in their so peculiar priviledge. *Polydor Virgil* making mention of it, saith because *Clericis affines* [o]. But in my poore opinion haply thus. Because an evident great favour and benefit redounded to Clergy-men in the enjoying of this priviledge, in that notwithstanding their conviction before the secular Magistrate, they might escape without punishment (at least of death, and losse of Member) in case they were able canonically to purge themselves before their Ordinary. And because also by the Canon-law, it belonged to the Church and ecclesiasticall Judge to handle the plea of Clergie, namely whether the offender be indeed (as in word he affirmes himselfe to be) a Clerke [p]. Therefore, in favour of lay men, who could not but take it much to heart to see Clerkes by this their immunity to escape, they themselves the whilest for want of it, suffering; and no lesse in favour of life; the secular Magistrates admitting and conniving at their plea, or their Ordinaries plea for them, of Clergy, permitted them as Clerkes to have the benefit of Clergy, in case (to colour over the matter) they could but read like a Clerke (the Booke being made as it were *Umpire* betweene the two Judges:) the Ordinaries in the interim, for the inlargement of their Jurisdiction readily condiscending, and after common practice had in processe of time given it the force of a Custome and so of a law, being constrained to make no difference in this point of Clerks and Laics that would pray their Clergy, but to challenge, claime and require them all alike, so far forth (namely in such cases) as the Statutes of the land have not disallowed nor restrained the same. *Ita mihi videtur, correctione alterius melius me sentientis semper salva.* And so inclining towards an end of this discourse, I desire you to hearken to the last of my five *Particulars.*

n Hist. ecclef. Angl.

o Hist. Angl. lib. 26.

p C. Si Iudex. de senten. excom. lib. 6.

5. *Particular.* *The declining and waning of this Priviledge by degrees, and restrained condition thereof with us at this day.* To demonstrate which I will tye my selfe to speake even wholly out of the Statutes and Canons of this our Realme: ordering them so, as that out of them you may see this point historically lead along from beginning to end. Turning then with me the old saying *Religio peperit divitias, & filia devoravit matrem,* into *Immunitas peperit impunitatem, & filia &c* [q]. you shall see this plainly verified in the subsequent story. If you have beene versed in *Beckets* story, you cannot but know that this immunity stood then generally accused of begetting impunity, and instances of it are there given in some Clerkes that escaped punishment altogether, or, if any, suffered but slight paines nothing answerable to the quality of their faults by vertue of this exemption, which thing caused the Kings so eager oppugning thereof. Now no course or provision (that I can find) was taken for remedying this abuse either by the Church or State afterwards, untill that *Boniface* aforesaid in the yeare 1261. made and set out a *provinciall Constitution* [r] commanding and injoyning Bishops in their Diocesses to erect and have one or more Prison or Prisons for the safe keeping of Clergy-malefactors. Providing withall that if any Clerke be so incorrigible, and accustomed to commit wickednesse, such as for which, if he were a layman, he should by the lawes of the land suffer death, that he shall be adjudged to perpetuall imprisonment, &c. This *Constitution,* whether for want of execution, or because it was not penall enough, did not afterwards generally serve turne to keepe Clerkes within compasse, as may be gathered out of the very second Statute [s] that makes mention of this priviledge. For there, to the end the King should not need to provide any other remedy therein, he admonisheth and enjoyneth the Prelates, upon the faith which they owe to him, and for the common profit and peace of the Realme, that Clerkes convict of felony delivered over to the Ordinary shall not be delivered without due purgation: which argueth a remissnesse this way in Ordinaries in former time. This Stat. being made in the yeare 1275. within three yeares after, namely *Ann. Dom.* 1278. the Prelates assembled in Convocation, consult, conclude upon and make a *Constitution* [t] providing against the tooeasie enlargement of criminous Clerkes, and the admission of slight and slender purgations for them, and injoyning a solemnity and wary exactnesse to be used therein, so that no occasion of offence be offered to the King or his Ministers through the non observance of this *Constitution.* Had not both these last mentioned Stat. and Constit. laine neglected without execution, as it should seeme (by the preamble of the Stat. 23. *Hen.* 8. *c.* 1.) they did, they might haply have beene the last that needed to have beene made of this

q Ut partus ille viperinus, de quo Plinius. lib. 10. c. 62.

r Cap. Item Statuimus de pœnis. in Provincial.

s 3 Ed. 1. cap. 2.

t Cap. Clerici de Purgatio. Canon. in Provincial.

nature.

nature. But becaufe they wrought not that good effect which was hoped and expected, therefore in the 25. of *Ed.* 3. another Stat. *(viz. c.* 1.) is inacted, and (as I gather by it) upon this occafion, *viz.* Becaufe that Clerkes were fuffered, by Ordinaries, upon flight purgations, to be inlarged and difmiffed, to their incouragement to offend againe, therefore the fecular Magiftrates debarred them their Clergy, and *fine delectu perfonarum,* punifhed them and laymen all alike. Now complaint being made hereof in Parliament by the Prelates, this Stat. was agreed upon and made, whereby for redreffe of the injury offered to the Church and Church-men, provifion is firft made for the priviledge of it and them, and then enfueth a promife made in their behalfe by the then Archbifhop of *Cant.* (*Simon Iflep*) to the King, that he will make a convenient Ordinance, whereby Clericall offenders delivered to the Ordinaries fhall be fafely kept and duely punifhed, fo that no Clerke fhall take courage to offend for default of correction. The performance of which his pro-mife you fhall finde recorded and teftified by a Succeffor of his, the *Author* of the *Anti-quitates Britannicæ,* in the life of the fame *Simon* pag. 244. under the yeare of Grace 1351. As alfo by *Harpsfield* in his *Ecclef. Hift. p.* 532. whofe fevere Conftitution made in that behalfe, if you defire to fee, although you will not finde it (I know not why) incorporated into *Linwoods Provincial,* yet is it extant amongft the Provinciall Conftitutions placed and annexed at the latter end of the Legatine Conftitutions, in fome Bookes (in mine *Fol.* 150.) I mufe therefore why the Stat. 4. *H.* 4. *c.* 3. fhould about 50. yeares after the date of it, call for fuch a Conftitution, as if it had beene yet unmade, and the old promife of the Archbifhop not hitherto performed. For fo the Stat. intimates, in fo much as the then Archbifhop *Thomas Arundell* was faine to renew the promife in Parliament, which notwith-ftanding was neither by himfelfe nor by any other fucceeding Archbifhop performed, as is teftified and avouched by the forecited Stat. 23. *H.* 8. *c.* 1. And thus much of the firft part of the *Apothegme. Immunitas peperit impunitatem.*

Great now had the patience of the King and State beene in expecting the reformation of fuch abufes as grew by reafon of this ecclefiafticall priviledge, and a long time had the fecular arme forborne to apply a temporall, but more terrible remedie and animadverfion. So that now, fith neither the former Conftitutions of the Church could keepe the Clergie in awe (as indeed how is it likely they fhould, the Authors of them not having *gladii poteftatem* [u] ?) neither the ingeminated threats of applying a temporall remedy to curbe their extravagancies, would make them and others, partakers with them in their priviledge, to beware, it was now high time to clip the wings of this mafterleffe liberty by reftraint. For untill the fourth yeare of *H.* 7. we fhall finde no Act of Parliament that hath any whit derogated or taken away from this priviledge. But then (which brings on the latter part of the Apothegme. *Filia devoravit matrem*) becaufe that in confidence and truft of the priviledge of the Church, divers perfons had beene the more bold to commit murder, rape, robbery, theft and all other mifchievous deeds, becaufe they have beene continually ad-mitted to the benefit of the Clergie, as often as they did offend in any of the premiffes (as the preamble of the Stat. 4. *H.* 7. *c.* 13. runneth) therefore, for avoiding of fuch boldneffe, it is enacted that the benefit of Clergie fhall be but once allowed to any per-fon not being within orders, and that convicted perfons (to the end, as I fuppofe, it may be knowne whether they have had their Clergy once before, or not) fhall be marked with the letter *M.* for murder, or *F.* for any other felony, and that to be done openly in the Court, before he be delivered to the Ordinary. Thus for Lay-clerkes. Now for Clerkes in orders, it alfo provides, that if upon their fecond asking of their Clergie, they have not their letters of orders, or a certificate from their Ordinary witneffing the fame, ready to fhow, or doe produce the one or the other by a day given them by the Juftices to bring them in, then to loofe the benefit of their Clergie as he fhall doe that is with-out orders.

[u] Duaren de facr. ecclef. minifter. & benef. lib. 1. c. 4.

This Act (it fhould appeare) was not ftrict enough to bridle the infolencies of fome Clergie-men and others that bare themfelves upon the priviledge of Clergie. In the 23d yeare therefore of the next King (*H.* 8.) his reigne, the Parliament having in the pream-ble of the Stat. 23. *ejufd. H. cap.* 1. enumerated many feverall promifes iterated and made by the prelates to take courfe within themfelves, and by their owne power and authority without any need of the States helpe to fuppreffe the infolencies of fuch malefactors, as upon confidence of Clergy dared the committing of almoft whatfoever foule enormities and outrages, and declared how thefe promifes were fruftrate and came to none effect, and withall complained of the many abufes of Ordinaries in and about purgations. For remedy, they inact that Clergy fhall be taken quite away from all perfons that are not within holy orders, which fhall commit petit treafon, wilful murder, and many the like felonies. And as for perfons in orders, none (faith the Statute) that fhall be convict of any the felonies therein mentioned fhall be fuffered to make purgation before his Ordi-nary, but fhall remaine and abide in perpetuall prifon under the keeping of the Ordi-nary, unleffe he become bound with fureties (fuch as the Stat. there alloweth and ac-cepteth of) for his good abearing, with certaine other claufes and provifoes. Amongft which one is for the degrading of Clerkes convict, and fending them to the Kings bench, there to fuffer judgement to dye, as lay-men. You fee this priviledge now brought pretty low, yet it ftoopes lower, and now comes to be almoft quite eclipfed. For befides many feve-rall Acts of Parliament [*] between the laft fpoken of, and the 28. *H.* 8. *c.* 1. taking it away from

[*] 23. H. 8. c. 11. & 25. H. 8. c. 3. & 5.

from divers forts of felonies. By this Act of 28. *H. 8. 1.* Clerkes in orders are brought under the fame paines and penalties that others be, which being but temporall, and made to endure onely unto the laft day of the next Parliament, when that time came about, was by the Stat. 32. *H. 8. cap. 3.* as good and beneficiall for the common wealth made perpetual. By which laft Act, over and above, in expreffe words, it is decreed that Clerkes in orders, in fuch manner as lay-clerkes are wont to be, fhall be burnt in the hand for fuch felonies as they may or ought to have their Clergie for.

This priviledge being brought thus low rofe up no more. For after the laft mentioned Stat. came that of 1. *Ed. 6. c. 12.* where as large an enumeration is made what offences fhall exclude their Authors of their Clergie, as in the former. It fuffered yet daily further reftraint. For afterwards Statutes upon Statutes, one at the heele, and in the necke of another take it from this and tother offender, as *Raftals Kalender*, in *verbo Clergy* will fully direct, as alfo will *Lambards Eirenarcha. pag. 540.* and fo forward, to which I referre you. For

Conveniunt cymbæ vela minora meæ.

And now, to fet before you that which principally hath divefted and outed the Church of her Jurifdiction over fuch as were and are to reape benefit by this priviledge, and to fhew unto you how the ancient courfe of the law in the point of delivering Clerkes to their Ordinaries to be purged, came to be altered. I have to acquaint you that the Stat. of 18. *Eliz. c. 6.* (the caufes and motives for making whereof are in the preamble expreffed, amongft the reft, to be thefe, *viz.* the avoyding of fundry perjuries and other abufes in and abour the purgation of Clerkes convict delivered to the Ordinaries) hath quite taken away purgation, untill that time ever accuftomed, ordaining withall that no Man, that fhall be allowed his Clergie, fhall be committed to the Ordinary, but prefently enlarged (after allowance of Clergy and burning in the hand:) Providing neverthelefle that the Juftices for the Offenders further correction, may retaine him in prifon for a time. Thus have you feene how this priviledge hath declined and beene brought downe to the prefent defpicable condition wherein it is with us at this day. Remaines fo meane, as by them the once flourifhing eftate of it will hardly gain beleefe. Truly then

Quod fuit in pretio, fit nullo denique honore.

Quarles Hift. of Jonah, Meditat. 10.

Suffer me to conclude this difcourfe with his fweet meditation, who making Gods mercy the fubject of his contemplation, in allufion to this practice and allowance of Clergy to convicted Prifoners, thus ejaculates.

Like pinion'd prifoners at the dying tree,
Our lingring hopes attend and waite on thee;
(Arraign'd at Juftice barre) prevent our doome;
To thee with joyful hearts we cheerly come;
Thou art our Clergy; Thou that deareft booke,
Wherein our fainting eyes defire to looke.
In thee we truft to read (what will releafe us)
In bloudy characters, that name of Jefus.

Numb. XLIV.

Bulla fuper Canonizatione Domini Roberti Cantuar. Archiepifcopi miffa Domino Thomæ Comiti Lancaftriæ.

JOhannes Epifcopus fervus fervorum, &c. Dilecto filio Thomæ Comiti Lancaftriæ, &c. Porro circa id quod de Canonizatione fanctæ memoriæ Roberti nuper Cant. Archiepifcopi fupplicafti, Scire te volumus quod Romana mater ecclefia non confuevit fuper tanta caufa præfertim præcipitanter aliquid agere, quin potius tale negotium folempnis examinationis indagine ponderare, propter quod fi negotium ipfum credideris promovendum, oportet quod illud coram fratribus noftris in Confiftorio per folempnes perfonas ex parte Prælatorum Cleri & populi Anglicani vitam, merita, atque miracula ipfius Archiepifcopi atteftantium fpecialiter deftinatas folempniter proponatur, fupplicatione fubjuncta, ut inquifitio hujufmodi de vita mirabili, miraculis etiam & meritis gloriofis perfonis idoneis committatur, ut juxta exitum inquifitionis ipfius canonizatio fieri debeat vel omitti, &c.

Numb. XLV.

The Fees of the Earl of Glocefter in refpect of his Offices of Steward and Butler at the Inthronization Feaft of an Archbifhop.

ISta pertinent ad feod. Comitis Gloverniæ pro officio fenefcalli, die intronizationis cujufli-bet Archiepifcopi Cantuar. fi tamen fummonitus fuerit, & venerit ad faciendum fervitium fuum & non aliter.
Idem Comes habebit de Archiepifcopo vij robas de fearleto.
Item xxx. fextarios vini.   Item

Item l. libras ceræ ad luminare fuum proprium pro toto festo.

Item liberationem feni & avenæ ad lxxx equos per 2. noctes tantum.

Item discos & salsaria quæ affidebit coram Archiepiscopo ad primum ferculum.

Item post festum perendinationem trium dierum cum l. equis tantum, sumptibus Archiepis-copi, ubi idem Comes eligere voluerit de proximis maneriis dicti Archiepiscopi ad fan-guinem minuendum.

Ista pertinent ad feod. ejusdem Comitis, pro Officio Pincernar. die supradicto, si tamen, &c.

Idem Comes habebit vij robas de scarleto.

Item xx sextarios vini.

Item l. libras ceræ.

Item liberationem feni & avenæ ad lx equos per 2 noctes tantum.

Item cuppam qua serviet coram Archiep. die festi.

Item omnia dolia evacuata

Item habebit sex dolia si tot potata fuerint viz. subtus barram, in crastino festi computo re-cepto, & licet plura dolia sic potata fuerint, sex tantum inde habebit, & residuum Archie-piscopo remanebit.

Et nota quòd in intronizatione Roberti de Kilewardby Archiepiscopi, prædict' Comes habuit primò prædicta feoda : & tunc habuit unum mantellum cum penula. Et postea in intronizatione I. de Peckam Archiepiscopi habuit duos mantellos.

Ista maneria tenet prædict. comes pro dicto officio senescalli faciend. viz. Tonebregg, cum castro & handlo cum pertinen. & totam leucatam.

Ista maneria tenet prædict. comes pro officio Pincernar. viz. Bradestede. Vieleston. Horsmandenne. Melton & Pectes.

Numb.
XLVI.

Sudburiæ natus Simon jacet hic tumulatus
Martyrizatus nece pro republica stratus.
Heu scelus infernum, crux, exitiale, nefandum
Præsulis eximii corpus venerabile dandum
In rabiem vulgi ————

Numb.
XLVII.

The Record of Archbishop Winchelsey *his Inthronization, shewing in and after what forme the Archbishops of* Canterbury *anciently were inthronized: and thence intitled.*

Forma Inthronizationis Archiepiscopi.

Die Dominico post festum sancti Michaelis, viz. vj Non. Octob. Anno Dom. 1294. Archiepiscopus Inthronizatus fuit ab Henrico tunc Priore Ecclsiæ Christi Cantuar. forma sequenti.

EOdem die summo mane, conventus primam, & totum servitium usque ad magnam missam celebrarunt, & postea, cappis induti, in choro Dominum Archiepiscopum ex-pectarunt qui in manerio conventus apud Chertham illa nocte & per quinque dies præce-dentes moram fecerat continuam. Cumque venisset Archiepiscopus ad portam Cimiterii de equo descendit, & Prior sacris indutus pallium ipsius Archiepiscopi de manu cujusdam clerici ejusdem Archiepiscopi in panno mundo plicatum recepit, & dictum pallium deplicavit & illud Capellano prius cum Conventu revestito tradidit deferendum, qui in vase argenteo panno serico candidissimo cooperto pallium deplicatum, manu erecta, conventu præcedente coram Archiepiscopo & Priore ad magnum altare solempniter deportavit, & super illud posuit. Conventu verò in Choro remanente Archiepiscopus ante magnum altare se prostravit orando. Completa oratione & data populo benedictione, Cantor Te Deum incepit. Pallio verò su-per altare remanente, & conventu in choro Te Deum canente Archiepiscopus ad sedem suam ligneam in choro interim declinavit. Quo cantato, Prior, deinde singuli per ordinem ad al-tare accedentes pallium osculabantur deinde Archiepiscopum. Hiis peractis pallium in Ve-stiarium delatum est : & Archiepiscopus ad cameram suam declinavit. Cumque Dominus Rex de Sancto Augustino venisset, & Ecclesiam intrasset, Archiepiscopus solempnioribus pon-tificalibus in Vestiario indutus & pallio redimitus, cum Priore, & tribus Diaconis, & tribus Sub-diaconis Cardinalibus chorum intravit. Ad cujus introitum, Cantor Bs' * Deum time in-cepit, quod conventus solempniter decantavit. Interim verò Archiepisc. & Prior & prædicti Ministti Altaris stationem fecerunt retro magnum altare sub feretro beati Blasii coram sede marmorea versi ad Orientem. Rex verò juxta sedem prædictam stando cum multis nobili-bus Regni Archiepiscopum expectavit Rseio * verò percantato, Prior subjunxit collectam. Dominus qui de excelso cælorum. & dicta collecta, Prior Archiepiscopum usque ad prædictam sedem marmoream perduxit. Et facta modica statione coram sede, Prior subjunxit aliam collectam. Omnipotens sempiterne Deus. Dicta vero collecta, Prior dictum Archiepisco-pum inter brachia sua reverenter recepit, & ipsum in sede prædicta intronizavit per verba

Sedes lignea Ar-chiepiscopi.

Subdiaconi Car-dinales.
* lege, Reponso-rium.

Feretrum beati Blasii. Sedes marmorea.

* lege, Respon-sorio.

* P
sub-

ſubſcripta quæ legit in cedula quam manu tenebat. *In Dei nomine Amen. Authoritate. ejuſdem ego Henricus Prior iſtius Eccleſiæ Chriſti Cantuar. intronizo te Dominum Robertum Archiepiſcopum in hac Cant. Eccleſia, in qua idem Dominus noſter Jeſus Chriſtus cuſtodiat introitum tuum ex hoc nunc & uſque in ſeculum Amen.* Lecta cedula vocatiſque teſtibus, Prior rogavit quendam Notarium Publicum quod præmiſſa omnia in publicam formam redigeret, ad memoriam futurorum. Hiis peractis, octo monachi cantum Benedictus coram Archiepiſcopo in Cathedra ſedente ſub feretro ſancti Blaſii alternatim decantaverunt. Qno cantato, Prior collectam ſubjunxit. *Omnipotens ſempiterne Deus.* Qua dicta, Cantor Officium Miſſæ de Trinitate ſolempniter incepit. Archiepiſcopus coram ſede ſua verſus ad Orientem incepit *Gloria in excelſis,* & poſtea ibidem collectam miſſæ ſubjunxit, & lecto Evangelio, *Credo* ibidem incepit, & poſtea *Dominus vobiſcum* ibidem ſubjunxit. Cantato verò officio, de ſede ſua deſcendit, & ante magnum Altare venit, & oblationem panis & vini à Cantore prout moris eſt recepit, & extunc totam miſſam ibidem complevit, nec poſtea illo die ad ſedem ſuam eſt reverſus. Miſſa celebrata indulgentias populo conceſſit, & ſacris veſtibus in veſtiario exutus, cameram ſuam intravit, & veſtibus feſtivalibus ad aulam magnam in palatio ſuo declinavit pranſurus. Rege verò autem ingreſſo diſcubuerunt omnes & ſpendide ſunt refecti. Poſtmodum * vero Rex & Archiepiſcopus ac etiam omnes Prælati & Proceres cameram Archiepiſcopi in Palatio ſunt ingreſſi, ſpecies. ita Mſ. ――― prout moris eſt poſt cibum ſumpturi. Deinde Rex ad S. Auguſtinum rediit, & Archiepiſc. in camera ſua remanſit. Cæteri vero omnes ad propria cum gaudio ſunt reverſi. Prædictæ vero intronizationi interfuerunt Dominus Edwardus Rex Angliæ, & E. filius ſus, & E. frater ejuſdem Regis, ac etiam London'. Lincoln'. Hereford', Elyen', Norwicen', Roffen' & Dunelm' Epiſcopi. Et Glovec', Lincoln', Penebr', Mareſeal', Hereford' & Warewik' Comites, ac etiam innumeroſa multitudo aliorum Prælatorum & Procerum Regni.

Aula magna Palatii.
* *lege poſt prandium.*

Numb. XLVIII.

Charta Reſtitutionis Monachorum a Rege Johanne.

JOhannes Dei gratia Rex Angliæ, Dominus Hiberniæ, Dux Normanniæ & Aquitanniæ & Comes Andeg. Omnibus Vicecomitibus, & Forreſtariis, & Ballivis ſuis ſalutem. Præcipimus volentes quod Priorem & Monachos Cant. pacificè habere permittatis omnes libertates & liberas conſuetudines ſuas in Ballivis veſtris ſicut habuerunt tempore inchoatæ diſcordiæ inter nos & ipſos. Teſte meipſo apud Winton xx die Julii.

Numb. XLIX.

Carmen ſepulchrale Nicolai de Sandwico:

Reſpice: care: mere: rogo: defuncti: miſerere:
Sandwicenſis: vivens: frater: memor: en: ſis.
Qui: nunc: in: Limo: : e: ſtricte: jacet: ymo:
Dic: Pater: hinc: &: Ave: Deus: hunc: &: protegat: a: ve:
Omni: ne: baratri: penas: ſibi: ſentiat: atri:
Set: celi: ſolio: requieſcat: in: agmine: pio:
Omnis: orans: ita: letetur: perpete: vita: Amen.

Numb. L.

A Charter of Freedom from Tallage.

Anno Domini Mcclxix. fuit declaratum quod Abbas non debet talliari in Civitate ſub tali forma. Rogerus Abbas ſancti Aug. Cant. Prior Eccleſiæ Chriſti Cant. & Prior ſancti Gregorii, & magiſter Hamo Doge perquiſiverunt breve Domini Regis direct' Baronibus de ſcaccario quod Vicecomes Kanc' venire faceret 6. de diſcretioribus hominibus villæ Cant. & 6. tam milites quam alios liberos & legales homines de vicineto ejuſdem villæ per quos rei veritas melius ſciri poterit ad certificandum eoſdem Barones ſi prædicti Abbas &c. & eorum predeceſſores unquam talliari conſueverunt ratione tenementorum quæ habent in Cant. vel non. Et poſtea venit inquiſitio per Rogerum de Northwood, Ricardum de Pontefracto milites & alios qui dixerunt ſuper ſacramentum ſuum quod prædicti Abbas & Priores nunquam talliari conſueverunt cum Burgenſibus ejuſdem villæ ratione tenementorum ſuorum prædictorum. Dixerunt etiam quod anteceſſores prædicti Hamonis Doge ratione mercandiſarum ſuarum quas fecerunt in eadem Civitate talliari conſueverunt, ſed ipſe non quia nullas exercuit mercandiſas & ideo conceſſum eſt quod prædicti Abbas & Priores ab hujuſm' tallag' ſint quieti. Unde H. Rex Vicec. Cantii ſic. Conſtat nobis per inquiſitionem quam nuper fieri fecimus quod Abbas & alii ſuperiùs nominati nunquam conſueverunt talliari ratione tenementorum ſuorum quæ habent in eadem villa, quando cives ejuſdem Civitatis talliati fuerunt. Ideo tibi præcipimus quod de demanda quam facis per ſummonitionem ſcaccarii noſtri prædictis Abbati & Prioribus de tall' ratione tenementorum ſuorum quæ habent ibidem pacem habere permittas: Et averia ſua ſeu catella ſi quæ capta fuerint occaſione prædicta eis deliberari facias, &c.

A

A Petition to the Pope for Autority to create Notaries. Numb. LI.

Significat fanctitati veftræ Prior Ecclefiæ Chtifti Cant. quod per fedem Apoftolicam frequenter committuntur eidem Priori Caufæ & negotia audienda & difcutienda, ac etiam Delegatorun fententiæ exequendæ : propter quæ neceffarium eft fibi ufus & officium Tabellion' & quia in Civitate & Dioc. Cant. rariffimè haberi poteft copia tabellionum : fupplicat fanctitati veftræ Prior prædictus quod placeat vobis gratiofè concedere fibi poteftatem faciendi duos tabelliones.

A Grant of power delegated to the Prior of Chrift-Church by a Count Palatine, to create Notaries. Numb. LII. a.

VEnerabili in Chrifto Patri Priori Ecclefiæ Chrifti Cantuar. Baffyanus de Allyate de Mediolan' Dei gratia Comes Palatinus Salutem & debitam diligentiam in commiffis. Sagax humanæ naturæ difcretio, memoriâ hominum labilitate penfatâ, ne diuturnitate temporum quæ inter contrahentes aguntur oblivionis defectui fubjacerent, tabellionatus adinvenit officium, per quod contrahentium vota fcribuntur & fcripturæ minifterio poftmodum longum fervantur in ævum. Cum itaque ex parte veftra nobis extitit humiliter fupplicatum, ut vobis poteftatem creandi-tres tabelliones feu notarios publicos concedere dignaremur. Nos hujufmodi fupplicationibus in hac parte favorabiliter annuentes, præfatam poteftatem ufque ad dictum numerum paternitati veftræ authoritate nobis & anteceſſoribus noftris à divis Imperatoribus fuper conficiendis tabellionibus feu notariis publicis conceffa plenariè duximus concedendam, veftram paternitatem ad hujufmodi poteftatem obtinendam approbantes. Verum quia volumus quod forma folita in creatione notariorum obfervetur, ne minus idonei & infufficientes ad hujufmodi officium exercendum deputentur, diligenti examinatione præmiffa, eofdem quos creare volueritis per Pennam, Calamarium atque Cartam quæ tunc in manibus tenebitis præfentialiter inveftiatis, recepto prius ab eifdem tribus figillatim, facri Imperii nomine, fidelitatis folitæ, nec non & de ipfo tabellionatus officio fideliter & legaliter exercendo, corporali Juramento. Dantes & concedentes unicuique illorum trium authoritate vobis, tenore præfentium, ut fuperius exprimitur, conceffa, plenam licentiam & liberam poteftatem Inftrumenta, acta, prothocolla, & literas exemplandi, faciendi, copiandi & publicandi teftes recipiendi, & examinandi ac publicandi, teftamenta conficiendi apperiendi & approbandi, confeffiones fuper quibufcunque contractibus audiendi & recipiendi, & infinuandi & fcribendi ultimas decedentium voluntates, tutores & curatores dandi, alimenta decernendi, decretum interponendi & faciendi ac fcribendi quælibet alia Inftrumenta & fcripturas five contractus tam ultimarum voluntatum, quam quorumcunque aliorum negotiorum, & Tabellionatus officium libere, prudenter & fideliter ubilibet exercendi, & omnia alia & fingula fcribendi & faciendi, quæ ad fæpedictum officium fpectare nofcuntur vel etiam pertinere. Et ad unumquemque eorundem trium cum neceffe fuerit, in omnibus & fingulis fupradictis, & quæ ad officium prædictum pertinent liberè recurratur. Forma autem Juramenti per unumquemque eorundem trium talis erit, dicatur etiam fic cuilibet figillatim. Tu jurabis ad fancta Dei Evangelia quod nunquam eris contrarius Romanæ Ecclefiæ, nec imperio, nec nobis, nunquam falfam facies cartam. Teftamentum autenticum & omnia ea quæ autenticari debent non autenticabis in cartis abrafis, bombacinis vel papyris. Contractus verò, acta caufarum, teftamenta, donationes, & omnia ea quæ ad artem & officium notarii pertinent, prout audiveris & rogatus fueris, manu propria, cum tuo nomine & figno fcribes & autenticabis. Dicta quoque teftium bona fide, fine fraude fcribes & recipies, & generaliter omnia alia & fingula quæ ad ipfam artem & officium not' fpectant juxta fidelitatem & officii confuetudinem fideliter ac integraliter obfervare jurabis. In quorum omnium teftimonium & certitudinem pleniorem præfens privilegium in forma publici Inftrumenti fieri mandavimus per notarium infrafcriptum, & noftri figilli fecimus appenfione muniri. Dat' & act' Lugd. in Ecclefia majori, fub anno Domini Milleſimo trecenteſimo fexto, die v. menfis Martii, Indictione iv. tempore Domini Clemen. PP. quinti anno primo, præfentibus difcretis viris Albertino filio dicti Comitis laico & Vitale Fagiani clerico Medioln' Dioc. teftibus ad hoc fpecialiter vocatis & rogatis.

(marginal notes:) Caufæ conceffionis. Conceffio. Formalia creationis Notar. Forma Juramenti per notarium præftandi.

Et ego Willielmus Thomæ dicti Coci de Ros clericus Hereford. Dioc. publicus facri Romani Imperii authoritate Notar' omnibus prædictis interfui, & de dicti comitis mandato prefens privilegium fcripfi, & publicavi, meoque figno confueto fignavi rogatus.

A for-

A Forme *or* Faculty *of a* Notaries *creation by vertue of the
precedent delegation.*

HEnricus permiffione divina Prior Ecclefiæ Chrifti Cantuar. Dilecto fibi in Chrifto Johanni de Watford clerico Lincoln' Dioc. Salutem, & in agendis viam veritatis. Hü funt ad officia publica meritò promovendi, quos morum honeftas, literarum peritia & factorum exper entia fufficientes reddunt ad laborum faftigia, & folicitudines publicas fubeundas. Cum igitur Dominus Baffyanus de Alliate de Mediolano Comes Palatinus nobis poteftatem creandi tres tabelliones feu notarios publicos authoritate eidem Domino Baffiano & antecefforibus fuis à divis Imperatoribus fuper conficiendis tabellionibus feu notariis publicis conceffa, plenariè duxerit concedendam, prout in literis fuis patentibus inde confectis quarum tenor inferius defcribitur plenius continetur. Nofque virtute poteftatis ejufdem, cum exacta diligentiâ, fervatâ formâ in eifdem literis contenta, Ma' Richardum de Northon' Lincoln' Dioc', & Johannem de Berham Cantuarien. Dioc' Tabelliones feu Notarios publicos nuper creavimus, unumque adhuc creare, virtute poteftatis ejufdem, tabellionem feu notarium publicum valeamus : probitatis merita, & fagacitatis induftriam te idoneum redden' ad tabellionatus officium exercendum, quæ & quem, diligenti examinatione præmiffa in te invenimus, attendentes: recepto prius à te ad fancta Dei Evangelia corporaliter juramento fuper omnibus & fingulis articulis fervandis in prædictis patentibus literis contentis, & de tabellionatus officio fideliter & legaliter exercendo, te creamus Tabellionem & Notar' publicum, ac de eodem officio per Pennam, Calamarium atque Cartam quæ in manibus tenemus præfentialiter inveftimus authoritate qua fungimur memoratâ Dantes & concedentes tibi plenam licentiam & liberam poteftatem faciendi & exercendi omnia & fingula quæ in eifdem patentibus literis continentur, & ad Tabellionatus officium fpectare nofcuntur, vel etiam pertinere, & quod ad te, fi neceffe fuerit, in omnibus & fingulis fupradictis & quæ ad prædictum officium pertinent, liberè recurratur. Tenor autem prædictarum literarum talis eft. Venerabili in Chrifto Patri —— Priori Ecclefiæ Chrifti Cant. Baffianus de Alliate de Mediolano Dei gratia Comes Palatinus Salutem, &c. ut fupra. In cujus rei teftimonium & certitudinem pleniorem præmiffa per Hugonem de Byford notarium publicum infrafcriptum in hanc publicam formam redigi mandavimus & figilli noftri appenfione muniri. Dat' & act' apud Waleworth juxta Lamheth Anno Domini Millefimo trecentefimo nono, Indictione octava, vicefimo feptimo die menfis Martii, Præfentibus difcretis viris Johanne de Teneth, Hugone de fancta Margareta, Alexandro de Sandwico monachis Ecclefiæ noftræ prædictæ, Bertino de Twitham Ad. de Thrulegh armigeris noftris literatis teftibus ad hæc vocatis fpecialiter & rogatis.

Et ego Hugo de Byford Clericus Hereford. Dioc. publicus authoritate Imperiali notarius, præmiffis Juramenti præftationi, creationi & invefituræ conceffioni & dationi una cum teftibus prædictis, anno, indictione, die & loco prædictis præfens interfui, & ea omnia prout fupra fcribuntur fieri vidi & audivi, & ad mandatum dicti Domini Prioris in hanc publicam formam redegi, meoque figno confueto fignavi rogatus.

The Kings *writt forbidding fuch Notaries the exercife of their office, and damning the credit of their Inftruments, intituled.*

Breve de Officio Tabellionis authoritate Imperiali non exercendo.

REx Vic. &c. Ex parte Cleri & populi regni noftri gravis relatio noftris auribus infonuit & tumultus, quod licet regnum noftrum Angliæ ab omni fubjectione imperiali fit immune, & aborigenes mundi extiterit alienum, tanta tamen multitudo Notariorum authoritate imperiali officium publicum in Regno noftro prædicto, tam de hiis quorum cognitio ad nos & non ad alium pertinet, quam de aliis, exercentium crevit, quod nobis & juri coronæ noftræ grave exheredations periculum & incolis & habitatoribus dicti Regni noftri dampnum irrecuperabile præfumitur evenire, nifi remedium apponetur in hac parte. Nos igitur volentes hujufmodi dampnis & periculis prout Juramenti vinculo aftringimur pro viribus obviare, & dictum regnum noftrum inde exuere, prout decet, tibi præcipimus quod in fingulis locis infra Ballivam tuam ubi expedire videris publicè proclamari, & ex parte noftra firmiter inhiberi facias, ne quis hujufmodi Notarius, fub pœna quæ incumbit in caufis, contractibus, feu aliis negotiis officium notarii exerceat quoquo modo. Facias autem in dictis locis publicari & diftrictius inhiberi, ne qui Archiepifcopi, Epifcopi feu alii prælati vel eorum Miniftri inftrumentis hujufmodi Notariorum ex nunc faciend. fidem aliquam præbeant ullo modo. T. meipfo apud Weftm' xxvj. die April. Anno Regni noftri xiii.

A

A Composition made Anno 1242. between the Abbey of St. Austins, and the Priory of Christ-Church, about divers things, especially maritime customes at and about Minster and Sandwich.

NOverint universi præsens scriptum inspecturi quod cum inter viros religiosos Dominum Robertum Abbatem & Conventum S. Augustini ex parte una, & Dominum Rogerum Priorem & Capitulum Ecclesiæ Christi Cant. ex altera super terris, redditibus, consuetudinibus maritimis juribus variis & diversis agitata esset diutius materia questionis, tandem de communi voluntate & assensu partium, de consilio virorum prudentum amicabiliter in hunc modum conquievit, viz. quod Abbas & Conventus prænominati pro bono perpetuæ pacis concedunt quod Prior & Capitulum memorati terras & redditus de feodo S. Augustini quas dicebantur hactenus occupasse de cetero habeant tam in Cant. quam extra. Ita tamen quod æquivalentes terras ac redditus permutationis nomine alibi recipiant ab eisdem. Simili modo concedunt Prior & Capitulum memorati Abbati & Conventui prædictis in similibus similem permutationem. Ita tamen quod de cætero neutra pars terras vel redditus alterius partis intrabit, vel sibi appropriare præsumet, nisi licentia super hac petita prius & optenta.
Item pro bono pacis concessum est à Priore & Capitulo antedictis quod de cetero ad Fletum de Menster per flumen de Sandwico sit accessus per navigium & recessus, hoc adjecto, quod si in ipso flumine, ante dictum Fletum aliqua navis anchoram fixerit, vel levandæ navis, vel negotiandi, seu merces alias transferendi causa se ibidem exoneravit, dicti Prior & Capitulum consuetudines maritimas habeant. In Fleto autem antedicto nihil juris de cætero vendicabunt, sed omnes consuetudines & emolumenta libere percipient Abbas & Conventus prædicti ratione fundi in eodem. Ita tamen quod tenentes dictorum Prioris & Capituli liberi sint & quieti ab omni consuetudine de qua hactenus liberi esse consueverunt, nec dictum Fletum malitiosa ampliabunt Abbas & Conventus prædicti in dictorum Prioris & Capituli detrimentum. Simili modo provisum est quod Prior & Capitulum memorati omnes consuetudines maritimas habeant in portu de Sandwico ex utraque parte Fluminis, secundum tenorem & usum cartarum suarum infra terminos in ipsis cartis contentos, quia sic hactenus usi sunt. Ita tamen quod dicti Abbas & Conventus in villa sua de Stanore & in terris suis dominium habeant & usum consuetum: quod si in dicta villa de Stanor sive in terris dictorum Abbatis & conventus sive in flumine infra dictos terminos inter quascunque personas discordiæ vel contentiones emerserint, secundum qualitatem delicti justitia super his fiet sicut hactenus fieri consuevit.
Ultra locum autem qui vocatur Hennebrigge prope Stanor versus Clivesende, Ramesgate, Margate, Westgate, sive in aliis terris dictorum Abbatis & Conventus tam in Thaneto quam extra, & ex alia parte maris in tenemento ipsorum de Northborne Idem Abbas & Conventus omnes consuetudines maritimas ratione applicationis & terræ suæ percipient preterquam ut distinctum est. Ita quod in mari nil juris vel consuetudinis maritimæ percipient præterquam ut distinctum est ratione applicationis & terræ suæ, nec impedient nec procurabunt quo minus dicti Prior & Capitulum per suos Ministros in mari secundum tenorem cartarum suarum & usum, jura & consuetudines maritimas recipere & capere possunt, nec aliquam querent occasionem vel aliquid facient per quod dictorum Prioris & Capituli jura & consuetudines maritimæ infrà suos terminos maris & terræ in aliquo minuantur. Similiter dicti Prior & Capitulum ultra dictum locum qui dicitur Hennebrigge nil juris aut maritimæ consuetudinis quæ dictis Abbati & Conventui ratione applicationis & terræ suæ provenire possunt accipient, vel impedient nec procurabunt quo minus naves quæ applicare voluerint ad tetras dictorum Abbatis & Conventus applicent & consuetudines maritimas reddant quæ ipsis ratione applicationis & terræ suæ debent, nec aliquam quærent occasionem vel facient aliquid per quod dictorum Abbatis & Conventus jura & consuetudines in terris suis in aliquo minuantur sed locis suis utrique libere utantur consuetis. Item concedunt liberaliter Prior & Capitulum memorati quod in navicula ipsorum prædicti Abbas & Conventus & eorum familia propria ————— Item quoniam per clericos recusatos à Capitulo sancti Augustini & à Capitulo Ecclesiæ Christi Cant. aliquando ad monachatum admissos, & è converso, sepius consuevit discordiæ fomes seminari, concessum est ab utrisque quod de cætero ex causa culpæ vel defectus recusatus ab alterutro capitulo à neutro recipiatur.

Margin notes:
Fletum de Menster.
Villa de Stanore.
Hennebrigge. Clivesende. Ramsgate. Margate. Westgate.
Navicula Prior. & Convent.

*A Composition between the same houses about a Kay and house
at Fordwich.*

With such circumstances as are added by the Relator,
Thorne, St Auguftines Chronicler.

A lieger booke of Chrift-Church hath a copie of it in French.
Vidi.

*Caya & domus
apud Fordwich.*

ANno Domini Mcclxxxv. die Lunæ proximo poft feftum Tranflationis fancti Thomæ Martyris fedata eft difcordia quæ mota fuerat inter Abbatem fancti Auguftini & Priorem fanctæ Trinitatis de quadam caya & domo ædificata in quodam prato apud Forwicum per Priorem fanctæ Trinitatis, quæ ædificia Abbas fancti Auguftini deftrui præcepit, quibus iterum per Priorem ibidem ædificatis Abbas fecundo funditus evertit meremio & omnibus aliis ibidem inventis in Sturam. projectis. Unde ad prædictam litem pacificandam Domi-

*Epifcopus de
Verdun. Otes de
Granfonne. Ste-
phanu de Pence-
ftre & alii nobi-
les.*

nis Henrico Epifcopo de Verdun, Otes de Granfonne, Stephano de Penceftr' & aliis nobilibus per Dominum Regem ad hoc fpecialiter affignatis, fub hac forma conquievit, quod Prior pro fe & fuis Succefforibus : conceffit quod in prato verfus Ecclefiam in Oriente de cetero aliquam domum alicujus ædificii fine gratiâ & licentiâ Abbatis nunquam levabit. Et quia prædictus Prior non poteft bene effe fine domo fuper ripam de Fordwico pro fuis vinis & aliis fuis victualibus recipiendis & fervandis Abbas prædictus conceffit Priori & fuis fuccefforibus unam plateam in Fordwico fuper ripam fittuatam quæ tenet in longitudine ix. perticatas de xvj. pedibus & dimid. in latitudine xxij. pedes, reddendo inde Abbati S. Auguftini unam Rofam in fefto fancti Johannis Baptiftæ pro omnibus fervitiis, fectis Curiarum, & omnibus aliis demandis; donis, Judiciis, executionibus & omnibus aliis delictis Ibidem factis eidem Abbati femper falvis, ficut in aliis locis ejufdem villæ idem Abbas habet vel folet habere. Ita quod in dicto manfo aliquas mercandizas, res vel victualia præterquam propria bona ejufdem Prioris non recipiet nec permittet quoquo modo fore recepta. Pro hac autem conceffione Prior prædictus dedit Abbati & Ecclefiæ fuæ tres acras prati cum omnibus fuis pertinentiis in Fordwico unde una acra jacet ex latere prati elemofinar' fancti Auguftini, & aliæ duæ jacent partim in prato ubi domus prius fic fuit levata, & partim in aliis locis prope pratum Abbatis, ficut bundæ monftrant & teftantur, Reddendo inde Priori unam Rofam in fefto S. Johannis Baptiftæ pro omnibus fervitiis & demandis. Ordinatum fuit etiam quod borrer' & piles per Abbatem in curfu aquæ

Barrer. & Piles.

erectæ fuper calfetum ibidem per Cuftodem quinque portuum deponentur & illud calfetum per Abbatem & homines fuos de Fordwico reparatum fiat communis Abbati, Priori, & Communitati villæ prædictæ, à quibus omnibus perpetuis futuris temporibus ad fugandum & cariandum deber fuftentari. Nec licebit Priori & fuccefforibus fuis in eadem villa de cætero aliquid perquirere de tenura Abbatis fine ejus voluntate vel fuccefforum fuorum. Et quia per iftam compofitionem feu ordinationem totum pratum in quo continetur quædam walla

*Walla Cellerari
Ecclef.] Chrifti-
Cant.*

vocata walla feu cafea Cellerarii Ecclefiæ Chrifti Cant. quæ continet xx perticatas in longitnd. & viginti pedes in latitudine data fuerat Abbati & Conventui fine quacunque forprifa in excambium pro platea apud Fordwicum ubi domus Prioris & Conventus fanctæ Trinitatis fuit ædificata, nec poterant dicti Prior & Conventus extunc de Jure habere ufum dictæ wallæ ut prius habuerunt, fuper quo poftea inter partes controverfia orta per magnam compofitionem fequentem provifum fuerat quod walla feu cafea prædicta dictis Abbati & Priori communis ad cariandum & chaceandum quotiens neceffe habuerint, & fibi viderint expedire.

The Epitaphs upon some of the Priors.

Hic requiefcit in gratia & Mifericordia Dei Richardus Oxinden, quondam Prior hujus Ecclefiæ, qui ob. Aug. 4. 1338.

Hic requiefcit in gratia & mifericordia Dei Dominus Robertus Hathbrand quondam Prior hujus Ecclefiæ, qui obiit xvij. die Aug. Anno Domini Mccclxx. Cujus animæ propitietur Deus, Amen.

Hic jacet Johannes Fynch de Winchelfey quondam Prior hujus Ecclefiæ qui obiit 9. die Januarii ———— edificia conftructa & plura alia collata bona ———— cujus animæ ————

Hic jacet Dominus Thomas Chyllindenne quondam Prior hujus Ecclefiæ, Decretorum Doctor egregius, qui navem iftius Ecclefiæ cæteraque diverfa ædificia, quamplurima quoque opera laudabilia de novo fieri fecit. Pretiofa infuper ———— ecclefiaftica,

ſtica, multaquè privilegia inſignia huic Eccleſiæ acquiſivit, qui poſtquam Prioratum hujus Eccleſiæ Annis viginti. 25. ſeptimanis, & quinque diebus nobiliter rexiſſet,
tandem in die aſſumptionis beatæ Mariæ Virginis diem ſuum clauſit extremum.
Anno Domini 1411. Cujus animæ propitietur Deus. Amen.

Numb. LV. e.

Eſt nece ſubſtratus Jon Woodneſbergh tumulatus,
Hujus erat gratus Prior Eccleſiæ numeratus;
Quem colie ornatus hic tantus ubique novatus,
Per loca plura datus ſit ſumptus teſtificatus:
Auctor erat morum, probitatis, laudis honorum,
Largus cunctorum, cunctis dator ille laborum,
Quique Prioratum rexit ſub ſchemate gratum.
Annos hunc plenos per ſeptenos quoque denos:
Quadrigentenis Mil. ejus bis quoque denis
Annis ſeptenis Domini nondum ſibi plenis.
———— cum tibi Chriſte ———— agone
Quem precibus pone radiantis forte corone.

Numb. LV. f.

Preteriens flere diſcas, & dic: miſerere,
Et ne ſubſannes, quia victus morte Johannes,
Membris extenſis jacet hic Sariſburienſis:
Sic non evades, vindice morte cades.
Hic prior Eccleſiæ Doctorque fuit Theoriæ:
Wulſtani feſto feria quarta memor eſto
Mille quater centum x. v. dant documentum
Sint animæ merces, lux, decor & requies. Amen.

Hic requieſcit Dominus Thomas Elham quondam Prior hujus Eccleſiæ, Qui cum Ann. 2. Numb.
menſ. 11. & 4. dieb. honorificè vixiſſet, 20. Febr. 1440. obdormivit in Domino. LV. g.

Hic jacet reverendus pater Wilhelmus Selling hujus ſacroſanctæ Eccleſiæ Prior, ac ſacræ Numb.
Paginæ. Profeſſor, qui poſtquam hanc Eccleſiam per ann. 22. menſ. 5. & 24. d. optimè LV. h.
gubernaſſet migravit ad Dominum, die viz. paſſionis ſancti Thomæ Martyris, Anno 1494.

Doctor Theologus Selling Greca etque Latina
Lingua prædoctus hic Prior almus obit
Omnis virtutis ſpeculum, exemplar Monachorum,
Religionis honor, mitis imago Dei.
Adde quod ingenii rivorum tanta cucurrit
Copia cunctorum quantula rara virum.
Regius orator cujus facundia mulſit
Romanos Gallos Orbis & ampla loca.
Hujus preſidio res iſta domeſtica rata eſt,
Et redimita annis plurimis egregie.
Pervigil hic Paſtor damna atque incommoda cuncta
A grege commiſſo fortiter expulerat.
Dum brevi tumulo latet hoc, tota Anglia famam
Predicat, & tanto lugeat orba patre.
Huc iter omnis habens, ſtet, perlegat & memor ejus
Oret ut aſcendat ſpiritus alta poli.

Hic jacet reverendus Pater Thomas Goldſtone hujus ſacroſanctæ Eccleſiæ Prior, ac ſacræ Numb.
paginæ Profeſſor, qui poſtquam hanc Eccleſiam per annos 24. 8. menſ. & dies 16. LV. i.
optime gubernaſſet, migravit ad Dominum, 16. Septemb. Anno Dom. 1517. Cujus
animæ, &c.

Tangite vos Citharam plangentes carmine, mole
Hic jacet occulta Religionis honos.
Occubuit Doctor Thomas Goldſton vocitatus
Moles quem preſens ſaxea magna tenet.
Arripit hunc patrem mors pervigilemque Priorem
Sic rapitur quoque lux iſtius Eccleſiæ.
Grex ſibi commiſſus monachorum plangat eundem
Omiſſum Patrem, qui ſibi fautor erat.
Largus in expenſis fieri dat plura novata
Iſtius Eccleſiam veſtibus ornat idem.
Sic fuit ad Regni laudem canit Anglia largus
Totus & is mitis pauperibus fuerat

O vos spectantes hujus jam funera patris,
Nunc estis memores fundite quæso preces.
Requiescat in sancta Pace. Amen.

Numb.
LVI.

Aid lent to the Citty by John Woodnesborough Prior of Christ-Church.

Memorandum quòd xij die Julii Anno R. R. Hen. 5. Angl. tertio, Dominus Johannes Prior Ecclesiæ Christi Cant. ad instantiam & specialem rogatum Wmi Lane & Wmi Mason Ballivorum Civitatis Cant. fact. per Joannem Browne Plomer dictæ Civitatis Civem & armigerum ac plumbarium præfatæ Ecclesiæ permisit servientes suos cum villanis egredi cum armis & aliis instrumentis defensivis ad augendum numerum & populum Civitatis. Quandam vigiliam in Civitate observatam pro gente Francorum qui revertebantur a Domino Rege de Suthampton versus partes proprias postquam acceperant a Domino Rege quòd ad partes hujusmodi disponeret transmeare. Et pro parte dictorum Ballivorum & civium Civitatis per oraculum vivæ vocis dicti Johannis Browne nuncii sive procuratoris eorundem, Dompno Stephano de Sancto Laurentio Cellerario, ac Willielmo Molash tunc Custodi ac Capellano præfati Domini Prioris, sub fidelitate eorum est infallibiliter repromissum, Quòd nusquam pro isto facto in hominibus nostris aliquid juris vel clamei pro consimilibus negotiis aliquid in posterum super nos aut homines nostros futuris temporibus vendicabunt , & sub hac conditione Dominus Prior supra dictus de familiaribus suis ipsis accommodavit xvj. Lanc' cum omni apparatu honesto ac xxiiij. architenentes ad decorem & laudem civium prædictorum. Hoc idem fecerunt penes Abbatem S. Augustini die & Anno supradictis a quo ix. lanc' & xxiiij. architenen' ex præscripto habuerunt.

Numb.
LVII.

The forme of electing and installing the Prior of the Church of Canterbury.

STatuto die de Priore eligendo, congregatis omnibus fratribus in Capitulo, qui ad Capitulum commod' poterint venire ; Dominus Archiepiscopus Capitulum intrabit cum solo Capellano suo, & proposito breviter verbo Dei, tanget de negotio electionis Prioris. Deinde præcipiet in virtute obedientiæ & sub pœna excommunicationis majoris ipso facto incurrendæ, ne aliquis amore, favore vel odio nominet aliquem in Priorem nisi illum quem magis idoneum & in spiritualibus & temporalibus esse crediderit circumspectum. Subsequenter D. Archiepiscopus examinabit personaliter totum conventum per singula capita. Et Capellanus suus scribet in rotulo nomina nominantium & nominatorum. Postea D. Archiepisc. deliberabit & conferet apud se illo die secundum Dominum & sanam & sanctam conscientiam suam, & prout in extremo judicio reddere voluerit rationem, de numero, zelo & merito nominantium, & idoneitate nominatorum in Priorem. In crastino verò Dominus Archiepisc. in pleno Capitulo illum quem major & sanior pars Capituli nominaverit, in Priorem nominabit publicè ita dicens. Invocato nomine & auxilio sanctæ Trinitatis & gloriosæ virginis matris Christi, & omnium Sanctorum hujus Ecclesiæ nostræ Patronorum, ad laudem & honorem eorundem, fratrem N. de N. nominamus vobis Priorem. Nominatus verò statim surget , & in medio Capituli insufficientiam suam humiliter & instanter allegabit. Et statim præcentor incipiet. Te Deum Laudamus. Quo incepto, omnes surgent, & conventu præcedente , & Domino Archiepisc. & Priore sequentibus ibunt in Ecclesiam solempniter cantantes Te

Stallum Prioris. Deum. Et cum venerit in Chorum Dominus Archiepisc. statim installabit Priorem in stallo suo ex parte Boreali. Quo facto Prior prosternat se super formam. Postea Dominus Archiepisc. in primo stallo chori ex parte australi expectabit quousque Te Deum percantetur. Quo finito, subjunget Dominus Archiepisc. Kyriel. Christel. Kyriel. Pater noster. Et ne nos. Salvum fac servum tuum. Esto ei Domine turris fortitudinis. Nihil proficiat inimicus in eo. Domine exaudi orationem meam. Domine vobiscum. Oremus. Omnipotens sempiterne Deus miserere famulo tuo N. & dirige eum secundum tuam clementiam in viam salutis eternæ, ut te donante tibi placita capiat, & tota virtute perficiat per Christum Dominum nostrum. Dicta itaque collecta omnes redibunt in Capitulum, tam Dominus Archiepisc. quam Prior &

Locus Prioris in conventus ordine quo supra. Et cum venerint in Capitulum antequam Dominus Archiepisc.
Capitulo. sedeat, ponat Priorem in locum suum juxta sedem Archiepiscopi ex parte boreali. Et hiis expletis, Dominus Archiep. data benedictione conventui & populo redeat ad cameram suam in Palatio, & Conventus ad servitium divinum. Si verò Dominus Archiepisc. agens in remotis, non possit personaliter interesse electioni Prioris, tunc committet vices suas duobus fratribus de Capitulo Cant. ad audiendum & examinandum vota singulorum, sicut supra continetur. Et ipsi duo fratres scribent nomina nominantium & nominatorum in Priorem. Et hujusmodi nomina in scriptis mittent vel portabunt Domino Archiepisc. sub sigillo communi Capituli ubicunque fuerit citra mare vel ultra. Et Dominus Archiepiscopus habita deliberatione & facta collatione ut præmittitur committet iterum vices suas alicui fratri de eodem Capitulo Cant. ad nominandum in Capitulo Priorem, & ipsum installandum in choro & ponendum in Capitulo in loco suo, juxta formam superius annotatam.

A Charter

O

A Charter of Archbishop Theobald, *inhibiting the Archdeacons of* Canterbury *from medling with the Capitular Concerns of the Convent.*

Numb.
LVIII.

Theobaldus Dei gratia Cant. Archiepisc. Angliæ Primas. W. Priori & Conventui ejusdem ecclesiæ, Salutem. Cum grande Conversationis monasticæ detrimentum esse dinoscitur, contra usum ecclesiarum, & contra statua regulæ Monachorum capitulo clericos quasi de Jure admisceri: iccirco ne quis clericorum sive Cant. Archidiaconus sive alius vestrum quoquo modo habeat capitulum prohibemus. Si vero vobis Archidiaconus vester necessarius fuerit, & eum vocaveritis, tunc demum non differat, & ad vos venire, & vobis, si opus est, pro viribus auxiliari. Quotiens autem ipse à vobis accersitus vel Archiepiscopum comitatus sive in cœna Domini, sive alliis opportunis temporibus in vestrum venerit Capitulum, more prædecessorum suorum Archidiaconorum, Asketini scilicet, Willielmi, & Helewisi qui nos precesserunt semper in suppeditaneo sedis Archiepiscopi sedeat, nec occasione hac vel alia in Capitulo vestro juris quippiam se habere arbitretur, &c.

Personal Grant of Jurisdiction to the Arch-deacons.

Numb.
LIX.

Ricardus Dei gratia Cant. Archiepisc. totius Angliæ Primas & Apostolicæ sedis Legatus, Universis Christi fidelibus ad quos præsentes literæ pervenerint, salutem. Cum dilectus filius Herbertus Archidiaconus noster plura ad Archidiaconatum suum de Jure debere pertinere vendicaret, de quibus nobis non constabat. Intuitu probitatis suæ & sincera affectione quam circa personam ipsius gerimus, hæc ei personaliter concessimus, sine omni prejudicio Cant. ecclesiæ & Successorum nostrorum. Institutiones viz. & Destitutiones Decanorum, præhabito consilio nostro. Custodiam vacantium ecclesiarum ad nostram donationem non pertinentium, & omnes fructus dum vacaverint inde provenientes liberè & absolutè. Placita etiam ecclesiastica & omnia emolumenta inde provenientia tam de Dominiis nostris quam Monachorum ecclesiæ Cant. in Archidiaconatu Cant. constitutis. Omnia etiam emolumenta de placitis Archidiaconatus sui ubicunque agitentur. Ita tamen quòd si modum circa homines Episcopor. vel Monachorum excesserit, nobis excessus correctionem reservavimus. Cognitionem etiam de causis matrimonior. cum accusantur usque ad definitivum calculum, & si dirimendum fuerit matrimonium, id nobis reservavimus. Institutiones etiam personarum in ecclesiis vacan' quæ ad nostram specialiter non pertineant donationem: cum extra provinciam fuerimus: cum autem præsentes fuerimus & persona aliqua instituenda prius oblata fuerit Archidiacono, dummodo hoc non fuerit procuratum, cum eam ad nos introduxerit, honorem ei in facto suo conservabimus. Omnes autem per nos instituti tam in ecclesiis de dominio nostro & Monachorum, quam in aliis, per Archidiaconum vel ejus Officialem introducentur in corporalem possessionem ecclesiarum in quibus fuerint instituti. Hæc autem omnia præscripta sub præsentis scripti & sigilli nostri testimonio duximus redigenda, ut sicut ea præfato Archidiacono nostro sunt à nobis personaliter concessa ita ejus personæ illibata conserventur. His testibus M[ro] Gerardo Walerano Archid. Baiocen. M[ro] Petro Blesen, &c.

The Chapters Confirmation of the Parsonages of Hakinton *and* Tenham *appropriated to the Archdeaconry of* Canterbury *by* Stephen Langton *the Archbishop.*

Numb.
LX. a.

UNiversis sanctæ matris ecclesiæ filiis præsentes literas inspecturis. I. Prior & Conventus ecclesiæ Christi Cant. Salutem in Domino. Ad universitatis vestræ notitiam volumus pervenire nos cartam venerabilis patris nostri Domini S. Dei gratia Cant. Archiepiscopi totius Angliæ Primatis & sanctæ Romanæ ecclesiæ Cardinalis inspexisse sub hac forma. Universis sanctæ matris ecclesiæ filiis præsentes literas inspecturis. S. permissione divina Cant. Archiepisc. totius Angliæ Primas & sanctæ Romanæ ecclesiæ Cardinalis salutem in Domino. Curæ pastoralis officium commissum laudabiliter prosequemur, si mentis acumen & manus exercitium ad ea quæ honorem Dei & ecclesiæ profectum respiciunt solicitius convertamus. Ea propter Cantuariensis ecclesiæ quæ Metropolis est, cui authore Domino deservimus, in omnibus quæ secundum Deum possumus augmentare volentes honorem, & supplere defectus, advertimus diligenter quod ecclesia illa quæ inter alias ecclesias Anglicanas obtinet principatum, ut pote quæ aliarum mater est & magistra, non nisi unum habet Archidiaconum, cujus Archidiaconatus proventus ita fuerunt hactenus tenues & exiles quod ipse, qui authoritate tantæ ecclesiæ inter alias plus habere dinoscitur honoris, vix habere de suo possit ad expensas & sumptus necessarios competentes. Volentes igitur defectum hujusmodi qui in scandalum ecclesiæ nostræ redundat salubri provisione supplere

Dignitas ecclesiæ Cantuar.

* R ecclesias

ecclefias de Tenham & Hackinton, quæ ad patronatum noftrum fpectare nofcuntur, de voluntate & affenfu Capituli noftri, monachorum fcilicet ecclefiæ Chrifti Cant. in Capitulo exiftentium Archidiaconatui ipfi duximus in perpetuum uniendas, decernentes ut qui pro tempore Archidiaconatum illum obtinuerint ecclefias prædictas, tanquam de corpore ipfius Archidiaconatus liberè poffideat & quietè. Ad hoc cum actenus temporibus noftris de confuetudine fit obtentum quod Officialis nofter Decanos conftituerit in Diocefi Cant. qui conftituti ftatim tenebantur Cantuar. Archidiacono refpondere, volumus & de voluntate & affenfu prædicti Capituli noftri ftatuimus ut de cetero Archidiaconi Cant. qui pro tempore fuerint Decanos conftituant, & amoveant pro fuæ voluntatis arbitrio prout melius viderint expedire in Dioc. memorata, & fibi refpondeant ficut decet, cum abfurdum fit ut alius eos conftituat quam is qui eis debeat præeffe, & cui refpondere tenentur, præfertim cum ipfis referentibus corrigere debent cæterorum errata. Ut igitur hæc omnia perpetuis temporibus ftabilem obtineant firmitatem præfenti fcripto figillum noftrum duximus apponendum. Actum Anno Domini Milefimo ducentefimo vicefimo feptimo. menfe Decembris. Nos igitur hæc omnia ficut prememorato venerabili patre noftro S. Cantuarienfi Archiepifcopo piè & rationabiliter provifa funt & conceffa, quantum in nobis eft, rata habemus & accepta. In cujus rei teftimonium præfenti fcripto figillum noftrum appofuimus. Actum Anno Domini Millefimo ducentefimo vicefimo feptimo, menfe Decemb.

Numb. LX. b. *An enlargement of the fame Archdeacons Jurifdiction by the fame Archbifhop.*

S. Dei gratia Cant. Archiepifcopus totius Angliæ Primas & fanctæ Romanæ ecclefiæ Cardinalis. Dilectis filiis univerfis ecclefiarum Rectoribus per Cant. Dioc. conftitutis Salutem, gratiam & benedictionem. Ad univerfitatis veftræ notitiam volumus pervenire nos in Cantuarienfi capitulo conftitutos, de affenfu & voluntate ipfius Capituli, Prioris I. & Conventus ecclefiæ Chrifti Cant. conceffiffe dilecto filio, magiftro S. de Langton Archid. Cantuar. & fuccefforibus fuis, ut omnes ecclefiæ parochiales Cant. Dioc. tam ad noftram quam ad Capituli noftri donationem fpectantes, & earum Rectores, Capellani etiam tam perpetui quam annui, in morum correctione, & ecclefiarum vifitatione cæterifque omnibus ad Archidiaconi officium fdectantibus, eifdem in perpetuum fint fubjecti. Unde vobis mandamus quatenus præfato Archidiacono fuccefforibus fuis in premiffis de cetero intendatis. In cujus rei Teftimonium has literas noftras patentes vobis duximus tranfmittendas. Dat' Anno Domini Millefimo ducentefimo vicefimo feptimo, menfe Decembris.

Numb. LXI. *The fame Archbifhops Charter of Revocation of certain Churches in the times of Baldwin and Hubert his Predeceffors exempted from the Archdeaconry, intituled,*

Carta S. Archiepifcopi de Revocatione ecclefiarum exemptarum tempore Baldwini & Huberti, & de revocatione dignitatis Archidiaconatus.

UNiverfis fanctæ matris ecclefiæ filiis præfentes literas infpecturis S. permiffione divina Cant. Archiepifc. totius Angliæ Primas, & fanctæ Romanæ ecclefiæ Cardinalis Salutem in Domino. Sicut ea quæ rationabiliter provifa fuerint & ftatuta robur optinere debent perpetuæ firmitatis, fic fi q' fint contra rationis tramitem attemptata digna correctione convenit emendari. Cum igitur nobis conftet Archidiaconatum Cant. per abufum quorundam temporibus piæ recordationis Baldewini & Huberti prædecefforum noftrorum, necnon & noftris temporibus in magna parte fuiffe minus rationabiliter diminutum, quibufdam ecclefiis quæ ad noftram feu capituli noftri donationem pertinent Archidiaconi Cant. Jurifdictioni fe fubtrahentibus tam in morum correctione, quam in ecclefiarum vifitatione & ceteris pertinentibus ad officium Archidiaconi memorati. Nos volentes prædictum Archidiaconatum in ftatum meliorem & debitum reformare, de voluntate & affenfu totius Capituli noftri, in ipfo capitulo exiftentes ftatuimus, quod etiam præfenti fcripto duximus confirmandum, ut de cetero omnes ecclefiæ parochiales Cant. Dioc. tam ad noftram quam ad Capituli noftri donationem fpectantes, & earum Rectores Archidiacono Cantuar. quicunque pro tempore fuerit in perpetuum fint fubjecti, tam in morum correctione, quam in ecclefiarum vifitatione & ceteris omnibus quæ ad Archidiaconi officium fpectare nofcuntur, non obftante exceptione quæ facta fuiffe proponitur à memoratis antecefforibus noftris

Baldwino viz. Et Huberto occafione capellarum de Hakintun & Lamheth quas ipfi in præjudicium Cant. ecclefiæ conftruere nitebantur, præfertim cum talis exemptio potius fuerit velamen malitiæ quam libertas, & audaciam frequentius præftitit delinquendi, cum etiam eædem capellæ per fententiam Apoftolicam fuerint demolitæ, & fententiatum fuerit illa omnia irritanda quæ occafione ipfarum fuerat attemptata, ficut in refcripto Apoftolico contineri perfpeximus evidenter. Unde volumus & firmiter præcipimus omnibus Rectoribus

ctoribus ecclesiarum prædictis, & Capellanis eorum tam annuis quam perpetuis ut magistro Simoni Archidiacono Cant. & ejus successoribus Cant. Archidiaconis, in hiis quæ ad officium Archidiaconi pertinent decetero sint subjecti, debitam eis in omnibus reverentiam & obedientiam, tanquam Archidiaconis impendendo. In cujus Rei testimonium presens scriptum sigilli nostri munimine duximus roborandum. Actum Anno Domini M°. CC°. vicesimo septimo, mense Decembris. Valt.

A personall Composition betweene the Chapter and the same Archdeacon touching Jurisdiction in the Vacancy. Numb. LXII.

UNiversis sanctæ matris ecclesiæ filiis ad quos præsens scriptum pervenerit Rogerus Prior & Capitulum ecclesiæ Christi Cantuar. Salutem in Domino. Noverit universitas vestra quod cum contentio verteretur inter nos R. Priorem & Capitulum ecclesiæ Christi Cantuar. ex una parte & magistrum Simonem de Langeton Archidiaconum Cant. ex altera super quibusdam juribus ad Archiepiscopum Cant. dum vivit sine contradictione & im- *Jura Archie-* mediate spectantibus, viz. super institutionibus faciendis ad vacantes ecclesias, & super *piscopalia.* collationibus ecclesiarum vacantium authoritate concilii, ac etiam super cognitione causarum matrimonialium, quæ ipsius Archiepiscopi forum dum vivit immediate contingunt. Item super causis omnibus quæ moventur & moveri possunt inter Suffraganeos & Suffraganeorum subjectos totius provinciæ subjectæ ecclesiæ nostræ Christi Cant. tum per simplicem querimoniam, tum per appellationem factam vel faciendam ad ipsum Archiepiscopum dum vivit in omnibus casibus à Canone diffinitis, tum etiam in causis tuitionum appellationum factarum ad sedem Apostolicam inter eosdem & quoslibet totius provinciæ supradictæ, quatenus procedunt appellationes à cognitione ordinaria vel extraordinaria delegatione. Item super instituendo clerico seculari & pœnitentiario in eadem ecclesia, sic conquievit. viz. quod nos Prior & Capitulum concedimus pro bono pacis & intuitu personæ ipsius, prædicto mag. Simoni Archidiacono personaliter & ad vitam suam quod au- *Archidiacono* thoritate ecclesiæ nostræ Cant. Metropolitanæ, habeat, sede vacante, Institutiones infra *quæ concessa.* Diocesf. & extra, collationes ecclesiarum vacantium authoritate concilii, & cogniriones causarum matrimonialium. Ita tamen quod ex ista nostra concessione, nec quoad titulum, nec quoad fidem bonam, nec quoad aliquam præscriptionem inchoandam sive complendam in prædictis juribus post mortem ipsius Archidiaconi vel cessionem nullum nobis possit præjudicium generari. De illis verò quæ sunt circa personas Episcoporum quoad querelas de eis deponendis vel appellationes ab eis faciendas ad sedem Cant. & similiter de tuitionibus appellationum ab eis ad Dominum Papam interpositarum, sic est actum inter partes prædictas, quod dictus Archidiaconus (tenore præsentium) protestatur & confitetur se nullam vendicare jurisdictionem nec cohertionem aliquam faciendam in personis Episcoporum occasione alicujus querelæ contra eos motæ vel movendæ, vel ipsorum negligentiæ; nec *Quæ P. & Con-* vendicat appellationes factas à personis Episcoporum nec ab eorum Officialibus, ipsis Epis- *vent reservata.* copis existentibus extra regnum. Similiter nec tuitiones appellationum ab eisdem ad Dominum Papam factarum cum sint de sequela dictarum appellationum. Set ipsi Prior & Capitulum in prædictis quod suum est exequantur. Ecclesias autem vacantes quæ nostræ sunt donationis dabimus personis quibus videbimus expedire, & collatione facta significabimus Archidiacono instituendos eosdem, qui absque omni contradictione & examinatione personæ, & inquisitione de persona ac difficultate qualibet instituet sine mora, nisi evidens & manifestum quid appareat propter quod hoc facere non possit, dummodo super aliis articulis sicut moris est inquiratur. Magistro vero Willielmo penitentiario mortuo vel amoto de alio substituendo clerico seculari in Penitentiarium sic convenimus, quod de Prioris *Pœnitentiarius.* & Archidiaconi præficiatur assensu, qui tantum in ecclesia nostra & non alibi quotiens commode poterit injunctum sibi officium prout Dominus dederit salubriter exequetur. Ille autem Penitentiarius secularis providetur in supplementum fratrum nostrorum penitentiariorum deputatorum vel deputandorum à Capitulo, ita quod tam salubre negotium nullum defectum habeat vel neglectum. Invocationem verò brachii secularis contra personas excommunicatorum tam à nobis authoritate privilegii nostri quam ab aliis claves ecclesiæ contemnentium habeat Archidiaconus, & sic excommunicatos à nobis ad instantiam nostram faciat publicè denuntiari. Ista autem sic procedit compositio quod tantummodo *Compositio* ad tempus Archidiaconi supradicti durabit, ita quod post obitum ipsius vel cessionem *temporalis.* nullum hincinde præjudicium in aliquo generetur. Utraque verò pars hæc omnia supradicta bona fide promisit fideliter observare. Et ut hæc compositio ut prædictum est robur optineat, duplicatum est hoc scriptum in modum cyrographi, cujus una pars sigillo nostro signata penes dictum Archidiaconum remanebit; altera verò pars sigillo dicti Archidiaconi signata penes nos in testimonium residebit. Act' apud Cant. Anno Domini M°. CC°. xl. primo xij°. Kalen. Septembris.

A Mandate

Numb. LXIII. *A Mandate for putting the Abbot of S.* Radegund *in poffeffion of the Perfonage of* Alcham.

Magifter Hugo de Mortuo mari Dilecto fibi officiali Archidiacon' Cant. falutem in Domino. De mandato Domini mei Archiepifcopi Cant. vobis mando fpecialiter, Quatenus Abbatem fanctæ Radigundis nomine fuo & conventus fui in poffeffionem ecclefiæ de Alcham mittatis corporalem, & tueamini inductum contradictores & rebelles per cenfuram ecclefiafticam compefcendo. Dat' die Martis prox. ante feftum. S. Nicolai Anno Domini 1258.

Numb. LXIV. *The Charter of* Coenulph *King of* Mercia, *and* Cuthred *King of* Kent, *to the Abbefs and Nuns of* Liming.

✠ Difpenfante ac gubernante Domino Deo omnipotente, Ego Coenulph Rex Marciorum, & Cuthred frater meus Rex Cantuariorum Anno Dominicæ incarnationis Dccciiij. conceffimus venerabili Abbatiffæ Selethrythæ & fuæ familiæ ad ecclefiam fanctæ Mariæ femper virginis quæ fita eft in loco qui dicitur Limming, ubi paufat corpus beatæ Eadburgæ, aliquantulam terræ partem in Civitate Dorobernia ad neceffitatis refugium : hoc eft, vj. jugera pertinentia ad ecclefiam quæ fita eft in honore beatæ **Forte terminos.* Mariæ in Occidentali parte civitatis, & quorum termini fic cingere videntur. Ab oriente fluvius Stur. Ab occidente & ab auftro murus Civitatis. A ftatu ecclefiæ protenditur in Aquilonem emiffione virgarum circiter ut fertur quindecim. Si quis autem hanc noftram donationem infringere vel minuere temptaverit fciat fe rationem redditurum in die Judicii, nifi ante digna fatisfactione Deo & hominibus emendare voluerit. Et hæc teftium nomina quæ inferius fcripta funt.
✠ Ego Coenulfus Rex Merciorum hanc donationem meam cum figno crucis Chrifti confirmo.
✠ Ego Cuthredus Rex Cant. fig. crucis confirmo.
✠ Ego Aethelheardus gratia Dei archiep' confenfi & fub.
✠ Ego Aldulf Epifc' confenfi & fubfcripfi.
✠ Ego Dæneberht Epifc' con. & fub.

Numb. LXV. *Monumental Infcriptions in the Parifh-Churches in the City, and Suburbs of the City of* Canterbury. *In the Church of* St. Elphege,

> In Maidftone natus jacet hic Jon Piers vocitatus
> Ecclefiæ Rector Alphegi martyris almi.
>   Cujus protector fit Deus omnipotens.
> Qui legis hæc omnia pro te pro teque labora,
> Sic tibi proficies & amicus tui mihi fies.
> Cum feris à tergo fator es impavidus ergo.

Hic jacet Magifter Johannes Parmenter quondam Rector iftius Ecclefiæ qui obiit xx die menfis Octob. Anno Domini M. D. j. cujus &c.

Here lieth Sr. Robert Proveft Parfon of S. Alpheys, which died the 22. day of January, Anno Dom. 1487. Mercy Ihu'.

> Es teftis Chrifte quod non jacet hic lapis ifte
> Corpus ut ornetur fet fpiritus ut memoretur.

Hic jacet Mr. Johannes Lovelych Bacallarius in Legibus quondam rector iftius Ecclefiæ, qui obiit 6. die Sept. Anno Dom. 1438. Cujus &c.

Here lieth Richard Stuppeny bachelor of both lawes, who had by his wife Catherine 2. fonnes and 4. daughters, and departed this life the fixteenth day of Novemb. 1596.

> Lo here a view of thine eftate is fet before thine eye :
> For as thou art even fuch was he who here in grave doth lie.
> If vertuous life or faithfull friend could ought prevailed have,
> Then fhould not he who here lieth dead have layed here in grave.
> But death will not intreated be, it taketh hold on all :
> So that as all men come from earth, fo to the earth they fhall.
> Yet this the comfort is of them which now to Chrift pertain,
> That dying they do die to live with Chrift for ay to reigne.

Here lieth Henry Gosborne cetezen and Alderman of the towne of Canturbury, and fowre yeares at fundry times Mayre of the fame Cety the which deceafed the 22th day of April, the yeare of our Lord 1522. on whofe Sowle &c.

Richardus

Richardus Engeham de magna Cherte reliquit hanc lucem 7. die Feb. Anno Dom. 1568. cujus animæ &c.

> Qui tumulos cernis cur non mortalia fpernis?
> Tali namque domo clauditur omnis homo.

> Pray for the fawlys of John Caxton and of Jone
> And Ifabel that to this Church great good hath done
> In making new in the Chancell
> Of Dexkys and Setys afwell
> An Antiphon the which did bye
> With a table of the Martyrdome of St Alphye
> For thing much which did pay
> And departed out of this Life of October the 12. day.
> And Ifabel his fecond wiff
> Paffed to bliffe where is no Strife
> The xijt day to tell the trowth
> Of the fame moneth as our Lord knoweth
> In the yeare of our Lord God a thoufand fower hundred fowerfcore and five.

Hic jacet Johannes Colfol quondam clericus parochialis iftius ecclefiæ qui obiit 28. die menf. Maii. A. D. 1500. & anno gratiæ, cujus animæ &c.

Hic jacet Nicolaus Reve quondam Civis & Wexchandler Cantuar. qui obiit 28. die menf. Decemb. 1431. cujus &c.

Orate pro animabus Edmundi Staplegate & Ellenoræ at Pytte uxoris ejus.

> O ye good People that here go this way:
> Of your charitie to have in remembrance:
> For the fowle of Agnes Halke to pray
> Sometime here of acquaintance.
> In this Churchyard fo was her chance
> Firft after the hallowing of the fame.
> Afore all other here to begin the dance
> Which to all creatures is the loth game.
> The Tuifday next before Pentecoft
> The yeare of our Lord M. D. and two
> Whofe foule Ihu' pardon that of might is moft.

In the Church of St. George.

Hic requiefcit Dominus Johannes Lovell quondam Rector iftius ecclefiæ, qui obiit 24. die menfis Aprilis Anno Domini 1438. Cujus &c.

In the Church of St. Mary Bredman.

Orate pro Thoma Alcock quondam Rectore iftius ecclefiæ qui obiit in die fanctæ Crucis Anno Domini 1500. Cujus animam falvet paffio Chrifti.

Orate pro anima Domini Roberti Richmond olim hujus ecclefiæ Rectoris, qui obiit anno Domini 1524. decimo octavio die Julii.

Here lieth William Megg fometime Alderman of this city which deceafed the firft day of January Anno Domini 1519. On whofe fowle &c.

In St. Peter's.

> Thomas Ikham & Jone fa femme gifoint icy
> Dieu de falmes eit mercy.——— 1400.

Hic jacet Willielmus Ikham quondam civis & Balivus Civitat. Cantuar. qui obiit ——— Julii———1424.

Orate pro anima Wilhelmi Septvans militis & Elifabethe ux. ejus.

Orate pro bono ftatu Johannis Bigg armigeri ac Aldermanni Civitatis Cant. & Conftantiæ confortis fuæ, qui me vitrari fecerunt, Anno Domini 1473.

Et fpecialiter pro bono ftatu Willielmi Bygg ——— Civitatis Cant. & Johannæ confortis fuæ, & pro animabus parentum ac benefactorum eorum qui hoc lumen ——— Anno Dom. 1468.

In the Chancell.

Hic jacet Dominus Johannes Colley quondam Rector iftius ecclefiæ, qui obiit 22. die menfis Feb. Anno Domini 14 8. Cujus &c.

In the Body.

Hic jacet Magifter Johannes Syre quondam Rector ecclefiæ Sancti Petri Cant. qui obiit in fefto Sancti Pauli ad vincula, Anno Dom. 1436. cujus &c.

In the Church of St. Mary Magdalen.

Hic Jacet Johanna filia Johannis Hache quondam uxor Henrici Lynde de Cant. quæ obiit 21. die Novemb. Anno Domini 1417.

Hic jacet Chriftoferus Alcock Draper qui obiit 3. die menf. September. Anno Domini 1492.

Here lyeth buried the Body of Sybell Orchard Widow, late the Wife of Mr. Libby Orchard late of Mounckton Court, in the Ifle of Thanet deceafed, which Sybell dyed the 12. day of March. Anno Domini 1586.

In the Church of St. Andrew.

Of your charity pray for the foule of Edward Bolney Efquire, which deceafed the fecond day of January in the yeare of our Lord God 1517. whofe foule, &c.

Here lyeth buried the body of Stephen White Citizen of this City and the firft Iron-monger that ever was dwelling in the City of Canterbury who deceafed the 28th of May Anno Domini 1592. &c.

Orate pro anima Domini Willielmi Mellrofe rectoris ecclefiæ fanctæ Mariæ de Brod-man. *By it is his Device, being* W. M. *with a* Rofe *over head.*

Orate pro anima fratris Johannis Fanting Rectoris fanctæ Mariæ de Bredyn. *With his Picture, and* Det mater Chrifti Fanting John gaudia cœli.

In the Church of St. Mildred.

Orate pro anima Richardi Atwood.

Orate pro animabus Thomæ Wood armigeri cuftodis contra rotular. Hofpitii reveren-diffimi patris in Chrifto Domini ———— Maioris hujus Civitatis, qui in honore Jefu hanc capellam fieri fecit, & Margaretæ uxoris ejus filiæ Johannis Moyle armigeri. Orate pro eis.

Magifter Johannes Boold.————

Dominus Johannes Mawny————

Orate pro animabus Roberti Bennet & Crift.————

Orate pro animabus Johannis Boys :————

Orate pro animabus Johannis Pocot, & Johannis Pocot filii ejufdem.

In the Church of St. Paul.

Orate pro Ricardo-Wavere.

Orate pro anima Johannis Stace, & Conftanciæ uxoris ejus.

Orate pro animabus Johannis Gale & Chriftine uxoris.

Orate pro animabus Georgii Wyndbourne generofi & Katherinæ uxoris fuæ, qui quidem G. obiit. 5°. die Ap. Anno Dom. 1531. quorum &c.

Orate pro animabus Richardi Berne & Johannæ uxoris ejus.

Orate pro animabus Thomæ Pollard, & Jo.————

Sub ifto marmore tumulatur corpus Magiftri Edmundi Hovynden quondam vicarii hujus ecclefiæ, qui obiit 23. die Julii 1497. Cujus &c.

Epitaphium Johannis Twyne armigeri qui obiit 28 Novemb. 1581.

> Clauditur hoc tumulo Johannes ille Tuuynus,
> Qui docuit pueros verba latina loqui.
> Quique urbem hanc rexit Prætor turbante Viato
> Rem populi & Regni feditione vafra.
> Huic Deus in Chrifti mundato fanguine donet.
> Leta refurgenti Lector idemque tibi.
> Vivit Dominus.

In the Church of S. Mary Northgate.

Hic jacet Galfridus Holman armiger qui obiit 24. die menfis Januarii. Anno Dom. 1478. Cujus &c.

Hic

Hic jacet Walterus Garrade nuper Vicarius istius ecclesiæ, qui obiit 26. die mensis Augusti Anno Dom. 1498. cujus &c.

> All ye that stand upon my corse
> Remember that late Ralf Browne I was.
> Alderman and Mayre of this Cite.
> Jesu upon my soule have pite.

In the Church of Holy Crosse of Westgate.

Hic jacet Stephanus Mathew quondam pannarius istius villæ qui obiit 5. die Januar. Anno Dom. 1442. cujus animæ &c.

Hic jacet Dominus Willielmus Hall Capellanus. cujus &c.

Hic jacet Robertus Colt quondam pandoxator istius villæ qui obiit 6. die Decemb. Anno Dom. 1444. & Deonisia uxor ejus quæ obiit——quorum animabus &c.

Hic jacet Willielmus Colkyn qui obiit 3. die Aug. Anno Dom. 1440. cujus &c.

Of your charity pray for the soules of John Nayler and Robert Nayler his sonne late Aldermen of the City of Cant. which Robert died the 25. day of Decemb. Anno Dom. 1545. On whose soule &c.

Orate pro animabus Thomæ Ramsey & Margaretæ uxoris ejus, qui obiit 3. die mensis Maii Anno Dom. 1495.

Hic jacet Johannes Cornwell dier & Johanna ac Alicia uxores ejus, qui quidem Johannes obiit 30. die mens. Decemb. Anno Dom. 1492. quorum &c.

Of your charitie pray for the soule of Margaret Colpholl the wife of Thomas Colpholl, which Marg. died the first day of March Anno Dom. 1533. on whose &c.

Hic jacet Jacobus Hope Gentleman qui obiit 12. die Decemb. Anno Dom. 1458. cujus &c.

Hic jacet Christiana Crane quæ obiit 22. die. mens. Januar. Anno Dom. 1445. cujus &c.

Of your charitie pray for the soule of John Barber and Jone his Wife which John deceased the 10th day of Aprill in the yeare of our Lord God. 1533.

Hic—— Thomas Lynd primus Maior Cant. & Constantia uxor ejus —— Feb. 12. Anno Dom.——

Of your charitie pray for the soule of William Charnell first Chantery Priest of Ihesus, which deceased the 10th day of Decemb. Anno Dom. 1516.

Some of the Vicars of the place lie interred in the Chancell: as

Nicholas Chilton, who died anno 1400.
Robert Raynhull, who died anno 1416.
Patricius Gerard, who died anno 1458.

And hard by them one Clement Harding, batchelor of law, with these lines upon his monument.

> Multorum causas defendere quique solebat
> Hanc mortis causam evadere non potuit
> Doctus & indoctus moritur, sic respice finem
> Ut bene discedas quisquis es ista legens.

In the Church of St. Dunstan.

Hic jacet Edmundus Roper qui obiit 11. die Decemb. Anno Dom. 1433. cujus &c.

Pray for the soule of John Roper Esquire, sometime genurall Attorney to our Sovereigne Lord King Hen. 8. and Prygnatory of the bench of our said Sovereigne Lord, and for the soule of Jane his wife, daughter of St John Fyneux Knight chief Judge of England, which John died the 7th day of Aprill in the yeare of the Incarnation of Ihu' Christ 1524. on whose soules and all his antecessors soules Ihu' have mercy, Amen.

Hic jacet venerabilis vir Gulielmus Roper armiger filius & heres quondam Johonnis Roper armigeri & Margareta uxor. ejusdam Gul. filia quondam Thomæ Mori militis summi olim Angliæ Cancellarii Græcis Latinisque literis doctissima, qui quidem Gul. patri suo in officio prothonotariatus supremæ curiæ banci Regii successit, in quo cum annis 54. fideliter ministrasset idem officium filio suo primogenito Thomæ reliquit. Fuit is Gul. domi forisque munificens, mitis, misericors, incarceratorum, oppressorum & pauperum baculus. Genuit ex Margareta uxore (quam unicam habuit) filios duos & filias tres, ex iis vidit in vita sua nepotes, & pronepotes, uxorem in virili ætate amisit, viduatus uxore castissimè vixit annis 33. Tandem completis in pace diebus decessit in senectute bona ab omnibus desideratus, die quarto mensis Jan. Anno Christi Salvatoris 1577. ætatis verò suæ 82.

In

In the Church of St. Mary Bredin.

Hic expectat refurrectionem mortuorum corpus Johannis Hales filii Johannis Hales fecundarii Baronis de fcaccario Domini Regis, qui Johannes Hales filius obiit quarto die Maii Anno Domini 1532.

In the Church of St. Margaret.

In the Chancell.

Hic jacet Johannes Winter bis Maior Civitatis Cant. qui obiit decimo die Novembris 1470. cujus animæ propitietur Deus Amen, qui lampadem ante fummum altare prefentis ecclefiæ in perpetuam memoriam fanctiffimi corporis Domini noftri Jefu Chrifti illuminari conftituit ; (de qua re vide Teftamentum dicti Johannis Winter.) Quod firma five proficuum proveniens de duobus tenement' cum pertinen' apud yrencroffe in dicta parochia annui valoris 16ˢ folvantur cuftodibus bonorum ejufdem ecclefiæ annuatim in perpetuum ad fuftentationem unius lampadis ardere coram fummo altare in fumma cancella dictæ ecclefiæ, ac ad acquietandum cimiterium ejufdem ecclefiæ de 3ˢ provenien' annuatim de eodem cimiterio verfus Prior. & Conventum ecclefiæ Chrifti Cant. & refiduum dict. 16ˢ fideliter expendatur circa reparationem dictorum 2 tenementorum.

Here lyeth the body of Leonard Cotten Gent. who was Sheriff of the City of Cant. in the yeare of our Lord 1563. in the time of Thomas Giles Mayor, and was afterward himfelf Mayor of the fame City in the yeare of our Lord 1579. and departed this life in the yeare of God the 24th of Aprill 1605. being of the age of 80. yeares.

Pray for the foules of Thomas Fort and Elizabeth his Wife. On whofe foules, &c.

Hic jacet Johannes Hosbrand & Johanna ac Johanna uxores ejus, qui quidem Johannes obiit 1º die Octob. Anno Domini 1452. quorum animabus &c.

Richard Prat lyeth buried here
Sometime of Cant. Citizen and Draper.
And Alice his wife, &c.

Numb. LXVI. A Compofition betweene Saint Auguftines Abbey and the Citie of Canterbury about limits and liberties, intituled by Thorne

Compofitio cum Civibus Cant.

ANno Domini Millefimo Cclxviij°. in craftino Purificationis beatæ Mariæ, Anno Regni Regis Hen. filii Regis Johannis xlij°. apud Weftm' coram eodem Domino Rege, convenit ex confenfu ipfius Domini Regis inter Abbatem fancti Auguftini Cant. & Cives dictæ Civitatis fuper quibufdam contentionibus motis inter eos, viz. quod fi aliquis latro *Infangthef* captus fuerit cum manu opere, ita quod poffit vocari Infangthef, de porta Cimiterii Oc*Porta cimiterii* cidentalis fancti Auguftini ufque ad domum Henrici Fabri, & à domo H. Fabri ufque *Occidentalis.* ad domum Nicholai de le Berton, & deinde per vicum qui vocatur Loderflane ufque ad *Loderflane.* novam ftratam, & fic à nova ftrata ufque ad fanctum fepulchrum à dextris remanebit de *Nova ftrata.* cetero civibus & libertati Civitatis Cant. fine contradictione prædicti Abbatis vel fuccefforum fuorum vel ecclefiæ Sᵗⁱ Aug' imperpetuum, five qui captus fit, de hominibus Abbatis vel de libertate fua interius vel exterius fuerit. Et fi qualifcunque captus fuerit, qui fimiliter vocari debeat Infangthef in finiftra parte prædictorum bundarum & metarum, *Chaldane.* vel à fancto Sepulcro ufque Chaldane, quantum fuerit de feodo ipfius Abbatis ex utraque parte, & fimiliter à domo prædicti Henrici Fabri per viam qua itur apud Fifpole, ex *Fifpole.* utraque parte ufque ad Fifpole, fcilicet quiquid fit de feodo ipfius Abbatis, & fimiliter fi *Northome.* talis latro inventus fuerit in campis de Northome, & per vicum qui ducit ad portam S. Auguftini, de cetero remaneat prædicto Abbati & Succefforibus fuis & ecclefiæ fuæ in perpetuum. Ita quod fervientes ipfius Abbatis illos licitè capere poterint infra prædictas metas & bundas, & juftitiam facere de ipfis fecundum cartam fuam & legem & confuetudinem Angliæ, fine contradictione prædictorum civium vel heredum fuorum inperpetuum, five ille qui captus fuerit fit de villa vel de libertate prædictæ civitatis vel aliunde. Ita tamen quod propter iftam conventionem nihil depereat prædictis civibus de juribus fuis quæ habuerint in tenentibus prædicti Abbatis, qui manentes funt infra metas & bundas prædictas, quæ remaneant tam prædicto Abbati quam prædictis civibus, quin illi qui *Lot. Scot. Tallag.* mercandifas fecerint fint in Lot & Scot & in Tallag' & in defenfione ipforum contra omnes ficut prius fuerunt fine aliqua contradictione ipfius Abbatis vel Succefforum fuorum. Ita quod quando tallagium affeffum eft fuper eos, tallagium illud colligetur per vifum Ballivi Domini Abbatis fi intereffe voluerit, & fi non tunc licitè per Ballivos prædictæ Civitatis. Dicti etiam cives nihilominus infra metas prædictas & bundas habebunt per Coronatorem fuum vifum hominum mortuorum & vulneratorum, & præfentationem quæ pertinet ad coronam Domini Regis coram Juftic' in adventu fuo ficut prius habuerunt attachiac'

attachiac' & prifonam omnium eorum de quibus dictus Abbas non poteft facere Juftitiam in Curia fua & fi ille qui captus fuerit per prædictum Abbatem infra prædictas metas & bundas evaferit de prifona dicti Abbatis dicti cives non debebunt refpondere de ipfo efcapio coram Juftitiariis, fed dictus Abbas & fucceffores fui ipfos acquietabunt coram eifdem. Et conceffum eft hincinde quod fi aliqua contentio oriatur inter eos de aliquibus articulis quibus fortaffe dictus Abbas dicit fe ufum fuiffe, vel dicti cives dicunt fe habuiffe in feodo ipfius Abbatis, & non poffunt inter eos inde convenire fine aliquo placito, querens veniet ad curiam, & habebit breve Domini Regis ad vicecomitem quod per facramentum xij. tam militum quam aliorum liberorum & legalium hominum forinfecorum per quos rei veritas melius fciri poterit, & qui nec prædictum Abbatem nec prædictos cives aliqua affinitate contingant, inquirat rei veritatem de jure & ufu per illos xij. terminabitur contentio, quia utraque pars conceffit quod fine aliqua calumpnia tenebit fe contentum de hoc quod prædicti Jurati utrique parti dabunt per facramentum fuum.

Prifona Abbatis.

The Ordination of the Vicarage of St. Paul Cant.

Numb.
LXVII.

UNiverfis Chrifti fidelibus ad quos præfens fcriptum pervenerit, Magifter Hugo de Mortuo mari Officialis Curiæ Cantuar. gerens vices venerabilis patris Domini Bonifacii Dei gratia Cant. Archiepifcopi totius Angliæ Primatis in remotis agentis Salutem in domino fempiternam. Noveritis nos ad præfentationem magiftri Hamonis Doge Rectoris ecclefiæ fancti Pauli Cantuar. Virgilium de Alcham Capellanum ad Vicariam prædictæ ecclefiæ, de confenfu & affenfu venerabilis patris R. Dei gratia Abbatis S. Auguftini Cant. & ejufdem loci Conventus qui dictæ ecclefiæ veri funt patroni admififfe, ipfumque vicarium charitatis intuitu inftituiffe canonicè in eadem. Salvis tamen dicto magiftro Hamoni Rectori dictæ ecclefiæ & fucceforibus fuis ejufdem ecclefiæ Rectoribus octo marcis argenti annuis de fructibus dictæ Vicariæ ad Natal Domini, ad Pafcham, ad feftum Natalis beati Johannis Baptiftæ, & ad feftum beati Michaelis equaliter percipiendis. Et dictus Vicarius folvet procurationes Domini Archidiaconi, & alia omnia onera ordinaria fuftinebit. Habebit autem dictus Vicarius & percipiet nomine Vicariæ fuæ omnes obventiones, oblationes, cafus & alia Jura omnia ad dictam ecclefiam fancti Pauli aliquo modo fpectantia & pertinentia (exceptis bladis & fabis in campo) & fic eft ad præfens taxata vicaria fupradicta. In cujus Rei teftimonium prefentes literas ei fieri fecimus figillo Officialitatis Curiæ Cantuar. firmiter roborat'. Dat' Cantuar. 5. Id. Decemb. Anno Domini 1268.

Refervata Rectori.

Onera Vicarii.

Jura Vicarii.

The Ordination of the Vicarage of St. Mary Northgate Canterb.

Numb.
LXVIII.

Anno Domini 1346. Bonæ memoriæ Johannes Cant. Archiepifcopus Vicariam parochialis ecclefiæ beatæ Mariæ de Northgate Cant. religiofis viris Priori & Conventui fancti Gregorii Cant. appropriatæ, de expreffo dictorum Religioforum & Domini Thomæ Sheme Vicarii dictæ ecclefiæ confenfu in certis ordinavit portionibus, fub hac forma.

[Die 4. menf.
Novemb. Reg.
Ecclef. Cant]

QUod viz. idem Vicarius & fucceffores fui in dicta ecclefia Vicarii haberent & perciperent nomine Vicariæ prædictæ libere & abfque impedimento & contradictione dictorum religioforum omnes oblationes in primis miffis parochianorum dictæ ecclefiæ de Northgate defunctorum ubicunque fepeliendorum, in dicta ecclefia factas & faciendas, ac in fecundis miffis hujufmodi defunctorum parochianorum ibidem haberent illi oblationes factas & faciendas qui eas de Jure vel confuetudine habere deberent quodque dicti Vicarii omnes & omnimodas alias oblationes in dicta ecclefia de Northgate, & in quibufcunque locis infra fines, limites feu decimationes dictæ ecclefiæ fcituatis qualitercunque factas ac faciendas, feu ad eam vel in ea provenientes, feu inpofterum provenire valentes, oblationibus & obventionibus hofpitalis de Northgate Cant. duntaxat exceptis. Dictique Vicarii omnes decimas lanæ, agnorum, porcellorum, aucarum, pomorum, pirorum, canap', lini, fabarum & aliorum fructuum & herbarum in ortis five gardinis crefcentium, ac decimas Warenciæ five mader vulgariter nuncupat', infra dictam parochiam provenientes, necnon omnes alias minutas decimas ad dictam ecclefiam qualitercunque fpectantes, omnefque alios proventus, quos dictæ ecclefiæ Vicarii ab antiquo percipere confueverunt, perciperent & haberent, præterquam omnes maiores decimas (ad quatuor marcas annis fingulis æftimatas) ad dictam pertinentes ecclefiam, quas Religiofi præfati fibiipfis perpetuum refervarunt. Quodque Vicarii antedicti onus deferviendi præfatæ ecclefiæ in divinis, inventionifque librorum & ornamentorum dictæ ecclefiæ, cereorum proceffionalium, & unius lampadis in Cancello dictæ ecclefiæ ardere debentis, miniftrationifque panis, vini, luminar' & aliorum ad celebrationem divinorum neceffariorum ibidem, ac etiam folutionis decimarum ac aliarum impofitionum quarumcunque quæ Anglicanæ ecclefiæ imponi contingent pro medietate taxationis dictæ ecclefiæ, fuis fubirent fumptibus & expenfis. Præfati verò religiofi onus refectionis & reparationis Cancelli dictæ ecclefiæ intus & exterius, ac folutionis hujufmodi decimarum & impofitionum quarumcunque, pro alia mediate taxationis ipfius ecclefiæ, necnon cætera onera ordinaria & extraordinaria eidem ecclefiæ incumbentia

Jura Vicariæ.

Hofpitale de
Northgate
exceptum.

Refervata Religiofis.
Onera Vicarii.

Onera Religiofor.

* T

cumbentia feu incumbere debentia Vicariis dictæ ecclefiæ non afcripta fuperius, agnofcerent perpetuum & fublrent.

The Ordination of the Vicarage of Holy-Croffe of Weftgate, Cant.

JOhannes permiffione divina Cantuar. Archiepifcopus totius Angliæ Primas & Apoftolicæ fedis Legatus cunctis Chrifti fidelibus Salutem confequi fempiternam. Ex officii noftri debito Religiofos viros Priorem & Conventum Prioratus fancti Gregorii Cantuar. quibus ecclefia parochialis fanctæ Crucis de Weftgate Cant. appropriata effe dicitur, & Dominum Johannem dictum Sorges vicarium ejufdem ecclefiæ, ad exhibendum coram nobis ordinationem Vicariæ ejufdem ad judicium nuper fecimus evocari. Sed dictæ partes in termino ad præmiffa eis dato nullam ordinationem hujufmodi exhibere fe poffe, quia eam non habuerunt, allegarunt. Pars infuper dictorum Religioforum afferunt quod ipfi onera folutionis decimarum & aliarum impofitionum quarumcunque pro taxatione ipfius ecclefiæ, necnon alia onera ordinaria eidem incumbentia in præteritum agnoverunt, quodque ipfi nihil de fructibus, redditibus, proventibus feu obventionibus ecclefiæ præfatæ pro tempore dicti Vicarii perceperunt, quamvis aliorum vicariorum ejufdem ecclefiæ temporibus certam pecuniæ penfionem habere confueverunt & percipere ab eadem. Dictus etiam Vicarius afferuit quod ecclefiæ præfatæ commoditates quæcunque fibi pro fua fuftentatione congrua & oneribus fuæ Vicariæ incumbentibus vix fufficiunt his diebus, unde nos fuper vero valore annuo, omnium & fingulorum fructuum, redituum, proventuum, & obventionum ejufdem ecclefiæ in quibufcunque rebus confiftant, necnon de & fuper omnibus & fingulis eidem ecclefiæ incumbentibus oneribus, quæ viz. per dictos religiofos & quæ per Vicarium ipfius ecclefiæ folebant agnofci, fummarie & de plano, abfque ftrepitu & figurâ Judicii præmiffis finem volentes imponere, de confenfu dictarum partium inquifitionem in forma Juris fieri fecimus diligentem, quam judicialiter publicavimus & examinavimus in præfentia partium earundem. Demumque de confenfu dictorum Religioforum Vicariæ prædictæ Patronorum, Vicariam ecclefiæ memoratæ, ejus confideratis facultatibus, & ponderatis in ea parte undique ponderandis, ordinandum duximus modo infrafcripto, & taxandum & limitandum quid & quantum præfati Religiofi in futurum percipient ex fructibus, redditibus & proventibus ecclefiæ prelibatæ. Ordinamus fiquidem & ftatuimus quod dicti Religiofi & Succeffores eorum decimas omnium & fingulorum hortorum infra fines & limites parochiæ prædictæ conftitutorum ecclefiæ undecunque, necnon decimis cujufdem molendini Sheffotes-mill vulgariter nuncupati infra parochiam ejufdem ecclefiæ fcituati percipiant & habeant poft inftans feftum Nativitatis Sancti Johannis Baptiftæ temporibus fequuturis. Dictus autem Vicarius & Succeffores fui ibidem Vicarii habeant & teneant duas manfiunculas fubtus ecclefiam prædictam ex utraque ipfius parte fcituatas ad Vicarium ejufdem ecclefiæ antiquitus pertinentes, ceteras etiam decimas tam majores quam minores, necnon oblationes ac fructus, redditus, proventus & obventus omnes & fingulas ad dictam pertinentes ecclefiam feu inpofterum pertinere valentes caufa feu occafione quibufcunque dictis religiofis fuperius non afcripta percipiant, teneant, habeant ipfius ecclefiæ Vicarii in perpetuum fuæ nomine Vicariæ. Onus autem eidem deferviendi ecclefiæ in divinis ac miniftrationis, & exhibitionis panis, vini, luminar', & aliorum quæ ad celebrationem divinorum ibidem neceffaria fuerint per Rectores feu Vicarios locorum inveniendorum feu miniftrandorum de jure vel confuetudine in noftra Diocefi ufitata, ac etiam lotionis veftimentorum & ornamentorum dictæ ecclefiæ inventionifque feu exhibitionis ftraminis quo dicta fternatur ecclefia prout & quotiens opus fuerit, Vicarii ecclefiæ præfatæ fuis agnfcant & fubeant fumptibus & expenfis. Onera vero refectionis & reparationis Cancelli ejufdem ecclefiæ, inventionifque feu exhibitionis & reparationis librorum, veftimentorum & ornamentorum ejufdem quæ per ecclefiarum Rectores inveniri feu exhibiri vel reparari de Jure vel confuetudine debent aut folent ac infuper onus folutionis decimarum & aliarum impofitionum quarumcunque que dictam ecclefiam fecundum ejus taxationem vel aliter concernere inpofterum poterint feu debebunt, necnon & cætera onera ordinaria & extraordinaria ecclefiæ prædictæ qualitercunque incumbentia feu incumbere debentia Vicario ejufdem ecclefiæ qui erit pro tempore non afcripta fuperius, dicti Religiofi fubeant in perpetuum & agnofcant. Refervantes nobis & Succefforibus noftris Archiepifcopis Cantuarienfibus dictam Vicariam augmentandi & diminuendi fi & quando nobis aut eis videbitur expedire, plenariam poteftatem. In quorum teftimonum figillum noftrum fecimus hiis apponi. Dat. apud Saltwood quinto Id. Junii Anno Domini Milefimo trecentefimo quadragefimo feptimo, & noftræ tranflationis quarto-decimo.

Margin notes:
Refervata Religiofis.
Conceffa Vicario.
Onera Vicarii.
Onera Religiofor

The Ordination of the Vicarage of St. Dunftan, Cant.

UNiverfis tenore præfentium innotefcat, quod nos Walterus permiffione &c. facta inquifitione fuper valore fructuum & obventionum omnium ecclefiæ fancti Dunftani juxta Cant. quæ viris religiofis Priori & Conventui fancti Gregorii Cantuar' appropriatam effe dinofcitur : Vicarium ecclefiæ S. Dunftani ordinamus in hunc modum, ut viz. ejufdem

Margin note:
Jura Vicarii.

dem loci Vicarius qui pro tempore fuerit pro sua suftentatione & suorum omnes decimas minores, oblationes & cæteros proventus omnimodos percipiat, decima garbarum cujuscunque bladi in campis crescentis duntaxat excepta, quam præfatis Religiosis nomine Rectoriæ applicamus, ac ipsos hujusmodi garbarum decimas perpetuis futuris temporibus percipere debere decernimus ac etiam ordinamus. Onera vero tam ordinaria quam extraordinaria Cancelli, librorum & ornamentorum, quatenus ad Rectores locorum pertinere consueverunt per hanc nostram ordinationem plene agnoscent. Salva nobis potestate hanc nostram ordinationem interpretandi, declarandi, corrigendi, addendi seu detrahendi quotiens & quando nobis expedire videbitur. In cujus &c. Dat apud Mortlake decimo sexto Kalen' Augusti 1322.

Referervata Religiosis.
Onera eorum.

The tenor of the same Vicarages augmentation.

JOhannes permissione divina Cant. Archiepiscopus totius Angliæ Primas & Apostolicæ sedis Legatus, cunctis Christi fidelibus Salutem perennem. Ne perpetui ecclesiarum parochialium Vicarii, propter rerum inopiam, & suarum portionum tenuitatem egeant, nostro pastorali officio convenit remedium adhibere. Eapropter religiosos viros Priorem & Conventum sancti Gregorii Cant. ecclesiam sancti Dunstani Cant. in proprios usus habentes, ut Domino Stephano Vicario ecclesiæ antedictæ cujus Vicariæ præsentatio ad ipsos dicitur pertinere, sufficientes de ipsius ecclesiæ fructibus, proventibus & obventionibus portiones, unde ipse possit & Successores sui in dicta ecclesia Vicarii possint congruam sustentationem habere, & sibi incumbentia onera supportare, infra certum à nobis eis præfixum terminum assignarent, nostra authoritate legitima moneri fecimus & induci. Qui quidem religiosi quandam exhibuerunt ordinationem dictæ Vicariæ per bonæ memoriæ Walterum quondam Cant. Archiepiscopum prædecessorem nostrum factam in qua taliter continetur quod Vicarius dictæ ecclesiæ qui pro tempore fuerit decimas minores, oblationes & cæteros proventus ad dictam pertinentes ecclesiam, & provenientes undecunque ad eam debeat percipere & habere, decimis garbarum cujuscunque generis bladi de terris infra parochiam prædictæ ecclesiæ constitutis provenientibus dictis religiosis retentis. Sedidem Vicarius asserens dictas portiones in hujusmodi ordinatione Vicariæ contentas & assignatas eidem nullatenus sufficientes fore; judicialiter demum, post altercationes diutinas dictarum partium super sufficientia & insufficientia portionum dictæ Vicariæ assignatarum in ordinatione prædicta super valore eorum annuo de mandato nostro & consensu dictarum rum partium legitimè inquisito, compertum extitit portiones easdem per prædictum prædecessorem nostrum, ut præmittitur assignatas Vicariæ ipsius ecclesiæ quatuor marcis annis singulis duntaxat valere. Unde Commissarius noster in hujusmodi negotio rite procedens, auditis propositis & allegationibus partium earum, necnon depositionibus testium prædictorum hincinde rimatis plenarie & discussis, nihilque per partem religiosorum quare portiones dictæ Vicariæ augmentari non debeant & suppleri effectualiter proposito sive dicto, terminis successivis & variis ad hoc datis, concurrentibusque omnibus, & singulis quæ in ea parte requirebantur de Jure, in præsentia dictarum partium coram eo sufficienter comparentium, dictam vicariam augmentari debere pronuntiavit finaliter & decrevit Ipsisque Vicariis & Successoribus suis ibidem Vicariis ultra ordinationem nostri prædecessoris prædicti, ea rata manente, mansum dictæ Vicariæ quem Vicarii ejusdem inhabitare solent antiquitus, necnon & pensionem duarum marcarum sterlingorum annuam per Religiosos prædictos solvendarum sibi & successoribus suis ibidem Vicariis in festis Natalis Domini & sancti Johannis Baptistæ equalibus portionibus annuatim in dictæ assignatæ suæ portionis augmentum canonicè assignavit. Ordinavit insuper & decrevit quod idem Vicarius & sui successores in eadem ecclesia Vicarii futuris temporibus eidem ecclesiæ deserviant in divinis sustentationibusque cereorum, luminarium, ac panis & vini, pro celebratione missarum in eadem. Necnon in quibuscunque solutionibus decimarum & impositionibus aliis extraordinariis dictæ ecclesiæ ad quatuor marcas estimata onera pro medietate supportabunt. Præfatique religiosi refectiones & reparationes cancelli dictæ ecclesiæ, inventionemque librorum, vestimentorum & ornamentorum ad Rectores locorum pertinentes subibunt perpetim & agnoscent, reservata nobis & Successoribus nostris &c. Unde nos idem Johannes Archiepiscopus præmissa omnia & singula authoritate nostra ordinaria (ut præmittitur) ritè facta approbamus & tenore præsentium confirmamus. Dat' Cantuariæ, iijo. Cal. Augusti Anno Domini Millesimo,Cccmo. xlijo. & nostræ translationis nono.

Causæ augmentationis.
Augmentatio ipsa.
Onera Vicarii.
Onera Religiosor

A Record shewing the ancient Forme and Custome of payment of Tithes in Canterbury, taken out of the Archbishops principall Registry.

THomas permissione divina Cantuar. Archiepiscopus totius, &c. Dilectis in Christo filiis Commissario nostro Cant. generali & Archidiaconi Officiali Salutem, gratiam & benedictonem. Clamosa insinuatione quorundam Rectorum & Vicariorum ecclesiarum nostræ Civitatis ad aures nostras pervenit, quod licet ex antiqua & rationabili consuetudine tam in nostra Civitate quam alibi per totam Civitatem London' antiquitus observata & legitime præscripta

scripta, etiam in contradictorio judicio aliquotiens obtenta, pro quolibet hospitio seu domicilio dictæ nostræ Civitatis pro decem solidis sterlingorum per unum annum conducto, quadrantem, & si pro viginti solidis hujusm' hospitium seu domus per annum conducatur, obolum, & pro hospitio pro quadraginta solidis per annum conducto denarium, & si hospitium hujusm' pro majori summa per annum conductum fuerit, plus, juxta summam seu portionem prædict', inhabitantes & conducentes domos & hospitia hujusmodi, qualibet die dominica per annum, & singulis etiam festis solempnibus, & præcipuè Apostolorum quorum etiam vigiliæ per annum jejunantur, Deo & Ecclesiæ in cujus parochia domus seu ædificia hujusmodi situantur offerre debeant & tenentur. Sunt tamen non-

Oblationes.

Decimæ personales.

nulli dictæ nostræ Civitatis qui tam obligationes suas hujusmodi Ecclesiis eorum parochialibus ac Rectoribus & Vicariis earundem vigore dictæ consuetudinis debitas, quam decimas eorum Personales de lucro negotiationum suarum provenientes & Ecclesiis quarum sunt parochiani debitas injustè subtrahunt & subtrahere moliuntur, ac decimas hujusmodi solvere contradicunt, objicientes contra Rectores & Vicarios hujusmodi decimas petentes consuetudinem non solvendi decimas supradictas, quam Canones vocant corruptelam, & plerumque quod deterius est confederatis & coadunatis pluribus conditionis similis, per illicitas conventiculas contra decimas hujusmodi exigentes ex præcogitatâ malitiâ gratis insurgunt, & quatenus in eis est Rectores & Vicarios sic petentes injustè opprimunt & jurium Ecclesiasticorum subtractiones diversis modis adaugent contra canonicas sanctiones, in animarum suarum grave periculum & libertatis Ecclesiasticæ læsionem manifestam. Nos igitur animabus nostrorum subditorum prospicere & morbo hujusmodi pestifero quantum à Canone est permissum mederi cupientes. Vobis con' & utrique vestrum di' committimus & mandamus firmiter injungendo, quatenus in singulis Ecclesiis dictæ nostræ Civitatis omnes & singulos decimas & oblationes hujusmodi injustè subtrahentes, & eas debitè non solventes, diebus dominicis & festivis intra missarum solempnia, cum major affuerit populi multitudo, authoritate nostra peremptoriè moneatis & efficaciter inducatis, quod de eorum decimis seu oblationibus subtractis Ecclesiis quarum sunt Parochiani, infra unius mensis spatium à tempore monitionis vestræ continuè numerandum satisfaciant competenter. Et quod de cætero subtrahentes hujusmodi suas decimas & oblationes quatenus ad eos attinet fideliter persolvant ut tenentnr, sub pœnâ excommunicationis majoris quam in contravenientes & monitionibus vestris non parentes in hac parte, mora & culpa eorum in ea parte præcedentibus per vos volumus canonicè fulminari, & sic excommunicatos publicè nuntiari. De nominibus verò hujusmodi subtrahentium cum omni diligentia & cautela plenius inquiratis seu inquiri faciatis in singulis Parochiis Ecelesiarum dictæ nostræ Civitatis, in quibus per ipsarum Ecclesiarum Rectores & Vicarios fueritis congrue requisiti. De die verò receptionis presentium, monitionisque & executionis vestrarum in hac parte factarum modo & forma, ac de nominibus subtrahentium hujusmodi, necnon de omni eo quod feceritis & inveneritis in hac parte, nos cum per partem dictorum Rectorum & Vicariorum fueritis congruè requisiti certificetis, per vestras literas patentes, seu certificet alter vestrum qui præsens mandatum fuerit executus per suas literas patentes harum serim continentes. Dat 'in palatio nostro Cant. xiiij. die mensis Aprilis Anno Domini Millesimo Cccmo. nonagesimo septimo, & nostræ translationis anno primo.

Numb. LXXI. b. *Another Record to the same purpose, taken out of the Registry of the Consistory at* Cant. *being a deposition or witnesses examination taken in a suite, Anno* 1457. *there commenced, for tithes, by the then Parson of* St. Elphege, Cant.

THomas Proude de Parochia sancti Elphegi Civitatis Cantuar. ætatis L. annorum & ultra, liberæ conditionis ut dicit, interrogatus an sit consuetudo in Civitate Cant. quod omnes & singuli parochiani cujuscunque Parochiæ tenentur offerre diebus dominicis & aliis diebus solemnibus quorum vigiliæ jejunantur secundum valorem redditus domuum, hoc est, si domus solvat xx s. obolum, & si xl s. denarium, & sic secundum ratam ascensive & descensive, dicit quod sic. Interrogatus quomodo scit, dicit quod ita ipse observavit, & obtulit, & sic vidit observari toto tempore suo, ac etiam sic audivit à tempore & per tempus cujus contrarii memoria hominum non existit à prædecessoribus suis ita observatum fuisse. Interrogatus an novit aliquam constitutionem in hac parte latam dicit quod audivit quod sic, & quod virtute illius constitutionis ac consuetudinis prædictæ quidam magister Galfridus Langbrok nuper Vicarius sancti Dunstani extra muros Civitatis Cantuar. contra Johannem Belsyre parochianum suum in casu consimili per sententiam diffinitivam victoriam obtinuit. Interrogatus insuper an Curati dictæ Civitatis præsentes & prædecessores sui pro temporibus suis, & præsertim dictus dominus Johannes Permenter Rector sancti Elphegi fuerunt & sunt in possessione seu quasi juris percipiendi & habendi hujusmodi oblationes ab inhabitantibus & occupantibus domos & hospitia infra suam parochiam modo & forma præmissis, dicit quod sic. Iterrogatus per quantum tempus, dicit quod de notitia, & scientia suis per x. xx. xxx. xl. annos, & de auditu suo per lx. annos, & per tempus cujus contrarii

trarii

trarii memoria hominum non exiſtit, & nunquam audivit de contrario uſque ad litem hanc motam.

Theſe things are con-teſted by *William Sellow* and *John Merſh* both of that Pariſh.

The Copy of an ancient Mſ. ſhewing and ſetting forth the forme of ſome Numb.
kinde of Law-trialls amongſt the Engliſh-Saxons. LXXII.

f

IN nomine Dei ſummi regis æterni. Plerumque etenim contingere ſolet ut res poſſeſſæ hereditatis acquiſitæ in contentionem pleriſque & altercationis conflictum deveniunt niſi cum idoneis teſtibus & ſubſcriptionibus ſapientium & fidelium perſonarum teſtimoniis tractata & confirmata fuerint. Quapropter ſapientes ſalubrem conſilium prudentium quærunt, & cyrographorum cautionibus & heroicorum virorum teſtimoniis confirmantur ne impoſterum aliquibus altercationibus vel ſcrupulo falſi ſuſpitionis corrumpuntur, aut nebulo ignorantiæ in aliquo fuſcetur. Idcirco etenim Oſwlf Dei gratia Dux atque Princeps Oſwlſ. Dux atque Princeps Provinciæ Orientalis Cantiæ circa ſuæ propriæ hereditatis jura tractare ſtuduit. Et hoc Provinciæ Orientalis Cantiæ. coram beatæ memoriæ Wlfredo Archiepiſcopo, coramque Abbatis Wernotho atque Feolgeldo ceteriſque fideliſſimis & religioſiſſimis Ceolſtano, viz. Aethelhuno atque Heremodo presbyteris Eccleſiæ Chriſti, nec non ſæpe coram ſociis ſuis & amicis fidiſſimis, qualiter poſt diſceſſionem ſuam circa hereditatem ſuam impoſterum agere voluiſſe, id eſt, ut poſt dies uxoris ſuæ & filii ejus Eardwlfi, filiæ quoque ſuæ Ealfthrythæ ad Eccleſiis Dei omnia dare Deo & ſanctis ejus ſibi in ſempiternam hereditatem ſub eorum teſtimonia dare præcepit ſicut in altera kartula manifeſte & lucide comprobatur. Sed tamen poſt obitum Oſwlfi Ducis ſurrexit excitata à quibuſdam quæſtio & contentio magno circa hereditatem Oſwlfi contra uxorem ejus Beornthrythæ cujus altercationis conflictum neque à Domino Archiepiſcopo nec ab aliquibus perſonis inferioribus ullo modo ſedare potuit, ſed utrique partes ad ſynodale concilium advocari & invitari jubebantur, & cum ad ſynodum deveniſſent & diligenti inveſtigatione veritatis ſententia utrarumque partium à ſancto ſynodo quæ facta eſt in loco præclaro æt aeclea querendo examinaretur, inventum eſt nihil juſtius nec rectius eſſe poſſe conſtare quam ſic perſeverare hereditatem Oſwlfi ſicut ipſe Oſwlf prius proprio arbitrio per omnia donare coram prædictis teſtibus decreverat, atque ita hoc etiam ab illo ſancto ſynodo perpetuae perdurare dejudicatum eſt. Inſuper etiam ſancta illa ſynodus decrevere ſtatuit ut illa altercatio nunquam amplius per aliquam inquietudinis diſcordiam poſt illum diem & deinceps excitando moveretur, & hoc cum ſigno ſanctæ crucis Chriſti perenniter perdurare conſcripſerunt. Et ſi quis poſthæc alicujus perſonis homo Diabolica inſtigatus temeritate inſurrexerit qui hoc Kanonica & ſynodalia decreta infringere temptaverit à ſocietate ſanctorum omnium, & à cœtu congregationis & communionis ipſorum ſciret ſe eſſe alienatum ſynodali judicio ſtatuerunt. Sed heu pro dolor ille antiquus venenatiſſimus ſerpens qui protuplauſtu piacula indidit, & humanum genus ſibi per hæc ſubdidit, ceu cælydra infeſta & peſtifera in quorundam pectore adhuc turgeſcit, & ad excitandas ſeditiones diſcordiaſque committendas poſt curricula quantorum annorum id eſt xxxiiij iterum eccleſiam Chriſti & hereditatem ſanctorum ejus adgravere ac depravere impia niſu ac prava voluntate conatus eſt, atque illam prædict' altercationis conflictum renovare & excitare poſt ſynodalia decreta, Synodale concilium apud Cantuariam. ac probabilium patrum ſanctiones ſtuduit. Quamobrem congregata multitudine ſpiritalium ſeculariuque perſonum in Dorovernia Civitate, anno dominicæ incarnationis Dcccxliiij. in dict. Aethelwlfo Regi præſente atque Aethelſtano filio ejus Ceolnotho quoque Archimetropolitano Archiepiſcopo, necnon Tatnoth presbitero electo ad Epiſcopalem Dorobrevis. ſedem Dorobrevi, id eſt, civitatis Hrofi, cum Principibus, Ducibus, Abbatibus & cunctis generalis dignitatis optimatibus inter quas etiam ille venenatiſſimus anguis cognomento Aethelwulf ad turbandum & inquietandum eccleſiam Dei deveniens, ſicut ſepe progenies & parentes ejus fecerunt, prolatis falſis machinamentis è latebris cordis ſuæ dicens hereditatem Oſwlfi Ducis cum auro & argento patris ſui Aethelheah eſſe comparatum, & per hoc ſpoliare eccleſiam Dei & ſanctos cœnubias ad quas hereditas illa pertinebat cum pravis ſequacibus niſus eſt. Tunc ille Archiepiſcopus Ceolnoth & familia ejus id eſt eccleſiæ Chriſti illa per ordinem replicavit qualiter in illo ſancto ſynodo de illo reconciliatum & dejudicatum eſt. At ille nolens adquieſcere, neque judicio ſynodis & probabilium patrum ſanctionibus neque adſertione & veredica voce Epiſcopi vel alicujus perſonis tunc etenim à ſapientibus & prudentibus trutinatum ac dijudicatum eſt familiam eccleſiæ Chriſti, Juridici examinis priſca formula. & familiam æt. Folcanſtane, familiam quoque at Dobrum, necnon & familiam æt Liminge adquos hereditas illa pertinebat juſto juramenta hereditatem illam ſibi ipſis contra hereditatem Aethelheahes caſtigare, nam & ita fecerunt. Juraverunt xxx homines de familiis prædictis, xij presbeteri, ceteri communi gradus & ſic etiam illa altercatio utrarumque partium perenniter ſedari decretum eſt, & illa altercatio nunquam amplius per aliquam inquie- Anathema in tudinis diſcordiam poſt diem illum excitando moveatur, & firmiter decreverunt ut ſub ana- violatores. thematis vinculo eſſet nodatus qui hanc reconciliationem in aliquo irritum faceret, ſicut & ille excommunicatus conſtat à conſortio ſanctorum omnium & à communione ſynodalis concilii & familiis noſtris eccleſiæque Dei alienus exiſtat qui hoc Kanonica Statuta &ſynodalia præcepta infringere ſtuduit, niſi digne Deo & hominibus præſumptionis ſuæ conamen emendare voluerit, & hoc ſigno ſanctæ crucis Chriſti roborando omnes pariter conſcripſerunt.

* u ✠ Ego

✠ Ego Aethelwlf Deo difpenfante Rex Occidentalium Anglorum hanc prædictam reconciliationem familiæ Chrifti & hereditatis Ethelheahes, & omnem altercationis conflictum qui inter fe concitatum habuerunt fedatum effe demonftrans, & hoc cum fapientibus meis figno fanctæ crucis Chrifti perenni titulo roborabo & fubfcribo quorum fubter in fcedula liquefcunt vocabula.

✠ Ego Aethelwlf Dux coa' & fub'. ✠ Ego Aethelheah con. & fub.
✠ Ego Cynewlf con. & fub. ✠ Ego Aethelheah con. & fub.
✠ Ego Lulling con. & fub. ✠ Ego Gisfhard con. & fub.

✠ Ego Ceolnoth gratia Dei Metropolitanus Archiepifc. cum presbyteris & familia fua hoc id eft figno fanctæ crucis Chrifti roborando fubfcripfi.

✠ Ego Alchhere Dux con. & fub. ✠ Ego Freothoric con. & fub.
✠ Ego Aethelwlf Dux con.& fub. ✠ Ego Denemod con. & fub.
✠ Ego Freothoric Ab' con' &fub'. ✠ Ego Beornfreth con. & fub.
✠ Ego Aethelmond con. & fub. ✠ Ego Osfere con.
✠ Ego Aethelred con. & fub.

Hæc funt etiam nomina familiæ Chrifti & illius familiæ æt Folcanftane nec non æt Dobrum, atque æt Liminge qui hanc jurationem juraverunt, quorum nomina fubter adnotantur.

✠ Ego Abba pr' con. & fub. ✠ Ego Sygeanod con. & fub.
✠ Ego Brunheard pr' con. & fub. ✠ Ego Wihtred con. & fub.
✠ Ego Hunred pr' con. & fub. ✠ Ego Willmund con. & fub.
✠ Ego Hyfenod pr' con. & fub. ✠ Ego Beornmod con. & fub.
✠ Ego Wigmund pr' con. & fub. ✠ Ego Cynwlf.
✠ Ego Eof pr' con. & fub. ✠ Ego Willhere.
✠ Ego Degmund pr' con. & fub. ✠ Ego Berhtnoth.
✠ Ego Wealdhere pr' con. & fub. ✠ Ego ———
✠ Ego Aethelred pr' con. & fub. ✠ Ego Ceolbald con.
✠ Ego Cichus con. & fub. ✠ Ego Alchhere.
✠ Ego Sigemund con. & fub. ✠ Ego Duddel.
✠ Ego Bornfred con. & fub. ✠ Ego Ethelhere.
✠ Ego Wynna con. & fub. ✠ Ego Nothhere.

The Foundation of the prefent Church of Holy-Crofs *of* Weftgate *in* Canterbury (*or as it is in the Original entituled*) Fundatio novæ Ecclefiæ de Weftgate.

Numb. LXXII.

Ricardus Dei Gratia Rex Angliæ & Franciæ, Dominus Hiberniæ, omnibus ad quos præfentes literæ pervenerint, falutem. Sciatis quod nos confiderantes, qualiter Venerabilis Pater *Simon* Archiepifcopus Cantuar. pro fortificatione claufuræ civitatis noftræ Cantuarienf. incœpit fieri facere unam novam portam loco cujufdam antiquæ debilis portæ vocatæ *Weftgate* : fuper quam quidem antiquam portam habebatur una antiqua Ecclefia parochialis vocata *Ecclefia S. Crucis de Weftgate*, quam dilecti nobis in Chrifto Prior & Conventus S. Gregorii in fuburbio civitatis noftræ tenuerunt in proprios ufus; & quæ quidem Ecclefia & antiqua porta poftratæ, ac parochiani ibidem de Ecclefia fua parochiali improvifi exiftunt, ut fumus veraciter informati de gratia noftra fpeciali conceffimus & licentiam dedimus pro nobis & heredibus noftris, quantum in nobis eft, dilectis Thomæ Hall, Johanni Gate, Wilhelmo al. Wood, Roberto Plomer, Richardo Tanner, Adæ Jolyf, Thomæ Cokker, Thomæ Spile, quod ipfi unam placeam terræ cum pertinent : in Civitate noftra prædicta, quæ quidem placea de nobis tenetur in capite in liberum Burgageum, ut dicitur, & continet quatuordecim virgas & quatuor pedes in longitudine & fex virgas & quatuor pedes in latitudine, dare poffint & affignare eifdem Priori & Conventui, Habend. & Tenend. fibi & fuccefforibus fuis de nobis & heredibus noftris per fervitia inde debita & confueta in perpetuum. Et eifdem Priori & Conventui quod ipfi dictam placeam cum pertinent. de prædictis Thoma Johanne, Wilhelmo, Roberto, Ricardo, Adam, Thoma, Thoma recipere poffint & tenere fibi & fuccefforibus fuis in formâ prædictâ, & in eadem placea unam novam Ecclefiam parochialem in honore fanctæ Crucis, & dicta antiqua Ecclefia fua erat, & unum cæmiterium facere, & id & eandem Ecclefiam, cum fic facta fuerit, appropriare & in proprios ufus tenere dictis Priori & Conventui & Succefforibus fuis prædictis eifdem modo & forma, quibus iidem Prior & Conventus tenuerunt priorem Ecclefiam fupradictam, & ad fuftenendum eadem onera, quæ ratione ejufdem tenebantur fuftinere in perpetuum. Tenore præfentium fimiliter licentiam dedimus fpecialem, ftatuto de terris & tenementis ad manum mortuam non ponendis edito, feu eo quod dicta placea cum pertinent. de nobis tenetur in liberum Burgageum, ut prædictum eft, non obftante nolentes quod prædicti Thomas, Johannes, Wilhelmus, Robertus, Richardus, Adam, Thomas, Thomas, vel heredes fui aut præfati Prior & Conventus aut fucceffores fui, ratione ftatuti prædicti vel aliorum præmifforum, per nos vel heredes noftros vel heredum noftrorum quofcunque occafionentur moleftentur in aliquo feu graventur. In cujus rei Teftimonium has literas noftras fieri fecimus patentes. Tefte meipfo apud Weftmonafterium decimo die Martij, Anno Regni noftri tertio W. S.

The

The Patent or Commission of the Commissary of Canterbury.

FRater I. Archiepisc. &c. Magistro Martino &c. Salutem. Quia quocunque auctoritas nostra se protendit ad incumbentia nobis onera exequenda simul & semel personaliter adesse nequivimus, illos nonnunquam in partem solicitudinis accepimus de quorum fide & industria plenam in Domino fiduciam reportamus. Hinc est quod de tuæ circumspectionis & fidei plenitudine confidentes, officium Commissar. Cant. tibi cum omnibus Juribus & Jurisdictionibus ad ipsum officium qualitercunque spectan' committimus per præsentes, ut tam prudenter quam fideliter in omnibus liberè authoritate nostra exercere valeas officium memoratum, & ad te tanquam nostrum in nostra Diocesi Commissarium generalem in his quæ ad ipsum pertineant officium recurratur. In cujus &c. Dat' apud Mortlake 3. Non. Maii Anno Dom. 1282. Consecrationis nostræ quarto.

Revocatio Jurisdictionis ecclesiarum exemptarum.

WAlter. permissione divina Cant. Archiep. totius Angliæ Primas. Dilecto filio Commiss. nostro Cant. salutem, gratiam, & benedictionem. Quia tam de Jure communi quam de consuetudine in nostra Civitate & Diocesi omnis Jurisdictio spiritualis ad nos authoritate Diocesana dinoscitur pertinere, jurisdictionem omnimodam quam rectores ecclesiarum sanctorum Martini & Elphegi Cant. & de Reculver, Monketon, Adesham, Ickham, Eastry, Dale, Godmersham, Saltwood, Westwell, Charing, Woodchurch, Wittresham, Northfleet & Pageham, necnon de Maidestan, & de Bocton subtus le Blen nostræ Diœcesis, ex nostra conniventia in parochiis ecclesiarum suarum singulariter exercuerunt, in derogationem Juris nostri & ecclesiæ nostræ, certis ex causis ad nos jamdudum revocavimus, ipsam jurisdictionem per nostros officiales seu Commissarios exercendam fore decernentes. Vobis committimus & mandamus quatenus omnimoda jurisdictione in parochiis ecclesiarum prædict' & earum qualibet ac capellarum dependentium ab eisdem & subditis earundem, de cetero utamini vice nostra prout Commissarii Cant. seu alii quicunque uti consueverint in eisdem temporibus retroactis. Contradictores & rebelles per censuras ecclesiasticas compescendo. In cujus Rei testimonium Sigillum nostrum præsentibus est appensum. Dat apud Lambeth 15. Kal. April. Anno Dom. 1317.

The Epilogue to his Countrymen.

IF, by your good acceptance of these my Labours for the City, I may receive encouragement to proceed in my endeavours, it is in my thoughts, by Gods assistance, in convenient time, to doe somewhat in like kinde for you in the Country. In the meane time, for that recourse which some of you have had unto me for satisfaction and information to what Saints their Churches were at first commanded, conceiving that it may give content both to them and others of you, who (not out of any either superstitious or riotous instinct, I hope, but for those good and pious ends which the first Institution of the Encænia had regard unto *) are desirous to reduce that ancient laudable Custome, sometime consonant to Canon*, of observing those Feasts of Dedication, now, through ignorance most what, I suppose, of their Saints names, generally in these parts laid aside; conceiving it, I say, an acceptable thing to revive and restore to each Parochial Church and Chappell the forgotten name and memory of such Saint or Saints, as at their dedication (upon such or like grounds as are judiciously rendred and laid down elsewhere *) were given (and are therefore proper) to them: having used my best diligence for a full Collection of those of Canterbury-Diocesse from good Record, I shall here leave it with you in pawne, and as a pledge unto you of those my future endeavours for your further content hereafter, if God permit.

Encænia.
* Namely, not onely the encouragement of others to the like acts of piety and devotion, by a thankfull commemoration of his or their bounty and munificence who had either founded or endowed the Church; but also the manifestation and maintenance of Christian Union, Charity, and good society, by a kind of Love Feast.
‖ Cap. Ex scripturis. de Feriis in Provincial.
* Hooker. Ecclesiastic. Polity. lib. 5. num. 13.

Canterbury-Deanrie.

S. Alphege.
S. Andrew.
S. Mary-Bredman.
S. Mary-Bredin.
S. Mary-Castle.
Holy-Crosse of Westgate
S. Edmund of Ridingate
S. George of Newingate — Within the City.
S. John.
S. Margaret.
S. Mary Magdalen.
S. Mary of Northgate.
S. Mary of Queningate.
S. Michael or Burgate.
S. Mildred.
S. Peter.
All-Sains.

S. Dunstan.
S. Martin. — In the Suburbs.
S. Paul.

S. Cosmas and Damian. Bleane.
S. Mary. Fordwich.
S. Mary. Little Hardres.
S. Michael. Herbaldowne.
S. Nicholas. Herbaldowne.
S. Stephen. Hackington.
S. Mary. Natyndon.
S. Nicolas. Sturrey.
S. Nicolas. Thannington. Milton.

Sandwich-Deanrie.

S. Clement.
S. Iames.
S. Mary. — in Sandwich.
S. Peter.
S. Mary Barfrestone.
Bettishanger.
S. Pancrace. Colred.
S. Leonard. Deale.
S. Mary. Eastry.
S. Augustine. Eastlongdon.
S. Peter and Paul. Eithorne.
S. George. Ham.
S. Clement. Knolton.

S. Martin. Great Mongeham.
S. Augustine. Norborne.
S. Mary. Ripple.
S. Nicholas. Ringwold.
S. Andrew. Sibertswold. Sutton.
S. Nicholas. Sholden.
S. Andrew. Tilmanstone.
S. Mary. Westlangdon.
All Saints. Waldershare.
S. Peter and Paul. Worth.
S. Mary. Walmer.
S. Mary. Woodnesborough.

Westbere-Deanrie.

All Saints. Birchington.
S. Mary. Minster.
S. Mary Magdalen. Mounkton.
S. Giles. Sarre.
S. Iohn Baptist.
S. Lawrence.
S. Nicholas. — in Thanet.
S. Peter.
S. Mary. Chistlet.

S. Martin. Hearne.
S. Mary;
Holy Croffe. } - Hoth.
S. Mary. Reculver.
S. Elphege. Seafalter.
S. Iohn Baptift. Swalcliffe.
All Saints. Weftbere.
All Saints. Whitftable.

Bridge-Deanrie.
S. Innocents. Adifham.
S. Nicholas. Afh.
S. Iohn Baptift. Barham.
S. Peter. Beaksbourne.
S. Iohn Evangelift. Ickham.
S. Giles. Kingftone.
S. Vincent. Littlebourne.
S. Peter. Molafh.
S. Mary. Bifhopsbourne.
S. Peter. Bridge.
S. Mary. Brooke.
All Saints. Boughton Alulph.
S. Mary. Chartam.
S. Cofmas and Damian. Challocke.
S. Mary. Chilham.
All Saints. Chillenden.
S. Mary. Crondall.
Elmeftone.
S. Lawrence. Godmerfham.
Holy Croffe-Goodneftone;
S. Peter and Paul. Great-Hardres;
S. Mary. Nonington.
All Saints. Petham.
S. Mary. Patricksbourne.
S. Mildred. Preston.
S. Mary Stodmerfh.
S. Iames. Staple.
All Saints. Stourmouth.
S. Mary. Stelling.
S. Andrew. Wickhambruex.
S. Mary. Wingham.
S. Gregory and S. Martin. Wy.
S. Bartholomew. Waltham.
S. Margaret. Wemingfwold.

Dover-Deanry.
S. Antonine. Alkham.
S. Peter. Bewsfield.
S. Andrew. Buckland.
S. Peter. Charlton.
S. Martin. Cheriton.
S. Mary. Capleferne.
S. Peter and S. Paul. Ewell.
S. Mary and S. Eanfwith. Folkftone.
S. Margaret. at Cliffe.
S. Martin. Gufton.
S. Nicholas. Newington.
S. Laurence. Hougham.
S. Michael. Hawkinge.
S. Iames.
S. Iohn.
S. Mary.
S. Nicholas. } In Dover.
S. Peter,
S. Mary. Liden;
S. Peter and S. Paul. River.
S. Peter. Swinkfield.
S. Peter. Weft-cliffe.

Ealaam-Dehnrie.
S. Martin. Acris.
S. Mary. Braborne.
S. Margaret. Bircholt.

S. Mary Magdalen. Denton.
S. Mary. Ealham.
S. Iames. Elmefted.
S. Peter. Horton.
S. Mary. Haftinglegh.
S. Mary & S. Eadburgh. Liminge.
S. Leonard. Hith.
S. Mary. Poftling.
S. Ofwald. Padlefworth.
S. Peter and S. Paul. Saltwood.
All Saints. Stanford.
S. Mary. Stowting.
S. Martin. Woodton.

Charing-Deanrie.
S. Mary. Afhford.
S. Nicholas. Boughton Malherb.
S. George. Bennenden.
All Saints. Biddenden.
S. Peter and Paul. Charing.
S. Mary. Great Chart.
S. Mary. Little Chart.
S. Dunftan. Cranebrooke.
S. Mary. Eaftwell.
S. Mary. Egerton.
S. Mary Frittenden.
S. Peter and Paul. Hedcorne.
S. Mary. Hothfield.
S. Mary. Halden.
S. Lawrence. Hawkherft.
S. Mary. Kennington.
S. Peter. Newenden.
S. Blafe Pet.
S. Mary. Pevington.
S. Nicholas. Pluckley.
S. Mary. Rolvinden.
S. Michael. Smarden.
S. Nicholas. Sandherft.
S. Mildred. Tenderden.
S. Mary. Weftwell.

Lim-Deanrie.
S. Martin. Aldington.
S. Peter and S. Paul. Appledoore.
S. Romwald. Bonington.
S. Peter and S. Paul. Bilfington.
All Saints. Burmefh.
S. Eanfwith. Brenfet.
S. Auguftine. Brookland.
S. Peter and S. Paul. Dimchurch.
S. Mary. Eboney.
S. Thomas Martyr. Fairfield.
S. Mary Hinxhill.
All Saints. Hope.
S. Leonard. Herft.
S. George. Ivechurch.
S. Mary. Kenarton.
S. Michael. Knigfnorth.
S. Stephen. Lim.
S. Peter and Paul. Newchurch.
S. Mary. Orlaftone.
S. Mary Magdalen. Rokinge.
S. Lawrence.
S. Martin.   } in New Romney.
S. John Baptift.
S. Nicholas.   } the prefent Church
S. Clement. Old Romney.
S. Mary. Sevington.
S. Mary. Sellinge.
S. Peter and Paul. Shadoxherft;
S. Mary. Smeth.
S. Auguftine. Snave.
S. Mary. Stone.
S. Dunftan. Snafgate.
S. Mary. Weft-Hith.
S. Mary. Willesborongh.
All-Saints. Lyd.
S. Mary's Church. In the Merfh.

S. John Baptift. Merfham.
S. Matthew. Warhorne.
All Saints. Wood Church.
S. John Baptift. Wittrefham.

Sutton-Deanrie.
S. Margaret. Bromefield.
S. Peter. Bredherft.
Holy Crofs. Barfted.
All Saints, Boxley.
S. Peter. Boughton Monchenfey.
S. Michael. Chart.
S. Martin. Detling.
S. Peter and Paul. Eaft-Sutton.
S. Dunftan. Frenfted.
S. Mary. Goodherft.
S. Iohn Baptift. Harietfham.
All Saints. Hollingbourne.
S. Margaret. Hucking.
S. Mary. Lenham.
S. Nicholas. Leeds.
Loofe.
S. Mary. Langley.
S. Nicholas. Linton.
All Saints. } Maide. { Colledge Church.
S. Faith. } ftone. { Parifh Church.
S. Michael. Marden.
S. Mary. Sutton Vallence.
All Saints. Stapleherft.
S. Mary. Thornham.
S. Nicholas. Otham.
All Saints. Ulcombe.
S. Giles. Wormfhill.

Sittingborne-Deanry;
Bicknore.
S. Iohn Baptift. Bredgate.
S. Peter and Paul. Borden.
S. Bartholomew. Bobbing.
S. Laurence. Bapchild.
All Saints. Eaftchurch.
S. Michael. Hartlip.
S. Margaret. Halftow.
All Saints. Iwade.
S. Katherine. Kingfdowne.
S. Clement. Leifdowne.
S. Trinity. Milton.
All Saints. Morton.
S. Mary. S. Sexburgh. Minfter.
S. Mary. S. Croffe. Milkfted.
S. Mary. Newington.
S. Trinity. Queenborough.
S. Margaret. Rainham.
S. Nicholas. Rodmerfham.
S. Mary Magdalen. Stockbury;
S. Michael. Sittingbourne.
S. Giles. Tong.
S. Iohn Baptift. Tonftall.
S. Mary. Upchurch.
S. Margaret. Witchling.
Wardon.

Ofpringe-Deanrie.
Buckland.
S. Peter and Paul. Boughton Blean.
S. Leonard. Badlefmere.
S. Mary Magdalen. Davington.
S. Iohn Baptift. Doddington.
S. Mary. Eaftling.
S. Mary. Feverfham.
S. Bartholomew. Goodneftone.
All Saints. Graveney.
S. Michael. Hearnhill.
S. Thomas Apoftle. Hartey.
S. Mary. Luddenham.
S. Lawrence. Leaveland.
S. Peter and Paul. Linfted.
S. Mary. Norton.
S. Peter and-Paul. Newenham.
S. Peter. Ore.
S. Lawrence. Otterden.
S. Peter and Paul. Ofpringe.
S. Katherine. Prefton.
S. Mary. Selling.
S. Iames. Sheldwich.
S. Mary. Stallesfield.
S. Mary. Tenham.
S. Michael. Throuleigh;

FINIS.

The TABLE.

Note: *The Letter A prefixed before the Number of the Page, directs to that Page in the* Appendix.

A.

Abbats-mill   24
Adisham   A 36, A 47
Aelmsland   A 48
Aghne   A 37
Aid, lent to the City by the Monks   147, A 64
Aldermanry, an Office   52
Aldington   A 38, A 44
All-Saints Church   167
Andres-gate   164
S. Andrew's Church   165, A 70
Apostolicæ Sedis Legatus, that Title when first given to the Archbishop   123
Appledore, the Mershes there inned,   147, the Manor   A 48
Archbishoprick at Litchfield   119
Archbishops. Their Antiquity in the Church, 113, number in England, 115. A Catalogue of the Archbishops of Cant. 116, the Form of their Inthronization, 139, A 57, their Palace at Canterbury   101
Archdeaconry of Cant. when erected, 34, 150, enlarged   156, A 65
Archdeacons. A Catalogue of them, 150, three at one time in the Diocess, 154, their House, 156, their Fees for inducting Bishops   162
Archery, commended   75, &c.
Arch-flamins   114
Arundel. Sir William his Monument   A 33
Atwood. A Family in Canterbury   166
St. Augustin's Abby, when and wherefore, and by whom founded, &c. 25, A 6, Ethelbert's Tower, 31, St. Pancrace Chappel, 32, Churchyard, 33, a common-way thro' that, 9, Common Seals of the Abby, 149, Composition with the City   167, A 72
Authentick Seals   145

B.

Bailiffs of Canterbury   179
Ballock Lane   170
Barbican   19
Barham   A 37
Barnacle-Cross   81
Barton-mill, 25, Manor, 47, A 38, Prison   144
Barton Elizabeth, called the Holy Maid of Kent, her Impostures   37
Beausherne   47
Berewick   A 57
Berksore   A 40
Bertha   52
Bilsington Priory and Parsonage   134
Binne   A 37
Binnewith, 55, a Family so named   ibid. 72
Bishop of S. Martin   34, 150
Bishoprick, the note of a City   121
Bishops Titular   57
Black Prince. His Chapel, 97, his Monument, 100, his Chantry-Priests House   7

Blean Wood, 45, A 40, Vicarage   62, A 15
Bocholt   A 37
Bocking   A 39
Bocton   A 45, A 48
Bovyton   A 40
Boxley   A 51
Bradestede   A 46
Bramling   A 36
Break-pot Lane   59
Bredgar-College   136
Brewers-Lane   15, 68
Bridewell   73
British-Bricks   4, 32, 34
Broke   A 40, A 52
Brotewell   A 37, A 39
Browns, a Family, Alderman of West-gate   52
Bulstake   79
Burgate, 9, the Ward   79
Burial, and Burning of the Dead in Cities forbidden, 26, 118, when first used in Christ's Church   118
Burn   A 37, A 44
Burricestune   A 51
Byri   A 37

C.

Cair, what it signifies   5
Cair-Medwag   13
Caldecote-Manor   131, A 40
Calvels, a Family in Canterbury   36
Canterbury. The Antiquity of it, 1, 21, 181, A 23, Names of it, 1, Famous in the Roman-times, 2, Survey of it in Doomsday-Book, 2, A 1, anciently a Hundred, 53, 54, commended by Malmesbury, 81, spoiled by the Danes, 84, 128, the cause of its Decay, 125, made a County per se, 181, the Ecclesiastical Government, 171, the Temporal Government, 178, the Liberties of it   A 3
Canterbury-Lane   170
Capgrave, John   68
Subdeacon-Cardinals at Christ-Church   129
The Castle   18
The Cathedral Church. Its Foundation, 151, a Monastery, 83, built by the Romans, 84, dedicated to our Saviour, 84, burnt and re-edified, 85, enlarged, 87, dedicated to the Holy Trinity, 87, The Campanile, 88, 103, Body new built, 89, 147, a Survey of the present Church, 90, S. Dunstan's Steeple, 91, Arundel Steeple, 91, Martyrdom, 91, Lady Chapel, 92, S. Michael's Chapel, 92, the Quire, 92, Hangings, 93, Altars, 94, Becket's Chapel and Crown, 95, Vestry and Sacrist, ib. Treasury, Dean's Chapel, Library, Windows, 96, Undercroft, French-Church, Black Prince's Chapel, Lady Chapel, 97, Becket's Tomb, Chapter-House, Cloister, 98, Monuments, Font, 99, Church-gate, 104, Cimitery-gate, School-House, 105, Honors, Infir-

*X

The TABLE.

Infirmary, 106, Dortor, 108, Refectory, ib. Celerar, Sacrist, Chamberlane, Treasurer, 109, Court-gate, 110, North-hall, 111, Steward's Court, Almnery, 112, Mint-yard, the Grammar School, 113, Benefactors to this Church, ib. Burial of Archbishops procured to it, 117, The several Seals, 87, 126
Chantery-Lane   36
Chanter of Christ-Church,   147
Chapters Rural   173
Charters before King Withred's time questionable   5
Charing   A 37, A 45
Chart   A 37, 38, 48
Chartham   A 48
Cheap, what it signifies   81
Cheyham   A 39
Chiches, a Family in Canterbury, 79, Alderman of Burgate, 53, Bailiff   180
Churches, before the Conquest, mostly of Wood 86, 163
In Church-matters Laics punished for intermeddling   135
Church-Yards, their beginning in England 118
City, the note of a Bishop's See   121, 122
Clavering   A 11
Clement's Lane   107
Clergy, the Privilege so called   A 49
Clyve   A 50
Cloth-market   68, 80
Cokins, a Family in Canterb. 60, Aldermen of Worthgate, 53, Bailiffs of the City   180
Cokins, Hospital and Lane   60, 170
Combewell   A 51
Commissary of Canterbury, his Office   173
Compositions, between Christ-Church and St. Augustin, 88, A 61, A 62, A 23, between the City and St. Augustin, A 72, between the Archbishop and Archdeacon, 160, between the Hospital of Poor Priests and the Parson of St. Margaret's, A 21, between Christ-Church and the Gray-Friars, A 13, between Christ-Church and the Archdeacon   A 67
Conduit at Canterbury   138
Consistory-Court at Canterbury   173
Controversy between the Archbishop and the Monks of Christ-Church, 127, between the Achdeacon and the Monks there, 154, 157 158, between the King and the Monks of St. Augustin, 155, between the Archdeacon and Commissary, 159, between the Archb. and Archdeacon, 160, between the City and St. Augustin's 9, between the City and St. Gregory's   49
Copton   A 39
Cowlings   A 38
Cotton's Hospital   75
Court-Christian   178
Courts of Record   145
Crinemelne-Lane   55
Croydon Hospital and School   138
Cumbe   A 37

D
THe Danes spare St. Augustin's Abby, 28, besiege and take the City, &c. 84, 128
Dapeschecourt, Sir Eustace   A 16
Davington   133
Dean of Christ-Church, 139, Deans of the new Foundation   149
Deans Rural   175

Decani Christianitatis   175
Dedications of the Churches in Kent   A 79
Dei Gratia, the Stile of the Archbishop   136
Derent   A 46
Diepham   142, A 40, A 41
Digges, a Family in Canterbury, 55, Aldermen of Newingate   53
Ditch about Canterbury   17
Doccomb   A 40
Dodingdale, Manery and Tithery   40 A 9
Doge Hamon, his Chantery, &c.   36, 167
Doomsday-Book, why so called   2
Dorobrevis   A 77
Dover, whence so called   21
Dungeon, the Manor and Hill   75
St. Dunstan's Church, 168, Vicarage, A 74, his Shrine searched   120, A 24
Durolevum   13

E.
Arhede,   A 46
Eastry   A 37, A 41, A 47
Ebbeny   A 38
Ecclesiastical Government of the City   171
Ecclesiecdici   173
St. Edmund's Church   11, 169
Eghethorn   A 38
Einsford   A 46
St. Elphege-Church   163
Old Epitaphs rare in England   123
Eshe   A 41
Etheredeshith   A 38
Royal Exchange at Canterbury   63, A 16, A 17
Eylwearton   A 39

F.
Airs, 124, at Christ-Church   135
Fairfield   A 41
Fawkshall   97, A 40
Fearnlege   A 38, A 52
Feversham, Town and Abby   124, 155
Fineux, Sir John   68, 69, A 33, A 71, A 18
Firmin's Barton   41
Fishmanschurch   80, 164
Fish-Market   80, 170
Fog, Sir Thomas   A 32, 33
Folkstane   A 38, A 39
Fraternities   58, 168
Freningham   A 41, A 50
Friers Augustin, 67, Black, 57, Gray   54

G.
Ates of the City   9
Gedding   A 36, A 37
Geferscipes, what   178
St. George his Church, 164, Gate   10
Guildhall   66
Gilingham   A 45
Godmersham   A 37, A 39, A 41, A 48
Goggeshall   A 39
Graveney   A 37, A 50
St. Gregory's Priory   48
Guildford Hospital   138
Guildford, John   A 32

H
Adleigh   A 38, A 39
Hakynton   47, 156, A 65
Halstow   A 41
Haltone   A 40
Hamme   A 38
Harges   A 37
Haut, Edmund   A 32
Hearn   131
Hengam

The TABLE.

Hengam, Odmar   A 32
K. *Henry* IV. his Monument   100
Herbaldown : the Original of the Name, 45,
   the Church of St. *Nicolas* there   44
Hermitage at Northgate   16
Heth   A 38, A 52
Hliden   A 36
Holy *Croſs* Church, 15, 168, The Vicarage en-
   dowed   A 74
Holingborn   A 39, A 48
Horſelegh   A 39
Hoſpitals {
   of St. *Jacob*   41
   of St. *Johns*   50
   of St. *Laurence*   39
   of *Poor Prieſts*   71 A 19
   of St. *Thomas* at *Eaſtbridge* 60, A 19
   of St. *Nicolas Herbaldbwn*, 42, the
     Chantry of it, A 10, of *Jeſus* 47
   of *Barton*   ib.
   of *Mayners*   74
   of *Cotton*   75
Hottewell   73
Hubert de Burgh   6
Hulecumb   A 47
Huntindune   A 50

I.

Ickham   A 37, A 38, A 47
   Jews in *Canterbury*, 65, *Jury* Lane   ib.
Illegh   A 39
Johan, Lady *Mohun*   100
St. *John's* Church and Lane   166
Iſabella, Counteſs of *Athol*   100

K.

Kingsbridge }   23
Kingſmill }

L.

Laling   A 39
   Lambert's Lane   15, 68
Lambeth   A 36
Langdone A 37, Abby there   A 51
Langport   A 52
Lazar-houſes about *Canterbury*   42
Leanham,   12, 14, A 38, A 52
Leed's Caſtle   136
Leiſdown   A 40
Liberties of *Canterbury*   A 3
Liminge Nonnes, 163, Manor   A 41
Little-Chert   A 48
Little-pet Lane   65
Liveland   52
Livingsborn Chantery   6, A 17
Loder's Lane   A 72
Longport   36
Loſe   A 38, A 50
Lukedale Chantry   35, A 8

M.

Maideſton Hoſpital and College, 128,
   133, 135, Manor   A 45
Maiors of *Canterbury*   181
Malling   A 38, A 46
Manumiſſion   A 32
St. *Margaret's* Church   169, A 19
Market-Field   80
St. Martins by *Canterbury*, 34, 150, by *Dover*,
   123, 134
St. *Mary Bredin* Church   169
St. *Mary Bredman*   164
St. *Mary Caſtle*   165
St. *Mary Magdalen*   165
St. *Mary Northgate*   167

St. *Mary Queningate*   16, 164
Mead-Lane   55
Medmilne   72
Melton   A 37
Mepham   A 38, A 41, A 50
Mercats in the City and Suburbs   80
Merſey   A 39
Merſham   A 39, A 48
Merſteham   A 39
St. *Michael's* Church   164
St. *Mildreds*   166
Mills upon the *Stour*   23
Milton   A 39
Minchen Wood, *i. e. Nonnes* Wood   37
Mints at *Canterbury*   64, 113
Monksdane   40
Monkton   134, A 38, A 41, A 47
Mortimer, Sir *Robert*   142
Mote   35

N.

Newingate, 10, the Ward   67
   Newington by *Sittingborn*   14
Newington   A 39
New-ſtreet   36, A 72
Niwenden   A 52
North-fleet   A 46
North-gate, 16, Ward   69
Norwood   A 45, A 47
Notaries   145, A 59, 60,
Noviomagus   12
Nunhelmeſtun   A 36

O.

Oaten-Hill   80
   Orſgariſwick   A 37
Orpintune   A 50
Oſterland   A 38
Otteford   22 A 37, *bis* A 46
Out-aliens Way   12

P.

Pageham   A 36
   St. *Pancrace* Chapel   32
Pavement of the City   80, A 22
St. *Paul's* Church, 167, and Vicarage,   A 73
Pechings   A 38
Peckham   A 38, A 50
Periodeutai   173
St. *Peter's* Church   164
Petham   A 44
Pikenot-Ally   170
Pluckly   A 45
Pocock's Lane   170
Polres, Aldermen of *North-gate*, 53, Bailiffs of
   the City   180
Pomœrium, what   18
Porta machecollata   16
Portreve of *Canterbury*   178
Portſota   53
Poſterns   17
The Poultry   79
Præfect of *Canterbury*   178
Preſtantune   A 38
Preſton   A 39, A 52
Prior of *Chriſt-Church* had a Key at *Fordwich*,
   146, A 62, a Lord Prior, 147, 150, his Ele-
   ction and Inſtallation   150, A 64
Priſon, 15, called the *Spech-houſe*   66
Prohibitions oppoſed as a Grievance   131
Provoſt of *Canterbury*   178

The TABLE.

Q.

Queningate, 16, Lane   103

R.

Raculver, 121, 131, A 38, A 40 A 43, A 45
St. Radegund's Abby   A 51
Rethercheap   81
Ridingate, 10, Ward   75
Risbergh   A 39
River of Stour   20
Rochester, Bishoprick   153
The Roman Way between London and Canterbury   12
Roking   A 37
Roper, a Family in Canterbury   168, A 71
Rush-Market   80

S.

Sændling   A 50
Salcocks Lane   170
Salthill   80
Saltwood   A 52
Sandherst   A 57
Sandwich   83, A 39, A 40, A 47
School at Canterbury, 105, A 33, at St. Martin's, 35, of the Jews   65
Seals not used here before the Conquest   87
Septvans, a Family   A 32, A 69
St. Sepulchre's Nunnery, 36, Church   38
Seasalter   A 41, A 48
Shafford's Mill   24
Shaldeford   A 37
Sheldwich   A 37
Shepeshank Lane   170
Slindone   A 40
South-Church   A 37
Spech-house Lane   66, 67
Staple of Wool in Canterbury   69
Staple-Gate, 69, a Family   69
Stystede   A 39, A 40
Stodmarsh   71, A 18
Stoursæt   21, A 44
Stouting   A 39
Summagium bosci   37
Sunderherst   A 46
Sunnewings Lane   170
Surling   A 50
Synods   172

T.

Tallage   144, A 58
Templars-House in Canterbury   70
Tenham   156, A 65, A 45
Terrings   A 38
Terstane   A 40
St. Thomas-Hill   47
Thorholt-Wood   131
Thorough-hall Lane   80
Thurrock   A 39
Tiernes, Aldermen of Worthgate   53
Tierne-crouch, (i.e. Cross)   11, 169
Tilmannestane   A 47
Tithes, how paid in Canterbury   171, A 75, 76
Totius Angliæ Primas   122

V.

Vagniacæ   13
Ulcomb   127

W.

Wales laid to the Province of Canterbury   127
The City-Wall   4, &c. 163
Wardmore   53
The City divided into Wards   52
Ware Lane   170
Waterlock Lane   70
Watling Street   11
Welle   A 48
Werehorn   A 39, A 49
West-cliffe   A 41
Westerham   A 41
West-Gate, 14, Mill, 24, Street, 51, Ward, 54
Westwell   89, A 24, A 41
Wheat Market   80
Willards Lane   170
Winchepe   81
Windows at Christ-Church   96, A 24
Wingham-College, 128, Manor   A 44
Winulphus, (i.e. Mayner's) Hospital   A 36
Wodeton   A 36
Worthgate   11, 71
Wroteham   A 46
Wye College   137
Wyke   35

Y.

Yelverton-Tithery   156

F I N I S.

The ERRATA *of the* FIRST PART.

PAge 3 line 1, read Hamo. p. 4 l. 50, r. therein set out. p. 29 l. 46, *Thorn* saies. p. 37 l. 31, r. Papalins. p. 44 l. 22, r. of Gardins. p. 49 l. 4, r. had other. p. 55 l. 7, r. which signifies. p. 68 l. 40, r. Convent. p. 71 l. 43, r. by the same. p. 101 l. 49, r. Palace. p. 152 l. ult. r. was. p. 155 l. 5, r. Alianors. p. 158 l. 39, r. *Robert Kilwardby's*. p. 190 l. 22, r. so much more.

The ERRATA *of the* APPENDIX *to the* First Part.

Pag. 1. In the Margin l. Alit. prati *Brady*. p. 3 l. 37, ac l. de. *ibid.* l. 45, l. die. p. 6 l. 31, l. sive Ecclesiasticæ sive sæculari. p. 9 l. 6 l. vel. *Ibid.* l. 48, l. erunt. p. 10 l. 12, l. vestræ. p. 12 l. 52, l. perscrutando, *ib.* l. 55, l. aliquam. p. 13 l. 50, l. subjiciet. *ib.* l. 59, l. minime. *ibid.* l. 62, l. super his cum religiosis. l. 64 *dele* cum his. p. 14 l. 42, l. eorum. p. 17 l. 29, l. vacat'. p. 27 l. 2, l. cui. *ibid.* l. 3, delicta. *ibid.* l. 8, l. Rachaeli. *ibid.* l 15, l. Christe. p. 28 l. 28, l. Cui. p. 29 l. 2, l pertranseunt. *ibid.* l. 15, l. superasti. *ibid.* l. 18, l. Marias. p. 30 l. 36, l. invida. p. 34 l. 58, l. molestastis. p. 36 l. 22, l. Commissarii. p. 37 l. 13, l. Aghne, Orgariswick, Treon. *ibid.* l. 57, l. quandam. p. 41 l. 38, l. maneriis. p. 44 l. 17, l. VIIs. *ibid.* l. 5, l. VII. p. 47 l. 37, l. XX. p. 52 l. 35, l. Monachorum. p. 49 l. 51, l. Canon. p. 53 l. 52, r. Clarendon. p. 58 l. 18, ingressi, species.----- Ita MS. prout, l. ingressi. -----prout. add in the Margin. Species MS. *ibid.* l. 21, l. suus. p. 60 l. 46, l. Origines. *ibid.* l. 49, l. exheredationis. p. 61 l. 24, l. malitiose. 62 in the Margin, l. Stephanus. p. 62 l. 9, l. Fordwicum. *ibid.* l. 31, l. barrer. p. 65 l. 10, l. aliis. *ibid.* l. 29, l. Cognitionem. p. 68 l. 34, l. meq; p. 69 l. 4, l. Octavo. p. 71 l. 46, l. general. *ibid.* l. 51, l. Johannis. p. 73 l. 43, l. eas. p. 74 l. 46, l. agnoscant. p. 79 l. 34, r. commended. *ib.* l. 66, r. East-Langdon. p. 80 l. 67, r. Eleham Deanry.

PLATES FROM *CANTUARIA SACRA*
BY
NICOLAS BATTELY

CantuarienfisEcclefiae
Cath:Facies occidentalis.

The West Prospect of the
Cathedral Church of
CANTERBURY.

In honorem Ecclesiae
Hanc Icona æri incidendam
curavit Thomas Archiepifcopus
Cantuarienfis.
Anno. 1703.

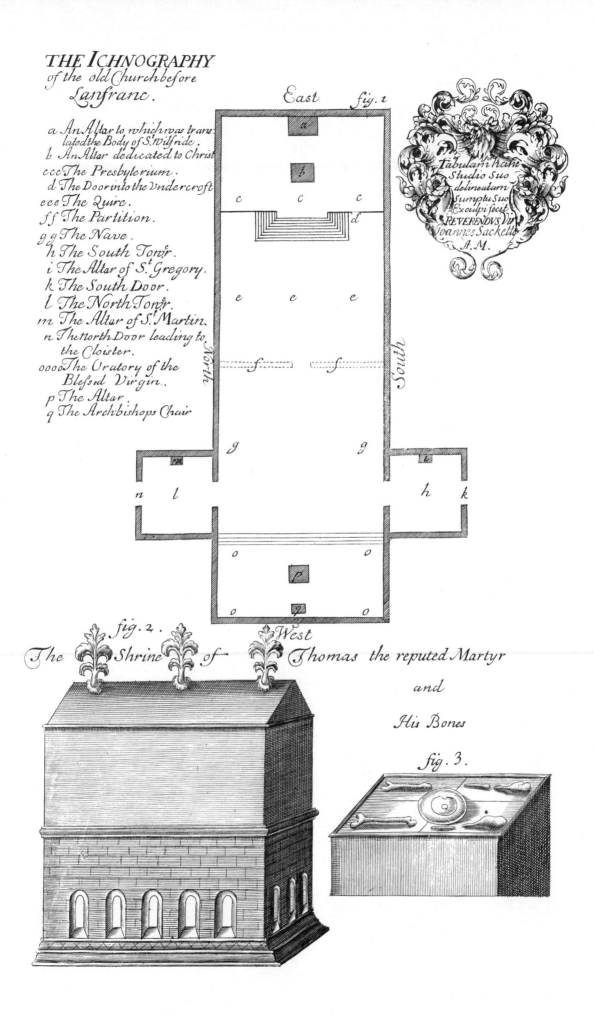

THE *I*CHNOGRAPHY
of the old Church before
Lanfranc .

East fig. 1

a *An Altar to which was trans-*
lated the Body of S.t Wilfride .
b *An Altar dedicated to Christ*
ccc *The Presbyterium .*
d *The Door into the Vndercroft*
eee *The Quire .*
ff *The Partition .*
g g *The Nave .*
h *The South Tower .*
i *The Altar of S.t Gregory .*
k *The South Door .*
l *The North Tower .*
m *The Altar of S.t Martin .*
n *The North Door leading to*
the Cloister .
oooo *The Oratory of the*
Blessed Virgin .
p *The Altar*
q *The Archbishops Chair*

North

South

West

fig. 2 .

The Shrine of Thomas the reputed Martyr

and

His Bones

fig. 3 .

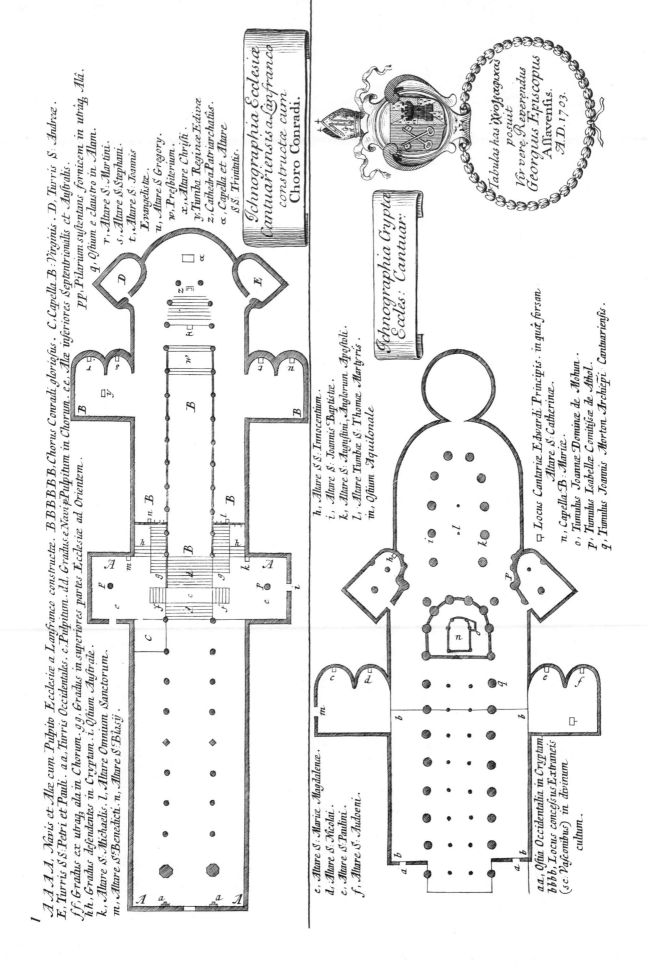

1

A A A A, Navis et Alæ cum Pulpito Ecclesiæ a Lanfranco constructæ. B B B B B B, Chorus Conradi gloriosus. C, Capella B: Virginis. D, Turris S: Andreæ.
E, Turris SS: Petri et Pauli. a a, Turris Occidentales. c, Pulpitum in Chorum. d d, Gradus e Navi Pulpitum in Chorum. e e, Alæ inferiores Septentrionalis et Australis.
f f, Gradus ex utraq; alâ in Chorum. g g, Gradus in superiores partes Ecclesiæ ad Orientem.
PP, Pilarum sustentans fornicem in utraq; Alâ.
h h, Gradus descendentes in Cryptam. i, Ostium Australe. q, Ostium e claustro in Alam.
k, Altare S: Michaelis. L, Altare Omnium Sanctorum.
m, Altare S: Benedicti. n, Altare S: Blasij.

r, Altare S: Martini.
s, Altare S: Stephani.
t, Altare S: Joannis Evangelistæ.
u, Altare S: Gregory.
w, Presbiterium.
x, Altare Christi.
y, Tumba Reginæ Ediuæ.
z, Cathedra Patriarchalis.
α, Capella et Altare SS: Trinitatis.

Ichnographia Ecclesiæ Cantuariensis a Lanfranco constructæ cum Choro Conradi.

Ichnographia Cryptæ Eccles: Cantuar:

h, Altare SS: Innocentium.
i, Altare S: Joannis Baptistæ.
k, Altare S: Augustini, Anglorum Apostoli.
L, Altare Tumbæ S: Thomæ Martyris.
m, Ostium Aquilonale.

c, Altare S: Mariæ Magdalenæ.
d, Altare S: Nicolai.
e, Altare S: Paulini.
f, Altare S: Audoeni.

a a, Ostia Occidentalia in Cryptam.
b b b b, Locus concessus Extraneis (sc. Vasconibus) in divinum cultum.

□, Locus Cantariæ Edwardi Principis. in quâ forsan. Altare S: Catherinæ.
n, Capella B: Mariæ.
o, Tumulus Joannæ Dominæ de Mohun.
P, Tumulus Isabellæ Comitissæ de Athol.
q, Tumulus Joannis Morton Archiepi: Cantuariensis.

Tabulas has Ἰχνογραφικας posuit Vir verè Reverendus Georgius Episcopus Assavensis. A.D. 1703.

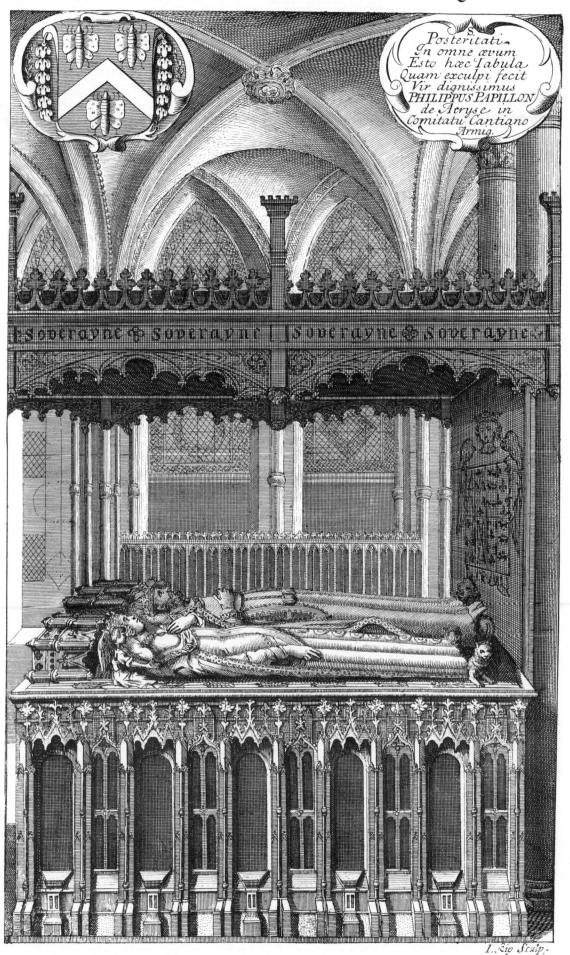

S.
Posteritati
In omne ævum
Esto hæc Tabula
Quam exculpi fecit
Vir dignissimus
PHILIPPUS PAPILLON
de Acryse in
Comitatu Cantiano
Armig.

I. Kip Sculp.

Tabulam hanc Sepulchralem
Illustrissimi Invictissimiq Principis,
EDWARDI, dicti NIGRI,
Vel ipso ære perenniorem
Honoratissimo Viro Iohanni Crisp Londinensi
Baronetto
Quam Ipse posuit,
Humillime Dedicat Consecratq,
Nicolaus Battely.

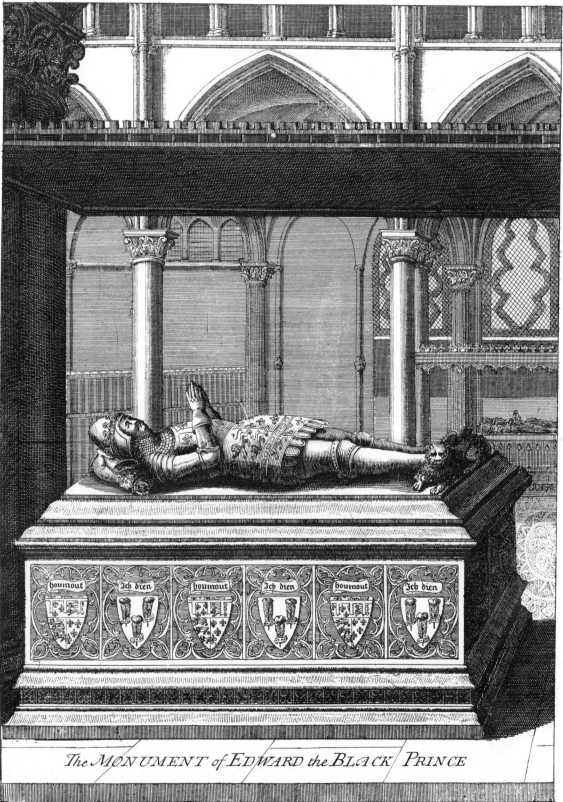

The MONUMENT *of* EDWARD *the* BLACK PRINCE

8

302

Viro Honorabili
Domino
EDWARDO NICHOLAS
Equiti Aurato Serenissimis,
Regibus CAROLO primo, et
secundo, Secretariorum vni
principalium, et è Secretio
ribus Consilijs.

Figuram hanc Tumuli Thomæ
Ducis Clarenciæ, Iohannis
Comitis Somersetiæ, et
Margaretæ eorundem Vxo
ris. D.D.D. F.S.

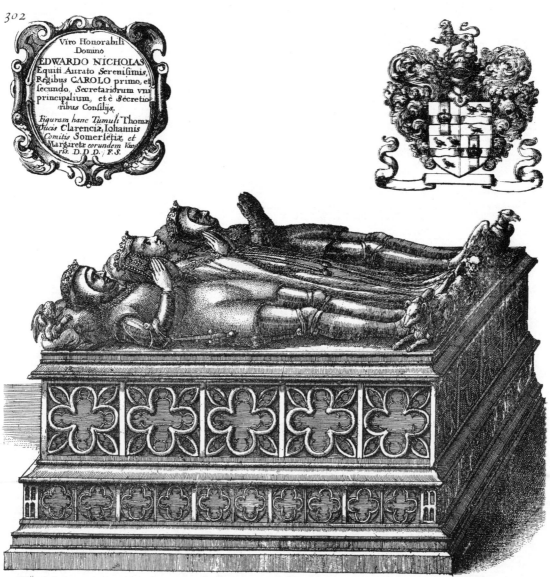

W.Hollar fecit.

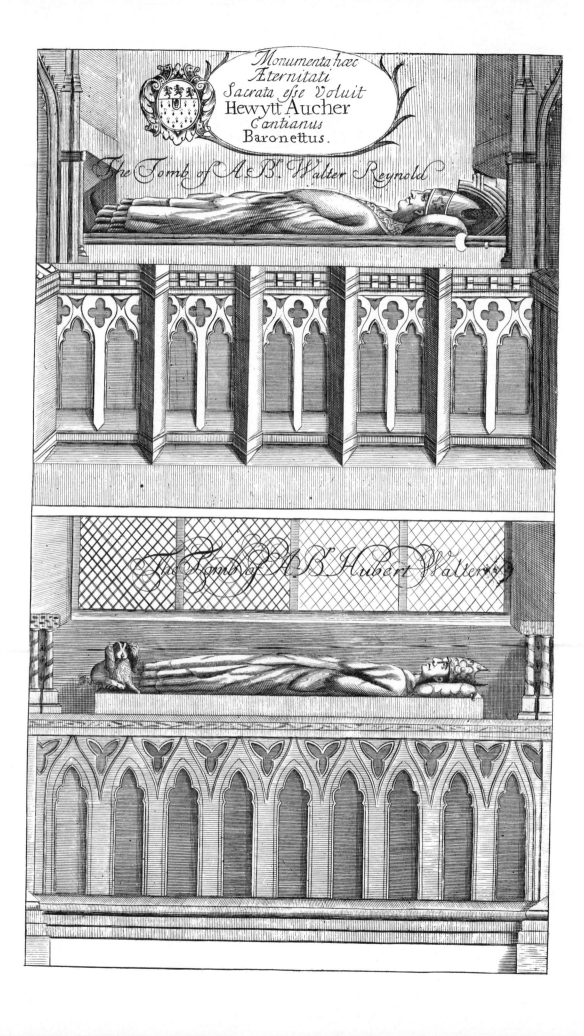

9

Monumenta hæc
Æternitati
Sacrata esse Voluit
Hewytt Aucher
Cantianus
Baronettus.

The Tomb of A. B. Walter Reynold

The Tomb of A. B. Hubert Walter

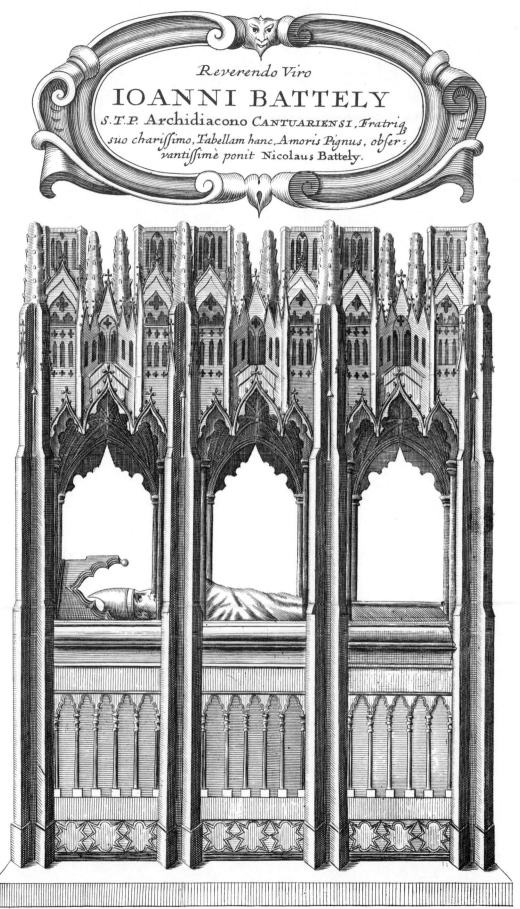

Reverendo Viro

IOANNI BATTELY

S.T.P. Archidiacono Cantuariensi, *Fratriꝗ*
ſuo chariſſimo, Tabellam hanc, Amoris Pignus, obſer=
vantiſſimè ponit Nicolaus Battely.

THE TOMB OF A=B.ᴾ IOHN STRATFORD.

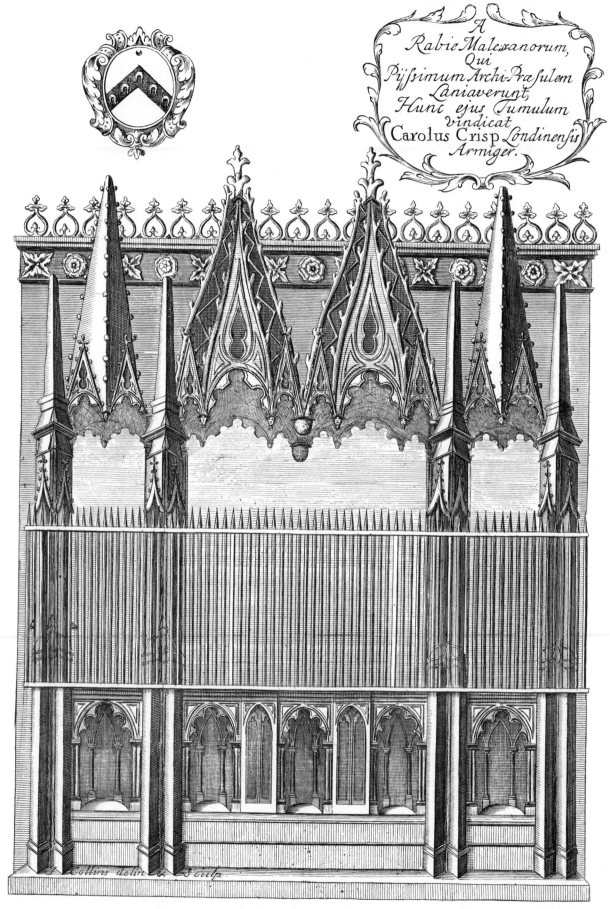

A
Rabie Malexanorum,
Qui
Piſsimum Archi-Præſulem
Laniaverunt,
Hunc ejus Tumulum
vindicat
Carolus Crisp Londinenſis
Armiger.

THE TOMB OF A:Bᵖ. SIMON SVDBVRY.

Ornatissimæ Dominæ
Catherinæ Adrian
Relicta
Thomæ Adrian
nuper Londin: Arm.
Tabulam hanc
Gratitudinis ergo
L.M.Q.DD.C.Q.
N.B.

Ja. Collins delin et Sculp.

THE TOMB OF A.Bʳ WILLIAM COVRTNEY

THE TOMB OF A.Bʳ THEOBALD

In perpetuum grati animi Testimonium, Fabulam hanc
Reverendis summæque Benevolentiæ Viris,

THOMÆ BELK et GEORGIO THORP
S.T. PP. Ecclesiæ CHRISTI Cantuariensis Canoni‑
cis, Lubentissimè dedicat Nicolaus Battely.

THE TOMB OF A. B^p. IOHN KEMP

J. Collins delin & sculp.

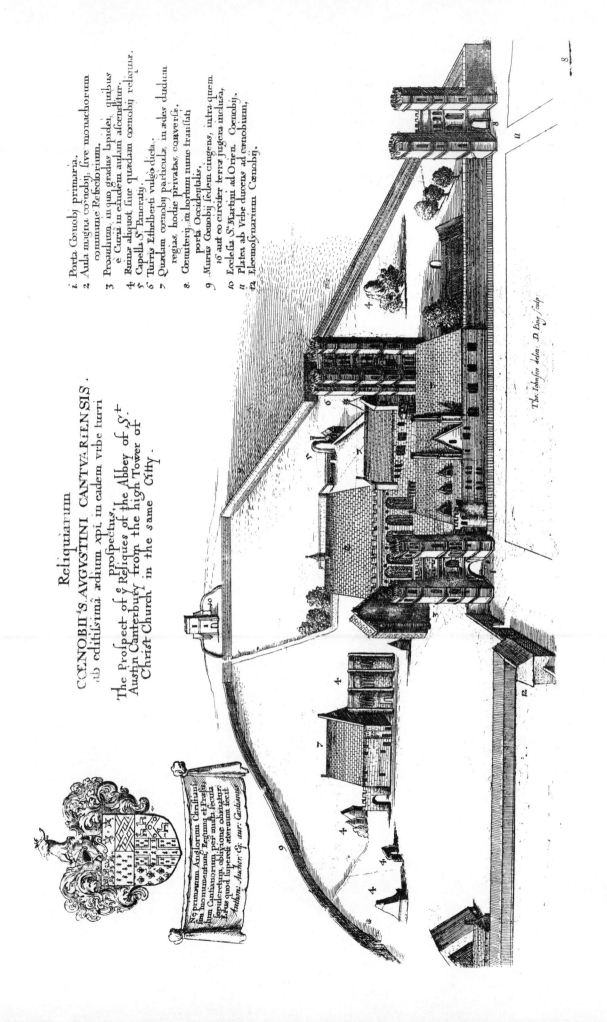

Reliquiarum

COENOBII's AVGVSTINI CANTVARiENSIS.
ab editiſsimâ ædium χρι in eadem vrbe turri
proſpectus.

The Proſpect of ẏ Reliques of the Abbey of S.t
Auſtin Canterbury from the high Tower of
Chriſt Church in the ſame Citty.

1. Porta Cœnobij, primaria.
2. Aula magna cœnobij, ſive monachorum commune Refectorium.
3. Proaulium, in quo gradus lapideî, quibus e Curiâ in eandem aulam aſcenditur.
4. Ruinæ aliquot ſive quædam cœnobij reliquiæ.
5. Capella S.t Pancratij.
6. Turris Ethelberti vulgò dicta.
7. Quædam cœnobij particulæ, in ædes dudum regias, hodie privatas, converſæ.
8. Gemiterij, in horum nunc tranſlati portâ Occidentalis.
9. Murus Cœnobij ſedem cingens, intra quem 16 aut eo circiter terræ jugera incluſa,
10. Eccleſia S.t Martini ad Orien. Cœnobij.
11. Platea ab vrbe ducens ad cœnobium,
12. Eleemoſynarium Cœnobij.

Tho: Johnſon delin: D. King ſculp: